Beginning VB.NET 2003

Thearon Willis
Jonathan Crossland
Richard D. Blair

WILEY

Wiley Publishing, Inc.

Beginning VB.NET 2003

Published by
Wiley Publishing, Inc.
10475 Crosspoint Boulevard
Indianapolis, IN 46256
www.wiley.com

Copyright © 2004 by Wiley Publishing, Inc., Indianapolis, Indiana

Published simultaneously in Canada

ISBN: 0-7645-5658-4

Manufactured in the United States of America

10 9 8 7 6 5 4

For general information on our other products and services or to obtain technical support, please contact our Customer Care Department within the U.S. at (800) 762-2974, outside the U.S. at (317) 572-3993 or fax (317) 572-4002.

Wiley also publishes its books in a variety of electronic formats. Some content that appears in print may not be available in electronic books.

Beginning VB.NET 2003

About the Authors

Thearon Willis

Thearon Willis, currently works as a senior consultant and develops intranet applications using ASP.NET, DHTML, XML, JavaScript, Visual Basic Script, VB COM components, and SQL Server. Over the years, Thearon has worked on a variety of systems from mainframe to client-server development.

Jonathan Crossland

Jonathan Crossland, is a co-author of *Professional Windows DNA*, *Professional VB.NET*, and *Beginning VB.NET*. He is currently working at Yokogawa Electric Corporation in the UK, where he is happily involved with the creation of software for the Batch manufacturing industry. Jonathan has been working in and out of various software technologies for eight years now, and spend most of his time in C# and ASP.NET. Jonathan also works with Visual Basic, Visual Basic .NET, and Web technologies such as JavaScript, DHTML, XML, ASP, and Web Services.

Richard D. Blair

Richard D. Blair (MCSD, MSCD.NET) was a Senior Solutions Developer/Architect for Empowered Software Solutions, Inc. (ESS). ESS is a Chicago-based consulting firm and a Microsoft Gold Certified Partner in e-Commerce. During his 14 years of experience, Richard helped clients streamline the electronic business process, expand access to vital information, and create usable systems.

Besides his consulting work, he also co-authored *Professional ASP XML*, *Beginning VB.NET*, *Professional VB.NET*, and served as Technical Reviewer on *Professional Design Patterns with VB.NET*, all published by Wrox Press. He also presented at DevDays99, the Wrox Developers Conferences, was an invited "Ask the Expert" at the Visual Studio .NET launch event in Chicago, and presented Visual Basic .NET 2003 at the launch events in Milwaukee and Indianapolis. Richard had a dual concentration bachelor's degree from the University of Michigan in English Literature and Theatre. So not only was he a Software Architect, he could play one on TV.

Richard D. Blair
July 29, 1966 to December 29, 2003.

Credits

Authors
Thearon Willis
Jonathan Crossland
Richard D. Blair

Senior Acquisitions Editor
Katie Mohr

Development Editor
Sydney Jones

Production Editor
Vincent Kunkemueller

Technical Editor
Todd Meister

Copy Editor
TechBooks

Senior Production Manager
Fred Bernardi

Editorial Manager
Mary Beth Wakefield

Vice President & Executive Group Publisher
Richard Swadley

Vice President and Executive Publisher
Robert Ipsen

Vice President and Publisher
Joseph B. Wikert

Executive Editorial Director
Mary Bednarek

Proofreading and Indexing
TECHBOOKS Production Services

Contents

Contents

Contents

Contents

Contents

Contents

Contents

Contents

Contents

Contents

Contents

Beginning VB.NET 2003

Introduction

Visual Basic .NET is Microsoft's latest version of the highly popular Visual Basic, a product based on the easy-to-learn BASIC language. Visual Basic .NET's strength lies in its ease of use and the speed at which you can put together your own applications for the Windows operating system.

In the past, Visual Basic has been used largely to create applications with a rich user interface including buttons, lists, and drop-down boxes. In this book, we will show you how to incorporate these things into your applications, and also show you where we think the future of programming for Windows will be.

With the introduction of Microsoft's .NET Framework there has never been a more exciting time to learn Visual Basic. For the first time, Visual Basic programmers have access to full object-orientation in their programs, a powerful technique for handling errors that arise and the ability to incorporate programs that exist on the Internet into their applications. Exciting times indeed!

This book will give you a thorough grounding in the basics of programming using Visual Basic .NET; from there the world is your oyster.

Who Is This Book For?

This book is designed to teach you how to write useful programs in Visual Basic .NET as quickly and easily as possible.

There are two kinds of beginners for whom this book is ideal:

❑   You're a beginner to programming and you've chosen Visual Basic .NET as the place to start. That's a great choice! Visual Basic .NET is not only easy to learn, it's also fun to use and very powerful.

❑   You can program in another language but you're a beginner to .NET programming. Again, you've made a great choice! Whether you've come from Fortran or Visual Basic 6, you'll find that this book quickly gets you up to speed on what you need to know to get the best from Visual Basic .NET.

What Does This Book Cover?

Visual Basic .NET offers a great deal of functionality in both tools and language. No book could ever cover Visual Basic .NET in its entirety—you would need a library of books. What this book aims to do is to get you started as quickly and easily as possible. It shows you the roadmap, so to speak, of what there is and where to go. Once we've taught you the basics of creating working applications (creating the windows and boxes, how your code should handle unexpected events, what object-oriented programming is, and how to use it in your applications, and so on) we'll show you some of the areas you might want to try your hand at next:

- ❑ Chapters 15 and 16 provide a taster of programming with databases and so cover Access, SQL Server, and ADO.NET

- ❑ Chapter 17 discusses how to use Web forms to create your own ASP.NET applications for the Web

- ❑ Chapter 18 provides a brief introduction to XML; a powerful tool for integrating your applications with others—regardless of the language they were written in

- ❑ Chapter 19 introduces you to Web services, a technology whereby functionality offered on the Internet can be accessed by your applications and seamlessly integrated into them

What Do I Need to Run Visual Basic .NET?

Apart from a willingness to learn, all you'll need for the first 14 chapters are a PC running Windows 2000, XP, or NT4 Server, Internet Explorer, and of course:

- ❑ Microsoft Visual Studio .NET

or

- ❑ Microsoft Visual Basic .NET Standard Edition

As the later chapters cover more advanced subject areas, you will need further software to get the best out of them:

- ❑ Chapter 15 requires Microsoft Access 2000.

- ❑ For Chapter 16, you will need to have access to SQL Server 7 or SQL Server 2000.

  If you don't have the full version of SQL Server 2000, you can use MSDE (Microsoft Data Engine) instead. MSDE is a cut-down version of SQL Server. A version compatible with SQL Server 7 is available with Office 2000 Professional and Premium editions and a version compatible with SQL Server 2000 is available with Office XP. The big difference between MSDE and the full version of SQL Server is that MSDE does not have a user interface—the good news is that this difference has no impact on the exercises in Chapter 16.

- ❑ Chapters 17 and 19 rely on ASP.NET technology so you will need IIS 5 (which comes with Windows 2000 and Windows XP).

Don't worry if you don't have these products already and want to wait a while before you purchase them. You should still find that you get a lot out of this book.

Conventions

We've used a number of different styles of text and layout in this book to help differentiate between the different kinds of information. Here are examples of the styles we used and an explanation of what they mean.

Try It Out **How Do They Work?**

1. Each step has a number.

2. Follow the steps through.

3. Then read *How It Works* to find out what's going on.

> **These boxes hold important, not-to-be forgotten, mission-critical details that are directly relevant to the surrounding text.**

Background information, asides, and references appear in text like this.

Bullets appear indented, with each new bullet marked as follows:

❑   Words that appear on the screen or in menus such as the File or Window, are in a similar casing to the one you would see on a Windows desktop

❑   Keys that you press on the keyboard such as *Ctrl* and *Enter*, are in italics

Code has several styles. If it's a word that we're talking about in the text—for example, when discussing a `For ... Next` loop, it's in this `font`. If it's a block of code that can be typed as a program and run, then it's also in a gray box:

```
Private Sub btnAdd_Click(ByVal sender As System.Object, _
         ByVal e As System.EventArgs) Handles btnAdd.Click

    Dim n As Integer
    n = 27

    MessageBox.Show(n)

End Sub
```

Sometimes we'll see code in a mixture of styles, like this:

```
Private Sub btnAdd_Click(ByVal sender As System.Object, _
         ByVal e As System.EventArgs) Handles btnAdd.Click

    Dim n As Integer
    n = 27

    n = n + 2

    MessageBox.Show(n)

End Sub
```

In cases like this, the code with a white background is the code we are already familiar with; the line highlighted in gray is a new addition to the code since we last looked at it.

Customer Support

We always value hearing from our readers, and we want to know what you think about this book: what you liked, what you didn't like, and what you think we can do better next time. You can send us your comments by e-mail to feedback@wrox.com. Please be sure to mention the book title in your message.

How to Download the Sample Code for the Book

When you visit the Wrox site, `http://www.wrox.com/`, simply locate the title through our Search facility or by using one of the title lists. Click on Download in the Code column or on Download Code on the book's detail page.

The files that are available for download from our site have been archived using WinZip. When you have saved the attachments to a folder on your hard drive, you need to extract the files using a de-compression program such as WinZip or PKUnzip. When you extract the files, the code is usually extracted into chapter folders. When you start the extraction process ensure that your software (WinZip or PKUnzip) is set to use folder names.

Errata

We've made every effort to make sure that there are no errors in the text or in the code. However, no one is perfect and mistakes do occur. If you find an error in one of our books, like a spelling mistake or a faulty piece of code, we would be very grateful to have your feedback. By sending in errata, you may save another reader from hours of frustration, and of course, you will be helping us provide even higher quality information. Simply e-mail the information to support@wrox.com; your information will be checked and if correct, posted to the errata page for that title or used in subsequent editions of the book.

To find errata on the Web site, go to `http://www.wrox.com/`, and simply locate the title through our Advanced Search or title list. Click on the Book Errata link, which is below the cover graphic on the book's detail page.

E-mail Support

If you wish to directly query a problem in the book with an expert who knows the book in detail then e-mail support@wrox.com, with the title of the book and the last four numbers of the ISBN in the subject field of the e-mail. A typical e-mail should include the following things:

❑　The title of the book, last four digits of the ISBN (6584), and page number of the problem in the Subject field

❑　Your name, contact information, and the problem in the body of the message

We won't send you junk mail. We need the details to save your time and ours. When you send an e-mail message, it will go through the following chain of support:

❑　Customer Support—Your message is delivered to our customer support staff, who are the first people to read it. They have files on most frequently asked questions and will answer anything general about the book or the Web site immediately.

❏ Editorial—Deeper queries are forwarded to the technical editor responsible for that book. They have experience with the programming language or particular product and are able to answer detailed technical questions on the subject.

❏ The Authors—Finally, in the unlikely event that the editor cannot answer your problem, they will forward the request to the author. We do try to protect the author from any distractions to their writing; however, we are quite happy to forward specific requests to them. All Wrox authors help with the support on their books. They will e-mail the customer and the editor with their response, and again all readers should benefit.

The Wrox Support process can only offer support to issues that are directly pertinent to the content of our published title. Support for questions that fall outside the scope of normal book support, is provided via the community lists of our `http://p2p.wrox.com/` forum.

p2p.wrox.com

For author and peer discussion join the P2P mailing lists. Our unique system provides programmer to programmer contact on mailing lists, forums, and newsgroups, all in addition to our one-to-one e-mail support system. If you post a query to P2P, you can be confident that it is being examined by many Wrox authors and other industry experts who are present on our mailing lists. At `p2p.wrox.com` you will find a number of different lists that will help you, not only while you read this book, but also as you develop your own applications. Particularly appropriate to this book are the beginning_vb and vb_dotnet lists.

To subscribe to a mailing list just follow these steps:

1. Go to `http://p2p.wrox.com/`.
2. Choose the appropriate category from the left menu bar.
3. Click on the mailing list you wish to join.
4. Follow the instructions to subscribe and fill in your e-mail address and password.
5. Reply to the confirmation e-mail you receive.
6. Use the subscription manager to join more lists and set your e-mail preferences.

Why This System Offers the Best Support

You can choose to join the mailing lists or you can receive them as a weekly digest. If you don't have the time, or facility, to receive the mailing list, you can search our online archives. Junk and spam mails are deleted and your own e-mail address is protected by the unique Lyris system. Queries about joining or leaving lists, and any other general queries about lists, should be sent to listsupport@p2p.wrox.com.

Welcome to Visual Basic .NET

The goal of this third edition is to help you come up to speed with the Visual Basic .NET language even if you have never programmed anything before. You will start slowly, and build on what you learn. So take a deep breath, let it out slowly, and tell yourself you can do this. No sweat! No kidding!

Programming a computer is a lot like teaching a child to tie their shoes. Until you find the correct way of giving the instructions, not much gets accomplished. Visual Basic .NET is a language in which you can tell your computer how to do things. But like a child, the computer will only understand if you explain things very clearly. If you have never programmed before, this sounds like an arduous task, and sometimes it is. However, Visual Basic .NET gives you a simple language to explain some complex things. Although it never hurts to have an understanding of what is happening at the lowest levels, Visual Basic .NET frees the programmer from having to deal with the mundane complexities of writing Windows programs. You are free to concentrate on solving problems.

Visual Basic .NET helps you create solutions that run on the Microsoft Windows operating system. If you are looking at this book, you might have already felt the need or the desire to create such programs. Even if you have never written a computer program before, as you progress through the *Try It Outs* in this book, you will become familiar with the various aspects of the Visual Basic .NET language, as well as its foundation in Microsoft's .NET Framework. You will find that it is not nearly as difficult as you have been imagining. Before you know it, you will be feeling quite comfortable creating a variety of different types of programs with Visual Basic .NET. Also, as the name implies, Visual Basic .NET can be used to create applications for use over the Internet and newly incorporated into Visual Studio .NET 2003 for its ability to create smart device applications (Pocket PCs and SmartPhones). However, while learning any new technology, you have to walk before you can run, so you begin by focusing on Windows applications before extending your boundaries to other platforms.

In this chapter, we will cover the following subjects:

- ❑ The installation of Visual Basic .Net 2003
- ❑ A tour of the Visual Basic .Net Integrated Development Environment (IDE)
- ❑ How to create a simple Windows program
- ❑ How to use and leverage the integrated help system

Windows Versus DOS Programming

A Windows program is quite different from its ancient relative, the MS-DOS program. A DOS program follows a relatively strict path from beginning to end. Although this does not necessarily limit the functionality of the program, it does limit the road the user has to take to get to it. A DOS program is like walking down a hallway; to get to the end you have to walk down the hallway, passing any obstacles that you may encounter. A DOS program would only let you open certain doors along your stroll.

Windows on the other hand, opened up the world of event-driven programming. Events in this context include, for example, clicking on a button, resizing a window, or changing an entry in a text box. The code that you write responds to these events. To go back to the hallway analogy: in a Windows program to get to the end of the hall, you just click on the end of the hall. The hallway can be ignored. If you get to the end and realize that is not where you wanted to be, you can just set off for the new destination without returning to your starting point. The program reacts to your movements and takes the necessary actions to complete your desired tasks (Visual Basic .NET).

Another big advantage in a Windows program is the abstraction of the hardware; which means that Windows takes care of communicating with the hardware for you. You do not need to know the inner workings of every laser printer on the market, just to create output. You do not need to study the schematics for graphics cards to write your game. Windows wraps up this functionality by providing generic routines that communicate with the drivers written by hardware manufacturers. This is probably the main reason that Windows has been so successful. The generic routines are referred to as the Windows Application Programming Interface (API).

Before Visual Basic 1.0 was introduced to the world in 1991, developers had to be well versed in C++ programming, as well as the rudimentary building blocks (Windows API) of the Windows system itself. This complexity meant that only the dedicated and properly trained individuals were capable of turning out software that could run on Windows. Visual Basic changed all of that, and it has been estimated that there are now as many lines of production code written in Visual Basic as in any other language.

Visual Basic changed the face of Windows programming by removing the complex burden of writing code for the user interface (UI). By allowing programmers to *draw* their own UI, it freed them to concentrate on the business problems they were trying to solve. Once the UI is drawn, the programmer can then add the code to react to events.

Visual Basic has also been extensible from the very beginning. Third-party vendors quickly saw the market for reusable modules to aid developers. These modules, or controls, were originally referred to as VBXs (named after their file extension). If you did not like the way a button behaved you could either buy or create your own. However, these controls had to be written in C or C++. Database access utilities were some of the first controls available. Version 5 of Visual Basic introduced the concept of ActiveX that allowed developers to create their own ActiveX controls.

When Microsoft introduced Visual Basic 3.0, the programming world changed again. Now you could build database applications directly accessible to users (so-called front-end applications) completely with Visual Basic. There was no need to rely on third-party controls. Microsoft accomplished this task with the introduction of the Data Access Objects (DAO), which allowed programmers to manipulate data with the same ease as manipulating the user interface.

Versions 4.0 and 5.0 extended the capabilities of version 3.0 in order to allow developers to target the new Windows 95 platform. Crucially they also made it easier for developers to write code, which could then be manipulated to make it usable to other language developers. Version 6.0 provided a new way to access databases with the integration of ActiveX Data Objects (ADO). ADO was developed by Microsoft to aid Web developers using Active Server Pages to access databases. With all of the improvements to Visual Basic over the years, it ensured its dominant place in the programming world. It helps developers write robust and maintainable applications in record time.

With the release of Visual Basic .NET in February 2002, many of the restrictions that used to exist have been obliterated. In the past, Visual Basic has been criticized and maligned as a "toy" language, as it did not provide all of the features of more sophisticated languages such as C++ and Java. Now, Microsoft has removed these restrictions and made Visual Basic .NET a very powerful development tool. This trend continues with Visual Basic .NET 2003. Although not as drastic a change as from Visual Basic 6 to Visual Basic .NET, there are enough improvements in the language (including support for the .NET Framework 1.1) that Visual Basic .NET 2003 is a welcome upgrade and is a great choice for programmers of all levels.

Installing Visual Basic .NET

You may own Visual Basic .NET:

❑   As part of Visual Studio .NET, a suite of tools and languages that also includes C# (pronounced C-sharp) and Visual C++ .NET. Visual Studio comes in three flavors: Professional, Enterprise Developer, and Enterprise Architect. Each of these versions comes with progressively more tools for building and managing the development of larger enterprise wide applications.

❑   As the Standard Edition, which includes a cut down set of the tools and languages available with Visual Studio .NET.

Both enable you to create your own applications for the Windows platform. The installation procedure is straightforward. In fact, the Visual Basic .NET Install is smart enough to figure out exactly what your computer requires to make it work.

The descriptions that follow are based on installing Visual Studio .NET Professional. However, all of Visual Studio .NET's languages use the same screens and windows (and hence look very similar), so you would not be seeing much that you would not see anyway.

<u>**Try It Out**</u>   **Installing Visual Basic .NET**

1.   The Visual Basic .NET CD has an auto-run feature, but if the Setup screen does not appear after inserting the CD, you have to run setup.exe from the root directory of the CD. To do this, go to your Windows Start menu (usually found right at the bottom of your screen) and select Run. Then type d:\setup.exe into the Open box, where d is the drive letter of your CD drive. After the setup program initializes you will see the screen as shown in Figure 1-1.

2.   This dialog box shows the order in which the installation takes place. To function properly, Visual Basic .NET requires that several components and updates be installed on your machine. Step 1 is the Windows component update, so click on the Windows Component Update link; you will then be prompted to insert the Component Update CD that came with your Visual Studio .NET disks.

Depending on how your operating system is configured you may receive the following message like the one shown in Figure 1-2 before you install the pre-requisites.

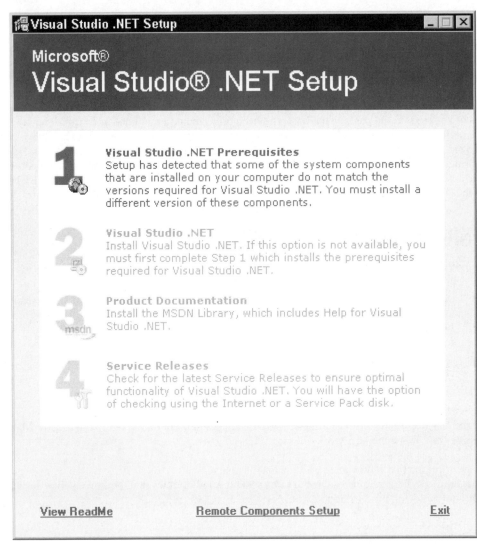

Figure 1-1

If you want to build Web applications locally you must install Internet Information Services (IIS) and Front Page Server Extensions. Clicking Setup Instructions takes you to a Web page with explicit instructions on how to install these components. You will have to restart the Visual Studio .NET / Visual Basic .NET installation after installing IIS. If you skip this step you will have to use a remote Web server to host your application.

3. The installation program then examines your system to see exactly which components have to be installed. Depending on the current state of your machine, this list could include any of the following items:

   ❑ Windows NT 4.0 Service Pack 6.0a

   ❑ Windows Installer 2.0

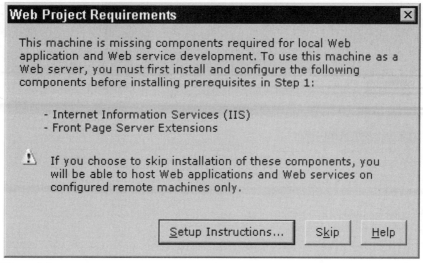

Figure 1-2

- Microsoft FrontPage 2000 Web Extensions Client
- Setup Runtime Files
- Microsoft Internet Explorer 6.0 with Service Pack 1
- Microsoft Data Access Components 2.7 with Service Pack 1
- Microsoft .NET Framework 1.1
- Microsoft Visual J# .Net Redistributable Package 1.1

If you don't know what some of those things are, don't worry about it. They are just Windows components that Visual Studio .NET or Visual Basic .NET requires.

4. After agreeing to the End User License agreement for the Prerequisite components, click Continue and the list of needed prerequisite components will be displayed.

Depending on what components you have already installed on your machine, your list of components that require updating may be different. For reference, these are the options on a completely patched version of Windows XP Professional that includes Internet Information Services.

5. Click Install Now! to begin the installation of the Prerequisites. After the Prerequisite install has finished, you will be returned to the initial Setup screen and step 2 will be enabled. You will now be able to install Visual Studio .NET, so click on Visual Studio .NET.

6. As with most installations you will be presented with an option list of components to install (see Figure 1-3). You can choose to install only the features that you need. For example, if your drive space is limited and you have no immediate need for Visual C++ .NET, you can exclude it from the installation. You will also be given the chance to select the location of items (although the defaults should suffice unless your particular machine has special requirements). Any option that is not chosen at the initial setup can always be added later as your needs or interests change.

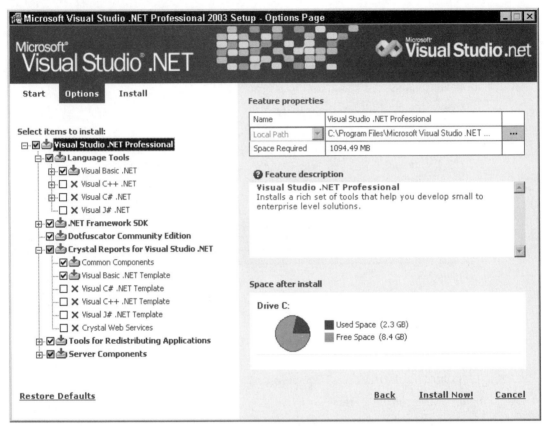

Figure 1-3

There are three sections of information given for each feature:

❑   The Feature properties section outlines where the required files will be installed and how much space will be needed to do this.

❑   The Feature description box gives you an outline of each feature and its function.

❑   Finally, the Space Allocation section illustrates how the space on your hard drive will be affected by the installation as a whole.

When you are running Visual Basic .NET, a lot of information is swapped from the disk to memory and back again. Therefore, it is important to have some free space on your disk. There is no exact rule for determining how much free space you will need, but if you use your machine for development as well as other tasks, anything less than 100MB free space should be considered a full disk.

7.   Once you have chosen all of the features you want, click Install Now! Installation will begin and you can sit back and relax for a bit. The setup time varies depending on how many features you chose to install. As a reference, the installation process took over an hour on a 650 MHz laptop computer with 256MB RAM, a 12GB hard drive, and running Windows XP Professional.

7. When installation is completed, you will see a dialog informing you that the installation has completed.

   Here you will see any problems that Setup encountered along the way. You are also given the chance to look at the installation log. This log provides a list of all actions taken during the installation process. Unless your installation reported errors, the installation log can safely be ignored. The Visual Studio .NET setup is nearly complete. Click Done to move on to installing the documentation.

8. Visual Studio .NET no longer includes the MSDN documentation as part of the installation. Instead it uses the separate MSDN Library installation routine. The big advantage in this is that one can always install the most current documentation regardless of what came out of your Visual Basic .NET box.

9. The MSDN Library installation is simple and straightforward and this section covers the highlights. After inserting disk one of the MSDN Library (assuming you are installing from CD) you will see the initial welcome screen.

10. This wizard interface guides you through the installation process. After gathering your License and User Information you will see the screen shown in Figure 1-4.

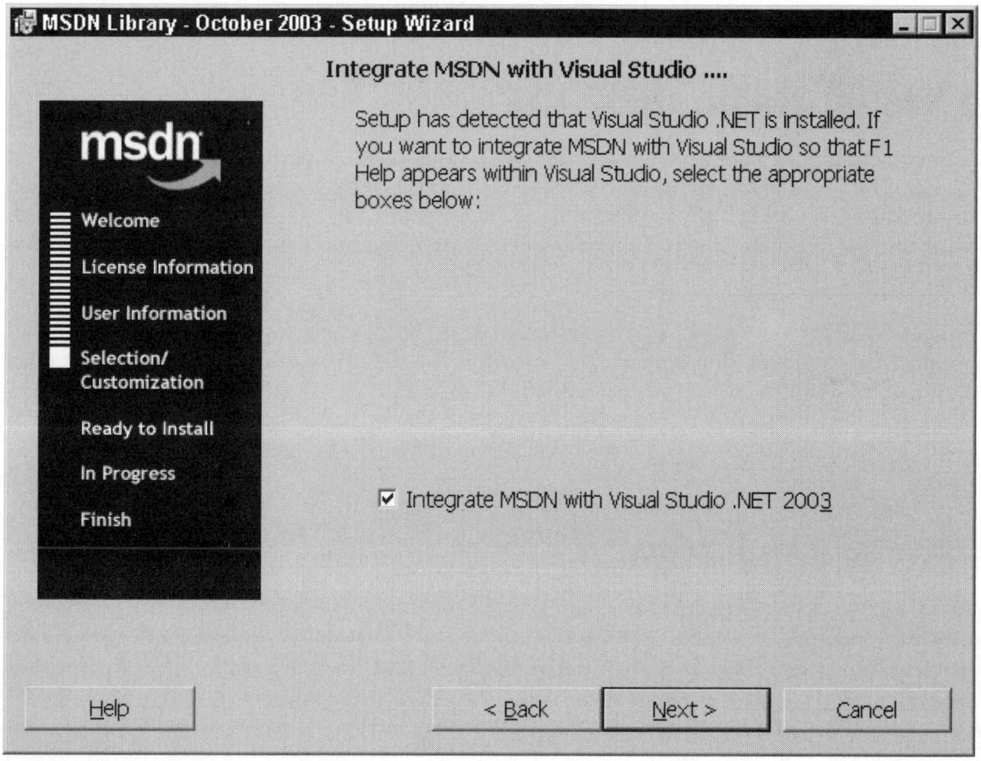

Figure 1-4

Make sure that the Integrate MSDN with Visual Studio .Net 2003 check box is checked so that Visual Studio .NET /Visual Basic .NET can find the MSDN documentation.

11. After clicking Next, you will be allowed to select the amount of the documentation you want to install. For example, if you did not install C++ there is probably little reason to install that documentation.

If you have the spare hard drive space, it is a very good idea to install the full documentation. MSDN does not always include specific examples or documentation for Visual Basic .NET; therefore you may find what you are looking for under SQL Server documentation, or even C#.

12. After the MSDN documentation has been installed you are returned to the initial setup screen again and the Service Releases option is now available.

It is a good idea to select Service Releases to check for updates. Microsoft has done a good job of making software updates available through the Internet. These updates can include anything from additional documentation to bug fixes. You will be given the choice to install any updates via a Service Pack CD or the Internet. Obviously, the Internet option requires an active connection. Since updates can be quite large, a fast connection is highly recommended.

Once you have performed the update process, Visual Basic .NET is ready to use. Now the real fun can begin! So get comfortable, relax, and let us enter the world of Visual Basic .NET.

The Visual Basic .NET IDE

You don't actually need the Visual Basic .NET product to write applications in the Visual Basic .NET language. The actual ability to run Visual Basic .NET code is included with the .NET Framework. You could actually just write all of your Visual Basic .NET using a text editor such as Notepad. You could also hammer nails using your shoe as a hammer, but that slick pneumatic nailer sitting there is probably a lot more efficient.

However, by far the easiest way to write in Visual Basic .NET is by using the Visual Studio .NET Integrated Development Environment, also known as the IDE. This is what you actually see when working with Visual Basic .NET—the windows, boxes, and so on. The IDE provides a wealth of features that are unavailable in ordinary text editors—such as code checking, visual representations of the finished application, and an explorer that displays all of the files that make up your project.

The Profile Setup Page

An IDE is a way of bringing together a suite of tools that make developing software a lot easier. Fire up Visual Basic .NET and see what you've got. If you used the default installation, go to your Windows Start menu and then Programs (All Programs on Windows XP and Windows Server 2003) ⇨ Microsoft Visual Studio.NET 2003 ⇨ Microsoft Visual Studio.NET 2003. A splash screen will briefly appear and then you should find yourself presented with the Start screen's My Profile tab, as shown in Figure 1-5.

This screen allows you to do some basic configuration of the IDE so that it serves you better. Since this IDE serves all the Visual Studio .NET languages, there are some settings to tailor it to our particular development interests. However, the default settings are acceptable for most users. Make any changes

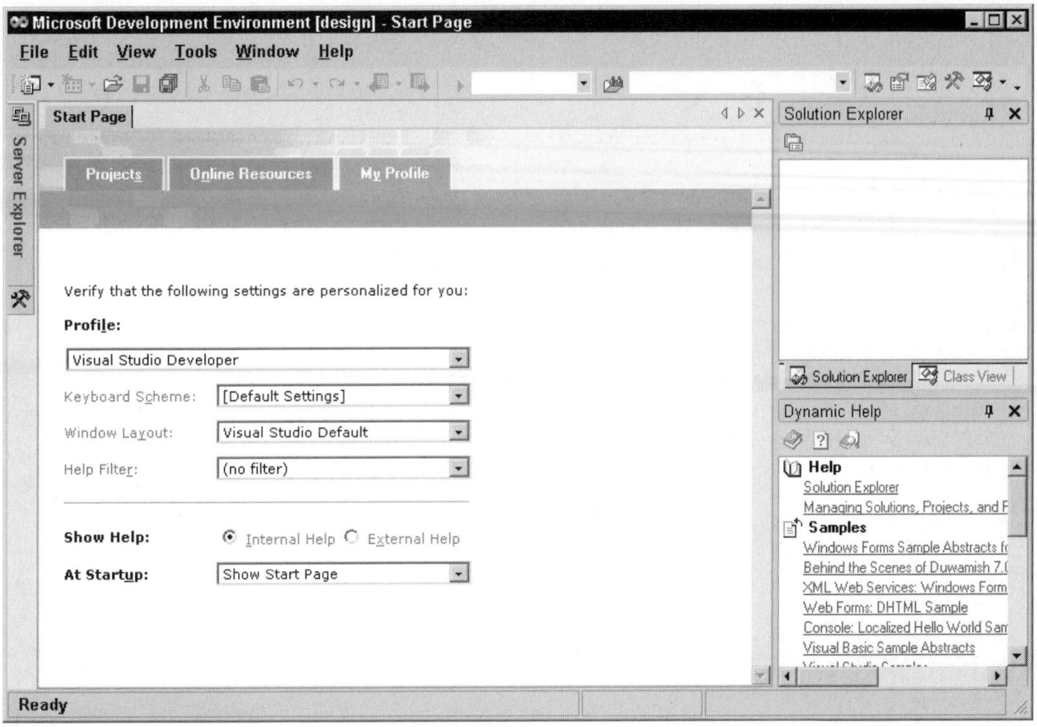

Figure 1-5

that you want and then click the Projects tab to be taken to that view. There you can create new projects and open existing projects.

The Projects Tab

By now, you may be a bit anxious to start writing some code. But first, take a look at the Projects tab on the Start Page and see what is there. Assuming that you have been following along while setting up Visual Studio .NET, your screen should now look something like Figure 1-6. Of course, since you have not created any projects yet, your project list will be empty. As you start creating projects, this list will grow and as you can see, the list contains the project name and the modified date. The project names are hyperlinks and clicking on a hyperlink for that project will open it up in the IDE.

Begin your exploration of the Visual Basic .NET IDE by looking at the toolbar and menu, which as you will learn are not really that different from toolbars and menus you have seen in other Microsoft software such as Word, Excel, and PowerPoint.

The Menu

Visual Studio .NET's menu is dynamic, meaning that items will be added or removed depending on what you are trying to do. While you are still looking at the Projects page, the menu bar will only consist of the

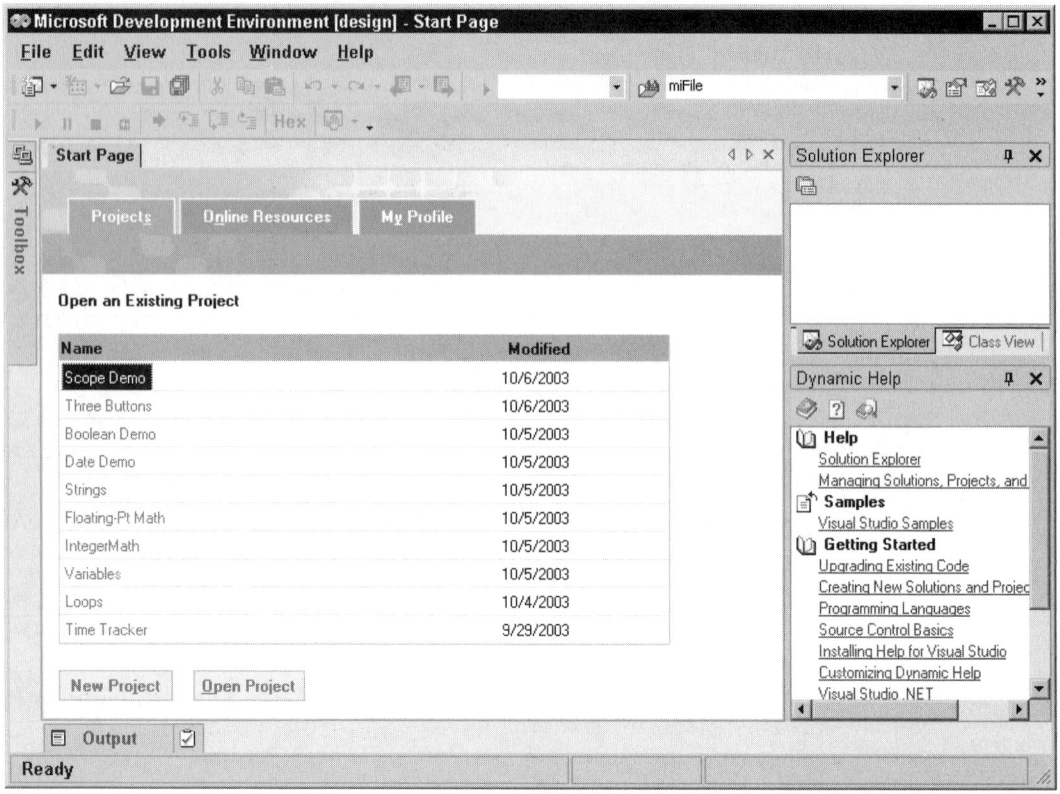

Figure 1-6

File, Edit, View, Tools, Window, and Help menus. However, when you start working on a project, the full Visual Studio .NET menu appears as shown in Figure 1-7.

Figure 1-7

At this point, there is no need to cover each menu topic in great detail. You will become familiar with each of them as you progress through the book. Here is a quick rundown of what activities each menu item pertains to:

❑ **File:** It seems every Windows program has a File menu. It has become the standard where you should find, if nothing else, a way to exit the application. In this case, you can also find ways of opening and closing single files and whole projects.

❑ **Edit:** The Edit menu provides access to the items you would expect: Undo, Redo, Cut, Copy, Paste, and Delete.

❑ **View:** The View menu provides quick access to the windows that make up the IDE, such as the Solution Explorer, Properties window, Output window, Toolbox, and so on.

❑ **Project:** The Project menu allows you to add various files to your application such as forms and classes.

❑ **Build:** The Build menu becomes important when you have completed your application and want to run it without the use of the Visual Basic .NET environment (perhaps running it directly from your Windows Start menu as you would any other application such as Word or Access).

❑ **Debug:** The Debug menu allows you to start and stop running your application within the Visual Basic .NET IDE. It also gives you access to the Visual Studio .NET debugger. The debugger allows you to step through your code while it is running to see how it is behaving.

❑ **Data**: The Data menu helps you to use information that comes from a database. It only appears when you are working with the visual part of your application (the [Design] tab will be the active one in the main window), not when you are writing code. Chapters 15 and 16 will introduce you to working with databases.

❑ **Format**: The Format menu also appears only when you are working with the visual part of your application. Items on the Format menu allow you to manipulate how the controls you create will appear on your forms.

❑ **Tools:** The Tools menu has commands to configure the Visual Studio .NET IDE, as well as links to other external tools that may have been installed.

❑ **Window:** The Window menu has become standard for any application that allows more than one window to be open at a time, such as Word or Excel. The commands on this menu allow you to switch between the windows in the IDE.

❑ **Help**: The Help menu provides access to the Visual Studio .NET documentation. There are many different ways to access this information (for example, via the help contents, an index, or a search). The Help menu also has options that connect to the Microsoft Web site to obtain updates or report problems.

The Toolbars

There are many toolbars available within the IDE, including Formatting, Image Editor, and Text Editor, which you can add to and remove from the IDE via the View ⇨ Toolbars menu option. Each one provides quick access to often-used commands, preventing you from having to navigate through a series of menu options. For example, the leftmost icon on the toolbar shown in Figure 1-8 (New Project) is available from the menu by navigating to File ⇨ New ⇨ Project.

The default toolbar (called Standard) appears at the top of the IDE as:

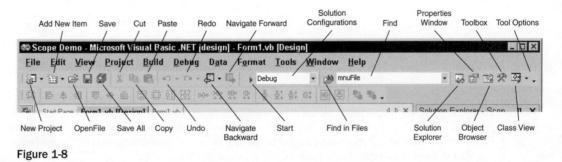

Figure 1-8

The toolbar is segmented into groups of related options, which are separated by a vertical bar. The first five icons provide access to the commonly used project and file manipulation options available through the File and Project menus, such as opening and saving files.

The next group of icons is for editing (Cut, Copy, and Paste). The third group of icons is for editing and navigation. The navigation buttons replicate functionality found in the View menu and allow you to cycle through the tabs at the top of the main window.

The fourth group of icons provides the ability to start your application running (via the blue triangle) and to specify build configurations. There are times when you want certain parts of your code only to appear in a debug version, a bit like a rough draft version of your application. For example, you may have code in your application that is only useful for tracking down problems in the application. When it is time to release your application to the world, you will want to exclude this code by setting the Solution Configurations settings to Release. You can also access the functionality offered by this group via the Build and Debug menus.

The next section allows you to locate parts of your code quickly. The simplest way to search is to type some text into the Find text box and press Enter. If the text is found, it will be highlighted in the central window. The Find in Files option allows you to specify more sophisticated searches, including matching the case of the text, looking in specific files or projects, and replacing the found text with new text. The search functionality can also be accessed via the Edit ➪ Find and Replace menu option.

The next group of icons provides quick links back to the Solution Explorer, Properties window, Object Browser, Toolbox, and Class view. If any of these windows are closed, clicking the appropriate icon will bring it back into view.

> *If you forget what a particular icon does, you can hover your mouse pointer over it so that a tooltip appears displaying the name of the toolbar option.*

You could continue to look at each of the other windows directly from the Start Page. But, as you can see they are all empty at this stage, and therefore not too revealing. The best way to look at the capabilities of the IDE is to use it while writing some code.

Creating a Simple Application

To finish your exploration of the Visual Basic .NET IDE you need to create a project, so that the windows shown earlier in Figure 1-6 actually have some interesting content for you to look at. You are now going to create a very simple application called HelloUser that will allow you to enter a person's name and display a greeting to that person in a message box.

Try It Out   Creating a HelloUser Project

1. Click on the New Project button on the Projects tab of the Start Page.

2. The New Project dialog box will open. Make sure you have Visual Basic Projects selected in the Project Types tree-view box to the left. Next, select Windows Application in the Templates box on the right. If you need to save this project to a location other than the default, be sure to enter it into the Location box. Finally, type HelloUser in the Name text box and click OK. Your New Project screen should look like Figure 1-9.

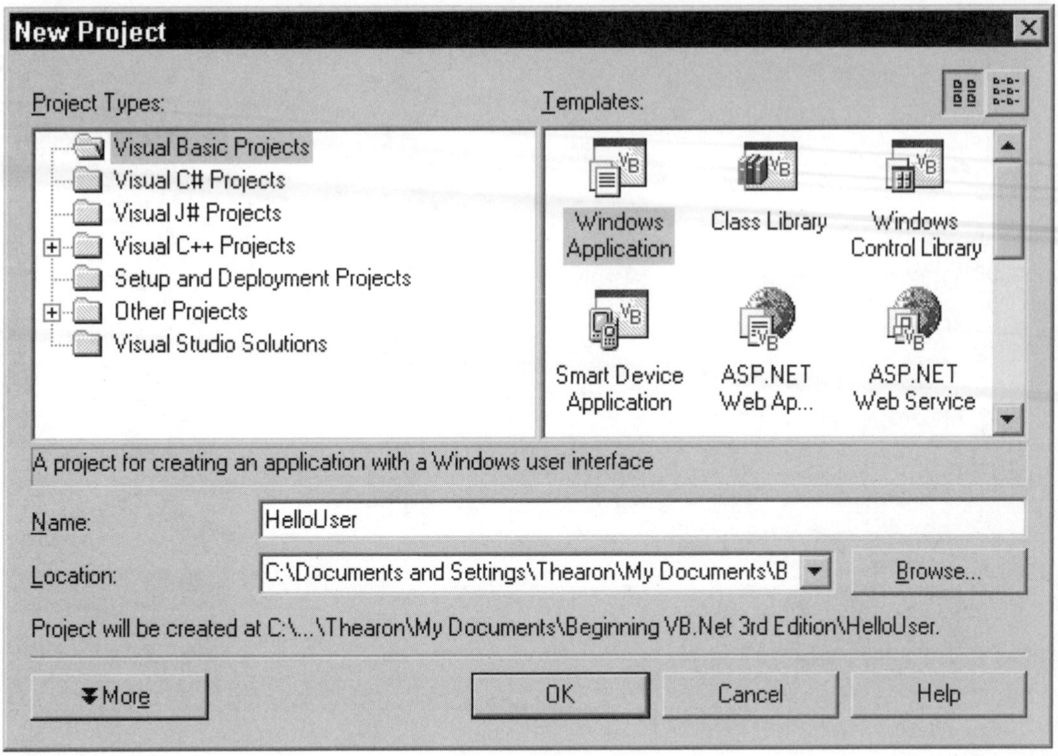

New Project

Project Types:
- Visual Basic Projects
- Visual C# Projects
- Visual J# Projects
- Visual C++ Projects
- Setup and Deployment Projects
- Other Projects
- Visual Studio Solutions

Templates:
- Windows Application
- Class Library
- Windows Control Library
- Smart Device Application
- ASP.NET Web Ap...
- ASP.NET Web Service

A project for creating an application with a Windows user interface

Name: HelloUser

Location: C:\Documents and Settings\Thearon\My Documents\B   Browse...

Project will be created at C:\...\Thearon\My Documents\Beginning VB.Net 3rd Edition\HelloUser.

[More]   [OK]   [Cancel]   [Help]

Figure 1-9

3. Visual Basic .NET will then create an empty Windows application for you. So far, your HelloUser program consists of one blank window called a Windows Form (or sometimes just a form), with the default name of Form1.vb, as shown in Figure 1-10.

Whenever Visual Studio .NET creates a new file, either as part of the project creation process or when you create a new file, it will use a name that describes what it is (in this case, a form) followed by a number.

Windows in the Visual Studio .NET IDE

At this point, you can see that the various windows in the IDE are beginning to show their purposes, and you should take a brief look at them now before you come back to the *Try It Out*. Note that if any of these windows are not visible on your screen, you can use the View menu to select and show them. Also if you do not like the location of any particular window you can move it by clicking on its title bar (the blue bar at the top) and dragging it to a new location. The windows in the IDE can float (stand out on their own) or be docked (as they appear in Figure 1-10). The following list introduces the available windows:

❑ **Server Explorer:** The Server Explorer gives you management access to the servers on your network. Here you can create database connections and view the services provided by the available servers. In Figure 1-10, the Server Explorer is a tab at the bottom of the Toolbox window.

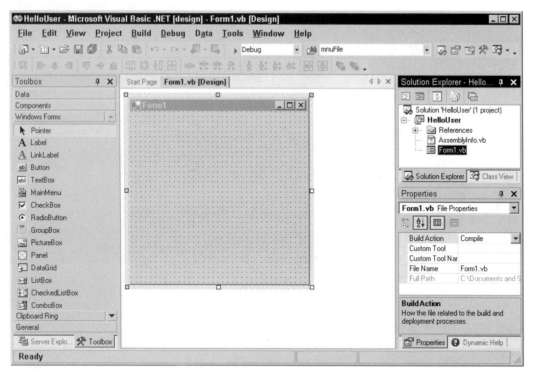

Figure 1-10

❑ **Toolbox:** The Toolbox contains reusable components that can be added to your application. These can range from buttons to data connectors to customized controls either purchased or developed by you.

❑ **Design Window:** The Design window is where a lot of the action takes place. This is where you will draw your user interface on your forms. This window is sometimes referred to as the Designer.

❑ **Solution Explorer:** The Solution Explorer window contains a hierarchical view of your solution. A solution can contain many projects while a project contains forms, classes, modules and components that solve a particular problem.

❑ **Class View:** The Class View window (shown as a tab at the bottom the Solution Explorer window) gives you a tree view of the classes in your program and shows the properties and methods that each contains. A class is a code file that groups data and the functions that manipulate it together into one unit. A property is data and a method is a function or subroutine.

❑ **Properties:** The Properties window shows what properties the selected object makes available. Although you can set these properties in your code, sometimes it is much easier to set them while you are designing your application (for example, drawing the controls on your form). You will notice that the File Name property has the value Form1.vb. This is the physical file name for the form's code and layout information.

❑ **Dynamic Help:** The Dynamic Help window (shown as a tab at the bottom of the Properties window) displays a list of help topics that relate to what has focus in the IDE. If you click on the form in the Design window and then open Dynamic Help, you will see a list of help topics relating to forms.

Creating a HelloUser Project (cont.)

1. Change the name of your form to something more indicative of what your application is. Click on Form1.vb in the Solution Explorer window. Then, in the Properties window, change the File Name property from Form1.vb to HelloUser.vb and press Enter, as shown in Figure 1-11. When changing properties you must either hit Enter or click off the property for it to take effect.

Figure 1-11

2. Notice that the form's file name has also been updated in the Solution Explorer to read HelloUser.vb.

3. Now click on the form displayed in the Design window; the Properties window will change to display the form's Form properties (instead of the File properties, which we have just been looking at). You will notice that the Properties window is dramatically different. The difference is the result of two different views of the same file. When the form name is highlighted in the Solution Explorer window, the physical file properties of the form are displayed. When the form in the Design window is highlighted, the visual properties and logical properties of the form are displayed.

The Properties window allows you to easily set a control's properties. Remember properties are a particular object's set of internal data. Properties usually describe appearance or behavior. In Figure 1-12, you can see that properties are grouped together in categories—Appearance (Header is not shown), Behavior, Configurations, Data, and Design are the ones shown here.

You can see that under the Appearance category (header not shown), even though we changed the file name of the form to HelloUser.vb, the text or caption of the form is still Form1. Also notice that the (Name) property under the Design category is still set to Form1. Unless this is changed any reference in the code to this form must refer to it as Form1.

4. Right now, the title (Text property) of your form (displayed in the bar at the top) is Form1. This is not very descriptive, so change it to reflect the purpose of this application. Locate the Text

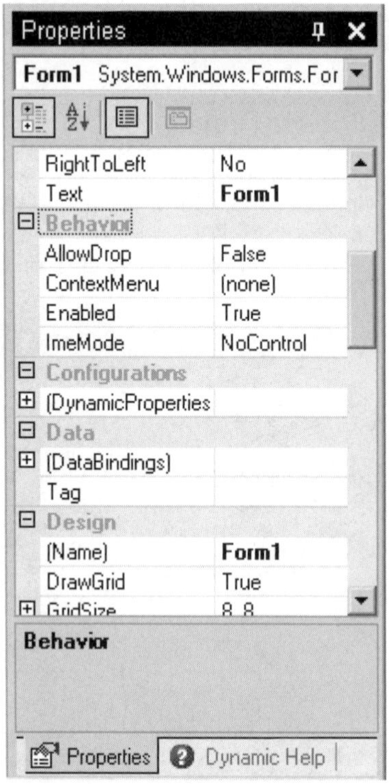

Figure 1-12

property in the Appearance section of the Properties window and change its value to Hello from Visual Basic .NET and press Enter. Notice that the form's title has been updated to reflect the change (see Figure 1-13).

If you have trouble finding properties, click the little AZ button on the toolbar toward the top of the Properties window. This changes the property listing from being ordered by category to being ordered by name.

5. You are now finished with the procedure. Click on the Start button on the Visual Studio .NET toolbar (the blue triangle) to run the application. As you work through the book, whenever we say "run the project" or "start the project," just click on the Start button. An empty window with the title Hello from Visual Basic .NET is displayed.

Notice how the grid patterns of dots have disappeared. These are displayed at design time to help place controls such as boxes, labels, and radio buttons onto your form. They're not needed (or even particularly desirable) at run time, so they're not shown.

That was simple, but your little application isn't doing much at the moment. Let us make it a little more interactive. To do this you are going to add some controls—a label, textbox, and two buttons to the form. This will let you see how the Toolbox makes adding functionality quite simple. You may be wondering at this point when you will actually look at some code. Soon! The great thing about Visual Basic .NET is that you can develop a fair amount of your application *without* writing any code. Sure, the code is still there, behind the scenes, but as you will see, Visual Basic .NET writes a lot of it for you.

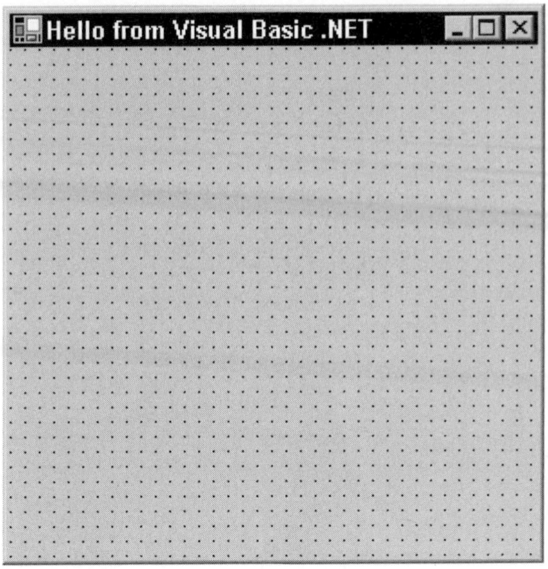

Figure 1-13

The Toolbox

The Toolbox is accessed via the View ⇨ Toolbox menu option, the Toolbox icon on the Standard menu bar, or by pressing *Ctrl+Alt+X*. Alternatively, the Toolbox tab is displayed on the left of the IDE and hovering your mouse over this tab will cause the Toolbox window to fly out, partially covering your form.

The Toolbox contains a tabbed view of the various controls and components that can be placed onto your form. Controls such as text boxes, buttons, radio buttons, and combo boxes can be selected and then *drawn* onto your form. For the HelloUser application, you will only be using the controls on the Windows Forms tab.

In Figure 1-14 you can see a partial listing of standard .NET controls for Windows Forms. The down arrow button to the right of the Clipboard Ring tab title actually scrolls the Windows Forms control list down as there are too many controls to fit. The up arrow button to the right of the Windows Forms tab scrolls the list up. Note that the order in which your controls appear may be different.

Controls can be added to your forms in any order, so it does not matter if you add the label control after the textbox or the buttons before the label.

Try It Out	Adding Controls to the HelloUser Application

1. Stop the project if it is still running, as you now want to add some controls to your form. The simplest way to do this is to click the X button in the top-right corner of the form. Alternatively, you can click on the blue square in the Visual Studio .NET IDE (which displays a tool tip of Stop Debugging if you hover over it with your mouse pointer).

2. Add a Label control to the form. Click Label in the Toolbox to select it. Move the cursor over the form's Designer. You'll notice that the cursor looks like a crosshair with a little floating letter A beneath it. Click and hold the mouse button where you want the top-left corner of the label and

Figure 1-14

drag the mouse to where you want the bottom right. (Placing controls on your form can also be accomplished by double-clicking on the required control in the Toolbox.)

3.   If the Label control you have just drawn is not in the desired location or is too big or too small, it really isn't a problem. Once the control is on the form you can resize it or move it around. Figure 1-15 shows what the control looks like after you place it on the form. To move it, click on the gray dotted border and drag it to the desired location. To resize it, click and drag on one of the white box "handles" and stretch the control in the needed direction. The corner handles resize both the horizontal and vertical dimension at the same time.

4.   After drawing a control on the form, we should at least configure its name and the text that it will display. You will see that the Properties window to the right of the Designer has changed to Label1, telling you that you are currently examining the properties for it. In the Properties window, set your new label's Text property to Enter Your Name and its (Name) property to lblName.

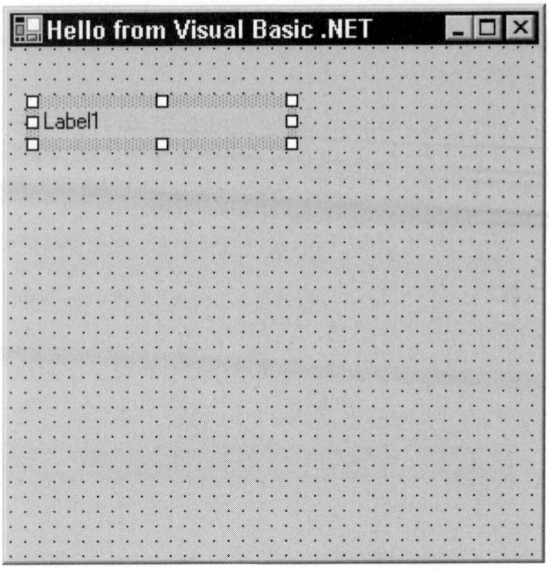

Hello from Visual Basic .NET `_ □ ✕`

□   □   □
□ Label1   □
□   □   □

Figure 1-15

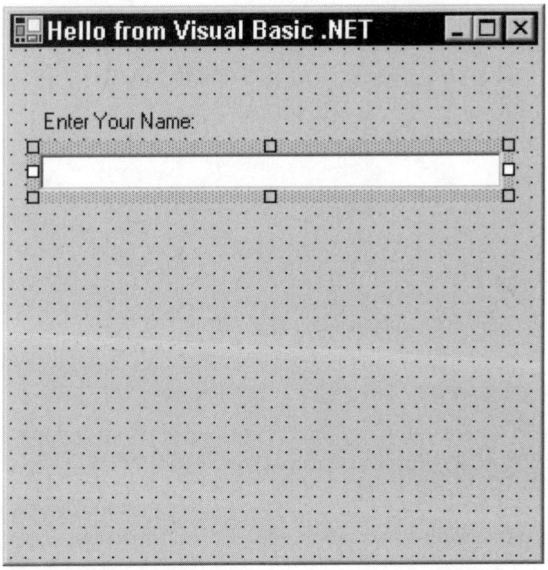

Hello from Visual Basic .NET `_ □ ✕`

Enter Your Name:
□   □   □

□   □

□   □   □

Figure 1-16

5.   Now, directly beneath the label, you want to add a textbox, so that you can enter a name. You are going to repeat the procedure you followed for adding the label, but this time make sure you select the TextBox from the toolbar. Once you have dragged-and-dropped (or double-clicked) the control into the appropriate position, use the Properties window to set its Name property to txtName and clear the Text property so that the textbox now appears to be blank as shown in Figure 1-16.

Notice how, out of the eight sizing handles surrounding the control, only two are shown in white. By default, the TextBox control cannot be made any taller than the absolute height necessary to contain the font that it will use to draw the text.

6. In the bottom left corner of the form, add a Button control in exactly the same manner as you added the label and textbox. Set its Name property to btnOK, and its Text property to & OK. Your form should now look similar to the one shown in Figure 1-17.

The ampersand (&) is used in the Text property of buttons to create a keyboard shortcut (known as a hot key). The letter with the & sign placed in front of it will become underlined (as shown in Figure 1-17) to signal users that they can select that button by pressing the Alt-letter key combination, instead of using the mouse (on some configurations the underline doesn't appear to the user until they press ALT). In this particular instance, pressing Alt+O would be the same as clicking directly on the OK button. There is no need to write code to accomplish this.

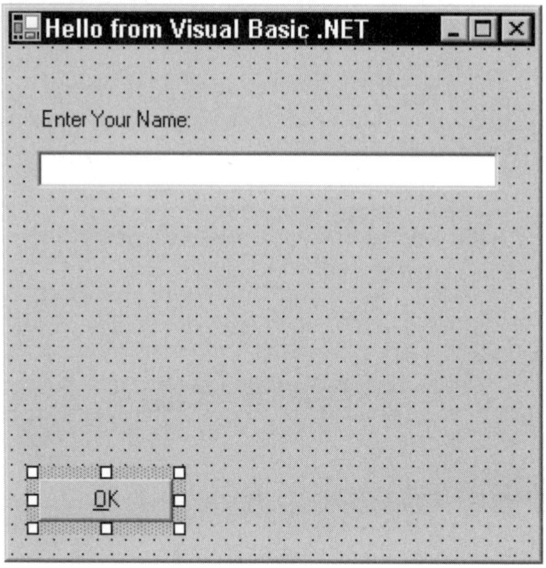

Figure 1-17

7. Now add a second Button control to the bottom right corner of the form and set the Name property to btnExit and the Text property to E&xit. Your form should look similar to Figure 1-18.

Now before you finish your sample application, let us briefly discuss some coding practices that you should be using.

Modified Hungarian Notation

You may have noticed that the names given to the controls look a little funny. Each name is prefixed with a shorthand identifier describing the type of control it is. This makes it much easier to understand what type of control you are working with when you are looking through the code. For example, say you had a control called simply Name, without a prefix of lbl or txt, you would not know whether you were working with a textbox that accepted a name or a label that displayed a name. Imagine if, in the previous

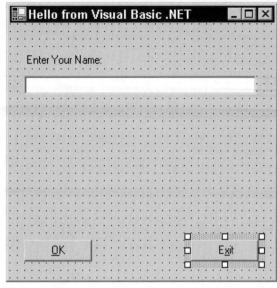

Figure 1-18

Try It Out, you had named your label Name1 and your textbox Name2—you would very quickly become confused. How about if you left your application for a month or two and then came back to it to make some changes?

When working with other developers, it is very important to keep the coding style consistent. One of the most commonly used styles used for controls within application development in many languages is Modified Hungarian notation. The notion of prefixing control names to identify their use was brought forth by Dr. Charles Simonyi. He worked for the Xerox Palo Alto Research Center (XPARC) before joining Microsoft. He came up with short prefix mnemonics that allowed programmers to easily identify the type of information a variable might contain. Since Dr. Simonyi is Hungarian, and the prefixes make the names look a little foreign, the name Hungarian Notation stuck. Because the original notation was used in C/C++ development, the notation for Visual Basic .NET is termed Modified. Table 1.1 shows some of the commonly used prefixes that you shall be using in this book.

Hungarian Notation can be a real time-saver when looking at code someone else wrote, or at code that you have written months past. However, by far the most important thing is to be consistent in your naming. When you start coding, pick a convention for your naming. It is recommended that you use the de facto standard Modified-Hungarian for Visual Basic .NET, but it is not required. Once you pick a convention, stick to it. When modifying someone else's code, use theirs. A standard naming convention followed throughout a project will save countless hours when the application is maintained. Now let's get back to the application. It's now time to write some actual code.

The Code Editor

Now that you have the HelloUser form defined, you have to add some code to actually make it do something interesting. You have already seen how easy it is to add controls to a form. Providing the

Table 1-1 Common prefixes in Visual Basic .Net

Control	Prefix
Button	cmd or btn
ComboBox	cbo
CheckBox	chk
Label	lbl
ListBox	lst
MainMenu	mnu
RadioButton	rdb
PictureBox	pic
TextBox	txt

functionality behind those on-screen elements is no more difficult. To add the code for a control, you just double-click on it. This will open the code editor in the main window, shown in Figure 1-19:

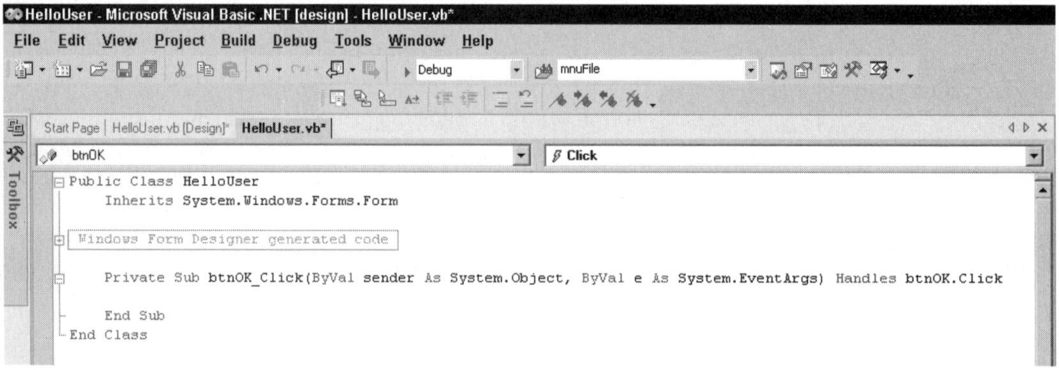

Figure 1-19

Notice that an additional tab has been created in the main window. Now you have the Design tab and the Code tab. You draw the controls on your form in the Design tab and you write code for your form in the Code tab. One thing to note here is that you have not created a separate file for the code. The visual definition and the code behind it both exist in the same file: HelloUser.vb. This is actually the reason why building applications with Visual Basic .NET is so slick and easy. Using the Design view you can visually lay out your application, and then using the Code view you add just the bits of code to implement your desired functionality.

You will also notice that there are two combo boxes at the top of the window. These provide shortcuts to the various parts of your code. If you pull down the one on the left you will see a list of all the objects within your application. If you pull down the one on the right you will see a list of all defined functions or subroutines for the object selected in the left combo box. If this particular form had a lot of code behind it, these pull-downs would make navigating to the desired area very quick—jumping to the selected area. However, since all of the code fits in the window, there are not a lot of places to get lost.

Now look at the code in the window. The code in Visual Studio .NET is set up into regions designated by the plus (+) and minus (–) buttons along the left side. These regions can be collapsed and expanded in order to simplify what you are looking at. If you expand the region labeled Windows Form Designer generated code, you will see a lot of code that Visual Basic .NET has automatically generated for you, which takes care of defining each of the controls on the form and how the form itself should behave. You do not have to worry about the code in this region, so collapse the Windows Form Designer generated code region once more and concentrate on the code you have to write.

Try It Out   **Adding Code to the HelloUser Project**

1. To begin adding the necessary code, click the Design tab to show the form again. Then double-click on the OK button. The code window will reopen with the following code. This is the shell of button's Click event and is the place where we enter the code that we want to run when we click on the button. This code is known as an event handler and sometimes is also referred to as an event procedure:

```
    Private Sub btnOK_Click(ByVal sender As System.Object, ByVal e As
System.EventArgs) Handles btnOK.Click

    End Sub
```

Due to the typographic constraints in publishing, it is not possible to put the Sub declaration on one line. Visual Basic .NET allows you to break up lines of code by using the underscore character (_) to signify a line continuation. The space before the underscore is required. Any whitespace preceding the code on the following line is ignored.

Sub is an example of a keyword. In programming terms, a keyword is a special word that is used to tell Visual Basic .NET to do something special. In this case, it tells Visual Basic .NET that this is a procedure. Anything that you type between the lines `Private Sub` and `End Sub` will make up the event procedure for the OK button.

2. Now add the highlighted code into the procedure:

```
    Private Sub btnOK_Click(ByVal sender As System.Object, ByVal e As
System.EventArgs) Handles btnOK.Click
    'Display a message box greeting the user
    MessageBox.Show("Hello," & txtName.Text & _
           "! Welcome to Visual Basic .NET.", _
           "HelloUser Message")
End Sub
```

Throughout this book, you will be presented with a code that you should enter into your program if you are following along. Usually, we will make it pretty obvious where you put the code, but as we go we will explain anything that looks out of the ordinary.

3. After you have added the code, go back to the Design tab, and double-click on the Exit button. Add the highlighted code to the btnExit _Click event procedure.

```
    Private Sub btnExit_Click(ByVal sender As System.Object, ByVal e As
System.EventArgs) Handles btnExit.Click
    'End the program and close the form
    Me.Close()
End Sub
```

You may be wondering what Me is. Me refers to the form. Just like the pronoun *me*, it is just a shorthand for referring to oneself.

4. Now that the code is finished, the moment of truth has arrived and you can see your creation. First though, save your work by using File ➪ Save from the menu, or by clicking the disk icon on the toolbar.

5. Now click on the Start button on the toolbar. You will notice a lot of activity in the Output window at the bottom of your screen. Provided you have not made any mistakes in entering the code, this information just lets you know what files are being loaded to run your application.

It is at this point that Visual Studio .NET will compile the code. Compiling is the activity of taking the Visual Basic .NET source code that you have written and translating it into a form that the computer understands. After the compilation is complete, Visual Studio .NET will run (also known as execute) the program and we'll be able to see the results.

If Visual Basic .NET encounters any errors, they will be displayed as tasks in the Task List window. Double-clicking on a task will transport you to the offending line of code. We will learn more about how to debug the errors in our code in Chapter 9.

6. When the application loads you will see the main form. Enter a name and click OK (or press the *Alt+O* key combination) (see Figure 1-20).

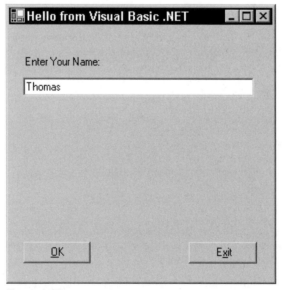

Figure 1-20

7. A window known as a message box appears, welcoming the person whose name was entered in the textbox on the form—in this case Thomas (see Figure 1-21).

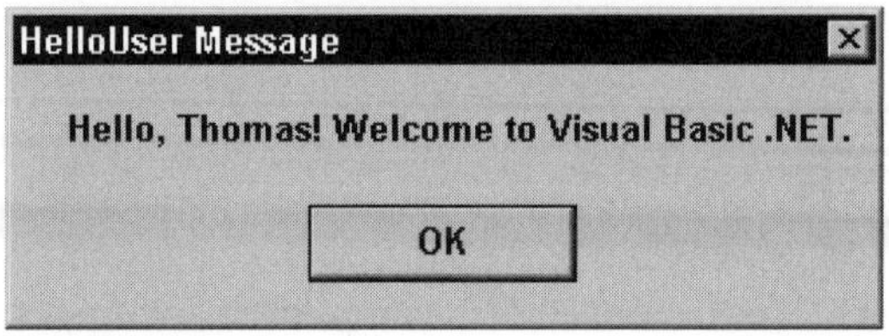

HelloUser Message ☒

Hello, Thomas! Welcome to Visual Basic .NET.

OK

Figure 1-21

8. After you close the message box by clicking the OK button, click on the Exit button on your form. The application will close and you will be brought back to the Visual Basic .NET IDE.

How It Works

The code that you added to the click event for the OK button will take the name that was entered in the text box and use it as part of the message that was displayed in Figure 1-21.

The first line of text entered in this procedure is actually a comment. Comments in Visual Basic .Net begin with a single quote (') and everything following is considered a comment.

The MessageBox.Show method displays a message box that accepts various parameters. As used in your code, you have passed the string text to be displayed in the message box. This is accomplished through the concatenation of string constants defined by text enclosed in quotes. Concatenation of strings is performed through the use of the ampersand (&) character.

In the code that follows, you have concatenated a string constant of "Hello," followed by the value contained in the Text property of the txtName text box control followed by a string constant of "! Welcome to Visual Basic .NET. ". The second parameter being passed to the MessageBox.Show method is the caption to be used in the title bar of the Message Box dialog box.

Finally, the underscore (_) character used at the end of the lines in your code below enables you to split your code onto separate lines. This tells the compiler that the rest of the code for the parameter is continued on the next line. This is really useful when building long strings as it allows you to view the entire code fragment in the code editor without having to scroll the code editor window to the right to view the entire line of code.

```
    Private Sub btnOK_Click(ByVal sender As System.Object, ByVal e As
System.EventArgs) Handles btnOK.Click
      'Display a message box greeting the user
      MessageBox.Show("Hello, " & txtName.Text & _
            "! Welcome to Visual Basic .NET", _
            "HelloUser Message")
    End Sub
```

The next procedure that you added code for was the Click event of the Exit button. Here you simply enter the code: Me.Close(). As explained earlier, the Me keyword refers to the form itself. The Close method of the form closes the form and releases all resources associated with it thus ending the program.

```
Private Sub btnExit_Click(ByVal sender As System.Object, ByVal e As
System.EventArgs) Handles btnExit.Click
'End the program and close the form
Me.Close()
End Sub
```

Using the Help System

The Help system included in Visual Basic .NET is an improvement over Help systems in previous versions. As you begin to learn Visual Basic .NET, you will probably become very familiar with the Help system. However, it is worthwhile to give you an overview, just to help speed your searches for information.

The Help menu contains the menu items shown in Figure 1-22:

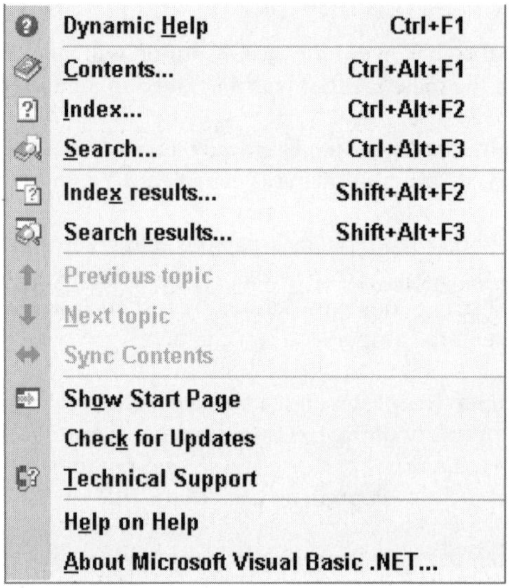

	Dynamic **H**elp	Ctrl+F1
	Contents...	Ctrl+Alt+F1
	Index...	Ctrl+Alt+F2
	Search...	Ctrl+Alt+F3
	Inde**x** results...	Shift+Alt+F2
	Search **r**esults...	Shift+Alt+F3
	Previous topic	
	Next topic	
	S**y**nc Contents	
	Sh**o**w Start Page	
	Chec**k** for Updates	
	Technical Support	
	H**e**lp on Help	
	About Microsoft Visual Basic .NET...	

Figure 1-22

As you can see this menu contains many more entries than the typical Windows application. The main reason for this is the vastness of the documentation. Few people could keep it all in their heads—but luckily, that is not a problem, as you can always quickly and easily refer to the Help system. Think of it as a safety net for your brain.

One really fantastic new feature is Dynamic Help. When you select the Dynamic Help menu item from the Help menu, the Dynamic Help window is displayed with a list of relevant topics for whatever you may be working on. If you followed the default installation and have not rearranged the IDE, the Dynamic Help is displayed as a tab behind the Properties window.

Let us say, for example, that you are working with a text box (perhaps the text box in the HelloUser application) and want to find out some information; you just select the textbox on our form or in the code window and you can see all the help topics that pertain to text boxes, as shown in Figure 1-23

Figure 1-23

The other help commands in the Help menu (Contents, Index, and Search), function just as they would in any other Windows application.

Summary

Hopefully, you are beginning to see that developing basic applications with Visual Basic .NET is not that difficult. You have taken a look at the IDE and saw how it can help you put together software very quickly. The Toolbox allows you to add controls quickly and easily to your programs. The Properties window makes configuring those controls a snap, while the Solution Explorer gives you a bird's eye view of the files that make up your project. You even wrote a little code.

In the coming chapters you will go into even more detail and get comfortable writing code. Before you go too far into Visual Basic .NET itself the next chapter will give you an introduction to the Microsoft .NET Framework. This Framework is what gives all of the .NET languages their ease of use, ease of interoperability, and simplicity in learning.

To summarize, you should now be familiar with:

- ❏ The Integrated Development Environment (IDE)
- ❏ Adding controls to your form in the Designer
- ❏ Setting the properties of your controls
- ❏ Adding code to your form in the code window

Exercises

At this point, you have not covered much about Visual Basic .NET, the language. So these exercises wouldn't be too difficult.

1.   What Modified-Hungarian prefix should you use for a combo box? A label? A textbox?

2.   (*This assumes you set the Help Filter to Visual Basic and Related.*) Open the Help System and search for MessageBox. Notice how many topics are returned. Change the Help Filter option on the My Profile screen, to No Filter. Repeat the search for MessageBox. Did the Help System return more or fewer topics?

3.   When creating a button, how would you make the button respond to a keyboard hot key?

The answers for these questions and those at the end of all the other chapters can be found in Appendix D.

2

The Microsoft .NET Framework

The .NET Framework provides an unprecedented platform for building desktop and Web applications with one or more languages. It is a definitive guide encompassing and encapsulating where we have come from as a development community and, of course, where we are going.

Today, .NET has been a real success in many respects, but its future was not all guaranteed. In fact, it was a large risk by Microsoft to move ahead with such a development when they did. Within the .NET Framework, a new language C# was born and a well-established Visual Basic was put to pasture. Not exactly a silver bullet for maintaining a customer base. In addition to the market share aspects, the entire company was involved in reshaping Microsoft's development tools and its future, which also illustrates the move by Microsoft. In fact, Microsoft risked a lot on this endeavor. It risked alienating a large development community. In general, developers around the world were somewhat skeptical of the Framework at first, including me.

When the first edition of this book was published, the Microsoft .NET Framework was being sent out, every fortnight. It was hard work learning evolving technology and writing about it. However, the overall concept has remained unchanged and it is this concept that has made the .NET Framework what it is today. The .NET Framework provides a very strong future and as you learn Visual Basic .NET, you will see some of its marvels.

In this chapter you will come across the following topics:

- ❑ Learn what the .NET Framework is
- ❑ Understand the .NET vision
- ❑ Learn why Microsoft dared to spend $2 billion on a single development project

Microsoft's Reliance on Windows

In terms of the great corporations of the world, Microsoft is still a new kid on the block. A fabulously rich and successful one, nonetheless the company has grown from nothing to a corporate superpower in a very short space of time.

What is perhaps more interesting is that although the origin of Microsoft can be traced back to the mid-1970s, it is really the Windows family of operating systems that has brought the company great success. Based on Presentation Manager for OS/2, Windows has seen many incarnations from Windows/286 to Windows XP, but the essential way that you use Windows and Windows applications has not changed in all that time. (Granted, there have been advances in the user interface and the hardware, but you still use the version of Excel included with Office XP in roughly the same way that you used the first version.)

The scary thing to Microsoft and its investors is that the pace of technological change means that in 2011, they cannot be sure that Windows is going to be as relevant as it is today. All it takes is one change in the way that people want to use computers and perhaps, just perhaps, the Windows platform's current incarnation may become obsolete.

It is unfair to say that Microsoft has been extremely lucky over the past 5 years in the way that it reacted to the new opportunities offered by the Internet. Yes, luck was involved, but do not underestimate the number of smart people working for that company! Once they discovered that companies like Netscape were making bucks with the Internet and identified the risk, they turned a gargantuan corporation on a dime and went after an unexplored market with teeth bared. So far, their gamble has paid off, but the announcement of the .NET Framework gives the impression that the strategists in Microsoft do not want to be scared like that again.

Luckily, for Microsoft, the applications that drove the adoption of the Internet worked well on a desktop operating system. Microsoft managed to adapt the Windows platform to provide the two killer Internet applications (e-mail and the Web) to the end user with a minimum of hassle, securing the Windows platform for another few years. It also delivered a number of great tools for developers, like ASP and IIS, and improved existing tools like Visual Basic and SQL, all of which made it easier for developers to build advanced Internet applications.

MSN 1.0

When the Internet started to become popular, Microsoft was trying to push the original incarnation of MSN. Rather than the successful portal that it is today, MSN was originally a proprietary dial-up service much like CompuServe. In the beginning, MSN did not provide access to the rich world of the Internet that we know today—it was a closed system. Let us call the original MSN, "MSN 1.0."

What MSN 1.0 did was to provide an opportunity for innovative companies to steal a march on Microsoft, which was already seen as an unshakable behemoth thanks to the combination of Windows and Office.

Imagine an alternative 1995 where Microsoft sticks to its guns with MSN 1.0, rather than plotting the course that brings it to where it is today. Imagine that a large computer manufacturer, like Dell, identifies this burgeoning community of forward-thinking business leaders and geeks called the Internet. Also say that Dell predicted that Microsoft's strategy is to usurp this community with MSN 1.0; in other words rather than cooperating with this community, Microsoft decides to crush it at all costs.

Now Dell needs to find a way to build this community. It predicts that home users and small businesses will love the Internet and so put together a very low cost PC. They need software to run on it and, luckily, predict that the Web and e-mail will be the killer applications of this new community. They find Linus Torvalds, who has been working on this thing called Linux since 1991 and they find Sun, which is keen to start pushing Java as a programming language to anyone who will listen. Another business partner builds a competent, yet usable, suite of productivity applications for the platform using Java. Another business partner builds easy-to-use connectivity solutions that allow the computers to connect to the Internet and other computers in the LAN, easily and cheaply.

Dell, Sun, and their selected business partners start pushing this new computer to anyone and everyone. The concept is a success and, for the first time since 1981, the dominance of the IBM-compatible PC is reduced, and sales of Microsoft products plummet. This is all because Microsoft did not move on a critical opportunity.

We all know that this did not happen, but there is nothing outlandish or crazy about this idea. It could have happened, and that is what scared Microsoft. It came very close to losing everything and .NET is its insurance against this happening again.

The .NET Vision

To understand .NET, you have to ignore the marketing hype from Microsoft and really think about what it is doing. With the first version of the framework and indeed even now, Microsoft appears to be pushing .NET as a platform for building Web services and large-scale enterprise systems. Although we cover Web services in Chapter 19, it is a tiny, tiny part of what .NET is about and, in my opinion, misinformation! In simple terms, .NET splits an operating systems platform, be it Windows, Linux, Mac, whatever, into two layers: a programming layer and an execution layer.

All computer platforms are trying to achieve roughly the same effect: to provide applications to the user. If I wanted to write a book, I would have the choice of using Star Office on Linux, or Word on Windows. However, I am using the computer in the same way, in other words the application remains the same irrespective of the platform.

It is a common understanding that software support is a large part of its success. Typically, the more high-quality software is available for a given platform, the larger the consumer adoption of that platform. The PC is the dominant platform because, back in the early-1980s, that is what the predominant target for software writers was. That trend has continued today and people are writing applications that run on Windows targets for the Intel ×86 type processors. The ×86 processor harks back to the introduction of the Intel 8086 processor in 1979 and today includes the Intel Pentium 4 processor and competitors like AMD's Athlon and Duron.

So without .NET, developers are still reliant on Windows, and Windows is still reliant on Intel. Although the relationship between Microsoft and Intel is thought to be fairly symbiotic, it is fair to assume that the strategists at Microsoft, who are feeling (rightly) paranoid about the future, might also want to lessen the dependence on a single family of chips, too.

The Windows/Intel combination (sometimes known as Wintel) is what is known as the execution layer. This layer takes the code and runs it—simple as that.

Although .NET targeted at the Windows platform, there is no reason why later versions of .NET cannot be directed at other platforms. Already, there are open-source projects, trying to recreate .NET for other platforms. What this means is that a program written by a .NET developer on Windows could run unchanged on Linux. In fact, between the first draft of this chapter and the time it went into editing, Miguel de Icaza, a prominent member of the Linux development community, began trying to put together the Ximian Mono project (www.go-mono.com/). This project is currently developing an open-source version of a C# compiler, a runtime for the Common Language Infrastructure (CLI, also known as the Common Intermediate Language—CIL), a subset of the .NET classes, and other .NET goodies independent of Microsoft's involvement.

.NET is a programming layer. It is totally owned and controlled by Microsoft. By turning all developers into .NET programmers rather than Windows programmers, software is written as .NET software, not Windows software.

To see the significance of this, imagine that a new platform is launched and starts eating up market share like crazy. Imagine that, like the Internet, this new platform offers a revolutionary way of working and living that offers real advantages. With the .NET vision in place, all Microsoft has to do to gain a foothold on this platform is develop a version of .NET that works on it. All of the .NET software now runs on the new platform, lessening the chance that the new platform will usurp Microsoft's market share.

In short, while Microsoft is a good innovator, what it is great at doing is taking someone else's bright idea and bringing it to the next level.

This Sounds Like Java

Some of this does sound a lot like Java. In fact, Java's mantra of "write once, run anywhere" fits nicely into the .NET doctrine. However, .NET is not a Java clone. Microsoft has a different approach.

To write in Java, developers were expected to learn a new language. This language was based on C++, and while C++ is a popular language, it is not the most popular language. In fact, the most popular language in terms of number of developers is Visual Basic and, obviously, Microsoft owns this. There are approximately 3 million Visual Basic developers worldwide, but bear in mind that this number includes Visual Basic professionals and also people who tinker with macros in the various Office products.

Whereas Java is "one language, many platforms," .NET is "many languages, one platform . . . for now." Microsoft wants to remove the barrier to entry to .NET by making it accessible to anyone who has used pretty much any language. The two primary languages for .NET are Visual Basic .NET and C#, and Visual Studio .NET comes supplied with both of these. (Other languages are in various stages of development, so developers should have no problems developing .NET applications in any language they feel comfortable with. A list of .NET language vendors can be found at www.gotdotnet.com/community/resources/default.aspx?ResourceTypeDropDownList =Language%20vendors.) Although C# is not C++, the developers of C++ should be able to migrate to C# with about the same amount of relearning that a Visual Basic 6 developer will have to do in order to move to Visual Basic .NET.

With Java, Sun attempted to build from the ground-up something so abstracted from the operating system that when you compare an application written natively in something like Visual C++ with a Java equivalent, it becomes fairly obvious that the Java version will run slower and not look as good in terms of user interface. In my opinion, Sun tried to take too big a bite out of the problem by straight away attempting to support everything, so that in the end it did not support one single thing completely.

Microsoft's .NET strategy is more like a military campaign. Firstly, it will use its understanding of the Windows platform to build .NET into something that will stand against a native C++ application. It will also try to bolster the lackluster uptake of Pocket PC with the Compact Framework. After its "won over the voters" on Windows, it may "invade" another platform, most likely Linux. This second stage will prove the concept that .NET applications can be ported from one platform to the next. After "invading and conquering Linux," it will move to another platform. Microsoft has been attempting to shake Solaris from the top spot in the server market for a long time, so it's likely that it'll go there next, probably with (and this is conjecture) as-yet-unannounced server products like SQL Server .NET and Exchange .NET.

If .NET works in the real world, you can expect to see the technology spreading across all facets of the industry: to the desktop, to servers, to network appliances, to set-top boxes, to PDAs, to cellphones, and so on. In fact, Microsoft has already announced and delivered versions of the Compact Framework designed for use with a Pocket PC.

Where Now?

Microsoft has bet its future on .NET. With developers writing software for the programming layer rather than an execution layer, it really does not matter whether Windows is the dominant platform in 2011 or Linux is, or whether something totally off the radar will be. If .NET works, developers will start calling themselves .NET developers, rather than C# developers and Visual Basic .NET developers. Eventually, Microsoft hopes we will simply call ourselves "developers."

The remainder of this chapter drills into the mechanics of .NET and takes a detailed look at how the whole thing works.

Writing Software for Windows

To understand how .NET works, look at how developers used to write software for Windows. The general principle is the same, only they had to do things in different ways to work with different technologies (COM, WIN32 API).

Any software that you write has to interact with various parts of the operating system in order to do its job. If the software needs a block of memory to store some data in, it interacts with the memory manager. To read a file from disk, you use the disk subsystem. To request a file from the network, you use the network subsystem. To draw a window on the screen, you use the graphics subsystem, and so on.

Where the system breaks down, as far as .NET is concerned, are that there is no commonality between the ways you use the subsystems on different platforms, despite the fact that platforms tend to have things in common. For example, even if you are writing an application for Linux, you may still need to use the network, disk, and screen subsystems. However, because different organizations developed these platforms, the way you open a file using the Linux platform may be different from the way you do it on Windows. If you want to move code dependent on one platform to another, you will probably have to rewrite portions of the code. You will also have to test the code to ensure it still works as intended.

Windows software communicates with the operating system and various subsystems using something called the Windows 32-bit Application Programming Interface, or Win32 API. Although object orientation was around at the time, this API was designed to be an evolution of the original Windows API, which predates the massive adoption of object-oriented techniques that are discussed in Chapter 10.

It is not easy to port API to other platforms, which is why (despite the fact that Linux has been around for 10 years) there is no version of the Win32 API for Linux. There is a cut-down version of the Win32 API for the Mac, but this has never received much of an industry following.

The Win32 API provides all basic stuff, but now and again, Microsoft extends the functionality of Windows with a new API. A classic example is the Windows Internet API, also known as the WinInit API. This API allows an application to download resources from a Web server, upload files to an FTP server, discover proxy settings, and so on. Again, it is not object oriented, but it does work.

A large factor in the success of early versions of Visual Basic is that it took the tricky-to-understand Win32 API calls and packaged them in a way that could be easily understood. Using the native Win32 API, it takes about a hundred lines of code to draw a window on the screen. The same effect can be achieved in Visual Basic with a few gestures of the mouse. Visual Basic represents an abstraction layer on top of the Win32 API that makes it easier for developers to use.

A long-time frustration for C++ developers was that a lot of the things that were very easy to do in Visual Basic remained not so much hard as laborious in C++. Conversely, developers like C++ because it gives them an amazing amount of control over how a program works, but at the cost that their programs take longer to write. Microsoft introduced the Microsoft Foundation Classes (MFC) because of this overhead, which, along with the IDE of Visual Studio, brought the ease of Visual C++ development a little towards that of Visual Basic.

The .NET Framework Classes

Unlike the Win32 API, .NET is totally object oriented. Anything you want to do in .NET, you are going to be doing with an object. If you want to open a file, you create an object that knows how to do this. If you want to draw a window on the screen, you create an object that knows how to do this. When you get to Chapter 10, you will discover that this is called encapsulation; the functionality is encapsulated in an object and you don't really care how it's done behind the scenes.

Although there is still the concept of subsystems in .NET, these subsystems are never accessed directly—instead they are abstracted away by the Framework classes. Either way, your .NET application will never talk directly to the subsystem (although you can do this if you really need or want to). Rather, you talk to objects that then talk to the subsystem. In Figure 2-1, the box marked System.IO.File is a class defined in the .NET Framework.

If you are talking to objects that talk to subsystems, do you really care what the subsystem looks like? Thankfully the answer is "no," and this is how Microsoft removes your reliance on Windows. If you know the name of a file, you use the same objects to open it whether you are running on Windows XP, a Pocket PC or, once the required Framework is released, Linux. Likewise, if you need to display a window on the screen, you do not care if it is on a Windows operating system or on a Mac.

The .NET Framework is actually a set of classes, called base classes. Although it is rather extensive, there are, at the time of writing, things not supported by .NET. This is because Microsoft needs to port everything from the old Win32 model to the new .NET model and some things are deemed more important than others.

Microsoft has developed the first release of .NET so that the vast majority of the functionality is in place. Developers moving from the old Win32 approach have to retrain great swathes of their knowledge to move to .NET as certain things are vastly different. Luckily, for you, as a reader of this book, you are likely to be a newcomer and so you will not have to go through the relearning process. You only have to learn it, without forgetting what you used to know!

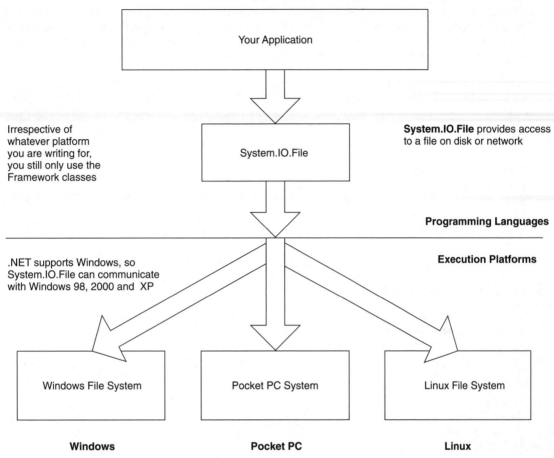

Irrespective of whatever platform you are writing for, you still only use the Framework classes

System.IO.File provides access to a file on disk or network

Programming Languages

Execution Platforms

.NET supports Windows, so System.IO.File can communicate with Windows 98, 2000 and XP

Figure 2-1

The class library itself is vast. There are several thousand objects available to developers, although in your day-to-day development you will only need to understand a handful of these to create some powerful applications.

The other wrinkle to this is that the classes are the same irrespective of the language used. So, if you are writing a Visual Basic .NET application, you use the same object as you would from within a C# application. That object will have the same methods, properties, and events, meaning that there is very little difference in capabilities between the two languages, since they both rely on the framework.

Executing Code

The class library is only half the equation. Once you have written the code that interacts with the classes, you still need to run it. This poses a tricky problem; to remove the reliance on the platform is to remove the reliance on the processor.

Whenever you write software for Windows, you are guaranteed that this code will run on an Intel ×86 chip. With .NET, Microsoft does not want to make this guarantee. It might be that the dominant chip in 2006 is a Transmeta chip, or something you have never even seen. What you need to do is abstract .NET away from the processor in a similar fashion to the way you abstracted .NET from the underlying subsystem implementations.

If you wrote an application with Visual Basic 6, you had to compile it into a set of ×86 instructions (collectively known as machine code or assembly) before you could deploy it. This machine code would then be installed and executed on any machine that supports ×86 instructions. Well, that is a mild oversimplification because the application also needs to have Windows around in order to run, but you get the idea.

Programming languages are somewhere in-between the languages that you and I speak every day and the language that the computer itself understands. The language that a computer uses is the machine code (sometimes called machine instructions). When you are using a PC with an Intel or competing processor, this language is more specifically known as ×86 machine instructions.

If you write an application with Visual Basic .NET, you still have to compile the code. However, you do not compile the Visual Basic .NET code directly into ×86 machine instructions as this would mean that the resulting program would only run on processors that support this language—in other words, the program would only run on Intel chips and their compatible competitors. Instead, compilation creates something called Microsoft Intermediate Language, or MSIL. This language is not dependent on any processor. It is a layer above the traditional machine code.

MSIL code will not just run on any processor as processors do not understand MSIL. In order to run the code, it has to be further compiled, as shown in Figure 2-2, from MSIL code into the native code that the processor understands.

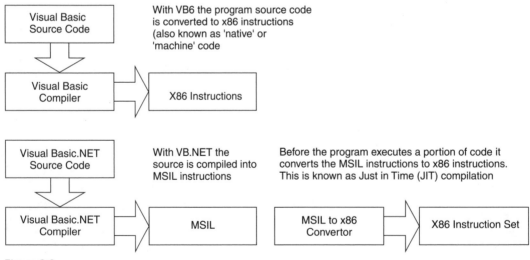

Figure 2-2

However, this approach also provides the industry with a subtle problem. In a world where .NET is extremely popular (some might say dominant), who is responsible for developing an MSIL-to-native compiler when a new processor is released? Is the new processor at the mercy of Microsoft's willingness to port .NET to the chip? Time, as they say, will tell!

Take a look at the thing that makes .NET work: the common language runtime.

Common Language Runtime

The common language runtime is the heart of .NET. The common language runtime takes your .NET application, compiles it into native processor code, and runs it. It provides an extensive range of functionality for helping the applications run properly, so look at each one in turn.

- ❏ Loading and executing code
- ❏ Application isolation
- ❏ Memory management
- ❏ Security
- ❏ Exception handling
- ❏ Interoperation

Do not worry if you do not understand what all these are—the following sections discuss all of them except for memory management. Memory management is quite a complex subject and is discussed in Chapter 11.

Loading and Executing Code

This part of the common language runtime deals with pulling the MSIL code from the disk and running it. It compiles the code from MSIL into the native language (machine code) that the processor understands.

Java also has a similar concept to MSIL known as byte code.

Application Isolation

One important premise of modern operating systems like Windows and Linux is that applications are isolated from one another. This is critically important from both security and stability standpoints.

Imagine that you have a badly written program and it crashes the PC. Should this happen? Instead, you only want the badly behaved program to crash, as you do not want other applications or even the operating system itself to be affected by a program running on it. For example, if your e-mail program crashes, you do not want to lose any unsaved changes in your word processor. With proper application isolation, one application crashing should not cause others to crash.

In some instances, even on Windows 2000, a badly behaved program can do something so horrendous that the entire machine crashes. This is commonly known as a Blue Screen of Death, or BSOD, so called because your attractive Windows desktop is replaced with a stark blue screen with a smattering of white text "explaining" the problem. This problem should be alleviated in .NET, but it is unlikely to be completely solved.

The other aspect to application isolation is one of security. Imagine that you are writing a personal and sensitive e-mail. You do not want other applications running on your computer to be able to grab the contents of the e-mail and pass it on to someone else. Traditionally, applications running in an isolated model cannot just take what they want. Instead, they have to ask if they can have something and, if they can, they are given it.

This level of application isolation is already available in Windows. .NET extends and enhances this functionality by further improving it.

Security

.NET has a powerful support for is the concept of code security. This was designed to give system administrators, users, and software developers a fine level of control over what a program can and cannot do.

Imagine that you have a program that scans your computer's hard disk looking for Word documents. You might think this is a useful program if it is the one that you run yourself in order to find documents that are missing. Now imagine that this program is delivered through e-mail and it automatically runs and e-mails copies of any "interesting" documents to someone else. You are less likely to find that useful.

This is the situation you find yourself in today with old-school Windows development. To all intents and purposes, Windows applications have unrestricted access over your computer and can do pretty much anything they want. That is why the Melissa and "I Love You" type viruses are possible—Windows does not understand the difference between a benign script file you write yourself, which looks through your address book and sends e-mails to everyone, and those written by someone else and delivered as viruses.

With .NET this situation will change because of the security features built into the common language runtime. Code requires "evidence" to run. This evidence can be policies set by you and your system administrator, as well as the origin of the code (for example, whether it came off your local machine, off a machine on your office network, or over the Internet).

Security is a very involved topic and is not covered in this book. However, you can find more information in *.NET Security Programming* (ISBN 0-471-22285-2).

Interoperation

Interoperation in the .NET Framework is achieved on various levels, which is not covered here. However, I must just point out some of the types of interoperation that it provides. One kind of interoperation is at the core of the framework where data types are shared by all managed languages. This is known as the Common Type System (CTS). This is a great improvement for language interoperability (see *The Common Type System and Common Language Specification* section).

The other type of interoperation is that of communicating with existing COM interfaces. Since a large application software base is written in COM, it was inevitable that .NET should be able to communicate with existing COM libraries. This is also known as COM interop.

Exception Handling

Exception handling is the concept of dealing with "exceptional happenings" when you are running the code. Imagine that you have written a program that opens a file on disk. What if that file is not there? Well, the fact that the file is not there is exceptional and you need to deal with it in some way. It could be that you crash, or you could display a window asking the user to supply a new filename. Either way, you have a fine level of control over what happens when an error does occur.

.NET provides a powerful exception handler that can "catch" exceptions when they occur and give your programs the opportunity to react and deal with the problem in some way. Chapter 11 talks about exception handling in more detail, but for now, think of exception handling as something provided by the common language runtime to all applications.

The Common Type System and Common Language Specification

One of the most important aspects of .NET that Microsoft has to get right is inter-language operation. Remember, Microsoft's motivation is to get any developer using any language using .NET, and in order for this to happen all languages should be treated equally. Likewise, applications created in one language have to be understood by other languages. For example, if I create a class in Visual Basic .NET, a C# developer should be able to use and extend that class. Alternatively, if I define a string in C#, I need to pass that to an object built in Visual Basic .NET, and make that object understand and manipulate the string successfully.

The Common Type System (CTS) allows software written in different languages to work together. Before .NET, the way that Visual Basic and C++ handled strings was done completely differently, meaning that each time you went from one to the other you had to go through a conversion process. With the Common Type System in place, Visual Basic .NET, C#, and other .NET languages use strings, integers, and so on, in the same way and therefore no conversion needs to take place.

In addition, the Common Language Specification (CLS) was introduced by Microsoft to make it easier for language developers to adapt their languages to make them compatible with .NET.

> *The Common Type System and Common Language Specifications are the foundation for this interoperation, but detailed discussion is unfortunately beyond the scope of this book.*

When talking to other .NET developers, it is likely that you will hear the term *managed code.* This simply describes code that runs inside the common language runtime. In other words, you get all of the advantages of the common language runtime such as the memory management and all of the language interoperability features previously mentioned.

Code written in Visual Basic .NET and C# is automatically created as managed code. C++ code is not automatically created as managed code because C++ does not fit well into the memory management scheme implemented by the common language runtime. You can, if you are interested, turn on an option to create managed code from within C++, in which case you use the term managed C++.

Hand-in-hand with managed code is managed data. As you can probably guess, this is data managed by the common language runtime, although in nearly all cases this data is actually objects. Objects managed by the common language runtime can easily be passed between languages.

Summary

This chapter introduced the Microsoft .NET Framework from the perspective of why Microsoft had chosen to radically change the way programs were written for Windows. You also saw that part of Microsoft's motivation for this was to move the dependence of developers from the execution platform (Windows, Linux, whatever) over to a new programming platform that it would always own.

After learning about why Microsoft developed .NET, you saw how writing for it is not much different from writing for Windows previously. You still have a layer that you program against; it is just that now, rather than being flat like the Win32 API, it is a rich set of classes. This chapter also discussed how these classes could be ported to other platforms, and how our applications could transfer across.

Finally, you looked at some of the more technical aspects of the .NET Framework, specifically the common language runtime.

To summarize, you should now understand:

❑ Microsoft's new business venure

❑ The goals of the .NET Framework

❑ The abstractions that the .NET Framework provides

❑ An introduction to the core of the .NET Framework

Exercises

1. What is the general premise behind .NET?
2. What is the similarity between .NET and Java?
3. What is the Framework Class Library?
4. How is application code compiled in .NET?

Writing Software

Now that you have gotten Visual Basic .NET up and running, and even written a simple but working program, you're going to look at the fundamentals behind the process of writing software and start putting together some exciting programs of your own.

In this chapter, you will:

- ❑   Learn about algorithms
- ❑   Learn to use variables
- ❑   Explore different data types including integers, floating-point numbers, strings, and dates
- ❑   Study scope
- ❑   Learn about debugging applications
- ❑   Learn more about how computers store data in memory

Information and Data

Information describes facts and can be presented or found in any format, whether that format is optimized for humans or for computers. For example, if you send four people out to survey cars at a particular intersection, at the end of the process you will end up with four handwritten tallies of the number of cars that went past.

Data is used to describe information that has been collated, ordered, and formatted in such a way that it can be directly used by a piece of computer software. The information you have (several notebooks full of handwritten scribbles) cannot be directly used by a piece of software. Rather, someone has to work with it to convert it into data, for example, the scribbles can be transferred to an Excel spreadsheet that can be directly used by a piece of software designed to analyze the results.

Algorithms

The computer industry is commonly regarded as one that changes at an incredible speed. Most professionals find themselves constantly retraining and re-educating to keep their skills sharp and up to date. However, some aspects of computing haven't really changed since they were first invented and perhaps won't change within our lifetimes. The process and discipline of software development is a good example of an aspect of computer technology whose essential nature hasn't changed since the beginning.

For software to work, you need to have some data to work with. The software then takes this data and manipulates it into another form. For example, software may take your customer database stored as ones and zeros on your computer's disk and make it available for you to read on your computer's monitor. The on-board computer in your car constantly examines environmental and performance information and continually adjusts the fuel mix to make the car run more efficiently. Your telephone service provider records the calls you make and generates bills based on this information.

The base underpinning all software is the algorithm. Before you can write software to solve a problem, you have to break it down into a step-by-step description of how the problem is going to be solved. An algorithm is independent of programming language and so, if you like, you can describe it to yourself either as a spoken language, or with diagrams, or with whatever helps you visualize the problem.

Imagine you work for a telephone company and you need to produce bills based on calls that your customers make. Here's an algorithm that describes a possible solution:

❑ On the first day of the month, you need to produce a bill for each customer you have.

❑ For each customer, you have a list of calls that the customer has made in the previous month.

❑ You know the duration of each call, and the time of day when the call was made. Based on this information, you can determine the cost of each call.

❑ For each bill, you total up the cost of each call.

❑ If a customer spends more than a preset limit, you give them a 10% discount.

❑ You apply sales tax to each bill.

❑ After you have the final bill, you need to print it.

Those seven points describe, fairly completely, an algorithm for a piece of software that generates bills for a telephone company. At the end of the day, it doesn't matter if you build this solution in C++, Visual Basic .NET, C#, Java, or whatever—the basic algorithms of the software never change. (However, it's important to realize that each of those seven parts of the algorithm may well be made up of algorithms.)

The good news for a newcomer to programming is that algorithms are usually easy to construct. There shouldn't be anything in the preceding algorithm that you don't understand. Algorithms always follow common-sense reasoning, although you may find yourself in a position in which you have to code algorithms that contain complex mathematical or scientific reasoning. It may not seem like common sense to you, but it will to someone else! The bad news is that the process of turning the algorithm into code can be arduous. As a programmer, learning how to construct algorithms is the most important skill you will ever obtain.

All good programmers respect the fact that the preferred language of the programmer is largely irrelevant. Different languages are good at doing different things. C++ gives the developer a lot of control over the way a program works; however, it's harder to write software in C++ than it is in Visual Basic .NET. Likewise, building the user interface for desktop applications is far easier to do in Visual Basic .NET than it is in C++. (Some of these problems do go away when using managed C++ with .NET, so this statement is less true today than it was a few years ago.) What you need to learn to do as a programmer is to adapt different languages to achieve solutions to a problem in the best possible way. Although when you begin programming you'll be "hooked" on one language, remember that different languages are focused toward developing different kinds of solutions. At some point in the future, you may have to take your basic skills as an algorithm designer and coder to a new language.

What Is a Programming Language?

In one way, you can regard a programming language as anything capable of making a decision. Computers are very good at making decisions, but they have to be fairly basic, for example: "Is four greater than three?" or "Is the car blue?"

If you have a complicated decision to make, the process of making that decision has to be broken down into simple parts that the computer can understand. You use algorithms to determine how to break down a complicated decision into simpler ones.

A good example of a problem that's hard for a computer to solve is recognizing peoples' faces. You can't just say to a computer, "Is this a picture of Dave?" Instead, you have to break the question down into a series of simpler questions that the computer can understand. The decisions that you ask computers to make, will have one of two possible answers: yes and no. You also refer to these possibilities as true and false and also as 1 and 0.

You might be looking at this as a limitation, and you're right so far as the intelligence of human beings goes, but it's not a limitation when it comes to building software. In software terms, you cannot make a decision based on the question, "How much bigger is 10 compared to 4?" Instead, you have to make a decision based on the question, "Is 10 bigger than 4?" The difference is subtle, yet important—the first question does not yield an answer of yes or no, whereas the second question does.

Of course, a computer is more than capable of answering the first question, but this is actually done through an operation; in other words, you have to actually subtract 4 from 10 to use the result in some other part of your algorithm.

You are using Visual Basic .NET for a language, but the important aspects of programming are largely language independent. Understanding that any software, no matter how flashy, whizzy it is, or which language it is written in, is made up of *methods* (functions and subroutines: the lines of code that actually implement the algorithm) and *variables* (place holders for the data the methods manipulate) is key.

Variables

A variable is something that you store a value in as you work through your algorithm. You can then make a decision based on that value (for example, "Is it equal to 7?", "Is it more than 4?") or you can perform operations on that value to change it into something else (for example, "Add 2 to the value", "Multiply it by 6", and so on).

Working with Variables

Before you get bogged down in code for a moment, look at another algorithm:

❑　Create a variable called "n" and store in it the value "27"

❑　Add 1 to the variable called "n" and store it

❑　Display the value of variable "n" to the user

In this algorithm, you're creating a variable called n and storing in it the value 27. What this means is that there's a part of the computer's memory that is being used by the program to store the value 27. That piece of memory keeps storing that value until you change it or tell the program that you don't need it any more.

In the second bullet point, you're performing an add operation. You're taking n and adding 1 to its value. After you've performed this operation, the piece of memory given over to storing n contains the value 28.

In the final bullet point, you want to tell the user what the value of n is. So, you read the current value from memory and write out to the screen.

Again, there's nothing about the algorithm there that you can't understand. It's just common sense! However, the Visual Basic .NET code looks a little more cryptic.

Try It Out   Working with Variables

1. Create a new project in Visual Studio .NET by selecting File ➪ New ➪ Project from the menu. When asked, select Windows Application from the right-hand pane and enter the project name as **Variables** (see Figure 3-1)

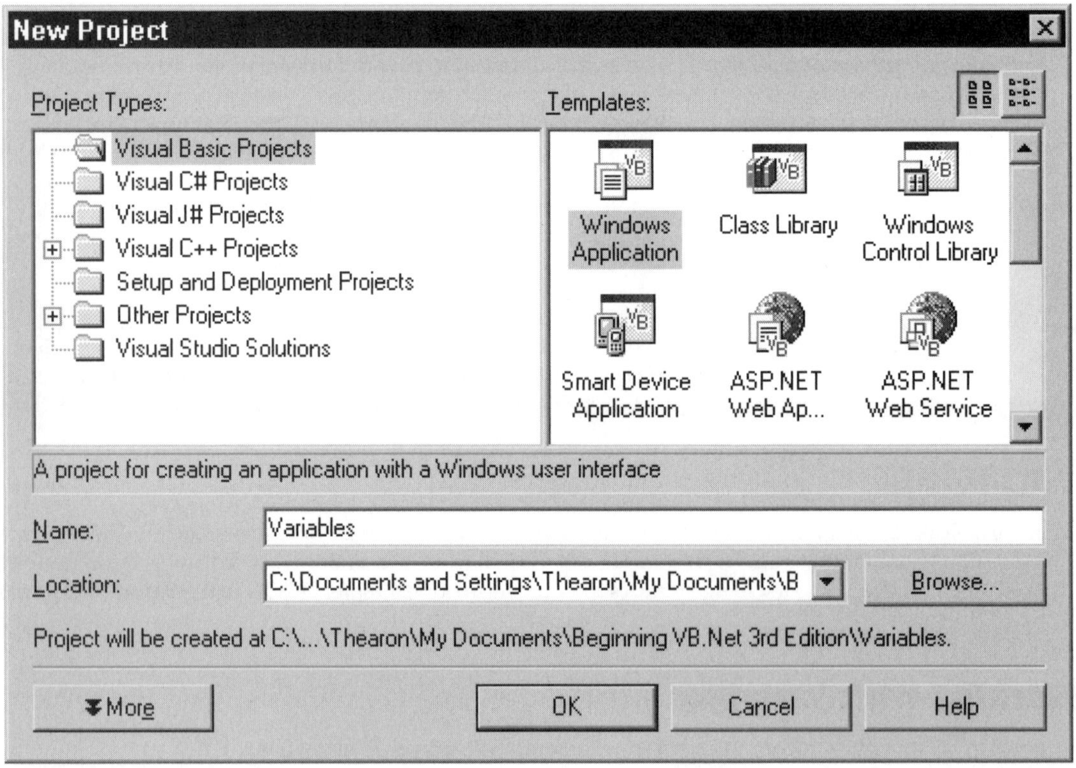

Figure 3-1

2. Make Form1 a little smaller and add a Button control from the Toolbox to it. Set the button's Text property to **Add 1 to n** and its Name property to **btnAdd**. Your form should look like Figure 3-2

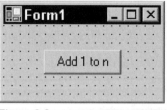

Figure 3-2

3.   Double-click the button to open the `btnAdd_Click` event handler. Add the following code to it:

```
Private Sub btnAdd_Click(ByVal sender As System.Object, _
          ByVal e As System.EventArgs) Handles btnAdd.Click
    Dim n As Integer
    n = 27
    n = n + 1
    MessageBox.Show("Value of n + 1 = " & n, "Variables")
End Sub
```

4.   Run the project, click on the Add 1 to n button, and you'll see a message box like the one in Figure 3-3.

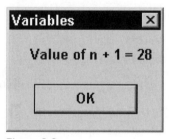

Figure 3-3

How It Works

The program starts at the top and works its way down, one line at a time, to the bottom. The first line defines a new variable, called n:

```
Dim n As Integer
```

Dim is a keyword. A keyword is a word that has a special meaning in Visual Basic .NET that is used for things such as commands. Dim tells Visual Basic .NET that what follows is a variable definition.

Its curious name harks back to the original versions of BASIC and is short for "dimension", as in "make some space for".

As Integer tells Visual Basic .NET what kind of value you want to store in the variable. This is known as the data type. For now, all you need to know is that this is used to tell Visual Basic .NET that you expect to store an integer (whole number) value in the variable.

The next line sets the value of n:

```
n = 27
```

. . . or, in other words, store the value 27 in the variable n.

The next statement is a bit of a conceptual loop, but simply adds one to n:

```
n = n + 1
```

What this line actually means is "store the current value of n plus 1 back into n."

The final line displays a message box with the text Value of n + 1 = and the current value of n. You've also set the title of the message box to Variables to match the project name:

```
MessageBox.Show("Value of n + 1 = " & n, "Variables")
```

Comments and Whitespace

When writing software code, you must be constantly aware that you or someone else may have to change that code in the future. Therefore, you should try to make it as easy to understand as possible.

Comments

Comments are ignored by the Visual Basic .NET compiler, which means you can write whatever you like in them, be it English, C#, PERL, Farsi, whatever. What they're supposed to do is help the developer reading the code understand what each part of the code is supposed to be doing.

All languages support comments, not just Visual Basic .NET. If you're looking at C# code, for example, you'll find that comments start with a double-forward-slash (//).

What's a good way of knowing when you need a comment? Well, it's different for different situations, but a good rule of thumb is to think about the algorithm. The program in the previous *Try It Out* had this algorithm:

❑   Define a value for n

❑   Add 1 to the value of n

❑   Display the new value of n to the user

You can add comments to the code from that example to match the steps in the algorithm:

```
' define a value for n...
Dim n As Integer
n = 27
' add 1 to the value of n...
n = n + 1
' display the new value of n to the user...
MessageBox.Show("Value of n + 1 = " & n, "Variables")
```

In Visual Basic .NET, you begin our comments with an apostrophe (') and then anything on the same line following that apostrophe is your comment. You can also add comments onto a line that already has code, like this:

```
n = n + 1 ' add 1 to the value of n...
```

This works just as well, as only comments (and not code) follow the apostrophe. Notice that the comments in the preceding code, more or less, match the algorithm. A good technique for adding comments is to write a few words explaining the stage of the algorithm that's being expressed as software code.

Comments are primarily used to make the code easier to understand either to a new developer who's never seen your code before, or to you when you haven't reviewed your code for a while. The purpose of a comment is to point out something that might not be immediately obvious, or to summarize code to enable the reader to understand what's going on without having to ponder over each and every line.

You'll find that programmers have their own guidelines about how to write comments. If you work for a larger software company, or your manager/mentor is hot on coding standards, then they'll dictate what formats your comments should take and where you should and should not add comments to the code.

Whitespace

Another important aspect of writing readable code is to leave lots of whitespace. In the last example, there is a blank line before each comment. This implies to anyone reading the code that each block is a unit of work, which it is.

You'll be coming back to the idea of whitespace in the next chapter when you discuss controlling the flow through our programs using special code blocks, but you'll find that the use of whitespace varies between developers. For now, remember not to be afraid to space out your code—it'll greatly improve the readability of your programs, especially as you write long chunks of code.

The compiler ignores white space and comments, so there are no performance differences between code with lots of white space and comments, and code with none.

Data Types

When you use variables, it's a good idea to know ahead of time the things that you want to store in them. So far in this chapter, you've seen a variable that holds an integer number.

When you define a variable, you want to tell it the type of data that should be stored in it. As you might have guessed, this is known as the data type and all meaningful programming languages have a vast array of different types to choose from. The data type of a variable has a great impact on how the computer will run your code. In this section, you'll take a deeper look at how variables work and how they might impact the performance of your program.

Working with Numbers

When you work with numbers in Visual Basic .NET, you'll be working with two kinds of numbers: integers and floating-point numbers. Both have very specific uses. Integer numbers are, usually, not much use for math-type calculations, for example, calculating how much money you have left on your mortgage or calculating how long it would take to fill a swimming pool with water. For these kinds of calculations, you're more likely to use floating-point variables for the simple reason that it's possible to represent decimal numbers using these, whereas you can't represent with integer variables (which can only hold whole numbers).

Oddly, you'll find that in your day-to-day activities, you're far more likely to use integer variables than floating-point variables. Most of the software that you write will use numbers to keep track of what is going on, rather than performing calculations.

For example, imagine you write a program that displays customer details on the screen. Let's also say that you have 100 customers in your database. When the program starts you'll display the first customer on the screen. You also need to keep track of which customer is being displayed, so that when the user says, "Next, please", you'll actually know which one is next.

Because a computer is more comfortable working with numbers than with anything else, you'll usually find that each customer has been given a unique number. This unique number will, in virtually all cases, be an integer. What this means is that each of your customers will have a unique integer number between 1 and 100 assigned to them. (You can choose any number range you want. For example, I might want to start at 48 and make all of my customers' IDs a factor of 6, so I'd have 48, 54, 60, 66, 72 and so on.) In your program, you'll also have a variable that stores the ID of the customer that you're currently looking at. When the user asks to see the next customer, you add one to that ID ("increment by one") and display the new customer.

You'll see how this kind of thing works as you move on to more advanced topics, but for now rest assured that you're more likely to use integer numbers than floating-points. Take a look now at some common operations.

Common Integer Math Operations

In this section, you create a new project for our math operations.

Try It Out   Common Integer Math

1. Create a new project in Visual Studio .NET by selecting File ⇨ New ⇨ Project from the menu. When asked, select Windows Application from the right pane (refer to Figure 3-1) and enter the project name as **IntegerMath**.

2. Using the Toolbox, add a new Button control to the Form1 as before. Set its Name property to **btnIntMath** and its Text property to **Math Test**. Double-click it and add this code to the new Click event handler that will be created:

```
Private Sub btnIntMath_Click(ByVal sender As System.Object, _
          ByVal e As System.EventArgs) Handles btnIntMath.Click
    ' define n...
    Dim n As Integer
    ' try adding numbers...
    n = 16
    n = n + 8
    MessageBox.Show("Addition test..." & n, "Integer Math")
    ' try subtracting numbers...
```

```
    n = 24
    n = n - 2
    MessageBox.Show("Subtraction test..." & n, "Integer Math")
    ' try multiplying numbers...
n = 6
    n = n * 10
    MessageBox.Show("Multiplication test..." & n, "Integer Math")
    ' try dividing numbers...
    n = 12
    n = n / 6
    MessageBox.Show("Division test..." & n, "Integer Math")
    End Sub
```

3. Run the project. You'll be able to click through to four message boxes, as shown in Figure 3-4.

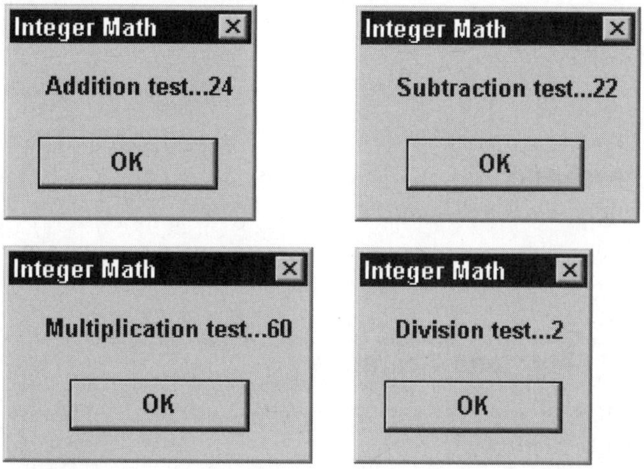

Figure 3-4

How It Works

Hopefully, none of the code you've seen should be too baffling. You've already seen the addition operator before. Here it is again:

```
    ' try adding numbers...
    n = 16
    n = n + 8
```

So, all you're saying is this:

❑   Let n be equal to the value 16.

❑   Then, let n be equal to the current value of n (which is 16) plus 8.

As you can see from the message box you get a result of 24, which is correct.

The subtraction operator is a minus (–) sign. Here it is in action:

```
    ' try subtracting numbers...
    n = 24
    n = n - 2
```

Again, same deal as before:

- ❑ Let n be equal to the value 24.
- ❑ Let n be equal to the current value of n (which is 24) minus 2.

The multiplication operator is an asterisk (*). Here it is in action:

```
' try multiplying numbers...
n = 6
n = n * 10
```

Finally, the division operator is a forward slash (/). Here it is in action:

```
' try dividing numbers...
n = 12
n = n / 6
```

Integer Math Shorthand

You can perform the same operations without having to write as much code by using *shorthand operators* (assignment operators) and although they look a little less logical than their more verbose counterparts, you'll soon learn to love them.

Try It Out   Using Shorthand Operators

1. Go back to Visual Studio .NET and open `Form1.vb` again. Change the highlighted lines:

```
Private Sub btnIntMath_Click(ByVal sender As System.Object, _
            ByVal e As System.EventArgs) Handles btnIntMath.Click
    ' define n...
    Dim n As Integer
    ' try adding numbers...
    n = 16
    n += 8
    MessageBox.Show("Addition test..." & n, "Integer Math")
    ' try subtracting numbers...
    n = 24
    n -= 2
    MessageBox.Show("Subtraction test..." & n, "Integer Math")
    ' try multiplying numbers...
    n = 6
    n *= 10
    MessageBox.Show("Multiplication test..." & n, "Integer Math")
    ' try dividing numbers...
    n = 12
    n /= 6
    MessageBox.Show("Division test..." & n, "Integer Math")
    End Sub
```

2. Run the project. You'll get the same results as in the previous *Try It Out*.

How It Works

To use the shorthand version you just rearrange the code and drop one of the ns. Here is the old version:

```
n = n + 8
```

...and here's the new version:

```
n += 8
```

The Problem with Integer Math

The main problem with integer math is that you can't do anything that involves a decimal. For example, you can't do this:

```
' try multiplying numbers...
n = 6
n = n * 10.23
```

...or rather, you can actually run that code but you won't get the result you were expecting. Because n has been defined as a variable designed to accept an integer only, the result is rounded up or down to the nearest integer. In this case, although the actual answer is 61.38, n will be set to the value 61. If the answer were 61.73, n would be set to 62.

Likewise, a similar problem occurs with division. Here's another piece of code:

```
' try dividing numbers...
n = 12
n = n / 7
```

This time the answer is 1.71. However, because the result has to be rounded up in order that it can be stored in n, you end up with n being set equal to 2. As you can imagine, if you were trying to write programs that actually calculated some form of value, you'd be in big trouble, as every step in the calculation would be subject to rounding errors.

In the next section, you'll look at how you can do these kinds of operation with floating-point numbers.

Floating-Point Math

So, you know that integers are not good for mathematical calculations because most calculations of these types involve a decimal component of some description. Later in this chapter, you'll see how to use floating-point numbers to calculate the area of a circle, but for now I'll just introduce the concepts.

Try It Out   Floating Point Math

1. Create a new Windows Application project in Visual Studio .NET called **Floating-Pt Math**. As before, place a button on the form, setting its name to **btnFloatMath** and its Text to **Double Test**.

2. Double-click btnFloatMath and add the following code:

```
Private Sub btnFloatMath_Click(ByVal sender As System.Object, _
        ByVal e As System.EventArgs) Handles btnFloatMath.Click
    ' define n...
    Dim n As Double
    ' try multiplying numbers...
```

```
n = 45.34
n *= 4.333
MessageBox.Show("Multiplication test..." & n, "Floating Points")
' try dividing numbers...
n = 12
n /= 7
MessageBox.Show("Division test..." & n, "Floating Points")
End Sub
```

3. Run the project and you'll see the results shown in Figure 3-5.

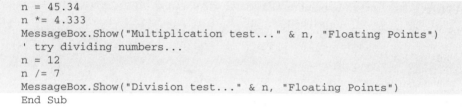

Figure 3-5

4. Be sure to save this project, you'll be returning to it later in the chapter.

How It Works

Perhaps the most important change in this code is the way you're defining n:

```
Dim n As Double
```

Rather than saying As Integer at the end, you're saying As Double. This tells Visual Basic .NET that you want to create a variable that holds a double-precision floating-point number, rather than an integer number. This means that any operation performed on n will be a floating-point operation, rather than an integer operation.

However, there's no difference in how either of these operations are performed. Here, you set n to be a decimal number and then multiply it by another decimal number:

```
' try multiplying numbers...
n = 45.34
n *= 4.333
```

When you run this, you get a result of 196.45822, which, as you can see, has a decimal component and therefore you can use this in calculations.

Of course, floating-point numbers don't have to have an explicit decimal component:

```
' try dividing numbers...
n = 12
n /= 7
```

This result still yields a floating-point result because n has been set up to hold such a result. You can see this by our result of 1.71, which is the same result you were looking for back when you were examining integer math.

Other States

Floating-point numbers can also hold a number of other states. Specifically, these are:

- ❏ NaN—which means "not a number"
- ❏ Positive infinity
- ❏ Negative infinity

We won't show how to get all of the results here, but the mathematicians among you will recognize that .NET will cater to their advanced math needs.

Single-Precision Floating-Point Numbers

I've been saying double-precision floating-point. In .NET, there are two main ways to represent floating-point numbers depending on your needs. Because in certain cases the decimal components of floating-point numbers can zoom off to infinity (pi being a particularly obvious example), there has to be some limit at which the computer will stop keeping track of the decimal component. These are usually related to the size of the variable, which is a subject discussed in much more detail towards the end of the chapter. There are also limits on how large the non-decimal component can be.

A double-precision floating-point number can hold any value between $-1.7 \times 10,308$ and $+1.7 \times 10,308$ to a great level of accuracy. On the other hand, a single-precision floating-point number can only hold between -3.4×1038 and $+3.4 \times 1038$. Again, still a pretty huge number, but this holds decimal components to a lesser degree of accuracy—the benefit being that single-precision floating point numbers require less memory.

You should avoid using double-precision numbers unless you actually require more accuracy than the single-precision allows. This is especially important in very large applications where using double-precision numbers for variables that only require single-precision numbers could slow up your program significantly.

The calculations you're trying to perform will dictate which type of floating-point number you wish to use. If you want to use a single-precision number, use `As Single` rather than `As Double`, like this:

```
Dim n As Single
```

Working with Strings

A string is a collection of characters and you use double quotes to mark its beginning and end. You've seen how to use strings to display the results of simple programs on the screen. Strings are commonly used for exactly this function—telling the user what happened and what needs to happen next. Another common use is storing a piece of text for later use in an algorithm. You'll see lots of strings throughout the rest of the book. So far, you've used strings like this:

```
MessageBox.Show("Multiplication test..." & n, "Floating Points")
```

`"Multiplication test..."` and `"Floating Points"` are strings; you can tell because of the double quotes (`"`). However, what about n? The value contained within n is being converted to a string value that can be displayed on the screen. (This is a pretty advanced topic that's covered later in the chapter, but for now concentrate on the fact that a conversion is taking place.) For example, if n represents the value 27, to display it on the screen it has to be converted into a string two-characters in length. Take a look at some of the things you can do with strings.

Try It Out   Using Strings

1.   Create a new Windows Application using the File ➪ New ➪ Project menu option. Call it **Strings**.

2.   Using the Toolbox, draw a button called **btnStrings** on the form and set its Text property to **Using Strings**. Double-click it and then add this code:

```
Private Sub btnStrings_Click(ByVal sender As System.Object, _
          ByVal e As System.EventArgs) Handles btnStrings.Click
    ' define a string...
    Dim s As String
    s = "Hello, world!"
    ' display the result...
    MessageBox.Show(s, "Strings")
End Sub
```

3.   Run the project. You'll see a message like the one in Figure 3-6.

Figure 3-6

How It Works

You can define a variable that holds a string using a similar notation to that used with the number variables, but this time using `As String`:

```
' define a string...
Dim s As String
```

You can also set that string to have a value, again as before:

```
s = "Hello, world!"
```

You need to use double quotes around the string value to delimit the string, meaning to mark where the string begins and where the string ends. This is an important point, because these double quotes tell the

Visual Basic .NET compiler not to compile the text that is contained within the string. If you don't include the quotes, Visual Basic .NET treats the value stored in the variable as part of the program's code, and this causes all kinds of problems.

With the value Hello, world! stored in a string variable called s, you can pass that variable to the message box whose job it is to then extract the value from the variable and display it. So, you can see that strings can be defined and used in the same way as the numeric values you saw before. Now look at how to perform operations on strings.

Concatenation

Concatenation means linking something together in a chain or series. If you have two strings that you join together, one after the other, you say they are concatenated. You can think of concatenation as addition for strings.

Try It Out   **Concatenation**

1.   Open Form1.vb again, delete the old code, and add this new code:

```
Private Sub btnStrings_Click(ByVal sender As System.Object, _
          ByVal e As System.EventArgs) Handles btnStrings.Click
    ' define a string...
    Dim s1 As String
    s1 = "Hello"
    ' define another string...
    Dim s2 As String
    s2 = ", world!"
    ' define a final string and concatenate...
    Dim s As String
    s = s1 & s2
' display the result...
MessageBox.Show(s, "Strings")
End Sub
```

2.   Run the project. You'll see the same results as shown in Figure 3-6.

How It Works

In this *Try It Out* you have two strings s1 and s2:

```
    ' define a string...
    Dim s1 As String
    s1 = "Hello"
    ' define another string...
    Dim s2 As String
    s2 = ", world!"
```

After this you're free to define a third string (s) and you use the & operator to concatenate the two previous strings:

```
    ' define a final string and concatenate...
    Dim s As String
    s = s1 & s2
```

What you're saying here is "let s be equal to the current value of s1 followed by the current value of s2". By the time you call MessageBox.Show, s will be equal to "Hello, world!", hence you get the same value as before.

Using the Concatenation Operator Inline

You don't have to define variables to use the concatenation operator. You can use it on the fly.

Try It Out   Using InlineConcatenation

1.   Open Form1.vb once more and remove the existing code, replacing it with this:

```
Private Sub btnStrings_Click(ByVal sender As System.Object, _
          ByVal e As System.EventArgs) Handles btnStrings.Click
   ' define a variable...
   Dim n As Integer
   n = 26
   ' display the result...
   MessageBox.Show("The value of n is: " & n, "Strings")
End Sub
```

2.   Run the code. You'll see the same results as shown in Figure 3-7.

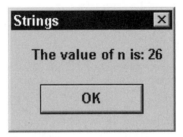

Figure 3-7

How It Works

You've already seen the concatenation operator being used like this in previous examples. What this is actually doing is converting the value stored in n to a string so that it can be displayed on the screen. Look at this line:

```
MessageBox.Show("The value of n is: " & n, "Strings")
```

The portion that reads, "The value of n is:" is actually a string, but you don't have to define it as a string variable. Visual Basic .NET calls this a string literal, meaning that it's a literal value contained in the code that doesn't change. When you use the concatenation operator on this string together with n, n is converted into a string and tacked onto the end of "The value of n is:". The result is one string passed to MessageBox.Show that contains both the base text and the current value of n.

More String Operations

You can do plenty more with strings! Take a look at some of them now. The first thing you'll do is to look at a property of the string that can be used to return its length.

Try It Out   **Returning the Length of a String**

1.   Using the designer for `Form1`, add a TextBox control called **txtString** to the form, clear its Text property, and change the Text property of the button to **Length**. Rearrange the controls so that they look like Figure 3-8.

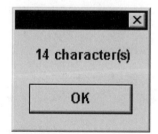

Figure 3-8

2.   Double-click the Button control to open its `Click` event handler. Replace whatever code is there with this:

```
Private Sub btnStrings_Click(ByVal sender As System.Object, _
          ByVal e As System.EventArgs) Handles btnStrings.Click
    ' get the text from the text box...
    Dim myString As String
    myString = txtString.Text
    ' display the length of the string...
    MessageBox.Show(myString.Length & " character(s)")
End Sub
```

3.   Run the project and enter some text into the text box.

4.   Click the Length button and you'll see results like those in Figure 3-9.

Figure 3-9

How It Works

The first thing you do in the event handler is extract the text from the text box and store it in a variable called `myString`:

```
Private Sub btnStrings_Click(ByVal sender As System.Object, _
          ByVal e As System.EventArgs) Handles btnStrings.Click
    ' get the text from the text box...
    Dim myString As String
    myString = txtString.Text
```

Once you have the string, you can use the Length property to get an integer value that represents the number of characters in it. Remember, as far as a computer is concerned, characters include things like spaces and other punctuation marks:

```
    ' display the length of the string...
    MessageBox.Show(myString.Length & " character(s)")
End Sub
```

Substrings

Common ways to manipulate strings in a program include using a set of characters that appears at the start, a set that appears at the end, or a set that appears somewhere in between. These are known as substrings.

In this *Try It Out* you build on our previous application and get it to display the first three, last three, and middle three characters.

Try It Out   Working with Substrings

1.   If the Strings program is running, close it.

2.   Change the Text property of the button to **Split**. Then, using the code editor for **Form1.vb**, change the code as follows:

```
Private Sub btnStrings_Click(ByVal sender As System.Object, _
            ByVal e As System.EventArgs) Handles btnStrings.Click
    ' get the text from the text box...
    Dim myString As String
    myString = txtString.Text
    ' display the first three characters...
    MessageBox.Show(myString.Substring(0, 3))
    ' display the last three characters...
    MessageBox.Show(myString.Substring(myString.Length - 3))
    ' display the middle three characters...
    MessageBox.Show(myString.Substring(3, 3))
End Sub
```

3.   Run the project. Enter the word **Cranberry** in the text box.

4.   Click the Split button and you'll see three message boxes one after another as shown in Figure 3-10.

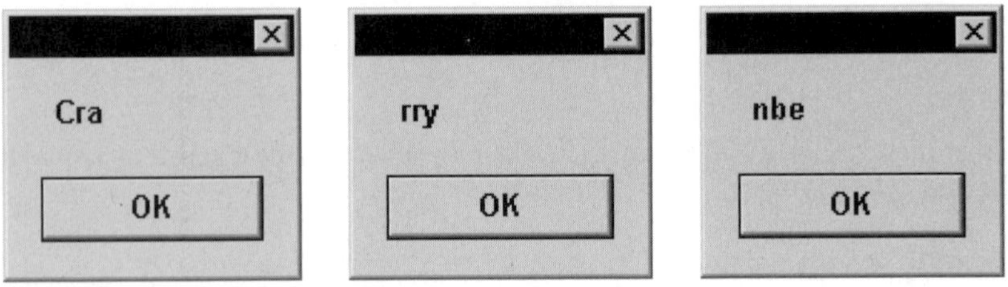

Figure 3-10

5.   Make sure you save this project somewhere safe.

How It Works

The `Substring` method lets you grab a set of characters from any position in the string. The method can be used in one of two ways. The first way is to give it a starting point and a number of characters to grab. In the first instance, you're telling it to start at character 0 and grab 3 characters:

```
' display the first three characters...
MessageBox.Show(myString.Substring(0, 3))
```

In the second instance, you're providing only one parameter. This tells `Substring` to start at the given position and grab everything right up to the end. In this case, you're using `Substring` in combination with `Length`, so you're saying, "Grab everything from three characters in from the right of the string to the end."

```
' display the last three characters...
MessageBox.Show(myString.Substring(myString.Length - 3))
```

Finally, you're using the first form of the method again to start three characters in from the start and grab three characters:

```
' display the middle three characters...
MessageBox.Show(myString.Substring(3, 3))
```

Formatting Strings

Often when working with numbers you'll need to alter the way they are displayed as a string. Figure 3-10 shows how a division operator works. In this case, you don't really need to see 14 decimal places—two or three would be fine! What you need to do is format the string so that you see everything to the left of the decimal point, but only three digits to the right.

Try It Out   Formatting Strings

1. Open up the Floating-Pt Math project that you saved previously in this chapter.

2. Open the code editor for `Form1` and make the following changes:

```
Private Sub btnFloatMath_Click(ByVal sender As System.Object, _
            ByVal e As System.EventArgs) Handles btnFloatMath.Click
    ' define n...
    Dim n As Double
    ' try dividing numbers...
    n = 12
    n /= 7
    ' display it without formatting:
    MessageBox.Show("Without formatting: " & n)
    ' create a new, formatted string...
    Dim s As String
    s = String.Format("{0:n3}", n)
    ' display the new string...
    MessageBox.Show("With formatting: " & s)
End Sub
```

Notice that in addition to the new code at the end, you've removed the multiplication code immediately after n is defined as a Double.

3. Run the project. The first message box will display a result of 1.71428571428571.

4. When you click OK, the second message box will display a result of 1.714.

How It Works

The magic here is in the call to `String.Format`. This powerful method allows the formatting of numbers. The key is all in the first parameter as this defines the format the final string will take:

```
s = String.Format("{0:n3}", n)
```

You passed `String.Format` two parameters. The first `"{0:n3}"` is the format that you want. The second parameter n is the value that you want to format.

The 0 in the format tells `String.Format` to work with the zeroth data parameter, which is just a cute way of saying "the second parameter", or n. What follows the colon is how you want n to be formatted. You said n3, which means: floating-point number, three decimal places. You could have said n2 for: floating-point number, two decimal places.

Localized Formatting

When building .NET applications, it's important to realize that the user may be familiar with cultural conventions that are uncommon to you. For example, if you live in the United States, you're used to seeing the decimal separator as a period (.). However, if you live in France the decimal separator is actually a comma (,).

Windows can deal with such problems for us based on the locale settings of the computer. If you use the .NET Framework in the correct way, by and large you'll never need to worry about this problem.

Here's an example—if you use a formatting string of n3 again, you are telling .NET that you want to format the number with thousands separators and also that you want the number displayed to three decimal places (1,714.286).

Note: The equation changed from 12 / 7 to 12000 / 7 to allow the display of the thousands separator (,).

Now, if I tell my computer that I want to use French locale settings, if I run the *same code* (I make no changes whatsoever to the application itself), I'll see 1 714,286.

You can change your language options by going to the Control Panel and clicking the Regional and Language Options icon and changing the language to French.

In France, the thousands separator is a space not a comma. Likewise, the decimal separator is a comma not a period. By using `String.Format` appropriately, you can write one application that works properly regardless of how the user has configured the locale settings on the computer.

Replacing Substrings

Another common string manipulation replaces occurrences of one string with another. To demonstrate this, you'll build an application that replaces the string "Hello" with the string "Goodbye."

Try It Out   Replacing Substrings

1. Open the Strings program you were working with before.

2. In Form1, change the Text property of btnStrings to **Replace** and change the code in its Click event handler to this:

```
Private Sub btnStrings_Click(ByVal sender As System.Object, _
        ByVal e As System.EventArgs) Handles btnStrings.Click
    ' get the text from the text box...
    Dim myString As String
    myString = txtString.Text
    ' replace the string...
    Dim newString As String
    newString = myString.Replace("Hello", "Goodbye")
    ' display the new string...
    MessageBox.Show(newString)
    End Sub
```

3. Run the project and enter **Hello world!** into the text box.

4. Click the button. You should see a message box that says Goodbye World!

How It Works

Replace works by taking the substring to look for as the first parameter and the new substring to replace it with whatever it finds it as the second parameter. Once the replacement has been done, a new string is returned that you can display in the usual way.

```
newString = myString.Replace("Hello", "Goodbye")
```

You're not limited to a single search and replace within this code. If you enter Hello twice into the text box and click the button, you'll notice two Goodbyes. However, the case is important—if you enter hello, it will not be replaced.

Using Dates

Another really common data type that you'll often use is Date. This data type holds, not surprisingly, a date value.

Try It Out   Displaying the Current Date

1. Create a new Windows Application project called **Date Demo**.

2. In the usual way, use the Toolbox to draw a new button control on the form. Call it **btnDate** and set its Text property to Show Date.

3. Double-click the button to bring up its Click event handler and add this code:

```
Private Sub btnDate_Click(ByVal sender As System.Object, _
        ByVal e As System.EventArgs) Handles btnDate.Click
    ' get the current date and time...
    Dim theDate As Date
```

```
    theDate = Date.Now()
    ' display it...
    MessageBox.Show(theDate, "Date Demo")
End Sub
```

4.   Run the project and click the button. You should see something like Figure 3-11 depending on the locale settings on your machine.

```
Date Demo                    X

      05/10/2003 07:33:43

             OK
```

Figure 3-11

How It Works

The Date data type can be used to hold a value that represents any date and time. After creating the variable, you initialized it to the current date and time using Date.Now:

```
' get the current date and time...
Dim theDate As Date
theDate = Date.Now()
```

Date data types aren't any different from other data types—although you can do more with them. In the next couple of sections, you'll see ways to manipulate dates and control how they are displayed on the screen.

Formatting Date Strings

You've already seen one way in which dates can be formatted. By default, if you pass a Date variable to MessageBox.Show, the date and time are displayed as shown in Figure 3-11.

Because this machine is in the United States, the date is shown in mm/dd/yyyy format and the time is shown using the 12-hour clock. This is another example of how the computer's locale setting affects the formatting of different data types. For example, if you set your computer to the United Kingdom locale, the date is in dd/mm/yyyy format and the time is displayed using the 24-hour clock, for example, 10/5/2003 19:33:43.

Although you can control the date format to the nth degree, it's best to rely on .NET to ascertain how the user wants strings to look and automatically display them in their preferred format. In the next *Try It Out*, you'll look at four useful methods that enable you to format dates.

Try It Out   Formatting Dates

1.   If the Date Demo program is running, close it.

2.   Using the code editor for Form1, find the Click event handler for the button and change the code to this:

```
Private Sub btnDate_Click(ByVal sender As System.Object, _
        ByVal e As System.EventArgs) Handles btnDate.Click
    ' get the current date and time...
    Dim theDate As Date
    theDate = Date.Now()
    ' display the date...
    MessageBox.Show(theDate.ToLongDateString, "Date Demo")
    MessageBox.Show(theDate.ToShortDateString, "Date Demo")
    ' display the time...
    MessageBox.Show(theDate.ToLongTimeString, "Date Demo")
    MessageBox.Show(theDate.ToShortTimeString, "Date Demo")
End Sub
```

3.   Run the project. You'll be able to click through four message boxes. The first message box will display the the long date and the second message box will display the short date. The third message box will display the long time while the last message box will display the short time.

How It Works

What you're seeing is the four basic ways that you can display date and time in Windows applications, namely long date, short date, long time, and short time. The names of the methods are self-explanatory!

```
    ' display the date...
    MessageBox.Show(theDate.ToLongDateString, "Date Demo")
    MessageBox.Show(theDate.ToShortDateString, "Date Demo")
    ' display the time...
    MessageBox.Show(theDate.ToLongTimeString, "Date Demo")
    MessageBox.Show(theDate.ToShortTimeString, "Date Demo")
```

Extracting Date Properties

When you have a variable of type Date, there are a number of properties that you can call to learn more about the date; let's look at them.

Try It Out   **Extracting Date Properties**

1.   If the Date Demo project is running, close it.

2.   Using the code editor, make these changes to the Click handler in Form1:

```
Private Sub btnDate_Click(ByVal sender As System.Object, _
        ByVal e As System.EventArgs) Handles btnDate.Click
    ' get the current date and time...
    Dim theDate As Date
    theDate = Date.Now()
    ' display the date/time details...
    MessageBox.Show("Month: " & theDate.Month, "Date Demo")
    MessageBox.Show("Day: " & theDate.Day, "Date Demo")
    MessageBox.Show("Year: " & theDate.Year, "Date Demo")
    MessageBox.Show("Hour: " & theDate.Hour, "Date Demo")
    MessageBox.Show("Minute: " & theDate.Minute, "Date Demo")
    MessageBox.Show("Second: " & theDate.Second, "Date Demo")
    MessageBox.Show("Day of week: " & theDate.DayOfWeek, "Date Demo")
    MessageBox.Show("Day of year: " & theDate.DayOfYear, "Date Demo")
End Sub
```

3. Run the project. If you click the button, you'll see a set of fairly self-explanatory message boxes.

How It Works

Again, there's nothing here that's rocket science. If you want to know the hour, use the Hour property. To get at the year, use Year, and so on.

Date Constants

In our previous *Try It Out*, you'll notice that when you called DayOfWeek you were actually given an integer value, as shown in Figure 3-12.

Figure 3-12

The date that you're working with, October 5, 2003, is a Sunday and although it's not immediately obvious, Sunday is 0. As the first day of the week is Sunday in the United States, you start counting from Sunday. However, there is a possibility that you're working on a computer whose locale setting starts the calendar on a Monday, in which case DayOfWeek would return 6. Complicated? Perhaps, but just remember that you can't guarantee that what you think is "Day 1" is always going to be Monday. Likewise, what's Wednesday in English is Mittwoch in German.

If you need to know the name of the day or the month in our application, a better approach is to get .NET to get the name for you, again from the particular locale settings of the computer.

Try It Out   Getting the Names of the Weekday and the Month

1. If the Date Demo project is running, close it.

2. Using the code editor, make these changes to the Click event handler:

```
Private Sub btnDate_Click(ByVal sender As System.Object, _
            ByVal e As System.EventArgs) Handles btnDate.Click
    ' get the current date and time...
    Dim theDate As Date
    theDate = Date.Now()
    ' display the weekday name...
    Dim s As String
    s = theDate.ToString("dddd")
    MessageBox.Show("Weekday name: " & s, "Date Demo")
    ' display the month name...
    s = theDate.ToString("MMMM")
    MessageBox.Show("Month name: " & s, "Date Demo")
End Sub
```

3. Run the project and click the button. You will see a message box that tells you the weekday name is Sunday and a second one that tells you that the month is October.

How It Works

When you used your `ToLongDateString` method and its siblings, you were basically allowing .NET to go away and look in the locale settings for the computer for the date format the user preferred. In this example, you're using the `ToString` method but supplying your own format string.

```
' display the weekday name...
Dim s As String
s = theDate.ToString("dddd")
MessageBox.Show("Weekday name: " & s, "Date Demo")
' display the month name...
s = theDate.ToString("MMMM")
MessageBox.Show("Month name: " & s, "Date Demo")
```

Usually, it's best practice not to use `ToString` to format dates because you should rely on the built-in formats, but here you're using the "dddd" string to get the weekday name and "MMMM" to get the month name. (The case is important here—"mmmm" won't work.)

To show this works, if the computer is set to use Italian locale settings, you get message boxes telling you the weekday name is Domenica and another telling you the month name is Ottobre.

Defining Date Literals

You know that if you want to use a string literal in your code, you can do this:

```
Dim s As String
s = "Woobie"
```

Date literals work in more or less the same way. However, you use sharp signs (#) to delimit the start and end of the number.

Try It Out   Defining Date Literals

1. If the Date Demo project is running, close it.

2. Using the code editor, make this change to the `Click` event handler:

```
Private Sub btnDate_Click(ByVal sender As System.Object, _
        ByVal e As System.EventArgs) Handles btnDate.Click
    ' define a date...
    Dim theDate As Date
    theDate = #5/5/1967 6:41:00 AM#
    ' display the date...
    MessageBox.Show(theDate.ToLongDateString & " " & _
    theDate.ToLongTimeString, "Date Demo")
End Sub
```

3. Run the project and click the button. You should see the message box shown in Figure 3-13.

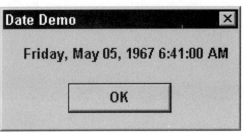

Figure 3-13

How It Works

When defining a date literal, it *must* be defined in mm/dd/yyyy format, regardless of the actual locale settings of the computer. You may or may not see an error if you try to define the date in the format dd/mm/yyyy. This is because you could put in a date in the format of dd/mm/yyyy (for example 06/07/2002) that is also a valid date in the required mm/dd/yyyy format. This requirement is to reduce ambiguity: does 6/7/2002 mean July 6th or June 7th?

> *In fact, this is a general truth of programming as a whole—there's no such thing as dialects when writing software. It's usually best to conform to North American standards. As you'll see through the rest of this book, this includes variables and method names, for example* GetColor *rather than* GetColour.

It's also worth noting that you don't have to supply both a date *and* a time—you can supply one, the other, or both.

Manipulating Dates

One thing that's always been pretty tricky for programmers to do is manipulate dates. You all remember New Year's Eve 1999, waiting to see if computers could deal with tipping into a new century. Also, dealing with leap years has always been a bit of a problem.

The next turn of the century that also features a leap year will be 2399 to 2400. In this section, you'll take a look at how you can use some of the methods available on the Date data type to adjust the date around that particular leap year.

Try It Out **Manipulating Dates**

1. If the Date Demo program is running, close it.

2. Using the code editor, find the `Click` event handler and make this change:

```
Private Sub btnDate_Click(ByVal sender As System.Object, _
        ByVal e As System.EventArgs) Handles btnDate.Click
    ' start off in 2400...
    Dim theDate As Date, changedDate As Date
theDate = #2/28/2400#
    ' add a day...
    changedDate = theDate.AddDays(1)
    MessageBox.Show(changedDate.ToLongDateString, "Date Demo")
    ' add some months...
    changedDate = theDate.AddMonths(6)
```

```
MessageBox.Show(changedDate.ToLongDateString, "Date Demo")
' subtract a year...
changedDate = theDate.AddYears(-1)
MessageBox.Show(changedDate.ToLongDateString, "Date Demo")
End Sub
```

3.　Run the project and click the button. You'll see three message boxes, one after another. The first message box will display the long date for 2/29/2400 while the second message box will display the long date for 8/28/2400. Finally, the final message box will display the long date for 2/28/2399.

How It Works

`Date` supports a number of methods for manipulating dates. Here are three of them:

```
' add a day...
changedDate = theDate.AddDays(1)
MessageBox.Show(changedDate.ToLongDateString, "Date Demo")
' add some months...
changedDate = theDate.AddMonths(6)
MessageBox.Show(changedDate.ToLongDateString, "Date Demo")
' subtract a year...
changedDate = theDate.AddYears(-1)
MessageBox.Show(changedDate.ToLongDateString, "Date Demo")
```

It's worth noting that when you supply a negative number to an `Add` method when working with `Date` variables, the effect is subtraction. (As you've seen by going from 2400 back to 2399.) The other important `Add` methods are `AddHours`, `AddMinutes`, `AddSeconds`, and `AddMilliseconds`.

Boolean

So far you've seen the `Integer`, `Double`, `Float`, `String`, and `Date` data types. The other one you need to look at is Boolean and, once you've done that, you've seen all of the simple data types that you're ever likely to use in our programs.

A Boolean variable can be either `True` or `False`. It can never be anything else, and is indicative of the binary nature of a computer, in that you're only ever dealing with 1s and 0s. Boolean values are really important when it's time for your programs to start making decisions, which is something you look at later on in this chapter and in much more detail in Chapter 4. But, it's worth taking a look at Booleans now.

Storing Variables

The most limited resource on your computer is typically its memory. It is important that you try to get the most out of the available memory. Whenever you create a variable, you are using a piece of memory so you must strive to use as few variables as possible and use the variables that you do have in the most efficient manner.

Today, absolute optimization of variables is not something you need to go into a deep level of detail about for two reasons. First, computers have far more memory these days, so the days when programmers tried to cram payroll systems into 32KB of memory are long gone. Second, the compilers themselves have a great deal of intelligence built in to help generate the most optimized code possible.

Binary

Computers use binary to represent everything. That means that whatever you store in a computer must be expressed as a binary pattern of ones and zeros. Take a simple integer, 27. In binary code, this number is actually 11011, each digit referring to a power of two. The diagram in Figure 3-14 shows how you represent 27 in the more familiar base-10 format, and then in binary.

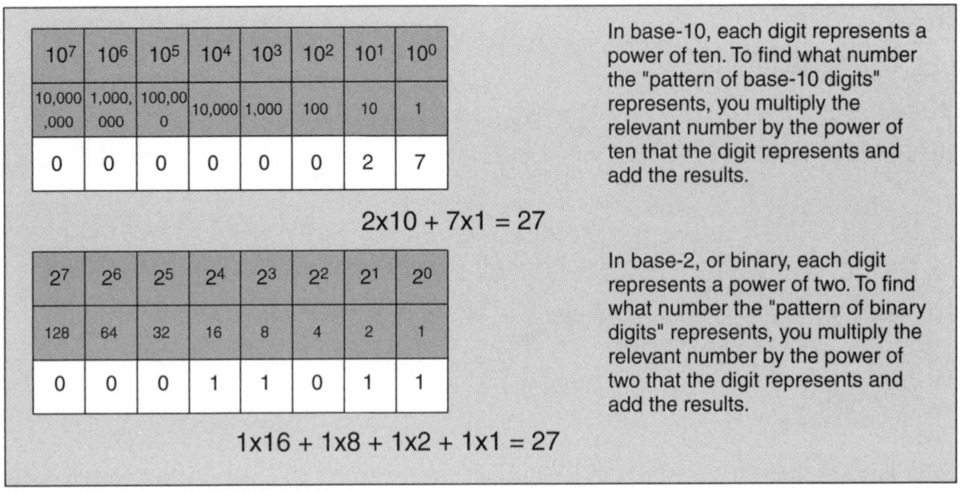

10^7	10^6	10^5	10^4	10^3	10^2	10^1	10^0
10,000,000	1,000,000	100,000	10,000	1,000	100	10	1
0	0	0	0	0	0	2	7

In base-10, each digit represents a power of ten. To find what number the "pattern of base-10 digits" represents, you multiply the relevant number by the power of ten that the digit represents and add the results.

$$2\times10 + 7\times1 = 27$$

2^7	2^6	2^5	2^4	2^3	2^2	2^1	2^0
128	64	32	16	8	4	2	1
0	0	0	1	1	0	1	1

In base-2, or binary, each digit represents a power of two. To find what number the "pattern of binary digits" represents, you multiply the relevant number by the power of two that the digit represents and add the results.

$$1\times16 + 1\times8 + 1\times2 + 1\times1 = 27$$

Figure 3-14

Although this may appear to be a bit obscure, look what's happening. In base-10, the decimal system that you're all familiar with, each digit fits into a "slot". This slot represents a power of ten—the first representing ten to the power zero, the second ten to the power one, and so on. If you want to know what number the pattern represents, you take each slot in turn, multiply it by the value it represents and add the results.

The same applies to binary—it's just that you're not familiar with dealing with base-2. To convert the number back to base-10, you take the digit in each slot in turn and multiply it by the number that the slot represents. Add all of the results together and you get the number.

Bits and Bytes

In computer terms, a slot is called a *bit* and the reason why there are eight slots/bits on the diagram is that there are eight bits in a byte. A byte is the unit of measurement that you use when talking about computer memory.

A *kilobyte*, or KB is 1,024 bytes. You use 1,024 rather than 1,000 because 1,024 is the 10th power of 2, so as far as the computer is concerned it's a "round number". Computers don't tend to think of things in terms of 10s like you do, so 1,024 is more natural to a computer than 1,000.

Likewise, a *megabyte* is 1,024 kilobytes, or 1,048,576 bytes. Again, that is another round number because this is the 20th power of 2. A *gigabyte* is 1,024 megabytes, or 1,073,741,824 bytes. (Again, think 2 to the power of 30 and you're on the right lines.) Finally, a *terabyte* is 2 to the 40th power and a *petabyte* is 2 to the 50th power.

So what's the point of all this? Well, it's worth having an understanding how computers store variables so that you can better design your programs. Let's imagine that your computer has 256 MB of memory. That's 262,144 KB or 268,435,456 bytes or (multiply by 8) 2,147,483,648 bits. As you write our software, you have to make the best possible use of this available memory.

Representing Values

Most recent computers are 32-bit, which means that they're optimized for dealing with integer values that are 32-bits in length. The number you just saw in the example was an 8-bit number. With an 8-bit number, the largest value you can store is:

```
1x128 + 1x64 + 1x32 + 1x16 + 1x8 + 1x4 + 1x2 + 1x1 = 255
```

A 32-bit number can represent any value between 0 and 4,294,967,296. Now, you know that if you define a variable like this:

```
Dim n As Integer
```

. . . you want to store an integer number. In response to this, .NET will allocate a 32-bit block of memory in which you can store any number between 0 and 4,294,967,296. Also, remember you only have a finite amount of memory and on our 256 MB computer; you can only store a maximum of 67,108,864 long numbers. Sounds like a lot, but remember that memory is for sharing. You shouldn't write software that deliberately tries to use as much memory as possible. Be frugal!

You also defined variables that were double-precision floating-point numbers, like this:

```
Dim d As Double
```

To represent a double-precision floating point number, you need 64-bits of memory. That means you can only store a maximum of 33,554,432 double-precision floating-point numbers.

Single-precision floating-point numbers take up 32-bits of memory, in other words half that of a double-precision number and the same as an integer value.

If you do define an integer, whether you store 1, 3,249 or 2,239,482,342 you're always using exactly the same amount of memory, 32-bits. The size of the number has no bearing on the amount of memory required to store it. This might seem incredibly wasteful, but the computer relies on numbers of the same type taking the same amount of storage. Without this, it would be unable to work at a decent speed.

Now look at how you define a string:

```
Dim s As String
s = "Hello, world!"
```

Unlike integers and doubles, strings do not have a fixed length. Each character in the string takes up two bytes, or 16-bits. So, to represent this 13-character string, you need 13 bytes, or 104 bits. That means that our computer is only able to store a little over two million strings of that length. Obviously, if the string is twice as long you can hold half as many, and so on.

A common mistake that new programmers make is not taking into consideration the impact the data type has on storage. If you have a variable that's supposed to hold a string, and you try to hold a numeric value in it, like this:

```
Dim s As String
s = "65536"
```

... you're using 5 bytes (or 40-bits) to store it. That's less efficient than storing the value in an integer type. To store this numerical value in a string, each character in the string has to be converted into a numerical representation. This is done according to something called *Unicode*, which is a standard way of defining the way computers store characters. Each character has a unique number between 0 and 65,535 and it's this value that is stored in each byte allocated to the string.

Here are the Unicode codes for each character in the string:

❑ "6"– ASCII code 54, binary 0000000000110110

❑ "5" – ASCII code 53, binary 0000000000110101

❑ "5" – ASCII code 53, binary 0000000000110101

❑ "3" – ASCII code 51, binary 0000000000110011

❑ "6" – ASCII code 54, binary 0000000000110110

Each character requires 16 bits, so to store a 5-digit number in a string requires 80 bits—five 16 bit numbers. What you should do is this:

```
Dim s As Integer
s = 65536
```

This stores the value as a single number binary pattern. An Integer uses 32 bits, so the binary representation will be 00000000000000010000000000000000, far smaller than the space needed to store it as a string.

Converting Values

Although strings seem natural to us, they're unnatural to a computer. A computer wants to take two numbers and perform some simple mathematical operation on them. However, a computer can perform such a vast number of these simple operations each second that you, as humans, get the results you want.

Let's imagine that a computer wants to add 1 to the value 27. You already know that you can represent 27 in binary as 11011. Figure 3-15 shows what happens.

As you can see, binary math is no different from decimal (base-10) math. If you try to add one to the first bit, it won't fit, so you revert it to zero and carry the one to the next bit. The same happens, and you carry the one to the third bit. At this point, you've finished and if you reckon up the value you get 28, as intended.

Any value that you have in your program ultimately has to be converted to simple numbers for the computer to do anything with them. To make the program run more efficiently, you have to keep the number of conversions to a minimum. Here's an example:

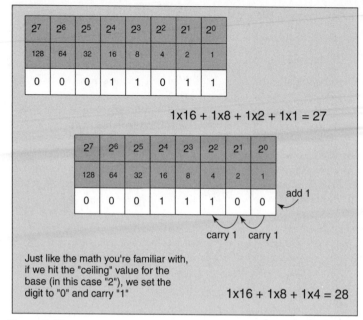

Figure 3-15

```
Dim n As String
n = "27"
n = n + 1
MessageBox.Show(n)
```

Let's look at what's happening:

❑   You create a string variable called n.

❑   You assign the value 27 to that string. This uses 4 bytes of memory.

❑   To add 1 to the value, the computer has to convert 27 to an internal, hidden integer variable that contains the value 27. This uses an additional 4 bytes of memory, taking the total to 6. However, more importantly, this conversion takes time!

❑   When the string is converted to an integer, 1 is added to it.

❑   The new value then has to be converted into a string.

❑   The string containing the new value is displayed on the screen.

To write an efficient program, you don't want to be constantly converting variables between different types. You only want to perform the conversion when it's absolutely necessary.

Here's some more code that has the same effect:

```
Dim n As Integer
n = 27
n = n + 1
MessageBox.Show(n)
```

- ❏ You create an integer variable called n.

- ❏ You assign the value 27 to the variable.

- ❏ You add 1 to the variable.

- ❏ You convert the variable to a string and display it on the screen.

In this case, you only have to do one conversion, and it's a logical one. MessageBox.Show works in terms of strings and characters so that's what it's most comfortable with.

What you have done is cut the conversions from two (string to integer, integer to string) down to one. This will make our program run more efficiently. Again, it's a small improvement, but imagine this improvement occurring hundreds of thousands of times each minute—you'll get an improvement in the performance of the system as a whole.

It is absolutely vital that you work with the correct data type for your needs. In simple applications like the ones you've created in this chapter, a performance penalty is not really noticeable. However, when you write more complex, sophisticated applications you'll really want to optimize your code by using the right data type.

Methods

A *method* is a self-contained block of code that "does something." They are *essential* for two reasons. Firstly, they break a program up and make it more understandable. Secondly, they promote code *reuse*—a topic you'll be spending most of your time on throughout the rest of this book.

As you know, when you write code you start with a high-level algorithm and keep refining the detail of that algorithm until you get the software code that expresses all of the algorithms up to and including the high-level one. A method describes a "line" in one of those algorithms, for example open a file, display text on screen, print a document, and so on.

Knowing how to break a program up into methods is something that comes with experience and, to add to the frustration, it's far easier to understand why you need to use methods when you're working on far more complex programs than the ones you've seen so far. In the rest of this section, I'll endeavor to show you how and why to use methods.

Why Use Methods?

In day-to-day use, you need to pass information to a method for it to produce the expected results. This might be a single integer value, a set of string values, or a combination of both. These are known as input values. However, some methods don't take input values, so having input values is not a requirement of a method. The method uses these input values and a combination of environmental information (for instance, facts about the current state of the program that the method knows about) to do something useful.

You say that when you give a method information, you pass it data. You also describe that data as parameters. Finally, when you want to use a method, you call it.

To summarize, you "call a method, passing in data through parameters."

The reason for using methods is to promote this idea of code reuse. The principle behind using a method makes sense if you consider the program from a fairly high level. If you have an understanding of all the algorithms involved in a program, you can find commonality. If you need to do the same thing more than once, you should wrap it up into a method that you can reuse.

Imagine you have a program that comprises a number of algorithms. Some of those algorithms call for the area of a circle to be calculated. Because *some* of those algorithms need to know how to calculate the area of a circle, it's a good candidate for a method. You write code that knows how to find the area of a circle given its radius, encapsulate it ("wrap it up") into a method, which you can reuse when you're coding the other algorithms. This means that you don't have to keep writing code that does the same thing—you do it once and reuse it as often as possible.

It might be the case that one algorithm always needs to work out the area of a circle with 100 for its radius, and another always needs to work out one with a radius of 200. By building the method in such a way that it takes the radius as a parameter, you can use the method from wherever you want.

> *With Visual Basic .NET, you can define a method using the* Sub *keyword or using the* Function *keyword.* Sub *is used when the method doesn't return a value and is short for subroutine.* Function *is used when the method returns a value.*

Methods You've Already Seen

The good news is that you've already been using methods. Consider this code that you wrote at the beginning of this chapter:

```
Private Sub btnAdd_Click(ByVal sender As System.Object, _
          ByVal e As System.EventArgs) Handles btnAdd.Click
    Dim n As Integer
    n = 27
    n = n + 1
    MessageBox.Show("Value of n + 1 = " & n, "Variables")
End Sub
```

That code is a method—it's a self-contained block of code that does something. In this case, it adds 1 to the value of n, and displays the result in a message box.

This method is a subroutine, so it starts with the Sub keyword and ends with the End Sub statement. Anything between these two statements is the code assigned to the method. Let's take a look at how you define the method:

```
Private Sub btnAdd_Click(ByVal sender As System.Object, _
          ByVal e As System.EventArgs) Handles btnAdd.Click
```

❑   First of all, you have the word Private. For now, you can ignore this, but it's something you'll learn more about in Chapter 4.

❑   Secondly, you have the keyword Sub to tell Visual Basic .NET that you want to define a subroutine.

❑   Thirdly, you have btnAdd_Click. This is the name of the subroutine.

❏ Fourthly, you have ByVal sender As System.Object, ByVal e As System.EventArgs. This tells Visual Basic .NET that the method takes two parameters—sender and e. We'll talk about this more later.

❏ Finally, you have Handles btnAdd.Click. This tells Visual Basic .NET that this method should be called whenever the Click event on the control btnAdd is fired.

Take a look at how you can build a method that displays a message box, and call the same method from three separate buttons.

Try It Out   Using Methods

1. Create a new Windows Application project. called **Three Buttons**.

2. Use the Toolbox to draw three buttons on the form, as shown in Figure 3-16.

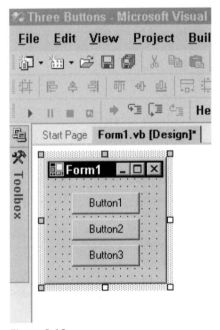

Figure 3-16

3. Double-click the top button (Button1) to create a new Click event handler. Add the highlighted code:

```
Private Sub Button1_Click(ByVal sender As System.Object, _
         ByVal e As System.EventArgs) Handles Button1.Click
    ' call our new method...
    SayHello()
End Sub
Sub SayHello()
    ' display a message box...
    MessageBox.Show("Hello, world!", "Three Buttons")
End Sub
```

4. Run the project and you'll see the form with three buttons appear. Click the topmost button and you'll see Hello world!

How It Works

As you know now, when you double-click a Button control in the designer, a new method is automatically created:

```
Private Sub Button1_Click(ByVal sender As System.Object, _
        ByVal e As System.EventArgs) Handles Button1.Click
...
End Sub
```

The `Handles Button1.Click` statement at the end tells Visual Basic .NET that this method should automatically be called when the `Click` event on the button is fired. As part of this, Visual Basic .NET provides two parameters, which you don't have to worry about for now. Outside of this method, you've defined a new method:

```
Sub SayHello()
    ' display a message box...
    MessageBox.Show("Hello, world!", "Three Buttons")
End Sub
```

The new method is called `SayHello`. Anything that appears between the two highlighted lines is part of the method and when that method is called, the code is executed. In this case, you've asked it to display a message box.

So, when the button is clicked you know that Visual Basic .NET will call the `Button1_Click` method. You then call the `SayHello` method. The upshot of all this is that when the button is clicked, the message box is displayed:

```
Private Sub Button1_Click(ByVal sender As System.Object, _
        ByVal e As System.EventArgs) Handles Button1.Click
    ' call our new method...
    SayHello()
End Sub
```

That should make the general premise behind methods a little clearer, but why did you need to break the code to display the message box into a separate method?

Try It Out   Reusing the Method

1. If the project is running, close it.

2. Now double-click the second button. Add this code to the new event handler:

```
Private Sub Button2_Click(ByVal sender As System.Object, _
        ByVal e As System.EventArgs) Handles Button2.Click
    ' call our method...
    SayHello()
End Sub
```

3. Flip back to the Design view and double-click the third button. Add this code:

```
Private Sub Button3_Click(ByVal sender As System.Object, _
            ByVal e As System.EventArgs) Handles Button3.Click
    ' call our method...
    SayHello()
End Sub
```

4. Now run the project and you'll notice that each of the buttons bring up the same message box.

5. Stop the project from running and find the SayHello method definition. Change the text to be displayed, like this:

```
Sub SayHello()
    ' display a message box...
    MessageBox.Show("I have changed!", "Three Buttons")
End Sub
```

6. Run the project again and you'll notice that the text displayed on the message boxes has changed.

How It Works

Each of the event handlers calls the same SayHello() method:

```
Private Sub Button1_Click(ByVal sender As System.Object, _
            ByVal e As System.EventArgs) Handles Button1.Click
    ' call our new method...
    SayHello()
End Sub
Private Sub Button2_Click(ByVal sender As System.Object, _
            ByVal e As System.EventArgs) Handles Button2.Click
    ' call our method...
    SayHello()
End Sub
Private Sub Button3_Click(ByVal sender As System.Object, _
            ByVal e As System.EventArgs) Handles Button3.Click
    ' call our method...
    SayHello()
End Sub
```

You'll also notice that the Handles keyword on each of the methods ties the method to a different control—Button1, Button2, or Button3.

What's really important (and clever!) here is that when you change the way that SayHello works, the effect you see on each button is the same. This is a really important programming concept. You can centralize code in your application so that when you change it in once place, the effect is felt throughout the application. Likewise, this saves you from having to enter the same or very similar code repeatedly.

Building a Method

In this section, you'll build a method that's capable of returning a value. Specifically, you'll build a method that can return the area of a circle if its radius is given. You can do this with the following algorithm:

❏   Square the radius

❏   Multiply it by pi

Try It Out   Building a Method

1. To try out this exercise, you can reuse the Three Buttons project you used before.

2. Add this code to define a new method (a function, as it returns a value):

```
' CalculateAreaFromRadius - find the area of a circle...
Function CalculateAreaFromRadius(ByVal radius As Double) As Double
    ' square the radius...
    Dim radiusSquared As Double
    radiusSquared = radius * radius
    ' multiply it by pi...
    Dim result As Double
    result = radiusSquared * Math.PI
    ' return the result...
    Return result
End Function
```

3. Now delete the existing code from the Button1_Click event handler, and add this code:

```
Private Sub Button1_Click(ByVal sender As System.Object, _
            ByVal e As System.EventArgs) Handles Button1.Click
    ' calculate the area of a circle with radius 100...
    Dim area As Double
    area = CalculateAreaFromRadius(100)
    ' print the results...
    MessageBox.Show(area, "Area")
End Sub
```

4. Run the project and click on Button1. You'll see something like Figure 3-17.

Figure 3-17

How It Works

First of all, you built a separate method called CalculateAreaFromRadius. You did this by using the Function...End Function block.

```
Function CalculateAreaFromRadius(ByVal radius As Double) As Double
    ...
End Function
```

Anything between Function and End Function is the "body" of the method and will only be executed when the method is called.

The `ByVal radius As Double` portion defines a parameter for the method. (You can ignore the `ByVal` for now. It means *by value*. As you become more experienced, you may want to pass in parameters by reference using `ByRef`. This is an advanced technique, and is beyond the scope of this book. In this case, you're telling it that you want to pass a parameter into the method called radius. In effect, this statement creates a variable called radius, just as if you had done this:

```
Dim radius As Double
```

In fact, there's a little more. The variable will be automatically set to the value passed through as a parameter, so if you pass 200 through as the value of the parameter, what you're effectively doing is this:

```
Dim radius As Double = 200
```

...or, if you pass 999 as the value of the parameter, you'd have this:

```
Dim radius As Double = 999
```

The `As Double` sitting at the end of the method tells Visual Basic .NET that this method will return a double-precision, floating-point number back to whoever called it:

```
Function CalculateAreaFromRadius(ByVal radius As Double) As Double
```

Now you can look at the method properly. First off, you know that to find the area of a circle you have this algorithm:

- ❏ Get a number that represents the radius of a circle
- ❏ Square the number
- ❏ Multiply it by pi (π)

And that's precisely what you've done:

```
' square the radius...
Dim radiusSquared As Double
radiusSquared = radius * radius
' multiply it by pi...
Dim result As Double
result = radiusSquared * Math.PI
```

The `Math.PI` in the previous code is a constant defined in Visual Basic .NET that defines the value of pi (π) for us. After the last line, you need to return the result to whoever called the method. This is done with this statement:

```
' return the result...
Return result
```

The code you added in `Button1_Click` calls the method and tells the user the results:

```
' calculate the area of a circle with radius 100...
Dim area As Double
```

```
        area = CalculateAreaFromRadius(100)
        ' print the results...
        MessageBox.Show(area, "Area")
```

The first thing to do is define a variable called `area` that will contain the area of the circle. You set this variable to whatever value `CalculateAreaFromRadius` returns. Using parentheses at the end of a method name is how you send the parameters. In this case, you're passing just one parameter and you're always passing the value 100.

After you call the method, you wait for the method to finish calculating the area. This area is returned from the method (the `Return` result line defined within `CalculateAreaFromRadius`) and stored in the variable area. You can then display this on the screen in the usual way.

Choosing Method Names

The .NET Framework has a few standards for how things should be named. This helps developers move between languages—a topic you talked about more in Chapter 2. Whenever you create a method, you should use Pascal casing. This is a format where the first letter in each word in the method is uppercase but nothing else is, for example:

❑   `CalculateAreaFromRadius`

❑   `OpenXmlFile`

❑   `GetEnvironmentValue`

You'll notice that when an acronym is used (in this case, XML), it *isn't* written in uppercase. This is to alleviate confusion for developers who may or may not know how something should be capitalized.

Parameters are always written in *camel casing*. (If you've ever seen Java, you'll be familiar with this.) To get camel casing, you do the same as Pascal casing but you don't capitalize the very first letter:

❑   `myAccount`

❑   `customerDetails`

❑   `updateDnsRecord`

Again, acronyms are not treated as a special case and so appear as a mix of upper and lowercase letters, just like in Pascal casing.

> *The name* camel casing *comes from the fact that the identifier has a hump in the middle, for example,* `camelCasing`. *Pascal casing comes from the fact that the convention was invented for use with the programming language Pascal.*

In Chapter 2, you saw that .NET isn't tied to a particular language. As some languages are case sensitive and others are not, it's important that you define standards to make life easier for programmers who may be coming from different programming language backgrounds.

Case sensitive means that the position of uppercase and lowercase letters are important. If Visual Basic .NET was case sensitive, `MYACCOUNT` would not be the same as `myAccount`. However, Visual Basic .NET is *not* a case-sensitive language, meaning that for all intents and purposes you can do whatever you like with respect to capitalization, in other words MYACCOUNT would be the same as mYacCounT.

Note that languages such as Java, C#, and C++ are case sensitive.

Scope

When introducing the concept of methods, I described them as self-contained. This has an important effect on the way that variables are used and defined in methods. Imagine you have these two methods, both of which define a variable called myName:

```
Sub DisplaySebastiansName()
    ' define a name...
    Dim myName As String
    myName = "Sebastian Blackwood"
    ' show a message box...
    MessageBox.Show(myName)
End Sub
Sub DisplayBlathazarsName()
    ' define a name...
    Dim myName As String
    myName = "Balthazar Keech"
    ' show a message box...
    MessageBox.Show(myName)
End Sub
```

Even though both of these methods use a variable with the same name, the "self-contained" feature of methods means that this is perfectly practicable and the variable names won't affect each other. Let's try it out.

Try It Out   **Scope**

1. Create a new Windows Application project called **Scope Demo**.

2. Add a button to the form called **btnScope** and double-click it. Add the highlighted code to the Click event handler:

```
Private Sub btnScope_Click(ByVal sender As System.Object, _
        ByVal e As System.EventArgs) Handles btnScope.Click
    ' run a method...
    DisplayBalthazarsName()
End Sub
Sub DisplaySebastiansName()
    ' define a name...
    Dim myName As String
    myName = "Sebastian Blackwood"
    ' show a message box...
    MessageBox.Show(myName, "Scope Demo")
End Sub
Sub DisplayBalthazarsName()
    ' define a name...
    Dim myName As String
```

```
    myName = "Balthazar Keech"
    ' show a message box...
    MessageBox.Show(myName, "Scope Demo")
End Sub
```

3. Run the project and you'll see the message box displaying the name Balthazar Keech when you click the button.

How It Works

What I'm trying to illustrate here is that even though you've used the same variable name in two separate places, the program still works as intended:

```
Sub DisplaySebastiansName()
    ' define a name...
    Dim myName As String
    myName = "Sebastian Blackwood"
    ' show a message box...
    MessageBox.Show(myName, "Scope Demo")
End Sub
Sub DisplayBalthazarsName()
    ' define a name...
    Dim myName As String
    myName = "Balthazar Keech"
    ' show a message box...
    MessageBox.Show(myName, "Scope Demo")
End Sub
```

When a method starts running, the variables that are defined within that method (in other words, between Sub and End Sub, or between Function and End Function) are given local scope. The *scope* defines which parts of the program can see the variable and *local* specifically means "within the method".

The myName variable technically doesn't exist until the method starts running. At this point, .NET and Windows allocate a member to the variable so that it can be used in the code. Firstly, you set the value and then you display the message box. Therefore, in this case as you're calling DisplayBalthazarsName, the variable is created the moment the method is called, you run the code in the method that alters the newly created version of myName, and when the method has finished, the variable is deleted.

You will see in the next chapter that scope can even be limited to loops within your sub routines and functions.

Summary

This chapter introduced the concept of writing software not just for Visual Basic .NET but also for all programming languages. I started by introducing the concept of an algorithm—the underpinnings of all computer software. I then introduced the concept of variables, and looked closely at the most commonly used data types: Integer, Double, String, Date, and Boolean. You saw how you could use these data types to perform operations such as mathematical operations, concatenation of strings, returning the length of a string, splitting text into substrings, retrieving the current date, and extracting date properties. You then looked at how variables are stored in the computer.

After this, you looked at methods—what they are, why you need them, how to create them, and how the variables you declare within our methods have local scope within that method and do not apply outside of it. We also described the difference between a function and a subroutine. Finally, we briefly discussed how to detect compilation errors in your programs.

To summarize, you should know:

- ❑ What an algorithm is and how it applies to software development.
- ❑ How to declare and use the most common types of variables.
- ❑ How to use the most common string functions when working with the String data type.
- ❑ How to use the Date data type and display dates and times so that they are automatically localized to the user's computer settings.
- ❑ How to create and use simple methods.

Exercises

1. What is camel casing?

2. Which variables are you more likely to use—variables that store integer values or variables that store decimal values?

3. How do you define a variable that contains character data?

4. Write a line of code that multiplies n by 64, using the shorthand operator.

5. What is an algorithm?

4

Controlling the Flow

In the previous chapter, you learned about algorithms and their role in programming. In this chapter, you're going to look at how you can control the flow through your algorithms so that you can make decisions like, "If X is the case, go and do A, otherwise do B." This ability to make decisions is known as *branching*. You'll also see how you can repeat a section of code (a process known as *looping*) a specified number of times, or while a certain condition applies.

Specifically, you'll learn more about:

❑   The `If` statement
❑   `Select Case`
❑   `For` loops
❑   `Do` loops

Making Decisions

Algorithms often include decisions. In fact, it's this decision-making ability that makes computers do what they do so well. When you're writing code you make two kinds of decisions. The first kind is used to find out what part of an algorithm you're currently working on or to cope with problems. For example, imagine you have a list of ten people and need to write a piece of code to send an e-mail to each of them. To do this, after sending each e-mail, you ask, "Have I finished?" If so, you quit the algorithm; otherwise you get the next person in the list. Alternatively, you might need to open a file and ask, "Does the file exist?" in that case you have to deal with both eventualities.

The second kind of decision is used to perform a different part of the algorithm depending on one or more facts. Imagine, when you're going through your list of ten people, that you want to send an e-mail to those who own a computer, but you'll telephone those who don't. As you look at each person, you use the fact that they do or don't own a computer, to choose what you should do.

These decisions are made in the same way, and it doesn't matter whether you have more of the first kind, more of the second kind or whatever. (You may, in practical use, discover that the first kind is more common.) Now, let's take a look at how to make a decision using the `If` statement.

The If Statement

The simplest way to make a decision in a Visual Basic .NET program is to use the `If...Then` statement.

Try It Out   **A Simple If...Then Statement**

1. Create a Windows Application project called **Simple If**. Add a button called **btnIf** to the form and set its Text property to **If**. Double-click btnIf and add the following code:

```
Private Sub btnIf_Click(ByVal sender As System.Object, _
            ByVal e As System.EventArgs) Handles btnIf.Click

    ' define a value for n...
    Dim n As Integer
    n = 27

    ' here's where we make a decision,
    ' and tell the user what happened...
    If n = 27 Then
        MessageBox.Show("'n' is, indeed, 27!")
    End If

End Sub
```

2. Now run the project and click the If button. You'll see the message box shown in Figure 4-1.

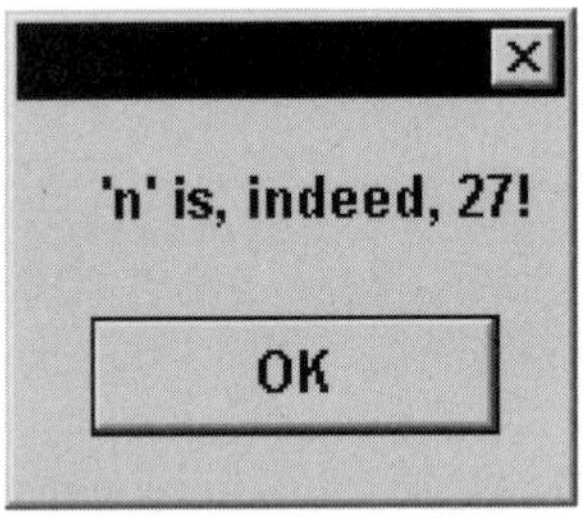

Figure 4-1

How It Works

After defining n and giving it the value `27`, you use an `If...Then` statement to determine what you should do next. In this case, you say, "If n is equal to `27`...":

```
    ' here's where you make a decision,
    ' and tell the user what happened...
    If n = 27 Then
        MessageBox.Show("'n' is, indeed, 27!")
    End If
```

The code block that follows this will be executed only if n equals 27. You end the code block with `End If`. Anything between `If` and `End If` is called only if the expression you're testing for is `true`.

So, as you walk through the code, you get to the If statement, and it's true. You drop into the code block that runs if the expression is true and the text is displayed in a message box.

Notice that the code within the If...End If block is automatically indented for you. This is to increase readability so that you can tell what code will run in the event of the condition being true. It's also good to add some whitespace before the If...Then statement and after the End If statement to further enhance readability.

A simple If block like the previous one, may also be written on one line, without an End If statement, for example:

```
If n = 27 Then MessageBox.Show("'n' is, indeed, 27!")
```

This works equally well—although you are limited to only one line of code within the If statement. So now you know what happens if your condition is true. But what happens if you fail the test and the result is false? You find out in the next *Try It Out*.

Try It Out   Failing the Test

1.   Make the following changes to the Simple If program:

```
Private Sub btnIf_Click(ByVal sender As System.Object, _
          ByVal e As System.EventArgs) Handles btnIf.Click

    ' define a value for n...
    Dim n As Integer
    n = 27

    ' here's where we make a decision,
    ' and tell the user what happened...
    If n = 1000 Then
        MessageBox.Show("'n' is, indeed, 1000!")
    End If

End Sub
```

2.   Run the code.

How It Works

In this case, the question, "Is n equal to 1000?" comes out false. The code block executes only if the statement is true, so it's skipped. If the statement were true, the line between the If and End If lines would have executed. However, in this instance the statement was false, so the next line to be executed was the first line directly following the End If line (which is the end of the Sub). In effect, the true code block is skipped.

The Else Statement

If you want to run one piece of code if the condition is true, and another piece if the condition is false, you use the Else statement. Expand on the previous *Try It Out* to see how it works.

Try It Out   The Else Statement

1.   Change the Simple If program so that it looks like this:

```
Private Sub btnIf_Click(ByVal sender As System.Object, _
          ByVal e As System.EventArgs) Handles btnIf.Click

    ' define a value for n...
    Dim n As Integer
    n = 27

    ' here's where we make a decision,
    ' and tell the user what happened...
    If n = 1000 Then
        MessageBox.Show("'n' is, indeed, 1000!")
    Else
        MessageBox.Show("'n' is not 1000!")
    End If

End Sub
```

2.   Run the code and you'll see the message box shown in Figure 4-2.

Figure 4-2

How It Works

The code following the `Else` statement runs if the condition in the `If` statement is not met. In this case the value of n is 27, but the condition being tested for is n = 1000, so the code after the `Else` statement is run:

```
    Else
        MessageBox.Show("'n' is not 1000!")
    End If
```

Allowing Multiple Alternatives with ElseIf

If you want to test for more than one condition, you need to make use of the `ElseIf` statement. Now take your SimpleIf program as an example to see how you can test for the value of n being 27 and 1000.

Try It Out   The ElseIf Statement

1.   Change the Simple If program so that it looks like this:

```
Private Sub btnIf_Click(ByVal sender As System.Object, _
        ByVal e As System.EventArgs) Handles btnIf.Click

    ' define a value for n...
    Dim n As Integer
    n = 27

    ' here's where we make a decision,
    ' and tell the user what happened...
    If n = 1000 Then
        MessageBox.Show("'n' is, indeed, 1000!")
    ElseIf n = 27 Then
        MessageBox.Show("'n' is 27!")
    Else
        MessageBox.Show("'n' is neither 1000 nor 27!")
    End If

End Sub
```

2.   Run the code and you'll see the message box shown in Figure 4-3:

Figure 4-3

How It Works

This time the code in the `ElseIf` statement ran because n met the condition n = 27. Note that you can still include the `Else` statement at the end to catch instances where n is neither 27 nor 1000, but something else entirely:

```
    ElseIf n = 27 Then
        MessageBox.Show("'n' is 27!")
    Else
        MessageBox.Show("'n' is neither 1000 nor 27!")
    End If
```

You can add as many `ElseIf` statements as you need to test for conditions. However, bear in mind that each `ElseIf` statement is executed as Visual Basic .NET attempts to discover whether the condition is true. This slows your program if you have a lot of conditions to be tested. If this is the case, you should try to put the statements in the order they are most likely to be executed, with the most common one at the top. Alternatively, you should use a `Select Case` block, which you will be looking at later in the chapter.

Nested If Statements

It's possible to nest an If statement inside another:

```
If n = 3 Then
    MessageBox.Show("n = 3")

    If x = 6 Then
        MessageBox.Show("x = 6")
    End If

End If
```

There's no real limit to how far you can nest your If statements. However, the more levels of nesting you have, the harder it is to follow what's happening in your code. So, try to keep the nesting of If statements to a minimum if you can.

Single-Line If Statement

The single-line form is typically used for short, simple tests, and saves space in the text editor. However, it doesn't provide the structure and flexibility of the multiline form and is usually harder to read:

```
If n = 3 Then MessageBox.Show("n = 3") Else MessageBox.Show("n is not 3")
```

You don't need an End If at the end of a single-line If...Then statement. Multiple statements can also be executed within a single line If...Then statement. All statements must be on the same line and must be separated by colons, as in the following example:

```
If n = 3 Then MessageBox.Show("n = 3") : n = n + 1 : Total += n
```

Comparison Operators

You know how to check whether a particular variable is equal to some value and execute code if this is the case. In fact, If is far more flexible than this. You can ask questions such as these, all of which have a true/false answer.

- ❏ Is n greater than 49?
- ❏ Is n less than 49?
- ❏ Is n greater than or equal to 49?
- ❏ Is n less than or equal to 49?
- ❏ Is name not equal to Ben?

When working with string values, most of the time you'll use the Equal To or Not Equal To operators. When working with numeric values (both integer and floating-point), you can use all of these arithmetic operators discussed in the previous chapter.

Using Not Equal To

You have not used Not Equal To yet, so test the Not Equal To operator with strings.

Try It Out   Using Not Equal To

1. Create a new Windows Application project called **If Demo**.

2. When the Form Designer for Form1 appears, add a TextBox control and a Button control. Set the Name property of the TextBox control to **txtName** and its Text property to **Ben**. Set the Name property of the button control to **btnCheck** and its Text property to **Check**. Your form should look like the one shown in Figure 4-4.

Figure 4-4

3. Double-click the button control to create its Click event handler. Add this code:

```
Private Sub btnCheck_Click(ByVal sender As System.Object, _
            ByVal e As System.EventArgs) Handles btnCheck.Click

    ' get the name from the text box...
    Dim name As String
    name = txtName.Text

    ' is the name Gretchen?
    If name <> "Gretchen" Then
        MessageBox.Show("The name is *not* Gretchen.", "If Demo")
    End If

End Sub
```

4. Run the project and click the Check button. You should see something similar to what is shown in Figure 4-5.

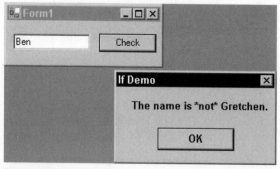

Figure 4-5

95

How It Works

The Not Equal To operator looks like this: <>. When the button is clicked, the first thing you do is to retrieve the name from the text box by looking up its `Text` property:

```
' get the name from the text box...
Dim name As String
name = txtName.Text
```

After you have the name, you use an `If` statement. This time, however, you use the Not Equal To operator rather than the Equal To operator. Also notice that you are comparing two string values.

```
' is the name Gretchen?
If name <> "Gretchen" Then
    MessageBox.Show("The name is *not* Gretchen.", "If Demo")
End If
```

The code between `Then` and `End If` executes only if the answer to the question asked in the `If` statement is `True`. You'll probably find this a bit of a heady principle, because the question you're asking is, "Is name not equal to `Gretchen`?" to which the answer is "Yes, the name is *not* equal to `Gretchen`." As the answer to this question is yes, or `True`, the code runs and the message box displays. However, if you enter `Gretchen` into the text box and click Check, nothing happens because the answer to the question is "No, the name *is* equal to `Gretchen`," therefore you have a no, or `False`, answer.

> If you try this, be sure to enter Gretchen with an uppercase G and with the rest of the letters in lowercase, otherwise the application won't work properly. You'll see why later.

An alternative way of checking that something does not equal something is to use the `Not` keyword. The condition in the `If` statement could have been written:

```
If Not name = "Gretchen" Then
```

Using the Numeric Operators

In this section you take a look at the four other comparison operators you can use. These are all fairly basic, so you'll go through this quite fast.

Try It Out   Using Less Than

1. If the project is running, close it. Open the Form Designer for `Form1` and change the Name property of the TextBox control to **txtValue.** Also, change the Text property to **10.**

2. Now replace the existing `Click` event handler code with this code:

```
Private Sub btnCheck_Click(ByVal sender As System.Object, _
        ByVal e As System.EventArgs) Handles btnCheck.Click

    ' get the number from the text box...
    Dim n As Integer
    Try
        n = txtValue.Text
    Catch
    End Try
```

```
' is n less than 27?
If n < 27 Then
    MessageBox.Show("Is 'n' less than 27? Yes!", "If Demo")
Else
    MessageBox.Show("Is 'n' less than 27? No!", "If Demo")
End If
```

```
End Sub
```

3. Run the project. Enter a number into the text box and you should be told whether it is less than or greater than 27 as shown in Figure 4-6.

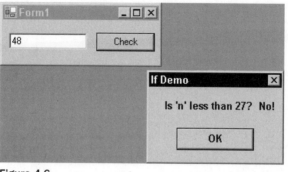

Figure 4-6

How It Works

First you get the value back from the text box. However, there is a slight wrinkle. As this is a text box, the end users are free to enter anything they like into it and if a series of characters that cannot be converted into an integer are entered, the program will crash. I've used an *exception handler* to make sure that I always get a value back. If the user enters something invalid, n remains 0, otherwise it will be whatever is entered:

```
' get the number from the text box...
Dim n As Integer
Try
    n = txtValue.Text
Catch
End Try
```

I'll introduce exception handlers properly in Chapter 9. For now, you can safely ignore it!

The Less Than operator looks like this: <. Here, you test to see whether the number entered was less than 27 and if it is, you say so in a message box, otherwise you say No:

```
' is n less than to 27?
If n < 27 Then
    MessageBox.Show("Is 'n' less than 27? Yes!", "If Demo")
Else
    MessageBox.Show("Is 'n' less than 27? No!", "If Demo")
End If
```

Here's something interesting though. If you actually enter 27 into the textbox and click the button, you'll see a message box that tells you n is not less than 27. The If statement said No and it's right. n is actually equal to 27 and the cutoff point for this operator is anything up to *but not including* the value itself. You can get around this problem with a different operator.

Try It Out   Using the Less Than Or Equal To Operator

1.   Change the If statement in the btnCheck_Click event handler as shown here:

```
Private Sub btnCheck_Click(ByVal sender As System.Object, _
             ByVal e As System.EventArgs) Handles btnCheck.Click

    ' get the number from the text box...
    Dim n As Integer
    Try
        n = txtValue.Text
    Catch
    End Try

    ' is n less than or equal to 27?
    If n <= 27 Then
        MessageBox.Show("Is 'n' less than or equal to 27? Yes!", _
                    "If Demo")
    Else
        MessageBox.Show("Is 'n' less than or equal to 27? No!", _
                    "If Demo")
    End If

End Sub
```

2.   Now run the project and enter 27 into the text box. Click on the Check button and you should see the results shown in Figure 4-7.

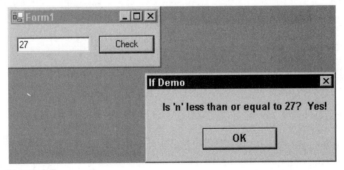

Figure 4-7

How It Works

The Less Than Or Equal To operator looks like this: <=. In this situation, you're extending the possible range of values up to include the value you're checking. So, in this case when you enter 27 you get the answer, Yes, n is less than or equal to 27. This type of operator is known as an *inclusive operator*.

The final two operators look really similar to this, so let's look at them now.

Using Greater Than and Greater Than Or Equal To

1. Open the `Click` event handler. Change the first `If` statement and add this second one:

```
Private Sub btnCheck_Click(ByVal sender As System.Object, _
            ByVal e As System.EventArgs) Handles btnCheck.Click

    ' get the number from the text box...
    Dim n As Integer
    Try
        n = txtValue.Text
    Catch
    End Try

    ' check n...
    If n > 27 Then
        MessageBox.Show("Is 'n' greater than 27? Yes!", _
                    "If Demo")
    Else
        MessageBox.Show("Is 'n' greater than 27? No!", _
                    "If Demo")
    End If
    If n >= 27 Then
        MessageBox.Show("Is 'n' greater than or equal to 27? Yes!", _
                    "If Demo")
    Else
        MessageBox.Show("Is 'n' greater than or equal to 27? No!", _
                    "If Demo")
    End If

End Sub
```

2. Run the program. This time enter a value of **99** and click the button. You'll see two message boxes one after the other when you click Check. The first message box will indicate that n is greater than 27 while the second message box will indicate that n is greater than or equal to 27.

How It Works

The Greater Than and Greater Than Or Equal To operators are basically the opposite of their Less Than counterparts. This time, you're asking, "Is n greater than 27?" and, "Is n greater than or equal to 27?" The results speak for themselves.

The And and Or Operators

What happens when you need your `If` statement to test more than one condition? For example, if you want to make sure that "n is less than 27 *and* greater than 10"? Or, how about checking that "name is 'Zoe' or 'Faye'?" You can combine operators used with an `If` statement with the `And` and `Or` operators.

Using the Or Operator

1. Open the Form Designer for `Form1`. Change the Name property of the text box to **txtName1** and set its Text property to **Zoe**.

2. Make the form slightly larger and add another TextBox control. Set its Name property to **txtName2** and its Text property to **Faye**. It should look like the one shown in Figure 4-8.

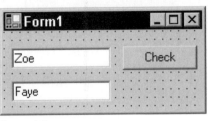

Figure 4-8

3.   Change `btnCheck`'s `Click` event handler to match this:

```
Private Sub btnCheck_Click(ByVal sender As System.Object, _
            ByVal e As System.EventArgs) Handles btnCheck.Click

    ' get the names...
    Dim name1 As String, name2 As String
    name1 = txtName1.Text
    name2 = txtName2.Text

    ' is one of them Zoe?
    If name1 = "Zoe" Or name2 = "Zoe" Then
        MessageBox.Show("One of the names is Zoe.", "If Demo")
    Else
        MessageBox.Show("Neither of the names are Zoe.", "If Demo")
    End If

End Sub
```

4.   Run the project. Click the button and you should see the results as shown in Figure 4-9.

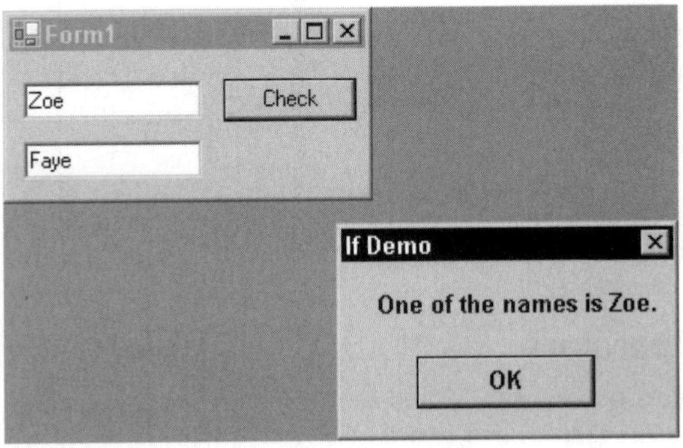

Figure 4-9

5.   Click OK to dismiss the message box and flip the names around so that the top one (txtName1) is **Faye** and the bottom one (txtName2) is **Zoe**. Click the button again and you'll see a message box indicating that one of the names is Zoe.

6.   Now, click on OK to dismiss the message box again and this time change the names so that neither of them is Zoe. Click the button and you should see a message box indicating that neither of the names is Zoe.

How It Works

The Or operator is a great way of building If statements that compare two different values in a single hit. In your Click event handler, the first thing you do is to retrieve both names and store them in variables name1 and name2:

```
' get the names...
Dim name1 As String, name2 As String
name1 = txtName1.Text
name2 = txtName2.Text
```

You'll notice that you've defined two variables on the same line. This is perfectly legitimate coding practice, although it can sometimes make the code look congested. The variables are separated with commas and notice that it's still important to use As to tell Visual Basic .NET what data type each of the variables is.

Once you have both names, you use the Or operator to combine two separate If statements. The question you're asking here is, "Is name1 equal to Zoe or is name2 equal to Zoe?" The answer to this question (providing that one of the text boxes contains the name Zoe) is, "Yes, either name1 is equal to Zoe or name2 is equal to Zoe." Again, it's a yes/no or True/False answer, even though the question is seemingly more complex:

```
' is one of them Zoe?
If name1 = "Zoe" Or name2 = "Zoe" Then
    MessageBox.Show("One of the names is Zoe.", "If Demo")
Else
    MessageBox.Show("Neither of the names are Zoe.", "If Demo")
End If
```

Using the And Operator

The And operator is conceptually similar to Or, except that both parts of the equation need to be satisfied.

Try It Out   Using the And Operator

1. Make this change to the btnCheck_Click event handler:

```
Private Sub btnCheck_Click(ByVal sender As System.Object, _
        ByVal e As System.EventArgs) Handles btnCheck.Click

    ' get the names...
    Dim name1 As String, name2 As String
    name1 = txtName1.Text
    name2 = txtName2.Text

    ' are both of them Zoe?
    If name1 = "Zoe" And name2 = "Zoe" Then
        MessageBox.Show("Both names are Zoe.", "If Demo")
    Else
        MessageBox.Show("One of the names is not Zoe.", "If Demo")
    End If

End Sub
```

2. Run the program. Click the button and a message box tells you that one of the names is not Zoe.

3. However, if you change both names so that they are both Zoe and click the button, you'll see the results as shown in Figure 4-10.

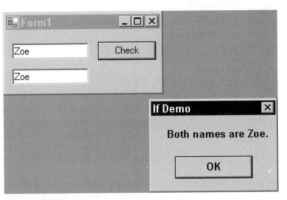

Figure 4-10

How It Works

After you've retrieved both names from the text boxes, you compare them. In this case, you're asking the question, "Is name1 equal to Zoe *and* is name2 equal to Zoe?" In this case, both parts of the If statement must be satisfied in order for the "Both names are Zoe" message box to be displayed:

```
' are both of them Zoe?
If name1 = "Zoe" And name2 = "Zoe" Then
    MessageBox.Show("Both names are Zoe.", "If Demo")
Else
    MessageBox.Show("One of the names is not Zoe.", "If Demo")
End If
```

More on And and Or

You've only seen And and Or used with strings. But, they can be used with numeric values, like this:

```
If a = 2 And b = 2.3 Then
    MessageBox.Show("Hello!")
End If
```

...or...

```
If a = 2 Or b = 2.3 Then
    MessageBox.Show("Hello, again!")
End If
```

Also, in Visual Basic, there's no realistic limit to the number of And operators or Or operators that you can include in a statement. It's perfectly possible to do this:

```
If a = 1 And b = 2 And c = 3 And d = 4 And e = 5 And f = 6 And g = 7 And _
    h = 1 And i = 2 And j = 3 And k = 4 And l = 5 And m = 6 And n = 7 And _
    o = 1 And p = 2 And q = 3 And r = 4 And s = 5 And t = 6 And u = 7 And _
    v = 1 And w = 2 And x = 3 And y = 4 And z = 5 Then
    MessageBox.Show("That's quite an If statement!")
End If
```

Although quite why you'd want to do that is beyond me!

Finally, it's possible to use parentheses to group operators and look for a value within a range. For example, say you want to check for the value of n being between 12 and 20 exclusive or between 22 and 25 exclusive. You can use the following If...Then statement:

```
If (n > 12 And n < 20) Or (n > 22 And n < 25) Then
```

There are many other combinations of operators, far more than I have room to go into here. Rest assured, if you want to check for a condition, there is a combination to suit your needs.

String Comparison

When working with strings and If statements, you often run into the problem of case sensitivity. A computer treats the characters "A" and "a" as separate entities, despite the fact that you consider them to be similar. This is known as *case sensitivity*—meaning that the case of the letters does matter when comparing strings. For example, if you run the following code, the message box would *not* be displayed.

```
Dim name As String
name = "Winston"
If name = "WINSTON" Then
    MessageBox.Show("Aha! You are Winston.")
End If
```

Because WINSTON is not strictly speaking the same as Winston due to the case being different, this If statement will not return a message. However, in many cases you don't actually care about the case, so you have to find a way of comparing strings and ignoring the case of the characters.

Try It Out   Using Case-Insensitive String Comparisons

1. Open the Form Designer for Form1 and delete the second text box.

2. Change the Name property of the first text box to **txtName** and the Text property to Winston.

3. Double-click the button to open its Click event handler. Add this code:

```
Private Sub btnCheck_Click(ByVal sender As System.Object, _
         ByVal ex As System.EventArgs) Handles btnCheck.Click

    ' get the name...
    Dim name As String
    name = txtName.Text

    ' compare the name...
    If String.Compare(name, "WINSTON", True) = 0 Then
        MessageBox.Show("Hello, Winston!", "If Demo")
    End If

End Sub
```

4. Run the project and click the button. You should see results like the ones shown in Figure 4-11.

Figure 4-11

5. Now, dismiss the message box and enter the name as wINsTON, or some other combination of upper and lower case letters and click the button. You should still see a message box that says "Hello, Winston!"

6. However, if you enter a name that isn't Winston, the message box will not be displayed when you click the button.

How It Works

Once you get the name back from the text box, you have to use a function to compare the two values rather than use the basic Equal To operator. In this instance, you're using the Compare method on System.String and giving it the two strings you want to compare. The first string is the value stored in name (which is the value entered into the text box), with the second string being "WINSTON". The last parameter that you supply is True, which tells Compare to perform a case-insensitive match, in other words it should ignore the differences in case. If you had supplied False for this parameter, the comparison would have been case sensitive, in which case you would have been no better off than using the vanilla Equal To operator:

```
' compare the name...
If String.Compare(name, "WINSTON", True) = 0 Then
    MessageBox.Show("Hello, Winston!", "If Demo")
End If
```

String.Compare returns a fairly curious result. It actually returns an integer, rather than a True or False value. This is because String.Compare can be used to determine *how* two strings are different rather than just a straightforward, "Yes, they are" or, "No, they're not." If the method returns 0, the strings match. If the method returns a value that is not 0, the strings do not match.

> String.Compare *returns an indication of how different two strings are in order to help you build sorting algorithms.*

Select Case

On occasion, you need to make a set of similar decisions like this:

❑   Is the customer called Darren? If so ... do this.

❑   Is the customer called Stephanie? If so ... do this.

❑   Is the customer called Cathy? If so ... do this.

❑   Is the customer called Zoe? If so ... do this.

❑   Is the customer called Edward? If so ... do this.

You can obviously do this with a set of If...Then statements. In fact, it would look a little like this:

```
If Customer.Name = "Darren" Then
        (do something)
ElseIf Customer.Name = "Stephanie" Then
        (do something)
ElseIf Customer.Name = "Cathy" Then
        (do something)
ElseIf Customer.Name = "Zoe" Then
        (do something)
ElseIf Customer.Name = "Edward" Then
        (do something)
End If
```

Using Select Case

What happens if you decide you want to check Customer.FirstName instead of Customer.Name? You'd have to change every If statement, which is a pain. Also, if Customer.Name turns out to be "Edward", you still have to go through the other four If statements, which is very inefficient. However, there is a better way!

Try It Out   **Using Select Case**

1.   Create a new Windows Application project. Call it **Select Demo**. Set the Text property of the form to **Select Case**.

2.   From the Toolbox, add a ListBox control to the form that appears and resize it so that it takes up the entire form.

3.   Change the Name property of the list box to **lstData**, and set its IntegralHeight property to False.

4.   You also want to make sure that the text box itself stretches with the form, so set its Anchor property to Top, Bottom, Left, Right. Your form should now look something like the one shown in Figure 4-12.

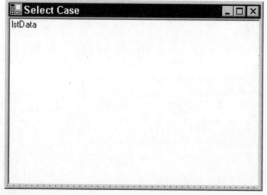

Figure 4-12

By default, when most controls are created they are glued at their top-left position, so that if the form is resized they remain in the same location and of the same size. Here the control is stuck to the relative right and bottom positions as well, so the list box grows or shrinks to fill the space between the fixed positions. To try out this anchoring feature, select the form itself in design mode and resize it. All the controls follow the size of the form.

5. With the lstData selected in the Form Designer, look at the Properties window and select the Items property. Click the ellipsis button to the right of the property and in the String Collection Editor that appears, add the five names on separate lines as shown in Figure 4-13.

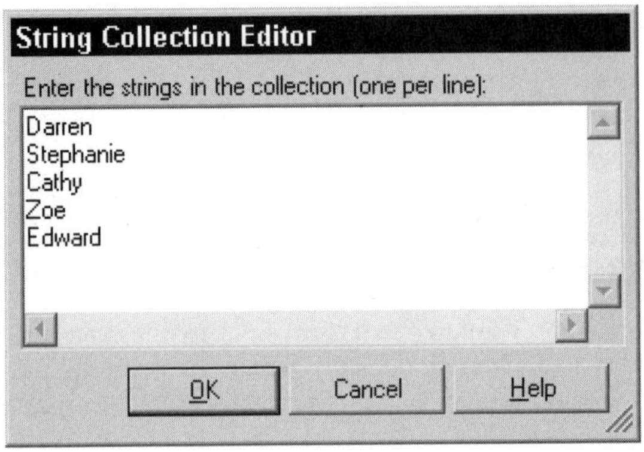

Figure 4-13

6. Click OK to save changes, and the names are added to your list box. Now double-click lstData to create a new `SelectedIndexChanged` event handler and add this code:

```
Private Sub lstData_SelectedIndexChanged(ByVal sender As _
            System.Object, ByVal e As System.EventArgs) _
            Handles lstData.SelectedIndexChanged
```

```
' what did we choose?
Dim name As String
name = lstData.Items(lstData.SelectedIndex)

' use a select case to do something...
Dim favoriteColor As String
Select Case name

    Case "Darren"
        favoriteColor = "Madras Yellow"

    Case "Stephanie"
        favoriteColor = "Starck Purple"

    Case "Cathy"
        favoriteColor = "Morning Mist"

    Case "Zoe"
        favoriteColor = "Evil Black"
```

```
        Case "Edward"
            favoriteColor = "Meeting Room Gray"

    End Select
    ' display a message box...
    MessageBox.Show(name & "'s favorite color is " & favoriteColor, _
                    "Select Demo")

End Sub
```

7. Run the project. Whenever you click one of the names, a message box will appear as shown in Figure 4-14.

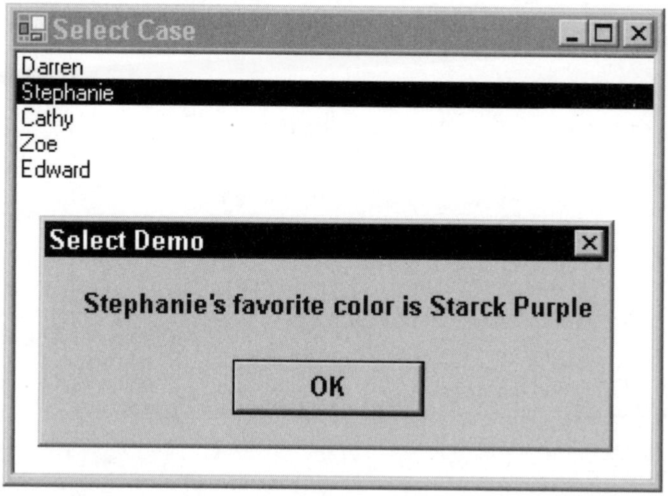

Figure 4-14

How It Works

The first thing you need to do in the `SelectedIndexChanged` handler is work out which name was selected. You do this by finding the item in the list that matches the current value of the `SelectedIndex` property:

```
' what did we choose?
Dim name As String
name = lstData.Items(lstData.SelectedIndex)
```

Once you have that, you start a `Select Case...End Select` block. To do this, you need to supply the variable that you're matching against; in this case, you're using the name that was selected in the list.

Inside the `Select Case...End Select` block, you define separate `Case` statements for each condition to be checked against. In this example, you have five and each one is set to respond to a different name. If a match can be found, Visual Basic .NET executes the code immediately following the relevant `Case` statement.

For example, if you clicked Darren, the message box would display Madras Yellow as his favorite color, because Visual Basic .NET would execute the line, `favoriteColor = "Madras Yellow"`. Clicking on Zoe would display Evil Black as her favorite color, as Visual Basic .NET would execute `favoriteColor = "Evil Black"`:

```
' use a select case to do something...
Dim favoriteColor As String

Select Case name

    Case "Darren"
        favoriteColor = "Madras Yellow"

    Case "Stephanie"
        favoriteColor = "Starck Purple"

    Case "Cathy"
        favoriteColor = "Morning Mist"

    Case "Zoe"
     favoriteColor = "Evil Black"

    Case "Edward"
        favoriteColor = "Meeting Room Gray"

End Select
```

After the `Select Case...End Select` block, you display a message:

```
MessageBox.Show(name & "'s favorite color is " & favoriteColor, _
                "Select Demo")
```

So how do you get out of a `Select Case...End Select` block? Well, as you're processing code that's beneath a `Case` statement, if you meet another `Case` statement Visual Basic .NET jumps out of the block and down to the line immediately following the block. Here's an illustration:

❑   The user clicks Stephanie. The `SelectedIndexChanged` event is activated and you store `"Stephanie"` in name.

❑   You reach the `Select Case` statement. This is set to compare the value in name with one of the five supplied names.

❑   Visual Basic .NET finds a `Case` statement that satisfies the request and immediately moves to `favoriteColor = "Stark Purple"`

❑   Visual Basic .NET moves to the next line. This is another `Case` statement, and seeing that you're already in one, you move to the first line after the `Select Case...End Select` block and display the message box.

`Select Case` is a powerful and easy-to-use technique for making a choice from several options. However, you must leave the block as soon as another `Case` statement is reached.

Case-Insensitive Select Case

Just like If, Select Case is case sensitive; prove it to yourself in the next *Try It Out*.

Using Case-Sensitive Select Case

1. Open the Form Designer for Form1. Locate the Items property for the list box and open the String Collection Editor again.

2. Change all the names so that they appear all in uppercase letters as shown in Figure 4-15.

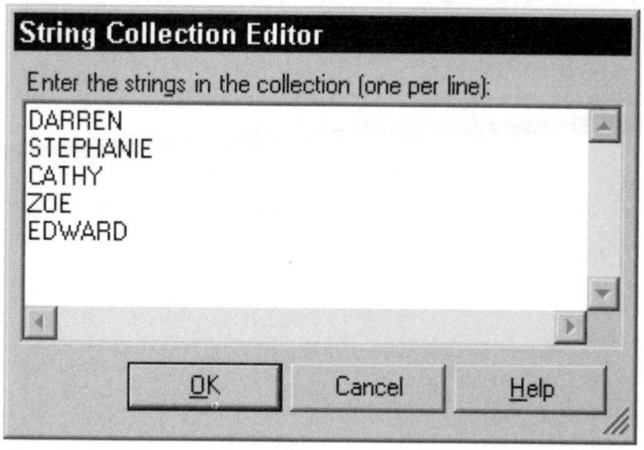

Figure 4-15

3. Click OK to save your changes and run the project. You'll notice that whenever you click a name, the message box doesn't specify a favorite color as shown in Figure 4-16.

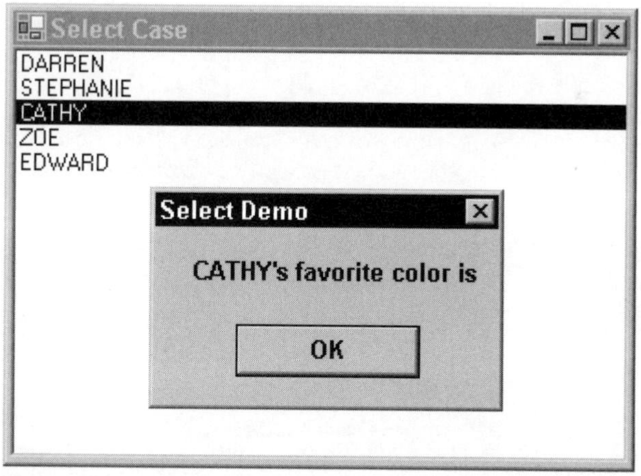

Figure 4-16

How It Works

Select Case performs a case-sensitive match, just like If. This means that if you provide the name CATHY or EDWARD to the statement, there won't be a corresponding Case statement because you're trying to say:

```
If "CATHY" = "Cathy"
```

...or...

```
If "EDWARD" = "Edward"
```

Earlier in the chapter, you took a look at how you can use the `String.Compare` method to perform case-insensitive comparisons with `If` statements. With `Select Case`, you can't use this method, so if you want to be insensitive towards case, you need to employ a different technique.

Try It Out   Case-Insensitive Select Case

1. Open the code editor for `Form1` and make these changes to the event handler for `SelectedIndexChanged`. Pay special attention to the `Case` statements—the name that you're trying to match *must* be supplied in all lower case letters:

```vb
Private Sub lstData_SelectedIndexChanged(ByVal sender As _
          System.Object, ByVal e As System.EventArgs) _
          Handles lstData.SelectedIndexChanged

    ' what did we choose?
    Dim name As String
    name = lstData.Items(lstData.SelectedIndex)

    ' use a select case to do something...
    Dim favoriteColor As String

    Select Case name.ToLower

        Case "darren"
            favoriteColor = "Madras Yellow"

        Case "stephanie"
            favoriteColor = "Starck Purple"

        Case "cathy"
            favoriteColor = "Morning Mist"

        Case "zoe"
            favoriteColor = "Evil Black"

        Case "edward"
            favoriteColor = "Meeting Room Gray"

    End Select
    ' display a message box...
    MessageBox.Show(name & "'s favorite color is " & favoriteColor, _
                "Select Demo")

End Sub
```

2. Run the project and try again. This time you will see that the message box includes the favorite color of the person you click as shown in Figure 4-17.

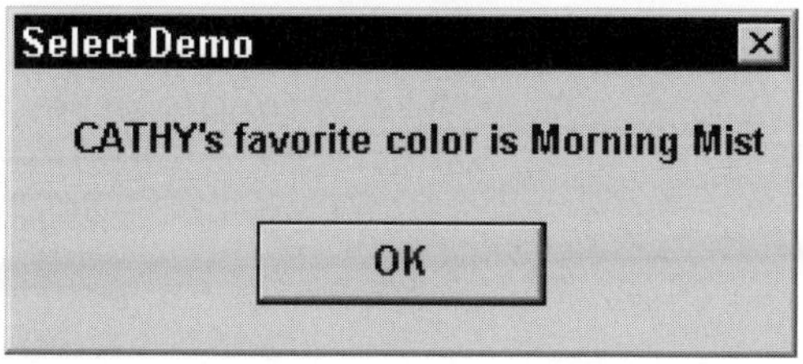

Figure 4-17

How It Works

To make the selection case insensitive, you have to convert the `name` that you are given into all lowercase letters. This is done using the `ToLower` method:

```
Select Case name.ToLwer
```

This means that whatever string you're given (whether it's `"DARREN"` or `"dARrEN"`) you always convert it to all lowercase (`"darren"`). However, when you do this you have to make sure that you're comparing apples to apples, which is why you had to convert the values you're checking against in the `Case` statements to all lowercase too. Therefore, if you are given `"DARREN"`, you convert this to `"darren"`, and then try to find the `Case` that matches `"darren"`:

```
Case "darren"
    favoriteColor = "Madras Yellow"

Case "stephanie"
    favoriteColor = "Starck Purple"

Case "cathy"
    favoriteColor = "Morning Mist"

Case "zoe"
    favoriteColor = "Evil Black"

Case "edward"
    favoriteColor = "Meeting Room Gray"

End Select
```

Finally, once you have the favorite color, you display a message box as usual.

You could have done the opposite of this and converted all the names to uppercase and used `name.ToUpper` *instead of* `name.ToLower`.

Multiple Selections

You're not limited to matching one value inside a `Select Case...End Select` block. You can also match multiple items. In the next *Try It Out*, you'll change the application so that you report the sex of whoever you click on.

Multiple Selections

1. Open the code editor for `Form1` and change the code in the `SelectedIndexChanged` handler to this:

```
Private Sub lstData_SelectedIndexChanged(ByVal sender As _
          System.Object, ByVal e As System.EventArgs) Handles _
          lstData.SelectedIndexChanged

    ' what did we choose?
    Dim name As String
    name = lstData.Items(lstData.SelectedIndex)

    ' use a select case to do something...
    Select Case name.ToLower

        Case "darren", "edward"
            MessageBox.Show("Male", "Select Demo")

        Case "stephanie", "cathy", "zoe"
            MessageBox.Show("Female", "Select Demo")

    End Select

End Sub
```

Note that you've removed the line that declared `favoriteColor` *and the one that displayed the favorite color message box.*

2. Run the project and click on one of the names. You will see results as shown in Figure 4-18.

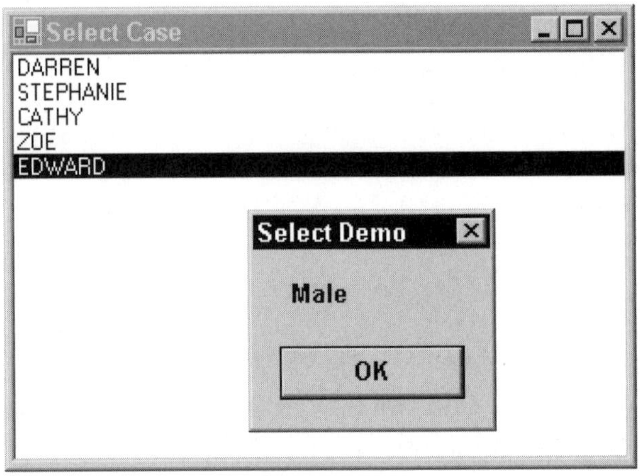

Figure 4-18

How It Works

The code you use to get back the name and initialize the `Select Case` block remains the same. However, in each `Case` statement you can provide a list of possible values separated with commas. In the first one, you look for darren *or* edward. If either of these matches, you run the code under the Case statement:

```
Case "darren", "edward"
    MessageBox.Show("Male", "Select Demo")
```

In the second one, you look for stephanie *or* cathy *or* zoe. If any of these three match, you again run the code under the Case statement:

```
Case "stephanie", "cathy", "zoe"
    MessageBox.Show("Female", "Select Demo")
```

It's important to realize that these are all *or* matches. You're saying "one *or* the other", not "one *and* the other".

The Case Else Statement

So what happens if none of the Case statements that you've included is matched? You saw this before when demonstrating the case-sensitive nature of Select Case.

Try It Out   Using Case Else

1. In the lstData_SelectedIndexChanged event handler, add this code:

```
Private Sub lstData_SelectedIndexChanged(ByVal sender As _
System.Object, ByVal e As System.EventArgs) Handles _
        lstData.SelectedIndexChanged

    ' what did we choose?
    Dim name As String
    name = lstData.Items(lstData.SelectedIndex)

    ' use a select case to do something...
    Select Case name.ToLower

        Case "darren", "edward"
            MessageBox.Show("Male", "Select Demo")

        Case "stephanie", "cathy", "zoe"
            MessageBox.Show("Female", "Select Demo")

        Case Else
            MessageBox.Show("I don't know the sex of this person.", _
                        "Select Demo")

    End Select

End Sub
```

Before running the project, use the String Collection Editor to add the name **OLLIE** to the list.

2. Click OK to save your changes and run the project. Click OLLIE and you will see results like the one shown in Figure 4-19.

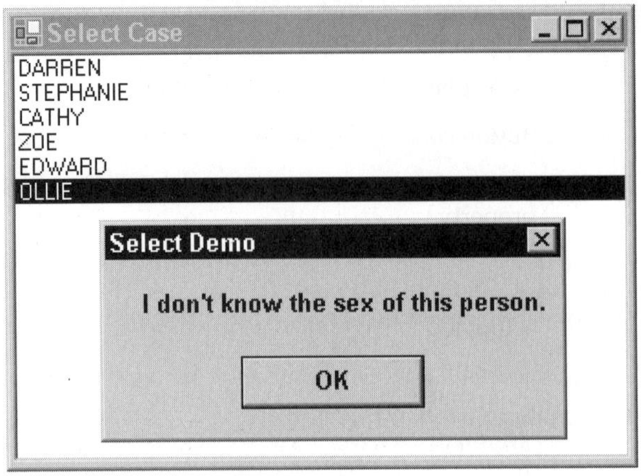

Figure 4-19

How It Works

The `Case Else` statement is used if none of the other supplied `Case` statements match what you're looking for. As there isn't a `Case "ollie"` defined within the block, you default to using whatever is underneath the `Case Else` statement. In this instance, you display a message box indicating that you do not know the sex of the person who's been selected.

Different Data Types with Select Case

In this chapter, you used `Select Case` with variables of type `String`. However, you can use `Select Case` with all basic data types in Visual Basic .NET, such as `Integer`, `Double`, and `Boolean`.

In day-to-day work, the most common types of `Select Case` are based on `String` and `Integer` data types. However, as a general rule, if a data type can be used in an `If` statement with the Equals (=) operator, it will work with `Select Case`.

Loops

When writing computer software, you often need to perform the same task a several times to get the effect you want. For example, you might need to create a telephone bill for *all* customers, or read in 10 files from your computer's disk.

To accomplish this, you use a *loop*, and in this section, you'll take a look at the two main types of loop available in Visual Basic .NET:

❑ **For loops** —These loops occur a certain number of times, for example exactly 10 times

❑ **Do loops**—These loops keep running until a certain condition is reached, for example until all of the data is processed

The For... Next Loop

The simplest loop to understand is the `For...Next` loop.

Building a For . . . Next Loop

1. Create a new Windows Application project called **Loops**.

2. Add a ListBox and a Button control to the form that appears.

3. Change the Name property of the list box to **lstData**. Also, set its IntegralHeight property to
False and its Anchor property to Top, Bottom, Left, Right. This enables you to resize the form at
runtime and still be able to easily view everything within the list box.

4. Change the Name property of the button to **btnGo**. Also, set its Text property to **Go** and change
its Anchor property to Top, Right. Your form should now look something similiar to the one
shown in Figure 4-20.

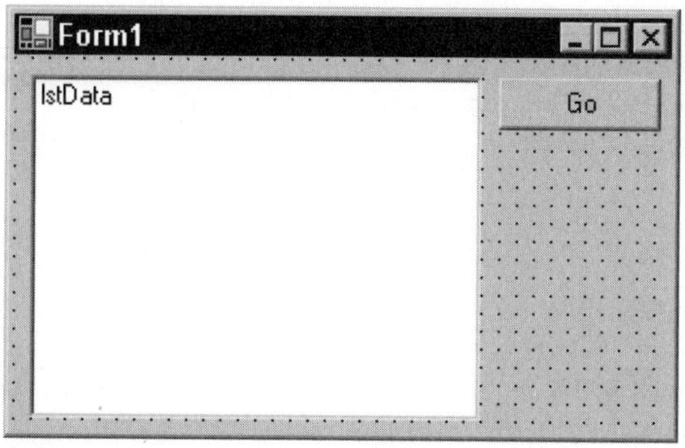

Figure 4-20

5. Double-click the Go button to create its Click event handler. Add this code:

```
Private Sub btnGo_Click(ByVal sender As System.Object, _
        ByVal e As System.EventArgs) Handles btnGo.Click

    ' loop...
    Dim n As Integer
    For n = 1 To 5
        ' add the item to the list...
        lstData.Items.Add("I'm item " & n & " in the list!")
    Next

End Sub
```

6. Run the project and click the Go button. You should see results like those in Figure 4-21.

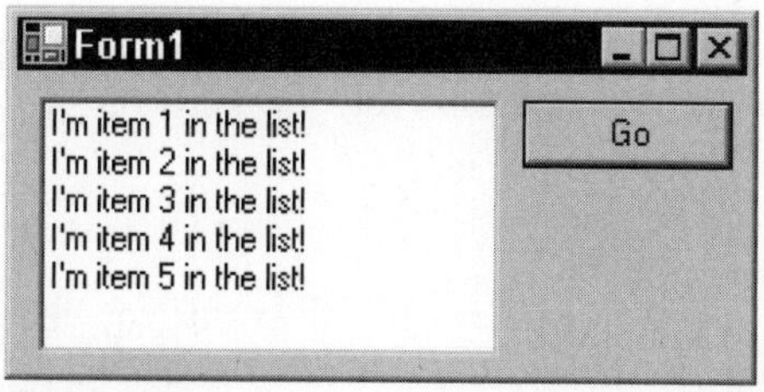

Figure 4-21

How It Works

First inside the `Click` event handler you define a variable:

```
' loop...
Dim n As Integer
```

Then you start the loop by using the `For` keyword. This tells Visual Basic .NET that you want to create a loop. Everything that follows the `For` keyword is used to define how the loop should act. In this case, you're giving it the variable you just created and then telling it to count *from* 1 *to* 5:

```
For n = 1 To 5
```

The variable that you give the loop (in this case, n) is known as the *control variable*. When you first enter the loop, Visual Basic .NET sets the control variable to the initial count value—in this case 1. After the loop starts, Visual Basic .NET moves to the first line within the `For` loop, in this case the line that adds a string to the list box:

```
' add the item to the list...
lstData.Items.Add("I'm item " & n & " in the list!")
```

This time, this line of codes add `I'm item 1 in the list!` to the list box. Visual Basic .NET then hits the `Next` statement, and that's where things start to get interesting:

```
Next
```

When the `Next` statement is executed, Visual Basic .NET increments the control variable by one. The first time `Next` is executed, 1 changes to 2. Providing that the value of the control variable is less than or equal to the "stop" value (in this case, 5), Visual Basic .NET moves back to the first line after the `For` statement, in this case:

```
' add the item to the list...
lstData.Items.Add("I'm item " & n & " in the list!")
```

This time, this line of code adds `I'm item 2 in the list!` to the list box. Again, after this line is executed, you run the `Next` statement. The value of n is now incremented from 2 to 3 and, because 3 is less than or equal to 5, you move back to the line that adds the item to the list. This happens until n is incremented from 5 to 6. As 6 is greater than the stop value for the loop, the loop stops.

> When you're talking about loops, you tend to use the term iteration. An iteration describes one movement from the `For` statement to the `Next` statement. Your loop has five iterations.

Step

You don't have to start our loop at 1—you can pick any value you like. You also don't have to increment the control value by 1 on each iteration—again, you can increment by any value you like.

Try It Out   Using Step

1.   Make the following changes to the code in the `Click` event handler for `btnGo`:

```
Private Sub btnGo_Click(ByVal sender As System.Object, _
            ByVal e As System.EventArgs) Handles btnGo.Click

    ' loop...
    Dim n As Integer
        For n = 4 To 62 Step 7
            ' add the item to the list...
            lstData.Items.Add(n)
        Next

End Sub
```

2.   Run the project and click the Go button. You will see results like those in Figure 4-22.

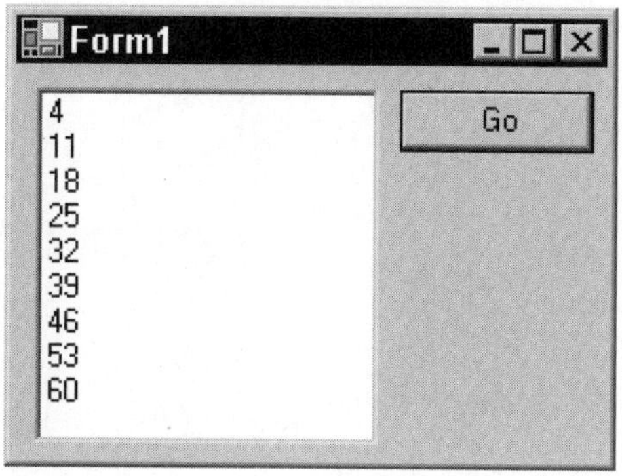

Figure 4-22

How It Works

The magic in this example all happens with this statement:

```
For n = 4 To 62 Step 7
```

Instead of using 1 as the start value, you're using 4. This means that on the first iteration of the loop, n is set to 4, and you can see this by the fact that the first item added to the list is indeed 4. Also, you've used the `Step` value to tell the loop to increment the control value by 7 on each iteration rather than by the default 1. This is why, by the time you start running the second iteration of the loop, n is set to 11 and not 5.

Although you gave `For` a stop value of 62, the loop has actually stopped at 60 because the stop value is a *maximum*. After the ninth iteration, n is actually 67, which is more than 62 and so the loop stops.

Looping Backwards

By using a `Step` value that's less than 0, you can make the loop go backwards rather than forward.

Looping Backwards

1.   Change the `Click` event handler for `btnGo` to this:

```
Private Sub btnGo_Click(ByVal sender As System.Object, _
          ByVal e As System.EventArgs) Handles btnGo.Click

    ' loop...
    Dim n As Integer
    For n = 10 To 1 Step -1
        ' add the item to the list...
        lstData.Items.Add(n)
    Next

End Sub
```

2.   Run the project and click the Go button. You should see results like the one shown in Figure 4-23.

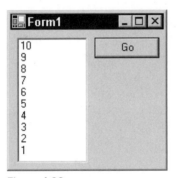

Figure 4-23

How It Works

If you use a negative number, like -1, For tries to add -1 to the current control value. Adding a negative number has the effect of subtracting the number, so n goes from its start value of 10 to its new value of 9 and so on until the stop value is reached.

The For Each...Next Loop

In practical, day-to-day work, it's unlikely that you'll use For...Next loops as illustrated here. Because of way the .NET Framework typically works, you'll usually use a derivative of the For...Next loop called for For Each...Next loop.

In the algorithms you design, whenever a loop is necessary, you'll have a set of things to work through and usually this set is expressed as an *array*. For example, you might want to look through all of the files in a folder, looking for ones that are over a particular size. When you ask the .NET Framework for a list of files, you are returned an array of objects, each object in that array describing a single file. In the next *Try It Out*, you'll change your Loops application so that it returns a list of subfolders contained in the root folder on our computer.

Looping Through Folders

1. Go to the top of the code for `Form1.vb` and add this namespace import declaration:

```
Imports System.IO

Public Class Form1
      Inherits System.Windows.Forms.Form
```

2. Change the `Click` event handler for `btnGo` to this:

```
Private Sub btnGo_Click(ByVal sender As System.Object, _
          ByVal e As System.EventArgs) Handles btnGo.Click

    ' get a list of subfolders...
    Dim subfolders() As DirectoryInfo
    subfolders = New DirectoryInfo("c:\").GetDirectories
    ' loop...
    Dim subfolder As DirectoryInfo
    For Each subfolder In subfolders
        ' add the item to the list...
        lstData.Items.Add(subfolder.FullName)
    Next

End Sub
```

3. Run the project and click the Go button. You should see a list of folders that are at the root of your C drive.

How It Works

`DirectoryInfo` is a class in the .NET Framework that enables you to learn more about the folders on the local computer and on computers on the network. To use the `DirectoryInfo` class in code, you must add a *namespace import declaration* (as `DirectoryInfo` is actually found in the `System.IO` namespace and its full "name" is `System.IO.DirectoryInfo`):

```
Imports System.IO
```

In this case, you use it to return an array of `System.IO.DirectoryInfo` objects, each one representing one folder in the root of the computer's C drive:

```
    ' get a list of subfolders...
    Dim subfolders() As DirectoryInfo
    subfolders = New DirectoryInfo("c:\").GetDirectories
```

Now that you have an array, you need a control variable for the loop. This control variable must be of the same type as the items in the array itself. As you've created an array of `DirectoryInfo` objects, your control variable is also a `DirectoryInfo` object:

```
    Dim subfolder As DirectoryInfo
```

The principle with a `For Each...Next` loop is that for each iteration you'll be given the "thing" that you're supposed to be working with. You need to provide a source of "things" (in this case, your array of `DirectoryInfo` objects) and a control variable into which the current "thing" can be put:

```
For Each subfolder In subfolders
```

What this means is that on the first iteration, `subfolder` is equal to the first item in the `subfolders` array (in my case, `"c:\Database Backups"`). You then add that item to the list box:

```
' add the item to the list...
lstData.Items.Add(subfolder.FullName)
```

As with normal `For...Next` loops, for every iteration of the loop you're given a `DirectoryInfo` object and you use the `FullName` property of this object to get the path of the folder, which you then add to the list.

The Do...Loop Loops

The other kind of loop you can use is one that keeps happening until a certain condition is met. These are known as `Do...Loop` loops and there are a number of variations.

The first one we'll introduce is the `Do Until...Loop`. This kind of loop keeps going until something happens. For this exercise, you're going to use the random number generator that's built into the .NET Framework, and as you haven't seen this yet, I'll introduce it using a `For...Next` loop before you look at `Do Until...Loop`.

Try It Out   **Using the Random Number Generator**

1. Open the code editor for `Form1` and make the following changes to the `Click` event handler for `btnGo`:

```
Private Sub btnGo_Click(ByVal sender As System.Object, _
        ByVal e As System.EventArgs) Handles btnGo.Click

    ' create a random number generator...
    Dim random As New Random()

    ' loop...
    Dim n As Integer
    For n = 1 To 10
        ' add the item...
        lstData.Items.Add(random.Next(25))
    Next

End Sub
```

2. Run the project and click the Go button. You'll see something similiar to the results shown in Figure 4-24. Keep in mind that since we are using the random number generator your results will be somewhat different.

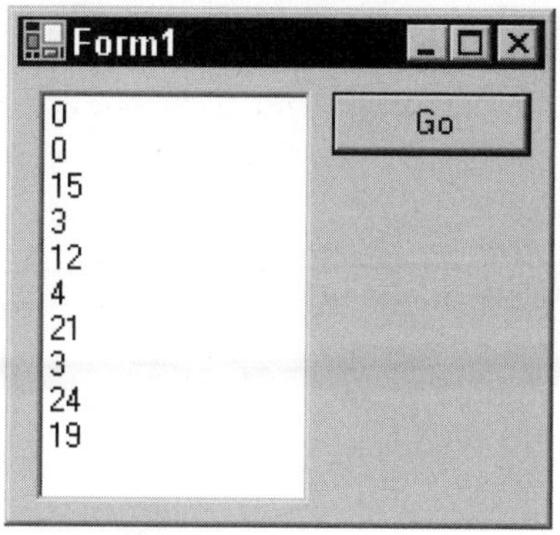

Figure 4-24

How It Works

To use the random number generator, you first need to create an instance of one:

```
' create a random number generator...
Dim random As New Random()
```

Once you have that, you can simply call the Next method of Random to get hold of random numbers. In this case, you've passed 25 as a parameter to Next, meaning that any number returned should be between 0 and 24 inclusive—as the number you supply must be one larger than the biggest number you ever want to get as the bounds that you ask for are non-inclusive. You do this in a loop so that you end up with a set of ten numbers rather than just one:

```
For n = 1 To 10

    ' add the item...
    lstData.Items.Add(random.Next(25))

Next
```

The Do Until...Loop

Now that you know how the random number generator works, let's create a loop that will keep generating random numbers *until* it produces the number 10. When you get the number 10, you'll stop the loop.

Try It Out   Using the Do Until...Loop

1. In the btnGo_Click event handler, make these changes to the code:

```
Private Sub btnGo_Click(ByVal sender As System.Object, _
        ByVal e As System.EventArgs) Handles btnGo.Click

    ' clear the list...
    lstData.Items.Clear()
```

```
' create a random number generator...
Dim random As New Random()

' loop...
Dim randomNumber As Integer = 0
Do Until randomNumber = 10
    ' get a random number...
    randomNumber = random.Next(25)
    ' add the item...
    lstData.Items.Add(randomNumber)
Loop

End Sub
```

2. Run the project and click the Go button. You'll see results similar to the results shown in Figure 4-24.

3. Keep clicking the Go button. You'll see that the number of elements in the list is different each time.

How It Works

A Do Until...Loop keeps running the loop until the given condition is met. When you use this type of loop, there isn't a control variable *per se*, rather you have to keep track of the current position of the loop yourself—let's see how you do this. You begin by clearing the list box (which is full of data after each time you click the Go button) and initializing the random number generator:

```
' clear the list...
lstData.Items.Clear()

' create a random number generator...
Dim random As New Random()
```

You then create your equivalent of a control variable:

```
' loop...
Dim randomNumber As Integer = 0
```

Next, you set up the loop and tell it that you want to keep running the loop until randomNumber is equal to 10:

```
Do Until randomNumber = 10
```

With each iteration of the loop, you ask the random number generator for a new number between 0 and 24 and store it in randomNumber. You also add the number that you got to the list:

```
' get a random number...
randomNumber = random.Next(25)
' add the item...
lstData.Items.Add(randomNumber)
```

The magic happens when you get to the Loop statement. At this point, Visual Basic .NET returns not to the first line within the loop, but instead to the Do Until line. When execution returns to Do Until, the expression is evaluated. Provided it returns False, the execution pointer moves to the first line within the loop. However, if `randomNumber` is `10`, the expression returns `True` and instead of moving to the first line within the loop, you continue at the first line immediately after `Loop`. In effect, the loop is stopped.

Do While . . . Loop

The conceptual opposite of a `Do Until...Loop` is a `Do While...Loop`. This kind of loop keeps iterating while a particular condition is `True`. Let's see it in action.

Try It Out   Using the Do While . . . Loop

1.   Make this change to `btnGo_Click`:

```
Private Sub btnGo_Click(ByVal sender As System.Object, _
            ByVal e As System.EventArgs) Handles btnGo.Click

    ' clear the list...
    lstData.Items.Clear()

    ' create a random number generator...
    Dim random As New Random()

    ' loop...
    Dim randomNumber As Integer = 0
    Do While randomNumber < 15
        ' get a random number...
        randomNumber = random.Next(25)

        ' add the item...
        lstData.Items.Add(randomNumber)
    Loop

End Sub
```

2.   Run the project and click the Go button. You'll see something similar to the results shown in Figure 4-25.

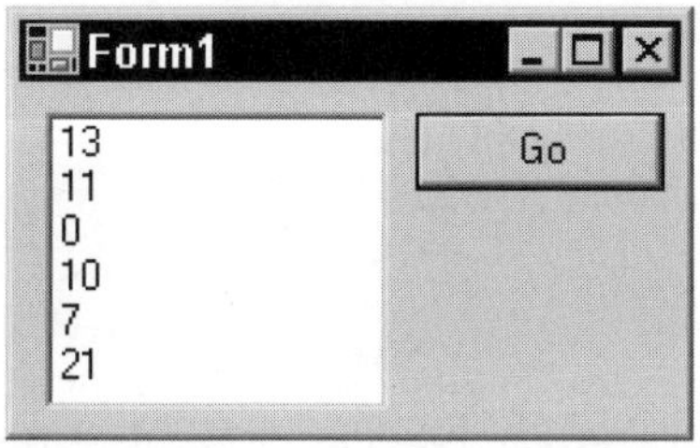

Figure 4-25

3.   If you keep pressing the Go button, the loop keeps going until the random number generator produces a number greater than or equal to `15`.

How It Works

A `Do While...Loop` keeps running so long as the given expression remains `True`. As soon as the expression becomes `False`, the loop quits. When you start the loop, you check to make sure that randomNumber is less than 15. If it is, the expression returns True and you can run the code within the loop:

```
Do While randomNumber < 15

    ' get a random number...
    randomNumber = random.Next(25)

    ' add the item...
    lstData.Items.Add(randomNumber)

Loop
```

Again, when you get to the Loop statement Visual Basic .NET moves back up to the Do While statement. When it gets there, it evaluates the expression again. If it's True, you run the code inside the loop once more. If it's False (because randomNumber is greater than or equal to 15), you continue with the first line after Loop, effectively quitting the loop.

Acceptable Expressions for a Do...Loop

You might be wondering what kind of expressions you can use with the two variations of Do...Loop. If you can use it with an If statement, you can use it with a Do...Loop. For example, you can write this:

```
Do While n > 10 And n < 100
```

...or...

```
Do Until (n > 10 And n < 100) Or b = True
```

...or...

```
Do While String.Compare(stringA, stringB) > 0
```

In short, it's a pretty powerful loop!

Other Versions of the Do...Loop

It's possible to put the Until *expression* or While *expression* statements after Loop rather than after Do. Consider these two loops:

```
Do While n < 3
    n += 1
Loop
```

...and...

```
Do
    n += 1
Loop While n < 3
```

At first glance it looks like the While n < 3 has just been moved around. You might think that these two loops are equivalent—but there's a subtle difference. Suppose the value of n is greater than 3 (4 say) as these two Do loops start. The first loop will not run at all. However, the second loop will run *once*. When the `Loop While n < 3` line is executed, the loop will be exited. This happens despite the condition saying that n must be less than 3.

Now consider these two Do Until loops:

```
Do Until n = 3
    n += 1
Loop
```

...and...

```
Do
    n += 1
Loop Until n = 3
```

Again, although at first glance it looks like these two loops are equivalent, they're not and behave slightly differently. Let's say that n is 3 this time. The first loop isn't going to run, as n already meets the exit condition for this loop. However, the second loop will run *once*. Then when you execute `Loop Until n = 3` the first time, n is now 4. So you go back to the start of the loop and increment n to 5, and so on. In fact, this is an example of an infinite loop (something we'll discuss later in this chapter) and will not stop.

> *When you use* Loop While *or* Loop Until, *you are saying that, no matter what, you want the loop to execute at least once. In general, I find it's best to stick with* Do While *and* Do Until, *rather than use* Loop While *and* Loop Until.

You may also come across a variation of Do While...Loop called the While...End While. This convention is a throwback to previous versions of Visual Basic, but old-school developers may still use it with .NET code, so it's important that you can recognize it. These two are equivalent, but you should use the first one.

```
Do While n < 3
    n += 1
Loop
```

...and...

```
While n < 3
    n += 1
End While
```

Nested Loops

You might need to start a loop even though you're already working through another loop. This is known as *nesting*, and is similar in theory to the nesting that you saw when you looked at If statements. In this *Try It Out*, you'll see how you can create and run through a loop, even though you're already working through one.

Using Nested Loops

1. Change the code from your last *Try It Out* to this:

```
Private Sub btnGo_Click(ByVal sender As System.Object, _
            ByVal e As System.EventArgs) Handles btnGo.Click

    ' clear the list...
    lstData.Items.Clear()

    ' loop1...
    Dim n As Integer
    Dim m As Integer
    For n = 1 To 2
        ' loop2...
        For m = 1 To 3
            lstData.Items.Add(n & ", " & m)
        Next
    Next

End Sub
```

2. Run the program and click the Go button. You should see results that look like those shown in Figure 4-26.

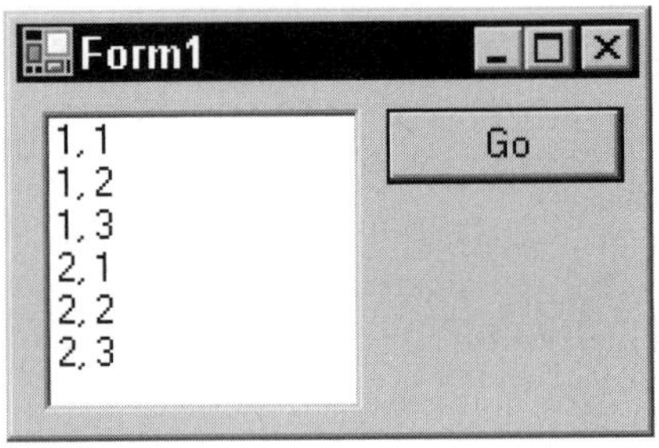

Figure 4-26

How It Works

This code is really quite simple. Our first loop iterates n from 1 to 2, and the second loop iterates m from 1 to 3. Within the second loop, you have a line of code to display the current values of n and m:

```
For n = 1 To 2
    ' loop2...
    For m = 1 To 3
        lstData.Items.Add(n & ", " & m)
    Next
Next
```

Each For statement must be paired with a Next statement, and each Next statement that you reach always "belongs" to the last created For statement. In this case, the first Next statement you reach is for the 1 To 3 loop, which results in m being incremented. When the value of m gets to be 4 you exit the loop.

After you've quit the second, inner loop, you hit another Next statement. This statement belongs to the first For statement, so n is set to 2 and you move back to the first line within the first, outer loop—in this case, the other For statement. Once there, the loop starts once more. Although in this *Try It Out* you've seen two For...Next loops nested together, you can nest Do While loops and even mix them, so you can have two Do loops nested inside a For loop and vice versa.

Quitting Early

Sometimes you don't want to see a loop through to its natural conclusion. For example, you might be looking through a list for something specific and, when you find it, there's no need to go through the remainder of the list.

In this exercise, you'll revise your program that looked through folders on the local drive, but this time when you get to c:\ Program Files, you'll display a message and quit.

Try It Out   Quitting a Loop Early

1.   Find the Click event handler for btnGo and change the code to this:

```
Private Sub btnGo_Click(ByVal sender As System.Object, _
            ByVal e As System.EventArgs) Handles btnGo.Click

    ' get a list of subfolders...
    Dim subfolders() As DirectoryInfo
    subfolders = New DirectoryInfo("c:\ ").GetDirectories

    ' loop...
    Dim subfolder As DirectoryInfo
    For Each subfolder In subfolders
        ' add the item to the list...
        lstData.Items.Add(subfolder.FullName)

        ' have we got to c:\ program files?
        If String.Compare(subfolder.FullName, _
            "c:\ program files", True) = 0 Then

            ' tell the user...
            MessageBox.Show("Found it!", "Loops")

            ' quit the loop...
            Exit For

        End If
    Next

End Sub
```

2.   Run the program and click the Go button. You'll see something similar to the results shown in Figure 4-27.

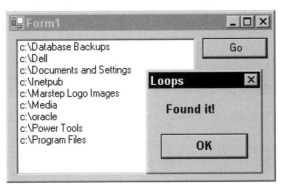

Figure 4-27

How It Works

This time, with each iteration you use the String.Compare method that we discussed earlier to check the name of the folder to see if it matches c:\Program Files:

```
' have you got to c:\program files?
If String.Compare(subfolder.FullName, _
    "c:\program files", True) = 0 Then
```

If it does, the first thing you do is display a message box:

```
' tell the user...
MessageBox.Show("Found it!", "Loops")
```

After the user has clicked OK to dismiss the message box, you use the Exit For statement to quit the loop. In this instance, the loop is short-circuited and the Visual Basic .NET moves to the first line after the Next statement.

```
' quit the loop...
Exit For
```

Of course, if the name of the folder doesn't match the one you're looking for, you keep looping. Using loops to find an item in a list is one of their most common uses. Once you've found the item you're looking for, using the Exit For statement to short-circuit the list is a very easy way to improve the performance of your application.

Imagine you have a list of a thousand items to look through. You find the item you're looking for on the tenth iteration. If you don't quit the loop after you've finished working with the item, you're effectively asking the computer to look through another 990 useless items. If, however, you do quit the loop early, you can move on and start running another part of the algorithm.

Quitting Do . . . Loops

As you might have guessed, you can quit a Do . . . Loop in more or less the same way.

Quitting a Do...Loop

1. Change the Click event handler for btnGo to this:

```
Private Sub btnGo_Click(ByVal sender As System.Object, _
        ByVal e As System.EventArgs) Handles btnGo.Click

    ' start looping...
    Dim n As Integer = 0
    Do While n < 10
        ' add n to the list...
        lstData.Items.Add(n)
        ' add one to n...
        n += 1

        ' do we need to quit?
        If n = 3 Then
            Exit Do
        End If
    Loop

End Sub
```

2. Run the project and click the Go button. You'll see a list containing the values 0, 1, and 2.

How It Works

In this case, because you're in a Do...Loop, you have to use Exit Do rather than Exit For. However, the principle is exactly the same. Exit Do will work with both Do While...Loop and Do Until...Loop loops.

Infinite Loops

When building loops you can create something called an *infinite loop*. What this means is a loop that, once started, will never finish. Consider this code:

```
Dim n As Integer = 0
Do
    n += 1
Loop Until n = 0
```

This loop will run *once*. Then when you execute Loop Until n = 0 the first time, n is 1. So you go back to the start of the loop again and increment n to 2, and so on. What's important here is that it will never get to 0. The loop becomes infinite, and the program won't crash (at least not instantly), but it may well become unresponsive.

If you suspect a program has dropped into an infinite loop, you'll need to force the program to stop. With Windows 2000, this is pretty easy. If you are running your program in Visual Studio .NET, flip over to it, and select Debug ⇨ Stop Debugging from the menu. This will immediately stop the program. If you are running your compiled program, you'll need to use Task Manager. Press *Ctrl+Alt+Delete* and select Task Manager. Your program should show as Not Responding. Select your program in the Task Manager and click End Task. Eventually this opens a dialog asking if you want to kill the program stone dead, so click End Task again.

In some extreme cases, the loop can take up so much processing power or other system resources that you won't be able to open Task Manager or flip over to Visual Studio. In these cases, you can persevere and try to use either of these methods; or you can reset your computer and chalk it up to experience.

Visual Studio .NET automatically saves the program files before running the application, so you're unlikely to lose any of your program code should you have to reset. However, that may not be true of other applications, so it's a good idea to make sure that you don't have other programs open while running code.

In some cases, it's perfectly acceptable to create infinite loops deliberately. However, you must take care to ensure that you use the appropriate Exit Do so that the program will end at some point.

Summary

In this chapter, you took a detailed look at the various ways that programs can make decisions and loop through code. You first saw the alternative operators that can be used with If statements and examined how multiple operators could be combined by using the And and Or keywords. Additionally, you examined how case-insensitive string comparisons could be performed.

You then looked at Select Case, an efficient technique for choosing one outcome out of a group of possibilities. Next you examined the concept of looping within a program and introduced the two main types of loops: For loops and Do loops. For loops iterate a given number of times, or the derivative For Each loop can be used to automatically loop through a list of items in an array. Do While loops iterate while a given condition remains True, whereas Do Until loops iterate until a given condition becomes True.

In summary, you should know how to use:

- ❑   IF, elseif And else statements to test for multiple conditions
- ❑   Nested IF statements
- ❑   Comparison operators and the String.Compare method
- ❑   The Select Case statement to perform multiple comparisons
- ❑   For...Next and For...Each loops
- ❑   Do...Loop and Do While...Loop statements

Exercises

1.   What are the six possible arithmetic operators that can be used with an If statement?
2.   How do you do case-insensitive string comparisons?
3.   What kind of loop is appropriate for iterating through items in an array?
4.   How can you exit a loop early?
5.   Why is a Select Case statement useful?

5

Working with Data Structures

In this chapter, you will see some ways in which you can work with complex sets of data. You start by learning about the array, which is used to hold lists of similar data. For example, you may create an array of friends' names (and you do exactly that later in this chapter). The chapter then discusses how enumerations can be used to allow a previously defined set of values to be made available (preventing you from supplying an invalid value). Constants are the next topic, and you will see how they improve the maintainability of your code by replacing recurring literal values. You then move on to working with structures (which are similar to classes), and then you see how you can build powerful collection classes for working with, maintaining, and manipulating lists of complex data.

Understanding Arrays

A fairly common requirement when writing software is the ability to hold lists of similar or related data. You can provide this functionality by using an array. Arrays are just lists of data that have a single data type. For example, you might want to store a list of friends' age in an integer array or their names in a string array.

In this section, you take a look at how to define, populate, and use arrays in your applications.

Defining and Using Arrays

When you define an array, you're actually creating a variable that has more than one dimension. For example, if you define a variable as a string, as follows, you can only hold a single string value in it:

```
Dim s As String
```

However, with an array you create a kind of multiplier effect with a variable, so you can hold more than one value in a single variable. An array is defined by entering the size of the array after the variable name. So, if you wanted to define a string array of length 10, you'd do this:

```
Dim s(9) As String
```

The reason why you use (9) instead of (10) to get an array of length 10 is explained in detail later. For now it is simply because numbering in an array starts at zero, so one to you is zero in an array, two to you is one in an array, and so on.

Once you have an array, you can access individual elements in it by providing an index value between 0 and a maximum possible value—this maximum possible value happens to be one less than the total size of the array.

So, to set the element with index 2 in the array, you'd do this:

```
s(2) = "Disraeli"
```

To get that same element back again, you'd do this:

```
MessageBox.Show(s(2))
```

What's important is that other elements in the array are unaffected when you set their siblings. So, if you do this:

```
s(3) = "Winston"
```

...s(2) remains set to "Disraeli".

Perhaps the easiest way to understand what an array looks like and how one works is to write some code that uses them.

Try It Out   Defining and Using a Simple Array

1. Using Visual Studio .NET, click the File menu and choose New ⇨ Project. In the New Project dialog box, create a new Windows Application called **Array Demo**.

2. When the Designer for Form1 appears, add a ListBox control to the form. Using the Properties window set its Name property to **lstFriends** and its IntegralHeight property to **False** (this tells the list box not to resize, but to show partial items).

3. Now add a Button control to the form. In this case, set its Name property to **btnGo** and set its Text property to **Go**. Your form should now look something like Figure 5-1.

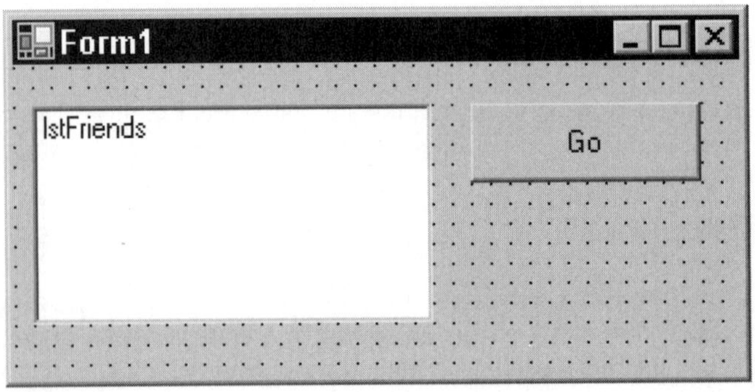

Figure 5-1

4. Double-click the Go button. Add this code:

```
Private Sub btnGo_Click(ByVal sender As System.Object, _
        ByVal e As System.EventArgs) Handles btnGo.Click
    ' define an array to hold friends in...
    Dim friends(4) As String
    ' store the name of each friend...
    friends(0) = "Jonathan"
    friends(1) = "Richard"
    friends(2) = "Thearon"
    friends(3) = "Sharon"
    friends(4) = "Micheal"
    ' add Jonathan to the list...
    lstFriends.Items.Add(friends(0))
End Sub
```

5. Run the project. Click the Go button and you will see a screen like the one in Figure 5-2.

Figure 5-2

How It Works

When you define an array you have to specify both a data type and a size. In this case, you're specifying an array of type `String` and also defining an array size of 5:

```
Private Sub btnGo_Click(ByVal sender As System.Object, _
        ByVal e As System.EventArgs) Handles btnGo.Click
    ' define an array to hold friends in...
    Dim friends(4) As String
```

The way the size is defined is a little quirky. You have to specify a size one less than the final size you want. (You learn why in a minute.) So here, you have used the line:

```
Dim friends(4) As String
```

In this way, you end up with an array of size 5. Another way of expressing this is to say that you have an array comprising 5 elements.

Once done, you have your array and you can access each item in the array by using an index. The index is given as a number in parentheses after the name of the array. Indexes start at zero and go up to one less than the number of items in the array. The following example sets all five possible items in the array to the names:

```
' store the name of each friend...
friends(0) = "Jonathan"
friends(1) = "Richard"
friends(2) = "Thearon"
friends(3) = "Sharon"
friends(4) = "Micheal"
```

In a similar way to how you can use an index to set the items in an array, you use an index to get items back out. In this case, you're asking for the item at position 0, which returns the first item in the array, namely Jonathan:

```
' add Jonathan to the list...
lstFriends.Items.Add(friends(0))
End Sub
```

The reason the indexes and sizes seem skewed is because the indexes are zero-based and in typical human logic you tend to number things from 1. In an array definition, specify the size of the array as the upper-index bound, or rather the highest possible index that the array will support. Likewise, when putting items into or retrieving items from an array, adjust the position you want down by one to get the actual index—for example, the fifth index is actually at position 4, the first index is at position 0, and so on.

Using For Each . . . Next

One common way to work with arrays is by using a For Each...Next loop. This loop was introduced in Chapter 4, but you used them with collections returned from Framework classes. Now look at how you use For Each...Next with an array.

Try It Out   Using For Each . . . Next with an Array

1. If the program is running, close it. Open the code editor for Form1 and change the btnGo_Click event procedure so that it now looks like this:

```
    ...
    friends(4) = "Micheal"
    ' go through each friend...
    Dim friendName As String
    For Each friendName In friends
        ' add each one to the list...
        lstFriends.Items.Add(friendName)
    Next
End Sub
```

2. Run the project and click Go. You'll see a screen like the one in Figure 5-3.

Figure 5-3

How It Works

Previously, you saw the `For Each...Next` loop iterate through a collection returned from the Framework. In this example, it is used in an array. The principle is similar—you have to create a control variable that is of the same type as the array and gives this to the loop when it starts. The internals behind the loop move through the array starting at element 0 until it reaches the last element. For each iteration, you can examine the value of the control variable and do something with it—in this case, you add the name to the list.

Also, notice that the items are added to the list in the same order that they appear in the array. That's because `For Each...Next` goes through from the first item to the last item as they are defined.

Passing Arrays as Parameters

It's extremely useful to be able to pass an array (which could be a list of values) to a function as a parameter. In this section, you look at how to do this.

Try It Out   Passing Arrays as Parameters

1. Open the code editor for Form1. Move the loop into a separate function, like this:

```
Private Sub btnGo_Click(ByVal sender As System.Object, _
        ByVal e As System.EventArgs) Handles btnGo.Click
    ' define an array to hold friends in...
    Dim friends(4) As String
    ' store the name of each friend...
    friends(0) = "Jonathan"
    friends(1) = "Richard"
    friends(2) = "Thearon"
    friends(3) = "Sharon"
    friends(4) = "Micheal"
End Sub
Sub AddFriendsToList(ByVal friends() As String)
    ' go through each friend...
    Dim friendName As String
    For Each friendName In friends
        ' add each one to the list...
        lstFriends.Items.Add(friendName)
    Next
End Sub
```

2. Now, change the code in `btnGo_Click` so that it reads as follows:

```
...
friends(4) = "Micheal"
' show the friends...
AddFriendsToList(friends)
End Sub
```

3. Run the project and click Go. You'll see the same results as shown in Figure 5-3.

How It Works

The trick here is to tell the function that the parameter is expecting an array of type `String`. You do this by using empty parentheses, like this:

```
Sub AddFriendsToList(ByVal friends() As String)
```

If you specify an array but don't define a size (or upper bound value) you're telling Visual Basic .Net that you don't know or care how big the array is. That means that you can pass an array of any size through to `AddFriendsToList`. Here, you're sending your original array:

```
friends(4) = "Micheal"
' show the friends...
AddFriendsToList(friends)
```

But, what happens if you define another array of a different size?

Try It Out   Adding More Friends

1. Open the code editor for Form1 and add this code to the `btnGo_Click` method:

```
...
friends(4) = "Micheal"
' store more friends...
Dim moreFriends(1) As String
moreFriends(0) = "Zita"
moreFriends(1) = "Seth"
' show the friends...
AddFriendsToList(friends)
AddFriendsToList(moreFriends)
End Sub
```

2. Run the project and click Go. You will see the form shown in Figure 5-4.

How It Works

What you have done here is proven that the array you pass as a parameter does not have to be of a fixed size. You created a new array of size 2 and passed it through to the same `AddFriendsToList` function.

As you're writing code, you can tell whether a parameter is an array type by looking for empty parentheses in the IntelliSense pop-up box, as illustrated in Figure 5-5.

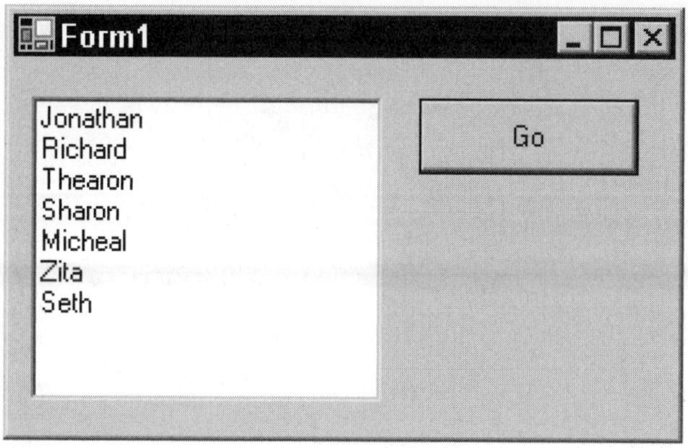

Jonathan
Richard
Thearon
Sharon
Micheal
Zita
Seth

Go

Figure 5-4

```
'show the friends...
AddFriendsToList(friends)
AddFriendsToList(more|
    AddFriendsToList (friends()As String)
End Sub
```

Figure 5-5

Not only are you informed that friends is an array type, but you also see that the data type of the array is String.

Sorting Arrays

It is sometimes useful to be able to take an array and sort it. In this section, you will see how you can take an array and sort it alphabetically.

Try It Out **Sorting Arrays**

1. Open the code editor for Form1 and find the AddFriendsToList method. Add this code:

```
Sub AddFriendsToList(ByVal friends() As String)
    ' sort it...
    Array.Sort(friends)
    ' go through each friend...
    ...
```

2. Run the project and click Go. You'll see Form1 with the array sorted alphabetically.

How It Works

All arrays are internally implemented in a class called System.Array. In this case, you want to use a shared method on that class called Sort, which takes a single parameter, namely the array you want to sort. Depending on the data type used by the array, the Sort method will then do as its name suggests and sort it for you. This case uses a string array and you get an alphanumeric sort.

If you were to attempt to use this technique on an array containing integer or floating-point values, the array would be sorted in numeric order.

Going Backwards

For Each...Next will only go through an array in one direction. It starts at position 0 and loops through to the end of the array. If you want to go through an array backwards (from the length—1 position to 0) you have to use a standard For...Next loop.

Try It Out   Going Backwards

1. In Form1 remove the second array definition and the second call to AddFriendsToList so you have what you had before:

```
Private Sub btnGo_Click(ByVal sender As System.Object, _
    ByVal e As System.EventArgs) Handles btnGo.Click
    ' define an array to hold friends in...
    Dim friends(4) As String
    ' store the name of each friend...
    friends(0) = "Jonathan"
    friends(1) = "Richard"
    friends(2) = "Thearon"
    friends(3) = "Sharon"
    friends(4) = "Micheal"
    ' show the friends...
    AddFriendsToList(friends)
End Sub
```

2. Alter AddFriendsToList so that it now looks like this:

```
Sub AddFriendsToList(ByVal friends() As String)
    ' sort it...
    Array.Sort(friends)
    ' how big is the array?
    Dim upperBound As Integer = friends.GetUpperBound(0)
    ' go through each friend...
    Dim index As Integer
    For index = upperBound To 0 Step -1
        ' add each one to the list...
        lstFriends.Items.Add(friends(index))
    Next
End Sub
```

3. Run the project and click Go. You'll see the friends listed in reverse order. (The array is sorted, and the items are added to the list in reverse order, so you see them here in reverse order.)

How It Works

When you are given an array in AddFriendsToList, you don't know how big it actually is. You can, however, use the GetUpperBound method to find out how big it is. You pass a value of 0 to this method to get the upper bound of the first dimension in the array—in other words the highest index value that the array supports:

```
    ' how big is the array?
    Dim upperBound As Integer = friends.GetUpperBound(0)
```

Once you have that value, you can set up a `For...Next` loop that accesses each index in the array one at a time, and in reverse order:

```
' go through each friend...
Dim index As Integer
For index = upperBound To 0 Step -1
    ' add each one to the list...
    lstFriends.Items.Add(friends(index))
```

Traversing an Array in Random Order

You've seen how you can go through an array in one direction, and then back through it in another. Now let's look at how to go through the array in a random order.

Try It Out   Traversing in Random Order

1. Make these changes to `AddFriendsToList`:

```
Sub AddFriendsToList(ByVal friends() As String)
    ' sort it...
    Array.Sort(friends)
    ' how big is the array?
    Dim upperBound As Integer = friends.GetUpperBound(0)
    ' create a randomizer...
    Dim random As New System.Random()
    ' count ten items...
    Dim n As Integer
    For n = 1 To 10
        ' which index?
        Dim index As Integer = random.Next(upperBound)
        lstFriends.Items.Add(index & ": " & friends(index))
    Next
End Sub
```

2. Run the project and click the Go button. You will see something like Figure 5-6.

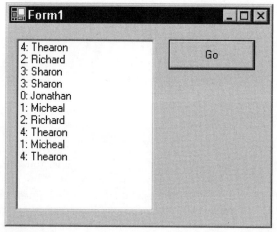

Figure 5-6

How It Works

The .NET random number generator (implemented in `System.Random`) can be used to create random numbers on demand. In this instance, for every iteration of the loop, you're asking the generator to give you a random number between 0 and upperBound—or the length of the array. The parameter passed to the `Random` class's `Next` method is exclusive, so you have to give it one more than the number you require:

```
Dim upperBound As Integer = friends.GetUpperBound(0)
' create a randomizer...
Dim random As New System.Random()
' count ten items...
Dim n As Integer
For n = 1 To 10
    ' which index?
    Dim index As Integer = random.Next(upperBound)
    lstFriends.Items.Add(index & ": " & friends(index))
```

Initializing Arrays with Values

It is possible to create an array in Visual Basic .NET and populate it in one line of code, rather than having to write specific lines to populate each item as shown here:

```
' store the name of each friend...
friends(0) = "Jonathan"
friends(1) = "Richard"
friends(2) = "Thearon"
friends(3) = "Sharon"
friends(4) = "Micheal"
```

Try It Out   Initializing Arrays with Values

1. Find the `btnGo_Click` event handler and make this change:

```
Private Sub btnGo_Click(ByVal sender As System.Object, _
        ByVal e As System.EventArgs) Handles btnGo.Click
    ' define an array to hold friends in...
    Dim friends() As String = {"Jonathan", "Richard", "Thearon", _
        "Sharon", "Micheal"}
    ' show the friends...
    AddFriendsToList(friends)
End Sub
```

2. Run the project. The program will behave just as it did before.

How It Works

The pair of braces {} allows you to set the values that should be held in an array directly. In this instance, you have five values to enter into the array, separated with commas. Notice that when you do this, you don't specify an upper bound for the array—instead you use empty parentheses. Visual Basic .NET prefers to calculate the upper bound for you based on the values you supply.

This technique can be quite awkward to use when populating large arrays. If your program relies on populating large arrays, you might want to use the method illustrated earlier—specifying the position and the value.

Understanding Enumerations

So far, the variables you've seen had virtually no limitations on the kinds of data you can store in them. Technical limits not withstanding, if you have a variable defined As Integer, you can put any number you like in it. Same with String and Double. However, you have seen a variable that has only two possible values: Boolean variables can be either True or False and nothing else.

Often when writing code you want to limit the possible values that can be stored in a variable. For example, if you have a variable that stores the number of doors that a car has, do you really want to be able to store 163,234?

Using Enumerations

Enumerations allow you to build a new type of variable, based on one of these data types: Integer, Long, Short, or Byte. This variable can be set to one value of a set of possible values that you define, and ideally prevents you from supplying invalid values. It is used to provide clarity in the code, as it can describe a particular value. In this section, you'll look at how to build an application that looks at the time of day and, based on that, can record a DayAction of one of these possible values:

❑   Asleep

❑   Getting ready for work

❑   Traveling to work

❑   At work

❑   At lunch

❑   Traveling from work

❑   Relaxing with friends

❑   Getting ready for bed

Try It Out   Using Enumerations

1. Using Visual Studio .NET, create a new Windows Application project called **Enum Demo**.

2. Enumerations are typically defined as a member of the class that intends to use them (though this does not have to be the case). When the Designer for Form1 opens, open the code editor for the form and add this to the top:

```
Public Class Form1
    Inherits System.Windows.Forms.Form
    ' enum...
    Public Enum DayAction As Integer
        Asleep = 0
```

```
            GettingReadyForWork = 1
            TravelingToWork = 2
            AtWork = 3
            AtLunch = 4
            TravelingFromWork = 5
            RelaxingWithFriends = 6
            GettingReadyForBed = 7
        End Enum
```

3. With an enumeration defined, you can create new member variables that use the enumeration as their data type. Add this member:

```
    ...
    End Enum
    ' members...
    Public CurrentState As DayAction
```

4. Flip back to the Designer for Form1. Change the Text property of Form1 to **What's Len Doing**? Now add a TrackBar control and a TextBox control to the form so that it looks like Figure 5-7.

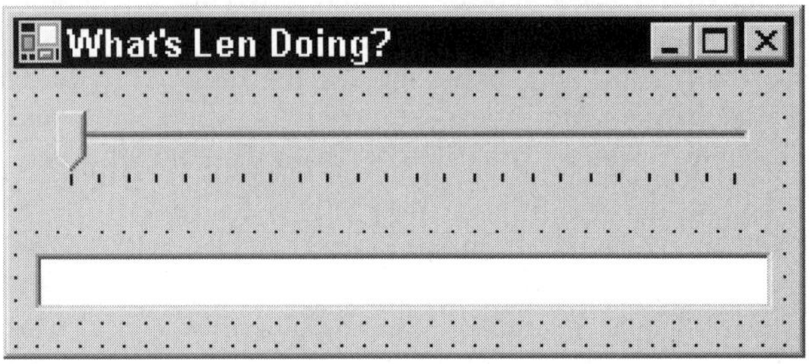

Figure 5-7

5. Using the Properties window, change the Name property of the track bar to **trkHour**. Set its Maximum property to 23 and its Minimum property to 0 (to cater for the 24-hour clock). In a similar fashion, change the Name property of the text box to **txtState**. Clear its Text property.

6. Double-click the background of the form to create a new Load event handler. Add this code:

```
Private Sub Form1_Load(ByVal sender As System.Object, _
            ByVal e As System.EventArgs) Handles MyBase.Load
    ' set the hour to the current hour...
    Me.Hour = Date.Now.Hour
End Sub
```

7. Now, add this property below the code you added in Step 3:

```
    ' Hour property...
    Public Property Hour() As Integer
        Get
            Return trkHour.Value
        End Get
```

```
Set(ByVal Value As Integer)
    ' set the hour...
    trkHour.Value = Value
    ' set the text...
    Dim statusText As String
    statusText = "At " & Value & ":00, Len is "
    ' update the display...
    txtState.Text = statusText
End Set
End Property
```

8.   Move over to the Designer again and double-click the track bar. Add this code to the new
Scroll event handler:

```
Private Sub trkHour_Scroll(ByVal sender As System.Object, _
        ByVal e As System.EventArgs) Handles trkHour.Scroll
    ' update the hour...
    Me.Hour = trkHour.Value
End Sub
```

9.   Run the project. You will be able to slide the track bar around and the text will update to reflect
the hour you select as shown in Figure 5-8.

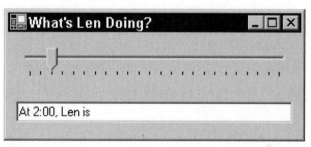

Figure 5-8

How It Works

In this application, the user will be able to use the track bar to choose the hour. You're then going to look
at the hour and determine which one of the eight states Len is in at the given time. To achieve this you
created a property called Hour that is set to the current hour when the application starts:

```
' set the hour to the current hour...
Me.Hour = Date.Now.Hour
```

You also set the same property when the thumb on the track bar is moved:

```
Private Sub trkHour_Scroll(ByVal sender As System.Object, _
        ByVal e As System.EventArgs) Handles trkHour.Scroll
    ' update the hour...
    Me.Hour = trkHour.Value
End Sub
```

When the Hour property is set, you form a string. You have not evaluated the Hour property to determine the state, but you will do this next:

```
' Hour property...
Public Property Hour() As Integer
    Get
        Return trkHour.Value
    End Get
    Set(ByVal Value As Integer)
        ' set the hour...
        trkHour.Value = Value
        ' set the text...
        Dim statusText As String
        statusText = "At " & Value & ":00, Len is "
        ' update the display...
        txtState.Text = statusText
    End Set
End Property
```

Determining the State

Now you look at determining the state when the Hour property is set. You can take the Integer value returned by the TrackBar control and use it to determine which value in your enumeration that it matches. This section demonstrates this and displays the value on your form.

Try It Out   Determining State

1. Open the code editor for Form1 and find the Hour property; add this code:

```
' Hour property...
Public Property Hour() As Integer
    Get
        Return trkHour.Value
    End Get
    Set(ByVal Value As Integer)
        ' set the hour...
        trkHour.Value = Value
        ' determine the state...
        Dim hour As Integer = Value
        If hour >= 6 And hour < 7 Then
            CurrentState = DayAction.TravelingToWork
        ElseIf hour >= 7 And hour < 8 Then
            CurrentState = DayAction.TravelingToWork
        ElseIf hour >= 8 And hour < 13 Then
            CurrentState = DayAction.AtWork
        ElseIf hour >= 13 And hour < 14 Then
            CurrentState = DayAction.AtLunch
        ElseIf hour >= 14 And hour < 17 Then
            CurrentState = DayAction.AtWork
        ElseIf hour >= 17 And hour < 18 Then
            CurrentState = DayAction.TravelingFromWork
        ElseIf hour >= 18 And hour < 22 Then
            CurrentState = DayAction.RelaxingWithFriends
```

```
        ElseIf hour >= 22 And hour < 23 Then
            CurrentState = DayAction.GettingReadyForBed
        Else
            CurrentState = DayAction.Asleep
        End If
        ' set the text...
        Dim statusText As String
        statusText = "At " & Value & ":00, Len is " & CurrentState
        ' update the display...
        txtState.Text = statusText
    End Set
End Property
```

2.   Run the project. You'll see something like Figure 5-9.

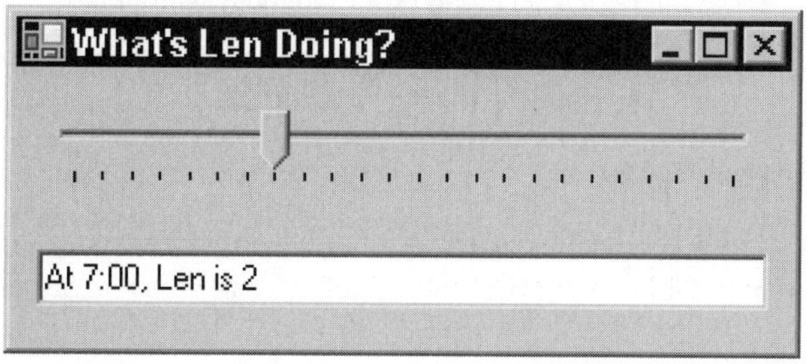

What's Len Doing?

At 7:00, Len is 2

Figure 5-9

3.   Here's a problem—the user doesn't know what 2 means. Close the project and find the following section of code within the Hour property:

```
' set the text...
Dim statusText As String
statusText = "At " & Value & ":00, Len is " & CurrentState
```

Change the last two lines to read as follows:

```
statusText = "At " & Value & ":00, Len is " & _
    CurrentState.ToString ()
```

4.   Now run the project and you'll see something like Figure 5-10.

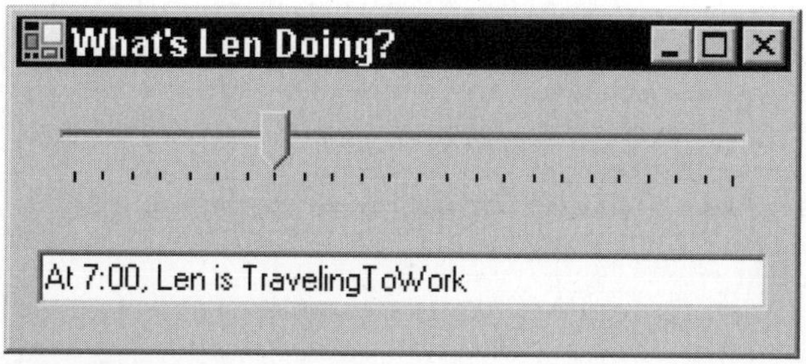

What's Len Doing?

At 7:00, Len is TravelingToWork

Figure 5-10

How It Works

As you typed the code in, you'd have noticed that whenever you tried to set a value against `CurrentState`, you were presented with a list of possibilities as shown in Figure 5-11.

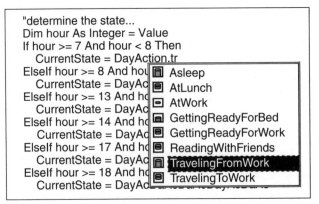

```
"determine the state...
Dim hour As Integer = Value
If hour >= 7 And hour < 8 Then
    CurrentState = DayAction.tr
ElseIf hour >= 8 And hou     ⬛ Asleep
    CurrentState = DayAc      ⬛ AtLunch
ElseIf hour >= 13 And hd     ⬛ AtWork
    CurrentState = DayAc      ⬛ GettingReadyForBed
ElseIf hour >= 14 And hd     ⬛ GettingReadyForWork
    CurrentState = DayAc      ⬛ ReadingWithFriends
ElseIf hour >= 17 And hd     ⬛ TravelingFromWork
    CurrentState = DayAc      ⬛ TravelingToWork
ElseIf hour >= 18 And hd
    CurrentState = DayAc
```

Figure 5-11

Visual Studio .NET knows that `CurrentState` is of type `DayAction`. It also knows that `DayAction` is an enumeration and that it defines eight possible values, each of which is displayed in the IntelliSense pop-up box.

Fundamentally though, because `DayAction` is based on an integer, `CurrentState` is an integer value. That's why the first time you ran the project with the state determination code in place you saw an integer at the end of the status string. At 11 A.M., you know that Len is at work, or rather `CurrentState` equals `DayAction.AtWork`. You defined this as 3, which is why 3 is displayed at the end of the string.

What we've done in this *Try It Out* is to tack a call to the `ToString` method onto the end of the string. This results in a string representation of `DayAction` being used, rather than the integer representation.

Enumerations are incredibly useful when you want to store one of a possible set of values in a variable. As you start to drill into more complex objects in the Framework you'll find that they are used all over the place!

Setting Invalid Values

One of the limitations of enumerations is that it is possible to store values against an enumeration that technically isn't one of the possible defined values. For example, if you change the `Hour` property so that rather than setting `CurrentState` to `Asleep`, you set it to 999:

```
ElseIf hour >= 22 And hour < 23 Then
    CurrentState = DayAction.GettingReadyForBed
Else
    CurrentState = 999
End If
' set the text...
```

```
Dim statusText As String
statusText = "At " & Value & ":00, Len is " & _
    CurrentState.ToString()
' update the display...
txtState.Text = statusText
```

If you build the project, you'll notice that Visual Basic .NET doesn't flag this as an error. Further, if you actually run the project, you'll see that the value for `CurrentState` is shown in the text box as 999.

So, you can see that you can set a variable that references an enumeration to a value that is not defined in that enumeration and the application will still "work" (as long as the value is of the same type as the enumeration). If you build classes that use enumerations, you have to rely on the consumer of that class being well behaved. One technique to solve this problem would be to disallow invalid values in any properties that used the enumeration as their data type.

Understanding Constants

Another good programming practice that you need to look at is the constant. Imagine you have these two methods, each of which does something with a given file on the computer's disk. (Obviously, I'm omitting the code here that actually manipulates the file.)

```
Public Sub DoSomething()
    ' what's the filename?
    Dim filename As String = "c:\Temp\Demo.txt"
    ' open the file...
    ...
End Sub
Public Sub DoSomethingElse()
    ' what's the filename?
    Dim myFilename As String = "c:\Temp\Demo.txt"
    ' do something with the file...
    ...
End Sub
```

Using Constants

The code defining a string literal gives the name of a file twice. This is poor programming practice because if both methods are supposed to access the same file, should that filename change, this change has to be made in two separate places.

In this instance, both methods are next to each other and the program itself is small, but imagine that you have a massive program where a separate string literal pointing to the file is defined in 10, 50, or even 1,000 places. If you need to change the filename you'll have to change it many times. This is exactly the kind of thing that leads to serious problems while maintaining software code.

What you need to do instead is define the filename globally and then use that global definition of the filename in the code, rather than using a string literal. This is known as a constant. This is, in effect, a special kind of variable that cannot be changed when the program is running.

Try It Out   Using Constants

1. Using Visual Studio .NET, creates a new Windows Application project. and call it **Constants Demo**.

2. When the Designer for Form1 opens, add three buttons. Set the Name property of the first one to **btnOne**, the second to **btnTwo**, and the third to **btnThree**. Change the Text property of each to **One**, **Two**, and **Three** respectively. Your form should look like Figure 5-12.

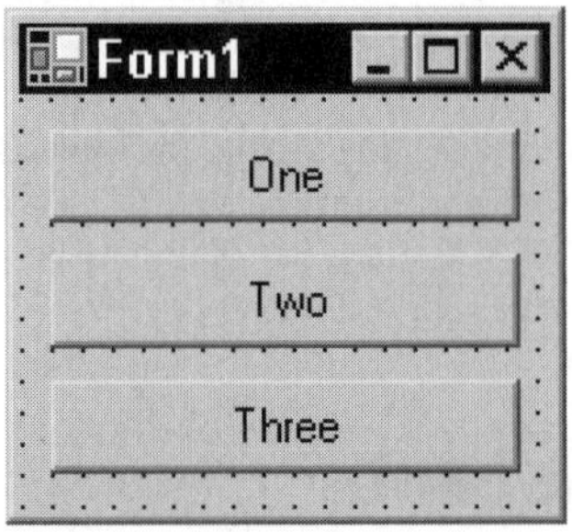

Figure 5-12

3. Now, at the top of the class definition, add this code:

```
Public Class Form1
    Inherits System.Windows.Forms.Form
    ' consts...
    Public Const MyFilename As String = "c:\Temp\Hello.txt"
```

4. Double-click button One in the Designer. Add this code:

```
Private Sub btnOne_Click(ByVal sender As System.Object, _
        ByVal e As System.EventArgs) Handles btnOne.Click
    ' use a constant...
    MessageBox.Show("1: " & MyFilename, "Constants Demo")
End Sub
```

5. Move over to the Designer again and double-click Two. Add this code:

```
Private Sub btnTwo_Click(ByVal sender As System.Object, _
        ByVal e As System.EventArgs) Handles btnTwo.Click
    ' use the constant again...
    MessageBox.Show("2: " & MyFilename, "Constants Demo")
End Sub
```

6. Finally, move over to the Designer and double-click Three. Add this code:

```
Private Sub btnThree_Click(ByVal sender As System.Object, _
        ByVal e As System.EventArgs) Handles btnThree.Click
    ' one more time...
    MessageBox.Show("3: " & MyFilename, "Constants Demo")
End Sub
```

7.   Run the project and click button One. You'll see the message box shown in Figure 5-13.

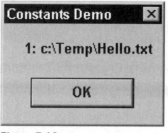

Figure 5-13

Likewise, you'll see the same filename if you click buttons Two or Three.

How It Works

A constant is actually a type of value that cannot be changed when the program is running. It is defined like a member is, but you add `Const` to the definition.

```
Public Class Form1
    Inherits System.Windows.Forms.Form
    ' consts...
    Public Const MyFilename As String = "c:\Wrox\Hello.txt"
```

You'll notice that it has a data type, just like a member, and you have to give it a value when it's defined. (Which makes sense, as you can't change it later.) You should define constants as members of the class, in the following way. Constants are available throughout the class definition. They are also available to other classes as they are shared by default. (You learn more about what *shared* means in Chapter 10.)

When you want to use the constant, refer to it just as you would refer a normal member:

```
Private Sub btnOne_Click(ByVal sender As System.Object, _
        ByVal e As System.EventArgs) Handles btnOne.Click
    ' use a constant...
    MessageBox.Show("1: " & MyFilename, "Constants Demo")
End Sub
```

Changing Constants

As mentioned before, the appeal of a constant is that it allows you to change a value that's used throughout a piece of code by altering a single piece of code. However, be aware that you can only change constants at design time, you cannot change their values at runtime. Look at how this works.

Try It Out   Changing Constants

1.   Change the value stored against `MyFilename`:

```
Public Class Form1
    Inherits System.Windows.Forms.Form
    ' consts...
    Public Const MyFilename As String = "c:\Chapter05\Welcome.txt"
```

2. Run the project. When you click any of the buttons you'll see that the new value of `MyFilename` is used as shown in Figure 5-14.

Figure 5-14

How It Works

This illustrates the power of constants—you can define a string literal value in a single location and then use that literal throughout the code. If the value of the literal has to change, you do it in one place and everything that used the old value automatically starts using the new value.

As a rule, constants should be used wherever you use a literal value more than once. However, this is a bit of overkill and developers tend to use constants whenever they need to store a reference to a resource that they use that might change at some point in the future. Filenames and instructions on how to connect to a database that an application needs are classic cases.

Different Constant Types

In this section, you've seen how to use a string constant, but you can use other types of variables as constants. There are some rules—basically a constant must not be able to change, so you should not store an object data type in a constant.

Integers are a very common form of constant. They can be defined like this:

```
Public Const HoursAsleepPerDay As Integer = 8
```

Also, it's fairly common to see constants used with enumerations, like this:

```
Public Const LensTypicalState As DayAction = DayAction.Asleep
```

Structures

Chapter 4 introduced the concept of creating your own classes for use in your applications. This section introduces structures.

Structures are very similar to classes, but have some subtle differences. As a rule of thumb, I would suggest that if you end up putting a lot of methods on a structure, it should probably be a class. It's also relatively tricky to convert from a structure to a class later on as the instantiation method is different, so choose once and choose wisely!

Building Structures

In terms of semantics, structures are known as value types and classes are known as reference types. This explains the difference in instantiation—you don't need to use the New keyword to instantiate an integer before you use it because it is a value type. Likewise, you do have to use the New keyword with a Form or other complex object because it is a reference type. Also, you cannot inherit from a structure—another important consideration when choosing whether to use a class or a structure.

Take a look at how you can build a structure.

Try It Out   Building a Structure

1. Using Visual Studio .NET, create a new Windows Application project. Call it **Structure Demo**.

2. When the project is created, use the Solution Explorer to add a new class called **Customer**.

3. When the code editor appears, add the following code:

```
Public Structure Customer
    ' members...
    Public FirstName As String
    Public LastName As String
    Public Email As String
End Structure
```

Note that you must ensure that you change Class *to* Structure *on the first and last lines!*

4. Open the Designer for Form1. Add four text boxes, four Label controls, and a button. Using the Properties window, change the properties as shown in Table 5.1.

Table 5-1 Setting Form1 properties

Control	Name	Property
First textbox	*txtName*	*Text = nothing*
Second textbox	*txtFirstName*	*Text = nothing*
Third textbox	*txtLastName*	*Text = nothing*
Fourth textbox	*txtEmailName*	*Text = nothing*
First label control	*lblName*	*Text = Name:*
Second label control	*lblFirstName*	*Text = First Name:*
Third label control	*lblLastName*	*Text = Last Name:*
Fourth label control	*lblEmailName*	*Text = E-mail:*
Button	*btnTest*	*Text = Test*

Your form should now look something like Figure 5-15.

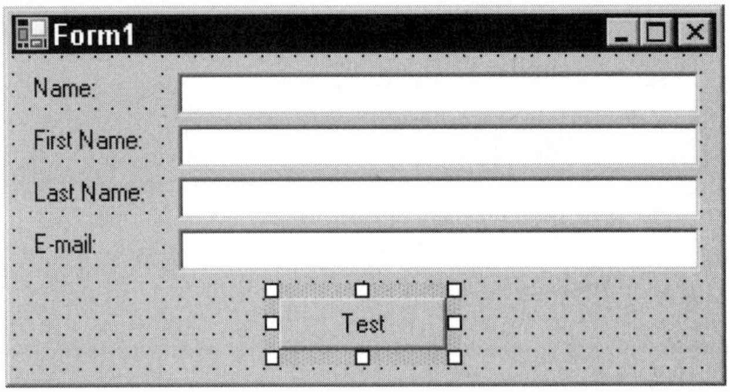

Figure 5-15

5. Double-click the button to create a new `Click` event handler. Add this code:

```
Private Sub btnTest_Click(ByVal sender As System.Object, _
        ByVal e As System.EventArgs) Handles btnTest.Click
    ' create a new customer...
    Dim testCustomer As Customer
    testCustomer.FirstName = "Amir"
    testCustomer.LastName = "Aliabadi"
    testCustomer.Email = "amir@pretendcompany.com"
    ' display the customer...
    DisplayCustomer(testCustomer)
End Sub
```

6. Next, add this procedure:

```
' DisplayCustomer - show the customer...
Public Sub DisplayCustomer(ByVal customer As Customer)
    ' update the fields...
    txtFirstName.Text = customer.FirstName
    txtLastName.Text = customer.LastName
    txtEmailName.Text = customer.Email
End Sub
```

7. Run the project and click the Test button. You'll see Figure 5-16.

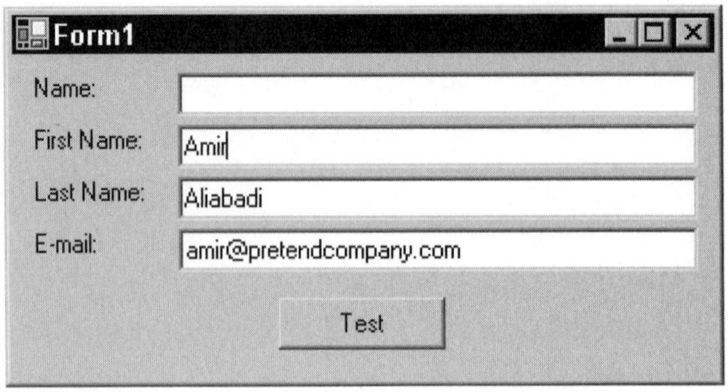

Figure 5-16

How It Works

A structure is conceptually very similar to a class.

The difference in definition is equally subtle: you use `Structure...End Structure` rather than `Class...End Class`.

```
Public Structure Customer
    ' members...
    Public FirstName As String
    Public LastName As String
    Public Email As String
End Structure
```

As you can see, structures can have public members just like classes have. They can also have private members, properties, and methods.

One important difference between structures and classes is that you don't have to create a structure with the `New` keyword before you can use it. In the `Click` handler code, you can see that you define a variable of type `Customer`, but you don't have to call `New`:

```
' create a new customer...
Dim testCustomer As Customer
testCustomer.FirstName = "Amir"
testCustomer.LastName = "Aliabadi"
testCustomer.Email = amir@pretendcompany.com
```

Adding Properties to Structures

Structures and classes are very similar. You can add properties to a structure just as you can with a class.

Try It Out   **Adding a Name Property**

1. Open the code editor for `Customer` and add this code below the members declaration code you added earlier:

```
' Name property...
Public ReadOnly Property Name() As String
    Get
        Return FirstName & " " & LastName
    End Get
End Property
```

2. Now, open the code editor for Form1. Find the `DisplayCustomer` method and add this code:

```
' DisplayCustomer - show the customer...
Public Sub DisplayCustomer(ByVal customer As Customer)
    ' update the fields...
    txtName.Text = customer.Name
    txtFirstName.Text = customer.FirstName
    txtLastName.Text = customer.LastName
    txtEmail.Text = customer.Email
End Sub
```

3. Run the project and click the Test button. You'll see that the top text box is populated, as shown in Figure 5-17.

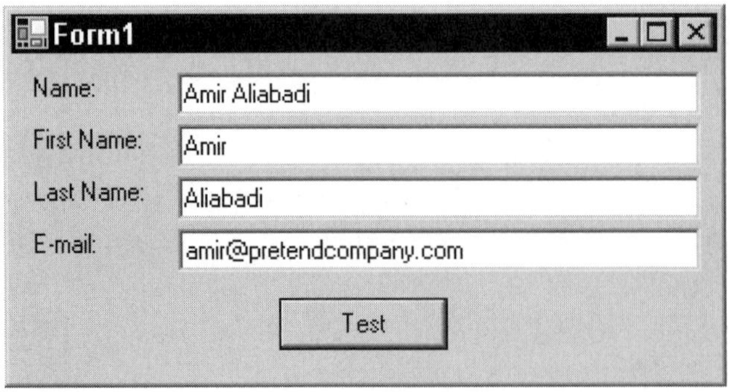

Figure 5-17

Working with Collections and Lists

One common construct you'll find used a lot in the Framework classes is the collection. These are conceptually similar to arrays; in other words they are a set of related information stored in a list of some sort, but they offer more flexibility to the developer using them. For example, imagine you need to store a set of `Customer` structures. You could use an array, but in some cases, the array might not be so easy to use.

If you need to add a new `Customer` to the array, you need to change the size of the array and insert the new item in the new last position in the array. (You learn more about how to change the size of an array later in this chapter.)

If you need to remove a `Customer` from the array, you need to look at each item in the array in turn. When you find the one we want, you have to create another version of the array one element smaller than the original array and copy everything but the one you want to delete into the new array. If you need to replace a `Customer` in the array with another customer, you need to look at each item in turn until you find the one we want and then replace it manually.

Using an Array List

The `System.Collections.ArrayList` provides a way to create an array that can be easily manipulated as you run your program. Look at using one of these now.

Try It Out   **Using an ArrayList**

1. Using the Designer for Form1, rearrange the form and add a new ListBox control. Change the Name property of the list box to **lstCustomers**. Change its IntegralHeight property to **False**. The form should now look something like Figure 5-18.

2. Open the code editor for Form1 and add this member to the top of the class definition:

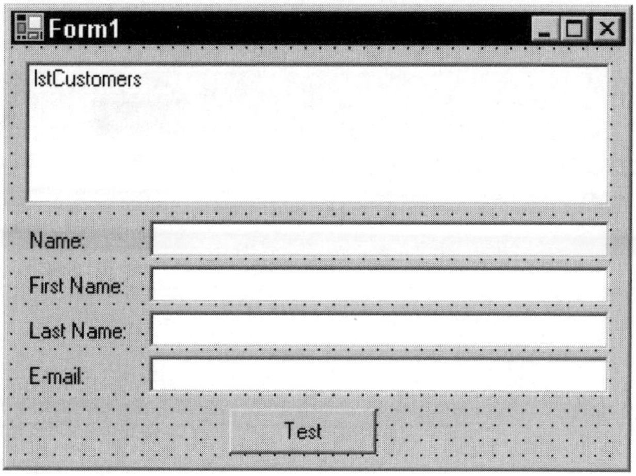

Figure 5-18

```
Public Class Form1
    Inherits System.Windows.Forms.Form
    ' members...
    Private_customers As New ArrayList()
```

3. Now, add this method to the `Form1` class:

```
' CreateCustomer - create a new customer...
Public Function CreateCustomer(ByVal firstName As String, _
    ByVal lastName As String, ByVal email As String) As Customer
    ' create the new customer...
    Dim newCustomer As Customer
    newCustomer.FirstName = firstName
    newCustomer.LastName = lastName
    newCustomer.Email = email
    ' add it to the list...
    _customers.Add(newCustomer)
    ' add it to the view...
    lstCustomers.Items.Add(newCustomer)
    ' return the customer...
    Return newCustomer
End Function
```

4. Next, find the `btnTest_Click` method and make these changes to the code:

```
Private Sub btnTest_Click(ByVal sender As System.Object, _
        ByVal e As System.EventArgs) Handles btnTest.Click
    ' create some customers...
    CreateCustomer("Amir", "Aliabadi", "amir@pretendcompany.com")
    CreateCustomer("Gretchen", "Aliabadi", _
                "gretchen@pretendcompany.com")
    CreateCustomer("Ben", "Aliabadi", "ben@pretendcompany.com")
End Sub
```

155

5. Run the project and click the Test button. You'll see Figure 5-19.

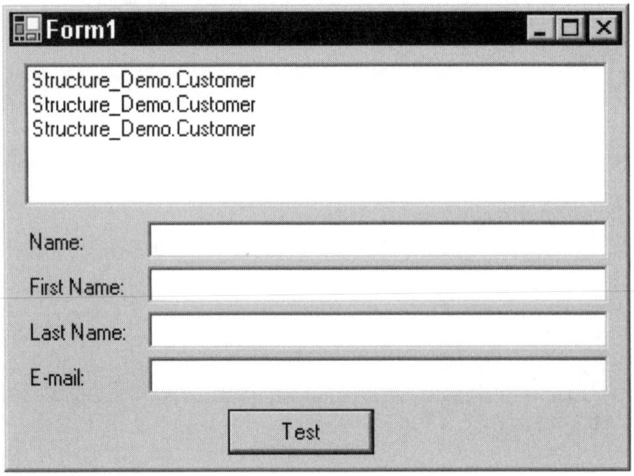

Figure 5-19

What I wanted to demonstrate here was that you are adding `Customer` structures to the list, but they are being displayed by the list as `Structure_Demo.Customer`; this is the full name of the class. The ListBox control accepts string values so by specifying that you wanted to add the `Customer` structure to the list box, Visual Basic .Net called the `ToString` method of the `Customer` structure. By default, the `ToString` method returns the structure name and not the contents that we wanted to see. So what you want to do is tweak `Customer` so that it can display something more meaningful. Once you do that, you'll see how the `ArrayList` works.

Try It Out   Overriding ToString

1. Open the code editor for `Customer` and add this method to the structure, ensuring that it is below the member declarations:

```
' ToString...
Public Overrides Function ToString() As String
    Return Name & " (" & Email & ")"
End Function
```

2. Run the project and click Test. You'll see Figure 5-20.

How It Works

Whenever a Customer structure is added to the list, the list box calls the `ToString` method on the structure to get a string representation of that structure. With this code, we override the default functionality of `ToString` so that rather than returning the full name of the structure, you get some interesting text:

```
' ToString...
Public Overrides Function ToString() As String
    Return Name & " (" & Email & ")"
End Function
```

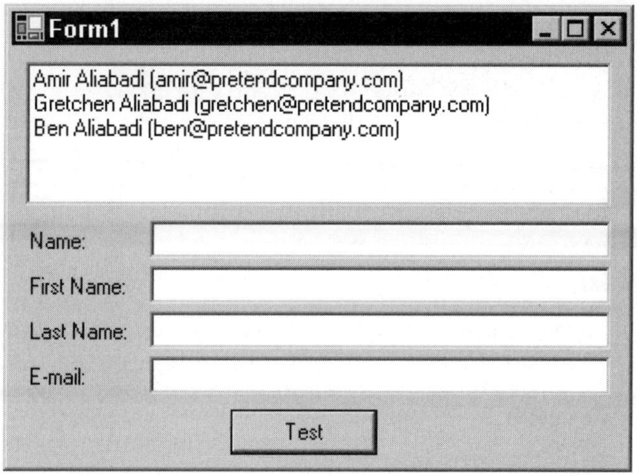

Figure 5-20

An `ArrayList` can be used to store a list of objects/structures of any type (in contrast to a regular array)—in fact, you can mix the types within an `ArrayList`, a topic we'll be talking about in a little while. What you've done is to create a method called `CreateCustomer` that initializes a new `Customer` structure based on parameters that it has passed:

```
' CreateCustomer - create a new customer...
Public Function CreateCustomer(ByVal firstName As String, _
    ByVal lastName As String, ByVal email As String) As Customer
    ' create the new customer...
    Dim newCustomer As Customer
    newCustomer.FirstName = firstName
    newCustomer.LastName = lastName
    newCustomer.Email = email
```

Once the structure has been initialized, we add it to the `ArrayList` stored in `customers`:

```
    ' add it to the list...
    _customers.Add(newCustomer)
```

You also add it to the list itself, like this:

```
    ' add it to the view...
    lstCustomers.Items.Add(newCustomer)
```

Finally, you can return the newly initialized `Customer` structure back to the caller:

```
    ' return the customer...
    Return newCustomer
End Function
```

With `CreateCustomer` defined, you can just call it to add new members to the `ArrayList` and to the list control:

```
Private Sub btnTest_Click(ByVal sender As System.Object, _
        ByVal e As System.EventArgs) Handles btnTest.Click
    ' create some customers...
    CreateCustomer("Amir", "Aliabadi", "amir@pretendcompany.com")
    CreateCustomer("Gretchen", "Aliabadi", _
                "gretchen@pretendcompany.com")
    CreateCustomer("Ben", "Aliabadi", "ben@pretendcompany.com")
End Sub
```

Deleting from an ArrayList

OK, so now you know the principle behind an `ArrayList`. You use it to do something that's traditionally hard to do with arrays but is pretty easy to do with an `ArrayList`, such as dynamically adding new values. Now let's look at how easy it is to delete items from an `ArrayList`.

Try It Out **Deleting Customers**

1. Using the Designer for Form1, add a new button. Change its Name property to **btnDelete** and its Text property to **Delete** as shown in Figure 5-21.

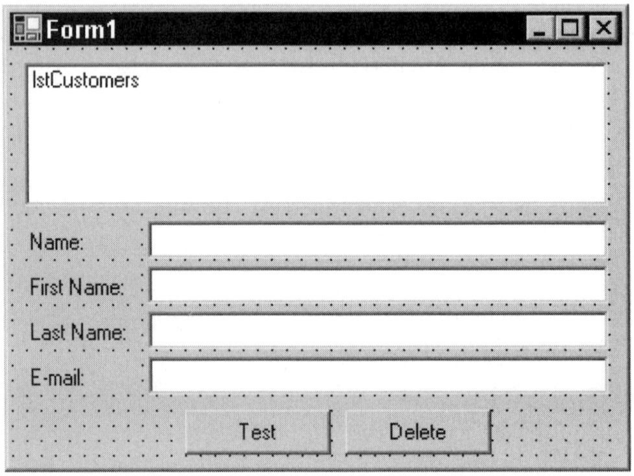

Figure 5-21

2. Double-click the Delete button. Add this code:

```
Private Sub btnDelete_Click(ByVal sender As System.Object, _
        ByVal e As System.EventArgs) Handles btnDelete.Click
    ' what customer to we want to select?
    If SelectedCustomer.IsEmpty = False Then
        ' ask the user...
        If MessageBox.Show("Are you sure you want to delete " & _
            SelectedCustomer.Name & "?", "Structure Demo", _
            MessageBoxButtons.YesNo, MessageBoxIcon.Question) _
            = DialogResult.Yes Then
```

```
                    ' store the customer that we want to delete...
                    Dim deleteCustomer As Customer = SelectedCustomer
                    ' remove it from the arraylist...
                    _customers.Remove(deleteCustomer)
                    ' remove it from the list view...
                    lstCustomers.Items.Remove(deleteCustomer)
                End If
            Else
                MessageBox.Show("You must select a customer.", _
                            "Structure Demo")
            End If
        End Sub
```

3. Next, add this property (below the section of code you added in Step 2):

```
Public ReadOnly Property SelectedCustomer() As Customer
    Get
        ' do we have a selection?
        If lstCustomers.SelectedIndex <> -1 Then
            ' return the selected customer...
            Return lstCustomers.Items(lstCustomers.SelectedIndex)
        End If
    End Get
End Property
```

Remember, adding the ReadOnly *keyword to a property definition prevents the developer from being able to change the value contained in the property.*

4. Finally, open the code editor for Customer and add this method:

```
' IsEmpty - are we populated?
Public Function IsEmpty() As Boolean
    If FirstName = "" Then
        Return True
    Else
        Return False
    End If
End Function
```

5. Run the project and click the Test button. *Do not* select a customer and click Delete. You'll see a message box indicating that you must select a customer.

6. Now select a customer and click Delete. You'll see a confirmation dialog similar to the one shown in Figure 5-22.

7. Click Yes and the person you selected will be removed from the list.

How It Works

The trick here is to build a property that will return the Customer structure that's selected in the list back to the caller on demand.

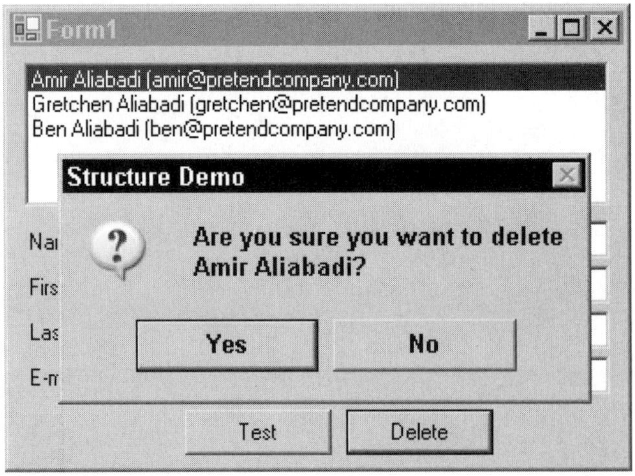

Figure 5-22

If no selection has been made in the list (or the list is empty) the ListBox control's SelectedIndex property will return −1. If you get a number other than this, an item has been selected and you can simply return this item back to the caller:

```
Public ReadOnly Property SelectedCustomer() As Customer
    Get
        ' do we have a selection?
        If lstCustomers.SelectedIndex <> -1 Then
            ' return the selected customer...
            Return lstCustomers.Items(lstCustomers.SelectedIndex)
        End If
    End Get
End Property
```

However, there is a problem. Due to the way structures work, the caller will be given a Customer structure that they can use regardless of whether or not one was actually selected. You need a way of determining whether or not a structure is empty, hence the IsEmpty method that you added to Customer:

```
' IsEmpty - are we populated?
Public Function IsEmpty() As Boolean
    If FirstName = "" Then
        Return True
    Else
        Return False
    End If
End Function
```

This method will return True if the FirstName member has not been populated or False if the member has been populated.

Inside the `Click` event for the Delete button, you can test to see if `SelectedCustomer` is empty, in other words whether or not a selection has been made:

```
' what customer to we want to select?
If SelectedCustomer.IsEmpty = False Then
```

If a selection has been made, you ask the user if they really want to go ahead with the deletion:

```
' ask the user...
If MessageBox.Show("Are you sure you want to delete "  & _
    SelectedCustomer.Name  & "?", "Structure Demo", _
    MessageBoxButtons.YesNo, MessageBoxIcon.Question) _
    = DialogResult.Yes Then
```

If the user does want to delete, you get a return value from `MessageBox.Show` equal to `DialogResult.Yes`. The `Remove` method of the ArrayList can then be used to remove the offending customer!

```
' remove it from the arraylist...
_customers.Remove(SelectedCustomer)
```

You also use a similar technique to remove the customer from the list box as well:

```
        ' remove it from the list view...
        lstCustomers.Items.Remove(SelectedCustomer)
    End If
Else
    MessageBox.Show("You must select a customer.", _
                    "Structure Demo")
    End If
End Sub
```

Showing Items in the ArrayList

For completeness, you'll want to add a quick piece of functionality to enhance the UI of your application. Here, you'll add code in the `SelectedIndexChanged` event for the Customers list. Every time you select a new customer, their details will be displayed in the text boxes on the form.

Try It Out   **Showing Details of the Selected Item**

  1. Using the Designer for Form1, double-click the list box. This will create a new `SelectedIndexChanged` event handler. Add this code:

```
Private Sub lstCustomers_SelectedIndexChanged(ByVal _
    sender As System.Object, ByVal e As System.EventArgs) _
    Handles lstCustomers.SelectedIndexChanged
    DisplayCustomer(SelectedCustomer)
End Sub
```

  2. Run the project and click the Test button to populate the list box. Now when you select items from the list they will appear in the fields at the bottom of the display, as shown in Figure 5-23.

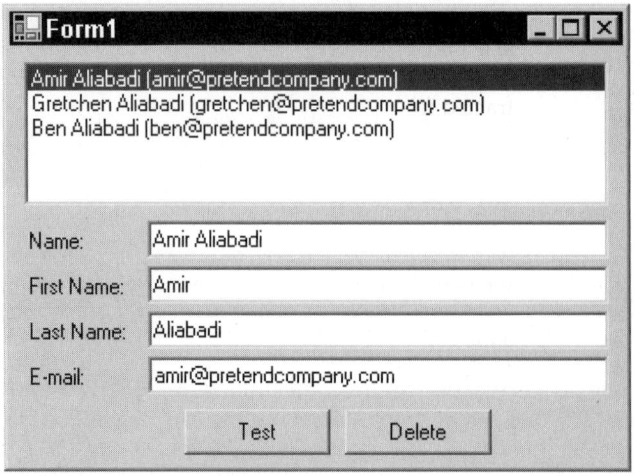

Figure 5-23

Collections

One thing that the .NET Framework uses all over the place is the collection. This is a way of easily creating ad hoc groups of similar or related items. If you take a look back at our Structure Demo code and peek into the `CreateCustomer` method, you'll notice that when adding items to the ArrayList and to the list box, you use a method called `Add`:

```
' add it to the list...
_customers.Add(newCustomer)
' add it to the view...
lstCustomers.Items.Add(newCustomer)
```

The code that deletes a customer uses a method called `Remove` on both objects:

```
' remove it from the arraylist...
_customers.Remove(SelectedCustomer)
' remove it from the list view...
lstCustomers.Items.Remove(SelectedCustomer)
```

Microsoft is very keen to see developers use the collection paradigm whenever they need to work with a list of items. It's also keen to see collections work in the same way irrespective of what they actually hold—which is why you use `Add` to add an item and `Remove` to remove an item, even though you're using a `System.Collections.ArrayList` object in one case and a `System.Windows.Forms.ListBox.ObjectCollection` object in another. This is something that Microsoft has taken a great deal of care over when building the .NET Framework. Consistency is good—it allows developers to map an understanding of one thing and use that same understanding with a similar thing. When designing the classes for use in your application, you should take steps to follow the conventions that Microsoft has laid down. For example, if you have a collection class and want to create a method that removes an item, call it `Remove` not `Delete`. Developers using your class will have an intuitive understanding of what `Remove` does because they're familiar with it. On the other hand, developers would "double-take" `Delete` because this has a different connotation.

One of the problems with using an `ArrayList` is that the developer who has an array list cannot guarantee that every item in the list is of the same type. Note that `ArrayList` makes no guarantees about the type of object (when I say object, I mean "object or structure") that it has a hold of. For this reason, each time an item is extracted from the `ArrayList`, the type should be checked to minimize the chances of causing an error.

The solution is to create a strongly-typed collection. This is a separate class that contains only objects of a particular type. They are very easy to create and, according to .NET best-programming standards as defined by Microsoft, the best way to create one is to derive a new class from `System.Collections.CollectionBase`, and add two methods (`Add` and `Remove`) and one property (`Item`):

❑ `Add` adds a new item to the collection

❑ `Remove` removes an items from the collection

❑ `Item` returns the item at the given index in the collection

Although you're going to be creating a strongly-typed collection class for holding structures, this technique works equally well for classes.

Creating CustomerCollection

In this *Try It Out* section you create a `CustomerCollection` class that is designed to hold a collection of `Customer` structures.

Try It Out   **Creating CustomerCollection**

1. Using the Solution Explorer, create a new class called **CustomerCollection**. Set the class to inherit from `CollectionBase`, and add a method such that your code now looks like this:

```
Public Class CustomerCollection
    Inherits System.Collections.CollectionBase
    ' Add - add a customer...
    Public Sub Add(ByVal newCustomer As Customer)
        Me.List.Add(newCustomer)
    End Sub
End Class
```

2. Then, add this method:

```
' Remove - delete a customer...
Public Sub Remove(ByVal removeCustomer As Customer)
    Me.List.Remove(removeCustomer)
End Sub
```

3. Open the code editor for Form1 and find the definition for the _customers member. Change its type from ArrayList to `CustomerCollection`:

```
Public Class Form1
    Inherits System.Windows.Forms.Form
    ' members...
    Private_customers As New CustomerCollection
```

4. Finally, run the project. The application should work as it did before.

How It Works

The `System.Collections.CollectionBase` class contains a basic implementation of a collection that can hold any object. In that respect it's very similar to an `ArrayList`. However, the advantage comes when you add your own methods to the class that inherits from `CollectionBase` as is the case with `CustomerCollection`.

Since you provided a version of `Add` that only accepts a `Customer` structure, it's impossible to put anything into the array that isn't a `Customer`. You can see there that IntelliSense is telling you that the only thing you can pass through to `Add` is a `Structure_Demo.Customer` structure.

Internally, `CollectionBase` provides you with a protected property called `List` that you can use to store items. That's precisely what you use when you need to add or remove items from the list:

```
' Add - add a customer...
Public Sub Add(ByVal newCustomer As Customer)
    Me.List.Add(newCustomer)
End Sub
' Remove - delete a customer...
Public Sub Remove(ByVal removeCustomer As Customer)
    Me.List.Remove(removeCustomer)
End Sub
```

The reason why you're supposed to build collections like this is that it's a .NET best practice. As a newcomer to .NET programming, you may not appreciate just how useful this is—but trust me—it is! Whenever you need to use a collection of classes that you build yourself, this technique is the right way to go.

Adding an Item Property

Back when collections were introduced, you read that you were supposed to add two methods and one property. You've seen the methods but not the property—look at it now.

Try It Out   Adding an Item Property

1. Open the code editor for `CustomerCollection` and add this code:

```
' Item - return a customer given an index...
Default Public Property Item(ByVal index As Integer) As Customer
    Get
        Return Me.List.Item(index)
    End Get
    Set(ByVal Value As Customer)
        Me.List.Item(index) = Value
    End Set
End Property
```

2. To verify that this works, open the code editor for Form1. Find the `SelectedCustomer` property and make this change:

```
' return the selected customer...
Return _customers(lstCustomers.SelectedIndex)
```

3. Run the project. Click the Test button and notice that when you select items in the list the details are shown in the fields as they were before.

How It Works

The Item property is actually very important as it gives the developer direct access to the data stored in the list, but maintains the strongly-typed nature of the collection.

If you look at the code again for SelectedCustomer, you'll notice that when you wanted to return the given item from within _customers, you didn't have to provide the property name of Item. Instead, _customers behaved as if it were an array:

```
' do we have a selection?
If lstCustomers.SelectedIndex <> -1 Then
    ' return the selected customer...
    Return_customers(lstCustomers.SelectedIndex)
End If
```

IntelliSense tells you to enter the index of the item that you require and that you should expect to get a Customer structure in return.

The reason you don't have to specify the property name of Item is that you marked the property as default by using the Default keyword:

```
' Item - return a customer given an index...
Default Public Property Item(ByVal index As Integer) As Customer
    Get
        Return Me.List.Item(index)
    End Get
    Set(ByVal Value As Customer)
        Me.List.Item(index) = Value
    End Set
End Property
```

A given class can only have a single default property, and that property must take a parameter of some kind. This parameter must be an index or search term of some description. The one used here provides an index to an element in an array. You can have multiple overloaded versions of the same property so you could provide an e-mail address rather than an index. This gives a great deal of flexibility.

What you have at this point is the following:

❑ A way of storing a list of Customer structures, and just Customer structures

❑ A way of adding new items to the collection on demand

❑ A way of removing existing items from the collection on demand

❑ A way of accessing members in the collection as if it were a normal array

Building Lookup Tables with Hashtable

So far, whenever you want to find something in an array or in a collection you have to provide an integer index representing the position of the item. It's quite common to end up needing a way of being able to look up an item in a collection when you have something other than an index. For example, you might want to find a Customer structure when you provide an e-mail address.

In this section you take a look at `System.Collections.Hashtable`. This is a special kind of collection that works on a *key-value* principle.

Using Hashtables

Each item in the collection is given a key. This key can be used at a later time to "unlock" the value. So, if I add Amir's `Customer` structure to the Hashtable, I'll be given a key that matches his e-mail address of `amir@pretendcompany.com`. If at a later time I come along with that key, I'll be able to find his record quickly.

As you know, all .NET objects are derived from an object called `System.Object`. This object itself provides a method called `GetHashCode`. This method is used to return an integer value that uniquely identifies the object. So, if you create a class of your own and generate 10 instances of that class, each call to `GetHashCode` will return a value that represents the object. More importantly, this value never changes for a given object, so if you call `GetHashCode` on an object called `MyObject`, you might get a value back of 27. On every subsequent call to `GetHashCode` on that object, you'll always get 27.

> *In the vast majority of cases, you'll never need to supply your own implementation of* `GetHashCode`.

Whenever you add an object to the Hashtable, it calls `GetHashCode` on the object to be added and uses this as the key. Likewise, whenever you want to retrieve an object from the Hashtable, it calls `GetHashCode` on the object to get a lookup key and matches that key against the ones it has in the list. When it finds it, it will return the related value to you.

Lookups from a Hashtable are very, very fast. Irrespective of the object you pass in, you're only matching on a relatively small integer ID.

> *An integer ID takes up 4 bytes of memory, so if you pass in a 100-character string (which is 200-bytes long), the lookup code only needs to compare 4 bytes, which makes everything run really quickly.*

Try It Out   Using a Hashtable

1. Open the code editor for `CustomerCollection`. Add this member to the top of the class definition:

```
Public Class CustomerCollection
    Inherits System.Collections.CollectionBase
    ' members...
    Private_emailHashtable As New Hashtable()
```

2. Next, add this read-only property:

```
' EmailHashtable - return the e-mail hashtable...
Public ReadOnly Property EmailHashtable() As Hashtable
    Get
        Return_emailHashtable
    End Get
End Property
```

3. Now, make this change to the `Add` property:

```
' Add - add a customer...
Public Sub Add(ByVal newCustomer As Customer)
    Me.List.Add(newCustomer)
    ' add to the hashtable...
    EmailHashtable.Add(newCustomer.Email, newCustomer)
End Sub
```

4. Next, add this alternative, overloaded version of `Item` that allows you to find a customer by giving an e-mail address:

```
' Alternative version of Item. Finds customer from e-mail address...
Default Public ReadOnly Property Item(ByVal email As String) _
        As Customer
    Get
        Return EmailHashtable.Item(email)
    End Get
End Property
```

5. Open the Designer for Form1, shrink the txtEmail control, and add a new button. Set the Name property of the button to **btnLookupEmail** and the Text property to **Lookup**, as shown in Figure 5-24.

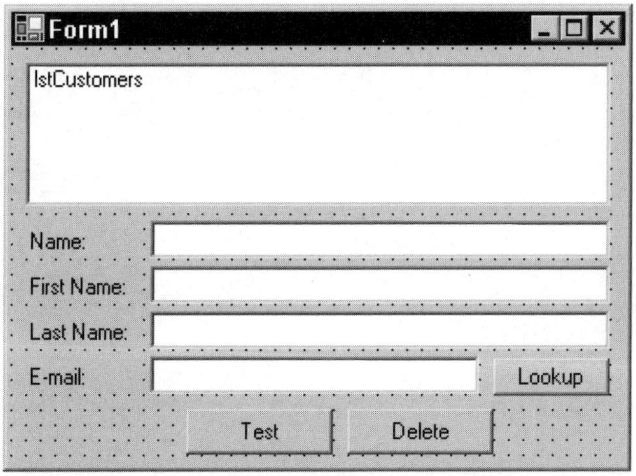

Figure 5-24

6. Double-click the Lookup button and add this code:

```
Private Sub btnLookupEmail_Click(ByVal sender As System.Object, _
        ByVal e As System.EventArgs) Handles btnLookupEmail.Click
    ' what e-mail address do we want to find?
    Dim findEmail As String = txtEmailName.Text
    ' lookup and display the customer by email...
    Dim foundCustomer As Customer
    foundCustomer = _customers(findEmail)
    If foundCustomer.IsEmpty = False Then
```

```
        ' show the customer's name...
        MessageBox.Show("The name is: " & foundCustomer.Name, _
                        "Structure Demo")
    Else
        ' display an error...
        MessageBox.Show( _
            "There is no customer with the e-mail address " & _
            findEmail & ".", "Structure Demo")
    End If
End Sub
```

7. Run the project and click the Test button. If you enter an e-mail address that does not exist into the E-mail text box and click Lookup, you'll see something like the message in Figure 5-25.

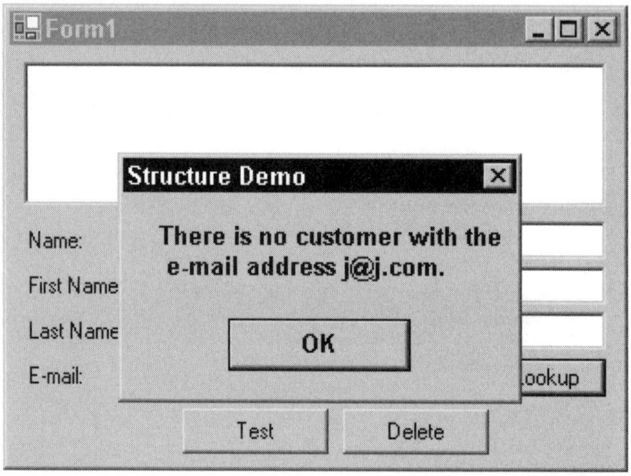

Figure 5-25

8. However, if you do enter one that exists, for example, ben@pretendcompany.com, the name of the customer will be shown in a message box.

How It Works

You've added a new member to the CustomerCollection class that can be used to hold a Hashtable:

```
' members...
Private_emailHashtable As New Hashtable()
```

Whenever you add a new Customer to the collection, you also add it to the Hashtable:

```
' Add - add a customer...
Public Sub Add(ByVal newCustomer As Customer)
    Me.List.Add(newCustomer)
    ' add to the hashtable...
    EmailHashtable.Add(newCustomer.Email, newCustomer)
End Sub
```

However, unlike the kinds of Add methods that you've seen earlier, this method takes two parameters. The first is the key—and you're using the e-mail address as the key. The key can be any object you like, but it must be unique. You cannot supply the same key twice. (If you do, an exception will be thrown.) The second parameter is the value that you want to link the key to, so whenever we give that key to the Hashtable, you get that object back.

The next trick is to create an overloaded version of the default `Item` property. This one, however, takes a string as its only parameter. IntelliSense will display the overloaded method as items 1 and 2 when you access it from your code.

This time you can provide either an index or an e-mail address. If you use an e-mail address you end up using the alternative version of `Item` and this defers to the `Item` property of the Hashtable object. This takes a key and returns the related item, providing the key can be found:

```
Default Public ReadOnly Property Item(ByVal email As String) _
       As Customer
   Get
       Return EmailHashtable.Item(email)
   End Get
End Property
```

So, at this point you have a collection class that not only enables you to look up items by index but also allows you to look up objects by e-mail address.

Cleaning Up: Remove, RemoveAt, and Clear

It isn't possible to use the same key twice in a Hashtable. Therefore, you have to take steps to ensure that what's in the Hashtable matches whatever is in the list itself.

Although you implemented your own `Remove` method, `CollectionBase` also implements `RemoveAt` and `Clear` methods. Whereas `Remove` takes an object, `RemoveAt` takes an index. You need to provide new implementations of those that also adjust the Hashtable.

Try It Out   Cleaning Up the List

1. Open the code editor for Form1. Find the `btnTest_Click` method and add this code to clear the two lists:

```
Private Sub btnTest_Click(ByVal sender As System.Object, _
         ByVal e As System.EventArgs) Handles btnTest.Click
    ' clear the lists...
    _customers.Clear()
    lstCustomers.Items.Clear()
    ' create some customers...
    CreateCustomer("Amir", "Aliabadi", "amir@pretendcompany.com")
    CreateCustomer("Gretchen", "Aliabadi",_
                   "gretchen@pretendcompany.com")
    CreateCustomer("Ben", "Aliabadi", "ben@pretendcompany.com")
End Sub
```

To demonstrate how this goes wrong, run the project and click the Test button. When the list has loaded, click the Test button again. An exception will be thrown telling you that the item has been used already as shown in Figure 5-26. (This illustrates my earlier point how a Hashtable can only contain one instance of a particular key.)

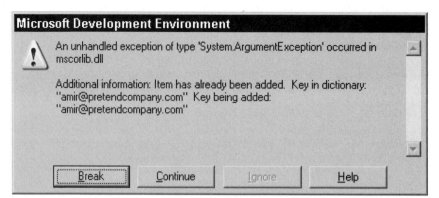

Figure 5-26

2. Click the Continue button. This will stop the debugging session.

3. Using the code editor, add this method to `CustomerCollection`:

```
' Clear - provide a new implementation of clear...
Public Shadows Sub Clear()
    ' get collectionbase to clear...
    MyBase.Clear()
    ' clear our hashtable...
    EmailHashtable.Clear()
End Sub
```

4. Next, make this change to `Remove`:

```
' Remove - delete a customer...
Public Sub Remove(ByVal removeCustomer As Customer)
    ' remove from our list...
    Me.List.Remove(removeCustomer)
    ' remove from the hashtable...
    EmailHashtable.Remove(removeCustomer.Email)
End Sub
```

5. Now, add this new version of `RemoveAt` to override the default functionality defined in `CollectionBase`:

```
' RemoveAt - remove an item by index...
Public Shadows Sub RemoveAt(ByVal index As Integer)
    Remove(Item(index))
End Sub
```

6. Run the project. Click Test to load the items and click Test again straight afterwards. This won't cause an exception to be thrown again.

How It Works

The exception isn't thrown the second time round because you are now making sure that the Hashtable and the internal list maintained by `CollectionBase` are properly synchronized. Specifically, whenever your `CustomerCollection` list is cleared using the `Clear` method, you make sure that the Hashtable is also cleared.

To clear the internal list maintained by `CollectionBase`, you ask the base class to use its own `Clear` implementation rather than trying to provide your own implementation. Straight after that, you call `Clear` on the Hashtable:

```
' Clear - provide a new implementation of clear...
Public Shadows Sub Clear()
    ' get collectionbase to clear...
    MyBase.Clear()
    ' clear our hashtable...
    EmailHashtable.Clear()
End Sub
```

You'll also find that when you delete items from the collection by using `Remove`, the corresponding entry is also removed from the Hashtable, because of the line added in Step 5 in the previous *Try It Out* section.

The `Shadows` keyword indicates that this `Clear` procedure should be used instead of the `Clear` in the base class. Even though they do here, the arguments and the return type do not have to match those in the base class procedure.

You don't need to worry too much about the details of Shadows and Overrides at this point as they are discussed in detail in Chapter 10.

Case Sensitivity

It's about this time that case sensitivity rears its ugly head again. If you run the project and click Test, you will see a message, something like the one shown in Figure 5-27, if you don't specify the e-mail address as lowercase characters.

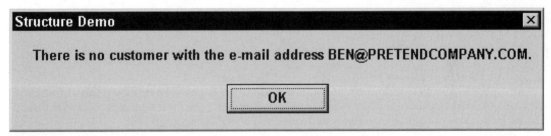

Structure Demo

There is no customer with the e-mail address BEN@PRETENDCOMPANY.COM.

OK

Figure 5-27

You need to get the collection to ignore case on the key. You do this by making sure that, whenever you save a key, you transform the e-mail address into all lowercase characters. Whenever you look up based on a key, you transform whatever you search for into lowercase characters too.

Try It Out   **Case Sensitivity**

1.   Open the code editor for `CustomerCollection` and make this change to the `Add` method:

```
' Add - add a customer...
Public Sub Add(ByVal newCustomer As Customer)
```

```
        ' add to the list...
      Me.List.Add(newCustomer)
        ' add to the hashtable...
      Dim useEmail As String
      useEmail = newCustomer.Email.ToLower
      EmailHashtable.Add(useEmail, newCustomer)
End Sub
```

2. Now, find the version of the `Item` property that takes an e-mail address and add this code:

```
Default Public ReadOnly Property Item(ByVal email As String) _
      As Customer
    Get
          ' use a lower case term...
          email = email.ToLower()
          Return EmailHashtable.Item(email)
    End Get
End Property
```

3. Next, find the `Remove` method and add this code:

```
' Remove - delete a customer...
Public Sub Remove(ByVal removeCustomer As Customer)
      ' remove from our list...
      Me.List.Remove(removeCustomer)
      ' remove from the hashtable...
      Dim useEmail As String
      useEmail = removeCustomer.Email.ToLower()
      EmailHashtable.Remove(useEmail)
End Sub
```

4. Run the project and click Test. Now if you enter the e-mail address in a non-matching case the lookup will still work.

How It Works

Back in Chapter 4 you saw how we could do case-insensitive string comparisons using the `String.Compare` method. You can't use this technique here because the Hashtable is handling the comparison and, ideally, you don't want to produce your own version of the comparison code that Hashtable uses just to do a case-insensitive match.

You can use the `ToLower` method available on strings. This creates a new string where all of the characters are transformed into the lower-case equivalent, so if you pass aMiR@pRETendCOMpany.COM you always get amir@pretendcompany.com out.

When you add an item to the collection, you can get `ToLower` to convert the e-mail address stored in the `Customer` structure so that it is always in lower case:

```
Dim useEmail As String
useEmail = newCustomer.Email.ToLower()
EmailHashtable.Add(useEmail, newCustomer)
```

Likewise, when you actually do the lookup, you also turn whatever value is passed in as a parameter into all lowercase characters:

```
' use a lower case term...
email = email.ToLower()
Return EmailHashtable.Item(email)
```

Providing you're consistent with it, what this does is to make uppercase characters "go away"—in other words you'll never end up with uppercase characters being stored in the key or being checked against the key.

> *This technique for removing the problem of uppercase characters can be used for normal string comparisons, but* String.Compare *is more efficient.*

Advanced Array Manipulation

At the beginning of this chapter the concept of arrays was introduced. I've left some of the more advanced discussions on arrays until later in the chapter, namely those involving adjusting the size of an array and multidimensional arrays.

Being able to manipulate the size of an array from code, and being able to store complex sets of data in an array is important, but with .NET it's far easier to achieve both of these using the collection functionality that the majority of this chapter discusses. These next two sections are included for completeness.

Dynamic Arrays

When using an array, if you want to change its size in order to add items, or clean up space when you remove items, you need to use the ReDim keyword to make it a dynamic array. This is a short form of, not surprisingly, redimension. You reuse the Array Demo project you used at the start of the chapter and tweak it so that you can add new friends to the array after the initial array has been created.

Try It Out   Using ReDim

1. Find and open the Array Demo project. Open the code editor for Form1 and replace the code in the AddFriendsToList method so that it looks like this:

```
Sub AddFriendsToList(ByVal friends() As String)
    ' add each friend...
    Dim friendName As String
    For Each friendName In friends
        ' add it...
        lstFriends.Items.Add("[" & friendName & "]")
    Next
End Sub
```

2. Run the project and click Go. Your form should look like Figure 5-28.

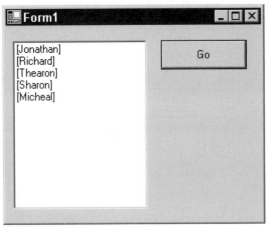

Figure 5-28

3. Now, close the project and make this change to btnGo_Click.

```
Private Sub btnGo_Click(ByVal sender As System.Object, _
        ByVal e As System.EventArgs) Handles btnGo.Click
    ' define an array to hold friends in...
    Dim friends() As String = {"Jonathan", "Richard", "Thearon", _
                                "Sharon", "Micheal"}
    ' make friends bigger!
    ReDim friends(6)
    friends(5) = "Zita"
    friends(6) = "Seth"
    ' show the friends...
    AddFriendsToList(friends)
End Sub
```

4. Run the project and click Go. You'll see the form as shown in Figure 5-29.

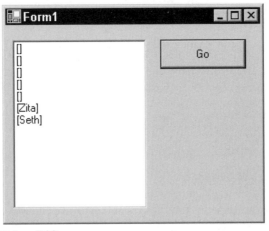

Figure 5-29

How It Works

After defining an array of length 5, you use the `ReDim` keyword to re-dimension the array to have an upper bound of 6, which, as you know, gives it a size of 7. After you do that, you have two new items in the array to play with—items 5 and 6:

```
' make friends bigger!
ReDim friends(6)
friends(5) = "Zoe"
friends(6) = "Faye"
```

Then, you can pass the resized array through to `AddFriendsToList`:

```
' show the friends...
AddFriendsToList(friends)
```

But, as you can see from the results, the values for the first five items have been lost. (This is why you wrapped brackets around the results—if the name stored in the array is blank you still see something appear in the list.) `ReDim` does indeed resize the array, but by default it will also clear the array.

You can solve this problem by using the `Preserve` keyword. When an array is re-dimensioned, by default all of the values in the array are cleared, losing the values you defined when you initialized the array in the first place.

Using Preserve

By including the `Preserve` keyword with the `ReDim` keyword, you can ask Visual Basic .NET not to clear the existing items. One thing to remember is that if you use `Preserve` to make an array smaller than it originally was, data will be lost from the eliminated elements.

Try It Out   Using Preserve

1. Open the code editor for Form1 and find the `btnGo_Click` method. Add the `Preserve` keyword to the `ReDim` statement:

```
Private Sub btnGo_Click(ByVal sender As System.Object, _
            ByVal e As System.EventArgs) Handles btnGo.Click
    ' define an array to hold friends in...
    Dim friends() As String = {"Jonathan", "Richard", "Thearon", _
                                "Sharon", "Michel"}
    ' make friends bigger!
    ReDim Preserve friends(6)
    friends(5) = "Zita"
    friends(6) = "Seth"
    ' show the friends...
    AddFriendsToList(friends)
End Sub
```

2. Run the project and click Go. You should now find that the existing items in the array are preserved, as shown in Figure 5-30.

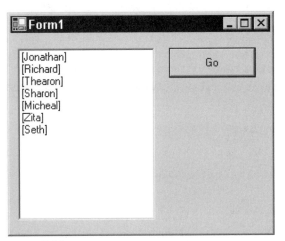

Figure 5-30

Summary

In this chapter, you saw some ways in which you could manage complex groups of data. You started by looking at the concept of an array, or rather, defining a special type of variable that's configured to hold a one-dimensional list of similar items rather than a single item.

You then looked at the concepts behind enumerations and constants. Both of these can be used to a great effect in making more readable and manageable code. An enumeration lets you define human-readable, common sense titles to basic variable types. So rather than saying "mode=3", you can say "mode=MyModes.Menu". Constants allow you to globally define literal values and use them elsewhere in your code.

You then looked at the structure. This is a relative of the class that you have already met, and is well suited for storing lists of information. After looking at these, you moved on to look at various types of collection, including the basic ArrayList and then saw how you could build your own powerful collection classes inherited from CollectionBase. Finally, you looked at the Hashtable class and covered some of the less-commonly used array functionality.

To summarize, you should know how to:

- ❏ Define and redimension fixed and dynamic string arrays
- ❏ Enumerate through arrays and find their upper dimension
- ❏ Define an enumeration of values using the Enum class
- ❏ Create and use structures to manipulate sets of related data
- ❏ Use an ArrayList to hold any type of object
- ❏ Use collections to manage sets of related data

Exercises

1. What is an array?

2. What's the difference between a structure and a class?

3. What's the best way to build a collection?

4. What is an enumeration?

5. What is a Hashtable?

6

Building Windows Applications

When Microsoft first released Visual Basic, developers fell in love with it because it made building the user interface components of an application very simple. Instead of having to write thousands of lines of code to display windows—the very staple of a Windows application—developers could simply "draw" the window on the screen.

In Visual Basic, a window is known as a *form*. With .NET, this form design capability has been brought to all of the managed languages as *Windows Forms*. You've been using these forms over the course of the previous five chapters, but you haven't really given that much thought to them—focusing instead on the code that we've written inside them.

In this chapter, you look in detail at Windows Forms and learn how you can use Visual Basic .NET to put together fully featured Windows applications. In particular, you will look at:

❑   Adding features such as buttons, text boxes, and radio buttons

❑   Creating a simple toolbar and code buttons to respond to events

❑   Creating additional forms in a Windows Forms application

❑   Deployment of a Windows application

   Note that, on occasion you'll hear developers refer to Windows Forms as WinForms.

Responding to Events

Building a user interface using Windows Forms is all about responding to *events* (such as `Clicks`), so programming for Windows is commonly known as *event-driven programming*. As you know, to build a form you paint controls onto a blank window called the Designer using the mouse. Each of these controls is able to tell you when an event happens, for example, if you run your program and click a button that's been painted onto a form, that button will say, "Hey, I've been clicked!" and give you an opportunity to execute some code that you provide to respond to that event.

Setting Up a Button Event

A good way to illustrate the event philosophy is to wire up a button. An example would be the `Click` event that is *fired* whenever the button is clicked. You have more events than just the `Click` event, although, in day-to-day practice it's unlikely you'll use more than a handful of these.

Using Button Events

1.   Start Visual Studio .NET and select File ➪ New ➪ Project from the menu. Create a Windows Application project called *Hello World* 2 and click OK.

2.   Scroll up the Properties window until you find the Text property for `Form1`. Change it to Hello, world! 2.0.

3.   From the Toolbox, select the Button control, and then drag and drop a button onto the form. Change its Text property to **Hello, world!** and its Name property to **btnSayHello**. Your button should look like the one shown in Figure 6-1.

Figure 6-1

4.   Double-click the button and add the following code in the code editor:

```
Private Sub btnSayHelloClick(ByVal sender As System.Object,
        ByVal e As System.EventArgs) Handles btnSayHello.Click

    ' say hello!
    MessageBox.Show("Hello, world!", Me.Text)

End Sub
```

5.   Drop down the list in the Class Name combo box at the top of the code window. You'll see the options shown in Figure 6-2.

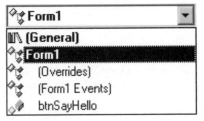

Figure 6-2

Notice that the last three items in the list are slightly indented. This tells you that (Overrides), (Form1 Events), and btnSayHello are all related to Form1. btnSayHello is a member of Form1. As you add more members to the form, they will appear in this list.

6. Before you continue, take a quick look at the list in the Method Name combo box to the right of the Class Name combo box. Drop it down, and you'll see the options shown in Figure 6-3. These options are described in the list that follows the figure.

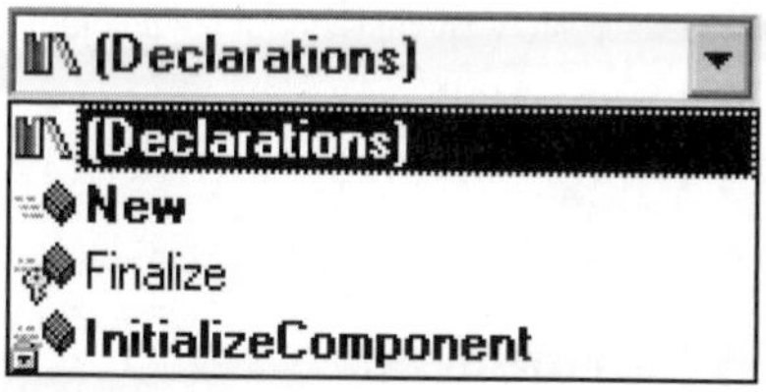

Figure 6-3

❑ The contents of the Method Name combo box change depending on the item selected in the Class Name combo box. The right list lets you navigate through items related to whatever you selected in the left. In this case, its main job is to show you the methods and properties that you added to the class.

❑ The (Declarations) entry takes you to the top of the class where you can change the definition of the class and add member variables.

❑ The Finalize method is quite interesting. Whenever an entry in the right list appears in faint (as opposed to bold) text, the method doesn't exist. However, selecting the object will make Visual Basic .NET create a definition for the selected function. In this case, if you select Finalize, Visual Basic .NET will create a new method called Finalize and add it to the class.

❑ You'll notice that Visual Basic .NET adds a small icon to the left of everything it displays in these lists. These can tell you what the item in the list actually is. A small purple square represents a method, a small blue square represents a member, four books stacked together represent a library, and three squares joined together with lines represent a class.

Visual Studio may also decorate these icons with other icons to indicate the way they are defined. For example, next to Finalize you'll see a small key, which tells you the method is protected. The padlock icon tells us the item is private.

It's not really important to memorize all of these now, but Visual Basic .NET is fairly consistent with its representations, so if you do learn them over time they will help you understand what's going on.

7. Select btnSayHello from the left list. Now, drop down the right list again, as shown in Figure 6-4.

Since the left list is set to btnSayHello, now the right list exclusively shows items related to that control. In this case, you have a huge list of events. One of those events, Click, is shown in bold because you provided a definition for this. If you select Click, you'll be taken to the method in Form1 that provides an event handler for this method.

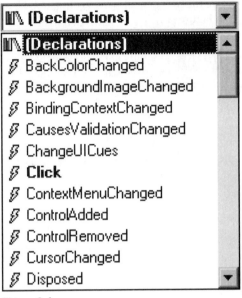

Figure 6-4

8.   Now add another event handler to the Button control. With btnSayHello still selected in the left list, select MouseEnter from the right list. A new event handler method will be created, and you need to add the following code to it:

```
Private Sub btnSayHello_MouseEnter(ByVal sender As Object, _
      ByVal e As System.EventArgs) Handles btnSayHello.MouseEnter

   ' change the text...
   btnSayHello.Text = "The mouse is here!"

End Sub
```

The MouseEnter event will be fired whenever the mouse pointer "enters" the control, in other words, crosses its boundary.

9.   To complete this exercise, you need another event handler. Select btnSayHello from the left list and select MouseLeave from the right list. Again, a new event will be created, so add this code:

```
Private Sub btnSayHello_MouseLeave(ByVal sender As Object, _
      ByVal e As System.EventArgs) Handles btnSayHello.MouseLeave

   ' change the text...
   btnSayHello.Text = "The mouse has gone!"

End Sub
```

The MouseLeave event will be fired whenever the mouse pointer moves back outside of the control.

10. Run the project. Move the mouse over and away from the control and you'll see the text change, as shown in Figure 6-5.

Figure 6-5

How It Works

Most of the controls that you use will have a dazzling array of events, although in day-to-day programming only a few of them will be consistently useful. For the Button control, the most useful is usually the Click event.

Visual Basic .NET knows enough about the control to automatically create the default event handlers for us. This makes our life a lot easier and saves on typing!

When you created your MouseEnter event and added your custom code, here's what you had:

```
Private Sub btnSayHello_MouseEnter(ByVal sender As Object, _
      ByVal e As System.EventArgs) Handles btnSayHello.MouseEnter
   ' change the text...
   btnSayHello.Text = "The mouse is here!"

End Sub
```

You'll notice that at the end of the method definition is the Handles keyword. This ties the method definition into the btnSayHello.MouseEnter subroutine. When the button fires this event your code will be executed.

Although previously you changed only the button's Text property at design time using the Properties window, here you can see that you can change it at runtime too.

As a quick reminder here, design time *is the term used to define the period of time that you actually require for writing the program, in other words, working with the Designer or adding code.* Runtime *is the term used to define the period of time when the program is running.*

Likewise, the MouseLeave event works in a very similar way:

```
Private Sub btnSayHello_MouseLeave(ByVal sender As Object, _
       ByVal e As System.EventArgs) Handles btnSayHello.MouseLeave

   ' change the text...
   btnSayHello.Text = "The mouse has gone!"

End Sub
```

Building a Simple Application

Visual Studio .NET comes with a comprehensive set of controls that you can use in your projects. For the most part, you'll be able to build all of your applications using just these controls, but in Chapter 13 you look at how you can create your own application.

Take a look at how you can use some of these controls to put together a basic application. In the following *Try It Out* you build a basic Windows application that lets the user enter text into a form. The application will count the number of words and letters in the block of text that they enter.

Building the Form

The first job is to start a new project and build a form. This form will contain a multi line text box where we can enter text. It will also contain two radio buttons that will give us the option of counting either the words or the number of characters in the text box. So let us get started.

Try It Out   Building the Form

1. Select File ➪ New ➪ Project from the Visual Basic .NET menu and create a new Windows Application project. Enter the project name as Word Counter and click OK.

2. Stretch the form until it looks like Figure 6-6 and use the Properties window to change the form's Text property to Word Counter.

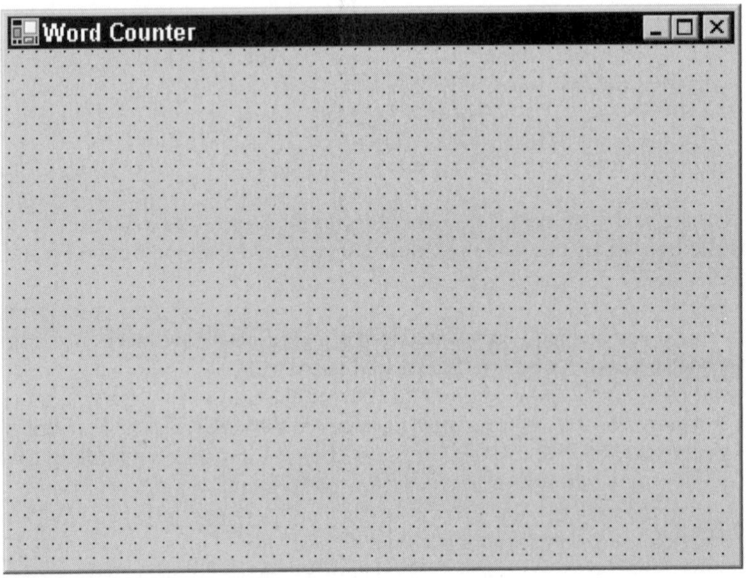

Figure 6-6

3. From the Toolbox, select the TextBox control and paint it onto the form. Now change the properties of the text box as shown in the following list:

    ❏   Set Name to txtWords

    ❏   Set Multiline to True

❑   Set ScrollBars to Vertical

❑   Leave the Text property blank.

4.   Note that when you changed the Multiline property, your six gray sizing handles around the control turned white. This means that you can now change the height of the text box. Stretch it until it occupies a lot more of the form.

5.   To tell the user what to do with the form you add a label. Select the Label control from the Toolbox, drag and drop it just above the text box. Change the Text property to **Enter some text into this box**, as shown in Figure 6-7.

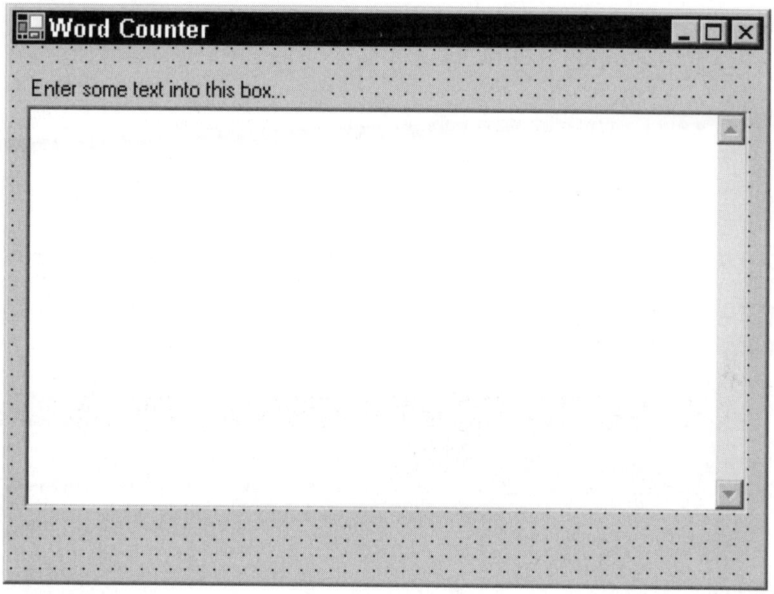

Figure 6-7

Strictly speaking, unless you're going to need to talk to the control from your Visual Basic .NET code, you don't need to change its Name property. With the text box, you need to use its properties and methods to make the application work. However, the label is just there for esthetics, so you don't need to change the name from Label1. (This depends on how fussy you are—some developers give every control a specific name, others give only to specific controls that really need a name.)

It's worth noting that if you are going to refer to a control from Visual Basic .NET code, it's bad practice not to give it a name, in other words you should never end up with a line like Button1.Text. *Developers should be able to determine what the control represents based on its name even if they've never seen your code before.*

6.   Your application is going to be capable of counting either the characters the user entered or the number of words. To allow the user to select the method they would prefer to use, you use two radio buttons. Draw two RadioButton controls onto the form next to each other below the text box. You need to refer to the radio buttons from your Visual Basic .NET code, so change the properties as shown in the following lists:

For the first radio button

- ❑ Set Name to radCountChars
- ❑ Set Checked to True
- ❑ Set Text to Chars

For the second radio button

- ❑ Set Name to radCountWords
- ❑ Set Text to Words

7. As the user types, you take the words that they enter and count up the words or characters as appropriate. You want to pass your results to the user, so add two new Label controls next to the RadioButton controls that you just added.

8. The first Label control (marked Label2) is just for esthetics, so change its Text property to **The results are:**. The second Label control will report the results, so you need to give it a name. Delete the value for its Text property (in other words make it blank) and enter the Name property as lblResults.

9. You also need a Button control that shows a message pop-up box, so add a Button control to the form. You don't strictly need this because the user can read the results on the form, but it illustrates a couple of important points. Change the Text property to Show Me! and the Name property to btnShowMe, as shown in Figure 6-8.

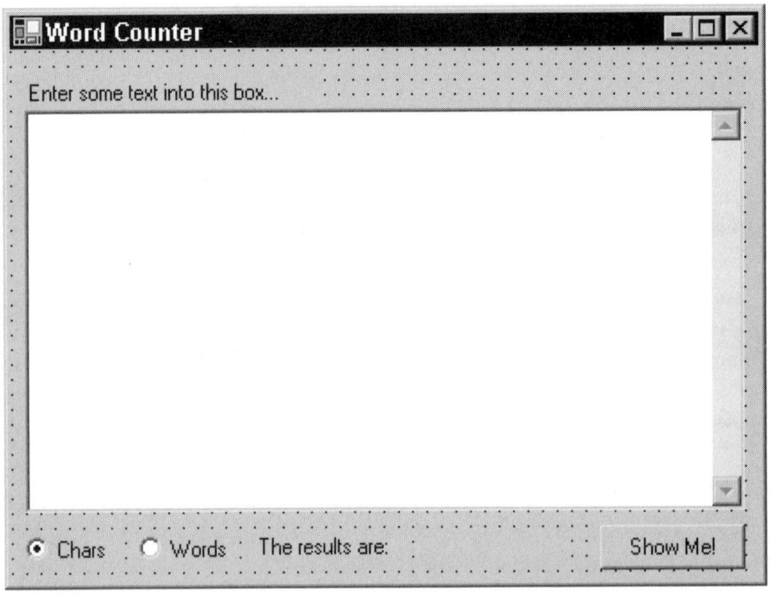

Figure 6-8

10. Finally, now that you have your form the way you want it, make sure you keep it that way. Make sure you select one of the controls and not the actual form, and then select Format ⇨ Lock Controls from the menu. This sets the Locked property of each of the controls to True and prevents them from accidentally being moved, resized, or deleted.

Counting Characters

With your form designed, build some event handlers to count the number of characters in a block of text that the user types. Switch to the form's code view by right clicking the form in the Solution Explorer and choosing View Code from the context menu.

Try It Out   Counting Characters

1. Since your application will be able to count words and characters, you build separate functions for each. In this *Try It Out* you write the code to count characters. Add this code to the bottom of Form1 just before the `End Class` statement:

```
' CountCharacters - count the characters in a block of text...
Public Function CountCharacters(ByVal text As String) As Integer

    ' return the number of characters...
    Return text.Length

End Function
```

2. Now you need to build an event handler for the text box. Double-click the TextBox control in the Form Designer and Visual Studio .NET will create a default handler for `TextChanged`. Add this code to it:

```
Private Sub txtWords_TextChanged(ByVal sender As System.Object, _
        ByVal e As System.EventArgs) Handles txtWords.TextChanged

    ' count the number of characters...
    Dim intChars As Integer = CountCharacters(txtWords.Text)

    ' report the results...
    lblResults.Text = intChars & "characters"

End Sub
```

3. Run the project. Enter some text into the text box and you'll see a screen like the one in Figure 6-9.

How It Works

Notice that whenever you type a character into the text box, the label at the bottom of the form reports the current number of characters. That's because the `TextChanged` event is fired whenever the user changes the text in the box. This happens when new text is entered, changes are made to existing text, and when old text is deleted. You should be "listening" for this event and whenever you "hear" it (or rather receive it), you call `CountCharacters` and pass in the block of text. As the user types text into the `txtWords` text box, the `Text` property is updated to reflect the text that has been entered. You can get the value for this property (in other words the block of text) and pass it to `CountCharacters`:

```
    ' count the number of characters...
    Dim intChars As Integer = CountCharacters(txtWords.Text)
```

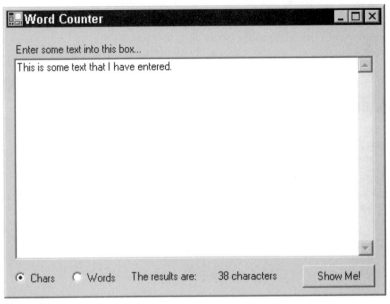

Figure 6-9

In return, it passes back an integer representing the number of characters:

```
' return the number of characters...
Return text.Length
```

After you have the number of characters, you need to update the lblResults control:

```
' report the results...
lblResults.Text = intChars & "characters"
```

Counting Words

Although building a Visual Basic .NET application is actually very easy, building an elegant solution to a problem requires a combination of thought, experience, and a bit of luck.

Take your application—when the Words radio button is checked, you want to count the number of words, whereas when Chars is checked you want to count the number of characters. This has three implications. First, when you respond to the `TextChanged` event you need to call a different method that counts the words, rather than your existing method for counting characters. This isn't too difficult. Second, whenever you select a different radio button, you need to change the text in the results from "characters" to "words" or back again. In a similar way, whenever the Show Me! button is pressed, you need to take the same result, but rather than displaying it in the Label control, you need to use a message box.

Now add some more event handlers and when you finish examine the logic behind the technique you used.

Try It Out   Counting Words

1. The first thing you want to do is add a function after `CountCharacters` that will count the number of words in a block of text:

```
' CountCharacters - count the characters in a block of text...
Public Function CountCharacters(ByVal text As String) As Integer

    ' return the number of characters...
    Return Text.Length
End Function
```

```
' CountWords - count the number of words in a block of text...
Public Function CountWords(ByVal text As String) As Integer

    ' is the text box empty?
    If txtWords.Text = "" Then Return 0

    ' split...
    Dim strWords() As String = text.Split(" ".ToCharArray())
    Return strWords.Length

End Function
```

2. Now, add this function:

```
' UpdateDisplay - update the display...
Public Function UpdateDisplay() As String

    ' what text do we want to use?
    Dim strCountText As String = txtWords.Text
    Dim strResultText As String

    ' do we want to count words?
    If radCountWords.Checked = True Then
        ' count the words...
        Dim intWords As Integer = CountWords(strCountText)

        ' return the text...
        strResultText = intWords & "words"

    Else

        ' count the chars...
        Dim intChars As Integer = CountCharacters(strCountText)

        ' return the text...
        strResultText = intChars & "characters"

    End If
    ' update the display...
    lblResults.Text = strResultText

End Function
```

This method deals with the hassle of getting the text from the text box and updating the display. It also understands whether it's supposed to find the number of words or number of characters by looking at the Checked property on the radCountWords radio button.

3. Now, instead of calling `CountCharacters` from within your `TextChanged` handler, you want to call `UpdateDisplay`. Make the following change:

```
Private Sub txtWords_TextChanged(ByVal sender As System.Object, _
        ByVal e As System.EventArgs) Handles txtWords.TextChanged

    ' something's changed... update the display...
    UpdateDisplay()

End Sub
```

4. Finally, you want the display to alter when you change the radio button from Chars to Words and vice versa. To add the `CheckedChanged` event, select radCountWords from the left drop-down list at the top of the code window and CheckedChanged from the right one, as shown in Figure 6-10.

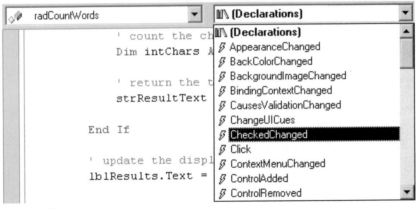

Figure 6-10

5. Add this code to the new event handler:

```
Private Sub radCountWords_CheckedChanged(ByVal sender As Object, _
        ByVal e As System.EventArgs) Handles radCountWords.CheckedChanged

    ' something's changed... update the display...
    UpdateDisplay()

End Sub
```

6. Repeat this step for `radCountChars`:

```
Private Sub radCountChars_CheckedChanged (ByVal sender As Object, _
        ByVal e As System.EventArgs) Handles radCountChars.CheckedChanged

    ' something's changed... update the display...
    UpdateDisplay()

End Sub
```

7. Run the project. Enter some text in the box and check Words. Notice how the display changes (see Figure 6-11).

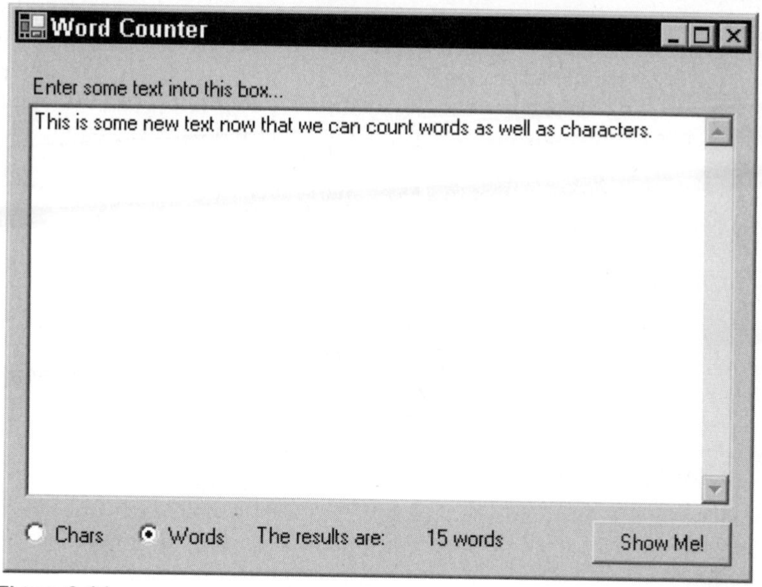

Figure 6-11

How It Works

Before you look at the technique you used to put the form together, take a quick look at CountWords:

```
' CountWords - count the number of words in a block of text...
Public Function CountWords(ByVal text As String) As Integer

    ' is the text box empty?
    If txtWords.Text = "" Then Return 0

    ' split...
    Dim strWords () As String = text.Split(" ".ToCharArray())
    Return strWords.Length

End Function
```

You start by checking to see whether the text box is empty; if no text has been entered you immediately return a value of 0.

The Split method of the String class is used to take a string and turn it into an array of string objects. Here, the parameter you passed is equivalent to the "space" character and so you're effectively telling Split to break up the string based on a space. This means that Split returns an array containing each of the words in the string. You return the length of this array, in other words, the number of words back to the caller.

Note that because this code uses a single space character to split the text into words, you'll get unexpected behavior if you separate your words with more than one space character or use the Return key to start a new line.

One of the golden rules of programming is that you never write more code than you absolutely have to. In particular, when you find yourself in a position where you are going to write the same piece of code twice, try to find a way that means you only have to write it once. In this example, you have to change the value displayed in lblResults from two different places. The most sensible way to do this is to split the code that updates the label into a separate function. You can then easily set up the TextChanged and CheckedChanged event handlers to call this method. The upshot of this is that you only have to write the tricky "get the text, find the results, and display them" routine once. This technique also creates code that is easier to change in the future and easier to debug when a problem is found.

You'll find as you build applications that this technique of breaking out the code for an event handler is something you'll do quite often.

Creating the Show Me! Button

To finish this exercise, you need to write code for the Show Me! button. All you're going to do with this button is display a message box containing the same text that's displayed on lblResults.

Try It Out   **Coding the Show Me! Button**

1.   From the code window for Form1, create a Click event handler for the button by selecting btnShowMe from the left drop-down list and then selecting Click from the right one. Then add this code:

```
Private Sub btnShowMe_Click(ByVal sender As System.Object, _
            ByVal e As System.EventArgs) Handles btnShowMe.Click

    ' display the text contained in the label...
    MessageBox.Show(lblResults.Text, "Word Counter")

End Sub
```

2.   Run the project. If you type something into the text box and click Show Me!, the same value will be displayed in the message box as appears in the results Label control, as shown in Figure 6-12.

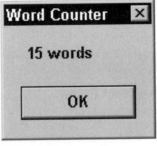

Figure 6-12

When you click the button, the code is selecting the Text property from the Label control and passing it to MessageBox.Show.

Creating Complex Applications

Normal applications generally have a number of common elements. Among these are toolbars and status bars. Putting together an application that has these features is a fairly trivial task in Visual Basic .NET.

In this next section, you build an application that allows you to make changes to the text entered into a text box, such as changing its color and making it all uppercase or lowercase.

The Text Manipulation Project

Now you are going to build an application that allows you to manipulate the text in a text box. You'll be using a ToolBar control to change the color of the text in your text box and also to change the case of the text to either all upper case letters or all lower case letters.

The StatusBar control will also be used in your project to display the status of your actions as a result of clicking on a button on the toolbar.

Our first step on the road to building your application is to create a new project.

Try It Out   Creating the Text Editor Project

1. Create a new Windows Application project and call it Text Editor.

2. Most of the time, Form1 isn't a very appropriate name for a form as it's not very descriptive. Right-click the form in the Solution Explorer, select Rename and change its name to TextEditor.vb as shown in Figure 6-13. Then press Enter to save the changes.

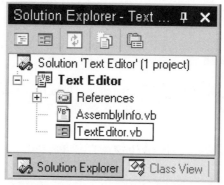

Figure 6-13

3. That is only half the battle—although you've renamed the form, you have not actually renamed the class that contains the form's implementation. To do this, select the form in the Designer and change its Name property to TextEditor.

4. Select View ⇨ Other Windows ⇨ Task List from the menu to bring up the Task List window as shown in Figure 6-14. It will display an error message saying that `Sub Main could not be found in TextEditor.Form1`, which makes sense because you just renamed it.

5. Double-click the error message and you'll be prompted to select a new startup class as shown in Figure 6-15. Select Text_Editor.TextEditor and click OK.

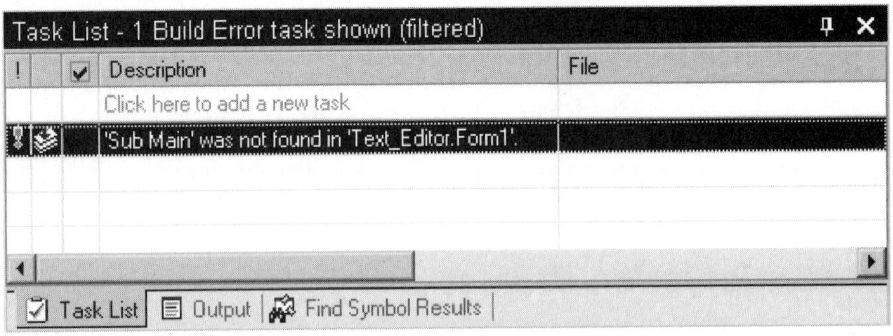

Figure 6-14

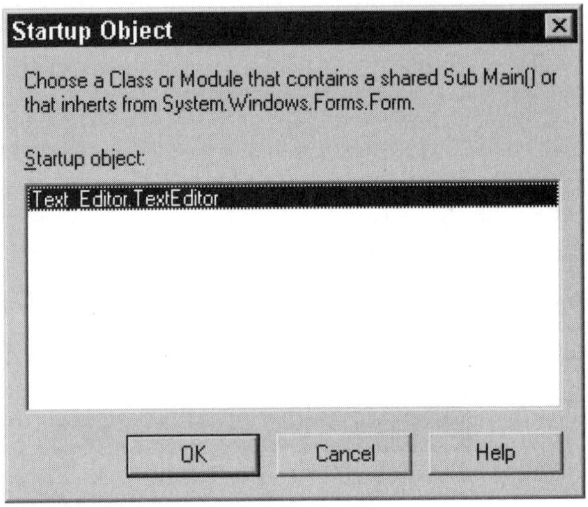

Figure 6-15

6. In the screenshots, I'm going to show the design window as quite small to save paper! You should explicitly set the size of the form by going to the Properties window of the form and setting the Size property to 600, 460.

In the next section you start building the fun part of the application.

Creating the Status Bar

Perhaps the most boring part of your project is the status bar, so you tackle this first. This is a panel that sits at the bottom of an application window and tells the user what's going on.

Try It Out   Adding a Status Bar

1. Open the Designer for the TextEditor form and select the StatusBar control from the Toolbox. Draw it anywhere on the form. You will find that it automatically glues itself to the bottom edge of the form and you'll only be able to change the height portion of its Size property. Make the Height property a little larger than the text. Set its Name property to statusBar and delete the value for the Text property. You'll get something like Figure 6-16.

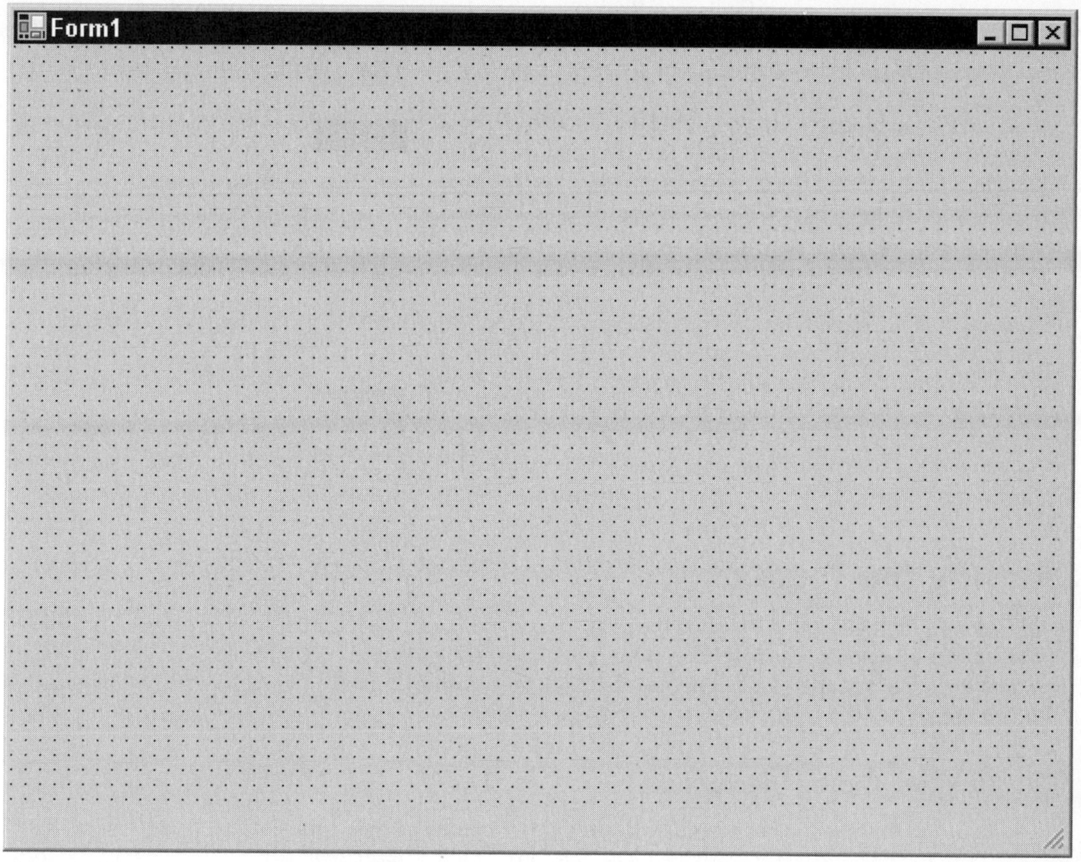

Figure 6-16

2. Open the code editor for the form and add the following code:

```
' StatusText - set the text on the status bar...
Public Property StatusText() As String
    Get
        Return statusBar.Text
    End Get
    Set(ByVal Value As String)
        statusBar.Text = Value
    End Set
End Property
```

There's no need to run the project at this point, so let's just talk about what you've done here.

How It Works

Visual Studio .NET has some neat features for making form design easier. One thing that was always laborious in previous versions of Visual Basic and Visual C++ was to create a form that would automatically adjust itself when the user changed its size.

In Visual Studio .NET, controls have the capability to dock themselves to the edges of the form. By default, the StatusBar control sets itself to dock to the bottom of the form, but you can change the docking location. So, when someone resizes the form, either at design time or at runtime, the status bar stays where you put it.

You may be wondering why you built a `StatusText` property to get and set the text on the status bar. Well, this comes back to abstraction. Ideally, you want to make sure that anyone using this class doesn't have to worry about how you've implemented the status bar. You might want to replace the .NET-supplied status bar with another control, and if this happens any user wanting to use your `TextEditor` class in their own applications (or developers wanting to add more functionality to this application later), would have to change their code to make sure it continued to work properly.

That's why you defined this property as `Public`. This means that anyone creating an instance of `TextEditor` to use its functionality in their own application can change the status bar if they want. If you don't want them to be able to change the text themselves, relying instead on other methods and properties on the form to change the text on their behalf, you mark it as `Private`.

As you work through this example, you'll see definitions of `Public` and `Private`. From this you'll be able to infer what functionality might be available to a developer using our `TextEditor` class.

Creating the Toolbar

To make up for the fact that building the status bar was so dull, you add the toolbar in this next *Try It Out*. The toolbar contains a collection of buttons that can be set to a normal style as seen in a lot of applications or to a flat style as seen in Visual Studio .Net 2003. In the following example, you will use the default style of normal.

Try It Out   Adding the Toolbar

1. Adding the toolbar is similar to adding the status bar. Select the ToolBar control from the Toolbox and draw it anywhere on the form. It will automatically dock at the top of the form.

2. Note that the Toolbar control doesn't display any sizing handles when it's selected. This is because the .NET Framework controls the size and position of the toolbars itself, and doesn't expect you to do it. To see if it is selected, look in the Properties window to make sure that the list at the top does indeed refer to the toolbar. If it doesn't, click the toolbar to make the selection.

3. Change the Name property of the toolbar to toolbar.

4. To add buttons to the toolbar you use a built-in editor. Find the Buttons property, select it, and left-click the ellipsis (...) to the right of (Collection).

5. You're going to add six buttons to the toolbar: Clear, Red, Blue, Uppercase, Lowercase, and About. Add the first one by clicking the Add button in the ToolBarButton Collection Editor.

6. The Collection Editor displays a properties palette much like the one that you're used to using. For each button you need to change its text, give it an icon, give it a name, and provide some explanatory ToolTip text. You add the icons in the next *Try It Out*, so just change these properties of ToolBarButton1:

    ❑   Set Name to toolbarClear

    ❑   Set Text to Clear

    ❑   Set ToolTipText to Clear the text box

The Collection Editor should look like Figure 6-17.

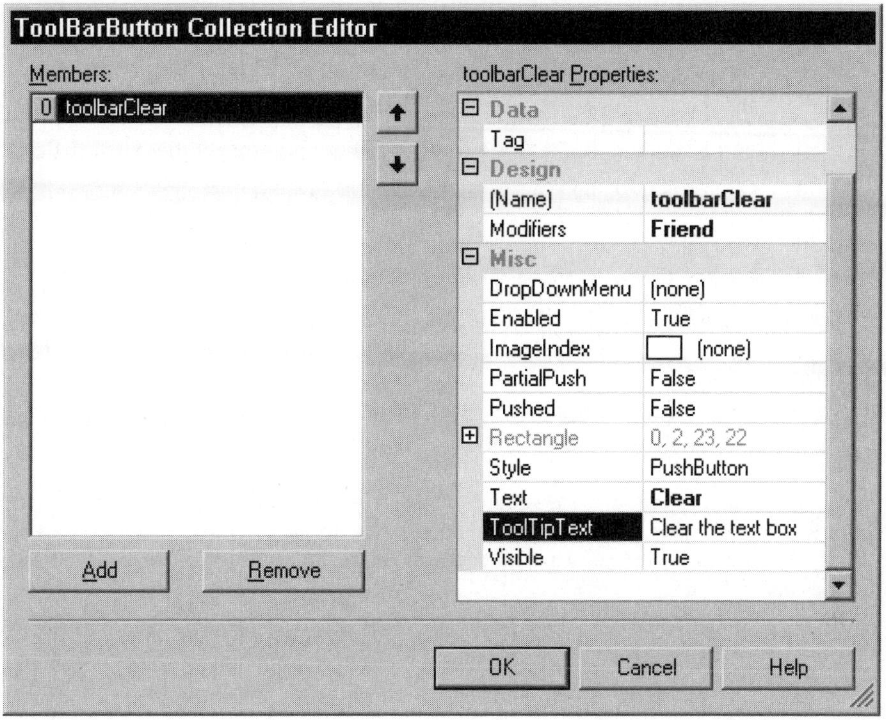

ToolBarButton Collection Editor

Members:

| 0 | toolbarClear |

toolbarClear Properties:

Data	
Tag	
Design	
(Name)	**toolbarClear**
Modifiers	**Friend**
Misc	
DropDownMenu	(none)
Enabled	True
ImageIndex	(none)
PartialPush	False
Pushed	False
Rectangle	0, 2, 23, 22
Style	PushButton
Text	**Clear**
ToolTipText	Clear the text box
Visible	True

Add   Remove

OK   Cancel   Help

Figure 6-17

7. Click the Add button again to add the Red button. Set the following properties:

- ❑ Set Name to toolbarRed
- ❑ Set Text to Red
- ❑ Set ToolTipText to Make the text red

8. Click the Add button again to add the Blue button. Set these properties:

- ❑ Set Name to toolbarBlue
- ❑ Set Text to Blue
- ❑ Set ToolTipText to Make the text blue

9. Click the Add button again to add the Uppercase button. Set these properties:

- ❑ Set Name to toolbarUppercase
- ❑ Set Text to Uppercase
- ❑ Set ToolTipText to Make the text uppercase

10. Click the Add button again to add the Lowercase button. Set these properties:

- ❑ Set Name to toolbarLowercase

❑   Set Text to Lowercase

❑   Set ToolTipText to Make the text lowercase

11.   Now you add a separator to make a space between the Lowercase button and the About button. Click Add and change the Style property to Separator. You don't need to change the name of the control unless you particularly want to.

12.   Click the Add button one last time to add the About button. Set these properties:

❑   Set Name to toolbarHelpAbout

❑   Set Text to About

❑   Set ToolTipText to Display the About box

13.   Finally, click the OK button to save the toolbar.

How It Works

Much like the StatusBar control, theToolbar control docks to a particular position on the form. In this case, it docks itself to the top edge of the form.

The seven controls (six buttons and one separator) that you added to the toolbar actually appear as full members of the `TextEditor` class, but it's unlikely in this application that you'll need to access them directly. Later, you see how you can respond to the `Click` event on the toolbar itself to determine when the button has been clicked.

The ToolTipText property enables .NET to display a ToolTip above the button whenever the user hovers the mouse over it. You don't need to worry about actually creating or showing a ToolTip; .NET does this for you.

At the moment your toolbar is looking pretty boring, so let's add some images.

Adding Images to the Toolbar

Now that you have added your buttons to the toolbar, you need to add some images to demonstrate the purpose of each button. While you can have buttons on the toolbar with text only, adding images to the buttons just makes for a nicer user interface and allows a user to quickly associate an image with an action without having to read the text on the button.

Try It Out   Finding Toolbar Pictures in the .NET Framework Samples

1.   The first thing you need to do is find the Microsoft Visual Studio .Net folder. This is usually under `c:\Program Files\`, but you may have to dig around to find it if you changed the default installation location.

2.   In the `Common7\Graphics\bitmaps` folder beneath it, you'll find numerous pictures in sub folders that you can use in your toolbar.

3.   In this project you use `NEW.BMP` for the Clear button, `DIAMOND.BMP` for the Red and Blue buttons (with the color changed for the Blue button), `BLD.BMP` for the Uppercase button, `JST.BMP` for Lowercase button, and `HELP.BMP` for the About button. `DIAMOND.BMP` has been renamed to `Red.bmp` and `Blue.bmp`.

4.   Browse the folders for the figures you want and copy them to a new Figures folder in your W project folder.

Icons can be created using Visual Studio .NET by simply right-clicking a project, and selecting Add ⇨ Add New Item. Choose Icon File from the Add New Item window, and give the icon a meaningful name. Select Open, and you will be presented with an icon editor that you can use to create your own icons.

Try It Out   Adding the Toolbar Pictures

1. Now you need to add the toolbar pictures to the project. The first step in doing this is to create an image list in which you can add the pictures. Open the Form Designer and locate the ImageList control in the Toolbox. Add it to your form.

2. You'll notice that the image list does not appear on the form, but appears in a new region at the bottom of the designer as shown in Figure 6-18. ImageList controls do not have a user interface at runtime, and in this region controls that do not have a UI appear.

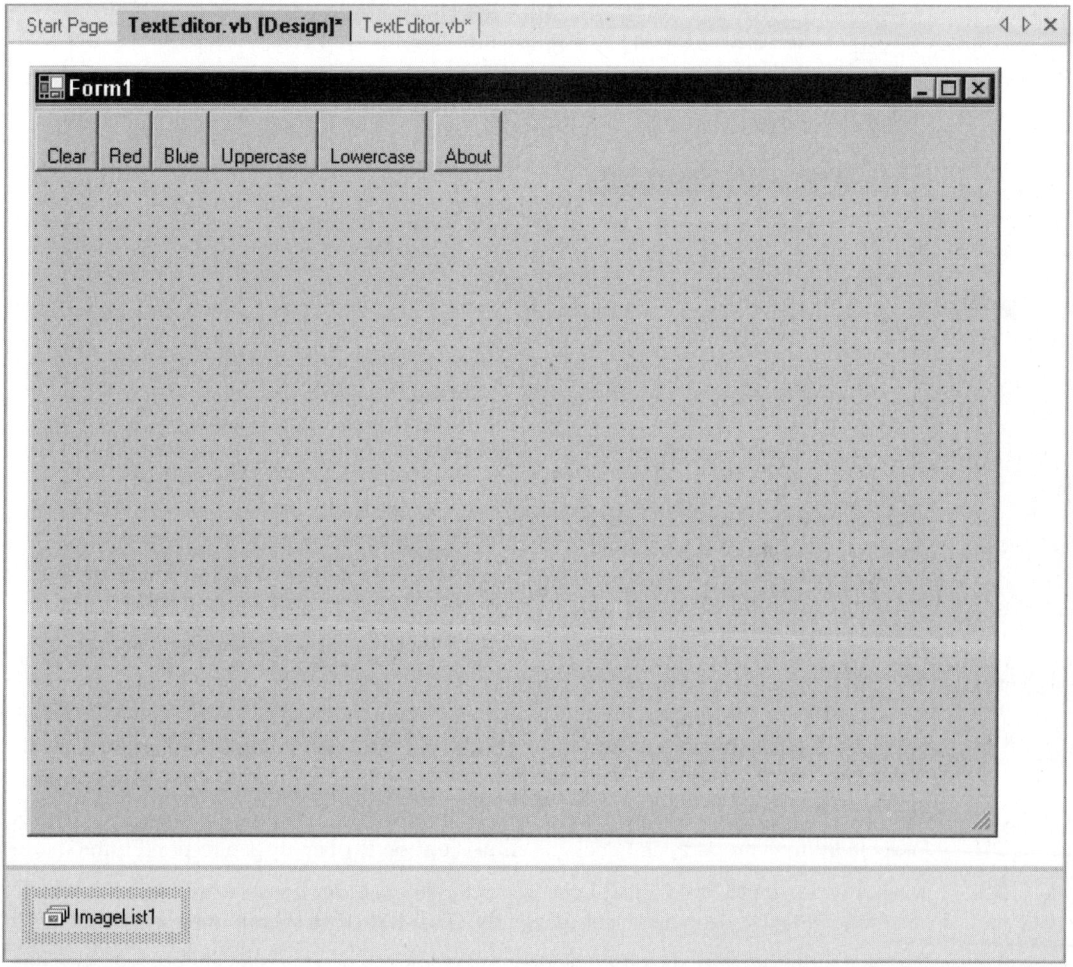

Figure 6-18

3. Change the Name property of the ImageList control to imglstToolbar.

4. Select its Images property. Again, you'll find an ellipsis button (...) next to (Collection). Click it.

5. Another Collection Editor window appears, but this time you're adding new images to the image list. Click Add.

6. The File Open dialog box appears. Browse to the correct folder using the Look in box.

7. The folder should appear. Select NEW.BMP and click Open.

8. Go through the same process to add the images for the Red, Blue, Uppercase, Lowercase, and About buttons (in that order). When you are done, your complete image collection should look like the one shown in Figure 6-19. Finally, click OK to dismiss the Collection Editor.

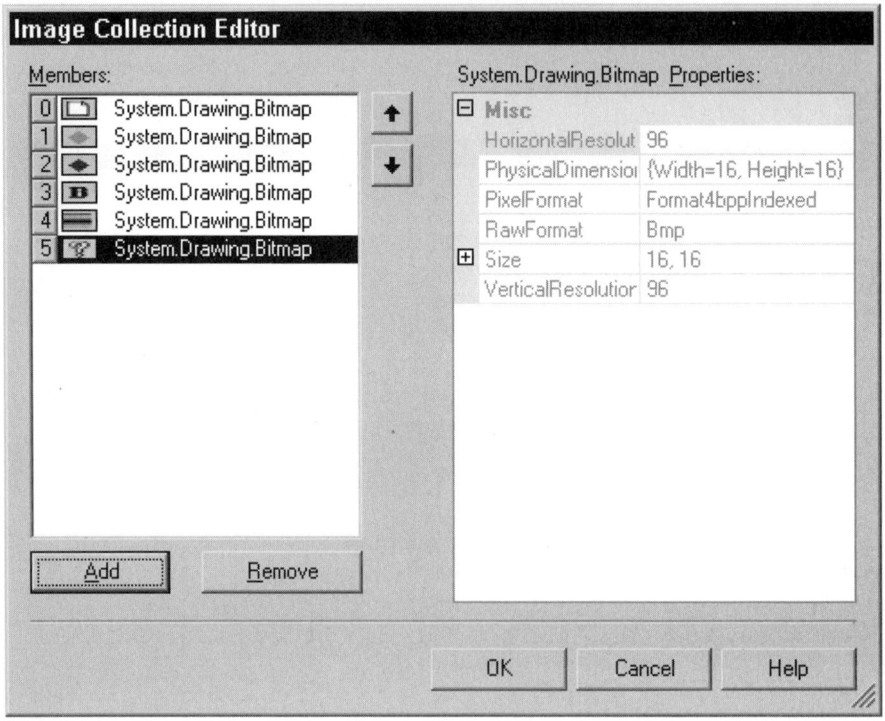

Image Collection Editor

Members:

0		System.Drawing.Bitmap
1		System.Drawing.Bitmap
2		System.Drawing.Bitmap
3	**B**	System.Drawing.Bitmap
4		System.Drawing.Bitmap
5		System.Drawing.Bitmap

System.Drawing.Bitmap Properties:

- **Misc**
  - HorizontalResolut 96
  - PhysicalDimensioi {Width=16, Height=16}
  - PixelFormat Format4bppIndexed
  - RawFormat Bmp
  - Size 16, 16
  - VerticalResolutior 96

Add   Remove

OK   Cancel   Help

Figure 6-19

9. Select the ToolBar control and find its ImageList property. Select imglstToolbar from the list. This action ties the ImageList control to the toolbar. You can now point each button to an image in the image list.

10. Find the Buttons property and click the ellipsis button to open the Collection Editor.

11. ToolbarClear should be selected. Drop down the ImageIndex property and select 0, which corresponds to the icon you've chosen for the Clear button as shown in Figure 6-20.

12. Repeat the process with the other buttons. When you've finished you should have buttons similar to those in Figure 6-21.

Finally, you can start working on the code!

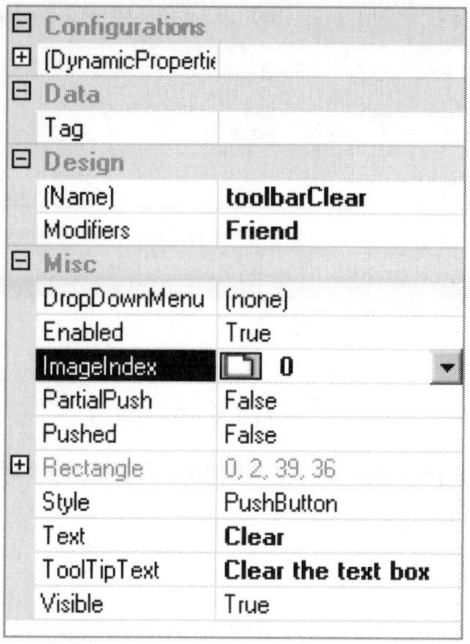
Configurations
(DynamicPropertie
Data
Tag
Design
(Name) toolbarClear
Modifiers Friend
Misc
DropDownMenu (none)
Enabled True
ImageIndex 0
PartialPush False
Pushed False
Rectangle 0, 2, 39, 36
Style PushButton
Text Clear
ToolTipText Clear the text box
Visible True

Figure 6-20

Clear
Red
Blue
B
Uppercase
Lowercase
About

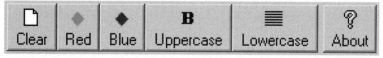

Figure 6-21

Creating an Edit Box

The first thing you want to do is create a text box that can be used to edit the text entered. The text box has a Multiline property, which by default is set to False. This property determines if the text box should have only one line or be resizable to contain multiple lines. When you change this property to True, the text box control can be resized to any size that you want and you can enter multiple lines of text in this control.

Try It Out Creating an Edit Box

1. Open the Designer for TextEditor form and draw a TextBox control in the center between the bottom of the toolbar and the top of the status bar.
2. Change the following properties of the TextBox control:
    - Set Name to txtEdit
    - Set Multiline to True
    - Set ScrollBars to Vertical
    - Clear the Text property so it is blank

Your form should now look like Figure 6-22.

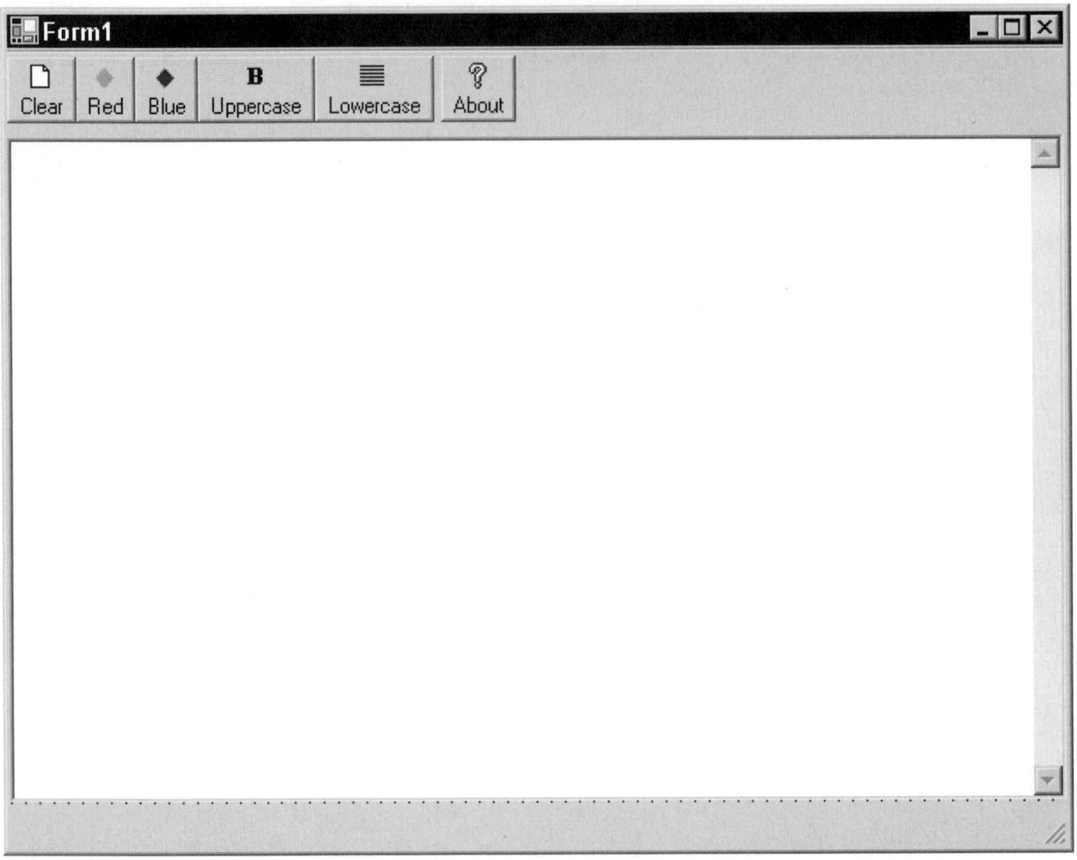

Figure 6-22

3. As you know, when the form changes size, the toolbar and status bar stay "locked" in their position. To make sure that the text box itself stretches with the form, set the Anchor property to Top, Bottom, Left, Right.

Clearing the Edit Box

In the following *Try It Out*, you're going to create a property called EditText that will get or set the text you're going to edit. Then, clearing the edit box will simply be a matter of blanking out the EditText property.

Try It Out   **Clearing txtEdit**

1. Add this code to TextEditor:

```
' EditText - gets or sets the text that we're editing...
Public Property EditText() As String
    Get
        Return txtEdit.Text
    End Get
```

```
        Set(ByVal Value As String)
            txtEdit.Text = Value
        End Set
    End Property
```

As you have done earlier, when you created a property to abstract away the action of setting the status bar text, you created this property to give developers using the TextEditor form the ability to get or set the text of the document irrespective of how you actually implement the editor.

2. You can now build ClearEditBox, the method that actually clears your text box. Add the following code:

```
' ClearEditBox - empties txtEdit...
Public Sub ClearEditBox()
' reset the EditText property...
    EditText = ""

    ' reset the font color
    txtEdit.ForeColor = System.Drawing.Color.Black

    ' reset the status bar...
    StatusText = "Clear text box"
End Sub
```

3. Now select txtEdit from the left drop-down list and TextChanged from the right list at the top of the code editor. Add this code:

```
Private Sub txtEdit_TextChanged(ByVal sender As Object, _
        ByVal e As System.EventArgs) Handles txtEdit.TextChanged
    ' reset the status bar...
    StatusText = "Ready"
End Sub
```

How It Works

The first thing you want to do is clear your text box. In the next *Try It Out,* you see how you can call ClearEditBox from the toolbar.

All this procedure does is set the EditText property to " ", set the ForeColor property of the text box (which is the color of the actual text) to black and place the text Clear text box in the status bar.

```
' ClearEditBox - empties txtEdit...
Public Sub ClearEditBox()
    ' reset the EditText property...
    EditText = ""

    ' reset the font color
    txtEdit.ForeColor = System.Drawing.Color.Black

    ' reset the status bar...
    StatusText = "Clear text box"
End Sub
```

As mentioned, EditText abstracts the action of getting and setting the text in the box away from our actual implementation. This makes it easier for other developers down the line to use your `TextEditor` form class in their own applications:

```
' EditText - gets or sets the text that we're editing...
Public Property EditText() As String
    Get
        Return txtEdit.Text
    End Get
    Set(ByVal Value As String)
        txtEdit.Text = Value
    End Set
End Property
```

As you type, the `TextChanged` event handler will be repeatedly called:

```
Private Sub txtEdit_TextChanged(ByVal sender As Object, _
        ByVal e As System.EventArgs) Handles txtEdit.TextChanged
    ' reset the status bar...
    StatusText = "Ready"
End Sub
```

Changing the status text at this point resets any message that might appear. For example, if the user has to type a lot of text and looks down to see *Clear text box*, he or she may be a little concerned. Setting it to Ready is a pretty standard way of informing the user that the computer is doing something or waiting. It does not mean anything specific.

Responding to Toolbars

The toolbar implementation in .NET is a little disappointing, since to make effective use of it you need to go through a number of hoops. The toolbar control does not provide a click event for each button in the Buttons collection. Instead, it provides a `ButtonClick` event for the entire toolbar and it is up to you to determine which button in the Buttons collection was clicked. When you look at building application menus in Chapter 8, you'll notice that menus are far easier to build.

Try It Out **Responding to Toolbar Clicks**

1. In the code window, select `toolbarClear` from the left drop down and then drop down the right list. You'll see the Text Editor screen shown in Figure 6-23.

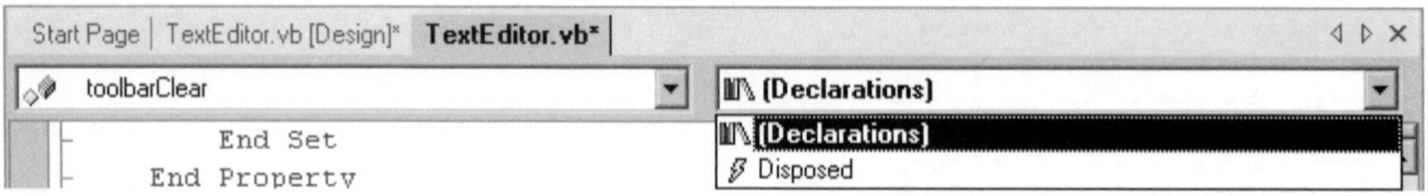

Figure 6-23

If you follow the convention that you have been used to, it's pretty logical to assume that the toolbar button control itself is capable of firing an event like `Click` that you could respond to.

Unfortunately, this isn't the case and you actually have to respond to a `ButtonClick` event on the ToolBar control itself.

2. Select toolbar from the left drop-down list and then select `ButtonClick` from the right one. You'll see something like this:

```
Private Sub toolbar_ButtonClick(ByVal sender As System.Object, _
        ByVal e As System.Windows.Forms.ToolBarButtonClickEventArgs) _
        Handles toolbar.ButtonClick

End Sub
```

The second parameter passed to this event handler is a `ToolBarButtonClickEventArgs` object. This object contains a property that refers to the actual button that was clicked. In order to find out which button actually was clicked, you need to try to match it to one of the other controls.

3. Add the following code to the procedure that was just inserted into your code window:

```
Private Sub toolbar_ButtonClick(ByVal sender As System.Object, _
        ByVal e As System.Windows.Forms.ToolBarButtonClickEventArgs) _
        Handles toolbar.ButtonClick

    ' do we want to empty the text box?
    If e.Button Is toolbarClear Then
        ClearEditBox()
    End If

End Sub
```

4. Now run the project. Type some text into the edit box and click any of the buttons except Clear—nothing will happen. Now click the Clear button. The box will become blank and the status bar will inform you that it has been cleared.

How It Works

The trick here is to use the `Is` operator. This operator allows matching of objects, so when you say:

```
If e.Button Is toolbarClear Then
```

...you're actually saying, "Is the button passed through from the `ToolbarButtonClickEventArgs` object the same as the reference you already have in `toolbarClear`?"

When you click any button other than the Clear button, this isn't true. However, when you click the Clear button it is true and so you call the `ClearEditBox` method.

Coding the Red Button

Now add the code that will make your Red button turn any text entered red. In this *Try It Out* you will create a procedure to turn the text in the text box red and then call that procedure from the ButtonClick event of the toolbar.

Try It Out   Coding the Red Button

1.   The first thing you have to do is create a function that will actually change the text red and update the status bar:

```
Public Sub RedText()
    ' make the text red...
    txtEdit.ForeColor = System.Drawing.Color.Red

    ' reset the status bar...
    StatusText = "The text is red"
End Sub
```

2.   Next, change the `toolbar_ButtonClick` method to look like this:

```
Private Sub toolbar_ButtonClick(ByVal sender As Object, _
        ByVal e As System.Windows.Forms.ToolBarButtonClickEventArgs) _
        Handles toolbar.ButtonClick

    ' do we want to empty the text box?
    If e.Button Is toolbarClear Then
        ClearEditBox()
        Exit Sub
    End If

        ' do we want to make our text red?
        If e.Button Is toolbarRed Then
            RedText()
            Exit Sub
        End If
End Sub
```

Adding the line of code, `Exit Sub`, in your `If` statements allows you to bypass processing the rest of the code in this procedure after you encounter the `If` statement that you need to execute. This just makes your code more efficient by not having to execute unnecessary code.

3.   Run the project and enter some text. Click the Red button, and the text's color will change from black to red, as shown in Figure 6-24. Notice that if you carry on typing into the box, the new text will also be red.

4.   Click on the Clear button to remove the text and revert the color of any new text to black.

How It Works

This *Try It Out* was really quite simple. All you did was to call the `RedText` function from your Red button. `RedText` used `System.Drawing.Color.Red` to set the ForeColor property of your text box to red:

```
    ' make the text red...
    txtEdit.ForeColor = System.Drawing.Color.Red
```

The Forecolor remains red until you set it to something else—so clicking the Clear button turns it back to black.

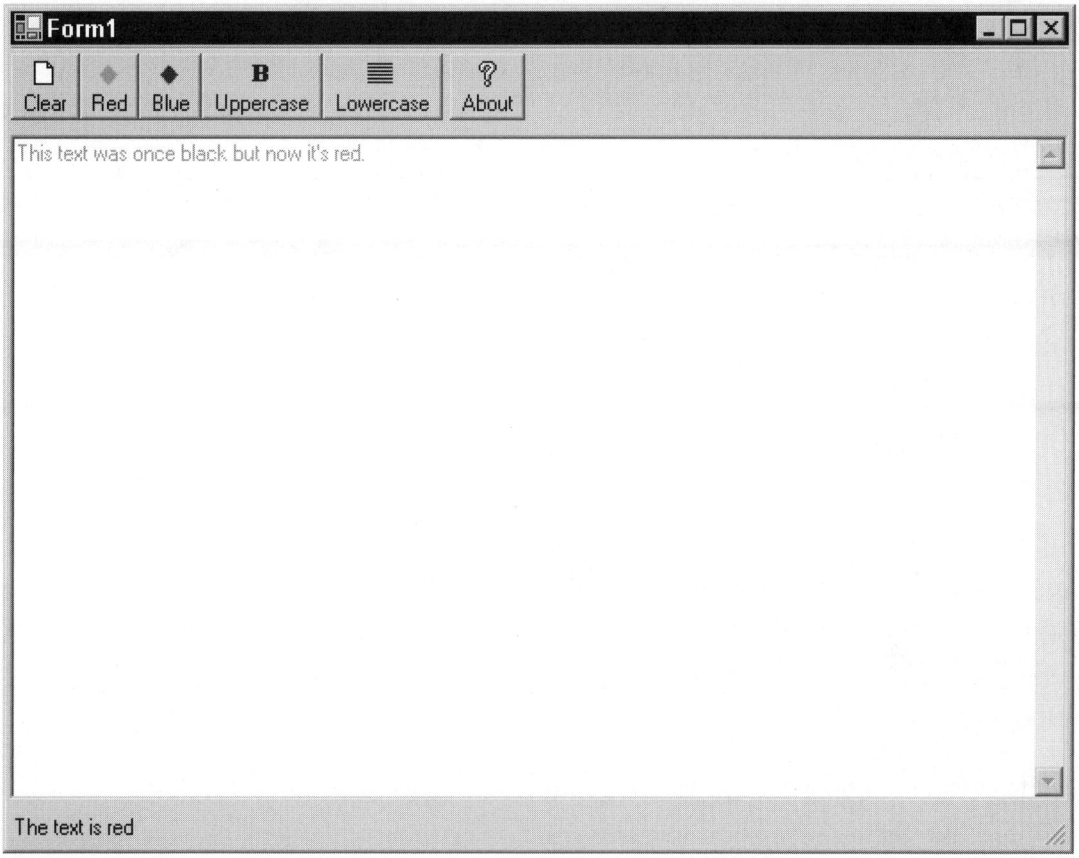

Figure 6-24

Coding the Blue Button

Let's see how you implement the Blue button. This *Try It Out* will be almost identical to the previous one.

Try It Out　　**Coding the Blue Button**

1.　Add the following `BlueText` function to the `TextEditor` form:

```
Public Sub BlueText()
    ' make the text blue...
    txtEdit.ForeColor = System.Drawing.Color.Blue

    ' reset the status bar...
    StatusText = "The text is blue"
End Sub
```

2. Now add this `If...Then` statement to `toolbar_ButtonClick`:

```
' do we want to make our text red?
If e.Button Is toolbarRed Then
    RedText()
    Exit Sub
End If
```

```
    ' do we want to make our text blue?
    If e.Button Is toolbarBlue Then
        BlueText()
        Exit Sub
    End If
```

```
End Sub
```

3. Run the project, and you'll see that the Blue button works in a similar fashion to the Red button, except it turns all our text blue.

Coding the Uppercase and Lowercase Buttons

The code for the Uppercase and Lowercase buttons is very similar, so look at them both now. You will be using the `EditText` property to change the case of the text in the text box. Remember that the `EditText` property returns a string so you will be making use of the built-in functions of the `String` class (`ToUpper` and `ToLower`) to convert the text to upper and lower case.

Try It Out   **Coding the Uppercase and Lowercase Buttons**

1. Add the following functions to your `TextEditor` form:

```
Public Sub UppercaseText()
    ' make the text uppercase...
    EditText = EditText.ToUpper

    ' update the status bar...
    StatusText = "The text is all uppercase"

End Sub

Public Sub LowercaseText()

    ' make the text lowercase
    EditText = EditText.ToLower

    ' update the status bar...
    StatusText = "The text is all lowercase"

End Sub
```

2. Now add this code to `toolbar_ButtonClick` to connect your `UppercaseText` and `LowercaseText` methods to their respective buttons:

```
' do we want to make our text blue?
If e.Button Is toolbarBlue Then
   BlueText()
   Exit Sub
End If
```

```
    ' do we want to make our text uppercase?
   If e.Button Is toolbarUppercase Then
      UppercaseText()
      Exit Sub
   End If

    ' do we want to make our text lowercase?
   If e.Button Is toolbarLowercase Then
      LowercaseText()
      Exit Sub
   End If
```

```
End Sub
```

3. Run the project and enter some text into the box in a mixture of lowercase and uppercase. Then click the Uppercase button to make it all uppercase as shown in Figure 6-25.

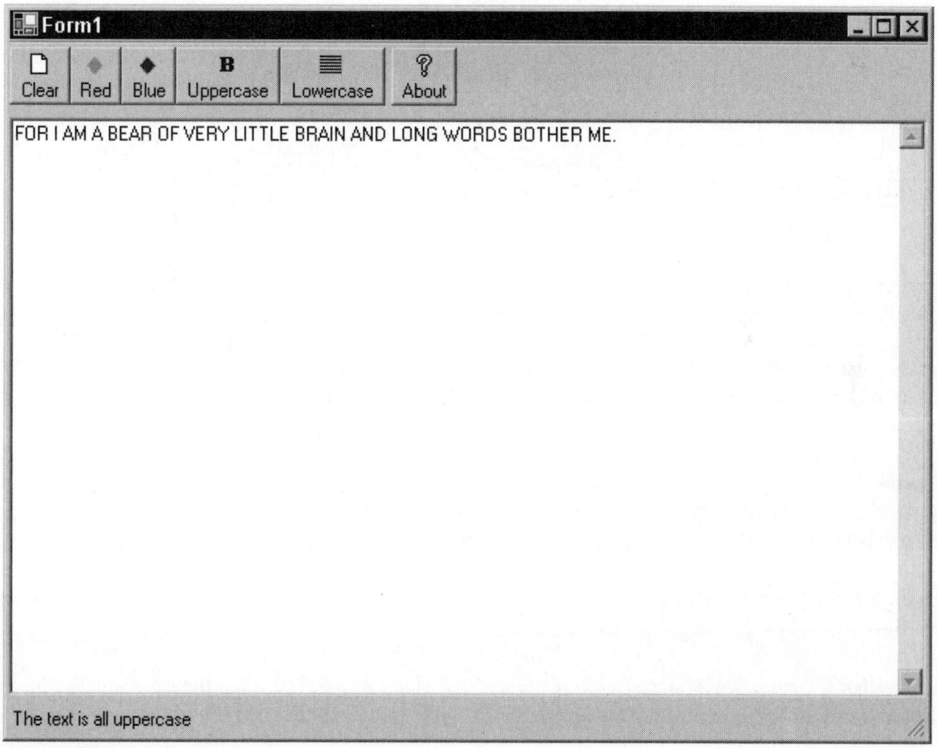

Figure 6-25

4. Click on the Lowercase button and all the text becomes lowercase.

How It Works

The code in this *Try It Out* is very simple; you have seen it all before. If the user clicks on the Uppercase button you call `UppercaseText`, which uses the `ToUpper` method to convert all the text held in `EditText` to uppercase text:

```
' make the text uppercase...
EditText = EditText.ToUpper
```

Likewise, if the user clicks on the Lowercase button you call `LowercaseText`, which uses the `ToLower` method to convert all the text held in `EditText` to lowercase text:

```
' make the text lowercase
EditText = EditText.ToLower
```

Understanding Focus

There's a problem with your Text Editor project. When you change the case using the Uppercase and Lowercase buttons, the entire text in the box is highlighted. This happens because the focus has been set to the TextBox control. The control that has focus is the control that is currently selected as shown in Figure 6-26. For example, if you have two buttons on a form, the code in the event handler for the button that has focus will be executed if you press *Return*.

Figure 6-26

If there are a number of text boxes on a form, any text you type will be entered into the textbox that currently has the focus.

You can move focus between controls at runtime by pressing the Tab key. For example, if the user of the form shown in Figure 6-26 pressed the Tab key, focus would jump to the *I do not* button. If the user pressed the Tab key again, focus would jump back to the *I have focus* button.

The order in which the focus moves between the controls on a form is not arbitrary. As you place controls on a form they are assigned a value for their `TabIndex` property. The first control to be placed on the form has a `TabIndex` of 0, the second 1, the third 2, and so on. This is the same order that the controls will have the focus as you tab through them. If you have placed all your controls on the form and are not happy with the resulting tab order, you can manually change it yourself by using the Properties window to set the `TabIndex` properties of the controls.

Note that although labels have a TabIndex property it is not possible to tab to them at runtime. Instead, the focus moves to the next control that can receive it, such as a text box or button.

Visual Basic .NET has a very handy feature for displaying the tab order of your controls. Select View ⇨ Tab Order and your form will look something like Figure 6-27.

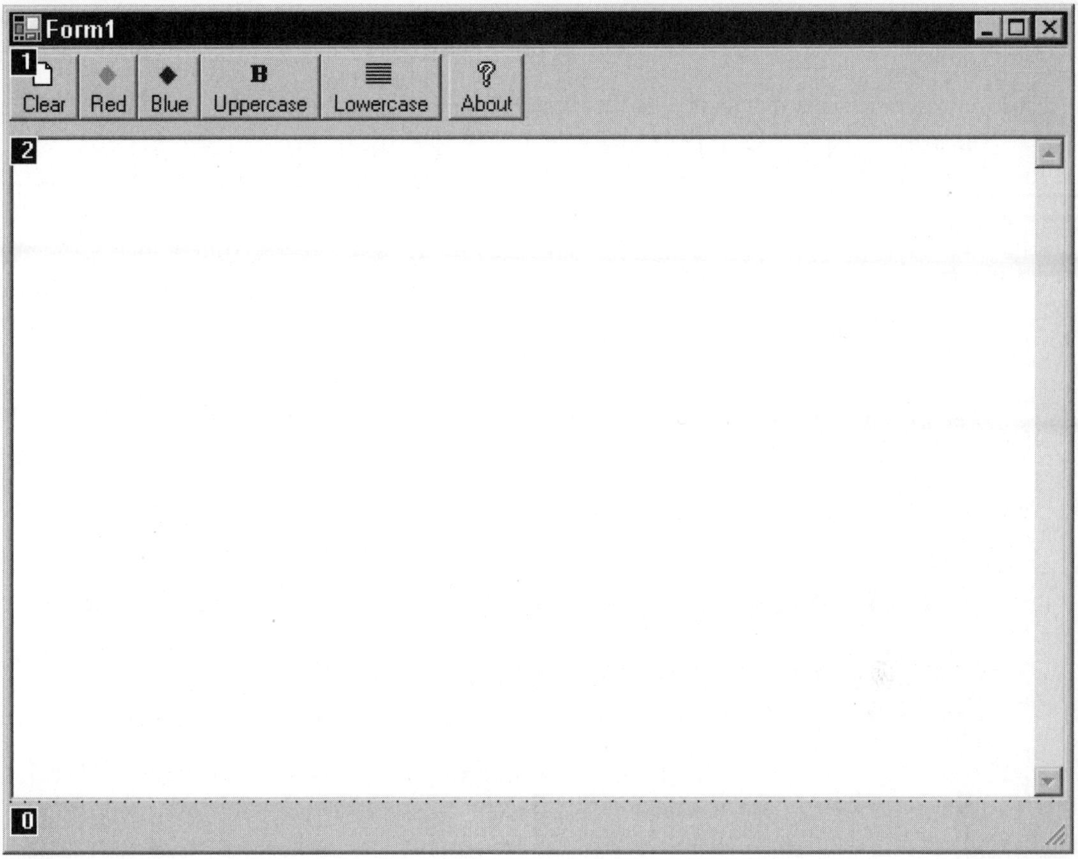

Figure 6-27

The tab order shown in the previous figure represents the order in which you placed your controls on the form. To remove the numbers just select View ⇨ Tab Order once more.

> *It is possible to assign shortcut keys to labels in a similar way in which shortcut keys can be assigned to menu items (see Chapter 8). With keyboard shortcuts on labels, pressing the shortcut key doesn't move the focus to the label, but it moves focus to the edit field (or other user input field) with a TabIndex, one greater than the label's TabIndex.*

Using Multiple Forms

All Windows applications have two types of windows—normal windows and dialog boxes. A normal window provides the main UI for an application. For example, if you use Word you use a normal window for editing your documents.

On occasion, the application will display a dialog box when you want to access a special feature. This type of window "hijacks" the application and forces you to use just that window. For example, when you select the Print option in Word, a dialog box appears, and from that point on you can't actually change the document—the only thing you can use is the Print dialog box itself. We call forms that do this *modal*.

Dialog boxes are discussed in more detail in Chapter 7. For now, you focus on adding additional forms to your application. The form that you add is a simple modal form.

Help About

Most applications have an About box that describes the application's name and copyright information. As you already have a toolbar button for this feature, wire it in now.

Try It Out   **Adding an About Box**

1.   To add a new form to the project, you need to use the Solution Explorer. Right-click the Text Editor project and select Add ⇨ Add Windows Form as shown in Figure 6-28. Enter the name of the form as About and click Open to create the new form.

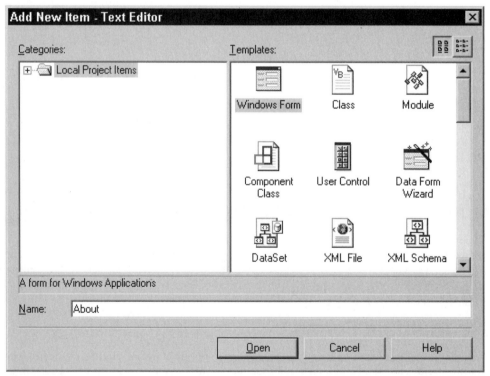

Figure 6-28

2.   When the form's Designer appears, set its Text property to About Wrox Text Editor.

3. Dialog boxes and About boxes traditionally appear centered over the application window. Look for the StartPosition property and change this to CenterParent. This will make the About box start in the correct place.

4. Another tradition about modal windows is that they usually cannot be sized—although thanks to the fact that .NET makes it far easier to create resizable forms, this tradition is likely to end. However, you want to make sure that your About box cannot be resized, so find the `FormBorderStyle` property and change it to `FixedDialog`.

5. Strangely, although you told the form that it is a `FixedDialog`, it still has minimize and maximize buttons. Find the `MinimizeBox` and `MaximizeBox` properties and change both to `False`.

6. Now you need to add two labels, a LinkLabel control (found in the Toolbox) and a button to the form. Add these components so the form looks like Figure 6-29.

Figure 6-29

Set these properties in your project as follows:

- ❑ Create a Label control. Name it Label1, and set these properties: Text = Wrox Text Editor; Font (Bold, Size = 10).
- ❑ Create a Label control. Name it lblVersion and set these properties: Text = Version.
- ❑ Create a LinkLabel control. Name it lnkWrox, and set these properties: Text = http://www.wrox.com.
- ❑ Create a Button control. Name it BtnOK and set these properties: Text = OK; DialogResult = OK.

7. To make the OK button the default button, select the form and change its AcceptButton property to btnOK. This means that when the user is looking at the dialog box, if they press the Enter key, the dialog box will be dismissed. (In effect, the `Click` event on the button is simulated.)

8. Double-click the form background to create a handler for the form's `Load` event. Add this code:

```
Private Sub About_Load(ByVal sender As System.Object, _
        ByVal e As System.EventArgs) Handles MyBase.Load
```

```
    ' set the version number...
    lblVersion.Text &= " " & Environment.Version.ToString()
```

```
End Sub
```

9. Now, return to the Form Designer and double-click the LinkLabel control. Add this code:

```
Private Sub lnkWrox_LinkClicked(ByVal sender As System.Object, _
        ByVal e As System.Windows.Forms.LinkLabelLinkClickedEventArgs) _
        Handles lnkWrox.LinkClicked

    ' run a Web browser and point it at wrox.com...
    System.Diagnostics.Process.Start("http://www.wrox.com/")

End Sub
```

10. You need to write a function that will display the About box, so add this to the `TextEditor` form:

```
' ShowAboutBox - display the about box...
Public Sub ShowAboutBox()
    Dim objAboutBox As New About()
    objAboutBox.ShowDialog(Me)
End Sub
```

11. Finally, you need to call `ShowAboutBox` from `toolbar_ButtonClick`:

```
    ' do we want to make our text lowercase?
    If e.Button Is toolbarLowercase Then
        LowercaseText()
        Exit Sub
    End If

        ' do we want to display the about box?
        If e.Button Is toolbarHelpAbout Then
            ShowAboutBox()
        End If

End Sub
```

12. Run the project and click on the About button. You should see the dialog and if you click the link, your default browser will start up and you'll be taken to www.wrox.com/:

How It Works

Each form in your application has to have its own class, so to create a new form you need to get Visual Basic .NET to create a new class. We create a new class called `About`.

When the form starts, it will fire the `Load` event. You take this opportunity to write the version number to the lblVersion control:

```
Private Sub About_Load(ByVal sender As System.Object, _
        ByVal e As System.EventArgs) Handles MyBase.Load

    ' set the version number...
    lblVersion.Text &= " " & Environment.Version.ToString()
End Sub
```

The shared property `Environment.Version` provides access to the version number of the current application. Version numbers in .NET have four components. The major and minor version numbers in this case are 1 and 1, and can be set by the developer. The next two numbers are the build and revision numbers, and are generated by Visual Basic .NET automatically as we compile. The `ToString` method can be used to combine all four components of the version number into a string with the format: *Major.Minor.Revision.Build*.

The LinkLabel control is a general-purpose control that can be used in your applications for a variety of different reasons. In this case, you're using it to visit a URL. This is done through the shared `System.Diagnostics.Process.Start` method. What this does is ask Windows to run the supplied "program." Thanks to the way that Web browsers integrate with Windows, when you try to run a URL as you are doing here, the default Web browser will open the URL for you:

```
Private Sub lnkWrox_LinkClicked(ByVal sender As System.Object, _
        ByVal e As System.Windows.Forms.LinkLabelLinkClickedEventArgs) _
        Handles lnkWrox.LinkClicked
    ' run a Web browser and point it at wrox.com...
    System.Diagnostics.Process.Start("http://www.wrox.com/")

End Sub
```

To display another window you have to create an instance of it. That's exactly what you've done in the `ShowAboutBox` method. Once you have an instance, you have to use the `ShowDialog` method to show it modally. You need to pass a reference to the owner form (in this case, the TextEditor form):

```
' ShowAboutBox - display the about box...
Public Sub ShowAboutBox()
    Dim objAboutBox As New About()
    objAboutBox.ShowDialog(Me)
End Sub
```

To dismiss the dialog box you rely on functionality built into the Button control. When you drew the button onto the About form, you set its `DialogResult` property to `OK`. If the button is on a modal dialog box this tells it that when it's pressed that modal dialog should be closed and the value in `DialogResult` (in this case, `OK`) should be passed back to the caller.

Deploying the Wrox Text Editor

Your Wrox Text Editor works well on your development machine, but how do you get it to the end user? This is where deployment comes into play. For the deployment of Windows applications, Visual Studio .NET provides access to the Windows Installer, which provides the following functionality:

- ❑ Allows the user to select features they wish to install at the time of installation

- ❑ Allows applications to be completely uninstalled

- ❑ Allows the repair of files, should a file become corrupted

- ❑ Allows files to be copied to the destination machine, adding registry entries and creating desktop shortcuts

- ❑ Allows rollbacks so that during an installation if a component fails to install, a rollback will occurs and the system will be left in the state it started in

In the next *Try It Out* you create a basic Setup project that can be used to install your Wrox Text Editor to other machines in a professional manner.

Try It Out   Creating an Installer

1. You start by adding a new project to your solution. Right-click Solution 'Text Editor' in the Solution Explorer and select Add ➪ Add New Project. Then click Setup and Deployment Projects to show the list of project templates shown in Figure 6-30.

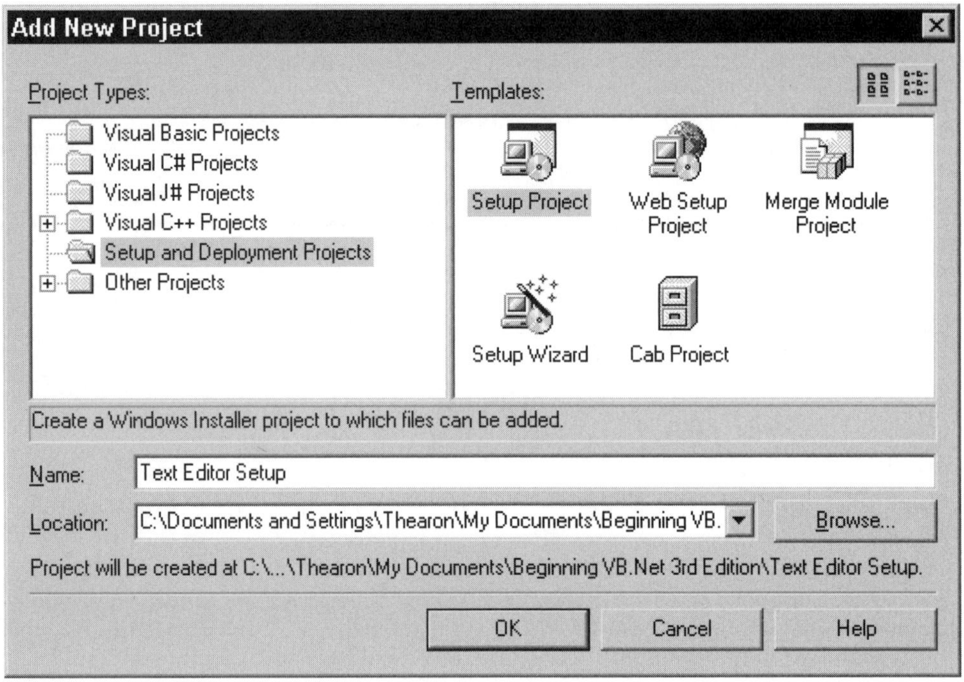

Figure 6-30

2. Select Setup Project, rename the project Text Editor Setup, and click the OK button. Only Setup Project is available in Visual Basic Standard Edition and this is the method you use to create an Installer.

3. Click the Text Editor Setup project in the Solution Explorer, then change the following properties in the Properties window as shown in Figure 6-31:

    ❑   Set Author to Wrox Author Team

    ❑   Set Description to Basic Text Editor

    ❑   Set Manufacturer to Wrox Press

    ❑   Set ManufacturerUrl to http://www.wrox.com/

    ❑   Set ProductName to Wrox Text Editor

    ❑   Set Title Wrox to Text Editor

Figure 6-31

4. Click the Text Editor Setup project in the Solution Explorer again. In the File System Editor select the Application Folder. Now go to the main menu bar and select the Action ➪ Add ➪ Project Output to display the dialog shown in Figure 6-32.

5. Ensure that Text Editor is displayed in the Project drop-down box. Next, select Primary output from the listbox and finally select (Active) for the configuration. Click the OK button to confirm these actions.

6. In the Solution Explorer right-click on Text Editor Setup and choose Build.

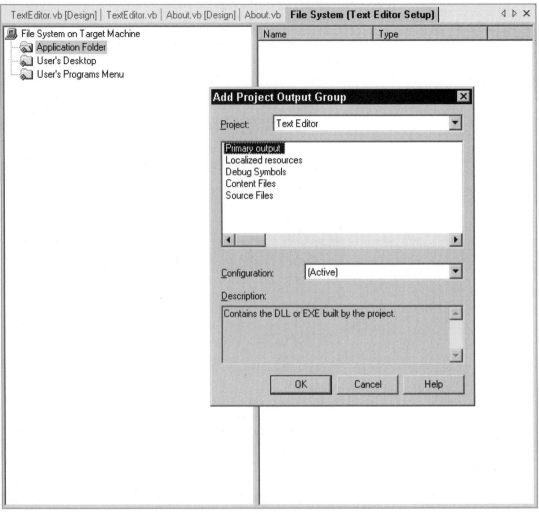

Figure 6-32

How It Works

Visual Studio makes it very easy to build an installation program that will help bundle your application for deployment. The first thing you did was to add a new setup project to our solution. Several different types of setup templates are available:

❏ *Setup Project*—This was the template chosen, and is designed to create Installer Packages for Windows applications, hence is best suited for the task at hand.

❏ *Web Setup Project*—This template provides a convenient way to deploy a Web site in a simple install package. It will not only encapsulate the Web pages themselves, but also handle any issues regarding registration and configuration of the Web site automatically. This is often used to allow an entire Web site to be downloaded or for deployment in multiple Web servers. We will not use this project in this chapter because we are deploying a Windows application.

❑   *Merge Module Project*—A Merge Module project creates an installer file for components that are to be used in multiple applications. This Merge Module can then be included in the Install Packages of each of the applications.

❑   *Cab Project*—This is used to create cabinet files. Cab files are used to compress single or multiple files together into a small distributable package. They are often used to distribute ActiveX controls from a Web server to a Web browser.

❑   *Setup Wizard*—This wizard provides a step-by-step walkthrough of the templates described above.

After choosing a setup project you changed various properties of the project relevant to your application, such as the name and author. These properties will be displayed when the text editor is being installed.

Next you told the installer that you wanted to add an application to the installer package. Here you chose several options:

❑   From the drop-down menu you chose which application you actually wanted to install—in this case it was the Text Editor.

❑   Next you chose what you wanted to install; in this case you only want the Primary output files. Other options include choosing debug symbols used for debugging, resources, the actual source code, or a help file for the user who is installing the application on the target machine.

❑   The default configuration (Active) will usually be sufficient. The other choices are Debug or Release. With Debug selected, the application is compiled along with additional information for the debugger to operate correctly. You use the Release configuration to install your applications on client's machines, as this does not include the debugger information, hence the application file is smaller and executes more quickly.

❑   Finally, you built the Installation package and are ready to deploy it to your users.

Deploying the Installer

The Installation Package is treated like any other project in Visual Studio .NET. On the first screen when you chose the template you also selected where you wanted the project to exist. If you look in the Debug directory (this is my current configuration) it will contain all of the files needed to deploy the Wrox Text Editor. These files could be deployed in many ways:

❑   Burning them on a CD-ROM

❑   Placing them on a shared network

❑   Compressing them and e-mailing them

❑   Through a distribution product like System Management Server (SMS)

The main point here is that the client machine needs access to all of the files in the directory, as shown in Figure 6-33, (Debug or Release) in order to actually do the install.

Name ▲	Size	Type	Date Modified	Attributes
Setup.Exe	108 KB	Application	3/19/2003 1:03 AM	A
Setup.Ini	1 KB	Configuration Settings	8/3/2003 11:20 AM	A
Text Editor Setup.msi	312 KB	Windows Installer Package	8/3/2003 11:21 AM	A

Figure 6-33

All that you need to deploy the solution are these files and a target computer with version 1.1 of the .NET Framework installed. Double-clicking on Setup.exe will start the install process and you will be greeted with the introduction screen of the Setup wizard.

The user simply follows the on-screen instructions to install the Wrox Text Editor.

We have covered the basic functionality here, but we've really only scratched the surface of how to deploy a Windows application. There are many other capabilities and options available within Visual Studio .NET that you can use to customize the way in which your application is deployed, to suit your needs and preferences.

Summary

This chapter discussed some of the more advanced features of Windows forms and the commonly used controls. It discussed the event-driven nature of Windows and showed three events that can happen to a button (namely `Click`, `MouseEnter`, and `MouseLeave`).

You created a simple application that allowed you to enter some text and then choose between counting the number of characters or the number of words by using radio buttons.

You then turned your attention to building a more complex application that allowed you to edit text by changing its color or its case. This application showed how easy it was to build toolbars and status bars. You even added an About box to display the version number and a link to the Wrox Web site.

Finally, you built an installation package that makes your application look professional and easy to deploy.

To summarize, you should now know how to:

❑   Write code to respond to control events

❑   Set properties on controls to customize their look and behavior

❑   Use the ToolBar and StatusBar controls

❑   Display other forms in your application

❑   Create a simple setup project to deploy your application

Exercises

1.   What event is fired when the mouse pointer crosses over a button's boundary to hover over it? What event is fired as it moves in the other direction, away from the button?

2.   How can you prevent your controls from being accidentally deleted or resized?

3.   What should you consider when choosing names for controls?

4.   What is special about the toolbar and status bar controls?

5.   How can you add a separator to your toolbar?

7

Displaying Dialog Boxes

Visual Basic .NET provides several built-in dialog boxes that help you to provide a rich user interface in your front-end applications. These dialogs provide the common user interface that is seen in most Windows applications. They also provide many properties and methods that allow you to customize these dialogs to suit your needs while still maintaining the standard look.

In this chapter, you will learn the following:

- ❑ Create a message box using different buttons and icons
- ❑ Create an Open dialog box that allows you to open files
- ❑ Create a Save dialog box that allows you to save files
- ❑ Create a Font dialog box that allows you to apply the selected font to text
- ❑ Create a Color dialog box that allows you to define and select custom colors
- ❑ Create a Print dialog box that will print text from your application

These dialogs boxes help you manage displaying messages to your users, opening and saving files, choosing fonts and colors, and printing documents. This chapter will explore these dialog boxes in depth and will show how you can use them in your Visual Basic .NET applications, to help you build a more professional looking application for your users.

The MessageBox Dialog box

The MessageBox dialog box is one of the dialog boxes you are likely to use most as a developer. This dialog box enables you to display custom messages to your users and accept their input regarding the choice that they have made. This dialog box is very versatile—you can customize it by displaying a variety of icons with your messages and by choosing which buttons to display.

In day-to-day operation of a computer, you have all seen message boxes that display one of the icons shown in Figure 7-1. In this section, you learn how to create and display message boxes that use these icons.

Figure 7-1

The first icon in Figure 7-1 has three member names: Error, Hand, and Stop. The second icon has only one member name, Question. The third icon has only two member names, Exclamation and Warning. The final icon in Figure 7-1 has two member names, Asterisk and Information.

When building a Windows application, there are times when you need to prompt the user for information or display a warning that something did not happen or something unexpected happened. For instance, suppose the user of your application has modified some data and is trying to close the application without saving the data. You could display a message box that carries an information or warning icon and an appropriate message—that they will lose all unsaved data. You could also provide OK and Cancel buttons to allow the user to continue or cancel the operation.

This is where the MessageBox dialog box comes in as it allows you to quickly build custom dialog boxes that will prompt the user for a decision while displaying your custom message, a choice of icons, and a choice of buttons. All of this functionality also allows you to display a message box to inform users of validation errors, and to display formatted system errors that are trapped by error handling.

Before you jump into some code, take a look at the MessageBox class. The MessageBox class contains public and protected methods inherited from the Object class. The Show method is called to display the MessageBox dialog box. The title, message, icons, and buttons displayed are determined by the parameters you pass to this method. This may seem complicated, but actually using MessageBox is very simple—as you will see in the following sections.

Available Icons for MessageBox

You saw the available icons in Figure 7-1. Table 7-1 outlines four standard icons that you can display in a message box. The actual graphic displayed is a function of the operating system constants and (in the current implementations at least) there are four unique symbols with multiple field names assigned to them.

Available Buttons for MessageBox

There are several buttons that you can display in a message box and Table 7-2 outlines them.

Setting the Default Button

Along with displaying the appropriate buttons, you can instruct the message box to set a default button for you. This allows the user to read the message and press the *Enter* key to specify the action for the default button. Table 7-3 outlines the available default button options.

Table 7-1 Icons available for MessageBox

Member Name	Description
Asterisk	Specifies that the message box displays an information icon
Information	Specifies that the message box displays an information icon
Error	Specifies that the message box displays an error icon
Hand	Specifies that the message box displays an error icon
Stop	Specifies that the message box displays an error icon
Exclamation	Specifies that the message box displays an exclamation icon
Warning	Specifies that the message box displays an exclamation icon
Question	Specifies that the message box displays a question mark icon
None	Specifies the message box will not display any icon

Table 7-2 Available buttons for MessageBox

Member Name	Description
AbortRetryIgnore	Specifies that the message box displays Abort, Retry, and Ignore buttons
OK	Specifies that the message box displays an OK button
OKCancel	Specifies that the message box displays OK and Cancel buttons
RetryCancel	Specifies that the message box displays Retry and Cancel buttons
YesNo	Specifies that the message box displays Yes and No buttons
YesNoCancel	Specifies that the message box displays Yes, No, and Cancel buttons

Table 7-3 Available default option buttons for MessageBox

Member Name	Description
Button1	Specifies that the first button in the message box should be the default button
Button2	Specifies that the second button in the message box should be the default button
Button3	Specifies that the third button in the message box should be the default button

The default button chosen is relative to the MessageBox buttons, from left to right. Therefore, if you have the Yes, No, and Cancel buttons displayed and you choose the third button to be the default, Cancel will be the default button. Likewise, if you choose the third button to be the default and you only have OK and Cancel buttons, the first button becomes the default.

Miscellaneous Options

There are a couple of other options in the `MessageBoxOptions` enumeration that can be used with the message box and are shown in Table 7-4:

Table 7-4 Miscellaneous options for MessageBox

Member Name	Description
DefaultDesktopOnly	Specifies that the message box be displayed on the active desktop
RightAlign	Specifies that the text in a message box will be right-aligned, as opposed to left-aligned, which is the default
RTLReading	Specifies that the text in a message box be displayed with the RTL (right-to-left) reading order; this only applies to languages that are read from right to left
ServiceNotification	Specifies that the message box be displayed on the active desktop. The caller is a Windows service notifying the user of an event.

The Show Method Syntax

You call the `Show` method to display the message box. The following code example displays the message box shown in Figure 7-2. Notice that the code specifies the text that is displayed in the message box as the first argument, followed by the text that is displayed in the title bar. Then you specify the buttons that should be displayed, followed by the type of icon that should be displayed alongside. Lastly, you specify the button that you want to set as the default button—in this case `Button1`.

To run this code, start a new Windows Application project, double-click the form in the Designer to generate the `Form1_Load` event, and place the following code inside that `sub`:

```
MessageBox.Show("My Text", "My Caption", MessageBoxButtons.OKCancel, _
        MessageBoxIcon.Information, MessageBoxDefaultButton.Button1)
```

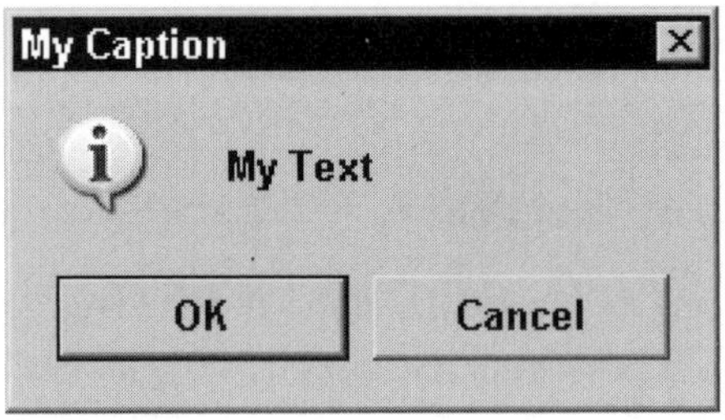

Figure 7-2

Now that you have seen the available icons, buttons, and default button fields, take a look at the `Show` method of the `MessageBox` class. The `Show` method can be specified in several ways, the more common syntaxes are shown in the following list:

❑   `MessageBox.Show(text)`

- ❑   `MessageBox.Show(text, caption)`

- ❑   `MessageBox.Show(text, caption, MessageBoxButtons)`

- ❑   `MessageBox.Show(text, caption, MessageBoxButtons,_MessageBoxIcon)`

- ❑   `MessageBox.Show(text, caption, MessageBoxButtons,MessageBoxIcon, MessageBoxDefaultButton)`

In the previous examples, *text* represents the message that will be displayed in the message box. This text can be static text (a literal string value) or can be supplied in the form of a string variable. These parameters are required:

- ❑   *Caption* represents either static text or a string variable that will be used to display text in the title bar of the message box. If this parameter is omitted then no text is displayed in the title bar.

- ❑   *MessageBoxButtons* represents the `MessageBoxButtons` enumeration. This parameter allows you to specify which of the available buttons will be displayed in the `MessageBox` dialog box.

- ❑   *MessageBoxIcon* represents the `MessageBoxIcon` enumeration. This parameter allows you to specify which of the available icons will be displayed in the `MessageBox` dialog box.

- ❑   *MessageBoxDefaultButton* represents the `MessageBoxDefaultButton` enumeration. This parameter allows you to specify which of the buttons will be set as the default button in the MessageBox dialog box.

All the syntax examples shown in the previous section return a value from the `DialogResult` enumeration, which indicates which button in the MessageBox dialog box was chosen. Table 7-5 shows the available members in the `DialogResult` enumeration.

Table 7-5 Members of the DialogResult enumeration

Member Name	Description
Abort	The return value is Abort, which is the result of clicking the Abort button
Cancel	The return value is Cancel, which is the result of clicking the Cancel button
Ignore	The return value is Ignore, which is the result of clicking the Ignore button
No	The return value is No, which is the result of clicking the No button
None	Nothing is returned, which means the dialog box continues running
OK	The return value is OK, which is the result of clicking the OK button
Retry	The return value is Retry, which is the result of clicking the Retry button
Yes	The return value is Yes, which is the result of clicking the Yes button

Example Message Boxes

Because there are multiple buttons that can be displayed in a MessageBox dialog box, there are multiple ways to display a dialog box and check the results. Of course, if you were displaying only one button using the message box for notification, you would not have to check the results at all and could use a very simple syntax.

Try It Out   Creating a Single Button MessageBox

1. Create a new Windows application project called SimpleMessageBox.

2. Next, you want to add a button control to the form that will open the MessageBox. Call this button btnShow, and set its text to Show.

3. The only code you have to add is the code to actually show the MessageBox dialog box. You want to add this code in the Click event for the btnShow button, so double-click this button in the Form Designer.

4. Enter the following code to the Click event in the code editor:

```
Private Sub btnShow_Click(ByVal sender As System.Object, _
                          ByVal e As System.EventArgs) Handles btnShow.Click
    MessageBox.Show("The print job has completed.", "Print Job Notification")
End Sub
```

5. Run the project. Execution of this code should produce the message box shown in Figure 7-3.

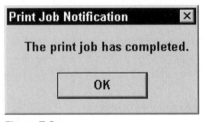

Figure 7-3

How It Works

The MessageBox.Show method opens this simple dialog box with the text and caption that you described:

```
MessageBox.Show("The print job has completed.", "Print Job Notification")
```

Notice that in the sample code you did not specify an icon to be used, nor did you specify a button to be displayed. The OK button is the default button that gets displayed when you do not specify a specific button.

Take a look at an example that contains two buttons.

Try It Out   Creating a Two Button MessageBox

1. Open the designer for the SimpleMessageBox again.

2. Go back to the Form Designer and add a text box. Set its Name to txtResult and clear the text field, so your form now looks like Figure 7-4.

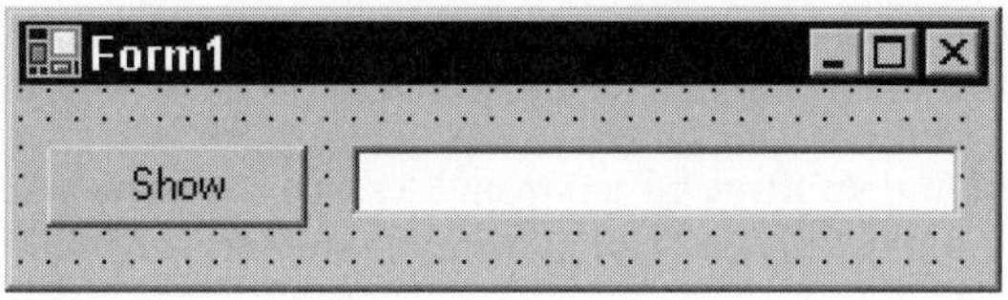

Figure 7-4

3. In code editor, change the code in the Click event for the btnShow button to:

```
Private Sub btnShow_Click(ByVal sender As System.Object, _
                          ByVal e As System.EventArgs) Handles btnShow.Click
    If MessageBox.Show("Your Internet connection will be closed now.", _
        "DUN Notification", _
        MessageBoxButtons.OKCancel, _
        Nothing, _
        MessageBoxDefaultButton.Button1) = DialogResult.OK Then
        txtResult.Text = "OK Clicked"
        ' Hangup the dial-up connection...
        ' Call some method here...
    Else
        txtResult.Text = "Cancel Clicked"
        ' Do nothing or we could place code here to be executed
        ' When the user chose the Cancel button
    End If
End Sub
```

4. Run the project. Execution of this code would produce the message box shown in Figure 7-5.

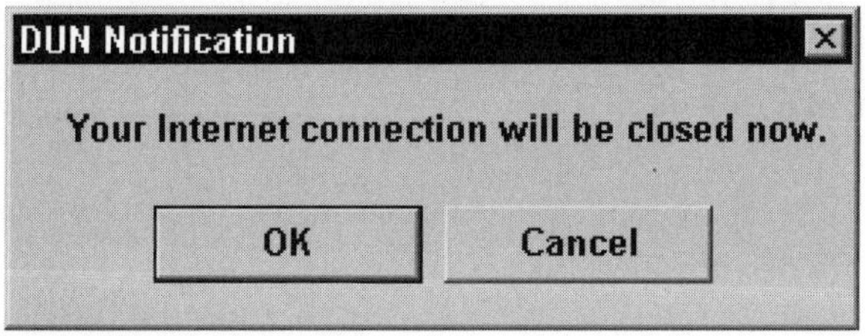

Figure 7-5

How It Works

The code uses the Show method of MessageBox again, but this time it is in an If statement to see if the OK button was chosen by the user.

```
If MessageBox.Show("Your Internet connection will be closed now.", _
    "DUN Notification", _
    MessageBoxButtons.OKCancel, _
    Nothing, _
    MessageBoxDefaultButton.Button1) = DialogResult.OK Then
```

Notice that you have specified that the OK and Cancel buttons are to be displayed in the dialog box and also that the OK button is to be the default button.

You have to specify something for the icon, this is required when you want to set the default button parameter. You did not want to display an icon so you have used the Nothing keyword.

Also notice that you check the results returned from MessageBox using DialogResult.OK. You could just as easily have checked for DialogResult.Cancel and written the If statement around this.

This is great if you only want to test the results of one or two buttons. But what happens when you want to test the results from a MessageBox dialog box that contains three buttons?

Try It Out   Testing a Three Button MessageBox

1.   Once again, open the designer for the SimpleMessageBox.

2.   Go to the Form Designer and change the code in the Click event for the btnShow button to:

```
Private Sub btnShow_Click(ByVal sender As System.Object, _
                          ByVal e As System.EventArgs) Handles btnShow.Click
    Dim intResult As DialogResult
    intResult = MessageBox.Show("The A drive is not ready." & _
        ControlChars.CrLf & ControlChars.CrLf & _
        "Please insert a diskette into the drive.", _
        "Device Not Ready", _
        MessageBoxButtons.AbortRetryIgnore, _
        MessageBoxIcon.Error, _
        MessageBoxDefaultButton.Button2)

    Select Case intResult
        Case DialogResult.Abort
            ' Do abort processing here...
            txtResult.Text = "Abort Clicked"
        Case DialogResult.Retry
            ' Do retry processing here...
            txtResult.Text = "Retry Clicked"
        Case DialogResult.Ignore
            ' Do ignore processing here...
            txtResult.Text = "Ignore Clicked"
    End Select
End Sub
```

3.   Run the project. The MessageBox dialog box shown in Figure 7-6 displays an icon and three buttons, where the second button is the default.

Figure 7-6

How It Works

The Show method returns a DialogResult, which is an Integer value. What you need to do in a case where there are three buttons is to capture the DialogResult in a variable and then test that variable.

In the following sample code, the first thing that you do is declare a variable as a DialogResult to capture the DialogResult returned from the MessageBox dialog box. Remember that the results returned from the dialog box are nothing but an enumeration of Integer values. Then you set the variable equal to that DialogResult.

```
Dim intResult As DialogResult
intResult = MessageBox.Show("The A drive is not ready." & _
    ControlChars.CrLf & ControlChars.CrLf & _
    "Please insert a diskette into the drive.", _
    "Device Not Ready", _
    MessageBoxButtons.AbortRetryIgnore, _
    MessageBoxIcon.Error, _
    MessageBoxDefaultButton.Button2)
```

Notice that the message in the Show method syntax is broken up into two sections separated with ControlChars.CrLf. This built-in constant provides a carriage-return-line-feed sequence, which allows you to break up your message and display it on separate lines.

Finally, you test the value of the intResult, and act on it accordingly:

```
Select Case intResult
    Case DialogResult.Abort
        ' Do abort processing here...
        txtResult.Text = "Abort Clicked"
    Case DialogResult.Retry
        ' Do retry processing here...
        txtResult.Text = "Retry Clicked"
    Case DialogResult.Ignore
        ' Do ignore processing here...
        txtResult.Text = "Ignore Clicked"
End Select
```

Here you write the name of the button selected in the text box to prove that the test actually works.

Now you have a general understanding of how the MessageBox dialog box works and you have a point of reference for the syntax. To familiarize yourself further with the MessageBox, try altering the values of the caption, text, MessageBoxButtons, MessageBoxIcon, and MessageBoxDefaultButton in the previous examples.

Be careful not to overuse the MessageBox dialog box and display a message box for every little message. This can be a real annoyance to the user. You must use common sense and good judgment on when a message box is appropriate. You should only display a MessageBox dialog box when you absolutely need to inform the user that some type of error has occurred or when you need to warn them of some type of possibly damaging action that they have requested. An example of the latter is shutting down the application without saving their work. You would want to prompt the user to let them know that, if they continue, they will lose all unsaved work and give them an option to continue or cancel the action of shutting down the application.

The OpenDialog Control

Most Windows applications process data from files, so you need a mechanism to open and save files. The .NET Framework provides the `OpenFileDialog` and `SaveFileDialog` classes to do just that. In this section you take a look at the OpenFileDialog dialog control, and in the next section you look at the SaveFileDialog control.

When you use Windows applications, such as Microsoft Word or Paint, you see the same standard Open dialog box. This does not happen by accident. There is a standard set of application programming interfaces (API) available to every developer that allows you to provide this type of standard interface; however, using the API can be cumbersome and difficult for a beginner. Fortunately, most of this functionality is already built into the .NET Framework so you can use it as you develop with Visual Basic .NET.

The OpenFileDialog Control

You can use OpenFileDialog as a .NET class—by declaring an instance of it in your code and modifying its properties in code, or as a control by dragging an instance of it onto the form at design time. In either case, the resulting object will have the same methods, properties, and events.

You can find the OpenFileDialog control in the Toolbox under the Windows Forms tab, where you can drag and drop it onto your project. Then, all you need to do is set the properties and execute the appropriate method. To use OpenFileDialog as a class you declare your own objects in order to use the dialog. Then you have control over the scope of the dialog box and can declare an object for it when needed, use it, and destroy it thereby using fewer resources.

This section focuses on using OpenFileDialog as a control. Once you have a better understanding of this dialog box and feel comfortable using it, you can then expand your skills and use OpenFileDialog as a class by declaring your own objects for it.

You can use OpenFileDialog by simply invoking its ShowDialog method, and this would produce results similar to the one shown in Figure 7-7.

The Properties of OpenFileDialog

While the dialog box shown in Figure 7-7 is the standard Open dialog in Windows, it provides no filtering. You see all file types listed in the window and are unable to specify a file type for filtering because no filters exist. This is where the properties of OpenFileDialog come in. You are able to set some of the properties before the Open dialog box is displayed, thereby customizing the dialog box to your needs.

Table 7-6 lists some of the available properties for the OpenFileDialog control.

The Methods of OpenFileDialog

Although there are many methods available in the OpenFileDialog, you will be concentrating only on the `ShowDialog` method in these examples. The following list contains some of the other available methods in OpenFileDialog:

❑   `Dispose` releases the resources used by the Open dialog box.

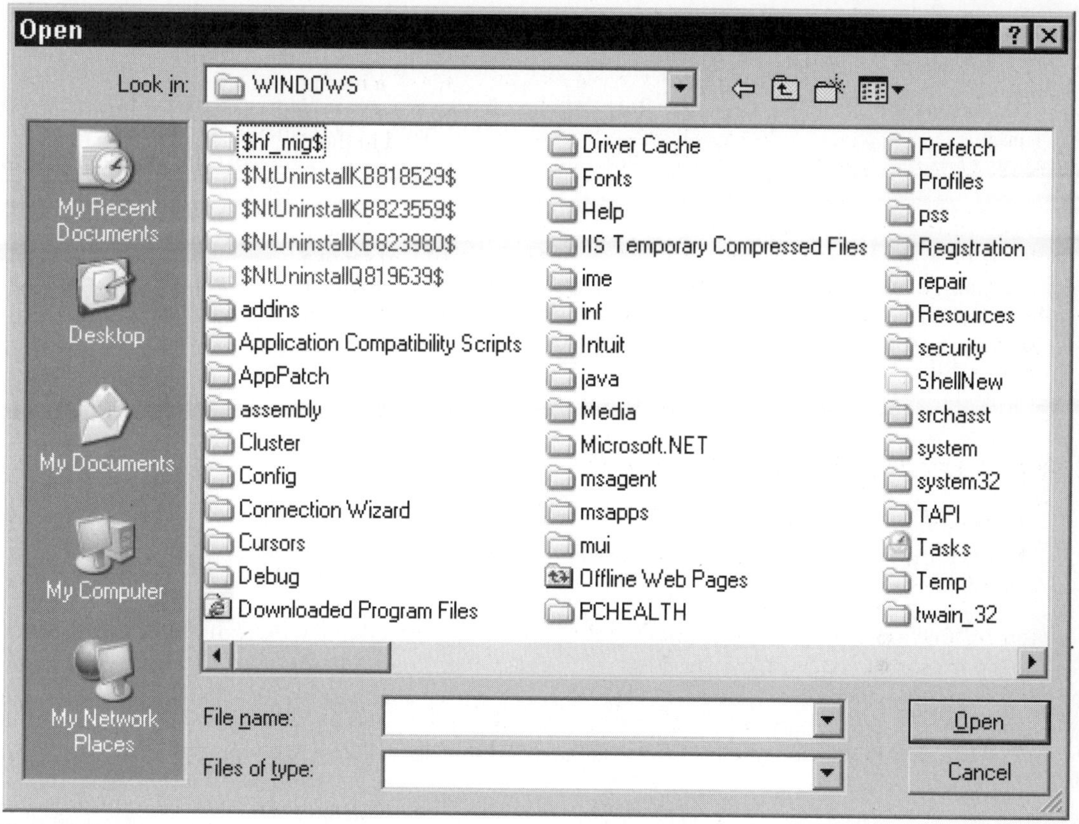

Figure 7-7

- ❏ OpenFile opens the file selected by the user with read-only permission. The file is specified by the FileName property.
- ❏ Reset resets all properties of the Open dialog box to their default values.
- ❏ ShowDialog shows the dialog box.

The ShowDialog method is straightforward as it accepts no parameters, so before calling the ShowDialog method you must set all the properties that you want. After the dialog box returns, you can query the properties to determine which file was selected, the directory, and the type of file selected. An example of the ShowDialog method is shown in the following code fragment:

```
OpenFileDialog1.ShowDialog()
```

The OpenFileDialog control returns a DialogResult of OK or Cancel, with OK corresponding to the Open button on the dialog box. This control does not actually open and read a file for you; it is merely a common interface that allows a user to locate and specify the file or files to be opened by the application. You need to query the OpenFileDialog properties that have been set by the control after the user clicks the Open button to determine which file or files should be opened.

Table 7-6 Properies of OpenFileDialog

Property	Description
AddExtension	Indicates whether an extension is automatically added to a filename if the user omits the extension. This is mainly used in the SaveFileDialog, which you will see in the next section.
CheckFileExists	Indicates whether the dialog displays a warning if the user specifies a file name that does not exist.
CheckPathExists	Indicates whether the dialog displays a warning if the user specifies a path that does not exist.
DefaultExt	Indicates the default file name extension.
DereferenceLinks	Used with shortcuts. Indicates whether the dialog returns the location of the *file* referenced by the shortcut or whether it returns the location of the shortcut itself.
FileName	Indicates the file name of the selected file in the dialog box.
FileNames	Indicates the file names of all selected files in the dialog. This is a read-only property.
Filter	Indicates the current file name filter string, which determines the choices that appear in the Files of type combo box in the dialog box.
FilterIndex	Indicates the index of the filter currently selected in the dialog box.
InitialDirectory	Indicates the initial directory displayed in the dialog box.
MultiSelect	Indicates whether or not the dialog box allows multiple files to be selected.
ReadOnlyChecked	Indicates whether the read-only check box is selected.
RestoreDirectory	Indicates whether the dialog box restores the current directory before closing.
ShowHelp	Indicates whether the Help button is displayed in the dialog box.
ShowReadOnly	Indicates whether the dialog contains a read-only checkbox.
Title	Indicates the title that is displayed in the title bar of the dialog.
ValidateNames	Indicates whether the dialog box should only accept valid WIN32 file names.

The StreamReader Class

Visual Basic .NET provides a StreamReader class that enables you to read data from a file. You can get the filename or names from the OpenFileDialog control and then use those file names with the StreamReader class to process those files.

The StreamReader class is implemented from the System.IO namespace so you must add this namespace to your project before it can be used. The following code fragment shows how this is done. In this discussion you do not need to enter the code in your project, we'll do that in the next *Try It Out* exercise. The `Imports` statement should be the very first line of code in your form class:

```
Imports System.IO
```

To use the `StreamReader` class, you must declare an object and set a reference to the `StreamReader` class as shown in the following code fragment, which passes a string to the `StreamReader` class that contains the path and filename of the file that you want to read. Setting your object to the `StreamReader` class in this way causes the `Stream_Reader` to actually open the file for processing:

```
Dim objReader As StreamReader = New StreamReader("C:\Temp\MyFile.txt")
```

After you have an object set to the `StreamReader` class, you are able to read from the file as shown in the next code fragment. This example reads the entire contents of the file into the `String` variable `strData`. You can also read one or more characters at a time, or read an entire line from the file by using the `StreamReader` methods.

```
strData = objReader.ReadToEnd()
```

After you have read all of the data from the file, you need to close the file and remove your reference to the `StreamReader` class, as shown in the next code fragment:

```
objReader.Close()
objReader = Nothing
```

The following list shows some of the methods available in the `StreamReader` class:

❑   `Close` closes `StreamReader` and releases any resources associated with the reader.

❑   `DiscardBufferedData` allows `StreamReader` to discard its current data.

❑   `Peek` returns the next available character without actually reading it from the input stream.

❑   `Read overloaded` reads the next character or next set of characters from the input stream.

❑   `ReadBlock` reads a maximum of count characters from the current stream and writes the data to buffer, beginning at index.

❑   `ReadLine` reads a line of characters from the current stream and returns the data as a string.

❑   `ReadToEnd` reads the stream from the current position to the end of the stream.

Using the OpenFileDialog Control

Now that you have had a look at the OpenFileDialog control and the `StreamReader` class you put this knowledge to use by coding a program that uses them both.

This program uses the OpenFileDialog control to display the Open File dialog box. You use the dialog box to locate and select a text file and then open the file and read its contents into a text box on your form using the `StreamReader` class.

Try It Out   Working with OpenFileDialog

1.   Create a new Windows Application project called Dialogs.

2.   To give your form a new name, go to In the Solution Explorer, right-click Form1.vb and choose Rename from the context menu. Then enter a new name of frmDialogs.vb. Set the properties of the form as shown in the following list:

   ❏   Set Size to 456, 304

   ❏   Set StartPosition to CenterScreen

   ❏   Set Text to Dialogs

3.   Since you are going to read the contents of a file into a text box, you want to add a text box to the form. You also want to add a button to the form so that you can invoke the Open File dialog box at will. Add these two controls to the form and set their properties according to the following list. Review Chapter 6 for details on setting property values:

   ❏   Name the text box txtFile and set the following properties: Anchor = Top,Bottom,Left,Right; Location = 8, 8; MultiLine = True; Size = 352, 264; Text = *nothing*.

   ❏   Name the Button control btnOpen and set the following properties: Anchor = Top,Right; Location = 368, 8; Size = 75, 23; Text = Open.

4.   When you have finished placing the controls on your form, your form should look similar to Figure 7-8.

Figure 7-8

The reason you anchored your controls in this example is that, when you resize or maximize your form, the text box is resized appropriately to the size of the form and the button stays in the upper right corner. You can test this at this point by running your project and resizing the form.

5. In the Toolbox, scroll down until you see the OpenFileDialog control and then drag it onto your form and drop it. The control will actually be added to the bottom on the workspace in the IDE.

   At this point, you could click the control in the workspace and then set the various properties for this control in the Properties window. However, accept the default name and properties for this control and set the various properties in code later.

6. Switch to the code for this form and change the class name from Form1 to frmDialogs.

7. Because you are going to use the StreamReader class in your project, you need to import the System.IO namespace. Add the following code to your form class as the first line of code:

```
Imports System.IO
```

8. Next, declare a string variable that will contain a default path and filename. You set this variable later in your code to the actual path and file name from the Open File dialog box. You can create the following file or use an existing text file:

```
Public Class frmDialogs
    Inherits System.Windows.Forms.Form

' Declare variable...
Private strFileName As String = "C:\Temp\Text Document.txt"
```

9. Now you need to write some code in the Click event for the btnOpen button. So bring up the button's Click event procedure by double clicking on the button on the form and add the following code. If your computer does not contain a Temp folder, substitute a folder of your choice:

```
Private Sub btnOpen_Click(ByVal sender As Object, _
        ByVal e As System.EventArgs) Handles btnOpen.Click
    ' Set the Open dialog properties...
    With OpenFileDialog1
        .Filter = "Text files (*.txt)|*.txt|All files (*.*)|*.*"
        .FilterIndex = 1
        .InitialDirectory = "C:\Temp\"
        .Title = "Demo Open File Dialog"
    End With

    ' Show the Open dialog and if the user clicks the OK button,
    ' load the file...
    If OpenFileDialog1.ShowDialog() = DialogResult.OK Then
        strFileName = OpenFileDialog1.FileName
        Dim objReader As StreamReader = New StreamReader(strFileName)
        txtFile.Text = objReader.ReadToEnd()
        objReader.Close()
        objReader = Nothing
    End If
End Sub
```

10. It's now time to test your code, so click the Start button.

11. Once your form is displayed, click the Open button to have the Open File dialog box displayed, as shown in Figure 7-9. The files you see will depend on the files in your Temp folder.

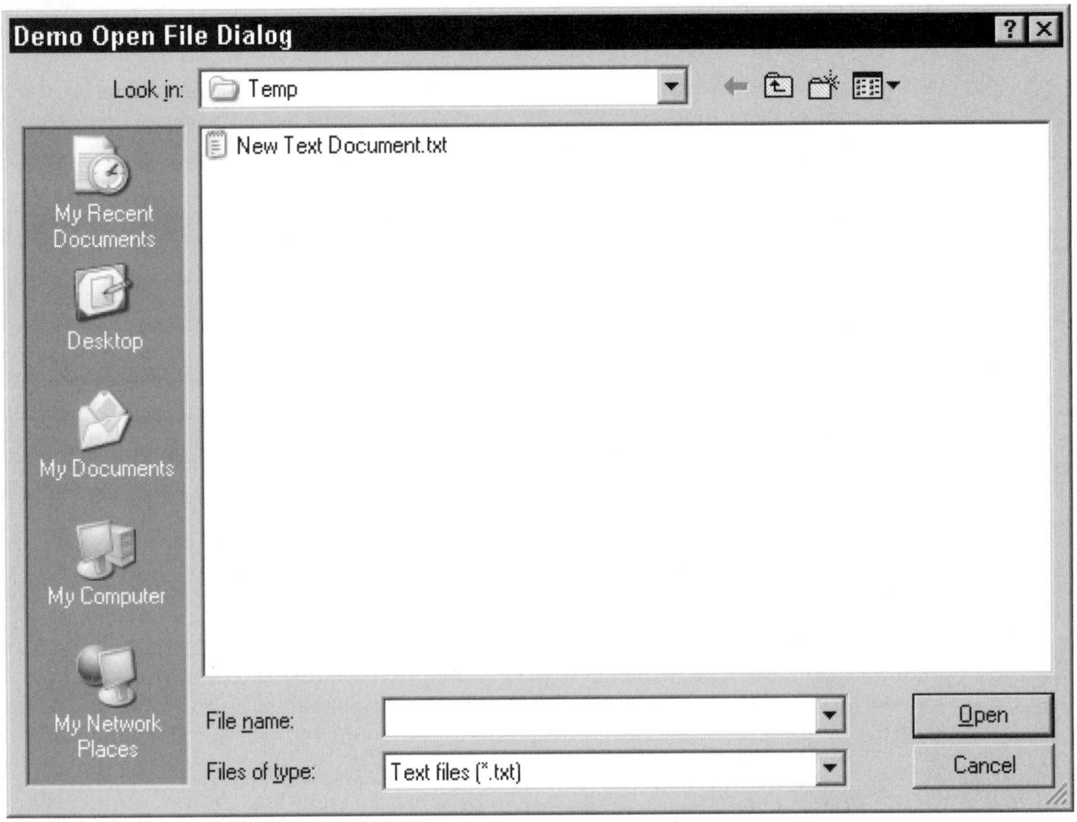

Figure 7-9

12. Notice the custom caption in the title bar of the dialog box; you specified this in your code. Also notice that the dialog box has opened in the Temp directory. If you click the Files of type combo box you will see two filters. Click the second filter to see all of the files in the Temp directory.

13. Now locate a text file and click that file. Then click on the Open button to have the file opened and the contents of that file placed in the text box on the form.

How It Works

Before displaying the Open File dialog box, you need to set some properties of OpenFileDialog1 so that the dialog box is customized for your application. You do this with a With statement. The With statement allows you to make repeated references to a single object without having to constantly specify the object name. You specify the object name once on the line with the With statement and then add all references to the properties of that object before the End With statement.

```
With OpenFileDialog1
```

The first property that you set was the Filter property. This property enables you to define the filters that are displayed in the Files of type combo box. When you define a file extension filter, you specify the filter description followed by a vertical bar (|) followed by the file extension. When you want the Filter property to contain multiple file extensions, as shown in the following code, you separate each file filter with a vertical bar as follows:

```
.Filter = "Text files (*.txt)|*.txt|All files (*.*)|*.*"
```

The next property that you set was the `FilterIndex` property. This property determines which filter is shown in the Files of type combo box. The default value for this property is 1, which is the first filter:

```
.FilterIndex = 1
```

Next, you set the `InitialDirectory` property. This is the directory that the Open File dialog box will show when it opens:

```
.InitialDirectory = "C:\Temp\"
```

Finally, you set the `Title` property. This is the caption that is displayed in the title bar of the dialog box:

```
.Title = "Demo Open File Dialog"
```

To show the Open File dialog box, remember that the `ShowDialog` method returns a `DialogResult` value because there are only two possible results and you can compare the results from the `ShowDialog` method to the `DialogResult.OK` constant. If the user clicks the Open button in the dialog box, the `ShowDialog` method returns a value of `OK` and if the user clicks the Cancel button, the `ShowDialog` method returns `Cancel`:

```
If OpenFileDialog1.ShowDialog() = DialogResult.OK Then
```

Next, you retrieve the path and filename that the user has chosen. This is contained in the `FileName` property of the OpenFileDialog control. The next line of code sets this path and filename in your variable `strFileName`:

```
strFileName = OpenFileDialog1.FileName
```

To read the file, you declare an object as a `StreamReader` and pass it the file that you want to open. This next line of code is doing just that, passing it the `strFileName` variable that now contains the file which you choose in the Open File dialog box:

```
Dim objReader As StreamReader = New StreamReader(strFileName)
```

This line of code reads the file to the end and places the results into the `Text` property of the txtFile text box in the form:

```
txtFile.Text = objReader.ReadToEnd()
```

Finally, you close the file and set the `StreamReader` object that you declared to `Nothing` to free up resources:

```
objReader.Close()
objReader = Nothing
```

There are many properties in this control that haven't been covered in this chapter and you should feel free to experiment on your own to see all of the possibilities that this dialog box has to offer.

The SaveDialog Control

Now that you can open a file with the OpenFileDialog control, take a look at the SaveFileDialog control so that you can save a file. Again, the SaveFileDialog can be used as a control or a class. Once you have mastered the SaveFileDialog as a control, you will not have any problems using SaveFileDialog as a class.

After you open a file, you may need to make some modifications to it and then save it. The SaveFileDialog control provides the same functionality as the OpenFileDialog control, except in reverse. It allows you to choose the location and filename to save a file.

The Properties of SaveFileDialog

Table 7-7 lists some of the properties that are available in the SaveFileDialog control.

The Methods of SaveFileDialog

The SaveFileDialog control exposes the same methods as exposed by the OpenFileDialog. If you want to review these methods, go back to *The Methods of OpenFileDialog* section. All the examples will use the ShowDialog method to show the Save File dialog.

The StreamWriter Class

Just as the OpenFileDialog control does not actually open and read a file, the SaveFileDialog control does not actually write to and close a file. For this you must rely on the StreamWriter class.

Visual Basic .NET provides a StreamWriter class that enables you to write data to a file. You get the file name from the SaveFileDialog control and give that file name to the StreamWriter class.

The StreamWriter class is also implemented from the System.IO namespace and so you must add this namespace to your project if you haven't already done so.

In order to use the StreamWriter class, you must declare an object and set a reference to the StreamWriter class as shown in the following code fragment. Notice that you pass a string to the StreamWriter class, which contains the path and filename of the file that you want to write to, and also a Boolean value indicating whether or not the StreamWriter should append the contents to the file. If this value is False, StreamWriter will completely replace the contents of the file. If this value is True, StreamWriter will append the contents to the end of the file. Setting your object to StreamWriter class in this way forces StreamWriter to actually open the file for processing:

```
Dim objWriter As StreamWriter = _
            New StreamWriter("C:\Temp\MyFile.txt", False)
```

After you have an object set to the StreamWriter class, you can write to the file as shown in the next code fragment. This example writes the entire contents of the string variable, strData, to the file

Table 7-7 Properties of SaveFileDialog

Property	Description
AddExtension	Indicates whether an extension is automatically added to a filename if the user omits the extension.
CheckFileExists	Indicates whether the dialog box displays a warning if the user specifies a file name that does not exist. This is useful when you want the user to save a file to an existing name.
CheckPathExists	Indicates whether the dialog box displays a warning if the user specifies a path that does not exist.
CreatePrompt	Indicates whether the dialog box prompts the user for permission to create a file if the user specifies a file that does not exist.
DefaultExt	Indicates the default file extension.
DereferenceLinks	Indicates whether the dialog box returns the location of the *file* referenced by the shortcut, or whether it returns the location of the shortcut itself.
FileName	Indicates the filename of the selected file in the dialog box. This is a read-only property.
FileNames	Indicates the filenames of all selected files in the dialog box. This is a read-only property that is returned as a string array.
Filter	Indicates the current file name filter string, which determines the choices that appear in the Files of type combo box in the dialog box.
FilterIndex	Indicates the index of the filter currently selected in the dialog box.
InitialDirectory	Indicates the initial directory displayed in the dialog box.
OverwritePrompt	Indicates whether the dialog box displays a warning if the user specifies a filename that already exists.
RestoreDirectory	Indicates whether the dialog box restores the current directory before closing.
ShowHelp	Indicates whether the Help button is displayed in the dialog box.
Title	Indicates the title that is displayed in the title bar of the dialog box.
ValidateNames	Indicates whether the dialog box should only accept valid WIN32 filenames.

referenced by the objWriter object:

```
objWriter.Write(strData)
```

After you have written the data to the file, you need to close the file and remove your reference to the StreamWriter class, as shown in the next code fragment:

```
objWriter.Close()
objWriter = Nothing
```

The following list shows some of the methods available in the `StreamWriter` class:

- ❑ `Close` closes `StreamWriter` and releases any resources associated with it.
- ❑ `Flush` clears all buffers for the current writer and causes any buffered data to be written to the underlying device.
- ❑ `Write Overloaded` writes the given data type to a text stream.
- ❑ `WriteLine Overloaded` writes data followed by a line terminator as specified by the overloaded parameters.

Using the SaveFileDialog Control

To see how to include the SaveFileDialog control in our project, you begin with the Dialogs project from the last *Try It Out* as a starting point and build upon it. In this exercise, you want to save the contents of the text box to a file.

You use the SaveFileDialog control to display a Save File dialog box that allows you to specify the location and name of the file. Then, using the `StreamWriter` object, you write the contents of the text box on your form to the specified file.

Try It Out   Working with SaveFileDialog

1. Open the Dialogs project from the last *Try It Out*.

2. On the form, add another button from the Toolbox and set its properties as follows:

- ❑ Set Name to btnSave
- ❑ Set Anchor to Top, Right
- ❑ Set Location to 368, 40
- ❑ Set Size to 75, 23
- ❑ Set Text to Save

3. In the Toolbox, scroll down until you see the SaveFileDialog control and then drag and drop it onto your form. The control will be added to the bottom on the workspace in the IDE.

4. Double-click the btnSave button to bring up its `Click` event and add the highlighted code:

```
Private Sub btnSave_Click(ByVal sender As Object, _
        ByVal e As System.EventArgs) Handles btnSave.Click

    ' Set the Save dialog properties...
    With SaveFileDialog1
        .DefaultExt = "txt"
        .FileName = strFileName
        .Filter = "Text files (*.txt)|*.txt|All files (*.*)|*.*"
        .FilterIndex = 1
        .InitialDirectory = "C:\Temp\"
        .OverwritePrompt = True
        .Title = "Demo Save File Dialog"
    End With
```

```
        ' Show the Save dialog and if the user clicks the Save button,
        ' load the file...
        If SaveFileDialog1.ShowDialog() = DialogResult.OK Then
            strFileName = SaveFileDialog1.FileName
            Dim objWriter As StreamWriter = _
                New StreamWriter(strFileName, False)
            objWriter.Write(txtFile.Text)
            objWriter.Close()
            objWriter = Nothing
        End If

End Sub
```

5. At this point, you are ready to test this code so run your project. Start with a simple test. Type some text into the text box on the form and then click on the Save button. The Save Dialog box will be displayed. Notice that the FileName combo box already has a file name in it. This is the file name that was set in the `strFileName` variable when we declared it in the previous *Try It Out*.

6. Enter another filename, but do not put a file extension on it. Then click the Save button and the file will be saved. To verify this, click the Open button on the form to invoke the Open File dialog box. You will see your new file.

7. To test the `OverwritePrompt` property of the SaveFileDialog control, enter some more text in the text box on the form and then click the Save button. In the Save File dialog box, choose an existing filename and then click the Save button. You will be prompted to confirm replacement of the existing file as shown in Figure 7-10. If you choose Yes, the file will be overwritten with the contents of the text box by the `StreamWriter` object. If you choose No, you will be returned to the Save File dialog box to enter another name.

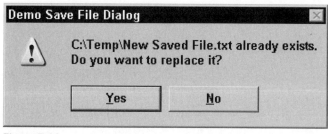

Figure 7-10

When the Open File or Save File dialog boxes are displayed, the context menu is fully functional and you can cut, copy, and paste files, as well as rename and delete them. There are other options in the context menu that vary depending on what software you have installed. For example, if you have WinZip installed, you will see the WinZip options on the context menu.

How It Works

Before displaying the Save File dialog box, you need to set some properties to customize the dialog to your application. The first property you set is the `DefaultExt` property. This property automatically sets the file extension if one has not been specified. For example, if you specify a filename of `NewFile` with no extension, the dialog box will automatically add .txt to the filename when it returns, so that you end up with a filename of NewFile.txt.

```
.DefaultExt = "txt"
```

The FileName property is set to the same path and filename as was returned from the Open File dialog. This allows you to open a file, edit it, and then display the same filename when you show the Save File dialog box. Of course, you can override this filename in the application's Save File dialog box.

```
.FileName = strFileName
```

The next three properties are the same as in the OpenFileDialog control and set the file extension filters to be displayed in the Save as type combo box and set the initial filter. You also set the initial directory where the dialog box shows the files:

```
.Filter = "Text files (*.txt)|*.txt|All files (*.*)|*.*"
.FilterIndex = 1
.InitialDirectory = "C:\Temp\"
```

The OverwritePrompt property accepts a Boolean value of True or False. When set to True, this property prompts you with a MessageBox dialog box if you choose an existing file name. If you select Yes, the existing file is overwritten and if you select No, you are returned to the Save File dialog box to choose another filename. When the OverwritePrompt property is set to False the file overwrites the existing files without asking for the user's permission.

```
.OverwritePrompt = True
```

The Title property sets the caption in the title bar of the Save File dialog box:

```
.Title = "Demo Save File Dialog"
```

After you have the properties set, you want to show the dialog box. The ShowDialog method SaveFileDialog control also returns a DialogResult, so you can use the SaveFileDialog control in an If statement and test the return value.

If the user clicks the Save button in the Save File dialog box, the dialog box returns a DialogResult of OK. If the user clicks the Cancel button in the dialog, the dialog box returns a DialogResult of Cancel. The following code tests for DialogResult.OK:

```
If SaveFileDialog1.ShowDialog() = DialogResult.OK Then
    strFileName = SaveFileDialog1.FileName
    Dim objWriter As StreamWriter = _
        New StreamWriter(strFileName, False)
    objWriter.Write(txtFile.Text)
    objWriter.Close()
    objWriter = Nothing
End If
```

The first thing that you want to do here is to save the path and filename chosen by the user in your strFileName variable.

Then you declare an object for the StreamWriter class and pass it to our string variable containing the path and file name. You also specify a value of False for the appended parameter so that StreamWriter completely replaces the contents of the file if it already exists, instead of appending the data to the end of the file.

Using the `Write` method of your `StreamWriter` object, you write the contents of the text box on your form to the file. Notice that you have passed the text box name and `Text` property as a parameter to the `Write` method.

Finally, you close the `StreamWriter` object and set it to `Nothing` to free up resources.

The FontDialog Control

Sometimes you may need to write an application that allows the user to choose the font in which they want their data to be displayed in. Or perhaps you may want to see all available fonts installed on a particular system. This is where the FontDialog control comes in; it displays a list of all available fonts installed on your system in a standard dialog that your users have become accustomed to.

Like the OpenFileDialog and SaveFileDialog controls, the `FontDialog` class can be used as a control by dragging it onto a form, or as a class by declaring it in code.

The FontDialog control is really easy to use; you just set some properties, show the dialog box, and then query the properties that you need.

The Properties of FontDialog

Table 7-8 lists some of its available properties.

Table 7-8 Properties of the FontDialog control

Property	Description
AllowScriptChange	Indicates whether the user can change the character set specified in the Script drop-down box to display a character set other than the one currently displayed.
Color	Indicates the selected font color.
Font	Indicates the selected font.
FontMustExist	Indicates whether the dialog box specifies an error condition if the user attempts to select a font or style that does not exist.
MaxSize	Indicates the maximum size (in points) a user can select.
MinSize	Indicates the minimum size (in points) a user can select.
ShowApply	Indicates whether the dialog box contains an Apply button.
ShowColor	Indicates whether the dialog box displays the color choice.
ShowEffects	Indicates whether the dialog box contains controls that allow the user to specify strikethrough, underline, and text color options.
ShowHelp	Indicates whether the dialog box displays a Help button.

The Methods of FontDialog

You will only be using one method (ShowDialog) of FontDialog in the forthcoming *Try It Out*. Other methods available include Reset, which allows you to reset all the properties to their default values.

Using the FontDialog Control

You can display the FontDialog control without setting any properties:

```
FontDialog1.ShowDialog()
```

The dialog box looks like Figure 7-11.

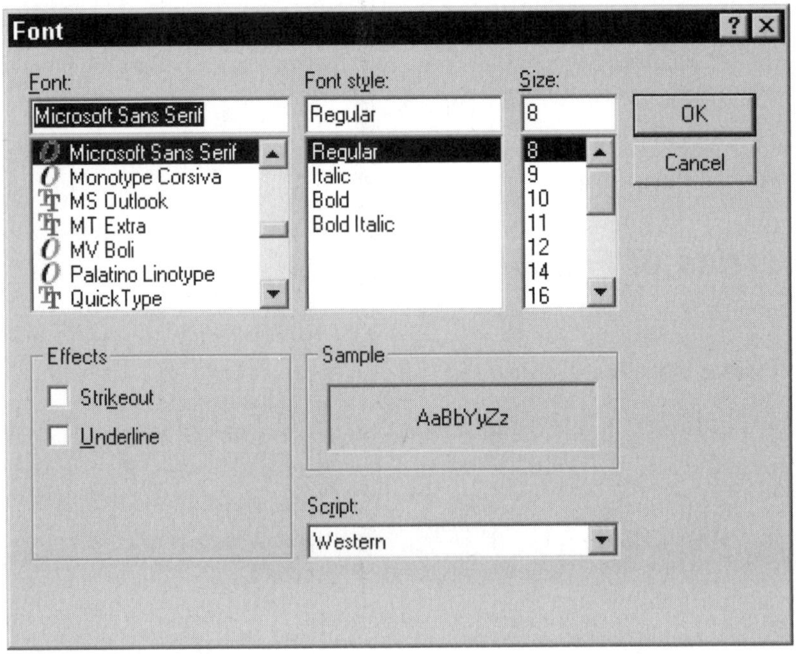

Figure 7-11

Notice that the Font dialog box contains an Effects section that enables you to check the options for Strikeout and Underline. However, color selection of the font is not provided by default. If you want this you must set the ShowColor property before calling the dialog box:

```
FontDialog1.ShowColor = True
FontDialog1.ShowDialog()
```

The ShowDialog method of this dialog box, like all of the ones that you have examined thus far, returns a DialogResult. This will be either DialogResult.OK or DialogResult.Cancel.

Once the dialog box returns, you can query for the Font and Color properties to see what font and color the user has chosen. You can then apply these properties to a control on your form or store them to a variable for later use.

Now that you know what the Font dialog looks like and how to call it, you use it in a *Try It Out*. You have to use the program from the last two *Try It Outs*, open a file, and have the contents of the file read into the text box on the form. You use the FontDialog control to display the Font dialog box, which allows you to select a font. Then you change the font in the text box to the font that you have chosen.

Try It Out   Working with FontDialog

1. Open the Dialogs project again.

2. On the form add another button from the Toolbox and set its properties according to the values shown in this list:

    ❑   Set Name to btnFont

    ❑   Set Anchor to Top, Right

    ❑   Set Location to 368, 72

    ❑   Set Size to 75, 23

    ❑   Set Text to Font

3. You also need to add the FontDialog control to your project, so locate this control in the Toolbox and drag and drop it onto the form in the workspace below the form. Accept all default properties for this control.

4. You want to add code to the Click event of the btnFont button, so double-click it and add the following code:

```
Public Sub btnFont_Click(ByVal sender As Object, _
          ByVal e As System.EventArgs) Handles btnFont.Click

    ' Set the FontDialog control properties...
    FontDialog1.ShowColor = True

    ' Show the Font dialog...
    If FontDialog1.ShowDialog() = DialogResult.OK Then
        ' If the OK button was clicked set the font
        ' in the text box on the form...
        txtFile.Font = FontDialog1.Font
        ' Set the color of the font in the text box on the form...
        txtFile.ForeColor = FontDialog1.Color
    End If

End Sub
```

5. Test your code. Click on the Start button. Once your form has been displayed, click on the Font button to display the Font dialog box as shown in Figure 7-12. Choose a new font and color and then click OK.

6. Now add some text in the text box on your form. The text will appear with the new font and color that you have chosen.

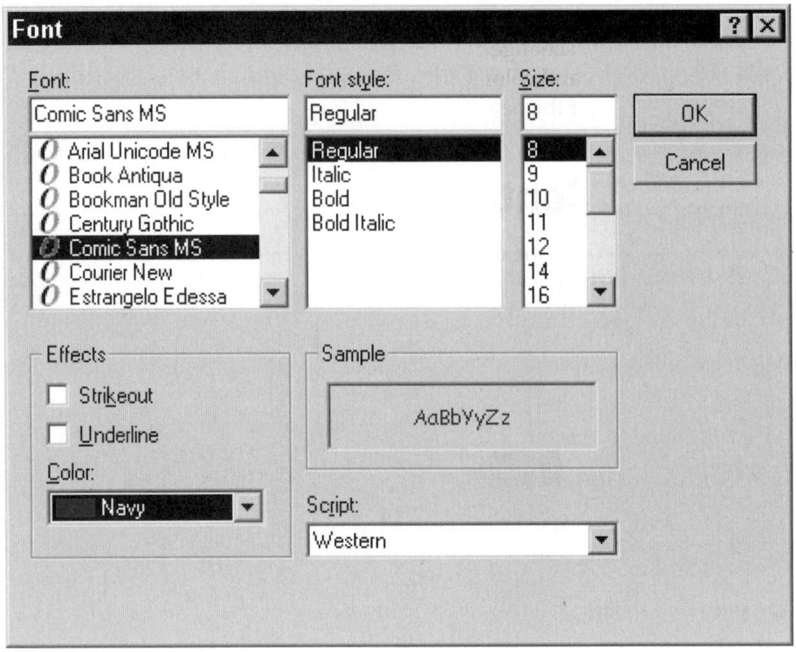

Figure 7-12

7. This same font and color will also be applied to the text that is inserted from a file. To demonstrate this, click the Open button on the form and open a text file. The text from the file is displayed in the same font and color that you chose in the Font dialog.

How It Works

You know that the Font dialog box does not show a Color box by default, so you begin by setting the ShowColor property of the FontDialog control to True so that the Color box is displayed:

```
FontDialog1.ShowColor = True
```

Next, you actually show the Font dialog box. Remember the DialogResult, so that you can compare the return value from the FontDialog control to DialogResult.OK. If the button that the user clicked was OK, you execute the code within the If statement:

```
If FontDialog1.ShowDialog() = DialogResult.OK Then
    ' If the OK button was clicked set the font
    ' in the text box on the form...
    txtFile.Font = FontDialog1.Font
    ' Set the color of the font in the text box on the form...
    txtFile.ForeColor = FontDialog1.Color
End If
```

You set the Font property of the text box (txtFile) equal to the Font property of the FontDialog control. This is the font that the user has chosen. Then you set the ForeColor property of the text box equal to the `Color` property of the FontDialog control, as this will be the color that the user has chosen. After these properties have been changed for the text box, the existing text in the text box is automatically updated to reflect the new font and color. If the text box does not contain any text, any new text that is typed into the text box will be of the new font and color.

The ColorDialog Control

Sometimes you may need to allow the user to customize the colors on their form. This may be the color of the form itself, a control, or of text in a text box. Visual Basic .NET provides the ColorDialog control for all such requirements. Once again, the ColorDialog control can also be used as a class—declared in code without dragging a control onto the Form Designer.

The ColorDialog control, shown in Figure 7-13, allows the user to choose from 48 basic colors.

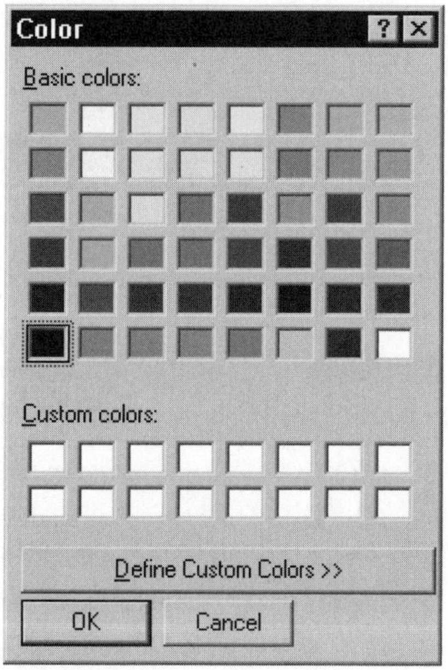

Figure 7-13

Notice that the users can also define their own custom colors, adding more flexibility to your applications. When the users click on the Define Custom Colors button in the Color dialog box, they can adjust the color to suit their needs (see Figure 7-14).

Having this opportunity for customization and flexibility in your applications gives them a more professional appearance, plus your users are happy because they are allowed to adjust their look.

The Properties of ColorDialog

Before you dive into some code, look at some of the available properties for ColorDialog control shown in Table 7-9.

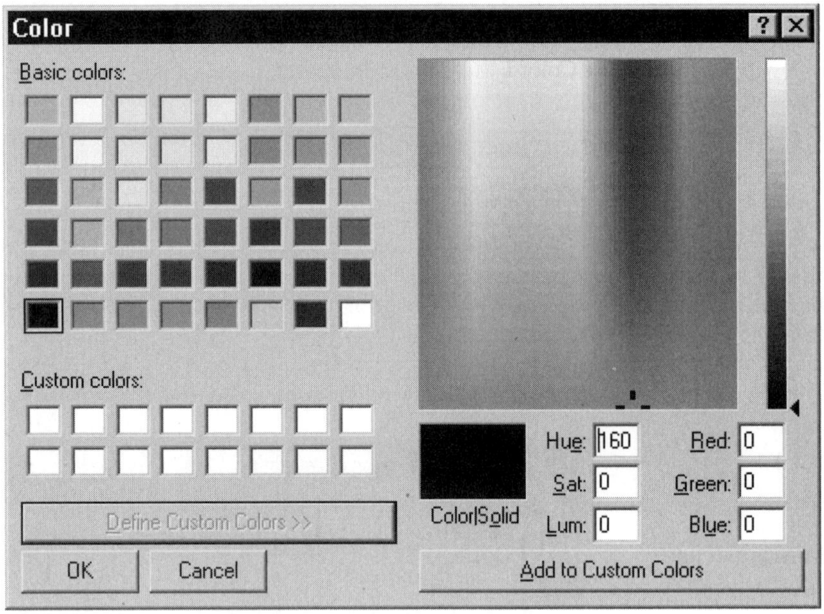

Figure 7-14

Table 7-9 Properties of the ColorDialog control

Property	Description
AllowFullOpen	Indicates whether the user can use the dialog box to define custom colors.
AnyColor	Indicates whether the dialog displays all available colors in the set of basic colors.
Color	Indicates the color selected by the user.
CustomColors	Indicates the set of custom colors shown in the dialog box.
FullOpen	Indicates whether the controls used to create custom colors are visible when the dialog box is opened.
ShowHelp	Indicates whether a Help button appears in the dialog box.
SolidColorOnly	Indicates whether the dialog box will restrict users to selecting solid colors only.

There aren't many properties that you need to worry about for this dialog, which makes it even simpler to use than the other dialogs that you have examined so far.

As with other dialog controls, ColorDialog has a Reset method and a ShowDialog method. You have already seen these methods in the previous examples and since they are the same they do not need to be discussed again.

Using the ColorDialog Control

All you need to do to display the Color Dialog box is to execute its `ShowDialog` method:

```
ColorDialog1.ShowDialog()
```

The ColorDialog control will return a `DialogResult` of `OK` or `Cancel`. Hence, you can use the previous statement in an `If` statement and test for a `DialogResult` of `OK`, as you have done in the previous examples that you have coded.

To retrieve the color that the user has chosen, you simply set the `Color` property to a variable or any property of a control that supports colors, such as the `ForeColor` property of a text box:

```
txtFile.ForeColor = ColorDialog1.Color
```

In the next *Try It Out*, you continue using the same project and make the ColorDialog control display the Color dialog box. Then you select a color. If the dialog box returns a `DialogResult` of `OK`, you change the color of the text on the buttons on the form.

Try It Out   Working with the ColorDialog Control

1. Open the Dialogs project.

2. On the form, add another button from the Toolbox and set its properties according to the values shown:

- ❑ Set Name to btnColor
- ❑ Set Location to 368, 104
- ❑ Set Size to 75, 23
- ❑ Set Text to Color

3. Next, add a ColorDialog control to your project from the Toolbox. It will be added to the workspace below the form and you will accept all default properties for this control.

4. Double-click `btnColor` to bring up its `Click` event procedure and add the following code:

```
Public Sub btnColor_Click(ByVal sender As Object, _
         ByVal e As System.EventArgs) Handles btnColor.Click

    ' Show the Color dialog...
    If ColorDialog1.ShowDialog() = DialogResult.OK Then
        ' Set the ForeColor property of all the controls on the form...
        btnOpen.ForeColor = ColorDialog1.Color
        btnSave.ForeColor = ColorDialog1.Color
        btnFont.ForeColor = ColorDialog1.Color
        btnColor.ForeColor = ColorDialog1.Color
    End If

End Sub
```

5. That's all the code you need to add. To test your changes to this project, click the Start button.

6. Once the form is displayed, click the Color button to display the ColorDialog. Choose any color that you want, or create a custom color by clicking the Define Custom Colors button. Once you have chosen a color, click the OK button in the Color dialog box.

7. The color of the text in each of the buttons has been changed to match the color that you chose.

8. Like the Font dialog box, you do not have to set the Color property of the ColorDialog control before displaying the Color dialog box again. It automatically remembers the color chosen and this will be the color that is selected when the dialog box is displayed again. To test this, click the Color button again and the color that you chose will be selected.

How It Works

This time you did not want to set any properties of the ColorDialog control, so you jumped right in and displayed it in an If statement to check the DialogResult returned by the ShowDialog method of this dialog box:

```
If ColorDialog1.ShowDialog() = DialogResult.OK Then
```

Within the If statement, you added the code necessary to change the text color of all of the buttons on the form. You did this by setting the ForeColor property of each button:

```
btnOpen.ForeColor = ColorDialog1.Color
btnSave.ForeColor = ColorDialog1.Color
btnFont.ForeColor = ColorDialog1.Color
btnColor.ForeColor = ColorDialog1.Color
```

The PrintDialog Control

Any application worth its salt will incorporate some kind of printing capabilities, whether it is basic printing or more sophisticated printing, such as allowing a user to print only selected text or a range of pages. In this last section of the chapter you explore basic printing. You take a look at several classes that help you to print text from a file.

Visual Basic .NET provides the PrintDialog control. It does not actually do any printing but enables you to select the printer that you want to use and set the printer properties such as page orientation and print quality. It also enables you to specify the print range. You will not be using this feature in this example, but it is worth noting that this functionality is available in the PrintDialog control as shown in Figure 7-15.

Like the previous dialog boxes that you have examined, the PrintDialog provides OK and Cancel buttons—thus its ShowDialog method returns a DialogResult of OK or Cancel. You can then use this in an If statement and test for the DialogResult.

The Properties of PrintDialog

Take a quick look at some of the properties provided in PrintDialog shown in Table 7-10.

Just like the other dialog boxes, PrintDialog exposes a ShowDialog method and a Reset method.

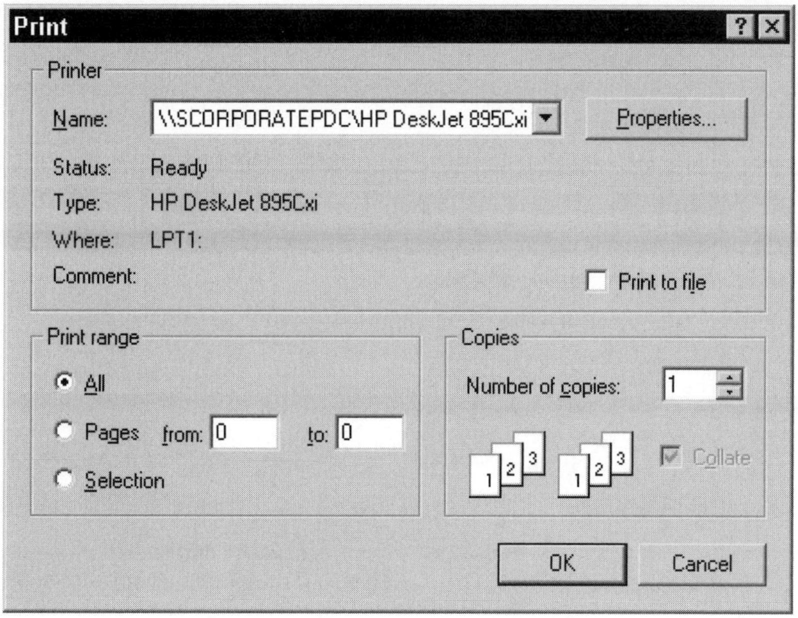

Figure 7-15

Table 7-10 Properties of the PrintDialog control

Property	Description
AllowPrintToFile	Indicates whether the Print to file check box is enabled.
AllowSelection	Indicates whether the Selection radio button is enabled.
AllowSomePages	Indicates whether the Pages radio button is enabled.
Document	Indicates the Print Document used to obtain the printer settings.
PrinterSettings	Indicates the printer settings that the dialog box will be modifying.
PrintToFile	Indicates whether the Print to file check box is checked.
ShowHelp	Indicates whether the Help button is displayed.
ShowNetwork	Indicates whether the Network button is displayed.

Using the PrintDialog Control

The only method that you will be using is the ShowDialog method, which will display the Print dialog box. As we mentioned earlier, the PrintDialog control merely displays the Print dialog box; it does not actually do any printing. The following code fragment shows how you display the Print dialog box:

```
PrintDialog1.ShowDialog()
```

The PrintDocument Class

To perform the task of actually printing, you rely on the PrintDocument class. This class requires the System.Drawing.Printing namespace, so you must include this namespace before attempting to define an object that uses the PrintDocument class.

The PrintDocument class sends output to the printer. You may be wondering from where PrintDocument gets its input. The answer to that question is the StreamReader class. (Remember this class from *The Open Dialog* section; you used this class to read text from a file.)

The Properties of the PrintDocument Class

Before you continue, take a look at some of the important properties of the PrintDocument class, listed in Table 7-11.

Table 7-11 Properties of the PrintDocument class

Property	Description
DefaultPageSettings	Indicates the default page settings for the document.
DocumentName	Indicates the document name that is displayed while printing the document. This is also the name that appears in the Print Status dialog box and printer queue.
PrintController	Indicates the print controller that guides the printing process.
PrinterSettings	Indicates the printer that prints the document.

The Print Method of the PrintDocument Class

The Print method of the PrintDocument class prints the document to the printer specified in the PrinterSettings property.

When you call the Print method of the PrintDocument class, the PrintPage event is raised for each page as it prints. Therefore, you need to create a procedure for that event and add an event handler for it. The procedure that you create for the PrintPage event does the actual reading of your text file using the StreamReader object that you define.

Now that you know a little bit about how printing works, look at how all this fits together in a *Try It Out*.

Again, you expand on the previous *Try It Outs* and implement printing into the same project. When you created this project in *The Open Dialog* section, you created a class-level variable that contained the path and name of the file that was opened. You use this variable in this *Try It Out*, so you will always print the last file opened or saved, as you also set this variable when you save a file.

Try It Out   Working with the PrintDialog Control

1. Open the Dialogs project.
2. On the form, add another button from the Toolbox and set its properties according to the values shown:
   - ❑ Set Name to btnPrint

❑ Set Anchor to Top, Right

❑ Set Location to 368, 136

❑ Set Size to 75, 23

❑ Set Text to Print

3. Now add a PrintDialog control to the project, dragging and dropping it from the Toolbox onto the form. It will be added to the workspace below the form and we will accept all default properties for this control.

4. The first thing that you want to add in your code is the required namespace for the `PrintDocument` class. Add this namespace to your code:

```
Imports System.IO
Imports System.Drawing.Printing
```

5. Next, you add a class-level object for the `StreamReader` class and an object for the font used for printing:

```
' Declare variable...
Private strFileName As String = "C:\Temp\Text Document.txt"
Private objStreamToPrint As StreamReader
Private objPrintFont As Font
```

6. Now add the following code to the `btnPrint_Click` event procedure:

```
Public Sub btnPrint_Click(ByVal sender As Object, _
        ByVal e As System.EventArgs) Handles btnPrint.Click

    ' Declare an object for the PrintDocument class...
    Dim objPrintDocument As PrintDocument = New PrintDocument()

    ' Set the DocumentName property...
    objPrintDocument.DocumentName = "Text File Print Demo"

    ' Set the PrintDialog properties...
    PrintDialog1.AllowPrintToFile = False
    PrintDialog1.AllowSelection = False
    PrintDialog1.AllowSomePages = False

    ' Set the Document property to the objPrintDocument object...
    PrintDialog1.Document = objPrintDocument

    ' Show the Print dialog...
    If PrintDialog1.ShowDialog() = DialogResult.OK Then
        ' If the user clicked on the OK button then set the
        ' StreamReader object to the file name in the strFileName
        ' variable...
        objStreamToPrint = New StreamReader(strFileName)

        ' Set the print font...
        objPrintFont = New Font("Arial", 10)

        ' Add an event handler for the PrintPage event of the
        'objPrintDocument object...
```

```
        AddHandler objPrintDocument.PrintPage, _
            AddressOf objPrintDocument_PrintPage

    ' Set the PrinterSettings property of the objPrintDocument
    ' object to the PrinterSettings property returned from the
    ' PrintDialog control...
    objPrintDocument.PrinterSettings = PrintDialog1.PrinterSettings

    ' Print the text file...
    objPrintDocument.Print()

    ' Clean up...
    objStreamToPrint.Close()
    objStreamToPrint = Nothing
  End If

End Sub
```

7. Remember that, when you call the `Print` method of the `PrintDocument` class the `PrintPage` event is raised. You need to create a procedure for this event, which will be responsible for actually reading from the file and sending data to the printer. Since the `objPrintDocument` object raises this event, you name this procedure using this object name, an underscore, and the event name. Enter the following code:

```
Private Sub objPrintDocument_PrintPage(ByVal sender As Object, _
            ByVal e As System.Drawing.Printing.PrintPageEventArgs)
    ' Declare variables...
    Dim sngLinesPerpage As Single = 0
    Dim sngVerticalPosition As Single = 0
    Dim intLineCount As Integer = 0
    Dim sngLeftMargin As Single = e.MarginBounds.Left
    Dim sngTopMargin As Single = e.MarginBounds.Top
    Dim strLine As String

    ' Work out the number of lines per page.
    ' Use the MarginBounds on the event to do this...
    sngLinesPerpage = _
       e.MarginBounds.Height / objPrintFont.GetHeight(e.Graphics)

    ' Now iterate through the file printing out each line.
    ' This assumes that a single line is not wider than the page
    ' width. Check intLineCount first so that we don't read a line
    ' that we won't print...
    strLine = objStreamToPrint.ReadLine()
    While (intLineCount < sngLinesPerpage And Not (strLine Is Nothing))
        ' Calculate the vertical position on the page...
        sngVerticalPosition = sngTopMargin + _
            (intLineCount * objPrintFont.GetHeight(e.Graphics))

        ' Pass a StringFormat to DrawString for the
        ' Print Preview control...
        e.Graphics.DrawString(strLine, objPrintFont, Brushes.Black, _
            sngLeftMargin, sngVerticalPosition, New StringFormat())
```

```
         ' Increment the line count...
         intLineCount = intLineCount + 1
         ' If the line count is less than the lines per page then
         ' read another line of text...
         If (intLineCount < sngLinesPerpage) Then
            strLine = objStreamToPrint.ReadLine()
         End If

    End While

    ' If we have more lines then print another page...
    If (strLine <> Nothing) Then
        e.HasMorePages = True
    Else
        e.HasMorePages = False
    End If

End Sub
```

8. You are now ready to test your code, so run the project.

9. Click on the Open button to open a file. This will cause the `strFileName` variable to be set with the path and filename that you just opened. Click the Print button to display the Print dialog box shown in Figure 7-16.

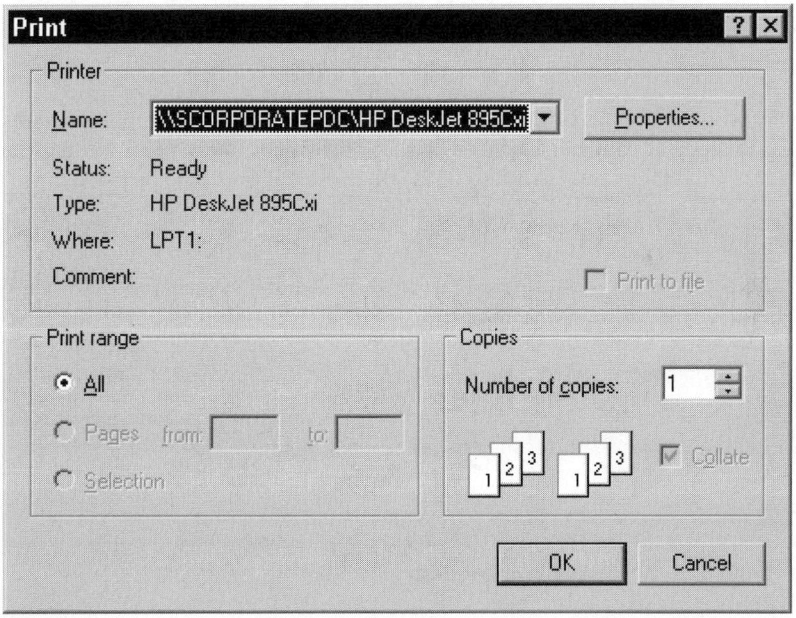

Figure 7-16

Notice that the Print to file check box as well as the Pages and Selection radio buttons are disabled. This is because you set the `AllowPrintToFile`, `AllSelection`, and `AllowSomePages` properties in the PrintDialog control to `False`.

If you have more than one printer installed, you can choose the name of the printer in the Name drop-down box. You can also click the Properties button to set the way your document will be printed. For example, you can choose between landscape and portrait printing.

10. Click the OK button in the Print dialog box to have the text file printed.

11. Now open the print queue for the printer that you specified by clicking Start on the task bar at the bottom of your screen and then clicking on Settings. Next, select Printers from the menu. This will open the Printers window shown in Figure 7-17.

Figure 7-17

12. Choose your printer and either double-click the icon or right-click the icon and select Open from the context menu. This causes the print queue for the printer to open. In the print queue, click the File menu and then Pause Printing. This will cause the printer to be paused.

You will need the appropriate permissions to pause the printer, such as being in the Administrators group.

13. Next, click on the Print button again to print the file that you opened. Now click on the print queue to see the document waiting to be printed. Notice the Document Name in the queue. This is the document name that we specified in the DocumentName property for the objPrintDocument object.

14. You have now finished testing. Click on the File menu in the print queue and then on the Pause Printing menu item to restart the printer and release the document for printing.

How It Works

You begin the btnPrint button's Click event procedure by declaring an object as a PrintDocument. You use this object to perform the actual printing:

```
Dim objPrintDocument As PrintDocument = New PrintDocument()
```

Next, you set the DocumentName property for the PrintDocument object. This will be the name that you see when the document is printing and also the name that is shown in the printer queue:

```
objPrintDocument.DocumentName = "Text File Print Demo"
```

Then you set some properties of the PrintDialog control. This will control the options on the Print dialog box. Since you are only doing basic printing in this example, you want the Print to file check box to be disabled along with the Pages and Selection radio buttons. The next three lines of code do this by setting these properties to `False`:

```
PrintDialog1.AllowPrintToFile = False
PrintDialog1.AllowSelection = False
PrintDialog1.AllowSomePages = False
```

With the PrintDialog control's properties set, you set its `Document` property equal to the `PrintDocument` object:

```
PrintDialog1.Document = objPrintDocument
```

Then you show the Print dialog box. So you execute the `ShowDialog` method of the PrintDialog control in an `If` statement as shown in the following code. Notice that you are also checking the `DialogResult` returned from the PrintDialog control:

```
If PrintDialog1.ShowDialog() = DialogResult.OK Then
```

If the user clicks on the OK button in the Print dialog box, you actually want to execute the code for printing. The first thing that you do is to set the `objStreamToPrint` object to a new `StreamReader` class and pass it the `strFileName` variable:

```
objStreamToPrint = New StreamReader(strFileName)
```

Remember that this variable is set to the path and filename every time you open or save a file. This will be the file that you print.

Next, you set the `objPrintFont` object to a valid font and font size. You have chosen an Arial font here and a font size of 10 points, but you could have put in any font and size that you wanted:

```
objPrintFont = New Font("Arial", 10)
```

You now add an event handler for the `PrintPage` event. Since the `objPrintDocument` object raises this event, you specify this object and the event. Then you specify the address of the `objPrintDocument_PrintPage` procedure:

```
AddHandler objPrintDocument.PrintPage,_
        AddressOf objPrintDocument_PrintPage
```

Next, you set the `PrinterSettings` property of the `objPrintDocument` object equal to the `PrinterSettings` property of the PrintDialog control. This specifies the printer used, page orientation, and print quality chosen by the user:

```
objPrintDocument.PrinterSettings = PrintDialog1.PrinterSettings
```

Then you call the `Print` method of the `objPrintDocument` object. Calling this method will raise the `PrintPage` event and the code inside the `objPrintDocument_PrintPage` procedure will be executed:

```
objPrintDocument.Print()
```

In the `objPrintDocument_PrintPage` procedure, you need to add two parameters: the first of which is the `sender`. Like every other procedure defined in this project, this argument is an `object` that lets you know what object called this procedure. The second parameter that you need to add is the `PrintPageEventArgs` object. The `PrintPage` event receives this argument and it contains data related to the `PrintPage` event such as margin boundaries and page boundaries.

```
Private Sub objPrintDocument_PrintPage(ByVal sender As Object, _
            ByVal e As System.Drawing.Printing.PrintPageEventArgs)
```

The first thing that you want to do in this procedure is to declare some variables and set their default values. Notice that you are setting the values for the `sngLeftMargin` and `sngTopMargin` variables using the `PrintPageEventArgs` that were passed to this procedure:

```
Dim sngLinesPerpage As Single = 0
Dim sngVerticalPosition As Single = 0
Dim intLineCount As Integer = 0
Dim sngLeftMargin As Single = e.MarginBounds.Left
Dim sngTopMargin As Single = e.MarginBounds.Top
Dim strLine As String
```

Next, you want to determine the number of lines that will fit on one page. You do this using the `MarginBounds.Height` property of `PrintPageEventArgs`. This property was set when you set the `PrinterSettings` property of the `objPrintDocument` to the `PrinterSettings` property of the PrintDialog control. You divide the `MarginBounds.Height` by the height of the font that was set in the `objPrintFont`:

```
sngLinesPerpage = _
        e.MarginBounds.Height / objPrintFont.GetHeight(e.Graphics)
```

Next, you read the first line from the text file and place the contents of that line in your `strLine` variable. Then you enter a loop to read and process all lines from the text file. You only want to process this loop while the `intLineCount` variable is less than the `sngLinesPerPage` variable and the `strLine` variable contains data to be printed:

```
strLine = objStreamToPrint.ReadLine()
While (intLineCount < sngLinesPerpage And Not (strLine Is Nothing))
```

Inside your `While` loop, you set the vertical position of the text to be printed. You calculate this position using the `sngTopMargin` variable and the `intLineCount` multiplied by the height of the printer font:

```
sngVerticalPosition = sngTopMargin + _
        (intLineCount * objPrintFont.GetHeight(e.Graphics))
```

Using the `DrawString` method of the `Graphics` class, you actually send a line of text to the printer. Here you pass the `strLine` variable (which contains a line of text to be printed), the font to be used when printing, the brush color to be used, the left margin, vertical position, and the format to be used:

```
e.Graphics.DrawString(strLine, objPrintFont, Brushes.Black, _
        sngLeftMargin, sngVerticalPosition, New StringFormat())
```

Next, you increment the line count on this page in the `intLineCount` variable:

```
intLineCount = intLineCount + 1
```

If the actual line count is less than the number of lines per page, you want to read another line from the text file to print. Then you go back to the beginning of your loop and process the next line of text:

```
If (intLineCount < sngLinesPerpage) Then
    strLine = objStreamToPrint.ReadLine()
End If

End While
```

Having completed your `While` loop, you then enter an `If` statement to test the value of `strLine`:

```
If (strLine <> Nothing) Then
    e.HasMorePages = True
Else
    e.HasMorePages = False
End If
```

If the `strLine` variable is not `Nothing`, then you have more printing to do so you set `HasMorePages` property to `True`, causing the `PrintPage` event to be fired again, and you will continue to read the text file and print another page.

If `strLine` is `Nothing`, then you have no more printing to do, so you set the `HasMorePages` property to `False`, causing the `Print` method of the `objPrintDocument` object to end processing and move to the next line of code within the `btnPrint_Click` event procedure.

Since the printing is complete, you clean up by closing the text file that was used for printing and freeing up the resources used by the `objStreamToPrint` object:

```
objStreamToPrint.Close()
objStreamToPrint = Nothing
```

Summary

This chapter has taken a look at some of the dialog boxes that are provided in Visual Basic .NET. You examined the MessageBox dialog box, and the OpenFileDialog, SaveFileDialog, FontDialog, ColorDialog, and PrintDialog controls. Each of these dialog boxes will help you provide a common interface in your applications for their respective functions. They also hide a lot of the complexities required to perform their tasks, allowing you to concentrate on the logic needed to make your application functional and feature-rich.

Although you used the controls from the Toolbox for all of these dialog boxes, except the MessageBox dialog box, remember that these controls can also be treated as normal classes. This means that the classes that these dialog boxes use expose the same properties and methods, whether you are using a control or using the class. You can define your own objects and set them to these classes, and then use the objects to perform the tasks that you performed using the controls. This provides better control over the scope of the objects. For example, you could define an object, set it to the OpenDialog class, use it, and then destroy it all in the same procedure. This method uses resources only in the procedure that defines and uses the OpenDialog class, and reduces the size of your executable.

To summarize, you should now know how to:

- ❑ Use the MessageBox dialog box to display messages
- ❑ Display icons and buttons in the MessageBox dialog box
- ❑ Use the OpenFileDialog control and StreamReader class to open files
- ❑ Use the SaveFileDialog control and StreamWriter class to save files
- ❑ Use the FontDialog control to set the font and color of text in a text box
- ❑ Use the ColorDialog control to set the color of the text on the buttons in your form
- ❑ Use the PrintDialog control and PrintDocument class to print from a text file

Exercises

1. Write the code to display a message box with a message and caption of your choice, using OK and Cancel buttons, but no icon. The Cancel button should be the default button.

2. How can you display the Open dialog box with a default file name already displayed?

3. How can you change the color of the text displayed in a text box using the Color dialog box?

4. When you save a file using the SaveFileDialog control and the file already exists, you are prompted to replace it. If you choose Yes, does the file actually get overwritten?

5. The Font dialog has been displayed and you have chosen a font, clicked the OK button and applied the font. When you display the Font dialog again, do you need to set the Font property to have the same font displayed as was previously selected?

Creating Menus

Menus are a part of every good application and provide not only an easy way to navigate within an application but also useful tools for working with that application. Take, for example, Visual Studio .NET. It provides menus for navigating various windows that it displays and useful tools for making the job of development easier through menus and context menus (also called pop-up menus) for cutting, copying, and pasting code. It also provides menu items for searching through code.

This chapter takes a look at creating menus in your Visual Basic .NET applications. You explore how to create and manage menus and submenus and how to create context menus and override the default context menus. Visual Studio .NET provides two menu controls in the Toolbox and you will be exploring both of these.

In this chapter you will:

- ❑ Create menus
- ❑ Create submenus
- ❑ Create context menus

Understanding Menu Features

The MainMenu control in Visual Studio .NET provides several key features. First and foremost, it provides a quick and easy way to add menus, menu items, and submenu items to your application. It also provides a built-in editor that allows you to add, edit, and delete menu items at the drop of a hat.

The menus that you create contain access keys, shortcut keys, checkmarks, and radiochecks.

Access Keys

An *access key* (also known as an accelerator key) enables you to navigate the menus using the *Alt* key and a letter that is underlined in the menu item. Once the access key has been used the menu will appear on the screen and the user can navigate through them using the arrow keys or the mouse.

Shortcut Keys

Shortcut keys enable you to invoke the menu item without displaying the menus at all. For example, you usually use a control key and a letter such as *Ctrl+X* to cut text.

Check Marks and Radiochecks

Check marks are either a checkmark symbol next to the menu item or, in the case of a radiocheck, a large dot next to the menu item. Both of these marks are indicators that the menu item is active. For example, if you click the View menu in Visual Studio .NET and then click the Toolbars menu item you see a submenu that has many submenu items, some of which have checkmarks. The submenu items that have checkmarks indicate the toolbars that are currently displayed. A radiocheck is more appropriate when you want to display a group of menu items and only want one menu item active at a time, just as we do with radio buttons.

Figure 8-1 shows many of the available features that you can incorporate into your menus. As you can see, this sample menu provides all the features that were just mentioned plus a separator. A separator provides a logical separation between groups of menu items.

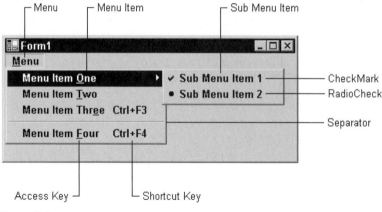

Figure 8-1

The previous figure shows the menu the way it looks when the project is being run. Figure 8-2 shows how the menu looks in Design mode.

Figure 8-2

The first thing that you'll notice when using the MainMenu control is that it provides a method to allow you to quickly add another menu, menu item, or submenu item. Each time you add one of these, another blank text area is added.

The second thing that you may notice is the absence of the shortcut keys, since they are not displayed in design mode.

The Properties Window

While you are creating or editing a menu, the Properties window displays the available properties that can be set for the menu being edited as shown in Figure 8-3, which shows the properties for the Menu Item. Notice that no shortcut key has been set for this menu item although it is to be displayed.

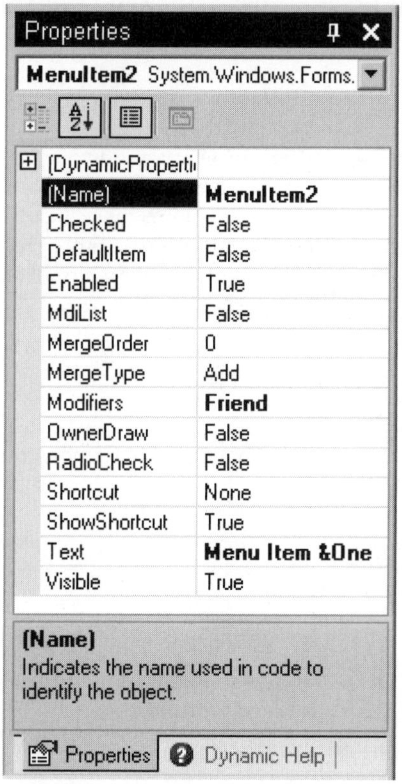

Properties	⇧ ✕
MenuItem2 System.Windows.Forms. ▼	

⊞ (DynamicPropertie	
[Name]	**MenuItem2**
Checked	False
DefaultItem	False
Enabled	True
MdiList	False
MergeOrder	0
MergeType	Add
Modifiers	**Friend**
OwnerDraw	False
RadioCheck	False
Shortcut	None
ShowShortcut	True
Text	**Menu Item &One**
Visible	True

[Name]
Indicates the name used in code to identify the object.

Properties | ❷ Dynamic Help

Figure 8-3

You can create as many menus, menu items, and submenu items as you need. You can even go as deep as you need to when creating submenu items by creating another submenu within a submenu.

> *Keep in mind though that if the menus are hard to navigate, or if it is hard to find the items your users are looking for, they will rapidly lose faith in your application.*

You should stick with the standard format for menus that you see in most Windows applications today. These are the menus that you see in Visual Studio .NET, Microsoft Word, or Microsoft Outlook. For example, you always have a File menu and an Exit menu item in the File menu to exit from the application. If your application provides cut, copy, and paste functionality then you would place these menu items in the Edit menu and so on.

The MSDN library that was installed with Visual Studio .NET contains a section on User Interface Design and Development. This section contains many topics that address the user interface and the Windows user interface. These should be explored for more details on Windows user-interface design-related topics.

The key is to make your menu look and feel like the menus in other Windows applications so the users can feel comfortable using your application. This way they do not feel like they have to learn the basics of Windows all over again. There will be menu items that are specific to your application but the key to incorporate them is to ensure that they fall into a general menu category that the users are familiar with or to place them in your own menu category. You would then place this new menu in the appropriate place in the menu bar, generally in the middle.

Creating Menus

Now, you move on and see how easy it is to create menus in your applications. In the following *Try It Out* you are going to create a form that contains a menu bar, two toolbars, and two text boxes. The menu bar will contain three menus: File, Edit, and View, and a few menu items and submenu items. This will enable you to fully demonstrate the features of the menu controls. Since there are a number of steps involved in building this application, this process will be broken down into several sections, the first of which is *Designing the Menus*.

Designing the Menus

You will be implementing code behind the menu items to demonstrate the menu and how to add code to your menu items, so let's get started.

Try It Out   Creating Menus

1. Create a new Windows Application project called Menus and click the OK button to have the project created. Refer to the *Responding to Events* section in Chapter 6 for detailed instructions on how to create a new project.

2. Set the properties of the form as outlined here:

    ❑   Set FormBorderStyle to FixedDialog

    ❑   Set MaximizeBox to False

    ❑   MinimizeBox to False

    ❑   Size to 300, 168

    ❑   StartPosition to CenterScreen

    ❑   Text to Menu Demo

3. Drag a MainMenu control from the Toolbox and drop it on your form. It will be automatically positioned at the top of your form as shown in Figure 8-4. The control will also be added to the

bottom of the development environment just like the dialog boxes discussed in Chapter 7. You can set the main properties of the MainMenu control there, but accept the default properties.

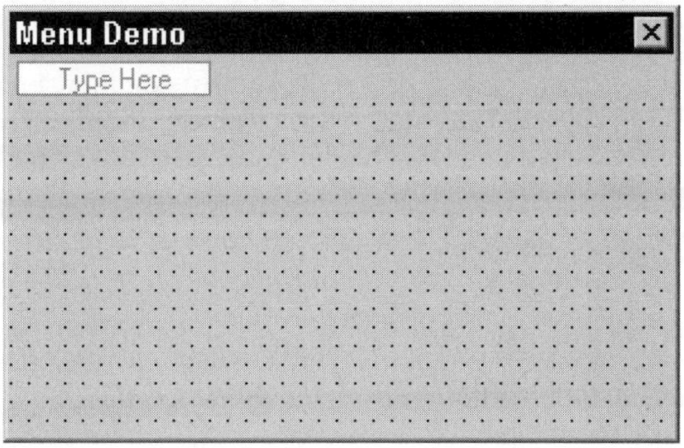

Figure 8-4

4. Enter the text **&File** in the box at the top of the form that says Type Here. This will become the File menu. Notice that the properties for this menu can be set in the Properties window. Accept the default properties for this menu.

An ampersand (&) in the menu name provides an access key for the menu or menu item. Once you have entered the menu name, the letter before which the ampersand appears will become underlined. This will allow this menu item to be accessed using the *Alt* key and the letter that is underlined. So for this menu, you will be able to access and expand the File menu by pressing *Alt+F*. You'll see this when you run your project later.

5. Notice that there is a box below and to the right of the menu that you just entered. This is only shown when the File menu is selected. This allows you to enter a new menu or a menu item. We want to enter a menu item of New, so type **&New** in the box below the File menu.

In the Properties window change the Name property of this menu item to **mnuFileNew**.

6. Now you enter a menu item separator. This is a line that separates the menu items, effectively grouping them together. The New menu item, is shown in Figure 8-5. Enter a dash (-). When you go to the next box, the dash will become a separator, filling the entire width of the menu.

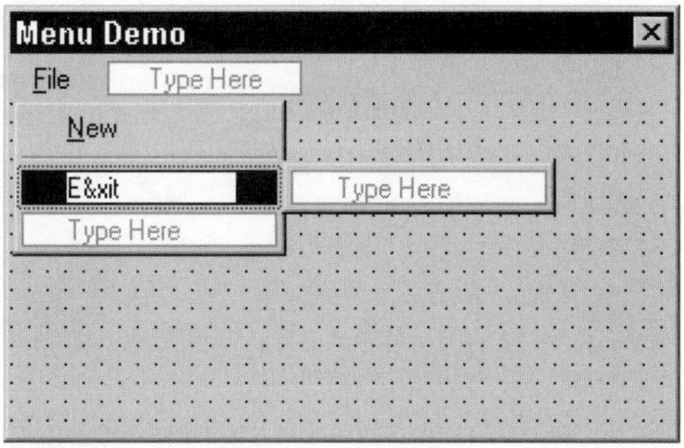

Figure 8-5

265

7. The next menu item that you add is Exit. In the box below the separator enter the text **&Exit**. Set the Name property of this menu item to **mnuFileExit** in the Properties window.

8. Now you add an Edit menu. In the box to the right of the File menu enter the text **&Edit** as shown in Figure 8-5. Accept all default properties for this menu.

9. The first menu item that you add here is the Undo menu item. Enter the text **&Undo** below the Edit menu. In the Properties window, enter a Name of **mnuEditUndo** and select *Ctrl+Z* in the ShortCut property drop-down list. This assigns a shortcut key for this menu item.

Remember that you will not see shortcut keys in the menu items at design time. They are only visible at runtime.

10. The next menu item that you want to add is a menu item separator. In the box below the Undo menu item enter a dash (-) and accept all default properties.

11. In the next box down, enter the text **&Cut** and set the Name property to **mnuEditCut**. Select *Ctrl+X* from the ShortCut drop-down list to assign the shortcut key for this menu item.

12. The next menu item that you add is Copy. Enter the text **&Copy**, set the Name property to **mnuEditCopy**, and assign a shortcut key of *Ctrl+C* in the ShortCut properties.

13. As you probably guessed, the next menu item is Paste. Enter the text **&Paste** in the next box, then set the Name property to **mnuEditPaste**, and assign a shortcut key of *Ctrl+V* in the ShortCut property.

14. You have to add another menu item separator, so enter a dash (-) in the next box and accept all default properties.

15. The final menu item in the Edit menu is Select All. Enter the text **&SelectAll**, set the Name property to **mnuEditSelectAll**, and assign a shortcut key of *Ctrl+A* in the ShortCut property. Your form should look like Figure 8-6.

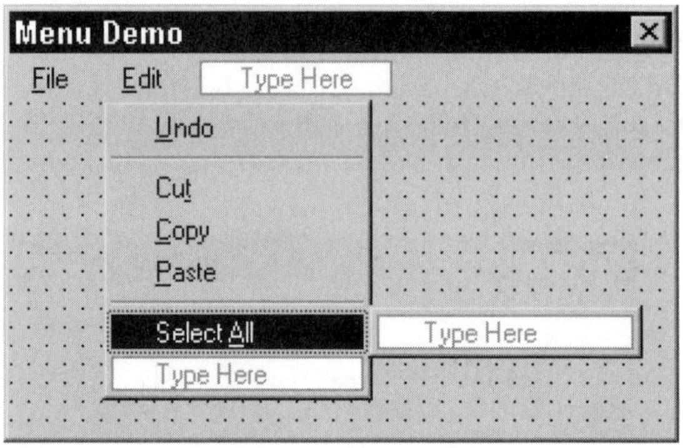

Figure 8-6

16. You have one final menu to add and that is the View menu. In the box next to the Edit menu enter **&View** and accept all default properties.

17. The one and only menu item under the View menu is Toolbars so enter the text **&Toolbars** and set the Name property to **mnuViewToolbars**.

18. You have to add two submenu items under the Toolbars menu item so in the box *next* to Toolbars enter the text **&Main**. Set the Name property to **mnuViewToolbarsMain** and set the Checked property to True. This causes this submenu item to be checked as shown in Figure 8-7.

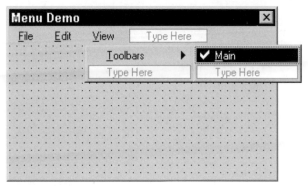

Figure 8-7

When you add a toolbar to this project, it will be displayed by default so this submenu item should be checked to indicate that the toolbar is displayed.

19. The next submenu item that you add is Formatting. Enter the text **&Formatting** in the box below Main and set the Name property to **mnuViewToolbarsFormatting**. Instead of a normal checkmark being displayed for this submenu item as shown previously, change the checkmark to a radiocheck to demonstrate how to set a radiocheck and see what it looks like in the menu. This setting causes a radio button mark to appear when this item is checked. Set the RadioCheck property to True.

Since this toolbar will not be shown by default, you need to leave the Checked property set to False.

Adding Toolbars and Controls

In this section you will add the toolbars and buttons for the toolbars that the application needs. The menus created in the previous section will control the displaying and hiding of these toolbars. You will also be adding a couple of TextBox controls that will be used in the application to cut, copy, and paste text using the toolbar buttons and menu items.

Try It Out   Adding Toolbars and Controls

1. You need to add two toolbars to the form, so locate the ToolBar control in the Toolbox and drag and drop it on your form. It automatically aligns itself to the top of the form below the menu and fills the width of the form. Set its Name property to **tbrMain**, its Appearance property to Flat.

2. Now add a second toolbar to the form in the same manner. It aligns itself under the first toolbar. Set the Name property to **tbrFormatting**, its Appearance property to Flat and set the Visible property to False, as you don't want this toolbar to be shown by default.

3. In order to add images to the toolbars you need to add an ImageList control to the form. Locate the ImageList control in the Toolbox and drag and drop it on your form. This control appears at the bottom of the development environment as shown in Figure 8-8 and you will accept the default name for this control.

Figure 8-8

4. You need to add some images to the ImageList control. The Images property of the ImageList control will contain a collection of images that will be placed on the toolbar buttons. Click the ellipsis button (...) for this property to invoke the Image Collection Editor.

5. Click the Add button to invoke the Open dialog. In the Look In combo box, navigate to the following folder: C:\Program Files\Microsoft Visual Studio.NET 2003\ Common7\Graphics\bitmaps\Tlbr_W95. (This assumes that Visual Studio .NET was installed in the default location. If you installed it in an alternative location, navigate to the Tlbr_W95 folder where you installed Visual Studio .NET.) In your production applications, icons will look better than bitmaps especially when the toolbar button is disabled.

6. Select the New.bmp image and click the Open button to have this image added to the Members list.

7. Click the Add button (Visual Studio will only allow you to add one at a time) again, and locate and select the following images to add them to the Members list. When you are done, your Image Collection Editor should look like the one shown in Figure 8-9.

- ❑ Undo.bmp
- ❑ Cut.bmp
- ❑ Copy.bmp
- ❑ Paste.bmp
- ❑ Lft.bmp
- ❑ Ctr.bmp
- ❑ Rt.bmp
- ❑ Jst.bmp

8. Click the OK button to close the Image Collection Editor. The images now contained in the ImageList control are available to any control on your form that supports images.

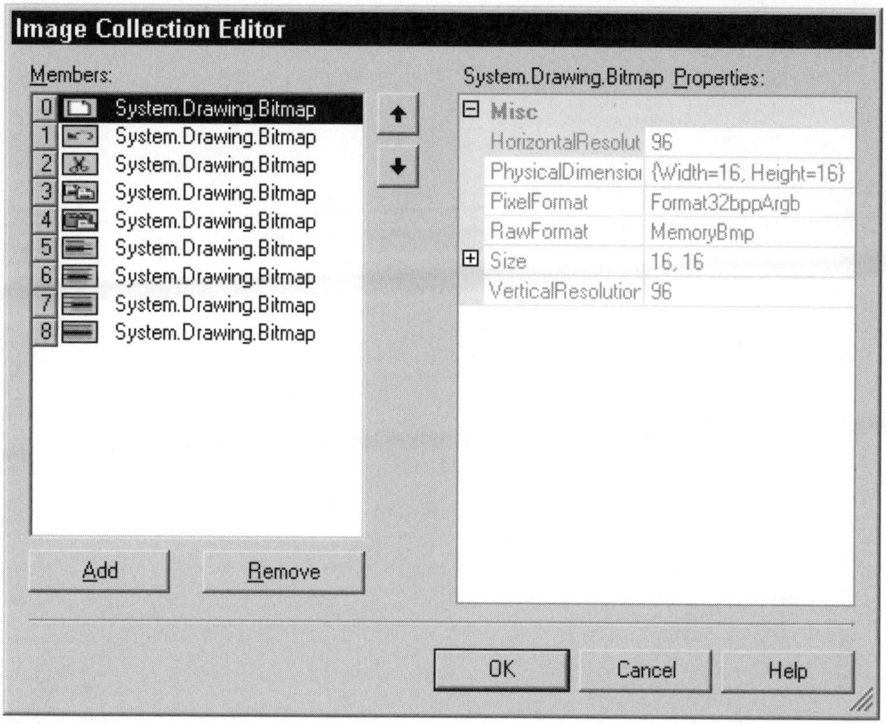

Figure 8-9

9. Click the main toolbar, tbrMain, and in the Properties window change the ButtonSize property to 16,16. This will make your buttons the same size as your images. You can set the ButtonSize property to any size that matches the images that you are using. Standard image sizes are 16×16 and 32×32 for toolbar buttons.

The Appearance property is set to Normal by default and provides raised buttons on the toolbar. Changing this property to Flat will cause the toolbar buttons to appear as flat buttons on the toolbar just as they appear in Visual Studio .NET. You can choose Normal or Flat. However, if you choose Flat, ensure that you set the Text property of each button to nothing or your buttons will appear as large as possible, with the text in the Text property displayed below the button image.

10. Click the ImageList property and select ImageList1 from the drop-down list. This assigns the ImageList1 control to your toolbar so you can access the images.

11. Click the ellipsis button for the Buttons property. The Buttons property will also contain a collection of buttons and invokes the ToolBarButton Collection Editor. The ToolBarButton Collection Editor is similar to the Image Collection Editor, though instead of a collection of images this editor allows you to add a collection of buttons. The buttons that you define here will use the images that you defined in the Image Collection Editor.

12. Click the Add button to add the first button. The properties for the button will be shown in the Properties window as illustrated in Figure 8-10.

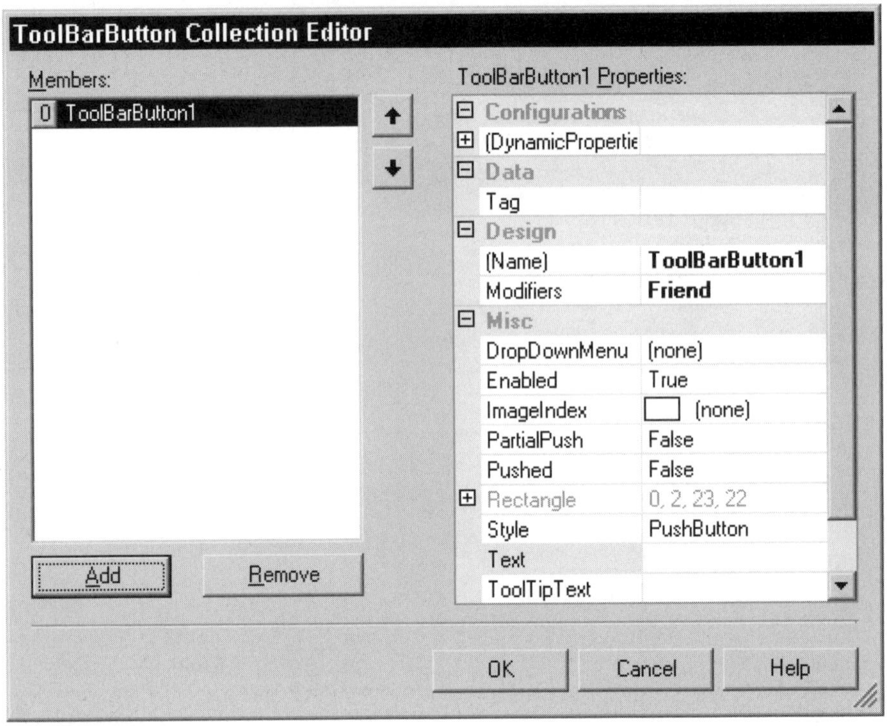

ToolBarButton Collection Editor

Members:

| 0 | ToolBarButton1 |

ToolBarButton1 Properties:

⊟ Configurations	
⊞ (DynamicPropertie	
⊟ Data	
Tag	
⊟ Design	
(Name)	**ToolBarButton1**
Modifiers	**Friend**
⊟ Misc	
DropDownMenu	(none)
Enabled	True
ImageIndex	(none)
PartialPush	False
Pushed	False
⊞ Rectangle	0, 2, 23, 22
Style	PushButton
Text	
ToolTipText	

Add   Remove

OK   Cancel   Help

Figure 8-10

13. In the Properties window, set the following properties for this button:

- ❑ Set Name to **tbnNew**
- ❑ Set ImageIndex to 0
- ❑ Set Text to *nothing*
- ❑ Set ToolTipText to **New**

14. Click the Add button again to add another button. Set the Style to Separator.

15. Add five more buttons and set their properties as shown in the following lists:

Button 1:

- ❑ Set Name to **tbnCut**
- ❑ Set ImageIndex to 2
- ❑ Set Text to *nothing*
- ❑ Set ToolTipText to **Cut**

Button 2:

- ❑ Set Name to **tbnCopy**
- ❑ Set ImageIndex to 3

❏ Set Text to *nothing*

❏ Set ToolTipText to **Copy**

Button 3:

❏ Set Name to **tbnPaste**

❏ Set ImageIndex to 4

❏ Set Text to *nothing*

❏ Set ToolTipText to **Paste**

Button 4:

❏ Set Style to Separator

Button 5:

❏ Set Name to **tbnUndo**

❏ Set ImageIndex to 1

❏ Set Text to *nothing*

❏ Set ToolTipText to **Undo**

16. Your completed collection should look like the one shown in Figure 8-11.

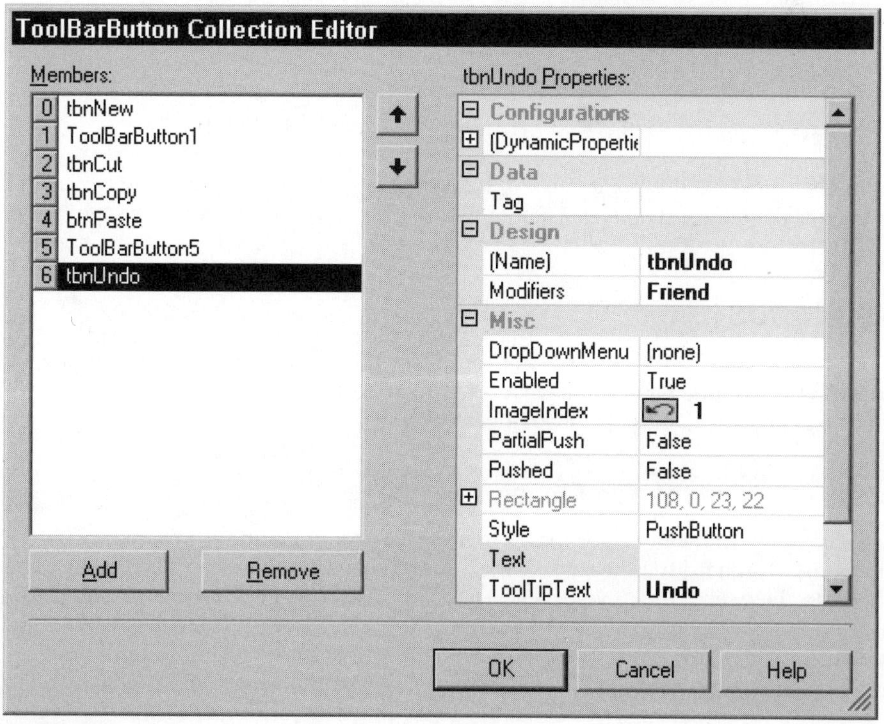

Figure 8-11

Chapter 8

17. Click the OK button to close the ToolBarButton Collection Editor and you will see the buttons, with images, on the toolbar.

18. Now click the second toolbar, tbrFormatting. In the Properties window set the ButtonSize property to 16, 16 and select ImageList1 as the ImageList property.

19. Click the ellipsis in the Buttons property to once again invoke the ToolBarButton Collection Editor.

20. Add four buttons and set their properties to 5 through 8, respectively. You are not concerned with the other properties as this toolbar is for demonstration purposes only, you will not be using it. When done, click the OK button to close the ToolBarButton Collection Editor.

21. Add two text-boxes to the form and accept their default properties. Their location and size are not important but they should be wide enough to enter text in. Your completed form should now look similar to the one shown in Figure 8-12.

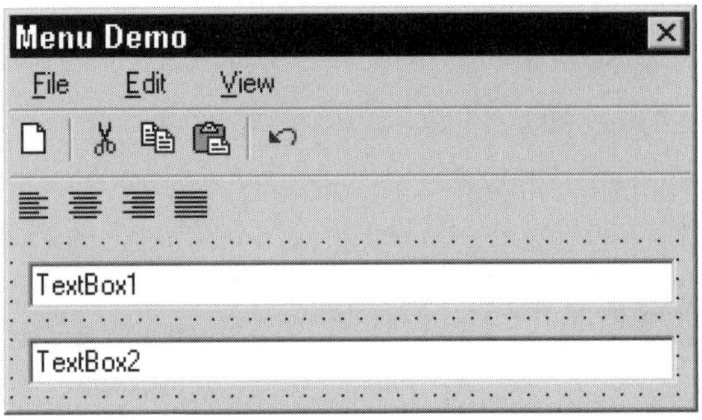

Figure 8-12

If you run your project at this point you will see the menus, the main toolbar, and two text boxes. The formatting toolbar is not visible at this point because the Visible property was set to False.

Coding Menus

Now that you have finally added all of your controls to the form, it's time to start writing some code to make these controls work. First, you have to add functionality to make the menus work. After you have done that you add code to make the main toolbar work.

Try It Out **Coding the File Menu**

1. Start by switching to the form class to view the code and adding a procedure for the New menu item. Click on the Class Name combo box and select mnuFileNew. Then in the Method Name combo box, select the Click event. The mnuFileNew_Click procedure will be added so add the following code to it:

```
Private Sub mnuFileNew_Click(ByVal sender As Object, ByVal e As _
                    System.EventArgs) Handles mnuFileNew.Click
    'Clear the textboxes
    TextBox1.Text = ""
```

272

```
        TextBox2.Text = ""
        'Set focus to the first textbox
        TextBox1.Focus()
    End Sub
```

2. Now add the procedure for the Exit menu item by selecting mnuFileExit from the Class Name box and Click from the Method Name box:

```
Private Sub mnuFileExit_Click(ByVal sender As Object, ByVal e As _
                    System.EventArgs) Handles mnuFileExit.Click
    'Close the form and end
    Me.Close()
End Sub
```

How It Works

It is a good practice to prefix your menu items with the prefix of mnu. It is also a good practice to specify not only the menu item name but also the menu that it belongs to as you have done here. This lets other developers quickly identify the menu item in code and know exactly what menu the menu item belongs to. This also becomes important when you have two menu items with the same name under different menus.

To clear the text boxes on the form in the mnuFileNew procedure add the following code to it. All you are doing here is setting the Text property of the text boxes to an empty string. The next line of code sets focus on the first text box by calling the Focus method of that text box:

```
Private Sub mnuFileNew_Click(ByVal sender As Object, ByVal e As _
                    System.EventArgs) Handles mnuFileNew.Click
    'Clear the textboxes
    TextBox1.Text = ""
    TextBox2.Text = ""
    'Set focus to the first textbox
    TextBox1.Focus()
End Sub
```

Now when you click the New menu item under the File menu, the text boxes on the form are cleared of all text and TextBox1 will be ready to accept text.

When you click the Exit menu item you want the program to end. In the mnuFileExit_Click procedure you added the following code. The Me keyword refers to the class where the code is executing and in this case refers to the form class. The Close method closes the form, releases all resources, and ends the program:

```
Private Sub mnuFileExit_Click(ByVal sender As Object, ByVal e As _
                    System.EventArgs) Handles mnuFileExit.Click
    'Close the form and end
    Me.Close()
End Sub
```

That takes care of the code for the File menu so move on to the Edit menu and add the code for those menu items.

Try It Out   **Coding the Edit Menu**

1. The first menu item in the Edit menu is the Undo menu item. Add the following code to the mnuEditUndo_Click event:

```
Private Sub mnuEditUndo_Click(ByVal sender As Object, ByVal e As _
                        System.EventArgs) Handles mnuEditUndo.Click
    'Declare a TextBox object and set it to the ActiveControl
    Dim objTextBox As TextBox = Me.ActiveControl

    'Undo the last operation
    objTextBox.Undo ()
End Sub
```

2. Add a procedure for the Click event of the Cut menu item and add this code:

```
Private Sub mnuEditCut_Click(ByVal sender As Object, ByVal e As _
                        System.EventArgs) Handles mnuEditCut.Click
    'Declare a TextBox object and set it to the ActiveControl
    Dim objTextBox As TextBox = Me.ActiveControl

    'Copy the text to the clipboard and clear the field
    objTextBox.Cut()
End Sub
```

3. The next menu item that you need to code is the mnuEditCopy menu item. Add the procedure for the Click event to your code:

```
Private Sub mnuEditCopy_Click(ByVal sender As Object, ByVal e As _
                        System.EventArgs) Handles mnuEditCopy.Click
    'Declare a TextBox object and set it to the ActiveControl
    Dim objTextBox As TextBox = Me.ActiveControl

    'Copy the text to the clipboard
    objTextBox.Copy()
End Sub
```

4. Add the procedure for the Click event to your code for the mnuEditPaste menu item. In this procedure add the following code:

```
Private Sub mnuEditPaste_Click(ByVal sender As Object, ByVal e As _
                        System.EventArgs) Handles mnuEditPaste.Click
    'Declare a TextBox object and set it to the ActiveControl
    Dim objTextBox As TextBox = Me.ActiveControl

    'Copy the data from the clipboard to the textbox
    objTextBox.Paste()
End Sub
```

5. The last menu item under the Edit menu is the Select All menu item. Add the procedure for the Click event of this menu item to your code:

```
Private Sub mnuEditSelectAll_Click(ByVal sender As Object, _
        ByVal e As System.EventArgs) Handles mnuEditSelectAll.Click
    'Declare a TextBox object and set it to the ActiveControl
    Dim objTextBox As TextBox = Me.ActiveControl

    'Select all text
    objTextBox.SelectAll()
End Sub
```

How It Works

You added the code for the Edit menu starting with the Undo item. Since you have two text boxes on your form, you need a way to determine which text box you are dealing with or a generic way of handling an undo operation for both text boxes. In this example, you go with the latter option and provide a generic way to handle both text boxes.

You do this by declaring a variable as an ActiveControl property of the form, which retrieves the active control on the form. This is the control that has focus:

```
Private Sub mnuEditUndo_Click(ByVal sender As Object, ByVal e As _
                        System.EventArgs) Handles mnuEditUndo.Click
    'Declare a TextBox object and set it to the ActiveControl
    Dim objTextBox As TextBox = Me.ActiveControl
```

It should be noted that the menu and toolbar are never set as the active control. This allows you to use the menus and toolbar buttons and always reference the active control.

Now that you have a reference to the active control on the form, you can invoke the Undo method as shown in the last line of code here. The Undo method is a method of the TextBox control and will undo the last operation in that text box if it can be undone.

```
    'Undo the last operation
    objTextBox.Undo()
End Sub
```

The ActiveControl property works fine in this small example since all you are dealing with is two text boxes. However, in a real-world application, you would need to test the active control to see if it supported the method that you were using (for example, Undo).

The next menu item under the Edit menu is Cut. The first thing that we do in this procedure is to again get a reference to the active control on the form and set it to the TextBox object that you declared.

Then you invoke the Cut method. This is a method of the TextBox control and will copy the selected text to the Clipboard and then remove the selected text from the text box:

```
Private Sub mnuEditCut_Click(ByVal sender As Object, ByVal e As _
                        System.EventArgs) Handles mnuEditCut.Click
    'Declare a TextBox object and set it to the ActiveControl
    Dim objTextBox As TextBox = Me.ActiveControl

    'Copy the text to the clipboard and clear the field
    objTextBox.Cut()
End Sub
```

Again, you declare a TextBox object and get a reference to the active control on the form for the Copy menu item. Then you invoke the Copy method to have the text in the active text box copied to the Clipboard:

```
Private Sub mnuEditCopy_Click(ByVal sender As Object, ByVal e As _
                       System.EventArgs) Handles mnuEditCopy.Click
   'Declare a TextBox object and set it to the ActiveControl
   Dim objTextBox As TextBox = Me.ActiveControl

   'Copy the text to the clipboard
   objTextBox.Copy()
End Sub
```

For the Click event for the Paste menu item, the first thing that you do is to get a reference to the active control by setting it to our TextBox object that you have declared. Then we invoke the Paste method, which will paste the text contents of the Clipboard into your text box:

```
Private Sub mnuEditPaste_Click(ByVal sender As Object, ByVal e As _
                       System.EventArgs) Handles mnuEditPaste.Click
   'Declare a TextBox object and set it to the ActiveControl
   Dim objTextBox As TextBox = Me.ActiveControl

   'Copy the data from the clipboard to the textbox
   objTextBox.Paste()
End Sub
```

Lastly, for the Select All item, you once again get a reference to the active control by setting it to the TextBox object that you declared. Then you invoke the SelectAll method, which will select all text in the text box that is active:

```
Private Sub mnuEditSelectAll_Click(ByVal sender As Object, _
        ByVal e As System.EventArgs) Handles mnuEditSelectAll.Click
   'Declare a TextBox object and set it to the ActiveControl
   Dim objTextBox As TextBox = Me.ActiveControl

   'Select all text
   objTextBox.SelectAll()
End Sub
```

Coding the View Menu and Toolbars

Now that you added the code to make the Edit menu items functional, the next step is to make the menu items under the View menu functional. You also add the code to make the toolbar buttons functional in this section.

Try It Out   **Coding the View Menu and the Main Toolbar**

1.   Add the mnuViewToolbarsMain_Click event procedure to your code and then add the following:

```
Private Sub mnuViewToolbarsMain_Click(ByVal sender As Object, _
        ByVal e As System.EventArgs) Handles mnuViewToolbarsMain.Click
    'Toggle the View\Toolbars\Main menu item Checked property
    mnuViewToolbarsMain.Checked = Not mnuViewToolbarsMain.Checked

    'Toggle the visibility of the Main toobar
    tbrMain.Visible = Not tbrMain.Visible
End Sub
```

2. You need to add the same type of code that you just added to the mnuViewToolbarsFormatting submenu item. So add the following code to its Click event procedure:

```
Private Sub mnuViewToolbarsFormatting_Click(ByVal sender As Object, _
        ByVal e As System.EventArgs) _
        Handles mnuViewToolbarsFormatting.Click
    'Toggle the View\Toolbars\Formatting menu item Checked property
    mnuViewToolbarsFormatting.Checked = Not _
    mnuViewToolbarsFormatting.Checked

    'Toggle the visibility of the Formatting toolbar
    tbrFormatting.Visible = Not tbrFormatting.Visible
End Sub
```

3. There's one last procedure that you need to add here and that is the procedure to implement the functionality for the main toolbar. Click the Class Name combo box and select tbrMain and in the Method Name combo box select the ButtonClick event. This is the event that gets activated when a toolbar button is clicked. Add the following code to this event procedure:

```
Private Sub tbrMain_ButtonClick(ByVal sender As Object, ByVal e As _
        System.Windows.Forms.ToolBarButtonClickEventArgs) _
        Handles tbrMain.ButtonClick
    Select Case tbrMain.Buttons.IndexOf (e.Button)
        Case 0 'New
            'Call the corresponding menu item
            mnuFileNew_Click(Nothing, Nothing)
        Case 1 'Separator
        Case 2 'Cut
            'Call the corresponding menu item
            mnuEditCut_Click(Nothing, Nothing)
        Case 3 'Copy
            'Call the corresponding menu item
            mnuEditCopy_Click(Nothing, Nothing)
        Case 4 'Paste
            'Call the corresponding menu item
            mnuEditPaste_Click(Nothing, Nothing)
        Case 5 'Separator
        Case 6 'Undo
            'Call the corresponding menu item
            mnuEditUndo_Click(Nothing, Nothing)
    End Select
End Sub
```

Testing Your Code

As your applications become more complex, testing your code becomes increasingly important. The more errors that you find and fix during your testing will help you to implement an application that is both stable and reliable for your users. This translates into satisfied users and earns a good reputation for you for delivering a quality product.

You not only need to test the functionality of your application but also to test various scenarios that a user might encounter or perform. For example, suppose you had a database application that gathers user input from a form and inserts them into a database. A good application will validate all user input before trying to insert the data into the database and a good test plan will try to break the data validation code. This will ensure that your validation code handles all possible scenarios and functions properly.

Try It Out   **Testing Your Code**

1. It's now time to test your code! Click the Run toolbar button and when your form loads, the only toolbar that you see is the main toolbar as shown in Figure 8-13.

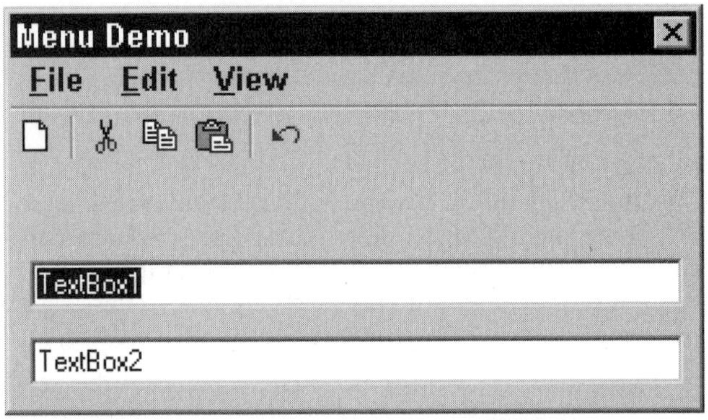

Figure 8-13

2. Notice that unlike most other applications, you do not immediately see the access keys. However, if you press the *Alt* key they will appear. Go ahead and press *Alt+E* to display the Edit menu. Notice that now you can see the shortcut keys that you did not see in the design mode shown in Figure 8-14.

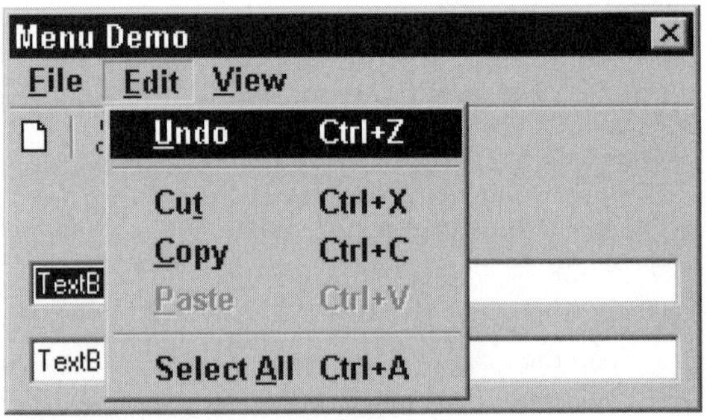

Figure 8-14

3. Click the View menu and then click on the Toolbars menu item. Notice that the Main submenu item is checked and the main toolbar is visible. Go ahead and click on the Formatting submenu item. The formatting toolbar is displayed along with the main toolbar.

4. If you click the View menu again and then click on the Toolbars menu item you will see that both the Main and Formatting submenu items are checked. Notice the difference in the check marks. The Main submenu item uses a checkmark while the Formatting submenu item uses a radiocheck.

   This was because you set the RadioCheck property to True for the Formatting submenu item. This demonstrates the different check marks that can be displayed in a menu.

The RadioCheck property has been used here for demonstration purposes. In a real world application, you would use this property for a group of menu items of which only one could be selected at a time.

5. Now test the functionality of the Edit menu. Click in the first text box and ensure that the text is not highlighted. Then click on the Edit menu and select the Select All menu item. Before selecting it though, take notice of the shortcut key for this menu item. Once you select the Select All menu item the text in the text box is highlighted.

   Now click in the second text box and ensure the text is not highlighted. Press the shortcut keys *Ctrl+A* and the text in the second text box will be highlighted. This demonstrates how the menu and shortcut keys work.

6. You now want to copy the text in the second text box while the text is highlighted. Hover your mouse over the Copy icon on the toolbar to view the tool tip. Now either click on the Copy icon on the toolbar or select the Edit ⇨ Copy menu item.

   Place your cursor in the first text box at the end of the current text, ensuring that the text is not highlighted. Then either click on the Paste icon on the toolbar or click on the Edit ⇨ Paste menu item. The text TextBox2 is pasted in the first text box behind the current text, as shown in Figure 8-15.

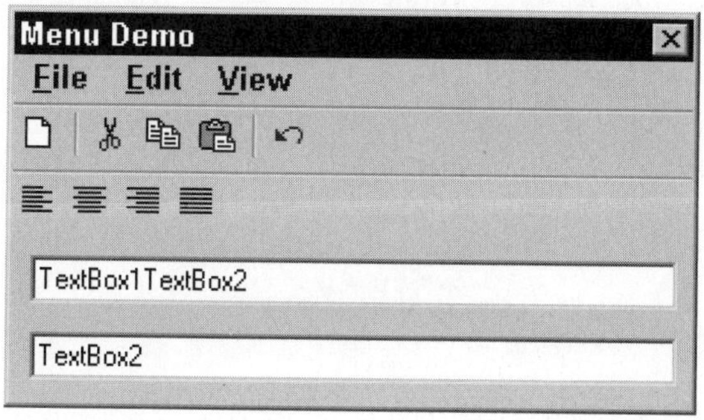

Figure 8-15

7. Now place your cursor in the second text box between the letters T and B and either click on the Paste icon on the toolbar or click on the Edit ⇨ Paste menu item. The text on the clipboard is inserted between the letters where your cursor is.

8. Click the Undo icon on the toolbar, or click the Edit ⇨ Undo menu item, or use the shortcut key combination of *Ctrl+Z* to undo the last operation in the text box. The text in the second text box is now restored to its previous state.

Place your cursor in the first text box and perform an undo operation. Notice that the text in the first text box is also restored to its previous state. If you perform an undo operation again, the text will be restored to the state before the undo and you will see the text TextBox1TextBox2 in the first text box.

9. The last item on the Edit menu to test is the Cut menu item. Highlight the text in the first text box by clicking on the Edit menu and selecting the Select All menu item. Then either click the Cut icon on the toolbar or click the Edit ⇨ Cut menu item. The text is copied to the Clipboard and is then removed from the text box.

    Place your cursor in the second text box and highlight the text there. Then paste the text in this text box. The text that was there has been replaced with the text that was cut from the first text box. This is how Windows' cut, copy, and paste operations work and, as you can see, there was very little code required to implement this functionality in your program.

10. Now click the File menu and choose the New menu item. The text in the text boxes is cleared. The only menu item left to test is the Exit menu item under the File menu. However, before you test that, take a quick look at context menus. Type some text in one of the text boxes. Now, right-click in that text box and you will see a context menu pop up as shown in Figure 8-16. Notice that this context menu appeared automatically; there was no code that you needed to add to have this done. This is a feature of the Windows operating system and Visual Studio .NET provides a way to override the default context menus, as you will see in the next section.

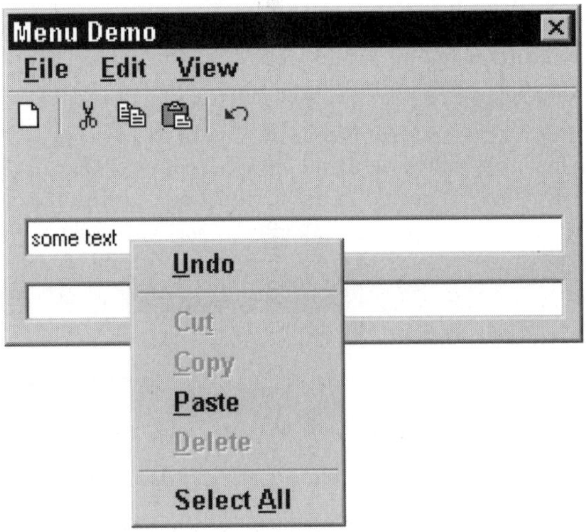

Figure 8-16

11. To test the last bit of functionality of your program, select the File ⇨ Exit menu item and your program will end.

How It Works

To begin with, you added the code to show and hide the toolbars on your form. The Main and Formatting submenu items are under the Toolbars menu item of the View menu. You added the procedures for these submenu items to your code just as you did for the menu items previously.

The first thing that you had to do was toggle the Checked property of the submenu item. You did this by setting the Checked property of the mnuViewToolbarsMain submenu item to not equal itself. Therefore, if the Checked property is set to True then this will cause it to be set to False and if it is set to False it will cause it to be set to True:

```
Private Sub mnuViewToolbarsMain_Click(ByVal sender As Object, _
        ByVal e As System.EventArgs) Handles mnuViewToolbarsMain.Click
    'Toggle the View\Toolbars\Main menu item Checked property
    mnuViewToolbarsMain.Checked = Not mnuViewToolbarsMain.Checked
```

The next line of code toggles the visibility of the main toolbar by using the Visible property, which also contains a True or False value. You set the Visible property not equal to itself, and so toggle it between True and False:

```
    'Toggle the visibility of the Main toolbar
    tbrMain.Visible = Not tbrMain.Visible
End Sub
```

You then added the same type of code to the mnuViewToolbarsFormatting submenu item. The first line of code toggles the mnuViewToolbarsFormatting submenu item by checking it or unchecking it and the second line of code toggles the visibility of the formatting toolbar.

Lastly, you added one further procedure that implemented the functionality for the main toolbar. When a toolbar button is clicked, the tbrMain_ButtonClick procedure is activated and the button that was clicked is passed in the ToolBarButtonClickEventArgs class. Remember that the buttons on the toolbar are a collection of buttons within the toolbar. The ToolBarButtonClickEventArgs class contains information about the button that was clicked in the Button property.

You can determine the exact button that was clicked by using a Select Case statement and assigning the index of the button that was clicked to the IndexOf method of the Buttons property of the toolbar. This will give you the exact index position of the button that was clicked. The Button property in the ToolBarButtonClickEventArgs class contains the index of the button in the Buttons collection that was clicked. This class is assigned to the parameter e in your procedure:

```
Private Sub tbrMain_ButtonClick(ByVal sender As Object, _
        ByVal e As System.Windows.Forms.ToolBarButtonClickEventArgs) _
        Handles tbrMain.ButtonClick
    Select Case tbrMain.Buttons.IndexOf (e.Button)
```

The first Case statement checks the index of the first button, which is the New button in the Buttons collection. The Buttons collection, like all other collections, is zero-based, meaning that the first button has an index of zero. If this is the button the user clicked, then you call the mnuFileNew_Click procedure passing it Nothing for the required arguments for that procedure. Since the mnuFileNew_Click procedure has two required arguments you need to pass something, and the Nothing keyword works fine. The mnuFileNew_Click procedure contains all of the logic necessary to clear the text boxes on the form.

The next Case statement merely documents the collection of buttons for you. This is the separator button between the New button and the Cut button:

```
Case 0 'New
    'Call the corresponding menu item
    mnuFileNew_Click(Nothing, Nothing)
Case 1 'Separator
```

The next three buttons in the Buttons collection represent the Cut, Copy, and Paste buttons. You check the index of the button in a `Case` statement and then call the appropriate menu procedure that corresponds to the button clicked:

```
Case 2 'Cut
    'Call the corresponding menu item
      mnuEditCut_Click(Nothing, Nothing)
Case 3 'Copy
    'Call the corresponding menu item
      mnuEditCopy_Click(Nothing, Nothing)
Case 4 'Paste
    'Call the corresponding menu item
    mnuEditPaste_Click(Nothing, Nothing)
```

There is a separator button between the Paste button and the Undo button. It's listed in the code merely to document it for you. The last `Case` statement in this code checks whether the button that was clicked was the Undo button. If it is, then you call the `mnuEditUndo_Click` procedure to perform an undo operation on the active text box:

```
Case 5 'Separator
Case 6 'Undo
    'Call the corresponding menu item
    mnuEditUndo_Click(Nothing, Nothing)
  End Select
End Sub
```

You can experiment with showing and hiding the toolbars by clicking the submenu items. Each time you click a submenu item, the corresponding toolbar is either shown or hidden and the check mark will either be shown or hidden.

Context Menus

Context menus are menus that pop up when a user clicks the right mouse button over a control or window. This provides the user with quick access to the most commonly used commands for the control that they are working with. As you just saw, the context menu that appeared provides you with a way to manage the text in a text box.

Context menus are customized for the control that you are working with and in the more complex applications, such as Visual Studio .NET or Microsoft Word, they provide quick access to the commands for the task that is being performed.

You saw that Windows provides a default context menu for the text box that you are working with and that you can override the default context menu if our applications dictate that you do so. For example, suppose that you have an application in which you want the user to be able to copy the text in a text box, but not actually cut or paste text in that text box. This would be an ideal situation to provide your own context menu to allow only the operations that you want.

Visual Studio .NET provides a ContextMenu control that you can place on your form and customize it just as you did the MainMenu control. However, the main difference between the MainMenu control and the ContextMenu control is that you can only create one top-level menu with the ContextMenu control. You can still create submenu items with the ContextMenu if you need to.

Most controls in the toolbox have a ContextMenu property that can be set to the context menu that you define. Then when you right-click that control, the context menu that you defined is displayed instead of the default context menu.

Some controls, such as the ComboBox and ListBox controls, do not have a default context menu. This is because they contain a list of items and not a single item like controls such as the TextBox control does. They do, however, have a ContextMenu property that can be set to a context menu that you define.

Creating Context Menus

Now that you know what context menus are, you are ready to learn how to create and use them in your Visual Basic .NET applications. In the next *Try It Out*, you will be expanding the code in the previous *Try It Out* section by adding a context menu to work with your text boxes. You add one context menu and use it for both text boxes. You could just as easily create two context menus, one for each text box, and have the context menus perform different functions.

Try It Out   Creating Context Menus

1. Open the Menus project if it is not already opened.

2. View the form in the designer and then click the toolbox to locate the ContextMenu control. Drag and drop it onto your form. It will be added at the bottom of the development environment just as the MainMenu and ImageList controls were.

3. On the form, click the text that says Context Menu, as shown in Figure 8-17 to have the first entry added. In the first text area, enter the text **Undo**. In the Properties window, set the Name property to **cmuUndo** and assign a shortcut key of *Ctrl+Z* in the ShortCut property.

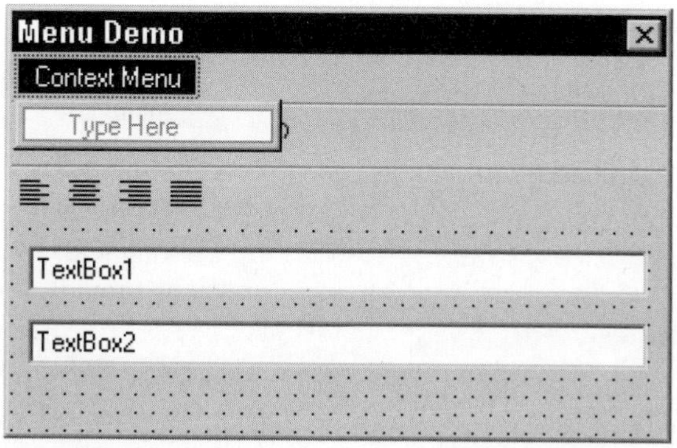

Figure 8-17

4. In the next text area, enter a dash (-) to create a separator bar between the menu items.

5. In the next few text areas enter the following menu items and set their properties accordingly:

   Cut menu item

   - ❑ Set Name to **cmuCut**
   - ❑ Set ShortCut to *Ctrl*+**X**
   - ❑ Set Text to **Cut**

   Copy Menu Item

   - ❑ Set Name to **cmuCopy**
   - ❑ Set ShortCut to *Ctrl*+**C**
   - ❑ Set Text to **Copy**

   Paste Menu Item

   - ❑ Set Name to **cmuPaste**
   - ❑ Set ShortCut to *Ctrl*+**V**
   - ❑ Set Text to **Paste**

   Separator Menu Item

   - ❑ Set Text to **-**

   Select All Menu Item

   - ❑ Set Name to **cmuSelectAll**
   - ❑ Set ShortCut to *Ctrl*+**A**
   - ❑ Set Text to **Select All**

6. When you are done, click on any part of the form and the context menu will disappear. (You can always make it reappear by clicking the ContextMenu control at the bottom of the development environment.)

7. Click the first text box and in the Properties window select ContextMenu1 in the drop-down list for the `ContextMenu` property. Repeat the same action for the second text box to assign a context menu in the `ContextMenu` property.

   Now test your context menu for look and feel. At this point, you haven't added any code to it but you can ensure that it looks visually correct. Run the application, then right-click in the first text box and you will see the context menu that you have just added, as shown in Figure 8-18. The same context menu will appear if you also right-click in the second text box.

8. Stop your program and switch to the code for your form so that you can add the code for the context menus. The first procedure that you want to add is that for the Undo context menu item. Bring up the `cmuUndo_Click` event procedure and add the following lines to it:

```
Private Sub cmuUndo_Click(ByVal sender As Object, ByVal e As _
                    System.EventArgs) Handles cmuUndo.Click
    'Call the corresponding menu item
    mnuEditUndo_Click(Nothing, Nothing)
End Sub
```

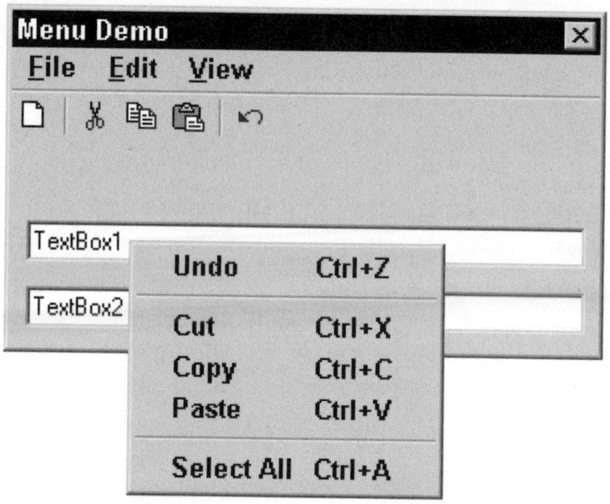

Figure 8-18

9. Next you insert the procedure for the Cut context menu item. Bring up the cmuCut_Click event procedure and add the code to call the mnuEditCut_Click procedure as follows:

```
Private Sub cmuCut_Click(ByVal sender As Object, ByVal e As _
                   System.EventArgs) Handles cmuCut.Click
   'Call the corresponding menu item
   mnuEditCut_Click(Nothing, Nothing)
End Sub
```

10. Insert the procedure for the Copy context menu item next (cmuCopy_Click). Add the code to call the mnuEditCopy_Click event as shown:

```
Private Sub cmuCopy_Click(ByVal sender As Object, ByVal e As _
                   System.EventArgs) Handles cmuCopy.Click
   'Call the corresponding menu item
   mnuEditCopy_Click(Nothing, Nothing)
End Sub
```

11. Insert the procedure for the Paste context menu item and add the code to call the mnuEditPaste_Click procedure as shown:

```
Private Sub cmuPaste_Click(ByVal sender As Object, ByVal e As _
                   System.EventArgs) Handles cmuPaste.Click
   'Call the corresponding menu item
   mnuEditPaste_Click(Nothing, Nothing)
End Sub
```

12. The last procedure that you need to add (cmuSelectAll_Click) is for the Select All context menu item. Add the code to call the mnuEditSelectAll_Click procedure as shown:

```
Private Sub cmuSelectAll_Click(ByVal sender As Object, ByVal e As _
                            System.EventArgs) Handles cmuSelectAll.Click
    'Call the corresponding menu item
    mnuEditSelectAll_Click(Nothing, Nothing)
End Sub
```

13. That's all the code that you need to add to implement your own context menu. Pretty simple huh? Now run your project to see your context menu in action and test it.

You can test the context menu by clicking on each of the context menu items shown. They will perform the same functions as their counterparts in the toolbar and Edit menu. Do you see the difference in your context menu from the one shown in Figure 8-16? Your context menu shows the shortcut keys and you have left out the Delete context menu item.

14. You need to add a procedure that can be called to toggle all of the Edit menu items, toolbar buttons, and context menu items from being enabled to disabled. They will be enabled and disabled based upon what should be available to the user. You call this procedure ToggleMenus, so stop your program and add the following procedure at the end of your existing code.

```
Private Sub ToggleMenus()

    'Declare a TextBox object and set it to the ActiveControl
    Dim objTextBox As TextBox = Me.ActiveControl

    'Toggle the Edit\Undo menu item
    mnuEditUndo.Enabled = objTextBox.CanUndo
    'Toggle the Undo context menu item
    cmuUndo.Enabled = objTextBox.CanUndo
    'Toggle the Undo toolbar button
    tbrMain.Buttons(6).Enabled = objTextBox.CanUndo

    'Toggle the Edit\Cut menu item
    mnuEditCut.Enabled = objTextBox.SelectionLength
    'Toggle the Cut context menu item
    cmuCut.Enabled = objTextBox.SelectionLength
    'Toggle the Cut toolbar button
    tbrMain.Buttons(2).Enabled = objTextBox.SelectionLength

    'Toggle the Edit\Copy menu item
    mnuEditCopy.Enabled = objTextBox.SelectionLength
    'Toggle the Copy context menu item
    cmuCopy.Enabled = objTextBox.SelectionLength
    'Toggle the Copy toolbar button
    tbrMain.Buttons(3).Enabled = objTextBox.SelectionLength

    'Toggle the Edit\Paste menu item
    mnuEditPaste.Enabled = _
        Clipboard.GetDataObject().GetDataPresent(DataFormats.Text)
    'Toggle the Paste context menu item
    cmuPaste.Enabled = _
        Clipboard.GetDataObject().GetDataPresent(DataFormats.Text)
    'Toggle the Paste toolbar button
    tbrMain.Buttons(4).Enabled = _
        Clipboard.GetDataObject().GetDataPresent(DataFormats.Text)
```

```
        'Toggle the Edit\Select All menu item
     mnuEditSelectAll.Enabled = objTextBox.SelectionLength < _
          objTextBox.Text.Length
     'Toggle the Select All context menu item
     cmuSelectAll.Enabled = objTextBox.SelectionLength < _
          objTextBox.Text.Length
   End Sub
```

That's it! All of that code will toggle the Edit menu items, the context menu items, and the toolbar buttons. Now all you need is to figure out when and where to call this procedure.

15. Since you are checking for only the two text boxes on your form, you can call the `ToggleMenu` procedure when the user moves the mouse in a text box. This way, you will toggle the Edit menu items and toolbar buttons when the user is in a text box and the code will be applied against the text box that you are in. To do this click the Class Name combo box, select TextBox1, and in the Method Name combo box select the `MouseMove` event. This inserts an empty procedure into your code. All you need to do here is to call the `ToggleMenus` procedure as shown:

```
Private Sub TextBox1_MouseMove(ByVal sender As Object, ByVal e As _
     System.Windows.Forms.MouseEventArgs) Handles TextBox1.MouseMove
     'Toggle the menu items and toolbar buttons
     ToggleMenus()
End Sub
```

16. Repeat this process for the second text box on the form. The code for this procedure is as follows:

```
Private Sub TextBox2_MouseMove(ByVal sender As Object, ByVal e As _
     System.Windows.Forms.MouseEventArgs) Handles TextBox2.MouseMove
     'Toggle the menu items and toolbar buttons
     ToggleMenus()
End Sub
```

17. Test your code again. Once the form has displayed, click in the first text box and ensure the text is not selected. Then right-click to display your context menu. Now the context menu has the appropriate menu items enabled as shown in Figure 8-19.

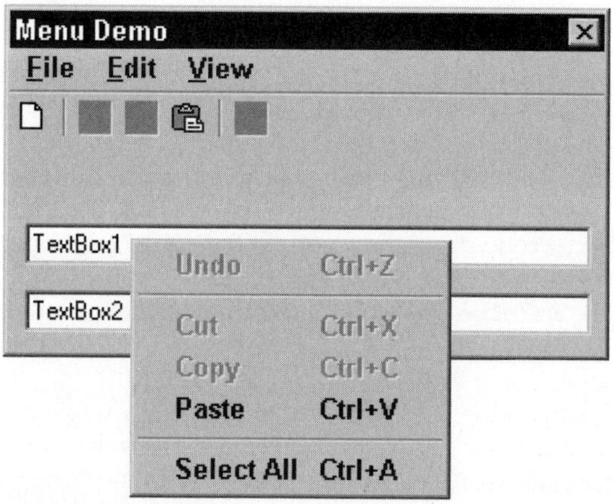

Figure 8-19

Notice also that the appropriate toolbar buttons are also enabled and disabled. If you click on the Edit menu, you will see that the appropriate menu items there are also enabled and disabled. If you click on the Select All menu item or context menu item, you will see the toolbar buttons change as well as the menu items under the Edit menu and context menu.

How It Works

Notice that you are using a different prefix of cmu for your names here. This will distinguish this menu item as a context menu item.

Since you had already written all of the code that these context menu items needed, all you had to do was to insert a call to the appropriate procedures. In the cmuUndo_Click procedure you added the following code, which calls the mnuEditUndo_Click procedure. You pass the Nothing keyword as the required parameters to that procedure:

```
Private Sub cmuUndo_Click(ByVal sender As Object, ByVal e As _
                     System.EventArgs) Handles cmuUndo.Click
    'Call the corresponding menu item
    mnuEditUndo_Click(Nothing, Nothing)
End Sub
```

This was repeated for all the items on the Edit menu with the different Click procedures being called.

Besides having the shortcut keys shown, there's one other difference that stood out when you first tested your context menu. Your context menu had all of its items enabled. To enable and disable the appropriate menu items, you needed to perform some basic checks before the context menu was displayed.

The first thing that you had to do in the ToggleMenus procedure was to declare an object and set it equal to the active TextBox control. You saw this in the last *Try It Out* and this object had all of the properties that the active text box had:

```
Private Sub ToggleMenus()
    'Declare a TextBox object and set it to the ActiveControl
    Dim objTextBox As TextBox = Me.ActiveControl
```

The first Edit menu item is Undo so you started there. The TextBox control has a property called CanUndo, which returns a True or False value indicating whether or not the last operation performed in the text box can be undone.

You use the CanUndo property to set the Enabled property of the Edit menu item. The Enabled property is set using a Boolean value, which works out great since the CanUndo property returns a Boolean value. The following code shows how you set the Enabled property of the Undo menu item.

You also want to toggle the Enabled property for the Undo context menu item and you use the CanUndo property for this too.

The toolbar also has an Undo button, and you want to enable or disable it also. Here you are specifying the main toolbar name, tbrMain, the Buttons collection, and the index of the item in the Buttons collection. Then you specify the Enabled property and set it to the CanUndo property of your TextBox object:

```
'Toggle the Edit\Undo menu item
mnuEditUndo.Enabled = objTextBox.CanUndo
'Toggle the Undo context menu item
cmuUndo.Enabled = objTextBox.CanUndo
'Toggle the Undo toolbar button
tbrMain.Buttons(6).Enabled = objTextBox.CanUndo
```

The next menu item in the Edit menu is the Cut menu item. This time you use the `SelectionLength` property of your TextBox object. `SelectionLength` returns the number of characters selected in a text box. You can use this number to act as `True` or `False` value because a value of `False` in Visual Basic .NET is `0` and a value of `True` is `1`. Since the value of `False` is always evaluated first, any number other than `0` evaluates to `True`.

Therefore, if no text is selected, the `SelectionLength` property will return `0` and you will disable the Cut menu item, Cut context menu item, and Cut toolbar button. If no text is selected you don't want to allow the user to perform this operation:

```
'Toggle the Edit\Cut menu item
mnuEditCut.Enabled = objTextBox.SelectionLength
'Toggle the Cut context menu item
cmuCut.Enabled = objTextBox.SelectionLength
'Toggle the Cut toolbar button
tbrMain.Buttons(2).Enabled = objTextBox.SelectionLength
```

The next menu item in the Edit menu is Copy menu item. Again, you use the `SelectionLength` property to determine whether any text is selected in the text box. If no text is selected, you do not want to allow the user to perform the copy operation and you disable the Copy menu items and toolbar button:

```
'Toggle the Edit\Copy menu item
mnuEditCopy.Enabled = objTextBox.SelectionLength
'Toggle the Copy context menu item
cmuCopy.Enabled = objTextBox.SelectionLength
'Toggle the Copy toolbar button
tbrMain.Buttons(3).Enabled = objTextBox.SelectionLength
```

The next menu item in the Edit menu is the Paste menu item. Setting the `Enabled` property of this menu item requires a little more work.

Using the Clipboard object you invoke the `GetDataObject` method, which retrieves the data that is on the Clipboard. Then using the `GetDataPresent` method, and passing it an argument of `DataFormats.Text`, you can determine whether the data on the Clipboard is text data.

The `DataFormat` class provides static clipboard data format names. The clipboard can contain text, images, and objects so you need a way to determine whether the data on the clipboard is text and this is it.

The `GetDataPresent` method returns a Boolean value indicating whether the clipboard contains data in text format. Using this return value you can set the `Enabled` property of the Paste menu item, context menu item, and the Paste toolbar button as shown in the following code:

```
'Toggle the Edit\Paste menu item
mnuEditPaste.Enabled = _
    Clipboard.GetDataObject().GetDataPresent(DataFormats.Text)
```

```
'Toggle the Paste context menu item
cmuPaste.Enabled = _
    Clipboard.GetDataObject().GetDataPresent(DataFormats.Text)
'Toggle the Paste toolbar button
tbrMain.Buttons(4).Enabled = _
    Clipboard.GetDataObject().GetDataPresent(DataFormats.Text)
```

*You can view the MSDN Library that is installed with Visual Studio .NET to see more information about
the* Clipboard *class and to view a complete list of its members.*

The last Edit menu item is the Select All menu item. Again, you use the SelectionLength property to
determine whether any text has been selected. If all of the text has been selected, then you set the
Enabled property to False, and set it to True at all other times. To do so you compare the length of the
selected text to the length of the text in the text box:

```
'Toggle the Edit\Select All menu item
mnuEditSellectAll.Enabled = objTextBox.SelectionLength < _
    objTextBox.Text.Length
'Toggle the Select All context menu item
cmuSellectAll.Enabled = objTextBox.SelectionLength < _
    objTextBox.Text.Length
End Sub
```

Summary

This chapter looks at how to implement menus and context menus. You saw how to implement toolbars,
although that was not the focus of the chapter. Through practical hands-on exercises you have seen how
to create menus, menu items, and submenu items. You have also seen how to add access keys and
shortcut keys to these menu items.

Since you used the Edit menu in the *Try It Outs* you have also seen how easy it is to implement basic
editing techniques in your application using the Clipboard object and the properties of the TextBox
control. You can see how easy it is to provide this functionality to your users—something users have
come to expect in every good Windows application.

You also explored how to create and implement context menus and to override the default context menus
provided by Windows. Since you had already coded the procedure to implement cut, copy, and paste
operations you simply reused these in your context menus.

Now that you have completed work in this chapter, you should know how to:

❑   Add a MainMenu control to your form and add menus, menu items, and submenu items

❑   Customize the menu items with a checkmark or radiocheck

❑   Add access keys and shortcut keys to your menu items

❑   Add a ContextMenu control to your form and add menu items

❑   Use the properties of the TextBox control to toggle the Enabled property of menu items

Exercises

1. How do you specify an access key for a menu item?
2. Can you specify any shortcut key that you want?
3. Can you specify checkmarks and radiochecks in a context menu?
4. Can you create submenu items in a context menu?
5. Can you create as many menu items as you want?

Debugging and Error Handling

Debugging is an essential part of any development project as it helps you find errors in your code and in your logic. Visual Studio .NET has a sophisticated debugger built right into the development environment. This debugger is the same for all languages that Visual Studio .NET supports. So once you have mastered debugging in one language, you can debug in any language that you can write in Visual Studio .NET.

No matter how good your code is, there are always going to be some unexpected circumstances that you have not thought of, which will cause your code to fail. If you do not anticipate and handle errors, your users will see a default error message about an unhandled exception that is provided by the common language runtime. This is not a user-friendly message and usually does not clearly inform the user about what is going on or how to correct it.

This is where error handling comes in. Visual Studio .NET also provides common error handling functions that are used across all languages. These functions allow you to test some code and catch any errors that may occur. If an error does occur, you can write your own user-friendly message that informs the user of what happened and how to correct it. You also get to control execution of your code at this point and allow the user to try the operation again if it makes sense to do so.

This chapter looks at some of the debugging features available in Visual Studio .NET and provides a walk through of debugging a program. You examine how to set breakpoints in your code to stop execution at any given point, how to watch the value of a variable change, and how to control the number of times a loop can execute before stopping. All of these can help you determine just what is going on inside your code. Finally, this chapter takes a detailed look at the structured error-handling functions provided by Visual Studio .NET.

In this chapter you will:

❑   Examine the major types of errors that you may encounter and how to correct them

❑   Examine and walk through debugging a program

❑   Examine and implement error handling in a program

Major Error Types

Error types can be broken down into three major categories: syntax, execution, and logic. This section will show you the important differences between these three types of errors and how to correct them.

Knowing what type of errors are possible and how to correct them will significantly speed up the development process. Of course, there are times when you just can't find the error on your own. Don't waste too much time trying to find errors in your code by yourself in these situations. Coming back to a nagging problem after a short coffee break can often help you crack it, otherwise ask a colleague to have a look at your code with you; two pairs of eyes are often better than one in these cases.

Syntax Errors

Syntax errors, the easiest type of errors to spot and fix, occur when the code you have written cannot be "understood" by the compiler because instructions are incomplete, supplied in unexpected order, or cannot be processed at all. An example of this would be declaring a variable of one name and misspelling this name in your code when you set or query the variable.

The development environment in Visual Studio .NET has a pretty sophisticated syntax-checking mechanism making it hard, but not impossible, to have syntax errors in your code. It provides instant syntax checking of variables and objects and will let you know immediately when you have a syntax error.

When you try to use a variable or object that you have not declared, the development environment will underline the variable or object name. This is your clue that a syntax error has occurred. If you hover your mouse over the syntax error, the development environment will display a ToolTip, as shown in Figure 9-1, informing you of the error.

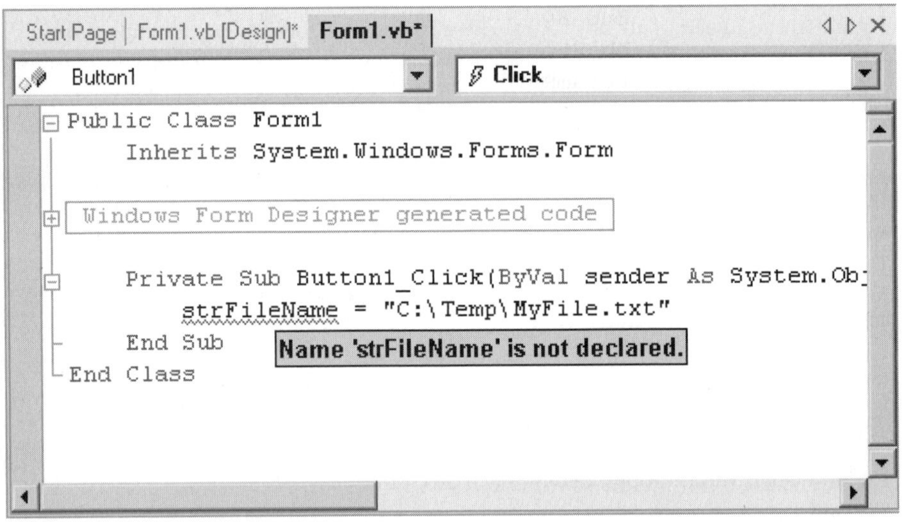

Figure 9-1

This highlighting of undeclared variables occurs only if you have not changed the Option Explicit option in the project Property Pages dialog box, which by default is turned on. This also assumes that you have not specified the `Option Explicit Off` statement in code, which overrides the Option Explicit option in the project Property Pages dialog box.

The Option Explicit option or the statement `Object Explicit On` forces you to declare all variables before using them. This means that Visual Studio .NET can provide guidance such as that shown in Figure 9-1, and also means that misspellings of variable names will be trapped by the compiler.

When this option or statement is turned off, all variables that are not explicitly declared are assumed to be of the `Object` data type. An `Object` data type can hold any type of value (for example, numeric or string) but it processes these values more slowly than the correct data type for the value being used. Therefore, it is good practice to always have the Option Explicit option turned on, which is the default.

The development environment also provides IntelliSense to assist in preventing syntax errors. IntelliSense provides a host of features such as providing a drop-down list of members for classes, structures, and namespaces as shown in Figure 9-2. This allows you to choose the correct member for the class, structure, or namespace that you are working with.

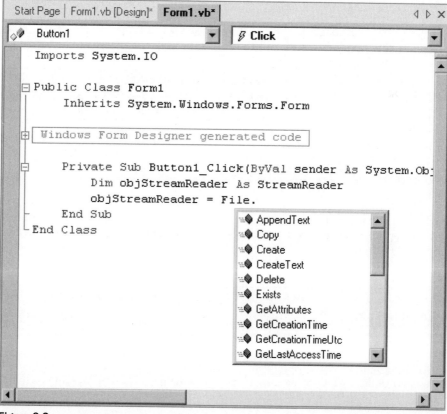

Figure 9-2

These IntelliSense features provide two major benefits. First, you do not have to remember all of the available members for the class. You simply scroll through the list to find the member that you want to work with. To select the member in the list that you want to work with, you press the *Tab* or *Enter* key, or double-click the member. Second, it helps to prevent syntax errors because you are less likely to misspell member names or try to use members that do not exist in the given class.

Another great feature of IntelliSense is that it provides a parameter list for the method that you are working with. IntelliSense will list the number, name, and type of the parameters required by the function, as shown in Figure 9-3. This is also a time saver, as you do not have to remember the required parameters for every class that you work with, or indeed search the product documentation for what you need.

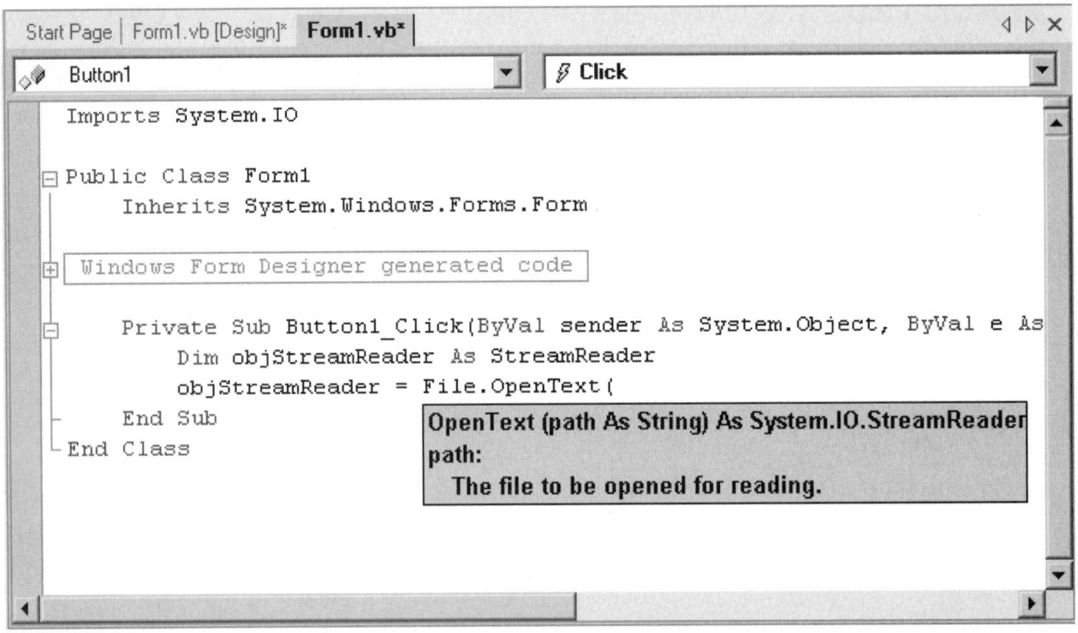

Figure 9-3

If the method is overloaded, that is, there are several methods with the same name but different parameters, a pop-up list enables you to scroll through the different options, as shown in Figure 9-4 for the `File.Open` method.

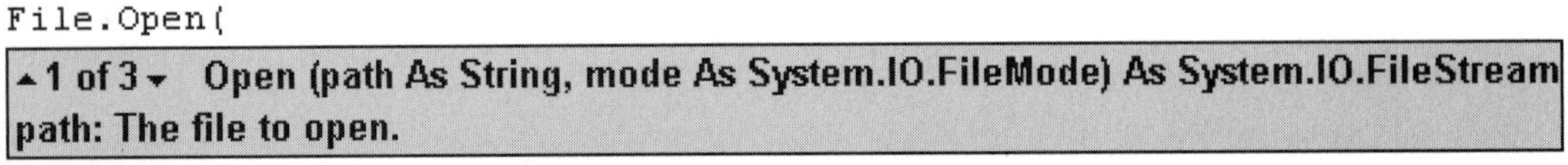

```
File.Open(
```

```
▲1 of 3 ▼  Open (path As String, mode As System.IO.FileMode) As System.IO.FileStream
path: The file to open.
```

Figure 9-4

Plenty of built-in features in the development environment can help prevent syntax errors. All you need to do is to be aware of these features and take advantage of them to help prevent syntax errors in your code.

Execution Errors

Execution errors (or *runtime errors*) are errors that occur while your program is executing. These errors are often caused because something outside of the application, such as a user, database, or hard disk, does not behave as expected.

Developers need to anticipate the possibility of execution errors and build appropriate error-handling logic. Implementing the appropriate error handling will not prevent execution errors, but will allow you to handle them either by gracefully shutting down your application or bypassing the code that failed and giving the user the opportunity to perform that action again. Error handling is covered later in this chapter.

The best way to prevent execution errors is to try anticipating the error before it occurs and to use error handling to trap and handle the error. You must also thoroughly test your code before deploying it.

Most execution errors can be found while you are testing your code in the development environment. This allows you to handle the errors and debug your code at the same time. You can then see what type of errors may occur and implement the appropriate error handling logic. Debugging is covered later in the *Debugging* section where you find and handle any execution errors that may crop up.

Logic Errors

Logic errors (or *semantic errors*) are errors that give unexpected or unwanted results because you did not fully understand what the code you were writing did. Probably the most common logic error is an infinite loop:

```
Private Sub PerformLoopExample()
    Dim n As Integer
    Do While n < 10
        ' some logic here
    Loop
End Sub
```

If the code inside the loop does not set n to 10 or above, then this loop will just keep going forever. This is a very simple example, but even experienced developers find themselves writing and executing loops where the exit condition can never be satisfied.

Logic errors can be the most difficult to find and troubleshoot, because it is very difficult to be sure that your program is completely free from logic errors.

Another type of logic error is when a comparison fails to give the result you expect. Say you made a comparison between a string variable set by your code from a database field or from the text in a file and the text entered by the user. You do not want the comparison to be case sensitive. You might write code like this:

```
If fileName = userInput.Text Then
     ...perform some logic
End If
```

However, if fileName is set to Index.HTML and userInput.Text is set to index.html, the comparison will fail. One way to prevent this logic error is to convert both fields being compared to either uppercase or lowercase. This way, the results of the comparison would be True if the user entered the same text as was contained in the variable, even if the case was different. The next code fragment shows how we can accomplish this:

```
If fileName.ToUpper = userInput.Text.ToUpper Then
     ...perform some logic
End If
```

The ToUpper method of the String class converts the characters in the string to all uppercase and returns the converted results. Since the Text property of a TextBox is also a string, you can use the same method to convert the text to all upper case. This would make the comparison in the previous example equal.

Since logic errors are the hardest errors to troubleshoot and can cause applications to fail or give unexpected and unwanted results, you must check the logic carefully as you code and try to plan for all possible errors that may be encountered by a user. As you become more experienced you will encounter and learn from the common errors that your users make.

One of the best ways to identify and fix logic errors is to use the debugging features of Visual Studio .NET. Using these features you can find loops that execute too many times or comparisons that do not give the expected result.

Debugging

Debugging code is a part of life—even experienced developers will make mistakes and need to debug their code. Knowing how to efficiently debug your code can make the difference between enjoying your job as a developer and hating it.

Creating a Sample Project

In this section, you take a look at some of the built-in debugging features in the Visual Studio .NET development environment. You write a simple program and learn how to use the most common and useful debugging features available.

You begin this process by creating a program that will use the OpenFileDialog class to display the Open File dialog box to allow users to choose a text file to open. You then open and read the chosen text file line by line using the StreamReader class and place the contents into a text box on the form. You keep track of the number of lines read and the current and previous files opened.

Try It Out   Creating a Sample Project to Debug

1. Create a new Windows Application project called **Debugging** and click the OK button to have the project created.

2. In the Solution Explorer window, change the form name from Form1.vb to **Debug.vb** and then set the form's properties as shown:

   ❑ Set FormBorderStyle to FixedDialog

   ❑ Set MaximizeBox to False

   ❑ Set MinimizeBox to False

   ❑ Set Size to 408, 304

   ❑ Set StartPosition to CenterScreen.

   ❑ Set Text to **Debug Demo**

3. Next, you want to add some basic controls to the form and set their properties, as shown in the following list:

   ❑ Create a TextBox control. Name it **txtData**, and set these properties: Location = 8, 8; Multiline = True; ScrollBars = Vertical; Size = 304, 192; Text = *blank*.

❑ Create a Button control named **btnOpen** and set these properties: Location = 320, 8; Size = 75, 23; Text = Open.

❑ Create a Button control named **btnClear** and set these properties: Location = 320, 40; Size = 75, 23; Text = Clear.

❑ Create a Label control named **lblLines** and set these properties: Location = 8, 208; Size = 152, 16; Text = Number of lines read: 0.

❑ Create a Label control named **lblLastFile** and set these properties: Location = 8, 232; Size = 296, 16; Text = Last file opened: None.

❑ Create a Label control named **lblCurrentFile** and set these properties: Location = 8, 256; Size = 296, 16; Text = Current file opened: None.

Your completed form should like Figure 9-5.

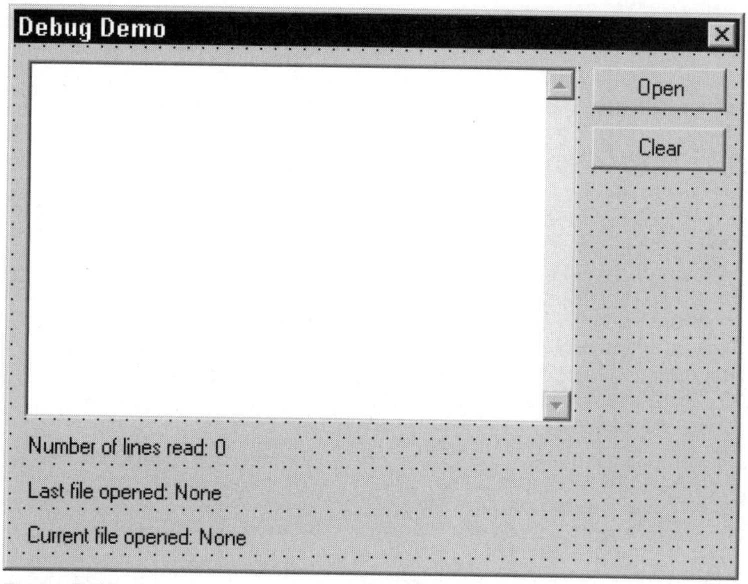

Figure 9-5

4. Add the following code to the top of the Debug.vb source:

```
' Namespace for StreamReader...
Imports System.IO
```

5. Add the following code just below the Windows Forms Designer generated code region:

```
    'Declare variables
    Dim strLastFileName As String = "None"

    Public Sub btnOpen_Click(ByVal sender As System.Object, ByVal e As
System.EventArgs) Handles btnOpen.Click
        ' Declare an object for the OpenFileDialog class...
        Dim objOpenFileDialog As OpenFileDialog = New OpenFileDialog
```

```vb
        ' Set the dialog properties...
    With objOpenFileDialog
        .Filter = "Text files (*.txt)|*.txt|All files (*.*)|*.*"
        .FilterIndex = 1
        .InitialDirectory = "C:\Temp\"
        .Title = "Open File"
        .CheckFileExists = False
    End With

    ' Show the dialog...
    If objOpenFileDialog.ShowDialog() = DialogResult.OK Then
        ' Process the file chosen...
        ProcessFile(objOpenFileDialog.FileName)
        ' Display the last file opened...
        lblLastFile.Text = "Last file opened: " & strLastFileName
        ' Display the current file opened...
        lblCurrentFile.Text = "Current file opened: " & _
                            objOpenFileDialog.FileName
        ' Save the new file as the last file opened...
        strLastFileName = objOpenFileDialog.FileName
    End If

    ' Clean up...
    objOpenFileDialog = Nothing
End Sub

Private Sub ProcessFile(ByVal strFileName As String)
    ' Declare an object for the StreamReader class...
    Dim objStreamReader As StreamReader

    ' Open the file...
    objStreamReader = File.OpenText(strFileName)

    ' Declare variables...
    Dim intLineCounter As Integer = 0
    Dim strCurrentLine As String, strCurrentData As String

    ' Loop through the file counting the lines and loading the
    ' text box...
    Do
        ' Read a line from the file...
        strCurrentLine = objStreamReader.ReadLine
        ' Increment the line counter
        intLineCounter += 1
        ' Concatenate the data to the strCurrentData variable...
        strCurrentData &= strCurrentLine & ControlChars.CrLf
    Loop Until strCurrentLine Is Nothing

    ' Load the text box...
    txtData.Text = strCurrentData

    ' Display the number of lines read...
    lblLines.Text = "Number of lines read: " & _
                        intLineCounter - 1
```

```
            ' Clean up...
            objStreamReader.Close()
            objStreamReader = Nothing
    End Sub

    Public Sub btnClear_Click(ByVal sender As System.Object, ByVal e As
System.EventArgs) Handles btnClear.Click
            ' Clear variables...
            strLastFileName = ""

            ' Clear form fields...
            txtData.Text = ""

            ' Reset the labels...
            lblLines.Text = "Number of lines read: 0"
            lblLastFile.Text = "Last file opened: None"
            lblCurrentFile.Text = "Current file opened: None"
    End Sub
```

How It Works

Most of this code is pretty familiar—the real purpose of it is to give you something to play with while debugging. The most interesting section of this code is the Do...Loop in the ProcessFile procedure:

```
    Do
            ' Read a line from the file...
            strCurrentLine = objStreamReader.ReadLine
            ' Increment the line counter
            intLineCounter += 1
            ' Concatenate the data to the strCurrentData variable...
            strCurrentData &= strCurrentLine & ControlChars.CrLf
    Loop Until strCurrentLine Is Nothing
```

The first line of code in this loop uses the StreamReader object objReader to read a line of text from the text file, and to set the variable strCurrentLine to the data that has been read. The next line of code increments the intLineCounter variable to reflect the number of lines read.

The last line of code is concatenating the data read into the variable strCurrentData. After each line of text that you concatenate to the strCurrentData variable, you place a carriage return and line feed character using the CrLf constant from the ControlChars class. This causes the text in your text box to appear on separate lines instead of all on one line. You need to do this because when the StreamReader class reads a line of text it returns the line to you without the carriage return and line feed characters. The rest of the code should be familiar to you from Chapter 8.

Setting Breakpoints

When trying to debug a large program you may find that you want to debug only a section of code, that is, you want your code to run up to a certain point and then stop. This is where breakpoints come in handy; they cause execution of your code to stop anywhere a breakpoint is defined. You can set breakpoints anywhere in your code and your code will run up to that point and stop.

Note that execution of the code will stop before *the line on which the breakpoint is set.*

You can set breakpoints when you write your code and you can also set them at runtime by switching to your code and setting the breakpoint at the desired location. You cannot set a breakpoint while your program is actually executing a section of code such as the code in a loop, but you can when the program is idle and waiting for user input.

When the development environment encounters a breakpoint, execution of your code halts and your program is considered to be in break mode. While your program is in break mode, a lot of debugging features are available. In fact, a lot of debugging features are only available to you while your program is in break mode. Figure 9-6 shows what happens when executing code reaches a breakpoint.

```
Start Page | Debug.vb [Design]  Debug.vb |                           ◁ ▷ ✕

 ⬦  btnOpen                    ▼   ⨏ Click                              ▼
               .Title = "Open File"                                    ▲
               .CheckFileExists = False
          End With

          ' Show the dialog...
 ⇨        If objOpenFileDialog.ShowDialog() = DialogResult.OK Then
               ' Process the file chosen...
               ProcessFile(objOpenFileDialog.FileName)
               ' Display the last file opened...
               lblLastFile.Text = "Last file opened: " & strLastFileName
               ' Display the current file opened...
               lblCurrentFile.Text = "Current file opened: " & _
                                     objOpenFileDialog.FileName
               ' Save the new file as the last file opened...
               strLastFileName = objOpenFileDialog.FileName
          End If                                                       ▼
 ◁                                                                ▷
```

Figure 9-6

You can set breakpoints by clicking the gray margin next to the line of code on which you want to set the breakpoint. When the breakpoint is set you will see a solid red circle in the gray margin and the line will be highlighted in red. When you are done with a particular breakpoint you can remove it by clicking the solid red circle. You see more of this in the *Try It Out* exercise in this section.

Sometimes you'll want to debug code in a loop, such as one that reads data from a file. You know that the first x number of records are good, and it is time consuming to step through all the code repetitively until you get to what you suspect is the bad record. A breakpoint can be set inside the loop and you can set a hit counter on it. The code inside the loop will execute the number of times that you specified in the hit counter and then stop and place you in break mode. This can be a real time saver and you will be taking a look at this in the next *Try It Out*. You can also set a condition on a breakpoint, such as when a variable contains a certain value or when the value of a variable changes. You also take a look at this in the *Try It Out*.

Before you begin, you should display the Debug toolbar in the development environment, as this will make it easier to quickly see and choose the debugging options that you want. You can do this in one of two ways. Either right-click an empty space on the current toolbar and choose Debug in the context menu or click View ➪ Toolbars ➪ Debug from the menu.

Try It Out   Working with Breakpoints

1.   The first thing to do is set a breakpoint in the openText_Click method—on the If statement that displays the Open File dialog, to be precise. To set the breakpoint, click on the gray margin to the left of the line where the desired breakpoint should be, as shown in Figure 9-7.

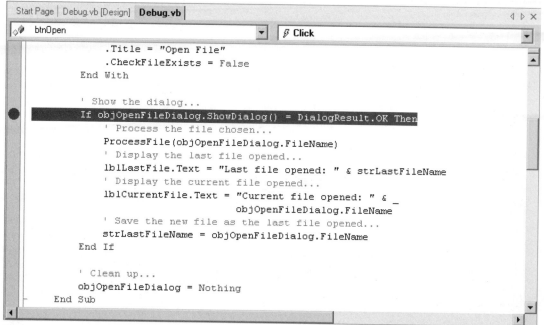

```
Start Page | Debug.vb [Design]  Debug.vb |                                    ◁ ▷ ×

⬦ btnOpen                                    ▾  ℬ Click                              ▾

                .Title = "Open File"
                .CheckFileExists = False
            End With

            ' Show the dialog...
●           If objOpenFileDialog.ShowDialog() = DialogResult.OK Then
                ' Process the file chosen...
                ProcessFile(objOpenFileDialog.FileName)
                ' Display the last file opened...
                lblLastFile.Text = "Last file opened: " & strLastFileName
                ' Display the current file opened...
                lblCurrentFile.Text = "Current file opened: " & _
                                      objOpenFileDialog.FileName
                ' Save the new file as the last file opened...
                strLastFileName = objOpenFileDialog.FileName
            End If

            ' Clean up...
            objOpenFileDialog = Nothing
        End Sub
◀                                                                                  ▶
```

Figure 9-7

2.   Now run the project.

3.   To get to the code where the breakpoint is set, click the Open button on your form. The code executes up to the breakpoint and the development environment window receives focus making it the topmost window. You should now see a yellow arrow on your breakpoint pointing to the line of code where execution has been paused and the entire line should be highlighted in yellow, as shown in Figure 9-8.

Also notice that there are a few new windows at the bottom of the development environment. What you see will vary depending on which windows you have specified to be shown—you can choose different ones using the tabs at the bottom.

Take a pause in the *Try It Out* to learn about some of the features of the IDE in debug mode.

The Breakpoints Window

You can display the Breakpoints window, if the tab is not shown, in the bottom-right of the IDE by clicking on the Breakpoints icon on the Debug toolbar or by clicking the Debug ⇨ Windows ⇨ Breakpoints. The Breakpoints window shows what line of code the current breakpoint is at, any conditions it has, and the hit count if applicable, as shown in Figure 9-9.

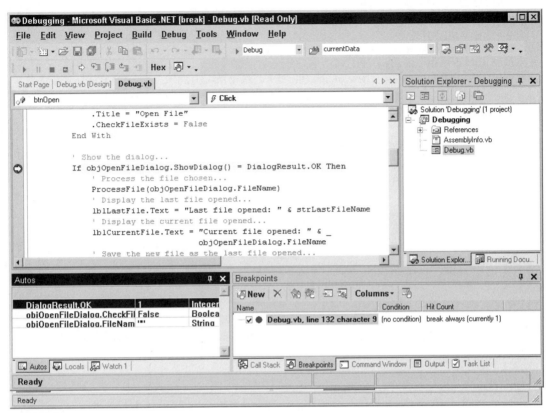

Figure 9-8

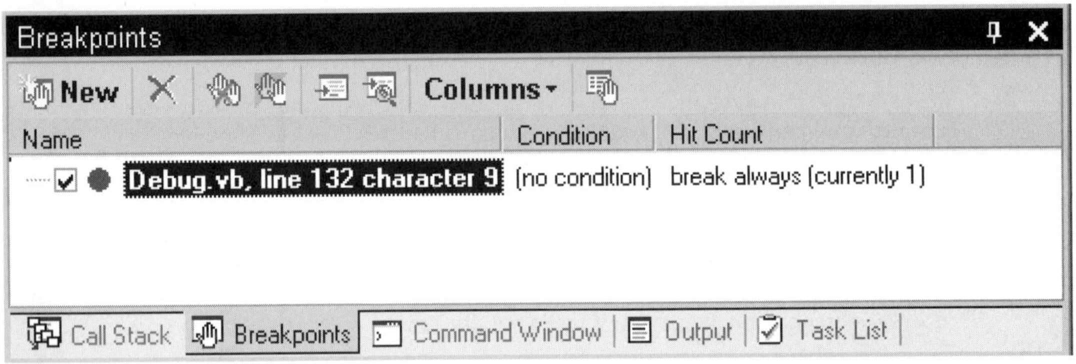

Figure 9-9

The Breakpoints window shows all of the breakpoints you have set, which in this case is only one. When a breakpoint is encountered, it will be highlighted as shown in Figure 9-9. In this window, you can set new breakpoints, delete existing breakpoints, and also change the properties of the breakpoints. You see more of this later in the chapter.

Useful Icons on the Debug Toolbar

In this *Try It Out*, you want to step through your code line by line. On the Debug toolbar there are three icons of particular interest to you as shown in Figure 9-10.

❑ The first icon is the *Step Into* icon. When you click this icon you can step through your code line-by-line. This includes stepping into any function or procedure that the code calls and working through them line by line.

❑ The second icon is the *Step Over* icon. This works in a similar way as Step Into, but you pass straight over the procedures and functions—they still execute, but all in one go. You then move straight on to the next line in the block of code that called the procedure.

❑ Last is the *Step Out* icon. This icon allows you to jump to the end of the procedure or function that you are currently in, and move to the line of code *after* the line that called the procedure or function. This is handy when you step into a long procedure and want to get out of it. The rest of the code in the procedure still gets executed, but we do not step through it.

Figure 9-10

There is one more really useful button worth adding to the toolbar —*Run To Cursor*. The Run To Cursor icon enables you to place your cursor anywhere in the code following the current breakpoint where execution has been paused and then click this icon. The code between the current breakpoint and where the cursor is positioned will be executed, and execution will stop on the line of code where the cursor is located.

To add this button, you right-click on any empty area of the toolbar and choose Customize from the context menu. In the Customize dialog click on the Commands tab, shown in Figure 9-11, and then click on Debug in the Categories list. In the Commands list click on Run To Cursor.

After you select Run To Cursor, you drag its icon from the Commands list onto the debug toolbar, to form a group of icons as shown in Figure 9-12 and then click the Close button to close the Customize dialog box.

You are now ready to continue working through the *Try It Out*.

Try It Out   **Working with Breakpoints (cont.)**

1. You ended the last step of the *Try It Out* at the breakpoint. Now click the Step Into icon. The Open File dialog should be displayed and should be the window with focus. Select a text file that you worked with in Chapter 8 and then click the Open button in the Open File dialog box.

If you didn't work through Chapter 8 then you need to create a text file, using something like Notepad, and save it in a suitable directory on your hard drive.

You should now be at the next line of code. This line of code calls the `ProcessFile` procedure and will process the file that you have selected:

```
ProcessFile(objOpenFileDialog.FileName)
```

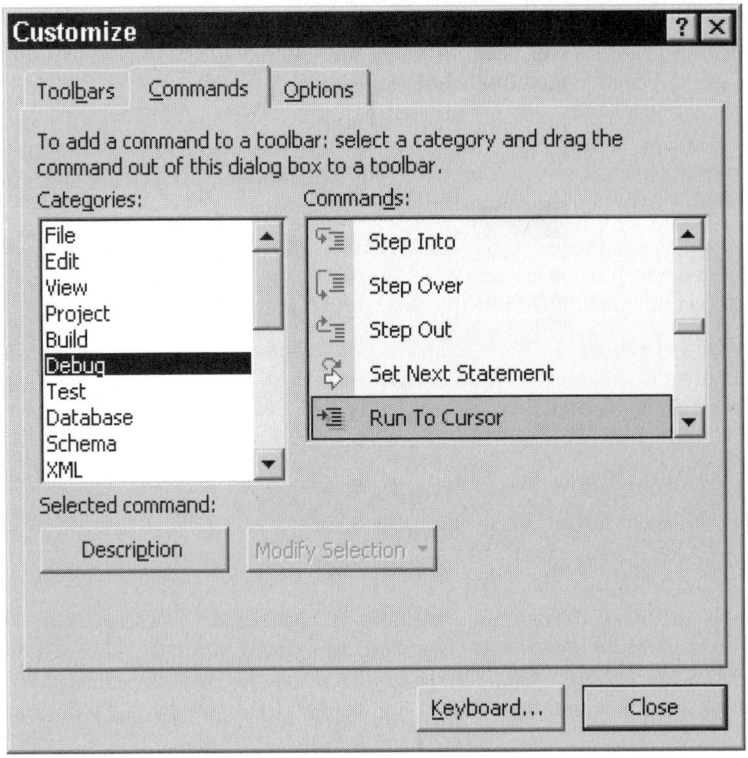

Customize

Toolbars	Commands	Options

To add a command to a toolbar: select a category and drag the
command out of this dialog box to a toolbar.

Categories:

File
Edit
View
Project
Build
Debug
Test
Database
Schema
XML

Commands:

Step Into
Step Over
Step Out
Set Next Statement
Run To Cursor

Selected command:

Description   Modify Selection

Keyboard...   Close

Figure 9-11

Figure 9-12

2. Click the Step Into icon again and you should be at the beginning of the `ProcessFile` procedure:

```
Private Sub ProcessFile(ByVal strFileName As String)
```

3. Click the Step Into icon once more and you should be at the first line of executable code, which is `objStreamReader = File.OpenText(strFileName)`. Since you do not want to see any of this code at this time, you are going to step out of this procedure. This will place us back on the line that called `ProcessFile`. We do this by clicking on the Step Out icon. Notice that you are taken out of the `ProcessFile` procedure and back to where the call originated.

4. Let's test one more icon. Place your cursor on the last line of code in this procedure (the one shown below). Then click on the Run To Cursor icon. All the code between the current line of code where execution is paused and the line of code where your cursor is will be executed, and the program will be paused again at the cursor.

```
objOpenFileDialog = Nothing
```

5. You want to continue processing as normal and have the rest of the code execute without interruption. If you hover your mouse over the Start icon on the toolbar you will notice that the Tool Tip has been changed from Start to Continue. Click on this icon to let the rest of the code run.

You should now see your completed form as shown in Figure 9-13. The labels of course will contain information that is relevant to the file that you opened.

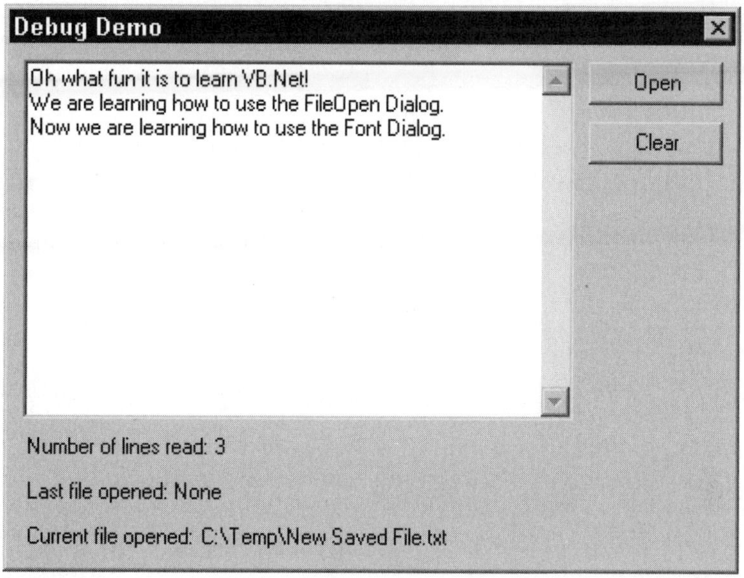

Figure 9-13

At this point, set another breakpoint in your code. This time you want to set a breakpoint in the Do loop of the ProcessFile procedure. In the next *Try It Out* you will be examining the Hit Count. The Hit Count allows you to define how many executions of a loop should be performed before the IDE stops execution of your code and puts it into break mode. This is useful for processing large files as you can read a certain number of records before you encounter a breakpoint.

Try It Out   Using the Breakpoint's Hit Count

1. Click on the left margin next to the following line of code to set the new breakpoint:

```
strCurrentLine = objStreamReader.ReadLine
```

2. In the Breakpoints window, click this breakpoint and then click on the Properties icon on the Breakpoints window's toolbar to invoke the Breakpoint Properties dialog box for this new breakpoint (see Figure 9-14).

3. The breakpoint you set will halt execution every time it is encountered. Change it to only break when the loop enters its third execution. You do this by clicking the Hit Count button to invoke the Breakpoint Hit Count dialog box. In the drop down in this dialog box, select *Break When The Hit Count Is Equal To* and then enter the number 3 in the text box displayed next to it as shown in Figure 9-15.

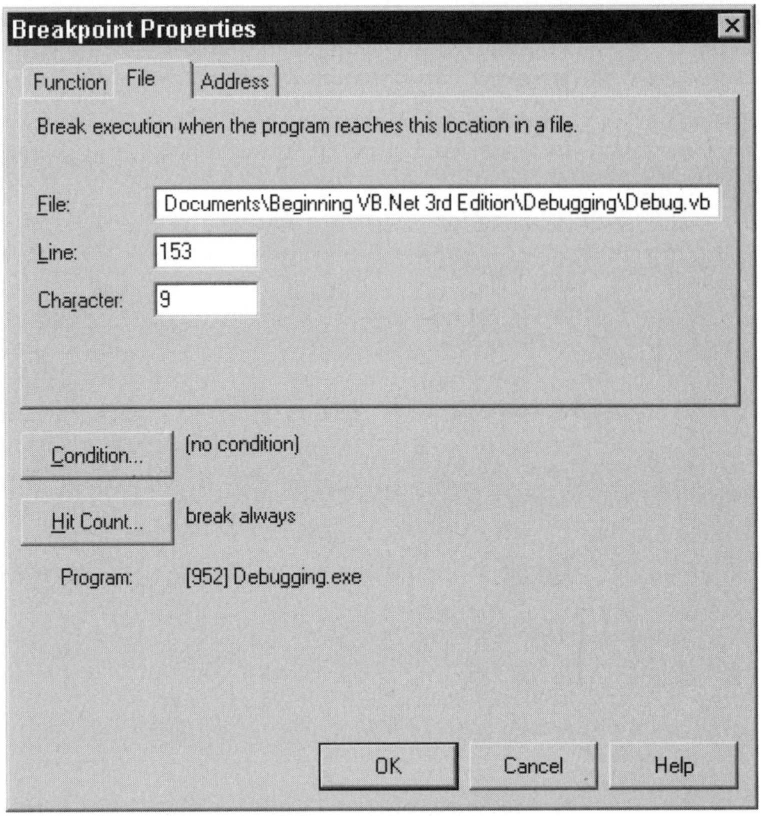

Breakpoint Properties ☒

Function | File | Address

Break execution when the program reaches this location in a file.

File: Documents\Beginning VB.Net 3rd Edition\Debugging\Debug.vb

Line: 153

Character: 9

Condition... | (no condition)

Hit Count... | break always

Program: [952] Debugging.exe

OK | Cancel | Help

Figure 9-14

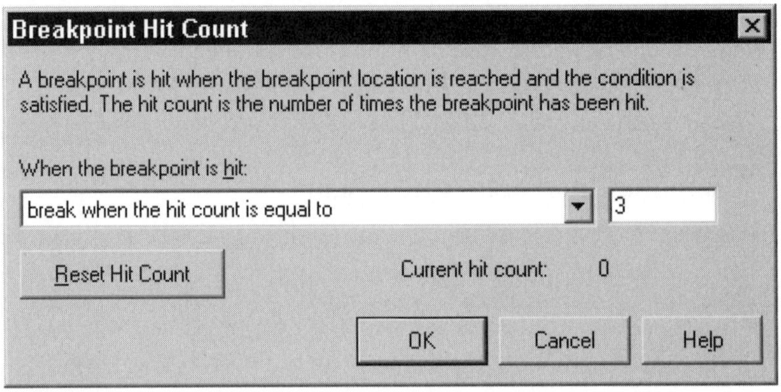

Breakpoint Hit Count ☒

A breakpoint is hit when the breakpoint location is reached and the condition is satisfied. The hit count is the number of times the breakpoint has been hit.

When the breakpoint is hit:

break when the hit count is equal to ▼ | 3

 Reset Hit Count | Current hit count: 0

OK | Cancel | Help

Figure 9-15

Click the OK button to close this dialog box and then click the OK button to close the Breakpoint Properties dialog box. Your program is still in run mode and just waiting to do something.

4. At this point, click on the Open button on the form. By clicking on the Open button you are again stopped at your first breakpoint.

5. This breakpoint is highlighted in the Breakpoints window and you no longer need it, so delete it. Click the Delete icon in the Breakpoints window and the breakpoint will be deleted. Your code is still paused at this point, so click the Continue button on the Debug toolbar.

6. The Open File dialog box is displayed and this time you want to choose a different text file. Ensure that this file has at least three lines of text in it and then click the Open button to have the file opened and processed.

7. You are now stopped at your breakpoint in the `ProcessFile` procedure as the loop enters its third execution. Notice that the Breakpoints window shows the hit count criteria that you selected and also the current hit count, as shown in Figure 9-16. If you hover your mouse pointer over any of the variables in this procedure, the current contents of the variables will be displayed in a ToolTip tip. This is a quick and handy way to see the contents of your variables while your code is paused.

This also works for properties of objects such as the text box on the form. If you hover your mouse over the Text property of the txtData text box, you will see the current contents of the text box. Notice that the content of the Text property is from the previous file that you opened, as you have not yet set it to the contents of the current file you are reading.

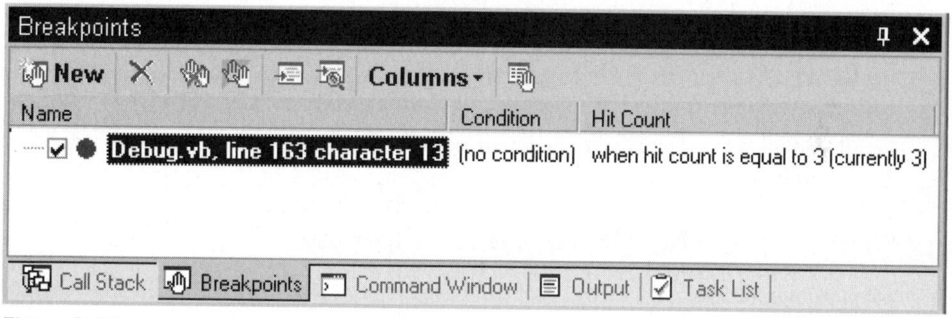

Figure 9-16

8. Now let your code continue executing by clicking on the Continue button on the Debug toolbar.

This time let's modify the properties of the only breakpoint that you have left.

Try It Out   Changing Breakpoint Properties

1. In the Breakpoints window click the Properties icon to invoke the Breakpoint Properties dialog box.

2. Click the Hit Count button to invoke the Breakpoint Hit Count dialog box. Notice the Reset Hit Count button. When you click this button you reset the hit counter for the next execution. Also, notice that this dialog box displays the current hit count.

3. You have to change the hit count back to its original setting so select *break always* in the drop-down box and then click the OK button to close this dialog box.

4. In the Breakpoints Properties dialog, you want to set a specific condition for this breakpoint so click on the Condition button to invoke Breakpoint Condition dialog box. Enter the condition as shown in Figure 9-17. This will cause this breakpoint to break only when the variable `intLineCounter` is equal to 3. Notice that you could also specify that the breakpoint would be activated when the value of a variable changes. Click the OK button to close the dialog box and then click the OK button in the Breakpoint Properties dialog box to close it.

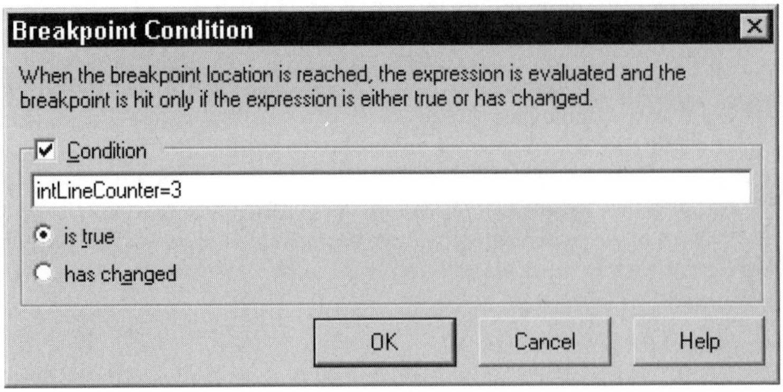

Breakpoint Condition ✕

When the breakpoint location is reached, the expression is evaluated and the breakpoint is hit only if the expression is either true or has changed.

☑ Condition

intLineCounter=3

◉ is true

○ has changed

OK   Cancel   Help

Figure 9-17

5. Now switch back to your form and open another file that has at least three lines of text. If you wish, this can be the file that you just opened. Once the `intLineCounter` variable is equal to 3, the breakpoint will be activated and the execution of the code will be paused at the line where the breakpoint is specified. Notice that this is actually our fourth time into the loop as the line of code that increments the `intLineCounter` variable is the next line of code.

6. Finally, go ahead and let your code finish executing by clicking the Continue button on the Debug toolbar.

Debugging Using the Command Window

The *Command window* (also known as the *Immediate window*) can be a very powerful ally when debugging your programs. It allows you to control the execution and outcome of your program by letting you query and set the values of variables. You can even write small amounts of code in the Command window to alter the outcome of your program such as closing objects or changing values. The Command window only allows you to enter code while your program is in break mode, but you can view the contents of the Command window at design time.

For instance, suppose you are debugging your program and you query the value of a variable. The results of that query are listed in the Command window. Once you stop executing your code you can view the Command window and see the results of the commands that you executed, allowing you to make any adjustments to your code as necessary. Let's see how you can use the Command window while debugging. In the following *Try It Out*, you use the Command window to query and set the value of various variables defined in your program. Once you are done, you stop your program and then display the Command window while you are in design mode.

Try It Out   **Using the Command Window**

1. If you previously stopped your program, start it again by clicking Start on the toolbar.

2. You should still have the breakpoint set. If not, set it on the following line of code and to break when `intLineCounter = 3`:

```
strCurrentLine = objStreamReader.ReadLine
```

3. Click the Open button on your form and open a text file that has at least three lines of text in it.

4. After the breakpoint has been activated, you can enter commands in the Command window. If you do not see the Command window at the bottom of the development environment, select Windows ⇨ Immediate from the Debug menu.

5. To query the value of variables in the Command window, you need to type a question mark followed by the variable name. Type: **?strCurrentData**, then press *Enter* to view the results as shown in Figure 9-18.

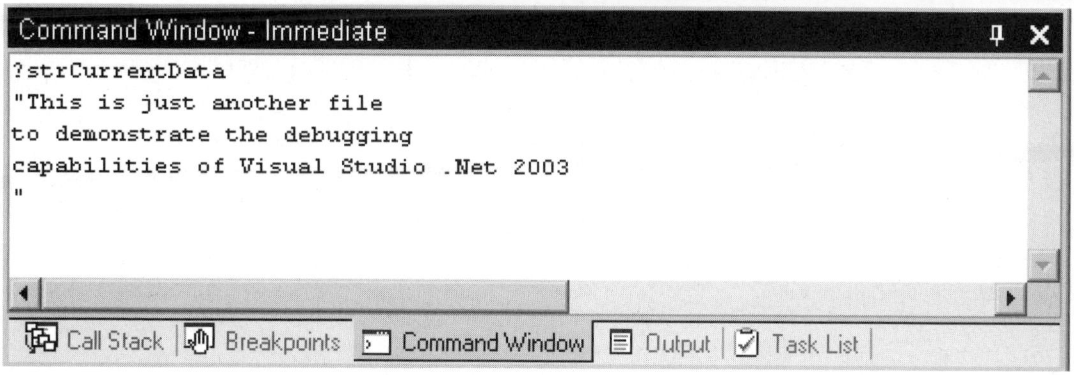

```
Command Window - Immediate                              ⊉ ✕
?strCurrentData
"This is just another file
to demonstrate the debugging
capabilities of Visual Studio .Net 2003
"
```
| 🔲 Call Stack | 🖐 Breakpoints | 📋 Command Window | 📄 Output | ☑ Task List |

Figure 9-18

6. To change the value of a variable, you type the variable name followed by an equal sign (=) followed by the value that you want it to be, just as you would normally set your variables in code. Take note of Figure 9-18. Since this is a string variable the results are returned in a pair of quotation marks (" "). Thus, if you want to change the value of this variable, you need to enclose the value in quotation marks as shown in Figure 9-19. Change the value of this variable to the phrase "debugging can be easy." Once you type in the text press *Enter* to have the value set.

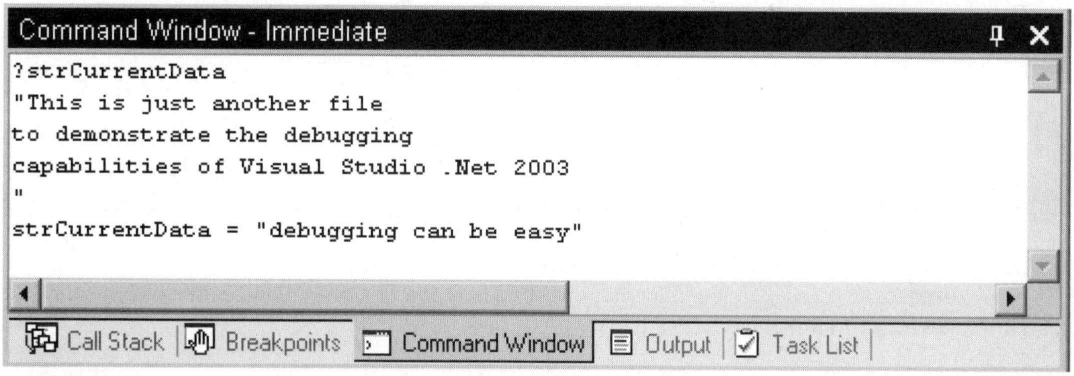

```
Command Window - Immediate                              ⊉ ✕
?strCurrentData
"This is just another file
to demonstrate the debugging
capabilities of Visual Studio .Net 2003
"
strCurrentData = "debugging can be easy"
```
| 🔲 Call Stack | 🖐 Breakpoints | 📋 Command Window | 📄 Output | ☑ Task List |

Figure 9-19

7. At this point, your code is still paused and you want to exit the loop. Skip over the rest of the code in the loop and start with the next line of code following the `Loop Until` statement. To do this, click the yellow arrow on the breakpoint and hold down the left mouse button. Then drag the arrow to the following line of code and release the left mouse button. The yellow arrow should now be on this line of code:

```
txtData.Text = strCurrentData
```

This method allows you to skip over code and not have it executed.

8. When you click the Continue button, execution of your code will start from this point forward. Go ahead and click the Continue button and let the rest of the code run. The text box on your form should show the phrase that you entered in the Command window.

9. End the program by clicking on the X in the upper right-hand corner of the form.

10. From the Debug menu in the development environment select Windows ➪ Immediate to have the Command window displayed. Notice that you will see all of the commands that you executed. This is very handy when you are debugging code and need to see what values certain variables contained.

You can clear the contents of the Command window by right-clicking in the window and choosing Clear All from the context menu.

Debugging Using the Watch Window

The Watch window provides a method for you to easily watch variables and expressions as the code is executing—this can be invaluable when you are trying to debug unwanted results in a variable. You can even change the values of variables in the Watch window. You can add as many variables and expressions as needed to debug your program. This provides a mechanism to watch the values of your variables change without any intervention on your part, as was needed when we used the Command window.

You can only add and delete a variable or expression to the QuickWatch dialog box when your program is in break mode. Therefore, before you run your program you need to set a breakpoint before the variable or expression that you want to watch. Once the breakpoint has been reached you can add as many Watch variables or expressions as needed.

In the following *Try It Out* you add the `intLineCounter` variable to the Watch window and also add an expression using the `intLineCounter` variable. This enables you to observe this variable and expression as you step through your code.

Try It Out   Using QuickWatch

1. Start your program again and if you have cleared the breakpoint that you have been using you need to set it again on the following line of code in the ProcessFile procedure, but this time do not set a condition:

```
strCurrentLine = objStreamReader.ReadLine
```

2. If you did not clear the breakpoint, you need to modify its condition. Bring up the Breakpoint Properties dialog box for the breakpoint using Debug ➪ Windows ➪ Breakpoints, highlight the desired breakpoint and click the Properties icon. Next, click the Condition button and in the

Breakpoint Condition dialog remove all the text from the text box. Click the OK button to close the dialog box and then click OK to close the Breakpoint Properties dialog box. This will cause this breakpoint to pause the program the first time it is encountered.

3. You can add a QuickWatch variable or expression only while your program is paused. You can pause the program before the breakpoint is encountered or you can wait until the breakpoint is encountered and the code is paused for you. Choose the latter. Click the Open button on the form and select a text file to open.

4. Once the breakpoint has been encountered, click the Debug menu and select QuickWatch to invoke the QuickWatch dialog box. Notice that the Expression drop-down box contains the variable where the breakpoint is currently set. You can enter a variable or expression at this point if you choose. However, to demonstrate another method click the Close button in the QuickWatch dialog box.

5. Now back in your code window, right-click the `intLineCounter` variable below the breakpoint and select QuickWatch from the context menu. Notice that this variable has not only been added to the Expression drop-down box but has also been placed in the Current value grid in the dialog, as shown in Figure 9-20. Click the Add Watch button to add this variable to the Watch window.

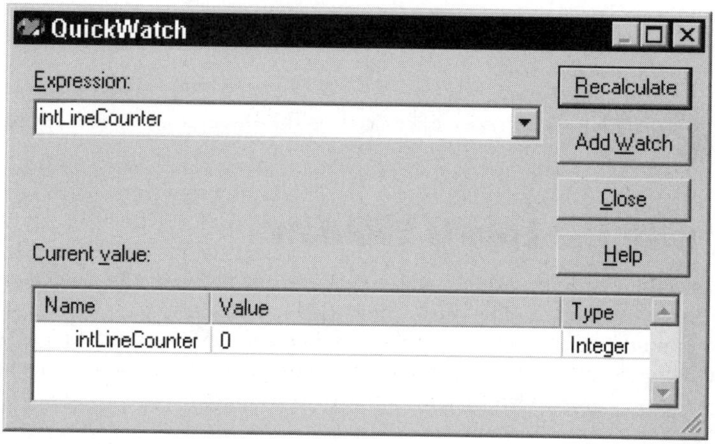

Figure 9-20

Note that if your computer displays the value as &H0, it means that Hex mode is switched on and values will be displayed in hexadecimal. Click the Hex button on the Debug toolbar to toggle this setting.

6. While you have the QuickWatch dialog box open, set an expression to be evaluated. Add the expression `intLineCounter = 1` in the Expression drop-down box. Then click the Add Watch button to have this expression added to the Watch window. Now close the QuickWatch dialog by clicking on the Close button.

7. If you do not see the Watch window at the bottom of the development environment, click on the Debug ⇨ Windows ⇨ Watch ⇨ Watch 1 menu item. You should now see a variable and an expression in the Watch window as shown in Figure 9-21.

The second watch expression that you added here returns a value of `True` when the `intLineCounter` variable equals 1, so Visual Studio .NET has set the Type to Boolean.

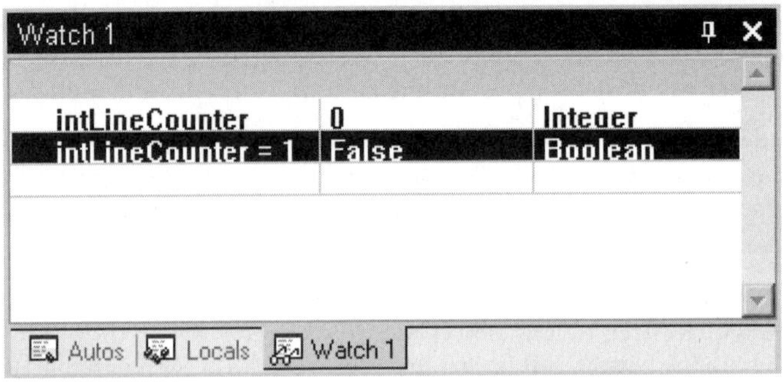

Figure 9-21

8. Step through your code line by line so that you can watch the value of the variable and expression change. Click on the Step Into icon on the Debug toolbar to step to the next line of code. Click once more to see the value of both the variable and expression in the Watch window change.

As you step through the loop in your code you will continue to see the value for the intLineCounter *variable change in the Watch window. When the value of the variable in the Watch window turns red, the value has just been changed. You can manually change the value anytime by entering a new value in the Value column in the Watch window.*

9. When you are done click the Continue icon on the Debug toolbar to let your code finish executing.

Debugging with the Locals Window

The *Locals window* is similar to the Watch window except that it shows all variables and objects for executing the current function or procedure. The Locals window also lets you change the value of a variable or object and the same rules that apply to the Watch window apply here. That is, the program must be paused before a value can be changed. The text for a value that has just changed also turns red, making it easy to spot the variable or object that has just changed.

The Locals window is great if you want a quick glance at everything that is going on in a function or procedure but not very useful for watching the values of one or two variables or expressions. The reason for this is that the Locals window contains all variables and objects in a procedure or function. Therefore, if you have a lot of variables and objects you will have to constantly scroll through the window to view the various variables and objects. This is where the Watch window comes in handy; it lets you watch just the variables that you need. In this *Try It Out*, you examine the contents of the Locals window in two different procedures. This will demonstrate how the contents of the Locals window change from one procedure to the next.

Try It Out   Using the Locals Window

1. To prepare for this exercise you need to have the same breakpoint set in the ProcessFile procedure that we have been working with. In addition, you need to set a breakpoint in the btnOpen_Click procedure at the following line of code:

```
With objOpenFileDialog
```

2. Run your program, if it is not still running, by clicking on the Start icon on the Debug toolbar. If you do not see the Locals window at the bottom of the development environment click Debug ⇨ Windows ⇨ Locals.

3. Notice that at this point the Locals window contains no variables or objects. This is because you have not entered a procedure or function. Click the Open button on the form and your breakpoint in the `btnOpen_Click` procedure will be encountered and execution will be paused.

4. Notice the various objects and their types listed in the Locals window. The first item in the list is Me, which is the form itself. If you expand this item you will see all the objects and controls associated with your form, as shown in Figure 9-22.

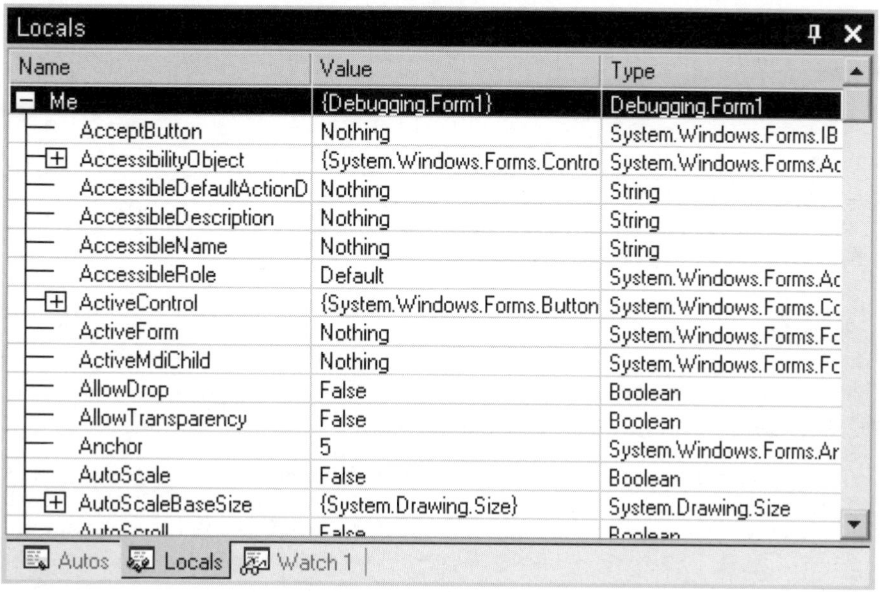

Locals			⊼ ✕
Name	**Value**	**Type**	
⊟ Me	{Debugging.Form1}	Debugging.Form1	
AcceptButton	Nothing	System.Windows.Forms.IB	
⊞ AccessibilityObject	{System.Windows.Forms.Contro	System.Windows.Forms.Ac	
AccessibleDefaultActionD	Nothing	String	
AccessibleDescription	Nothing	String	
AccessibleName	Nothing	String	
AccessibleRole	Default	System.Windows.Forms.Ac	
⊞ ActiveControl	{System.Windows.Forms.Button	System.Windows.Forms.Cc	
ActiveForm	Nothing	System.Windows.Forms.Fc	
ActiveMdiChild	Nothing	System.Windows.Forms.Fc	
AllowDrop	False	Boolean	
AllowTransparency	False	Boolean	
Anchor	5	System.Windows.Forms.Ar	
AutoScale	False	Boolean	
⊞ AutoScaleBaseSize	{System.Drawing.Size}	System.Drawing.Size	
AutoScroll	False	Boolean	

🖳 Autos 🖳 Locals 🖳 Watch 1

Figure 9-22

5. Now click on the Continue icon on the Debug toolbar and the Open File dialog will be displayed. Select a text file and click the Open button.

6. The next breakpoint that you encounter is in the `ProcessFile` procedure. Now take a look at the Locals windows and you will see different objects and variables. The one constant item in both procedures is Me, which is associated with the form.

7. If you step through a couple of lines of code in the loop where the breakpoint has paused your program, you will see the values in the Locals window change. This is the same behavior that you saw in the Watch window. You can continue to step through your code, or you can clear the breakpoint and click the Continue icon on the Debug toolbar to let your program run to completion.

After you change your build configuration from Debug to Release, debugging is no longer available; even if you have breakpoints set in your code they will not be encountered.

Error Handling

Error handling is an essential part of any good code. In Visual Basic .NET the error mechanism is based on the concept of exceptions that can be "thrown" to raise an error and "caught" when the error is handled. If you do not provide any type of error handling and an error occurs, your user will receive a message about an unhandled exception, which is provided by the common language runtime and then the program will terminate. This is not a user-friendly message and does not inform the user about the true nature of the error or how to resolve it. The unhandled error could also cause the user to lose the data that they were working with or leave the user and their data in an unknown state.

Visual Studio .NET provides *structured error-handling* statements that are common across all languages. In this section you examine structured error handling and how it can be incorporated into your programs with very little effort.

> *Structured error handling is a way to organize error handling in a structured way without the need for GoTo statements and the resulting spaghetti code.*

Structured error handling in Visual Studio .NET is handled with the `Try...Catch...Finally` blocks. You execute the code that might throw an exception in the `Try` block and handle anticipated errors in the `Catch` block. The `Finally` block is always executed and allows you to place any cleanup code here regardless of whether an error has occurred or not. If an error occurs that was not handled in the `Catch` block, the common language runtime will display its standard error message and terminate your program. Therefore, it is important to try to anticipate all possible errors for the code that is contained in the `Try` block.

Take a look at the syntax for the `Try...Catch...Finally` statement:

```
   [  trystatements ]
Catch [  exception [ As  type ] ] [ When  expression ]
   [  catchstatements ]
[ Exit Try ]
...
[ Finally
   [  finallystatements ] ]
End Try
```

❑   The *trystatements* argument in the syntax is used to specify the statements to be executed that may cause an error.

❑   The *exception* argument can be any variable name. It will be set to contain the value of the thrown error.

❑   The optional *type* argument specifies the type of class filter that the exception belongs to. If this argument is not supplied, your `Catch` block will handle any exception defined in the `System.Exception` class. Using this argument allows you to specify the type of exception that you maybe looking for. An example of a specific exception is `IOException`, which is used when performing any type of IO (input/output) against a file.

❑   The *expression* argument is any expression that describes a generic filter typically used to filter a specific error number. The expression used must return a Boolean value and the exception is handled only when the value evaluates to `True`. This is useful when you want to filter the exception handled to a specific error.

❏ The *catchstatements* are the statements that handle the error that has occurred.

❏ The `Exit Try` statement is used to break out of the error handling structure and execution of your code resumes after the `End Try` statement. This is optional and should only be used if you do not want the code following the `Finally` keyword to be executed.

❏ The *finallystatements* are the statements to be executed after all other processing has occurred.

You can have multiple `Catch` blocks. That means you can test for multiple errors using multiple `Catch` blocks and catchstatements within the same `Try` block. When an error occurs in trystatements, control is passed to the appropriate catchstatements for processing.

When you define a `Catch` block, you can specify a variable name for the exception and define the type of exception you want to catch, as shown in the following code fragment. This code defines an exception variable with a name of e and the type of the variable is defined as `IOException`. This example traps any type of IO exception that may occur when processing files and stores the error information in an object named e:

```
Catch e As IOException
    ...
    code to handle the exception goes here
    ...
```

When dealing with mathematical expressions, you can define and catch the various errors that you may encounter such as a divide-by-zero exception. You can also catch errors such as overflow errors that may occur when multiplying two numbers and trying to place the result in a variable that is too small for the result. However, in cases such as these it may be better to check for these sort of problems in advance—you should only use exceptions in exceptional circumstances.

Using Structured Error Handling

In the next *Try It Out* you add some structured error handling to the sample program that you have been working with. When you open a file for processing it is possible that you could encounter an error. For example, the file could be deleted before you open it or it could be corrupt, causing the open statement to fail. This code is a prime candidate for structured error handling. Another place where error handling can be incorporated is when you read the file. You can check for an end-of-file condition to ensure you do not try to read past the end of the file.

Try It Out   Structured Error Handling

1. Modify the code in the `ProcessFile` procedure as shown:

```
' Declare an object for the StreamReader class...
Dim objStreamReader As StreamReader

    Try
        ' Open the file...
        objStreamReader = File.OpenText(strFileName)
    Catch IOExceptionErr As IOException
        ' Display the messages...
        MessageBox.Show(IOExceptionErr.ToString)
        MessageBox.Show(IOExceptionErr.Message)
```

```
                ' Exit the procedure...
            Exit Sub
        End Try


        ' Declare variables...
        Dim intLineCounter As Integer = 0
        Dim strCurrentLine As String, strCurrentData As String

    ' Loop through the file counting the lines and loading the
    ' text box...
    Do
            Try
                ' Read a line from the file...
                strCurrentLine = objStreamReader.ReadLine
                ' Increment the line counter
                intLineCounter += 1
            Catch EndOfStreamExceptionErr As EndOfStreamException
                ' Display the message...
                MessageBox.Show(EndOfStreamExceptionErr.Message)
                ' Exit the Do loop...
                Exit Do
            Finally
                ' Concatenate the data to the strCurrentData variable...
                strCurrentData &= strCurrentLine & ControlChars.CrLf
            End Try
    Loop Until strCurrentLine Is Nothing
```

2. Save the project once more.

How It Works

The code you entered contains two error handlers. The first error handler that you have coded here contains only a Try block and a Catch block, both of which are required blocks of code in structured error handling. We have opted not to use the Finally block in this error handling routine:

```
Try
    ' Open the file...
    objStreamReader = File.OpenText(strFileName)
Catch IOExceptionErr As IOException
    ' Display the messages...
    MessageBox.Show(IOExceptionErr.ToString)
    MessageBox.Show(IOExceptionErr.Message)
    ' Exit the procedure...
    Exit Sub
End Try
```

The error that you want to trap is any error that may occur when you open a file, so you have placed your open statement in the Try block. Using the OpenText method of the File class you open the file that was returned in the Open File dialog box and set it to your StreamReader object.

The Catch block in your structured error handler will trap any IO exception that may occur, such as if the file does not exist or the file is corrupt. You defined the variable IOExceptionErr for the exception argument; as is the standard practice among most developers you use the exception name along with a suffix of Err. You then defined the type of exception that you want to test for and trap, which is an IOException.

You place your error handling code within the `Catch` block as you have done here. If an error should occur, you display two message boxes using the `MessageBox` class. Your code only sets the message in the `MessageBox` dialog boxes; accept the default values for the other arguments for the MessageBox dialog boxes.

The first line of code displays all available information about the error. The `ToString` method of the `IOException` class is used here and will return the full details of the exception. This message contains a lot of detail, which is really not of much use to an end user. You see this message when you test your code. The second line of code displays the `Message` property of the `IOException` class. This is a more meaningful message and one that the end user will understand. The last line of code in the `Catch` block (`Exit Sub`) exits the procedure. If any type of error occurs here, you cannot process the file so it only makes sense to exit the procedure, bypassing the rest of the code.

The next structured error handler in this procedure is inside the `Do` loop, which processes the contents of the file. This time you have coded the `Finally` block of the structured error handler:

```
Try
    ' Read a line from the file...
    strCurrentLine = objStreamReader.ReadLine
    ' Increment the line counter
    intLineCounter += 1
Catch EndOfStreamExceptionErr As EndOfStreamException
    ' Display the message...
    MessageBox.Show(EndOfStreamExceptionErr.Message)
    ' Exit the Do loop...
    Exit Do
Finally
    ' Concatenate the data to the strCurrentData variable...
    strCurrentData &= strCurrentLine & ControlChars.CrLf
End Try
```

The code in the `Try` block reads a line of text from the open text file and, if successful, increments the line count variable. The `Catch` block tests for and trap an end-of-stream exception using `EndOfStreamException` class. This class returns an exception when you attempt to read past the end of the stream in your text file. Again, you have specified the variable e as the exception argument. Within the `Catch` block, you display a message box using the MessageBox dialog box and display the Message property of the `EndOfStreamException` class. You then exit the `Do` loop and process the rest of the code in this procedure.

The `Finally` block contains the code that will be executed regardless of whether an error occurred. In this case, the code simply concatenates the data read in the `strCurrentLine` variable to the `strCurrentData` variable and places a carriage return line feed character at the end using the `CrLf` constant from the `ControlChars` class. At this point you are ready to test your code.

Try It Out   Testing Your Error Handlers

1. Click the Start icon on the toolbar.

2. You need to set a breakpoint and also add a watch for the `strFileName` variable in the `ProcessFile` procedure, so switch back to Visual Studio .NET.

3. Remember that the program must be in break mode before you can add a watch variable. Click Break All on the Debug toolbar or select the Debug ➪ Break All. In the `ProcessFile` procedure, find and right-click the `strFileName` variable. Then click on QuickWatch in the context menu to invoke the QuickWatch dialog box.

4. In the QuickWatch dialog box, the `strFileName` variable should be shown in the Expression drop-down box. Click the Add Watch button to add this variable to the Watch window and then click the Close button to close the QuickWatch dialog box.

5. Next, you set a couple of breakpoints in your structured error handlers. In the first error handler set a breakpoint on the following line of code by clicking in the gray margin to the left of this line:

```
objStreamReader = File.OpenText(strFileName)
```

6. Click the Continue icon on the toolbar or click the Debug ⇨ Continue.

7. On the form click the Open button to invoke the Open File dialog box and choose a text file. Click the Open button in the dialog box to open the file. Once your breakpoint has been encountered click on the Watch window to see the value of the `strFileName` variable.

   Simulate the effects of the file not being found. The most "realistic" way to do this is to rename or delete the file that you selected. An easier way is simply to change the value of the `strFileName` variable. To do this, click on the Value cell for `strFileName` in the Watch window and change the name of the file to something that does not exist by adding an extra letter or number in the file name. Click outside of the Value box in the Watch window to have the change take effect.

8. Step through your code for a few lines by clicking the Step Into icon on the toolbar.

   An error is raised because the file does not exist and the first line of code in the `Catch` block is executed. Remember that this line uses the `ToString` method of the `IOException` class, which returns the full details of the error. This message, shown in Figure 9-23, shows a lot of detail that is not really useful to the end user.

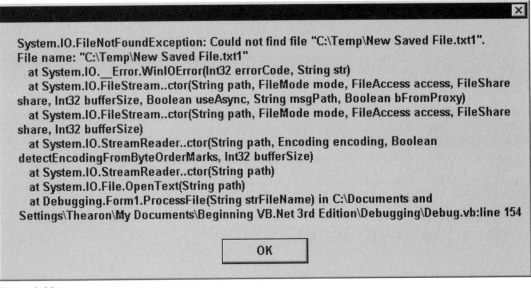

Figure 9-23

9.   Click the OK button in the message box to have the second message displayed. This next message is more user-friendly and gets to the point. The message in Figure 9-24 is the type of message that you want your users to see and one that they will understand. Of course, you would want to customize the message box to suit the error being displayed, such as displaying the appropriate caption and icon. Refer back to Chapter 7 for details on how to do this.

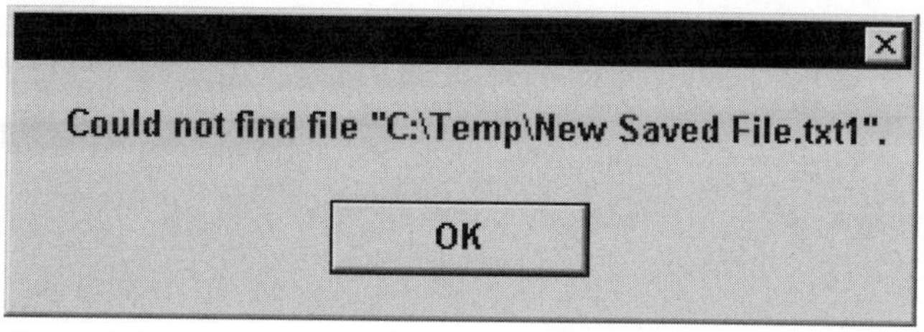

Could not find file "C:\Temp\New Saved File.txt1".

OK

Figure 9-24

10. Click the OK button in the second message to let your code run. Once you do this the next line of code is executed, which is the `Exit Sub` statement. Since you could not successfully open a file you want to bypass the rest of the code in this procedure, which is what you have done by placing the `Exit Sub` statement in your `Catch` block.

As you become more familiar with the types of errors that can occur, you will be able to write more sophisticated structured error handlers. This only comes with experience and testing. You will discover more errors and will be able to handle them only by thoroughly testing your code. The online documentation for most methods that you use in Visual Studio .NET will explain the errors that can arise when certain conditions occur. For example, the documentation for the `StreamReader.ReadLine` method explains that an `IOException` will occur on any I/O error.

Summary

This chapter looked at some useful debugging tools that are built into the Visual Studio .NET development environment. You saw how easy it is to debug your programs as you stepped through the various *Try It Out* sections.

Having thoroughly covered breakpoints, you saw how you can stop the execution of your program at any given point. As useful as this is, setting breakpoints with a hit counter in a loop is even more useful as you are able to execute a loop several times before encountering a breakpoint in the loop.

You also examined the various windows available while debugging your program, such as the Locals window and the Watch window. These windows provide you with valuable information about the variables and expressions in our program. You are able to watch the values change and are able to change the values to control the execution of our code.

You should know what types of major errors you may encounter while developing and debugging your code. You should be able to readily recognize syntax and execution errors and possibly correct them. While debugging a program for logic errors may be difficult at first, it does become easier with time and experience.

This chapter also covered structured error handling and you should incorporate this knowledge into your programs at every opportunity. Not only does it give you the opportunity to provide the user with a friendlier message when things go wrong, but it also helps you when debugging your code because you will have some basis to go on (for example, a message of the actual error and the precise location of the line of code that caused the error).

In summary, you should know the following:

❑ How to recognize and correct major types of errors

❑ How to successfully use breakpoints to debug your program

❑ How to use the Locals and Watch windows to see and change variables and expressions

❑ How to use the Command window to query and set variables

❑ How to use structured error handling

Exercises

1. How do you know when you have a syntax error in your code?

2. You know that you can set a breakpoint with a hit counter, but can you set a conditional breakpoint?

3. What information does the Locals window show?

4. If you are stepping through your code line by line, how can you bypass stepping through the code of a called procedure?

5. Can you define multiple Catch blocks in structured error handling?

6. When you use your program to open a file with a blank line, like this:

```
Line 1
Line 2

Line 4
```

You do not get the expected result—only the first two lines get displayed. Is this a syntax, execution, or logic error? How can you identify the problem? And what could you do to fix it?

10

Building Objects

You may have heard the term *object-oriented* a lot since you first started using computers. You may also have heard that it is a scary and tricky subject to understand. In its early years it was, but today's modern tools and languages make object-orientation (OO) a wonderfully easy-to-understand concept that brings massive benefits to software developers. This is mainly because languages such as Visual Basic, C++, and of course Visual Basic .NET and C# have matured to a point where they make creating objects and software that uses them very easy indeed. With these development tools, you will have no problem understanding even the most advanced object-oriented concepts and will be able to use them to build exciting object-based applications.

In this chapter, you'll look at object-orientation in detail and build on the foundations of the last chapter to start producing some cool Visual Basic .NET applications.

In this chapter, you will:

- ❑   Build a reusable object with methods and properties
- ❑   Inherit the object that you build in another object
- ❑   Override methods and properties in your base object
- ❑   Create your own namespace

Understanding Objects

An object is almost anything you can think of. We work with physical objects all the time: televisions, cars, customers, reports, light bulbs—anything. In computer terms, an object is a representation of a thing that we want to manipulate in our application. Sometimes, the two definitions, usefully map exactly onto each other. So, if you have a physical car object sitting in your driveway and want to describe it in software terms, you build a software car object that sits in your computer.

Likewise, if you need to write a piece of software that generates a bill for a customer, you may well have a Bill object and a Customer object. The Customer object represents the customer and may be capable of having a name, address, and also have the capability to generate the bill. The Bill object would represent an instance of a bill for a customer and would be able to impart the details of the bill and may also have the capability to print itself.

What is important here is the concept that the object has the intelligence to produce actions related to it—the Customer object can generate the bill. In effect, if you have a Customer object you can simply say to it: "Produce a bill for me." The Customer object would then go away and do all the hard work related to creating the bill. Likewise, once you have a Bill object you can say to it: "Print yourself." What you have here is two examples of object behavior.

Objects are unbelievably useful because they turn software engineering into something conceptually similar to wooden building blocks. You arrange the blocks (the objects) to build something greater than the sum of the parts. The power of objects comes from the fact that, as someone using objects, you don't need to understand how they work behind the scene. You're familiar with this with real-world objects too. When you use a mobile phone, you don't need to understand how it works inside. Even if you do understand how a mobile phone works inside—even if you made it yourself—it's still much easier to use the mobile phone's simple interface. The interface can also prevent you from accidentally doing something that breaks the phone. The same is true with computer objects—even if you build all the objects yourself, having the complicated workings hidden behind a simple interface can make your life much easier and safer.

Object-orientation was first explained to me by using a television metaphor. Look at the television in your lounge. There are several things you know how to do with it:

❏   Watch the image on the screen

❏   Change channel

❏   Change volume

❏   Switch it on or off

❏   Plug in a games console

What you don't have to do is understand how everything works to allow you to carry out these activities. If asked, I couldn't put together the components needed to make a modern television. I could, with a little research and patience, come up with something fairly basic, but nothing as complex as the one sitting in my lounge. However, I do understand how to use a television. I know how to change the channel, change the volume, switch it on and off, plug it in a Nintendo Game Cube, and so on.

Objects in software engineering work in basically the same way. Once you have an object you can use it and ask it do things without having to understand how the internals of it actually work. This is phenomenally powerful, as you'll see soon.

Software objects typically have the following characteristics:

❏   Identity—User: "What are you?" TV: "I'm a TV."

❏   State—User: "What channel am I watching?" TV: "You're watching Channel 4."

❏   Behavior—User: "Please turn up the volume to 50%." Then, we can use the State again—User: "How loud is the volume?" TV: "50%."

Encapsulation

The core concept behind object-orientation is encapsulation. This is a big word, but it's very simple to understand. What this means is that the functionality is wrapped up in a self-contained manner and that you don't need to understand what it's actually doing when you ask it to do something.

If you remember in Chapter 3, you built a function that calculated the area of the circle. In that function you encapsulated the logic of calculating the area in such a way that anyone using the function could find the area without having to know how to physically perform the operation. This is the same concept but taken to the next level.

> *Objects are often referred to as black boxes. If you imagine software objects as small plastic boxes with buttons on the top and connectors on the side, with a basic understanding of what the box does, together with a general understanding of how boxes generally plug together, you can build up a complex system with them without ever having to have the capability of building a box independently.*

Methods and Properties

You interact with objects through methods and properties. These can be defined as:

- ❏ *Methods* are ways of instructing an object to do something
- ❏ *Properties* are things that describe features of an object

A method was defined previously as a self-contained block of code that does something. This is true, but it is a rather simplistic definition. In fact the strict definition of a method applies only to OO and is a way to manipulate an object—a way to instruct it to perform certain behaviors. In previous chapters you created methods that instructed an object—in most cases a Form—to do something. When you create a Form in Visual Basic .NET, you are actually defining a new type of Form object.

So, if you need to turn on the TV, you need to find a method that does this because a method is something you get the object to do. When you invoke the method, the object itself is supposed to understand what to do to satisfy the request. To hammer the point home you don't care what it actually does, you just say, "Switch on." It's down to the TV to switch relays to deliver power, boot up the circuitry, warm up the electron gun, and all the other things that you don't need to understand!

> *Invoke means the same as call, but is more OO-friendly. It reminds us that we are invoking a method on something, rather than just calling a chunk of code.*

On the other hand, if you need to change the channel you might set the channel property. If you want to tune into Channel 10 you set the channel property to the value 10. Again, the object is responsible for reacting to the request and you don't care about the technical hoops it has to go through in order to do that.

Events

In Visual Basic .NET you listen for events to determine when something has happened to a control on a form. You can consider an event as something that an object does. In effect, someone using an object can listen to events, like a `Click` event on a button or a `PowerOn` event on a TV. When the event is received, the developer can take some action. Some old TVs take ages to warm up. In OO terms, there is the `SwitchOn` method that gets called on the TV object, when the TV has warmed up it raises a `PowerOn` event. You could then respond to this event by adjusting the volume to the required level.

An event might also be used when the performer of an action is not the only entity interested in the action taking place. For example, when you have the TV on you might go and get a drink during a commercial break. But while you're in the kitchen, you keep your ears open for when the program starts again. Effectively you are listening for a `ProgramResume` event. You do not cause the program to resume, but you do want to know when it does.

Visibility

To build decent objects you have to make them easy for developers to use. For example, internally it might be really important for your TV object to know what frequency the tuner needs, but does the person using the TV care? More importantly, do you actually want the developer to be able to change this frequency directly? What you're trying to do is make the object more "abstract."

Some parts of your object will be private, whereas other parts will be public. The public interface is available for others to use. The private part is what you expect the object itself to use internally. The logic for the object exists in the private part and may include methods and properties that are important, but that won't get called from outside the object. For example, a TV object might have methods for ConnectPower, WarmUp, and so on. These would be private and would all be called from the public SwitchOn method. Similarly, while there is a public Channel property there will probably be a private Frequency property. The TV could not work without knowing the signal frequency it was receiving, but the users are only interested in the channel.

Now that you understand the basics of object orientation, let's look at how we can use objects within an application.

You'll notice that some of the code samples you have seen in previous chapters included a line that looked similar to this:

```
lstData.Items.Add(n)
```

That's a classic example of object orientation! `lstData` is, in fact, an object. `Items` is a property of the `lstData` object. The `Items` property is an object in its own right and has an `Add` method. The period (`.`) tells Visual Basic .NET that the word to the right is a member of the word to the left. So, `Items` is a member of `lstData` and `Add` is a member of `Items`.

`lstData` is an instance of a class called `System.Windows.Forms.ListBox` (or just `ListBox`). This class is part of the .NET Framework you learned about in Chapter 2.

The `ListBox` class can display a list of items on screen and let a user choose a particular one. Again, here's the concept of encapsulation. You as a user of `ListBox` don't need to know anything about technologies involved in displaying the list or listening for input. You may not have even heard of GDI+, stdin, keyboard drivers, display drivers, or anything else that goes into the complex action of displaying a list on screen, yet you still have the capability to do it.

The `ListBox` is an example of an object that you can see. Users can look at a program running and know that there is a `ListBox` involved. Most objects in OO programming are invisible and represent something in memory.

What Is a Class?

A class is the definition of an object and is made up of the software code. This is effectively the circuitry inside the black box. If you want to build a software object, you have to understand how the internals work. You express those internals with Visual Basic .NET code. So, when the software developer using your object says, "Turn up the volume" you have to know how to instruct the amplifier to increase the output. (As an aside, remember that the amplifier is just another object. You don't necessarily need to know how it works inside. In OO programming, you will often find that one object is a load of other objects with some code to link them together—just as a TV is a load of standard components and a bit of custom circuitry.)

When you want to use an object you have to instantiate an instance of the class. So, if you have 50 TV objects, you have 50 instances of the TV class. Each of those instances has been created by instantiation, which is a fancy term for creating. Typically, you "create classes" and "instantiate objects." The difference is used to reduce ambiguity. Creating a class is done at design time when you're building your software and involves writing the actual code. Instantiating objects is done at runtime when your program is being used.

A classic analogy is the cookie cutter. You can go out to my workshop and shape a piece of metal in the shape of a Christmas tree. You do this once and put the cutter in a drawer in your kitchen. Whenever you need to create Christmas tree cookies, you roll some dough (the computer's memory) and stamp out however many you need. In effect you're instantiating cookies. You can reuse the cutter at a later date to create more cookies each the same as the ones before.

Once you've instantiated instances of the class to get the objects, you can manipulate the properties and methods defined on the class. For example, you can build a class once at design time that represents a television. However, you can instantiate two objects from that class—one to represent the TV in the lounge and one to represent the TV in the bedroom. Because both instances of the object share the same class, both instances have the same properties and methods. To turn on the TV you can call the SwitchOn method. To change the channel you can set the Channel property and so on.

Building Classes

You're now ready to start building classes. As you build your application you'll be using both classes developed by others (in particular, those in the .NET Framework) and your own. When you design an algorithm you will discover certain objects described. You need to abstract these real-world objects into a software representation. Here's an example:

1. Select a list of 10 customers from the database.

2. Go through each customer and prepare a bill for each.

3. When each bill has been prepared, print it on a printer.

For a pure object-oriented application (and with .NET you will end up using objects to represent everything) every real-world object will need a software object. For example:

❑   Customer—an object that represents a customer

❑   Bill—an object that represents a bill that is produced

❑   Printer—an object that represents a hardware printer that can be used to print the bill

Typically, while building an application, some of the classes you need will be included in the .NET Framework, others you will have to build yourself. In this case, although there's no specific Printer object, there are classes that deal with printing.

When you write software in .NET, you are given a vast set of classes called the Microsoft .NET Framework Classes. These classes describe virtually everything about the computing environment that you're trying to write software for. Writing object-oriented software for .NET is simply an issue of using objects that fit your needs and creating new objects if required.

For example, there are objects in the .NET Framework that provide printing functionality, and database access functionality. As your algorithm calls for both kinds of functionality, you don't need to write your own. If you need to print something, you create an object that understands how to print, tell it what you want to print, and then tell it to print it out. Again, this is encapsulation—you don't care how to turn your document into PostScript commands and send it down the wire to the printer; the object knows how to do this for itself.

In some cases, there are some objects that you need to represent that do not exist in the .NET Framework. In this example you need a Customer object and a Bill object.

Reusability

Perhaps the hardest aspect of object-oriented programming is to understand how to divide up the responsibility for the work. One of the most beautiful aspects of object-orientation is code reuse. Imagine a company has a need for several different applications: one to display customer bills, one to register a new customer, and one to track customer complaints. Well, in each of those applications you need to have a Customer object.

To simplify the issue, those three projects are not going to be undertaken simultaneously; you start by doing the first and when finished, you move on to the second and when you've finished that, you move on to the third. Do you want to build a new Customer class for each project, or you want to build the class once and reuse it in each of the other two projects?

Reuse is typically regarded as something that's universally good, although there is a tradeoff. Ideally, if you build a Customer class for one project, and another project you're working on calls for another Customer class, you should use the same one. However, it may well be the case that you can't just plug the class into another project for some reason. I say for some reason because there are no hard or fast rules when it comes to class design and reuse. It may also be the case that it's easier or more cost-effective to build simple classes for each project rather than trying to create one complex object that does everything. This might sound like it requires a degree in clairvoyance, but luckily it comes with experience! As you develop more and more applications you'll gain a better understanding of how to design great, reusable objects.

Each object should be responsible for activities involving itself and no more. As we've only discussed two objects: `Bill` and `Customer`, we'll only look at those.

The activity of printing a bill for telephone charges follows this algorithm:

- ❏ For a given customer, find the call details for the last period
- ❏ Go through each call and work out the price of each one
- ❏ Aggregate the cost of each call into a total
- ❏ Apply tax charges
- ❏ Print out the bill—the customer's name, address, and bill summary on the first page and then the bill details on subsequent pages

We only have two places where we can code this algorithm: the `Bill` object or the `Customer` object, so which one do you choose?

The calls made are really a property of the `Customer`. Basically, you are using these details to create a Bill. Most of the functionality would be placed in the `Bill` object. A `Customer` is responsible for representing a customer, not representing a bill. When you create a `Bill` object, you would associate it with a particular customer by using a `Cust` property, like this:

```
myBill.Cust = myCustomer
```

The `Bill` object would then know that it was a Bill for a given customer (represented by the `myCustomer` object) and could use the customer's details when creating a bill. You might want to change some other properties of the Bill such as where it will be mailed to, whether it should contain a warning because it is overdue, and so on. Finally, the Bill would have a `Print` method:

```
myBill.Print()
```

The `Bill` object would then consume (or use) a `Printer` object in order to print the bill.

Our First Object

Contrary to what I've said so far, you're not going to define an algorithm and then build objects to support it. For this rather academic example, I'm going to walk you through some of the features of a typical object, in this case, a car.

There are certain facts you might want to know about the object:

- ❏ What it looks like—a car includes things like make, model, color, number of doors, and so on. These aspects of the car will rarely change during the object's lifetime.
- ❏ Its capabilities—horsepower, engine size, cylinder configuration, and so on.
- ❏ What it's doing—whether it's stationary, moving forward or backwards, and its speed and direction.

❑ Where it is—the Global Positioning System (GPS) coordinates of its current position. This is effectively its position relative to another object (the planet Earth). Likewise, controls on forms have coordinates that describe their location relative to the form.

You might also want to be able to control the object, for example:

❑ Tell it to accelerate

❑ Tell it to decelerate

❑ Tell it to turn left

❑ Tell it to turn right

❑ Tell it to straighten up

❑ Tell it to do a three-point-turn

❑ Tell it to stop completely

There are three concepts of an object that you need to be aware of: identity, state, and behavior. We'll assume that the identity aspect is covered because you know what the class is, so the state and behavior are of interest here.

State

State describes facts about the object now. For example, a car's location and speed is part of its state. When designing objects, you need to think about what aspects of state you need to handle. It might not be useful to know a customer's speed, for example, but you might well want to know their current address.

State tends to be implemented as values inside an object. Some of these values will be publicly available through properties, and some will be private. Also, some aspects of state might be publicly readable but not changeable. For example cars have a speedometer that is readable to anybody using the car. But you can't change the car's speed by playing with the speedometer—you need to alter the car's behavior by using the brake or accelerating.

Behavior

While a car might have a read-only Speed property, it would have methods to accelerate and decelerate. When you call an object's method, you are telling your object to do something—so behavior is usually associated with methods. Properties can also be associated with behavior. When you set a property to a particular value you can trigger behavior. Behavior is usually implemented as a set of Visual Basic .NET statements that do something. This will usually involve one or both of the following:

❑ Changing its own state. When you call for the accelerate method on a car, it should get faster if it is capable of doing so.

❑ Somehow affecting the "world" outside the object. This could be manipulating other objects in the application, displaying something to the user, saving something to a disk, or printing a document.

In this chapter, you won't build all of the properties and methods discussed. Instead, you'll build a handful of the more interesting ones.

Try It Out   Creating a New Project and the Car Class

1. Start Visual Basic .NET and select File ⇨ New ⇨ Project from the menu.

2. When the New Project dialog box appears, select the Visual Basic .NET Console Application template and enter the name of the project as Objects. Click OK to create the project.

3. You now need to create a new class. This is done through the Solution Explorer, so right-click on the Objects project and select Add ⇨ Add Class. This will prompt you for a new class name, so enter Car.vb as the class name and click Open. The new class has been added to the Solution Explorer and the editor now shows the code listing for it, albeit empty.

Storing State

State describes what the object understands about itself, so if you give a car object some state, for example, "You are blue," you're giving the car object a fact: "The car I represent is blue."

So how do you actually manage state in your classes? Well, state is typically held in variables and you define those variables within the class. You see how to do this in a moment.

Usually, the methods and properties you build will either affect or use the state in some way. Imagine you've built a property that changes the color of the car. When you set that property, the variable that's responsible for storing the state will be changed to reflect the new value that it has been given. When you retrieve (Get) that property, the variable that's responsible for storing the state will be read and the current value will be returned to the caller.

In a way, then, properties are behavior. Under the hood, a public property has two methods: a Get method and a Set method. A simple Get method for the Color property will contain code to tell the caller what color the car is. A simple Set method for the Color property will set a value that represents the car's color. In a real application, though, Color would probably mean something more than just remembering a value. In a driving game the Set method of the Color property would need to change, for example, the color that the car had on the screen.

When a property has no behavior at all, you can cheat. In the next example, you create a Color "property" by declaring a Color variable and making it public. When done like this it is also called a field. Although this can be a useful and very fast technique for adding properties, declaring a field instead of the Property Get and Set is not actually recommended, but for this small example it is just fine.

Try It Out   Adding a Color Property

1. Open the Car.vb file if it's not already open and add this code:

```
Public Class Car
    Public Color As String
End Class
```

2. That's it! However, we do need a way of consuming the class so that we can see it working. Open `Module1.vb` and add this code:

```
Module Module1
    Sub Main()
        ' create a new car object...
        Dim myCar As Car
        myCar = New Car()
        ' set the Color property to "Red"...
        myCar.Color = "Red"
        ' show what the value of the property is...
        Console.WriteLine("My car is this color:")
        Console.WriteLine(myCar.Color)
        ' wait...
        Console.ReadLine()
    End Sub
End Module
```

3. Now run the project. A new window will appear similar to Figure 10-1.

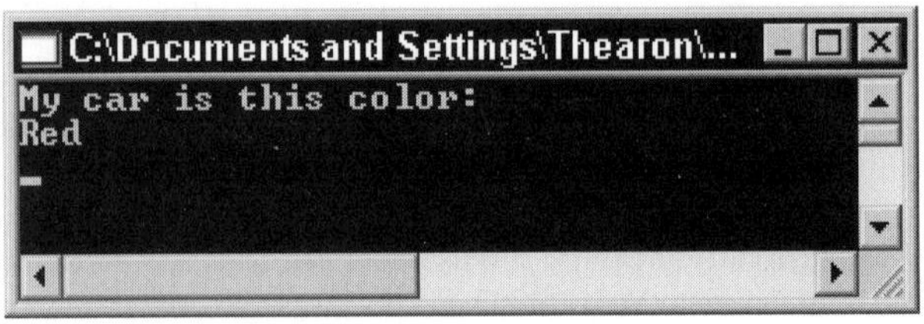

Figure 10-1

4. Press *Enter* to end the program.

How It Works

Defining the field is easy. The highlighted line

```
Public Class Car
    Public Color As String
```

...tells the class that you want to create a variable called `Color` and you want the field to hold a string of text characters. The use of the `Public` keyword when you declare the `Color` variable tells the class that the variable is accessible to people using the `Car` class, not only from within the class itself.

> *Variables defined in the location between the Public Class and End Class lines, but outside of a function, are known as member variables.*

Using the object is a little trickier and you do this from within `Module1.vb`. First, you have to instantiate an instance of the class. With the following lines, you create a variable called `myCar` and tell it that it's going to exclusively hold objects created using the `Car` class:

```
Sub Main()
    ' create a new car object...
    Dim myCar As Car
```

When you define the variable, it doesn't have an object instance associated with it, you are simply identifying the type of object. It's a bit like telling the computer to give you a hook that you can hang a Car object on, and call the hook myCar. You haven't hung anything on it yet—to do that you have to create an instance of the object. This is done using the New keyword like this:

```
myCar = New Car()
```

So, what you're saying here is: "let myCar refer to a newly created object instantiated from the class Car." In other words, "create a new car and hang it on the hook called myCar." You now have a Car object and can refer to it with the name myCar.

Note that in OO programming, the same object can be hanging on several different hooks at the same time and, therefore, have several different names. This seems confusing but in most cases it is a really intuitive way to work. Imagine how cool it would be if your keys could be on several hooks at the same time—they'd be so much easier to find!

After you have an object instance you can set its properties and call its methods. Here is how you set the Color property:

```
' set the Color property to "Red"...
myCar.Color = "Red"
```

Once the property has been set, it can be retrieved again as many times as you want or its value changed at a later point. Here, retrieval is illustrated by passing the WriteLine method on the Console class:

```
' show what the value of the property is...
Console.WriteLine("My car is this color:")
Console.WriteLine(myCar.Color)
' wait...
Console.ReadLine()
```

The Console.ReadLine line means that the program does not continue until you press *Enter*.

Console applications are a good way to test in-memory objects because you don't need to worry about setting up a user interface. You can just display lines of text whenever you want. The objects you build will work just as well in a Windows Application, though.

Even though this is not really a property from the point of view of a developer using the class, it works just like one. In fact, "real" properties are methods that look like variables to users of the class. Whether you use a method or a property really depends on what the users of your class will find easier. You'll start to see this in the next section.

Real Properties

Now that you've seen how to cheat, let's see how to do things properly. The property you saw can be set to pretty much anything. As long as it's a String it will be accepted. Also, setting the property doesn't do anything except change the object's internal state. Often you want to control what values a property can be set to, for example, you might have a list of valid colors that a car can be. Alternatively, you might want to associate a change to a property with a particular action. For example, when you change a channel on the TV you want it to do a bit more than just change its mind about what channel it's displaying. You want the TV to show a different picture! Just changing the value of a variable won't help here.

The simplest reason to use real properties is that you want to prevent the user of the class from directly changing the value. This is called a read-only property. The car's speed is a good example. If you are doing 60 mph, you cannot simply change the speed to a value you prefer. Rather, you want to use methods to control the speed (accelerate, decelerate) and keep a read-only property around called speed that will report on the current speed of the vehicle.

This is a good example of how a class that models a real-world object should behave like that real-world object. You can read the speed of a car from the speedometer, but you cannot change (write) the speed of the car by physically moving the needle around the dial with your finger. You have to control the car in another fashion, which you do by using the throttle to signal accelerate or decelerate methods.

What you need is a member variable that can only be seen or manipulated by the class itself. You accomplish this by using the `Private` keyword:

```
Public Color As String
Private _speed As Integer
```

Although you build this property in a little while, _speed is marked as `Private` and can, therefore, only be accessed by functions defined inside the class itself. Users of `Car` will not even be aware of its presence. Private members are `camelCased` rather than `PascalCased`, so that you can easily tell whether something is public or private when you use it. When a private variable maps directly to a public property, you prefix the variable name with an underscore (`_`).

Now you'll see how you can build a property that will give the user of the object read-only access to the car's speed.

Try It Out   Adding a Speed Property

1. To define a private variable use the `Private` instead of the `Public` keyword. Add this statement to `Car.vb`:

```
Public Class Car
    Public Color As String
    Private _speed As Integer
End Class
```

2. To report the speed, you need to build a read-only property. Add this code:

```
Public Class Car
    Public Color As String
    Private _speed As Integer
    ' Speed - read-only property to return the speed...
    ReadOnly Property Speed() As Integer
        Get
            Return _speed
        End Get
    End Property
End Class
```

3. Now, you build a method called `Accelerate` that will adjust the speed of the car by however many miles-per-hour you give it. Add this code after the `Speed` property:

```
Public Class Car
    Public Color As String
    Private _speed As Integer
    ' Speed - read-only property to return the speed...
    ReadOnly Property Speed() As Integer
        Get
            Return _speed
        End Get
    End Property
    ' Accelerate - add mph to the speed...
    Sub Accelerate(ByVal accelerateBy As Integer)
        ' adjust the speed...
        _speed += accelerateBy
    End Sub
End Class
```

4. To test the object, you need to make some changes to Module1.vb. Open the file and add this code in the place of what you had previously:

```
Sub Main()
    ' create a new car object...
    Dim myCar As Car
    myCar = New Car()
        ' report the speed...
    Console.WriteLine("The car's speed is:")
    Console.WriteLine(myCar.Speed)
    ' accelerate...
    myCar.Accelerate(5)
    ' report the new speed...
    Console.WriteLine("The car's speed is now:")
    Console.WriteLine(myCar.Speed)
    ' wait...
    Console.ReadLine()
End Sub
```

5. Now run the project. A new window will appear similar to Figure 10-2.

Figure 10-2

How It Works

The first thing you did was to define a private member variable called _speed.

```
Private _speed As Integer
```

By default, when the object is created _speed will have a value of zero because this is the default value for the data type Integer.

You then defined a read-only property that would return the current speed:

```
' Speed - read-only property to return the speed...
ReadOnly Property Speed() As Integer
    Get
         Return _speed
    End Get
End Property
```

When you define properties, you can either set them to be read-only (through the ReadOnly keyword), write-only (through the WriteOnly keyword), or both readable and writable by using neither. Reading a property is known as *getting* the value, whereas writing to a property is known as *setting* the value. The code between Get and End Get will be executed when the property is read. In this case, the only thing you're doing is returning the value currently stored in _speed.

You also created a method called Accelerate. As this method doesn't have to return a value you use the Sub keyword:

```
' Accelerate - add mph to the speed...
Sub Accelerate(ByVal accelerateBy As Integer)
    ' adjust the speed...
    _speed += accelerateBy
End Sub
```

The method takes a single parameter called accelerateBy that you use to tell the method how much to increase the speed. You'll notice that the only action of the method is to adjust the internal member _speed. In real life, the pressure on the accelerator along with factors such as wind speed and road surface will affect the speed. The speed will be an outcome of several factors—not something you can just change. You need some complex code to simulate this. Here we are just keeping things simple and showing how to use properties.

Accelerating a car is another example of encapsulation. To accelerate the car in a real-world implementation you need an actuator of some kind to further open the throttle until the required speed is reached. As consumers of the object you don't care how this is done. All you do care about is how to tell the car to accelerate.

Consuming this new functionality is simple. First, you create the object:

```
' create a new car object...
Dim myCar As Car
myCar = New Car()
```

Next, you write out the speed:

```
' report the speed...
Console.WriteLine("The car's speed is:")
Console.WriteLine(myCar.Speed)
```

Notice how you're using the read-only `Speed` property to get the current speed of the car. When the object is first created the internal `_speed` member will be set at 0.

Now you can call `Accelerate` and use it to increase the speed of the car:

```
' accelerate...
myCar.Accelerate(5)
```

Finally, you write out the new speed:

```
' report the speed...
Console.WriteLine("The car's speed is now:")
Console.WriteLine(myCar.Speed)
```

Read/Write Properties

So, why would you need to use the `Property` keyword to define properties that are both readable and writable if you can achieve the same effect with a line like this?

```
Public Color As String
```

Well, if you manually build the property using the `Property` keyword, you can write code that is executed whenever the property is called. This is extremely powerful.

For example, the `Property` keyword allows you to provide validation for new values. Imagine you had a property called `NumberOfDoors`. You wouldn't want this to be set to nonsense values like 0 or 23453. Rather, you would have some possible range. For modern cars this is going to go from 2 to 5.

This is an important consideration for developers building objects. It's imperative that you make life as easy as possible for a developer to consume your object. The fact that you deal with problems like making sure a car can't have 10 million doors is an important aspect of object design.

Likewise, you might not have the information to return to the consumer of your object when you are asked to return the property, and might have to retrieve the value from somewhere, or otherwise calculate it. You might have a property that describes the total number of orders a customer has ever made or the total number of chew toys a dog has destroyed in his life. If you build this as a property, you can intercept the instruction to "get" the value and find the actual value you require on demand from some other data store, such as a database or a Web service. You'll see this covered in later chapters.

For now, let's deal with the number of doors problem.

Try It Out   Adding a NumberOfDoors Property

1. The first thing you need to do is build a private member that will hold the number of doors. You're going to define this property as having a default of 5. Add this code in the `Car` class as indicated below:

```
Public Color As String
Private_speed As Integer
Private_numberOfDoors As Integer = 5
```

2. Now you can build a property that will get and set the number of doors, provided the number of doors is always between 2 and 5. Add this code to Car.vb directly beneath the Accelerate method:

```
' NumberOfDoors - get/set the number of doors...
Property NumberOfDoors() As Integer
    ' called when the property is "got"...
    Get
         Return _numberOfDoors
    End Get
    ' called when the property is "set"...
    Set(ByVal Value As Integer)
        ' is the new value between two and five?
        If Value >= 2 And Value <= 5 Then
            _numberOfDoors = Value
        End If
    End Set
End Property
```

In this chapter, you're going to ignore the problem of telling the developer if the user has provided an invalid value for a property. Ideally whenever this happens you need to throw something called an exception. The developer will be able to detect this exception and behave accordingly. (For example, if the user typed the number of doors as 9999 into a text box, the program could display a message box telling the user that they have provided an invalid value for the number of doors since no car has that many doors.) Exception handling is quite an advanced topic, which you learned in Chapter 9.

3. To test the property, you need to change Module1.vb by replacing the existing code with this new code as indicated here:

```
Sub Main()
    ' create a new car object...
    Dim myCar As Car
    myCar = New Car()
        ' report the number of doors...
    Console.WriteLine("The number of doors is:")
    Console.WriteLine(myCar.NumberOfDoors)
    ' try changing the number of doors to 1000...
    myCar.NumberOfDoors = 1000
    ' report the number of doors...
    Console.WriteLine("The number of doors is:")
    Console.WriteLine(myCar.NumberOfDoors)
    ' now try changing the number of doors to 2...
    myCar.NumberOfDoors = 2
    ' report the number of doors...
    Console.WriteLine("The number of doors is:")
    Console.WriteLine(myCar.NumberOfDoors)
    ' wait...
    Console.ReadLine()
End Sub
```

4. Try running the project. You should see Figure 10-3.

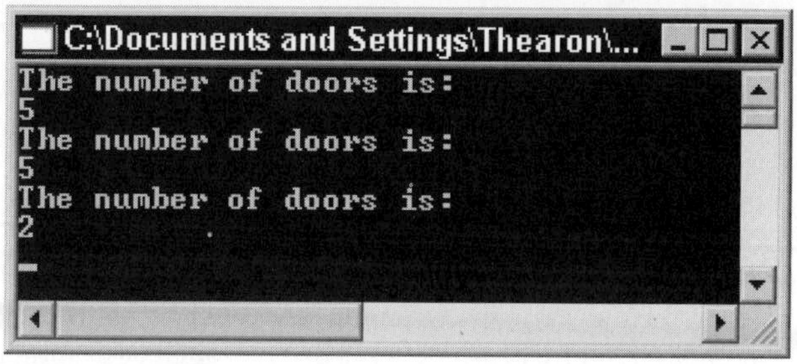

Figure 10-3

How It Works

The first thing you did was define a private member variable called _numberOfDoors. You also assigned the value 5 to this variable.

```
Private _numberOfDoors As Integer = 5
```

The motivation behind setting a value at this point is simple: you want _numberOfDoors to always be between 2 and 5. When the object is created, the _numberOfDoors will be assigned a value of 5. Without this assignment, _numberOfDoors would have a default value of 0. This would be inconsistent with the understanding that the number of doors must always be between 2 and 5 so you guard against it.

Next comes the property itself. The Get portion is simple—just return the value held in _numberOfDoors—but the Set portion involves a check to ensure that the new value is valid. The new value is passed in through a parameter called Value:

```
' NumberOfDoors - get/set the number of doors...
Property NumberOfDoors() As Integer
    ' called when the property is "got"...
    Get
        Return _numberOfDoors
    End Get
    ' called when the property is "set"...
    Set(ByVal Value As Integer)
        ' is the new value between two and five?
        If Value >= 2 And Value <= 5 Then
            _numberOfDoors = Value
        End If
    End Set
End Property
```

The test code you added to Module1.vb was not very complex. All you did was display the initial value of _numberOfDoors and then try to change it to 1000. The validation code in the _numberOfDoors property won't change _numberOfDoors if an inconsistent number is used, so when you report the number of doors again you find it hasn't changed from 5. Lastly, you try setting it to 2, which is a valid value, and this time when you report the number of doors you get an output of 2.

Even though read–write properties and public variables seem to work the same way, they are very different. When your Visual Basic .NET code is compiled, the compiled code sees property calls as a call to a method. Always using properties instead of public variables makes your objects more flexible and extendable. Of course, using public variables is easier and quicker. You need to decide what is most important in each case.

339

The IsMoving Method

When building objects you should always have the following question in the back of your mind. "How can I make this object easier to use?" For example, if the consumer needs to know if the car is moving what would be the easiest way to determine this?

One way would be to look at the Speed property. If this is zero, it can be assumed that the car has stopped. (Although on most cars the speed is not reported when the car is moving in reverse. So, assume you only have forward gears!) However, relying on the developer using the object to understand this relies on their having an understanding of whatever is being modeled. Common sense tells us that an object with a speed of "zero mph" is stationary, but should you assume anyone consuming the object shares your idea of common sense?

Instead, it's good practice to create methods that deal with these eventualities. One way you can solve this problem is by creating an IsMoving method.

Try It Out   Adding an IsMoving Method

1. All the IsMoving method needs in order to work is a simple test to look at the speed of the car and make a True or False determination as to whether it's moving. Add this code to Car.vb after the NumberOfDoors property:

```
' IsMoving - is the car moving?
Public Function IsMoving() As Boolean
    ' is the car's speed zero?
    If Speed = 0 Then
        Return False
    Else
        Return True
    End If
End Function
```

2. To test this method, make these changes to Module1.vb replacing the existing code with this new code as indicated:

```
Sub Main()
    ' create a new car object...
    Dim myCar As Car
    myCar = New Car()
    ' accelerate the car to 25mph...
    myCar.Accelerate(25)
    ' report whether or not the car is moving...
    If myCar.IsMoving = True Then
        Console.WriteLine("The car is moving.")
    Else
        Console.WriteLine("The car is not moving.")
    End If
    ' wait...
    Console.ReadLine()
End Sub
```

3. Now try running the project. A new window will appear similar to Figure 10-4.

Figure 10-4

How It Works

You created a simple method that examines the value of the Speed property and returns True if the speed is not zero, False if it is.

```
' IsMoving - is the car moving?
Public Function IsMoving() As Boolean
    ' is the car's speed zero?
    If Speed = 0 Then
        Return False
    Else
        Return True
    End If
End Function
```

Although this method is simple, it removes the conceptual leap required on the part of the consumer to understand whether or not the object is moving. There's no confusion as to whether or not the car is moving based on interpreting the value of one or more properties; one simple method returns a definitive answer.

Of course, before you go off building hundreds of methods for every eventuality, remember that paradoxically, the more methods and properties an object has, the harder it is to understand. Take care while designing the object and try to strike the right balance between too few and too many methods and properties.

You may be wondering why you used a method here when this is actually a property. All you are doing is reporting the object's state without affecting its behavior. There is no reason for not using a property here. However, using a method does remind users of the object that this value is calculated and is not a simple report of an internal variable. It also adds a bit of variety to your examples and reminds you how easy it is to add a method!

Constructors

One of the most important aspects of object design is the concept of a constructor. This is a piece of initialization code that runs whenever an object is instantiated. It's extremely useful for occasions when you need the object to be set up in a particular way before you use it. For example, it can be used to set up default values just as you did for the number of doors earlier.

Creating a Constructor

In this section you take a look at a simple constructor.

Try It Out   **Creating a Constructor**

1. For the sake of this discussion, you're going to remove the default value of 5 from the _numberOfDoors member. Make this change to Car.vb:

```
Public Class Car
    Public Color As String
    Private _speed As Integer
    Private _numberOfDoors As Integer
```

2. Now, add this method, which will form the constructor. Any code within this method will be executed whenever a Car object is created:

```
Public Class Car
    Public Color As String
    Private _speed As Integer
    Private _numberOfDoors As Integer
    ' Constructor...
    Sub New()
        ' set the defaults:
        Color = "White"
        _speed = 0
        _numberOfDoors = 5
    End Sub
```

   Setting the _speed to 0 here is actually redundant, as it will have that value already (since all Integer variables are set to 0 when they start), but it's included to make the example complete.

3. To test the action of the constructor, you're going to create a separate procedure that displays the car's details. Make these changes to Module1.vb.

```
Module Module1

    Sub Main()
        ' create a new car object...
        Dim myCar As Car
        myCar = New Car()
        ' display the details of the car...
        DisplayCarDetails(myCar)
        ' wait...
        Console.ReadLine()
    End Sub
    ' DisplayCarDetails - procedure that displays a car's details...
    Sub DisplayCarDetails(ByVal myCar As Car)
        ' display the details of the car...
        Console.WriteLine("Color:" & myCar.Color)
        Console.WriteLine("Number of doors:" & myCar.NumberOfDoors)
        Console.WriteLine("Current speed:" & myCar.Speed)
        Console.WriteLine()
    End Sub
End Module
```

4. Now try running the project and you should see an output similar to Figure 10-5.

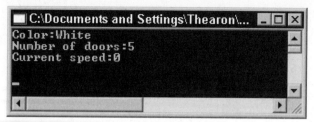

Figure 10-5

How It Works

The code in the constructor is called whenever an object is created. This is where you take an opportunity to set the values for the members:

```
' Constructor...
Sub New()
    ' set the defaults:
    Color = "White"
    _speed = 0
    _numberOfDoors = 5
End Sub
```

You see the results of the changes made to the properties when you run the project and see the details of the car displayed in the window. A constructor must always be a subroutine (defined with the Sub keyword) and must always be called New.

When you test the object you use a separate function called DisplayCarDetails in Module1.vb. This is useful when you need to see the details of more than one Car object or want to see the details of the Car object multiple times in your code.

Inheritance

Although the subject of inheritance is quite an advanced object-oriented programming topic, it is really useful. In fact, the .NET Framework itself makes heavy use of it and you have already created classes that are inherited from another class—every Windows form that you write is a new class that is inherited from a simple blank form (the starting point when you create a form).

Inheritance is used to create objects that have "everything another object has, but also some of their own bits and pieces." It's used to extend the functionality of objects, but doesn't require you to have an understanding as to how the internals of the object work. As I'm sure you understand, this is in line with your quest of building and using objects without having to understand how the original programmers put them together.

Inheritance enables you to, in effect, take another class and bolt on your own functionality, either by adding new methods and properties or by replacing existing methods and properties. What you're trying to do is move from a general car class to more specific variations—for example, sports car, SUV, van, and so on.

So, if you wanted to model a sports car it is likely that you would want to have a default number of doors as 2 instead of 5, and you might also like to have properties and methods that help you understand the performance of the car, such as `Weight` and `PowerToWeightRatio`, as shown in Figure 10-6.

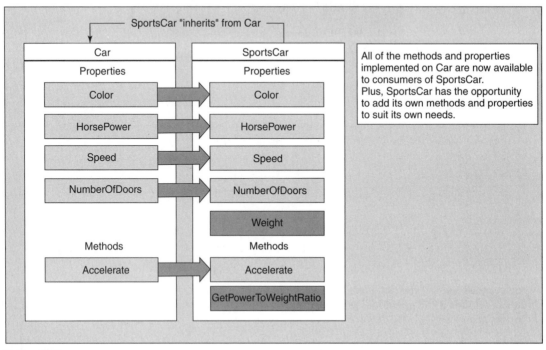

Figure 10-6

One thing that you need to understand about inheritance is the way that access to public and private members is controlled. Any public member like `Color` is accessible to derived classes. However, private members like `Speed` are not. This means that if `SportsCar` has to change the speed of the car, it has to do so through the properties and methods provided in `Car` itself.

Adding New Methods and Properties

To illustrate inheritance you need to create a new class called `SportsCar`, which is inherited from `Car` and enables you to see the power to weight ratio of your sports car.

Inheriting from Car

1.   For the purpose of this demonstration you need to add an additional public variable to `Car` that represents the horsepower of the car. Of course, if you want to make it really robust you would use a property and ensure a sensible range of values. But here, simplicity and speed wins out. Open `Car.vb` and add this line of code as indicated:

```
Public Class Car
    Public Color As String
    Public HorsePower As Integer
```

```
Private _speed As Integer
Private _numberOfDoors As Integer
```

2. Now, create a new class in the usual way by right-clicking the Objects project in the Solution Explorer and select Add ⇨ Add Class. Enter the name of the class as SportsCar and click Open.

3. To tell SportsCar that it's inherited from Car you need to use the Inherits keyword. Add this code to SportsCar.vb:

```
Public Class SportsCar
    Inherits Car
End Class
```

4. At this point, SportsCar now has all of the methods and properties that Car has. What you want to do now is add a new public variable called Weight:

```
Public Class SportsCar
    Inherits Car
    Public Weight As Integer
End Class
```

5. To test the new property you need to add some new code to Module1.vb. Pay close attention to the fact that you need to create a SportsCar object, not a Car object in order to get at the Weight property. Add this new code as indicated:

```
    ' display the details of the car...
    DisplayCarDetails(myCar)
    ' create a new SportsCar object...
    Dim mySportsCar As SportsCar
    mySportsCar = New SportsCar()
    ' set the horsepower and weight (kg)...
    mySportsCar.HorsePower = 240
    mySportsCar.Weight = 1085
    ' report the details...
    Console.WriteLine("Sports Car Horsepower:" & mySportsCar.HorsePower)
    Console.WriteLine("Sports Car Weight:" & mySportsCar.Weight)
    ' wait...
    Console.ReadLine()
End Sub
```

6. Try running the project and you'll see an output similar to that shown in Figure 10-7.

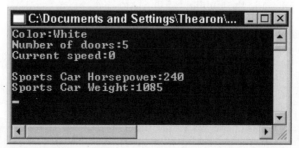

Figure 10-7

How It Works

The directive to inherit `SportsCar` from `Car` is done with the `Inherits` keyword:

```
Public Class SportsCar
    Inherits Car
```

At this point, the new `SportsCar` class contains all of the methods and properties in the `Car` class, but it cannot see or modify the private member variables. When you add your new property:

```
Public Weight As Integer
```

… you now have a new property that's only available when you create instances of `SportsCar` and not available to those creating plain instances of `Car`. This is an important point to realize—if you don't create an instance of `SportsCar`, you'll get a compile error if you try to access the `Weight` property. `Weight` isn't, and never has been, a property of `Car` (see Figure 10-6 for a clarification of this situation).

When you run the project you do indeed instantiate a new instance of `SportsCar`. This allows you to get and set the value for `Weight`.

Adding a GetPowerToWeightRatio Method

A `GetPowerToWeightRatio` method could be implemented as a read-only property (in which case you would probably call it `PowerToWeightRatio` instead), but for this discussion you'll add it as a method.

Try It Out   Adding a GetPowerToWeightRatio Method

1. For this method all you need to do is divide the horsepower by the weight. Add this code to `SportsCar.vb` as indicated below:

```
Public Class SportsCar
    Inherits Car
    Public Weight As Integer
    ' GetPowerToWeightRatio - work out the power to weight...
    Function GetPowerToWeightRatio() As Double
        ' do the calculation...
        Return CType(HorsePower, Double) / CType(Weight, Double)
    End Function
End Class
```

2. To see the results, add the highlighted line to `Module1.vb`:

```
' create a new SportsCar object...
Dim mySportsCar As SportsCar
mySportsCar = New SportsCar()
' set the horsepower and weight (kg)...
mySportsCar.HorsePower = 240
mySportsCar.Weight = 1085
' report the details...
Console.WriteLine("Horsepower:" & mySportsCar.HorsePower)
Console.WriteLine("Weight:" & mySportsCar.Weight)
Console.WriteLine("Power/weight:" & mySportsCar.GetPowerToWeightRatio)
```

```
    ' wait...
    Console.ReadLine()
End Sub
```

3. Run the project and you'll see something similar to Figure 10-8.

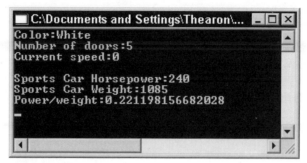

```
C:\Documents and Settings\Thearon\...  _ □ ×
Color:White
Number of doors:5
Current speed:0

Sports Car Horsepower:240
Sports Car Weight:1085
Power/weight:0.221198156682028
```

Figure 10-8

How It Works

Again, all you've done is add a new method to the new class called `GetPowerToWeightRatio`. This method then becomes available to anyone working with an instance of `SportsCar` as shown in Figure 10-9.

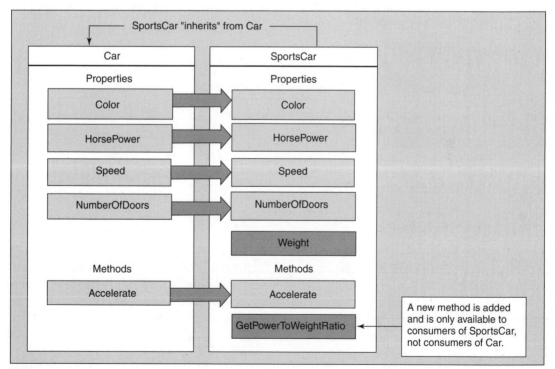

Figure 10-9

The only thing you have to be careful of is that if you divide an integer by an integer you get an integer result, but what you actually want here is a floating-point number. You have to convert the integer `HorsePower` and `Weight` properties to `Double` values in order to see the results:

```
Return CType(HorsePower, Double) / CType(Weight, Double)
```

Changing Defaults

In addition to adding new properties and methods, you might want to change the way an existing method or property works from that of the base class. In order to do this, you need to create your own implementation of the method or property.

Think back to the discussion on constructors. These are methods that are called whenever the object is created and let you get the object into a state where it can be used by a developer. In this constructor you set the default _numberOfDoors value to be 5. However, in a sports car this number should ideally be 2.

The class inherited from is known as the base class (which is `Car` in this example). If you want to replace an existing method or property with your own, the process is called *overriding*. In this next section you learn how to override the base class's constructor.

Try It Out   Overriding a Constructor

1. To override the constructor all you have to do is create your own constructor in the new `SportsCar` class. Add this code to `SportsCar`:

```
Public Class SportsCar
    Inherits Car
    Public Weight As Integer
    ' Constructor...
    Sub New ()
        ' change the defaults...
        Color = "Green"
        NumberOfDoors = 2
    End Sub
    ' GetPowerToWeightRatio - work out the power to weight...
    Function GetPowerToWeightRatio() As Double
        ' do the calculation...
        Return CType(HorsePower, Double) / CType(Weight, Double)
    End Function
End Class
```

2. To test the constructor you need to display the details of a `SportsCar`. So, add a call to `DisplayCarDetails` and pass in `mySportsCar`. Make this addition to `Module1.vb`.

```
Sub Main()

        ' create a new car object...
        Dim myCar As Car
        myCar = New Car
        ' display the details of the car...
```

```
        DisplayCarDetails(myCar)
        ' create a new SportsCar object...
        Dim mySportsCar As SportsCar
        mySportsCar = New SportsCar
        ' display the details of the sports car...
        DisplayCarDetails(mySportsCar)
        ' set the horsepower and weight (kg)...
        mySportsCar.HorsePower = 240
        mySportsCar.Weight = 1085
        Console.WriteLine("Sports Car Horsepower:" & mySportsCar.HorsePower)
        Console.WriteLine("Sports Car Weight:" & mySportsCar.Weight)
        Console.WriteLine("Power/weight:" & mySportsCar.GetPowerToWeightRatio)
        ' wait...
        Console.ReadLine()
End Sub
```

3. Now try running the project. You should see an output similar to Figure 10-10.

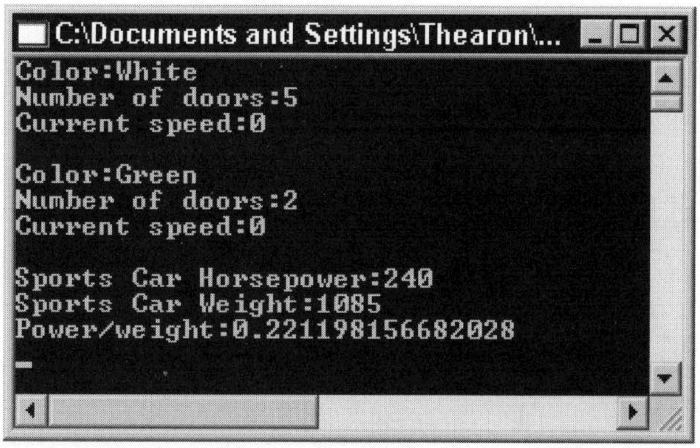

Figure 10-10

How It Works

The new constructor that you added to SportsCar runs after the existing one in Car. .NET knows that it's supposed to run the code in the constructor of the base class before running the new constructor in the class that inherits from it, so in effect it runs this code first:

```
' Constructor...
Sub New()
    ' set the defaults:
    Color = "White"
    _speed = 0
    _numberOfDoors = 5
End Sub
```

...and then runs this code:

```
' Constructor...
Sub New()
    ' change the defaults...
```

```
      Color = "Green"
      NumberOfDoors = 2
   End Sub
```

To summarize what happens:

1. The constructor on the base class `Car` is called

2. `Color` is set to `White`

3. `_speed` is set to `0`

4. `_numberOfDoors` is set to `5`

5. The constructor on the new class `SportsCar` is called

6. `Color` is set to `Green`

7. `NumberOfDoors` is set to `2`

Because you defined _numberOfDoors as a private member in `Car`, you cannot directly access it from inherited classes, just as you wouldn't be able to directly access it from a consumer of the class. Instead, you rely on being able to set an appropriate value through the `NumberOfDoors` property.

Polymorphism: Scary Word, Simple Concept

Another very common word mentioned when talking about object-oriented programming is polymorphism. This is, perhaps the scariest term, but one of the easiest to understand! In fact, you have already done it in the previous example.

Look again at the code for `DisplayCarDetails`:

```
' DisplayCarDetails - function that displays a car's details...
Function DisplayCarDetails(ByVal myCar As Car)
    ' display the details of the car...
    Console.WriteLine("Color:" & myCar.Color)
    Console.WriteLine("Number of doors:" & myCar.NumberOfDoors)
    Console.WriteLine("Current speed:" & myCar.Speed)
    Console.WriteLine()
End Function
```

The first line says that the parameter you want to accept is a `Car` object. But, when you call the object you're actually passing it a `SportsCar` object. Look at how you create the object and call `DisplayCarDetails`:

```
' create a new car object...
Dim mySportsCar As SportsCar
mySportsCar = New SportsCar()
' display the details of the car...
DisplayCarDetails(mySportsCar)
```

How can it be that if the function takes a `Car` object, you're allowed to pass it as a `SportsCar` object?

Well, *polymorphism* (which comes from the Greek for "many forms") means that an object can be treated as if it were a different kind of object, provided common sense prevails. In this case, you can treat a SportsCar object like a Car object because SportsCar inherits from Car. This act of inheritance dictates that anything a SportsCar object can do must include everything that a Car object can do; therefore, you can treat the two objects in the same way. If you need to call a method on Car, SportsCar must also implement the method.

This does not hold true the other way round. If you had a function defined like this:

```
Function DisplaySportsCarDetails(ByVal mySportsCar As SportsCar)
```

... you could not pass it a Car object. Car is not guaranteed to be able to do everything a SportsCar can do, because the extra methods and properties you add on to SportsCar won't exist on Car. SportsCar is a more specific type of Car.

So, to summarize, when people talk about polymorphism this is the action they are referring to—the principle that an object can behave as if it were another object without the developer having to go through too many hoops to make it happen.

Overriding More Methods

Although you've overridden Car's constructor, for completeness you should look at how to override a normal method.

To override a method you need to have the method in the base Car class. Because Accelerate shouldn't change depending on whether you have a sports car or a normal car and IsMoving was added for ease of use—and hence doesn't really count in this instance as it isn't a behavior of the object—you need to add a new method called CalculateAccelerationRate. Assume that on a normal car this is a constant, and on a sports car you change it so that it takes the power to weight ratio into consideration.

Try It Out   Adding Another Method

1.   Add this method below the IsMoving method in Car.vb.

```
' CalculateAccelerationRate - assume a constant for a normal car...
Function CalculateAccelerationRate() As Double
    ' if we assume a normal car goes from 0-60 in 14
    ' seconds, that's an average rate of 4.2 mph/s...
    Return 4.2
End Function
```

2.   Now to test the method, change the DisplayCarDetails procedure in Module1.vb to read like this:

```
' DisplayCarDetails - function that displays a car's details...
    Sub DisplayCarDetails(ByVal myCar As Car)
        ' display the details of the car...
        Console.WriteLine("Color:" & myCar.Color)
        Console.WriteLine("Number of doors:" & myCar.NumberOfDoors)
        Console.WriteLine("Current speed:" & myCar.Speed)
        Console.WriteLine("Acceleration rate:" & _
```

```
                myCar.CalculateAccelerationRate)
            Console.WriteLine()
    End Sub
```

3. Run the project and you'll get an output similar to Figure 10-11.

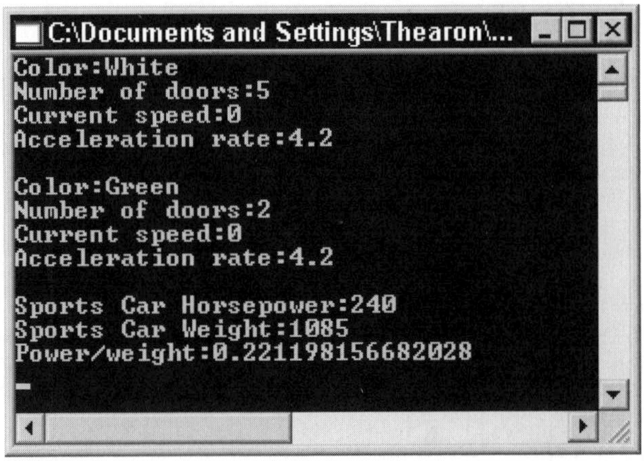

Figure 10-11

You've built a method on `Car` as normal. This method always returns a value of 4.2 mph/s for the acceleration rate.

Of course, our acceleration calculation algorithm is pure fantasy—no car is going to accelerate at the same rate irrespective of the gear, environment, current speed, and so on.

Try It Out   Overriding the New Method

1. To override the method you just have to provide a new implementation in `SportsCar`. However, there's one thing you need to do first. To override a method you have to mark it as `Overridable`. To do this, open `Car.vb` again and add the `Overridable` keyword to the method:

```
' CalculateAccelerationRate - assume a constant for a normal car...
Overridable Function CalculateAccelerationRate() As Double
    ' if we assume a normal car goes from 0-60 in 14
    ' seconds, that's a rate of 4.2 mph/s...
    Return 4.2
End Function
```

2. Now, you can create a method with the same name in `SportsCar.vb`. In order to override the method you must add the `Overrides` keyword before the method:

```
' CalculateAccelerationRate - take the power/weight into
' consideration...
Overrides Function CalculateAccelerationRate() As Double
    ' we'll assume the same 4.2 value, but we'll multiply it
    ' by the power/weight ratio...
    Return 4.2 * GetPowerToWeightRatio()
End Function
```

You didn't add the Overrides *keyword when you overrode the constructor because, basically, you didn't need to! Visual Basic .NET handled this for you.*

3. Before you can calculate the acceleration rate, you must first set the horsepower of your sports car. In Module1.vb, move the line of code that calls the DisplayCarDetails procedure after the lines of code that set the horsepower and weight, as shown below:

```
' create a new SportsCar object...
Dim mySportsCar As SportsCar
mySportsCar = New SportsCar
' set the horsepower and weight (kg)...
mySportsCar.HorsePower = 240
mySportsCar.Weight = 1085
' display the details of the sports car...
DisplayCarDetails(mySportsCar)
' report the details...
```

4. Now if you run the project you get an adjusted acceleration rate as shown in Figure 10-12.

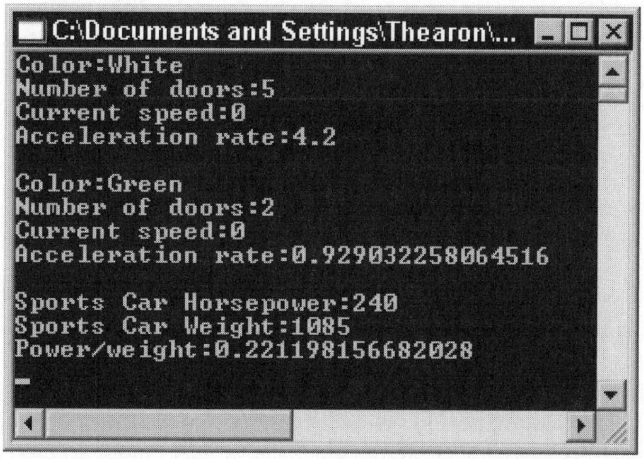

```
C:\Documents and Settings\Thearon\...
Color:White
Number of doors:5
Current speed:0
Acceleration rate:4.2

Color:Green
Number of doors:2
Current speed:0
Acceleration rate:0.929032258064516

Sports Car Horsepower:240
Sports Car Weight:1085
Power/weight:0.221198156682028
```

Figure 10-12

How It Works

Overriding the method lets you create your own implementation of an existing method on the object. Again, coming back to this concept of encapsulation, the object consumer doesn't have to know that anything is different about the object—they just call the method in the same way as they would for a normal Car object. This time, however, they get a different result rather than the constant value they always got on the normal Car object.

When you override a method, it's quite different from overriding a constructor. When you override a constructor the original constructor still gets called first. When you override a method, the original method only gets called if you specifically call it from inside the new method using Base.MethodName. *For example you could invoke* Base.CalculateAccelerationRate *from* SportsCar .CalculateAccelerationRate *to return a value of* 4.2.

Inheriting from Object

The final thing to look at, with respect to inheritance, is the fact that if you create a class without using the Inherits clause, the class will automatically inherit from a class called Object. This object provides you with a few methods that you can guarantee will be supported by every object you ever have. Most of these methods are beyond the scope of this book. However, the two most useful methods at this level are:

❑ ToString—this method returns a string representation of the object. You can override this to provide a helpful string value for any object, for example, you might want a person object to return that person's name. If you do not override it, it will return the name of the class name.

❑ GetType—this method returns a Type object that represents the data type of the object.

Remember, you do not have to explicitly inherit from Object. This happens automatically.

The Framework Classes

Although we discussed the .NET Framework in general in Chapter 2, let's take a look now at some aspects of the .NET Framework's construction that can help you when building objects. In particular, we want to take a look at namespaces and how you can create your own namespaces for use within your objects.

Namespaces

The .NET Framework is actually a vast collection of classes. There are around 3,500 classes in the .NET Framework all told, so how are you as developers supposed to find the ones that you want?

The .NET Framework is divided into a broad set of namespaces that group similar classes together. This limits the number of classes that you have to hunt through if you're looking for a specific piece of functionality.

These namespaces are also hierarchical in nature, meaning that a namespace can contain other namespaces that further group classes together. Each class must belong to exactly one namespace—it can't belong to multiple namespaces.

Most of the .NET Framework classes are lumped together in a namespace called System, or namespaces that are also contained within System. For example:

❑ System.Data contains classes related to accessing data stored in a database.

❑ System.Xml contains classes used to read and write XML documents.

❑ System.Windows.Forms contains classes for drawing windows on the screen.

❑ System.Net contains classes for communicating over a network.

The fact that namespaces exist means that all of the objects you've been using actually have longer names than the one's used in your software code. Until this point, you've been using a shorthand notation to refer to classes.

In fact, earlier when I said that everything has to be derived from `Object`, that was stretching it a bit. Because `Object` is contained within the `System` namespace, its full name is `System.Object`. Likewise, `Console` is actually shorthand for `System.Console`, meaning that this line:

```
Console.ReadLine()
```

...is actually the same as this line:

```
System.Console.ReadLine()
```

This can get a little silly, especially when you end up with object names like `System.Web.Services.Description.ServiceDescription`!

.NET automatically creates a shorthand version of all the classes within `System`, so you don't have to type `System.` all the time. Later, you'll see how you can add shorthand references to other namespaces.

Every class must be in exactly one namespace, but what about the classes we've made so far? Well, this project has a default namespace and your new classes are placed into this namespace.

Try It Out   Finding the Name of the Current Namespace

1. To see the namespace that you're using, right-click the Objects project in the Solution Explorer and select Properties.

2. The Root namespace entry in the Objects Property Pages window gives the name of the namespace that will be used for new classes as shown in Figure 10-13.

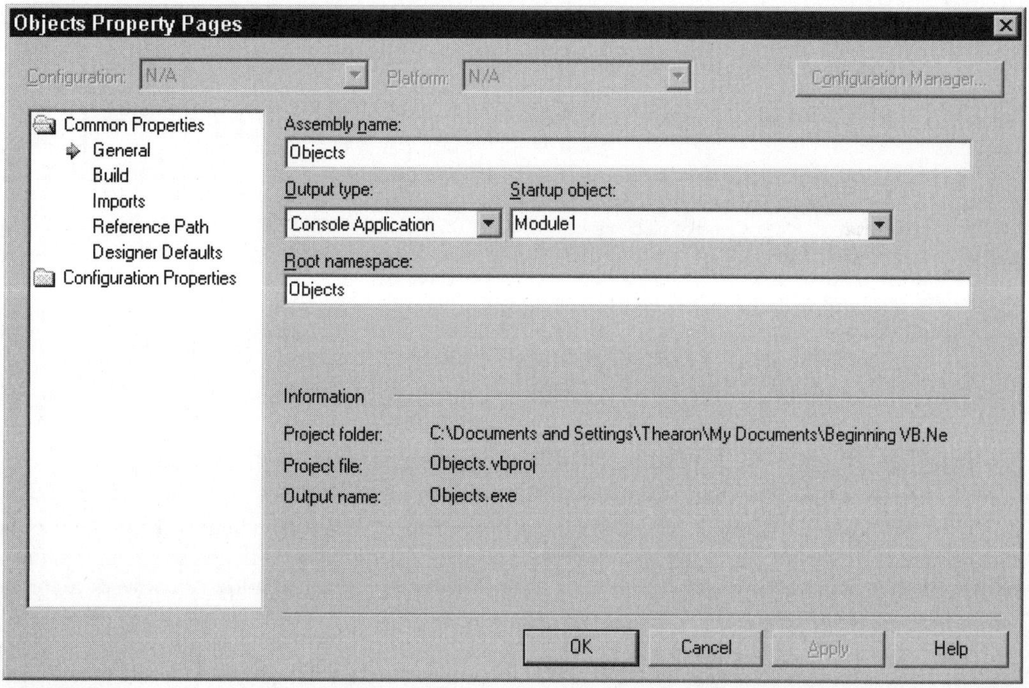

Figure 10-13

What this means is that your classes will have the text `Objects.` prefixed to them, like this:

❑ The `Car` class is actually called `Objects.Car`

❑ The `SportsCar` class is actually called `Objects.SportsCar`

> *As you may have guessed, .NET automatically creates a shorthand version of our classes too, so we can refer to* `SportsCar` *instead of having to type* `Objects.SportsCar`.

The motivation behind using namespaces is to make life easier for developers using your classes. Imagine that you give this project to another developer for use and they have already built their own class called `Car`. How do they tell the difference between their class and your class?

Well, yours will actually be called `Objects.Car`, whereas theirs will have a name like `MyOwnProject.Car` or `YaddaYadda.Car`. Namespaces remove the ambiguity of class names. Of course, I didn't choose a very good namespace because it doesn't really describe the classes that the namespace contains—I just chose a namespace that illustrated the purpose of the chapter.

The Imports Statement

Now you know you don't need to prefix your classes with `Car.` or `System.` as .NET automatically creates a shorthand version, but how do you do this yourself? The answer is the `Imports` statement!

If you go back to Chapter 4, you might remember this code from the top of a form:

```
Imports System.IO
Public Class Form1
    Inherits System.Windows.Forms.Form
```

as well as this code, behind a button on that form:

```
Private Sub btnGo_Click(ByVal sender As System.Object, _
            ByVal e As System.EventArgs) Handles btnGo.Click
    ' get a list of subfolders...
    Dim subfolders() As DirectoryInfo
    subfolders = New DirectoryInfo("c:\").GetDirectories
    ' loop...
    Dim subfolder As DirectoryInfo
    For Each subfolder In subfolders
        ' add the item to the list...
        lstData.Items.Add(subfolder.FullName)
    Next
End Sub
```

You used the `Imports System.IO` statement to import the `System.IO` namespace into your project. You needed to do this as you wanted to use the `DirectoryInfo` class. As stated in Chapter 4, the full name of this class is `System.IO.DirectoryInfo`, but because you had added a namespace import declaration you could just write `DirectoryInfo` instead.

All `Imports` statements must be written right at the top of the code file you want to use them in, before any other code.

The only drawback happens if you import two namespaces that have an identically named class or child namespace and Visual Basic .NET cannot tell what it is you are after (like `Car.Car` and `MyOwnProject.Car`). If this happens, you will be informed by Visual Basic .NET that the name is ambiguous—in which case the quickest and easiest thing to do is to specify the full name that you're after.

Creating Your Own Namespace

Namespaces are defined by wrapping the `Class...End Class` definition in a `Namespace...End Namespace` definition. By default, classes created in Visual Basic .NET are automatically assigned to a root namespace. Visual Studio .NET automatically names this root namespace based on the project name.

Creating a Namespace

1. Using the Solution Explorer, right-click the project and select Properties. The Root namespace field in the Common Properties ⇨ General pane option tells you the name. In this case, the root namespace name is `Objects`.

2. It's often recommended that you build your namespaces such that the full names of the classes you develop are prefixed with the name of your company. So, if my company was called `MyCodeWidgets`, ideally I would want my classes called `MyCodeWidgets.Car`. To do this, change Root namespace from `Objects` to `MyCodeWidgets` (see Figure 10-14). Then click the OK button to have this change applied to your project.

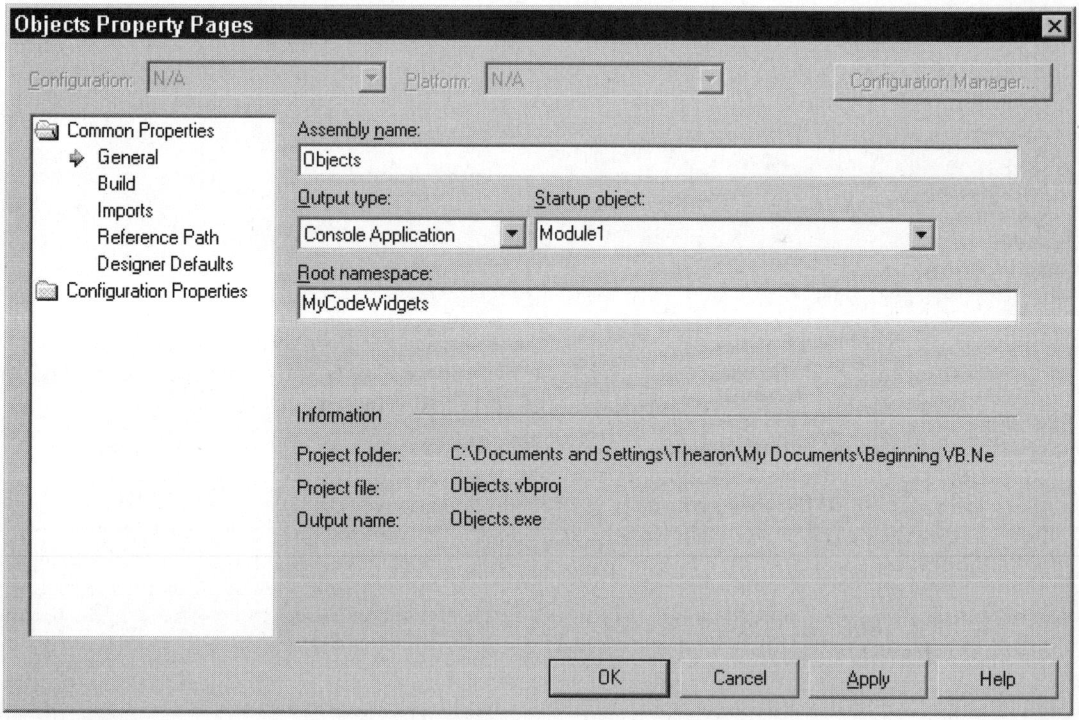

Objects Property Pages

Configuration: N/A	Platform: N/A	Configuration Manager...

Common Properties
→ General
  Build
  Imports
  Reference Path
  Designer Defaults
Configuration Properties

Assembly name:
Objects

Output type: | Startup object:
Console Application | Module1

Root namespace:
MyCodeWidgets

Information

Project folder: C:\Documents and Settings\Thearon\My Documents\Beginning VB.Ne
Project file: Objects.vbproj
Output name: Objects.exe

OK   Cancel   Apply   Help

Figure 10-14

3.   Visual Studio. NET's Object Browser is a useful tool that allows you to see what classes you have available in your project. You can find it by selecting View ⇨ Object Browser from the menu. When the Object Browser is displayed, the first item is usually the project. You can drill down into it to find your `Car` class (see Figure 10-15).

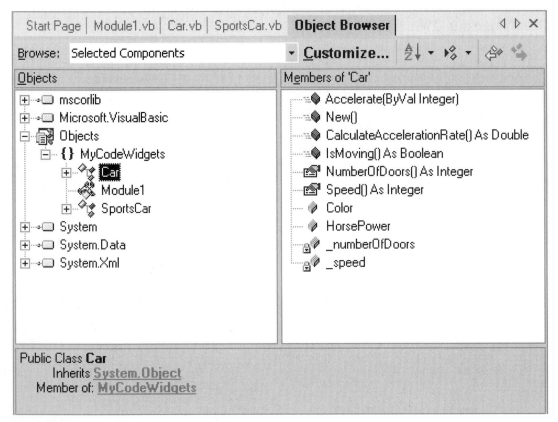

Figure 10-15

4.   Note that you can also see the methods, properties, and member variables listed for the class. Pertinent to this discussion, however, is the namespace. This is immediately above the class and is indicated by the icon containing the open and closed brace symbols ({ }).

So, that's fine, but imagine now you have two projects both containing a class called `Car`. You need to use namespaces to separate the `Car` class in one project from the `Car` class in another. Open the code editor for `Car` and add `Namespace CarPerformance` before the class definition and `End Namespace` after it. (I've omitted most of the code for brevity.)

```
Namespace CarPerformance
    Public Class Car
        . . .
    End Class
End Namespace
```

5. Now open the Object Browser again and you'll see a screen like the one in Figure 10-16.

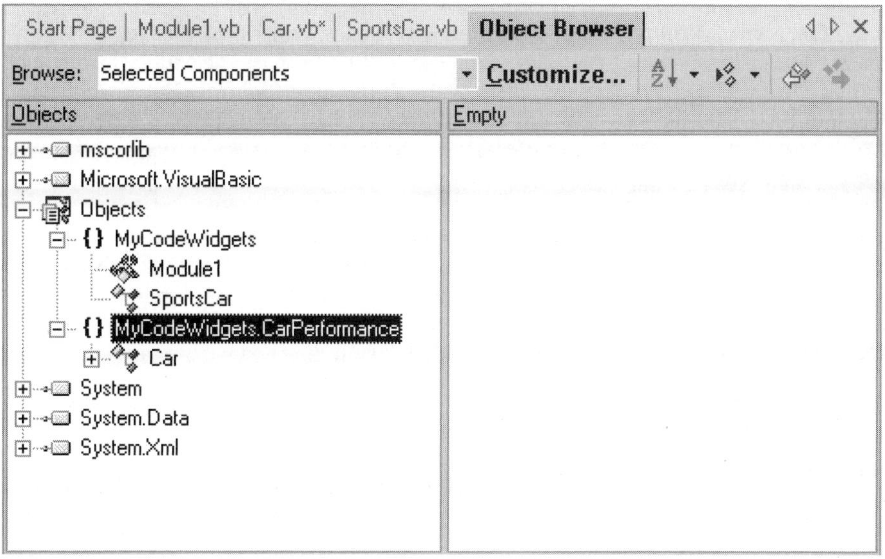

Figure 10-16

6. Since you have added the `CarPerformance` namespace to the `Car` class, any code that references the `Car` class will need to import that namespace in order to be able to access the shorthand methods of the `Car` class. Add this Imports statement to the very top of the `SportsCar` class and `Module1.vb` mode.

```
Imports MyCodeWidgets.CarPerformance
```

How It Works

What you've done is put `Car` inside a namespace called `CarPerformance`. As this namespace is contained within `MyCodeWidgets`, the full name of the class becomes `MyCodeWidgets .CarPerformance.Car`. If you put the classes of the other (imaginary) project into `CarDiagnostics` it would be called `MyCodeWidgets.CarDiagnostics.Car`.

Notice how Module1 still appears directly inside `MyCodeWidgets`. That's because you haven't wrapped the definition for Module1 in a namespace as you did with `Car`. Running your project at this point will produce the same results as before.

Inheritance in the .NET Framework

Inheritance is quite an advanced object-oriented topic. However, it's really important to include this here because the .NET Framework makes heavy use of inheritance.

One thing to understand about inheritance in .NET is that no class can inherit from more than one class. As everything must inherit from `System.Object` (the upshot of this is that everything must inherit from exactly one class. (Well, all except System.Object itself, but that's the exception that proves the rule.)

When I say that each class must inherit from exactly one class, I mean that each class can only mention one class in its Inherits clause. The class that it's inheriting from can also inherit from another class. So, for example, you could create a class called Porsche that is inherited from SportsCar. You could then say that it indirectly inherits from Car, but directly inherits from only one class—SportsCar. In fact, many classes indirectly inherit from lots of classes—but there is always a direct ancestry, where each class has exactly one parent.

Most of the classes that you will use in the .NET Framework, or that have been used so far, inherit some of their behavior from some other class. A good tool for viewing and learning about the different Namespace and Classes inside the .NET Framework is wincv.exe, as shown in Figure 10-17.

You can find wincv.exe off your Visual Studio .NET Install directory:

```
<drive>:\Program Files\Microsoft Visual Studio .NET 2003\SDK\v1.1\Bin
```

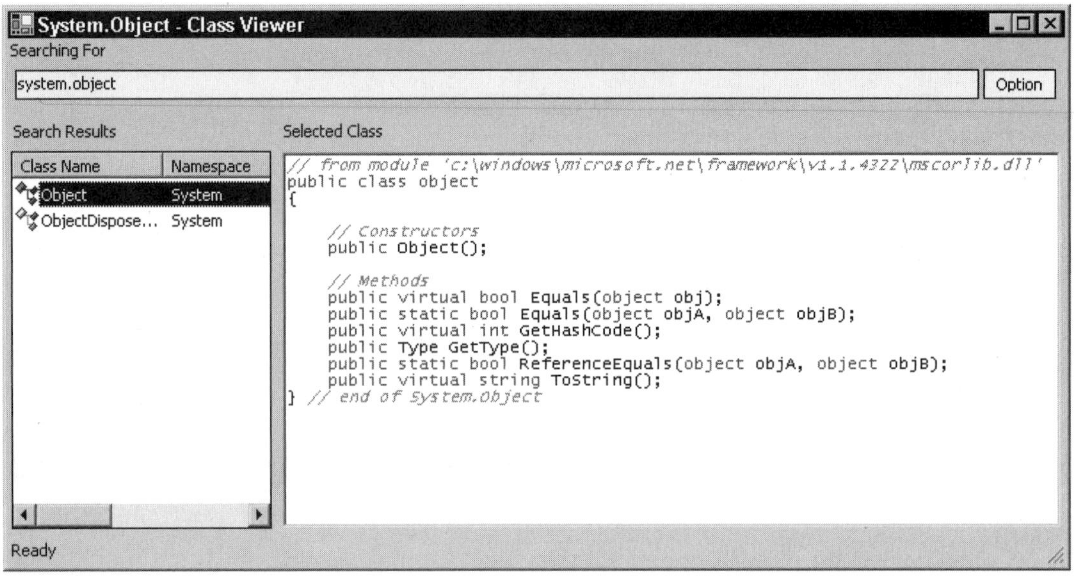

Figure 10-17

Summary

In this chapter, you looked at how to start building your own objects. You kicked off by learning how to design an object in terms of the properties and methods that it should support and then built a class that represented a car. You then started adding properties and methods to that class and used it from within your application.

Before moving on to the subject of inheritance you looked at how an object can be given a constructor—or rather a block of code that's executed whenever an object is created. Our discussion of inheritance demonstrated a number of key aspects of object-oriented design, including polymorphism and overriding.

To summarize, you should know how to:

- ❑   Create properties and methods in a class
- ❑   Provide a constructor for your class to initialize the state of your class
- ❑   Inherit another class
- ❑   Override properties and methods in the inherited class
- ❑   Create your own namespace for a class

Exercises

1.   What's the difference between a public and private member?
2.   How do you decide if something should be a property or a method? Give an example.
3.   What is a constructor? Why are they useful?
4.   What class do all other classes in .NET inherit from?
5.   What is overriding?

Advanced Object-Oriented Techniques

In the previous chapter, you looked at how you can build your own objects. Prior to that, you've been mostly using objects that already existed in the .NET Framework to build your applications. In this chapter, you'll be taking a look at some more object-oriented software development techniques.

In the first half of this chapter you create your own classes. This will be a single-tier application like the others we have discussed so far in this book. The idea of creating two-tier applications, as opposed to single-tier applications, will be introduced in Chapter 13. You will then learn about creating your own shared properties and methods. These are very useful when you want a method or property to apply to a class as a whole, rather than a specific instance of that class. Finally, you look at memory management in Visual Studio .Net and what you can do to clean up your objects properly.

Building a Favorites Viewer

In the first half of this chapter, you're going to build a simple application that displays all your Internet Explorer favorites and provides a button that you can click to open the URL in Internet Explorer. This application illustrates a key point regarding code reuse and some of the reasons why building code in an object-oriented fashion is so powerful.

Internet Shortcuts and Favorites

You're most likely familiar with the concepts of favorites in Internet Explorer. What you may not know is how Internet Explorer stores those favorites. In fact, the favorites list is available to all other applications—provided you know where to look.

Modern Windows 2000 and XP applications have the option of storing data in separate user folders within a folder called `C:\Documents and Settings`. In Figure 11-1 you can see that my computer has only one user folder—`Thearon`.

Default User is a special folder that Windows uses whenever a new user logs onto the computer for the first time and All Users contains items that are available to all users irrespective of who they log in as.

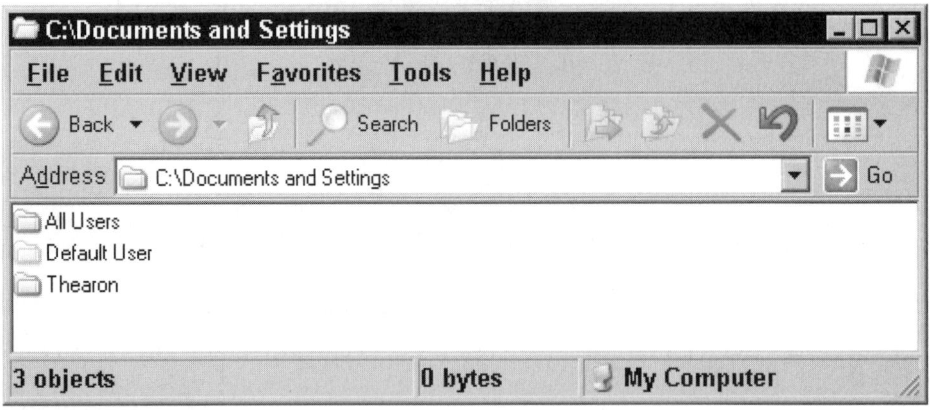

Figure 11-1

Depending on how the security of your computer is configured you may not be able to access this folder. Open the folder whose name matches the name that you supply when you log on. In the screenshots throughout this chapter, I've used `Thearon`. (If you cannot consistently open the folder, ask your system administrator to help you log in as a different user.) If you open this folder you'll find another group of folders. You'll see something like Figure 11-2 (though it may look different depending upon how your login is configured).

Figure 11-2

You'll notice that on my computer some of these folders appear as faint icons, whereas others appear as normal folders. My computer is configured to show all folders, so you may find that on your machine the faint folders do not appear as these are normally hidden. This doesn't matter because the one you're specifically looking for—`Favorites`—will appear whatever your system settings are.

This Thearon folder is where Windows stores a lot of folders that are related to the operation of your computer, for example:

- ❑ **Cookies** stores the cookies that are placed on the computer by Web sites that you visit
- ❑ **Desktop** stores the folders and links that appear on your desktop
- ❑ **Favorites** stores a list of Internet Explorer favorites
- ❑ **My Documents** stores the default location for storing Microsoft Office and other application data
- ❑ **Start Menu** stores a list of folders and links that appear when you press the Start button

It's the Favorites folder that you're interested in here, so open it. You'll see something like Figure 11-3 (obviously, this list will be different on your computer, as you'll have different favorites).

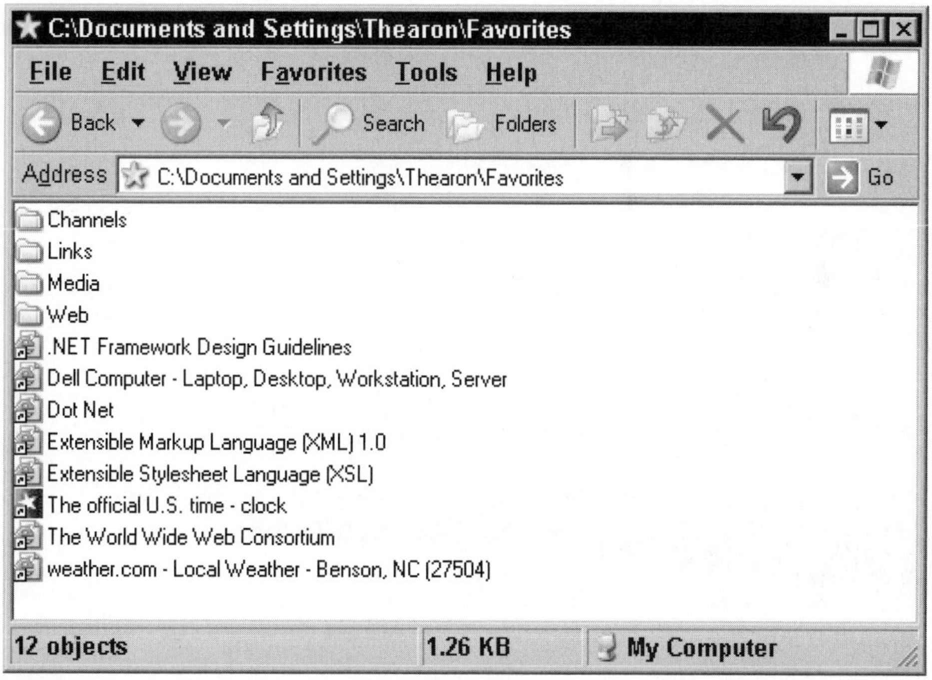

Figure 11-3

You'll notice that the links inside this folder relate to the links that appear in the Favorites menu in your browser. If you double-click one of those links you'll see that Internet Explorer opens and navigates to the URL that the favorite points to.

You can be fairly confident at this stage that, if you have a folder of links that appear to be favorites, you can create an application that opens this folder and can do something with the links—namely iterate through each of them, add them to a list, find out what URL they belong to, and provide a way to open that URL from our application. In our example, we're going to ignore the folders and just deal with the favorites that appear in the root Favorites folder.

Your final application will look like Figure 11-4.

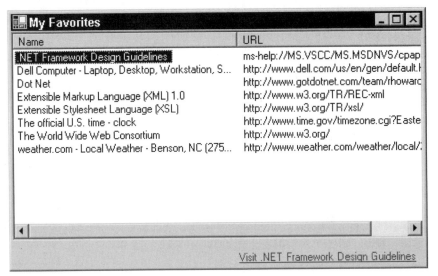

Figure 11-4

Using Classes

So far in this book you've built basic applications that do something, but most functionality that they provide has been coded into the applications' forms. Here, you're about to build some functionality that can load a list of favorites from the user's computer and provide a way to open Internet Explorer to show the URL. However, you do it in a way that means you can use the *list of favorites* functionality elsewhere.

The best way to build this application is to create a set of classes that include:

❑   A class called WebFavorite that represents a single favorite and has member variables such as Name and Url

❑   A class called Favorites that can scan the favorites list on the user's computer, creating a new WebFavorite object for each favorite

❑   A class called WebFavoriteCollection that contains a collection of WebFavorite objects

These three classes provide the *back-end* functionality of the application—in other words, all classes that do something but do not present the user with an interface. This isolates the code in the classes and allows you to reuse the code from different parts of the application—*code reuse*. You also need a *front end* to this application, which, in this case, will be a Windows form with a couple of controls on it.

In the next few sections, you build our classes and Windows application and come up with the application shown in Figure 11-4. You start by building the Windows Application project.

Try It Out   **Creating Favorites Viewer**

1.   Open Visual Studio .NET and create a new Visual Basic Windows Application project called Favorites Viewer.

2. When the Form Designer for Form1 appears, add a ListView control and a LinkLabel control to it, so that it resembles the form shown in Figure 11-4.

3. Select the ListView control and change these properties:

- ❑ Set Name to lstFavorites
- ❑ Set Anchor to Top, Bottom, Left, Right
- ❑ Set View to Details

4. Select the LinkLabel control and change these properties:

- ❑ Set Name to lnkUrl
- ❑ Set Anchor to Bottom, Left, Right
- ❑ Set TextAlign to Middle, Right

5. Select the lstFavorites control and select the Columns property in the Properties window. Click the ellipsis (...) button to display the ColumnHeader Collection Editor dialog box.

6. Click the Add button. Set these properties on the new column header:

- ❑ Set Name to hdrName
- ❑ Set Text to Name
- ❑ Set Width to 250

7. Click the Add button again to add a second column. Set these properties on the new column header:

- ❑ Set Name to hdrUrl
- ❑ Set Text to URL
- ❑ Set Width to 250

8. Click OK to close the editor.

9. Finally, change the Text property of the form to My Favorites and the StartPosition property to CenterScreen and your form should look similar to the one shown in Figure 11-5.

That's the basics of the form put together. Now look at how you can add the back-end classes. In the previous chapter you learned how to add classes to a Visual Studio .NET project, so you will use this feature to create the back end of your application.

Try It Out   Adding Classes

1. Using the Solution Explorer right-click Favorites Viewer. Select Add ⇨ Add Class from the menu to display the Add New Item dialog box. Select Class from the Templates list and give the class a name of WebFavorite. Your screen should look similar to Figure 11-6.

2. Click Open and the new class will be created.

All you've done so far is to create another class. For now, you need to turn your attention to actually putting some functionality into WebFavorite. In the next *Try It Out*, you start adding some methods and member variables to WebFavorite—the class that is used to instantiate objects that represent a single favorite.

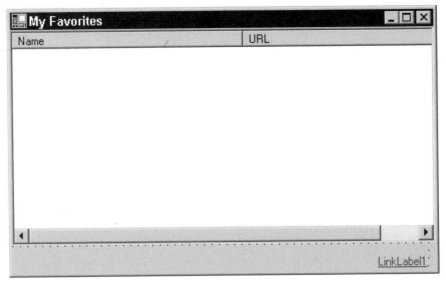

Figure 11-5

Figure 11-6

Try It Out   Building WebFavorite

1. Using the Solution Explorer, open the code editor for `WebFavorite` by right-clicking on it and selecting View Code if it is not already open.

2. Add this namespace import declaration to the top of the code listing:

```
Imports System.IO

Public Class WebFavorite
End Class
```

3. Then, add these two members at the top of the class:

```
Public Class WebFavorite

    ' members...
    Public Name As String
    Public Url As String
End Class
```

4. Next, add the following method:

```
' Load - open a .url file and populate ourselves...
Public Sub Load(ByVal fileInfo As FileInfo)

    ' firstly, set the name, but trim off the extension...
    Name = fileInfo.Name.Substring(0, _
        fileInfo.Name.Length - fileInfo.Extension.Length)

    ' open the file...
    Dim objFileStream As New FileStream(fileInfo.FullName, FileMode.Open)
    Dim objStreamReader As New StreamReader(objFileStream)

    ' go through each line...
    Do While True

        ' get a line...
        Dim strBuffer As String = objStreamReader.ReadLine
        If strBuffer Is Nothing Then Exit Do

        ' does the string start with "url="
        If strBuffer.StartsWith("URL=") Then

            ' set the url...
            Url = strBuffer.Substring(4)

            ' quit...
            Exit Do

        End If
    Loop
```

```
        ' close the file...
        objStreamReader.Close()
        objFileStream.Close()

    End Sub
```

5. Finally, add this method:

```
' Open - opens the favorite in IE...
Public Sub Open()
    System.Diagnostics.Process.Start(Url)
End Sub
```

Scanning Favorites

So that you can scan the favorites, you need to add a couple of new classes to the project. The first, WebFavoriteCollection, will be used to hold a collection of WebFavorite objects. The second, Favorites will physically scan the Favorites folder on the computer, create new WebFavorite objects, and add them to the collection.

Try It Out   Scanning Favorites

1. Using the Solution Explorer create a new class called WebFavoriteCollection. This class will be instantiated to an object that can hold a number of WebFavorite objects.

2. Add this code in your class:

```
Public Class WebFavoriteCollection
    Inherits CollectionBase

    ' Add - add items to the collection...
    Public Sub Add(ByVal Favorite As WebFavorite)
        List.Add(Favorite)
    End Sub

    ' Remove - remove items from the collection...
    Public Sub Remove(ByVal Index As Integer)
        If Index >= 0 And Index < Count Then
            List.Remove(Index)
        End If
    End Sub

    ' Item - get items by index...
    Public ReadOnly Property Item(ByVal Index As Integer) As WebFavorite
        Get
            Return CType(List.Item(Index), WebFavorite)
        End Get
    End Property

End Class
```

3. Create another new class called `Favorites`. This will be used to scan the Favorites folder and return a `WebFavoriteCollection` containing a `WebFavorite` object for each favorite in the folder. Start by adding this namespace declaration to the top of the code listing:

```
Imports System.IO

Public Class Favorites
End Class
```

4. Next, add this member:

```
Public Class Favorites

    ' members...
    Public FavoritesCollection As WebFavoriteCollection

End Class
```

5. You need a read-only property that can return the path to the user's Favorites folder. Add the following code within the `Favorites` class, below the code in the previous step and before the `End Class` statement:

```
' FavoritesFolder - returns the folder...
Public ReadOnly Property FavoritesFolder() As String
    Get
        Return _
        Environment.GetFolderPath(Environment.SpecialFolder.Favorites)
    End Get
End Property
```

6. Finally, you need a method that's capable of scanning through a folder looking for files. When it finds one, it will create a `WebFavorite` object and add it to the `Favorites` collection. You provide two versions of this method—one that automatically determines the path of the favorites by using the `FavoritesFolder` property and one that scans through a given folder. To do this add the following code to the `Favorites` class:

```
' ScanFavorites - look through the list of favorites...
Public Sub ScanFavorites()
    ScanFavorites(FavoritesFolder)
End Sub

Public Sub ScanFavorites(ByVal folderName As String)

    ' double-check... do we have a favorites list?
    If FavoritesCollection Is Nothing Then FavoritesCollection = New _
                WebFavoriteCollection()

    ' get the folder...
    Dim objScanFolder As New DirectoryInfo(folderName)

    ' look through each one...
```

```
        Dim objFavoriteFile As FileInfo
        For Each objFavoriteFile In objScanFolder.GetFiles

            ' is it a .url file?
            If String.Compare(objFavoriteFile.Extension, ".url", True) = 0 Then

                ' create a new webfavorite...
                Dim objWebFavorite As New WebFavorite
                objWebFavorite.Load(objFavoriteFile)

                ' add it to the collection...
                FavoritesCollection.Add(objWebFavorite)

            End If

        Next

    End Sub
```

To make all of this work, you need to get the Favorites Viewer project to create an instance of a
Favorites object, get it to scan the favorites, and add each one it finds to the list.

How It Works

There's a lot to take in there, but a good starting point is the WebFavoriteCollection class. This
illustrates an important best practice when working with lists of objects.

As you saw in Chapter 5, you can hold lists of objects in one of two ways—either by holding them in an
array or by holding them in a collection.

When building classes that work with lists, the best practice is to use a collection. You should build
collections that are also tied into using whatever types you're working with, so in this example you built
a WebFavoriteCollection class that exclusively holds a collection of WebFavorite objects.

You derived WebFavoriteCollection from System.Collections.CollectionBase. This
provides the basic list that the collection will use:

```
    Public Class WebFavoriteCollection
        Inherits CollectionBase
```

To fit in with the .NET Framework's way of doing things, you need to define three methods on a
collection that you build. The Add method adds an item to the collection:

```
    ' Add - add items to the collection...
    Public Sub Add(ByVal Favorite As WebFavorite)
        List.Add(Favorite)
    End Sub
```

The List property is a protected member of CollectionBase that only code within classes inheriting
from CollectionBase can access. You access this property to add, remove, and find items in the list.
You can see from the Add method here that you specified that the item must be a WebFavorite object.

This is why you're supposed to build collections using this technique—because you can only add objects of type `WebFavorite`, anyone who has hold of a `WebFavoriteCollection` object knows that it will only contain objects of type `WebFavorite`. This makes life much easier for them, because they will not get nasty surprises when they discover it contains something else, and therefore reduces the chance of errors. The `Remove` method that you built removes an item from the list:

```
' Remove - remove items from the collection...
Public Sub Remove(ByVal Index As Integer)
    If Index >= 0 And Index < Count Then
        List.Remove(Index)
    End If
End Sub
```

The `Item` method lets you get an item from the list when given a specific index:

```
' Item - get items by index...
Public ReadOnly Property Item(ByVal Index As Integer) _
    As WebFavorite
    Get
        Return CType(List.Item(Index), WebFavorite)
    End Get
End Property
```

Try It Out   Creating an Instance of a Favorites Object

1. In the form code, select (Overrides) in the Class Name combo box and select `OnLoad` in the Method Name combo box. Add this code:

```
Protected Overrides Sub OnLoad(ByVal e As System.EventArgs)

    ' create a favorites object...
    Dim objFavorites As New Favorites
    objFavorites.ScanFavorites()

    ' go through each favorite...
    Dim objWebFavorite As WebFavorite
    For Each objWebFavorite In objFavorites.FavoritesCollection

        ' add it to the list...
        Dim objItem As New ListViewItem
        objItem.Text = objWebFavorite.Name
        objItem.SubItems.Add(objWebFavorite.Url)
        lstFavorites.Items.Add(objItem)

    Next

End Sub
```

2. Run the project and you should see something like Figure 11-7.

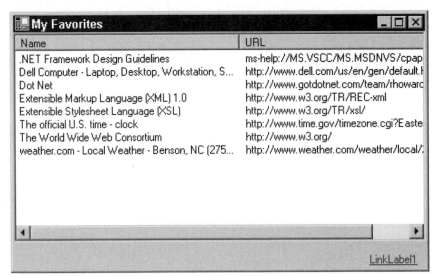

Figure 11-7

How It Works

So how do you populate this collection? Well, on the Favorites class you built a method called ScanFavorites. This takes a folder and examines it for files that end in .url. But, before you look at that you need to look at the FavoritesFolder property.

Since the location of the Favorites folder can change depending on the currently logged in user, you have to ask Windows where this folder actually is. To do this, you use the shared GetFolderPath method of the System.Environment class:

```
' FavoritesFolder - returns the folder...
Public ReadOnly Property FavoritesFolder() As String
    Get
        Return _
        Environment.GetFolderPath(Environment.SpecialFolder.Favorites)
    End Get
End Property
```

GetFolderPath can be used to return most of the special system folders available on the computer, including the location of the My Documents folder, the Program Files folder, and where Windows itself is installed. Look in the MSDN documentation under the GetFolderPath method of the Environment class for more information.

When the application asks us to load in the favorites from the disk, it calls ScanFavorites. The first version of this takes no parameters. It looks up the location of the user's Favorites folder and passes that to another version of the method:

```
' ScanFavorites - look through the list of favorites...
Public Sub ScanFavorites()
    ScanFavorites(FavoritesFolder)
End Sub
```

The first thing that this second version of the method does is to check to ensure that the `Favorites` member contains a `WebFavoriteCollection` object. If it doesn't, it creates one:

```
Public Sub ScanFavorites(ByVal folderName As String)

    ' double-check... do we have a favorites list?
    If FavoritesCollection Is Nothing Then FavoritesCollection = New _
                    WebFavoriteCollection()
```

The method then creates a `System.IO.DirectoryInfo` object that you can use to find the files:

```
    ' get the folder...
    Dim objScanFolder As New DirectoryInfo(folderName)
```

After you have that, you scan through each file in turn:

```
    ' look through each one...
    Dim objFavoriteFile As FileInfo
    For Each objFavoriteFile In objScanFolder.GetFiles
```

Whenever you come across a file, you check to make sure that the file's extension is `.url`. You use `String.Compare` to perform a case-insensitive match for you:

```
        ' is it a .url file?
        If String.Compare(objFavoriteFile.Extension, ".url", True) = 0 Then
```

If you find a file, you create a new `WebFavorite` object and call `Load`. You examine `Load` in a moment, but suffice it to say that this method opens the `.url` file and determines which URL the favorite actually points to:

```
            ' create a new webfavorite...
            Dim objWebFavorite As New WebFavorite()
            objWebFavorite.Load(objFavoriteFile)
```

After you have the new `WebFavorite` object, we add it to `FavoritesCollection`:

```
            ' add it to the collection...
            FavoritesCollection.Add(objWebFavorite)

        End If

    Next

End Sub
```

How It Works: WebFavorite

The next thing we need to examine is how the `WebFavorite` object populates itself when the `Load` method is called. The first thing to do is set the `Name` variable by taking the name of the file (for example `"The Register.url"`) and removing the extension. The `Substring` method of the string class lets you do this, and here you're saying, "Take a substring, starting at the zeroth or first character, and continue for the complete length of the string minus the length of the `Extension` property." This, in effect, removes the `.url` from the end. Notice that the array of `Char` variables that make up a string is zero-based, just like all the arrays that you've seen so far.

```
' Load - open a .url file and populate ourselves...
Public Sub Load(ByVal fileInfo As FileInfo)

    ' firstly, set the name, but trim off the extension...
    Name = fileInfo.Name.Substring(0, _
            fileInfo.Name.Length - fileInfo.Extension.Length)
```

After you have the name, you open the file and create a new `System.IO.StreamReader` object that lets you read data from the file line by line:

```
    ' open the file...
    Dim objFileStream As New FileStream(fileInfo.FullName, FileMode.Open)
    Dim objStreamReader As New StreamReader(objFileStream)
```

You then set up a loop and read a single line from the file per iteration. If this line comes back as blank or `Nothing`, you quit the loop as this signals the end of the file:

```
    ' go through each line...
    Do While True

        ' get a line...
        Dim strBuffer As String = objStreamReader.ReadLine
        If strBuffer Is Nothing Then Exit Do
```

When you have the line, you look to see whether it starts with the text `URL=`. If it does, you use `Substring` again, but this time you create a string starting at the fourth index (fifth character) of the string all the way until the end. Once you have the URL, you also quit the loop because there's no need to continue looking through the file when you have the data you need:

```
        ' does the string start with "url="
        If strBuffer.StartsWith("URL=") Then

            ' set the url...
            Url = strBuffer.Substring(4)

            ' quit...
            Exit Do

        End If

    Loop
```

After you're finished with the file, you close it and `StreamReader`:

```
    ' close the file...
    objStreamReader.Close()
    objFileStream.Close()

End Sub
```

So at this point you can create an instance of a `Favorites` object and ask it to scan through the favorites. You can also get a list of the favorites back. To finish off this discussion, this is what happens when the form is loaded.

How It Works: Loading Form1

First, you create a new `Favorites` object. Once you have the object, you ask it to scan the favorites by calling the `ScanFavorites` method. The effect here is that a new `WebFavoritesCollection` object will be created and filled, and will be accessible through the `FavoritesCollection` property:

```
Protected Overrides Sub OnLoad(ByVal e As System.EventArgs)

    ' create a favorites object...
    Dim objFavorites As New Favorites()
    objFavorites.ScanFavorites()
```

After `ScanFavorites` has finished, you take each favorite in turn and add it to the list:

```
    ' go through each favorite...
    Dim objWebFavorite As WebFavorite
    For Each objWebFavorite In objFavorites.FavoritesCollection

        ' add it to the list...
        Dim objItem As New ListViewItem()
        objItem.Text = objWebFavorite.Name
        objItem.SubItems.Add(objWebFavorite.Url)
        lstFavorites.Items.Add(objItem)

    Next

End Sub
```

That's it! Now you can display a list of the favorites that the user has installed on their machine. However, you can't actually view favorites so let's look at that now.

Viewing Favorites

You already built a method on `WebFavorite` called `Open` that contains code to open the favorite and run it. What you need to do now is to change your application so that when a favorite is selected from the list, the LinkLabel control at the bottom of the form is configured to report the name of the selected favorite and when this control is clicked, Internet Explorer opens to the URL of the favorite.

At the moment, when you add items to the list you're creating, configuring, and adding `ListViewItem` objects. When an item is selected from the list you can find only the currently selected `ListViewItem` object, and resolving this object to a `WebFavorite` that you can actually use is quite hard. What you want to do instead is to create a new class derived from `ListViewItem`. You can easily add a property to this new class that references a `WebFavorite` object and by virtue of the fact that it's derived from `ListViewItem`, we can add it to the list without any problems.

Try It Out   **Viewing Favorites**

1. Using the Solution Explorer, add a new class to the Favorite `Viewer` project called `WebFavoriteListViewItem`.

2. Next, set the class to inherit from `System.Windows.Forms.ListViewItem`, like this:

```
Public Class WebFavoriteListViewItem
    Inherits ListViewItem

End Class
```

3. Finally, add this member and this new constructor to the class:

```
Public Class WebFavoriteListViewItem
    Inherits ListViewItem
    ' members...
    Public Favorite As WebFavorite

    ' Constructor...
    Public Sub New(ByVal newFavorite As WebFavorite)

        ' set the property...
        Favorite = newFavorite

        ' set the text...
        Text = Favorite.Name
        SubItems.Add(Favorite.Url)

    End Sub

End Class
```

4. Open the code editor for Form1. At the top of the class definition add this member:

```
Public Class Form1
    Inherits System.Windows.Forms.Form

    ' members...
    Private _selectedFavorite As WebFavorite
```

5. Next, add this property:

```
' SelectedFavorite property...
Public Property SelectedFavorite() As WebFavorite
    Get
        Return _SelectedFavorite
    End Get
    Set(ByVal Value As WebFavorite)

        ' store the item...
        _SelectedFavorite = Value
```

```
            ' did we select anything?
            If Not _SelectedFavorite Is Nothing Then

                ' update the link label control...
                lnkUrl.Text = "Visit " & _SelectedFavorite.Name
                lnkUrl.Enabled = True

            Else

                ' disable the link...
                lnkUrl.Enabled = False

            End If

        End Set
End Property
```

6. From the left drop-down list of the Code Editor select lstFavorites. From the right list select
   Click. Add this code to the new event handler:

```
Private Sub lstFavorites_Click(ByVal sender As Object, _
        ByVal e As System.EventArgs) Handles lstFavorites.Click

    ' reset the selection...
    SelectedFavorite = Nothing

    ' go through each item looking for the selected one...
    Dim objItem As WebFavoriteListViewItem
    For Each objItem In lstFavorites.Items

        ' selected?
        If objItem.Selected = True Then

            ' store the selected item...
            SelectedFavorite = objItem.Favorite

            ' exit the loop...
            Exit For

        End If

    Next

End Sub
```

7. Next, find the OnLoad method. Remember to select (Overrides) from the left drop down at the
   top of the code editor, as you did previously. Make this change to the method:

```
Protected Overrides Sub OnLoad(ByVal e As System.EventArgs)

    ' create a favorites object...
    Dim objFavorites As New Favorites()
    objFavorites.ScanFavorites()
```

```
        ' go through each favorite...
        Dim objWebFavorite As WebFavorite
        For Each objWebFavorite In objFavorites.FavoritesCollection

            ' add it to the list...
            Dim objItem As New WebFavoriteListViewItem(objWebFavorite)
            lstFavorites.Items.Add(objItem)

            ' if this is the first item, select it...
            If lstFavorites.Items.Count = 1 Then

                ' select it...
                objItem.Selected = True
                SelectedFavorite = objWebFavorite

            End If

        Next

End Sub
```

8. Finally, from the left drop-down list of the code editor select lnkUrl and from the right list select LinkClicked. Add this code to the new event handler:

```
Private Sub lnkUrl_LinkClicked(ByVal sender As System.Object, _
    ByVal e As System.Windows.Forms.LinkLabelLinkClickedEventArgs) _
    Handles lnkUrl.LinkClicked

    ' do we have a selection?
    If Not SelectedFavorite Is Nothing Then

        ' show it...
        SelectedFavorite.Open()

    End If

End Sub
```

9. Run the project. You should now see that when a URL is selected from the list, the LinkLabel control changes to reflect the name of the selected item. If you click on the link, Internet Explorer should open the URL.

How It Works

The most important change here was altering the code so that `WebFavoriteListViewItem` objects were added to the list rather than `ListViewItem`. If you do not do this, then when you ask the list for the selected item you get the text (`.Net Framework Design Guidelines`, `Dell Computer—Laptop, Desktop, Workstation, Server`, etc.) rather than a `WebFavorite` object. If you get the text, you have to somehow find the related `WebFavorite` object from the list maintained by the `Favorites` object.

When you built `WebFavoriteListViewItem` you provided a new constructor. This not only stored the favorite in `Favorite` member, but also set the `Text` property of the item and added a new sub-item that the list used to display the URL of the link. Before you built the `WebFavoriteListViewItem` class, the functionality to add the link to the list was in the form's `OnLoad` event handler. You've moved it here to the constructor of the new class:

```
' Constructor...
Public Sub New(ByVal newFavorite As WebFavorite)

        ' set the property...
        Favorite = newFavorite

        ' set the text...
        Text = Favorite.Name
        SubItems.Add(Favorite.Url)

End Sub
```

The `SelectedFavorite` property is also quite important. This handles the updating of the LinkLabel control to report the currently selected favorite and also disables the control if no item is selected:

```
' SelectedFavorite property...
Public Property SelectedFavorite() As WebFavorite
      Get
            Return _SelectedFavorite
      End Get
      Set(ByVal Value As WebFavorite)

            ' store the item...
            _SelectedFavorite = Value

            ' did we select anything?
            If Not _SelectedFavorite Is Nothing Then

                  ' update the link label control...
                  lnkUrl.Text = "Visit " & _selectedFavorite.Name
                  lnkUrl.Enabled = True

            Else

                  ' disable the link...
                  lnkUrl.Enabled = False

            End If

      End Set
End Property
```

Finding the currently selected item from a ListView control can be done in several ways. You can ask for the selected item using the `ListView.SelectedItems` property or you can iterate through each of the items in the list looking for one that has its `Selected` property set to `True`. You used the second option in this case:

```
Private Sub lstFavorites_Click(ByVal sender As Object, _
        ByVal e As System.EventArgs) Handles lstFavorites.Click

    ' reset the selection...
    SelectedFavorite = Nothing
    ' go through each item looking for the selected one...
    Dim objItem As WebFavoriteListViewItem
    For Each objItem In lstFavorites.Items

        ' selected?
        If objItem.Selected = True Then
```

After you have it, you set the `SelectedFavorite` property and quit the loop. Remember, setting that property has the effect of updating the LinkLabel control:

```
        ' store the selected item...
        SelectedFavorite = objItem.Favorite

        ' exit the loop...
        Exit For

    End If

    Next

End Sub
```

Finally, when the LinkLabel control is clicked, you check to make sure that you do have a `SelectedFavorite` and, if you do, call its `Open` method:

```
Private Sub lnkUrl_LinkClicked(ByVal sender As System.Object, _
        ByVal e As System.Windows.Forms.LinkLabelLinkClickedEventArgs) _
        Handles lnkUrl.LinkClicked

    ' do we have a selection?
    If Not SelectedFavorite Is Nothing Then

        ' show it...
        SelectedFavorite.Open()

    End If

End Sub
```

An Alternative Favorite Viewer

You know that building separate classes promotes reuse, but let's prove that. If code reuse is such a hot idea, you should be able to build another application that can use the functionality in the classes to find and open favorites but without having to rewrite or change any of the code.

In this case, you might have given a colleague the Favorites, WebFavorite, and WebFavorite Collection classes, and that colleague should be able to build a new application that uses this functionality without having to understand the internals of how Internet shortcuts work or how Windows stores the user's favorites.

Building a Favorites Tray

In this section, you build an application that displays a small icon on the system tray. Clicking this icon will open a list of the user's favorites as a menu as shown in Figure 11-8. Clicking a favorite automatically opens Internet Explorer to the URL.

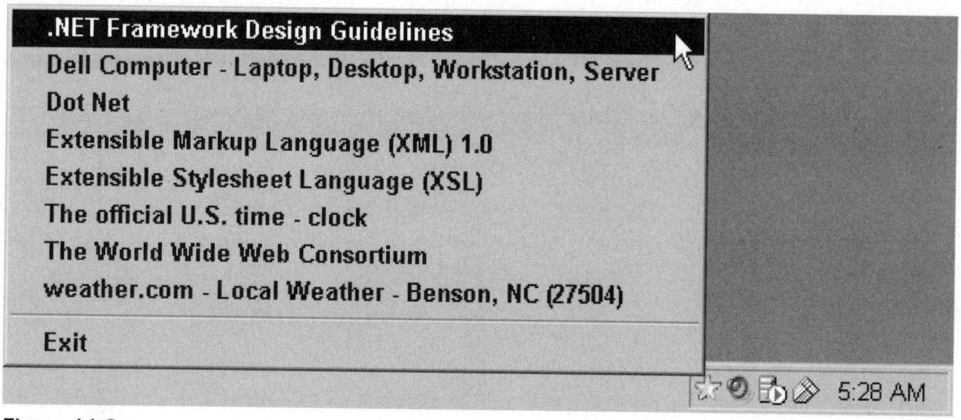

.NET Framework Design Guidelines
Dell Computer - Laptop, Desktop, Workstation, Server
Dot Net
Extensible Markup Language (XML) 1.0
Extensible Stylesheet Language (XSL)
The official U.S. time - clock
The World Wide Web Consortium
weather.com - Local Weather - Benson, NC (27504)

Exit

5:28 AM

Figure 11-8

To demonstrate this principle of reuse, you need to create a new Visual Basic .NET project.

Try It Out   **Building a Favorites Tray**

1. Using Visual Studio, select File ⇨ New ⇨ Project from the menu and create a new Visual Basic .NET Windows Application project called Favorites Tray.

2. When the Designer for Form1 appears, change the WindowState property to Minimized and change the ShowInTaskbar property to False. This will, effectively, prevent the form from being displayed.

3. Using the Toolbox, drag a NotifyIcon control onto the form. Set the Name property of the new control to icnNotify and set the Text property to Right-click me to view Favorites.

4. Next, open the code editor for Form1. Add the _loadCalled variable to the form:

```
Public Class Form1
    Inherits System.Windows.Forms.Form
    Private_loadCalled As Boolean = False
```

5. From the left drop-down list at the top of the code editor, select (Overrides) and from the right list select OnVisibleChanged. Add this code to the event handler:

```
Protected Overloads Overrides Sub OnVisibleChanged(ByVal _
                e As System.EventArgs)

    if _loadCalled = False Then
        Return
    End if
    ' if the user can see us, hide us...
    If Me.Visible = True Then Me.Visible = False

End Sub
```

6. You now need to design a new icon. (If you don't do this, the icon won't be displayed on the task bar and effectively our application won't do anything.) Using the Solution Explorer right-click on the Favorites Tray project and select Add ⇨ Add New Item. With Local Project Items selected in the Categories list, scroll down the Templates list and select Icon File, as shown in Figure 11-9. Enter the filename as Tray.ico and click Open.

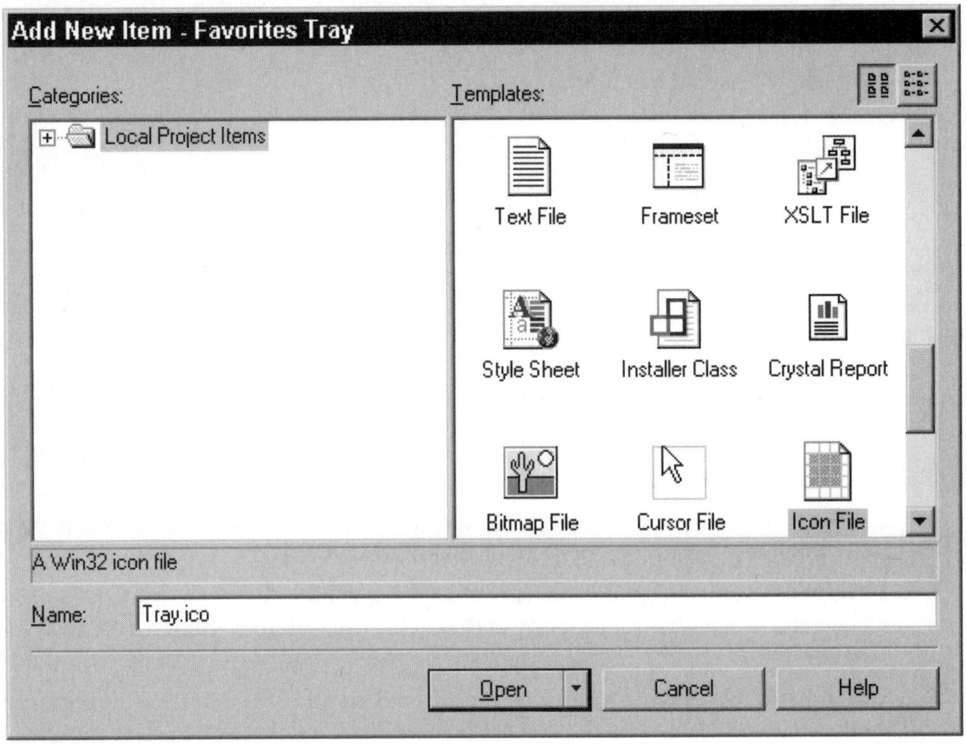

Figure 11-9

7. This displays Visual Studio .NET's Image Editor. You can use this to design new icons, new cursors, and new bitmap images for use in your applications. It's fairly intuitive to use, so I won't go through how you actually draw in much detail. In the toolbar you'll find a list of tools that you can use to design the icon, as shown in Figure 11-10.

8. Select Image ⇨ Show Colors Window to bring up the palette of colors shown in Figure 11-11, if they are not already displayed.

Figure 11-10

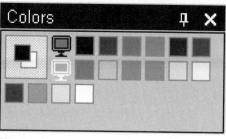

Figure 11-11

9. Before you start painting, you'll need to change the icon type. By default, Visual Studio .NET will create a 32×32 pixel icon, which is too large to fit on the tray. From the menu, select Image ⇨ New Image Type. Select 16×16, 256 colors and click OK.

10. This creates a new sub-icon within the image file, but you need to delete the main 32×32 icon, otherwise things will get confusing. From the menu again, select Image ⇨ Current Icon Image Types ⇨ 32×32, 16 colors. Then, immediately select Image ⇨ Delete Image Type from the menu.

11. If you're feeling creative, you can design your own icon for this application. On the other hand, you can do what I've done, which is to use a screen capture utility to take the favorites icon from Internet Explorer. My preferred utility is SnagIt (http://www.techsmith.com/), but a number of graphics programs offer this functionality.

12. Save the icon by selecting File ⇨ Save from the menu.

13. Go back to the Form Designer and select the icnNotify control. Use the Icon property in the properties list to open the icon you just created in the NotifyIcon control, as shown in Figure 11-12.

14. Try running the project now. You should discover that the tray icon will be added to your system tray as shown in Figure 11-13, but no window will appear.

15. Also, you'll notice that there appears to be no way to stop the program! Flip back to Visual Studio and select Debug ⇨ Stop Debugging from the menu.

16. When you do this, although the program will stop, the icon will remain in the tray. To get rid of it hover the mouse over it and it should disappear.

Windows only redraws the icons in the system tray when necessary, for example when the mouse is passed over it.

How It Works

Setting a form to appear minimized (WindowState = Minimized) and telling it not to appear in the taskbar (ShowInTaskbar = False) has the effect of creating a window that's hidden. You need a form to support the tray icon, but you don't need the form for any other reason. However, this is only half the

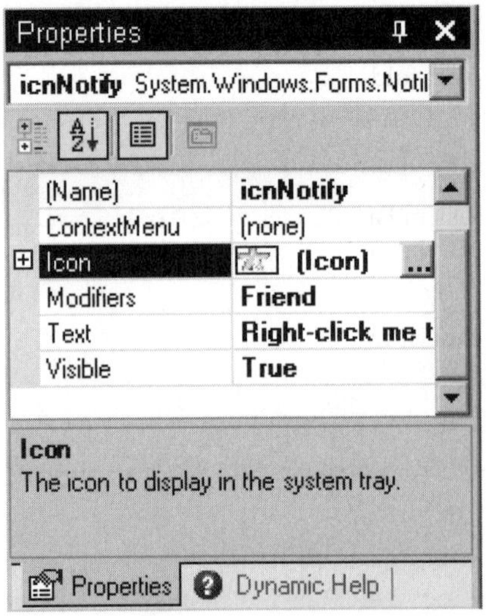

Properties ⧉ ✕

icnNotify System.Windows.Forms.Notif ▼

(Name)	**icnNotify**
ContextMenu	(none)
⊞ Icon	(Icon) ...
Modifiers	**Friend**
Text	**Right-click me t**
Visible	**True**

Icon
The icon to display in the system tray.

Properties ❷ Dynamic Help

Figure 11-12

Figure 11-13

battle because the form could appear in the *Alt+Tab* application switching list, unless you add the following code, which you already did:

```
Protected Overloads Overrides Sub OnVisibleChanged(ByVal _
            e As System.EventArgs)

    ' if the user can see us, hide us...
    If Me.Visible = True Then Me.Visible = False

End Sub
```

This event handler has a brute force approach that says, "If the user can see me, hide me."

Displaying Favorites

Now, let's look at how we can display the favorites. The first thing we need to do is to include the classes built in `Favorites Viewer` in this Favorites Tray solution. You can then use the `Favorites` object to get a list of favorites back and build a menu.

Try It Out   **Displaying Favorites**

1.   To display favorites, you need to get hold of the classes defined in the Favorites Viewer project. To do this you need to add the `Favorites`, `WebFavorite`, and `WebFavoriteCollection` classes to this solution.

Using the Solution Explorer, right-click the Favorites Tray project and select Add ⇨ Add Existing Item. Click the Browse button and find the `Favorites` class. This will be in the Favorites Viewer project folder. After clicking Open the class appears in the Solution Explorer. You can select multiple files at once by holding down the *Ctrl* key.

2. Repeat this for the other classes created in Favorties Viewer.

3. Now, create a new class in Favorites Tray by clicking the project once more and selecting Add ⇨ Add Class. Call the new class `WebFavoriteMenuItem`. This new class is pretty similar to the `WebFavoriteListViewItem` that you added in Favorites Viewer before.

4. Set the new class to inherit from `System.Windows.Forms.MenuItem`:

```
Public Class WebFavoriteMenuItem
    Inherits MenuItem

End Class
```

5. Add this member and method:

```
Public Class WebFavoriteMenuItem
    Inherits MenuItem

    ' members...
    Public Favorite As WebFavorite

    ' Constructor...
    Public Sub New(ByVal newFavorite As WebFavorite)

        ' set the property...
        Favorite = newFavorite

        ' update the text...
        Text = Favorite.Name

    End Sub

End Class
```

6. Unlike `ListViewItem`, `MenuItem` objects can react to themselves being clicked by overloading the `OnClick` method. From the left drop-down list in the code editor select (Overrides) and from the right drop-down list select `OnClick`. Add this code:

```
Protected Overrides Sub OnClick(ByVal e As System.EventArgs)
    ' open the favorite...
    If Not Favorite Is Nothing Then
        Favorite.Open()
    End If

End Sub
```

7. You need to do a similar trick to add an `Exit` option to your pop-up menu. Using the Solution Explorer create a new class called `ExitMenuItem` in the Favorites Tray project. Add the following code:

```
Public Class ExitMenuItem
    Inherits MenuItem

    ' Constructor...
    Public Sub New()
        Text = "Exit"
    End Sub

    ' OnClick...
    Protected Overrides Sub OnClick(ByVal e As System.EventArgs)
        Application.Exit()
    End Sub

End Class
```

8. Finally, you're in a position where you can load the favorites and create a menu for use with the tray icon. Add this member:

```
Public Class Form1
    Inherits System.Windows.Forms.Form

    ' members...
    Public Favorites As New Favorites()
```

9. From the left drop-down list select (Overrides) and from the right drop-down list select `OnLoad`. Now add the following code:

```
Protected Overrides Sub OnLoad(ByVal e As System.EventArgs)

    ' load the favorites...
    Favorites.ScanFavorites()

    ' create a new context menu...
    Dim objMenu As New ContextMenu()

    ' go through each favorite...
    Dim objFavorite As WebFavorite
    For Each objFavorite In Favorites.FavoritesCollection

        ' create a menu item and add it to the menu...
        Dim objItem As New WebFavoriteMenuItem(objFavorite)
        objMenu.MenuItems.Add(objItem)

    Next

    ' add a separator...
    objMenu.MenuItems.Add("-")
```

```
        ' then, add an exit option...
        objMenu.MenuItems.Add(New ExitMenuItem())

        ' finally, tell the tray icon to use this menu...
        icnNotify.ContextMenu = objMenu

    ' Set load flag
        _loadCalled = True
        Me.Hide()

End Sub
```

10. Run the project and the icon should appear on the tray. Right-click the icon and you'll be able to see a list of favorites as shown in Figure 11-14. Clicking on one will open Internet Explorer, while clicking on Exit will close the application.

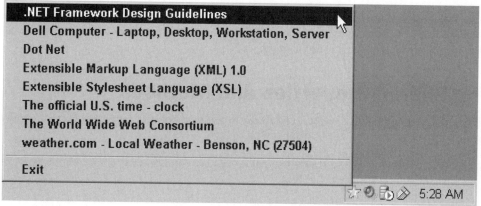

Figure 11-14

How It Works

One thing to note is because of the order of events you have to create a variable called _loadCalled. This variable makes sure that your favorites get loaded in the OnLoad method.

The WebFavoriteMenuItem is conceptually similar to the WebFavoriteListViewItem—in that you pass it a WebFavorite object and it configures itself. However, this class provides an OnClick method that you can overload. So, when the user selects the item from the menu you can immediately open up the URL:

```
Protected Overrides Sub OnClick(ByVal e As System.EventArgs)

    ' open the favorite...
    If Not Favorite Is Nothing Then
        Favorite.Open()
    End If

End Sub
```

The `ExitMenuItem` does a similar thing. When this item is clicked you call the shared `Application` `.Exit` method to quit the program:

```
' OnClick...
Protected Overrides Sub OnClick(ByVal e As System.EventArgs)
    Application.Exit()
End Sub
```

The important thing here is not the construction of the application itself, but rather the fact that you can reuse the functionality you built in a different project. This underlines the fundamental motive for reuse; it means you don't have to "reinvent the wheel" every time you want to do something.

The method of reuse described here was to add the existing classes to your new project, hence making a second copy of them. This isn't efficient as it takes up double the amount of storage needed for the classes, however, the classes are small so the cost of memory is minimal. It did save us from having to create the classes from scratch, allowing us to reuse the existing code, and it was very easy to do.

An alternative way of reusing classes is to create them in a class library. This class library is a separate project that can be referenced by a number of different applications so only one copy of the code is required. This is discussed in the next chapter.

Using Shared Properties and Methods

On occasion, you might find it useful to be able to access methods and properties that are not tied to an instance of an object, but are still associated with a class.

Imagine you have a class that stores the username and password of a user for a computer program. You might have something that looks like this:

```
Public Class User
    ' members...
    Public Username As String
    Private_password As String

End Class
```

Now imagine that the password for a user has to be of a minimum length. You create a separate member to store the length and implement a property like this:

```
Public Class User

    ' members...
    Public Username As String
    Private _password As String
    Public MinPasswordLength As Integer = 6

    ' Password property
    Public Property Password As String
        Get
            Return _password
```

```
        End Get
        Set(Value As String)
            If Value.Length >= MinPasswordLength Then
                _password = Value
            End If
        End Set
    End Property

End Class
```

That seems fairly straightforward. But now imagine that you have 5000 user objects in memory. Each `MinPasswordLength` takes up 4 bytes of memory, meaning that 20KB of memory is being used just to store the same value. Although 20KB of memory isn't a lot for modern computer systems, it's extremely inefficient and there is a better way.

Using Shared Procedures

Ideally, you want to store the value for the minimum password length in memory against a specific class once and share that memory between all of the objects created from that class as you do in the following *Try It Out*.

Try It Out   Using Shared Properties

1. Open Visual Studio .NET and create a new Visual Basic Windows Application project. Call it SharedDemo.

2. When the Designer for Form1 appears, change the Text property of the form to Shared Demo and then paint on a ListBox and a TrackBar control, as shown in Figure 11-15.

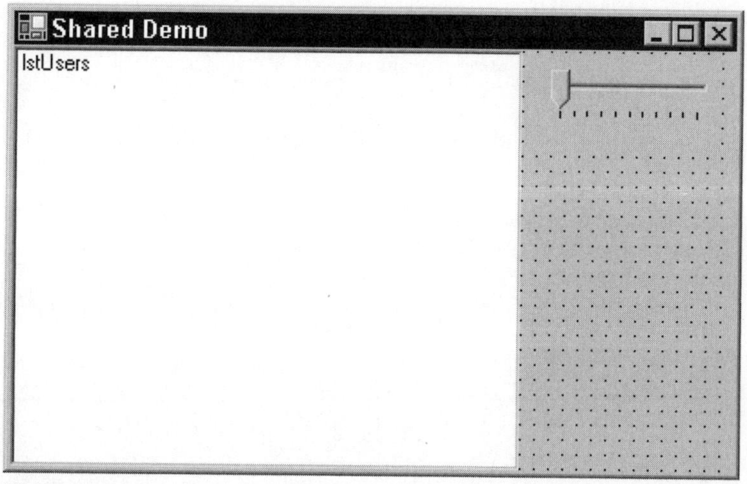

Figure 11-15

3. Set the Name property of the ListBox control to lstUsers.

4. Set the `Name` property of the TrackBar control to `trkMinPasswordLength` and set the Value property to 6.

5. Using the Solution Explorer create a new class named `User`. Add this code:

```
Public Class User

    ' members...
    Public Username As String
    Private _password As String
    Public Shared MinPasswordLength As Integer = 6

    ' Password property...
    Public Property Password() As String
        Get
            Return _password
        End Get
        Set(ByVal Value As String)
            If Value.Length >= MinPasswordLength Then
                _password = Value
            End If
        End Set
    End Property

End Class
```

6. Flip back to the Form Designer and double-click on the form background to create a new `Load` event handler. Add this code:

```
Private Sub Form1_Load(ByVal sender As System.Object, _
        ByVal e As System.EventArgs) Handles MyBase.Load

    Dim intIndex As Integer

    For intIndex = 1 To 100

        ' create a new user...
        Dim objUser As New User
        objUser.Username = "Fred" & intIndex
        objUser.Password = "password15"

        ' add it...
        arrUserList.Add(objUser)

    Next

    ' update the display...
    UpdateDisplay()

End Sub
```

7. You'll also need to add this member to `Form1.vb`:

```
Public Class Form1
    Inherits System.Windows.Forms.Form

    ' members...
    Private arrUserList As New ArrayList()
```

8.   Next, add this method to the `Form1` class:

```
Private Sub UpdateDisplay()

    ' clear the list...
    lstUsers.Items.Clear()

    ' add them...
    Dim objUser As User
    For Each objUser In arrUserList
        lstUsers.Items.Add(objUser.Username & ", " & objUser.Password & _
                " (" & objUser.MinPasswordLength & ")")
    Next

End Sub
```

9.   Flip back to the Form Designer and double-click the TrackBar control to create a new `Scroll` event handler. Add this code:

```
Private Sub trkMinPasswordLength_Scroll(ByVal sender As _
        System.Object, ByVal e As System.EventArgs) _
        Handles trkMinPasswordLength.Scroll

    ' set the minimum password length...
    User.MinPasswordLength = trkMinPasswordLength.Value

    ' update the display...
    UpdateDisplay()

End Sub
```

10.   Run the project. You should see a screen like the one shown in Figure 11-16.

11.   Slide the scrollbar and the list should update itself and the number in parentheses should change.

How It Works

To create a member variable, property, or method on an object that is shared, you use the `Shared` keyword.

```
Public Shared MinPasswordLength As Integer = 6
```

This tells Visual Basic .NET that the item should be available to all instances of the class.

Shared members can be accessed from within non-shared properties and methods, as well as shared properties and methods. For example, here's the `Password` property that can access the shared `MinPasswordLength` member:

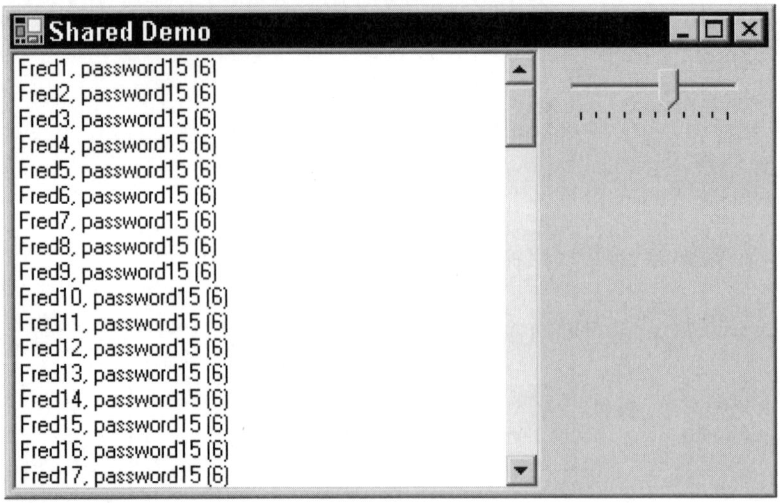

Figure 11-16

```
' Password property...
Public Property Password() As String
    Get
        Return _password
    End Get
    Set(ByVal Value As String)
        If Value.Length >= MinPasswordLength Then
            _password = Value
        End If
    End Set
End Property
```

What's important to realize here is that although the Password property and _password member "belong" to the particular instance of User, MinPasswordLength does not, therefore if it is changed the effect is felt throughout all the object instances built from the class in question.

In the form, UpdateDisplay is used to populate the list. You can again access MinPasswordLength as if it were a normal, non-shared public member of the User object:

```
Private Sub UpdateDisplay()

    ' clear the list...
    lstUsers.Items.Clear()

    ' add them...
    Dim objUser As User
    For Each objUser In arrUserList
        lstUsers.Items.Add(objUser.Username & ", " & objUser.Password & _
                " (" & objUser.MinPasswordLength & ")")
    Next

End Sub
```

At this point, we have a listing of users that shows that the `MinPasswordLength` value of each is set to 6 (refer to Figure 11-16).

Things start to get interesting when you move the slider and change `MinPasswordLength`. As this is a shared member you don't specifically *need* an instance of the class. Instead, you can set the property just by using the class name:

```
Private Sub trkMinPasswordLength_Scroll(ByVal sender As _
        System.Object, ByVal e As System.EventArgs) _
        Handles trkMinPasswordLength.Scroll

    ' set the minimum password length...
    User.MinPasswordLength = trkMinPasswordLength.Value

    ' update the display...
    UpdateDisplay()

End Sub
```

When building this method you may have noticed that after you had typed `User.`, Visual Studio .NET's IntelliSense popped up a list of members, including the `MinPasswordLength` property, as shown in Figure 11-17.

Figure 11-17

Shared members, properties, and methods can all be accessed through the class directly—you don't specifically need an instance of the class. (Actually, although you don't *need* one, if you have one you can use it, but it's not essential.)

When you change this member with code in the `Scroll` event handler, you update the display and this time you can see that the perceived value of `MinPasswordLength` has seemingly been changed for *all* instances of `User`, even though you only changed it in one place as shown in Figure 11-18.

Using Shared Methods

Although you've seen how to make a public member variable shared, you haven't seen how to do this with a method. In the following *Try It Out*, you look at an example of how to build a shared method that can create new instances of `User`. The main limitation with shared methods is that you can access only other shared methods and shared properties in the class in which it is defined.

This is a fairly artificial example of using a shared method as you could do the same job here with a customized constructor.

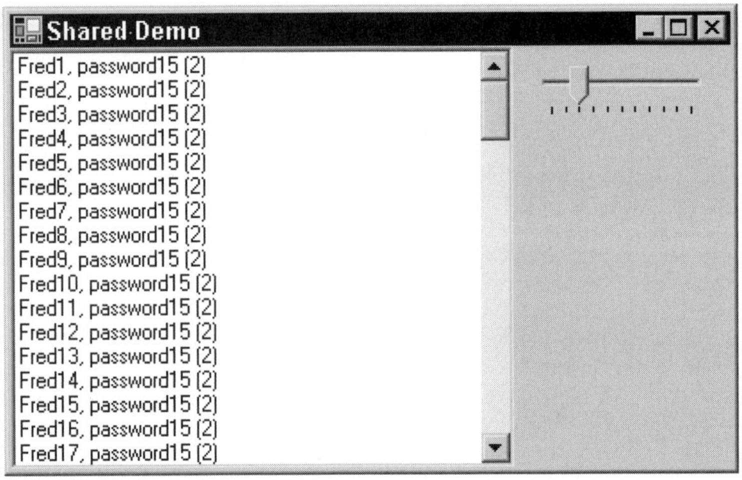

Figure 11-18

Try It Out   Using a Shared Method

1. Open the code editor for User. Add this code to the User class:

```
' CreateUser - create a new user...
Public Shared Function CreateUser(ByVal username As String, _
                ByVal password As String) As User
    ' create a new user...
    Dim objUser As New User()
    objUser.Username = username
    objUser.Password = password

    ' return it...
    Return objUser

End Function
```

2. Open the code editor for Form1 and find the Load event handler. Change the code so that it looks like this:

```
Private Sub Form1_Load(ByVal sender As System.Object, _
        ByVal e As System.EventArgs) Handles MyBase.Load

    Dim intIndex As Integer

    For intIndex = 1 To 100

        ' create a new user...
        Dim objUser As User
        objUser = User.CreateUser("Fred" & intIndex, "password15")

        ' add it...
        arrUserList.Add(objUser)
```

```
      Next

      ' update the display...
      UpdateDisplay()

   End Sub
```

3. You'll notice that as you type in the code, as soon as you type User., IntelliSense offers CreateUser as an option.

4. If you run the project you'll get the same results as the previous example.

How It Works

The important thing to look at here is the fact that CreateUser appears in the IntelliSense list after you type the class name. This is because it is shared and you do not need a specific instance of a class to access it.

You created the method as a shared method by using the Shared keyword:

```
' CreateUser - create a new user...
Public Shared Function CreateUser(ByVal username As String, _
                ByVal password As String) As User
```

One thing to consider with shared methods—you can only access members of the class that are also shared. You cannot access non-shared methods simply because you don't know what instance of the class you're actually running on. Likewise, you cannot access Me from within a shared method for the same reason.

Understanding Object-Oriented Programming and Memory Management

Object-orientation has an impact on how memory is used in an operating system. .NET is heavily object-oriented, so it makes sense that .NET would have to optimize the way it uses memory to best suit the way objects are used.

Whenever you create an object, you're using memory. Most of the objects you use have *state*, which describes what an object "knows." The methods and properties that an object has will either affect or work with that state. For example, an object that describes a file on disk will have state that describes its name, size, folder, and so on. Some of the state will be publicly accessible through properties. For example, a property called Size will probably return the size of the file. Some state will be private to the object and is used to keep track of what the object has done or what it needs to do.

Objects use memory in two ways. Firstly, something needs to keep track of the objects that exist on the system in memory. This is usually a task shared between you as an application developer and the common language runtime. If you create an object, you'll have to hold a reference to it in your program's memory so that you know where it is when you need to use its methods and properties. The common language runtime also needs to keep track of the object to determine when you no longer need it. Secondly, the common language runtime needs to allocate memory to the object so that the object can store its state. The more state an object has, the more memory it will need to use it.

The most expensive resource on a computer is the memory. I mean *expense* here in terms of what you get for your money. For $100, I can buy an 80GB hard disk, but for the same amount of money I can't buy 1GB of memory. Moreover, although I can, with relative ease, build a computer that supports thousands of gigabytes of storage, getting versions of Windows to use more than 4GB is a challenge. However, retrieving data from memory is thousands of times faster than retrieving it from disk so there's a tradeoff—if I need fast access I have to store it in memory, but there isn't much memory around.

When building an application you want to use as little memory as possible, so there's an implication that you want to have as few objects as possible and that those objects should have as little state as possible. The upside is that, today, computers have a lot more memory than they used to have, so as developers we can be more relaxed about our use of memory than our predecessors writing code 20 years ago!

The common language runtime manages memory in several distinct ways. First, it's responsible for creating objects at the request of the application. With a heavily object-oriented programming platform like .NET, this is going to happen all the time, so Microsoft has spent an awful lot of time making sure that the common language runtime creates objects in the most efficient way. The common language runtime, for example, can create objects far faster than its COM predecessor. Secondly, the common language runtime is responsible for cleaning up memory when it's no longer needed. In the developer community, the manner in which the common language runtime cleans up objects is one of the most controversial.

Imagine you're writing a routine that opens a file from disk and displays the contents on the screen. Well, with .NET you would use perhaps two .NET Framework objects to open the file and read its contents—namely `System.IO.FileStream` and `System.IO.StreamReader`. However, after the contents have been read, do you need the objects anymore? Probably not, so what you want to do is to remove your references to the objects and make the memory the objects were using available for creating more objects.

Imagine now that you don't remove your references to the objects. In this situation, the memory that the objects were using can't be used by anyone else. Now imagine that happening several thousand times. What happens is that the amount of memory that's being wasted keeps growing. In extreme circumstances the computer will run out of memory, meaning that other applications wouldn't ever be able to create any objects. This is a pretty catastrophic state of affairs.

We describe an object that is no longer needed but that holds onto memory as a *leak*. Memory leaks are one of the biggest causes of reliability problems on Windows, as when a program is no longer able to obtain memory, it will crash. There are plenty of system administrators out there who configure their servers to reboot on a daily or weekly basis just to reclaim memory that's no longer used.

With .NET this *should* never happen or, at the very least, to leak memory you would have to go to some pretty extreme steps. This is because of something called *garbage collection*. When an object is no longer being used, the *Garbage Collector* (GC) automatically removes the object from memory and makes the memory it was using available to other programs.

Garbage Collection

The Garbage Collector works by keeping track of how many parts of a program have a reference to an object. If it gets to the point where there are no open references to the object—it is deleted.

To understand this, think back to our discussion of scope in Chapter 3. Imagine you create a method and at the top of that method define a variable with local scope. That variable is used to store an object (it doesn't matter what kind of object is used for this discussion). At this point, one part of the program "knows" about the object's existence—that is, the variable is holding a reference to the object. When you return from the method, the variable will go out of scope and therefore the variable will "forget" about the object's existence, in other words, the only reference to the object is lost. At this point, no one "knows" about the object and so it can be safely deleted.

For an example, look at the following code:

```
Dim objObject As New MyObject
Console.WriteLine(objObject.GetType().FullName)
objObject = Nothing
```

This code snippet creates a new object from class `MyObject`, calls a method on it, and then removes the reference to the object. In this case, when you create the object, the `objObject` variable is the only thing that holds a reference to it. In the last line, `objObject` is set to `Nothing`, hence removing the only reference to the object. The Garbage Collector is then free to remove the reference to the object.

The Garbage Collector does not run constantly. Instead, it runs periodically based on a complex algorithm that measures the amount of work the computer is doing and how many objects might need to be deleted. When the Garbage Collector runs, it looks through the master list of all the objects the program has ever created and any that can be deleted are at this point.

In old school programming, programmers were responsible for deleting their own objects and had the freedom to say to an object, "You, now, clean yourself up and get out of memory." With .NET this ability is gone; rather an object will be deleted at some *indeterminate* time in the future.

Exactly when this happens is non-deterministic, in other words, as a developer you don't know when the Garbage Collector is going to run. This means that there is no immediate connection between the removal of the last reference to an object and the physical removal of that object from memory. This is known as *non-deterministic finalization*.

Understanding the Finalize Method

When the object is removed from memory, the object itself has an opportunity to run some "finalize" code by way of the `Finalize` method. The Garbage Collector calls this method when the object is about to be removed from memory and can be used to implement any last minute clean-up operations that the object has to do.

Try It Out   Exploring the Garbage Collector

1. Open Visual Studio .NET. Create a new Visual Basic Console Application by selecting the Console Application template as shown in Figure 11-19 (*not* a Windows Application), and call it FinalizeDemo.

2. Using the Solution Explorer, right-click on the FinalizeDemo project and select Add ⇨ Add Class. Call the class `MyObject`.

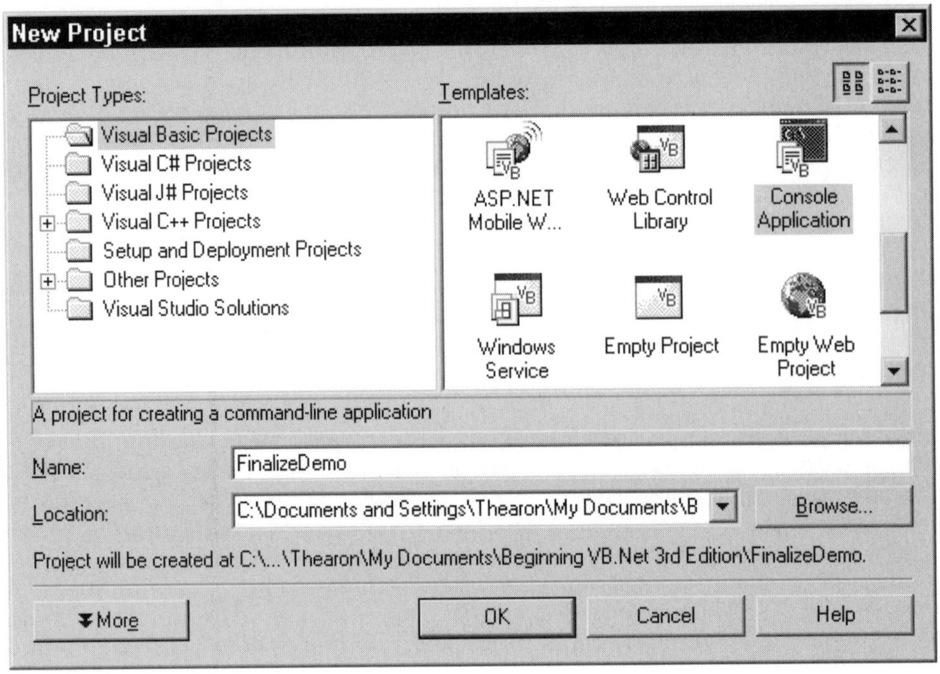

Figure 11-19

3. When the code editor appears, enter this code:

```
Public Class MyObject

    ' Constructor - called when the object is started...
    Public Sub New()
        Console.WriteLine("Object " & GetHashCode() & " created.")
    End Sub

    ' Finalize - called when the object is removed from memory...
    Protected Overrides Sub Finalize()
        MyBase.Finalize()

        ' tell the user we've deleted...
        Console.WriteLine("Object " & GetHashCode() & " finalized.")

    End Sub

End Class
```

4. Open the code editor for `Module1` and add this code to `Main`:

```
Sub Main()

    ' create five objects and add them to a list...
    Dim intIndex As Integer
```

```
        Dim arrList As New ArrayList

        For intIndex = 1 To 5
            arrList.Add(New MyObject)
        Next
        ' now delete the list, the objects now
        ' have no references...
        arrList.Clear()

        ' wait for the user to press return...
        Console.WriteLine("Press Return to collect the garbage...")
        Console.ReadLine()

        ' force a collect...
        GC.Collect()

        ' wait for the user to quit...
        Console.WriteLine("Press Return to quit...")
        Console.ReadLine()

    End Sub
```

5. Run the project and you'll see output shown in Figure 11-20.

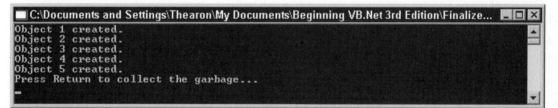

Figure 11-20

6. Press Return and you'll see the output shown in Figure 11-21.

```
C:\Documents and Settings\Thearon\My Documents\Beginning VB.Net 3rd Edition\Finalize...
Object 1 created.
Object 2 created.
Object 3 created.
Object 4 created.
Object 5 created.
Press Return to collect the garbage...

Press Return to quit...
Object 5 finalized.
Object 1 finalized.
Object 4 finalized.
Object 3 finalized.
Object 2 finalized.
```

Figure 11-21

How It Works

With `MyObject` you created a class that has a constructor and a finalizer. In each case, you used `Console.WriteLine` to report the status of the object to the user:

```
' Constructor - called when the object is started...
Public Sub New()
    Console.WriteLine("Object " & GetHashCode() & " created.")
End Sub

' Finalize - called when the object is removed from memory...
Protected Overrides Sub Finalize()
    MyBase.Finalize()

    ' tell the user we've deleted...
    Console.WriteLine("Object " & GetHashCode() & " finalized.")

End Sub
```

The `GetHashCode` method is guaranteed to be unique among objects of the same type. That means that if you call it from within `Console.WriteLine`, you can write the ID of the object that's being constructed or finalized.

Inside `Module1` you create five objects and add them to an array list. This means that each `MyObject` instance has one reference and this reference is stored internally in the `ArrayList` object:

```
Sub Main()

    ' create five objects and add them to a list...
    Dim intIndex As Integer
    Dim arrList As New ArrayList

    For intIndex = 1 To 5
        arrList.Add(New MyObject)
    Next
```

Once you have the objects stored in the array list, you call `Clear`. This removes the references to the objects completely, meaning that they are now candidates for Garbage Collection:

```
    ' now delete the list, the objects now
    ' have no references...
    arrList.Clear()

    ' wait for the user to press return...
    Console.WriteLine("Press Return to collect the garbage...")
    Console.ReadLine()
```

However, at this point, you see the information shown in Figure 11-20.

You can see that five objects have been created, but none of them has been finalized because the output doesn't contain any `Object nn finalized` messages.

You can force the Garbage Collector to collect the objects. But you should never do so because it's very bad practice! Garbage Collection is .NET's problem and you should leave it that way. However, I'm trying to show you what happens when garbage is collected, so we can get away with it here:

```
' force a collect...
GC.Collect()

' wait for the user to quit...
Console.WriteLine("Press Return to quit...")
Console.ReadLine()

End Sub
```

After `GC.Collect` has been called and the application is waiting again, you see the information you saw in Figure 11-21. This is really interesting! The messages appear after the `Press Return to quit` message. Even though you called `GC.Collect`, the actual collection hasn't physically happened until later on in the code. Also, notice that the objects have been removed in a seemingly random order. Remember, the `Finalize` method on the object is called just before the Garbage Collector removes it from memory. It's at this point that you display your message.

What this illustrates is that, even when you tell it to collect objects, there is no immediate link between removing the last reference to an object and `Finalize` being called. It happens some time in the future.

Releasing Resources

In some cases, objects that you build may need access to certain system and network resources, such as files and database connections. Using these resources requires a certain discipline to ensure that you don't inadvertently cause problems.

Here's an example—if you create a new file, write some data to it but forget to close it, no one else will be able to read data from that file. This is because you have an exclusive lock on the file; it doesn't make sense for someone to be able to read from a file when it's still being written to. You must take care to release system resources should you open them.

When an object has access to scarce system or network resources like this, it's important that the caller tells the object that it can release those resources as soon as they're no longer needed. For example, here's some code that creates a file:

```
' open a file...
Dim objFileStream As System.IO.FileStream("c:\myfile.txt", _
            System.IO.FileMode.Create)

' do something with the file...
...

' close the file...
objFileStream.Close
objFileStream = Nothing
```

As soon as you finish working with the file you call `Close`. This tells .NET that the consumer is finished with the file and Windows can make it available for other applications to use. This is known as "releasing the lock." When you clear the object reference by setting objFileStream = Nothing in the next line, this is an entirely separate action from calling Close.

The FileStream object releases the lock on the file when its Finalize method is called. However, as we've just learned, the time period between the instance of the FileStream object becoming a candidate for Garbage Collection (which happens when objFileStream = Nothing) and Finalize being called is non-deterministic. So, if you had not called Close, the file would have remained open for a period of time, which would have caused problems for anyone else who needed to use the file.

Using the AddText Method to Explain Exceptions

In the AddText method, you may have been wondering about this piece of code:

```
' have we been disposed?
If _isDisposed = True Then
    Throw New ObjectDisposedException("I_'ve been disposed!")
End If
```

In objects that support Dispose, it's important that each time before you try to access potentially disposed resources you check to make sure that they are still available. If they're not, you must use this code to throw an ObjectDisposedException exception. (Refer to Chapter 9 for a review of exceptions and error handling. However, remember that this is again another part of the best practice involved with Dispose.)

Defragmentation and Compaction

As the last part in its bag of tricks, the Garbage Collector is able to defragment and compact memory. In much the same way that your computer's hard disk needs periodic defragmentation to make it run more efficiently, so does memory. Imagine you create 10 small objects in memory, each about 1KB in size. Imagine that .NET allocates them all on top of each other so you end up taking up one 10KB piece of memory. (In reality, we don't usually care where objects exist in memory, so this discussion is a bit academic.)

Now imagine you want to create another object and this object is of medium size, say about 3KB. .NET will have to create this object at the end of the 10KB block. This means that you'll have allocated 13KB in total.

Now imagine that you delete every other small object, so now our 10KB block of memory has holes in it. Not much of a problem, but imagine you want to create another 3KB object. Although there's 5KB of space in the original block, you can't put it there because no gap is big enough. Instead, it has to go on the end, meaning your application is now taking up 16KB of memory.

What the Garbage Collector can do is defragment memory, which means that it removes the gaps when objects have been removed, as shown in Figure 11-22. The upshot of this is that your application uses memory more efficiently, meaning that applications take up less memory.

Although this may not seem like a big deal on a PC with 512MB of memory available, consider that .NET could potentially be running on much smaller devices where memory usage is a big deal, for example, a mobile device with 256KB of memory in total. Besides, imagine making 3,000 5KB savings as we have in

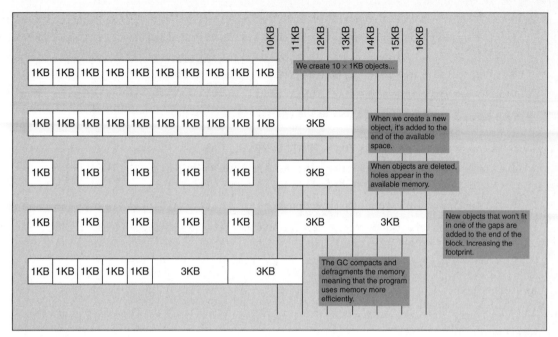

Figure 11-22

this example because then you've saved over 15MB of memory! Chapter 22 will introduce you to writing applications for mobile devices and to topics that you need to be aware of when coding for these devices.

Summary

In this chapter, you took a look at some more valuable techniques that you are able to use to assist the building of object-oriented software. Initially, you examined the idea of reuse. Specifically, you looked at classes that would allow you to examine the Internet Explorer favorites stored on the user's computer. You consumed these classes from two applications—one standard desktop application and also as a mini-application that exists on the system tray.

You then examined the idea of shared members, properties, and methods. Sharing these kinds of items is a powerful way to make common functionality available to all classes in an application.

Finally, you examined how consumers of objects should ensure that scarce systems resources are freed whenever an object is deleted by the Garbage Collector using the `Dispose` and `Finalize` methods.

To summarize, you should know how to:

❑ Build a class that inherits from the the `System.Collections.CollectionBase` namespace and add methods that allow you to add and remove objects from the collection and provide a property that allows an application to query for the number of items in the collection

❑   Use the collection class in your own application creating objects and adding them to the collection

❑   Use shared properties and methods in a class that can be shared among all instantiated instances of the class

❑   Properly dispose of resources to make efficient use of the Garbage Collector

Exercises

1. What's the advantage of using a class library?

2. In the Favorites Tray application, why did you create a new class that inherited from `System.Windows.Forms.MenuItem`?

3. Why do you create your own collections?

4. How much time usually elapses between an object no longer having references and the Garbage Collector cleaning it up?

5. What is the difference between `Dispose` and `Finalize`?

12

Building Class Libraries

In this chapter, you're going to look at building libraries of classes. This will gather together many of the concepts you've learned in this book, so let's have a quick review. So far you've learned a lot about developing Windows Applications by dragging controls onto forms, editing their properties, and adding code. When you edit a form in the Form Designer, you are actually designing a new class that inherits from the `System.Windows.Forms.Form` class. The first two lines of code in a Visual Basic .NET form will look something like this:

```
Public Class Form1
    Inherits System.Windows.Forms.Form
```

When you make changes to the form in the designer, the designer works out what code needs to be added to the class. You can view this code by opening up the Windows Form Designer generated code region. Then, when you run the program, an instance of this class is created—an object. Like most objects, the form has state and behavior—you can have variables and controls on the form (state) and you can perform actions when, for example, the user clicks a button on the form (behavior). In theory, you could write your forms without using the designer at all, but there are very few programmers who work this way while creating Windows forms.

Right from the start you've been creating classes. You've also looked at creating your own classes from scratch. Recall what you have studied about building objects in Chapter 10, where you created a project called Objects, which contained the classes `Car` and `SportsCar`. These classes are used in a Console application because it made the objects easier to test, but they would have worked just as well in a Windows Application. You could even have used them in a Web Application or Web Service. In fact one of the key benefits of using classes is that, once you've designed a good one, you can use it over and over again in different applications.

Understanding Class Libraries

In Chapter 11 you did use the same classes in two different applications. You built a favorites view in your application and a task bar application using the same underlying classes. You did this by creating the class in one application and then adding a copy of that code to the second. This was a quick and easy way of reusing code, but there were some problems with it:

❏ To use the class you need to have access to the source code file. One of the advantages of classes and objects is that they can be a "black box." Developers should not need to know what goes on inside the classes they use. It is often a good thing if they don't. Also, if you've developed a class, you might want to keep your source secret. You might be happy to let people use it, but not let them copy how it works or improve it, or even claim it as their own work.

❏ Every time the program that uses the class is compiled, the class needs to be compiled too. This is not really a problem if the application uses a few simple classes, but if it's using a lot of complex classes it will make compilation very slow. It will also make the resulting program very big because one EXE will include all of the classes.

❏ If you realize that there is a bug in the class or that there is a way to make it faster or more efficient, you need to make the change in lots of different places—in every application that uses the class.

The solution is class libraries. A *class library* is a collection of classes that compile to a file. You cannot run a class library, but you can use the classes in it from your applications. You can use a class library without the source code, it does not need to be recompiled when the application is compiled, and if the library changes, then the applications using it will automatically get the advantage of the improved code.

In this chapter, you will:

❏ Create your own class libraries and learn how to get information about existing libraries that are not part of the .NET Framework

❏ Learn to strong-name assemblies (compiled files) to ensure that all assemblies have a unique identity

❏ Register assemblies in a repository called the Global Assembly Cache (GAC) so that they can be shared between applications on the same computer

Creating a Class Library

These are instructions for creating a class library in Visual Studio .NET Professional or above.

Try It Out   **Creating a Class Library in Visual Studio .NET Professional or Above**

1. In Visual Studio .NET select File ➪ New ➪ Project.

2. Select Visual Basic Projects from the Project Types list and then choose the Class Library icon from the Templates list as shown in Figure 12-1. Enter the name MyFavorites.

3. Click OK. A new Class Library project will be created with a default class called `Class1.vb`. Right-click `Class1.vb` in the Solution Explorer and choose Delete.

How It Works

That was really easy. Let's just think about what Visual Studio .NET is doing during these two steps. First, you choose a Class Library project. The Template that you choose controls how Visual Studio .NET sets up the project. The most obvious difference is that when you start a Windows Application you get a blank form and a designer. The blank form is called `Form1.vb`. When you start a class library, you get no designer and a blank class called `Class1.vb`.

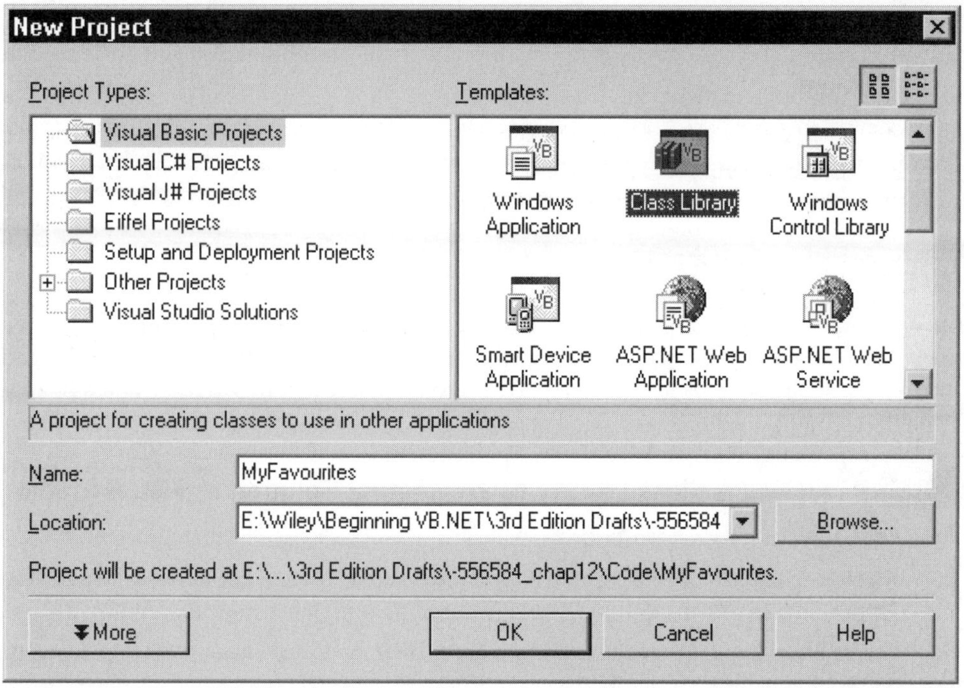

Figure 12-1

There are also more subtle differences. When you create a Windows Application, Visual Studio .NET knows that you will be compiling it into a program that can run. When you choose a Class Library, Visual Studio .NET knows that the resulting library will not be run on its own—so the choices you make here affect what Visual Studio .NET does when you build the project. You select a Class Library, meaning that Visual Studio .NET will build the project to a DLL file (dynamic link library).

After clicking OK, you delete the blank class that Visual Studio .NET generates. Having classes with the name `Class1` is not very helpful—it's much better to start from scratch with meaningful file and class names.

In Chapter 10 you created classes and used the same Visual Basic .NET class in two projects—Favorites Viewer and Favorites Tray. In the following sections, you will see how to convert these applications so that both of them use a copy of the same compiled class library. Of course, this is a somewhat unrealistic situation. Usually you would build a class library and application, rather than creating an application and then splitting it up into a smaller application and a class library. However, this will give you a good idea of how you would create a class library from scratch—and it will be much faster. First of all, open the Favorites Viewer project. Remember that this consists of the following files:

❑   `Favorites.vb`—contains the `Favorites` class

❑   `WebFavorite.vb`—contains the `WebFavorite` class

❑   `WebFavoriteCollection.vb`—contains the `WebFavoriteCollection` class

❑   `WebFavoriteListViewItem.vb`—contains the `WebFavoriteListViewItem` class

❑   `Form1.vb`—contains the `Form1` class, which represents the application's main form

❑   `AssemblyInfo.vb`—contains information about the assembly, which you don't need to worry about—yet!

Of these, the first three listed are also used in Favorites Tray. The remaining three are specific to this particular application. You want to build a class library that contains `Favorites`, `WebFavorite`, and `WebFavoriteCollection`.

Building a Class Library for Favorites Viewer

When you're writing Visual Basic .NET applications, a solution can contain multiple projects. At the moment you have one project in the solution—the Favorites Viewer application. You need to add a Class Library project to this solution and then move the classes from the Windows Application project to the Class Library project.

Try It Out   Adding a Class Library to an Existing Solution in Visual Studio .NET

1.   Open the Favorites Viewer project.

2.   Right-click the Solution "Favorites Viewer" line in the Solution Explorer and select Add ➪ New Project.

3.   Follow Steps 2 and 3 from the *Creating a Class Library in Visual Studio .NET Professional or Above* section, but name the project `FavoritesLib`.

How It Works

Adding a class library to an existing solution works in pretty much the same way as creating a new class library on its own in a solution—it is just a little easier to do it this way if you are adding a new class library to an existing solution.

Now you have two projects within your solution. You have a Windows Application and a class library. Currently, the class library is empty—and all the classes that you want to add to the class library are in the Windows Application project.

You have already seen how to add a new class to a Windows Application and you can add new classes to a class library in exactly the same way. You just right-click on the `FavoritesLib` project and select Add ➪ Add Class. You don't want to do that though—the classes already exist. The quickest way to move a class between two projects in the same solution is to drag and drop them.

Try It Out   Moving Classes Between Projects

1.   Select the `Favorites.vb` file in the Solution Explorer, as shown in Figure 12-2, and drag it onto the `FavoritesLib` project.

You may need to wait a second or two, but the `Favorites.vb` class file will be moved from the Favorites Viewer project to the `FavoritesLib` project. In addition to changing projects, the file is physically moved from the folder containing the Favorites Viewer project to the folder containing the `FavoritesLib` folder.

2.   Follow the same procedure for `WebFavorite.vb` and `WebFavoriteCollection.vb`.

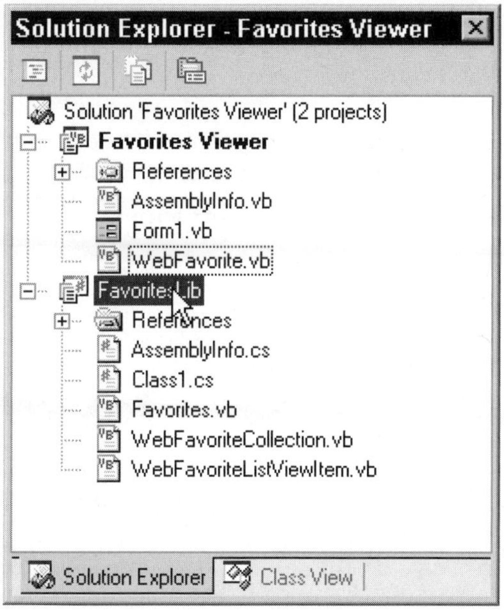

Figure 12-2

So, you now have a class library and a Windows Application. However, even though they are both contained in the same project they cannot see each other. If you try running the application now you will see a series of errors, as shown in Figure 12-3.

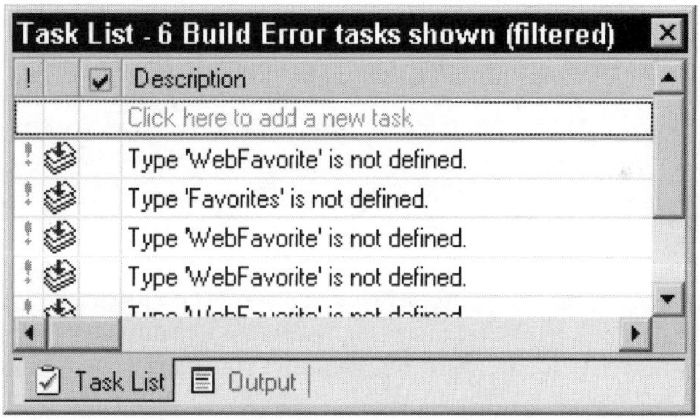

Figure 12-3

These errors are all caused by the same thing: the classes in Form1.vb and WebFavoriteListView.vb cannot see the classes in the class library. There are two stages to solving this problem:

❑ Add a reference to the Class Library project, so that the Windows Application knows to look for the compiled FavoritesLib.dll file that contains the classes. Previously, all code was compiled into one file so you didn't need to do this.

❑ Add an Imports statement to Form1 and WebFavoriteListView classes, so that they can use classes from the FavoritesLib namespace without giving a fully qualified name (that is, including the namespace as well as the class name). Previously, all classes were in the same namespace so you didn't need to do this. As you saw in Chapter 4, classes are by default given the same project name as their namespace.

If this doesn't seem very clear—don't worry! Both of these things are easy to do.

Try It Out   Adding a Reference to Another Project

1.   Right-click the Favorites Viewer project in the Solution Explorer and select Add Reference.

2.   Select the Projects tab and then double-click FavoritesLib in the list, as shown in Figure 12-4. FavoritesLib will be added to the Selected Components list at the bottom of the dialog box.

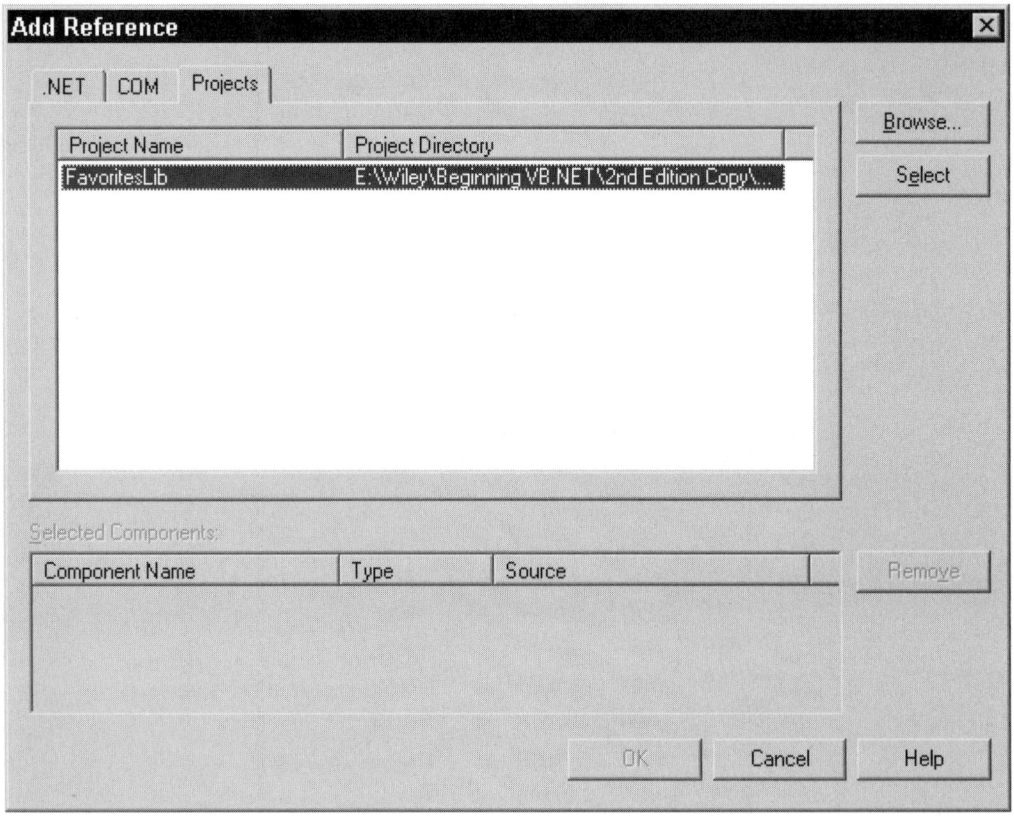

Add Reference

.NET | COM | Projects

Browse...

Project Name	Project Directory
FavoritesLib	E:\Wiley\Beginning VB.NET\2nd Edition Copy\...

Select

Selected Components:

Component Name	Type	Source

Remove

OK | Cancel | Help

Figure 12-4

3.   Now click OK. A reference to FavoritesLib will now appear in the Solution Explorer—under the References section for the Favorites Viewer project.

How It Works

By adding a reference, you tell Visual Studio .NET that the Favorites Viewer.exe file will require the FavoritesLib.dll file in order to run. Visual Studio .NET can use the classes exposed from

FavoritesLib in order to check the syntax of the code, so the automatic underlining of errors and so on will work correctly.

> *Whenever you want to use a class library you must add a reference to it. You can add references to projects within the solution or to compiled DLLs if you wish.*

However, if you try to run the application now, you will still get lots of errors because the classes in the Favorites Viewer application are trying to use classes in the FavoritesLib class library without giving a fully qualified name. Unless you specify otherwise, classes are given the same namespace name as the name of the project they are in. This means that the classes you moved from Favorites Viewer to FavoritesLib changed namespace too.

The easiest way to cope with this problem is to add an Imports statement to the top of the classes that rely on the class library. This is what you'll do in a minute, but remember that you do have two other choices:

❑ Use fully qualified names every time you want to access a class in the class library from a class in the application. This would have required quite a few changes.

❑ Change the namespace of either the classes in the application or the classes in the class library. If the namespace was the same for both projects, you would not need to use fully qualified names or have an Imports statement. However, because the two projects are quite different, it would not really be sensible to give both of them the same namespace.

Try It Out   **Adding an Imports Statement**

1.   Right-click Form1.vb in the Solution Explorer and select View Code. Notice that when the code refers to a class in FavoritesLib, the word is underlined in blue—because the class is unavailable—as shown in Figure 12-5.

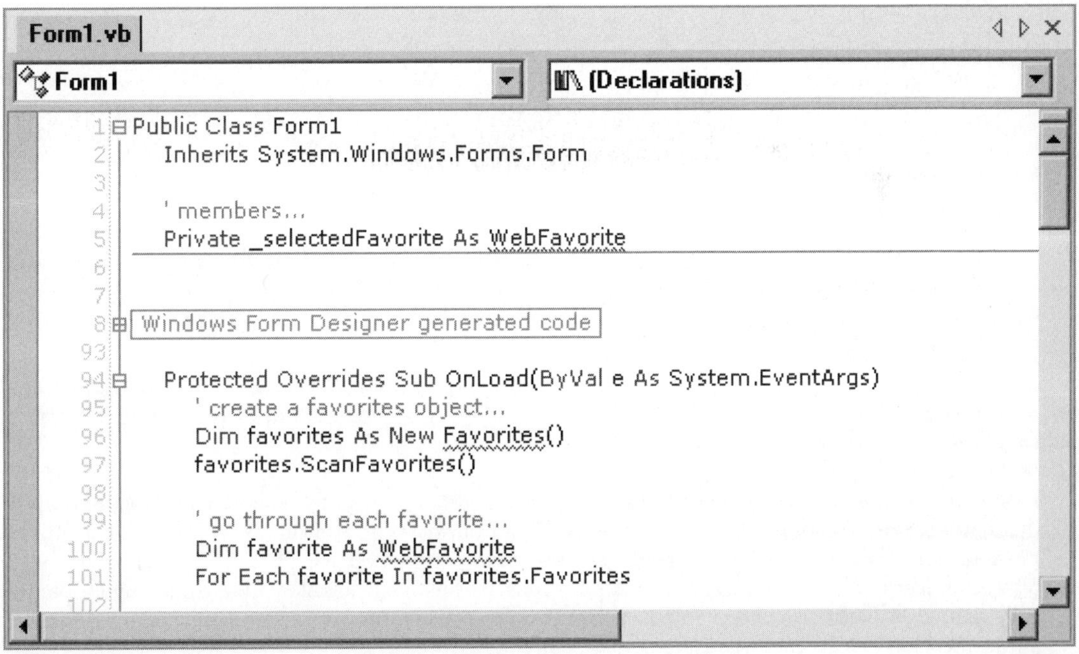

```
Form1.vb

Form1                                          (Declarations)

  1  Public Class Form1
  2      Inherits System.Windows.Forms.Form
  3
  4      ' members...
  5      Private _selectedFavorite As WebFavorite
  6
  7
  8      Windows Form Designer generated code
 93
 94      Protected Overrides Sub OnLoad(ByVal e As System.EventArgs)
 95          ' create a favorites object...
 96          Dim favorites As New Favorites()
 97          favorites.ScanFavorites()
 98
 99          ' go through each favorite...
100          Dim favorite As WebFavorite
101          For Each favorite In favorites.Favorites
102
```

Figure 12-5

2. Add the following line right at the top of the code file:

```
Imports FavoritesLib
```

3. Do the same thing for `WebFavoritesListViewItem.vb`.

How It Works

The Imports statement means that any time there is a reference to a class that is not qualified with a namespace, the Visual Basic .NET compiler will check the `FavoritesLib` namespace to see if a matching class exists there. Therefore, the compiler will be able to resolve the class name when you insert the `Imports` statement.

That's it! You have converted your Windows Application into a small client application and a class library. Run the application and it will work perfectly. You'll see results similar to those in Figure 12-6.

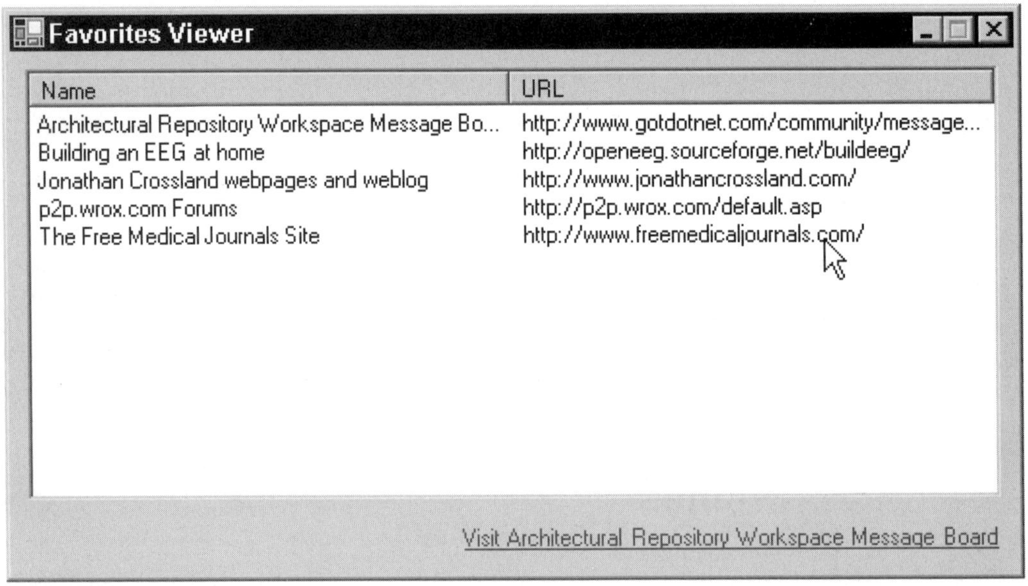

Figure 12-6

Note that when you ran this application, Visual Studio .NET compiled the class library to a DLL, then compiled the application to an EXE, and then ran the EXE. It needed to compile the DLL first because the compiler depends upon it while compiling the EXE.

In the previous demonstration you split your application into two tiers or layers. The class library is a tier that handles the concept of a favorite and obtains a list of my favorites from my computer. The other tier presents the favorites to the user and enables the user to perform actions on them. Class libraries are really a powerful tool for creating tiered applications, because they enable you to completely separate the code that exists in different tiers. You may often hear the term *n-tier design*. What this means is that an application has at least three separate tiers. Usually these three tiers are:

❏ A *data tier* concerned with obtaining raw data from a data source such as a database, text file, or your favorites folder and then writing data back. It generally doesn't worry about what the data means. It just enables you to read and write operations.

❏ A *business tier* concerned with applying certain business rules to the data retrieved from the data source or ensuring that data that is being written to the data source obeys these rules. For example, there may be certain sites that you would not want to list in your favorites viewer or you may want to ensure that URLs are valid before displaying them. The business tier may also contain code to manipulate or work with data—for example, the code needed to open a particular favorite.

❏ A *presentation tier* that displays the data to the user and lets them interact with it in some way. For example, you have a Windows Form that displays a list of favorites and a link button that lets users view them.

Your application is so small that there's no practical need to separate the data tier and the business tier. However, in a big application it can make the project far more manageable, even if it does mean spending a bit more time on design before the coding starts.

One of the great things about tiers is that you can mix and match tiers quite easily. For example, if a new browser becomes popular then you could change the data tier to read a different data format but still use the same presentation tier and business tier. This would be much easier if the data tier and business tiers were separate.

Soon, you are going to use your class library, which is really a combination of the business and data tiers in conjunction with a different presentation tier, namely the Favorites Tray application.

In this chapter you are working with existing projects so that you can concentrate specifically on class libraries rather than writing code. In most cases you would develop the class library first and then develop applications to use that library. Of course, as you were building the application you might decide to modify the library slightly. Using Visual Studio .NET you can do this very easily. When working in Visual Studio .NET you can make any changes you like to the code in the library and the change will instantly be available in the application.

Using Strong Names

Your complete solution now compiles to two files—a DLL and an EXE. You have written both files. Nobody else is writing applications that rely on the DLL and nobody else is going to change the DLL. In real life, this is often not the case. Often you use off-the-shelf DLLs or two separate developers are working on the DLL and the EXE.

For example, imagine that Kevin is working on `FavoritesLib.dll` and Simone is working on `Favorites Viewer.exe`. Kevin decides that `ScanFavorites` is not a very good name for a method and changes it to `LoadFavorites`. Then he recompiles the DLL. Later, Simone runs `Favorites Viewer.exe`. `Favorites Viewer.exe` tries to call `ScanFavorites` in the DLL but the method no longer exists. This generates an error and the program won't work.

Of course, Kevin shouldn't really have made the change to the DLL. He should have known that applications existed that required the `ScanFavorites` method. All too often, however, developers of libraries don't realize this. They make changes to DLLs that render existing software unusable.

Another possible scenario is that David is working on a system to manage favorites and he creates a file called `FavoritesLib` that is different from the one that Kevin developed. There is a danger that the two different DLLs will be confused and once again Favorites Viewer will stop working.

These DLL management problems have been a nightmare for Windows developers and it spawned the expression "DLL Hell." However, Visual Basic .NET goes a long way toward solving the problem. The problem is connected with two things:

❑ There can be several versions of a DLL and these can all work in different ways. It is not possible to tell the version from the filename alone.

❑ Different people can write DLLs with the same filename.

Strong named assemblies store information about their version and their author within the assembly itself. Because of this, it would be possible to tell the difference between the DLL used (when Favorites Viewer compiled) and the changed version. It would also be possible to tell the difference between Kevin's `FavoritesLib.dll` and David's `FavoritesLib.dll`. Strong naming can also store information about other properties that will help to uniquely identify an assembly; for example, the culture for which it was written, but you will concentrate on version and author.

Signing Assemblies

One way to certify who wrote an assembly is to sign it. To do this, you generate a key pair and sign the assembly with it. A key-pair is unique and, therefore, can identify the person or company who wrote an assembly. The principles behind assembly signing are quite advanced, but the actual practice is quite simple.

> *A strong-named assembly cannot reference a simple named assembly, as it would lose the versioning control that it enjoys.*

There are two steps involved in creating a strong-named or signed assembly:

❑ Create a key pair that you can use to sign your assembly.

❑ Apply this key pair to your assembly, so that it will be used to sign the assembly at the time of compilation.

Try It Out   Creating a Key Pair

1. First, you create a new key pair. From the Windows Start menu select Programs ➪ Microsoft Visual Studio .NET ➪ Visual Studio .NET Tools ➪ Visual Studio .NET Command Prompt.

2. Type the following into the Command Prompt that appears:

```
sn -k Testkey.snk
```

This will generate a key pair in the folder where the command is run (in this case, c : \).

How It Works

Running the Visual Studio .NET Command Prompt opens a DOS-style command window with the environment set up so that you can use the .NET command-line tools. You use this environment to run the Visual Basic .NET strong naming command. The k switch means that the command will generate a new key pair and write it to the specified file.

Now you have a key pair in the file c:\Testkey.snk. If you want to, you can move this to a more convenient location. After this, the next step is to use it to sign your assembly.

Try It Out   Signing the FavoritesLib Assembly

1. Open the `AssemblyInfo.vb` file in the FavoritesLib project, and add the following line:

```
<assembly:AssemblyKeyFileAttribute("c:\TestKey.snk")>
```

2. Build this project. The DLL will now be strong named.

How It Works

When you compile an assembly with an `AssemblyKeyFileAttribute`, it adds a copy of your public key to the assembly. It also adds a hash of the whole assembly, encrypted using the private key.

With public–private key cryptography, a message encrypted with one key can only be decrypted with the other key. You can't use the same key to encrypt and decrypt. You can give out a public key to a lot of people and they can encrypt messages with it. If you keep the private key secret, then nobody else will be able to read the encrypted messages—even if they have a copy of the public key.

You can also make this work the other way around. If you encrypt a message with the private key people can use the public key to decrypt it. If the decryption works and you haven't let somebody else get their hands on your private key, it proves that you wrote the message.

Part of the purpose of signing an assembly is to prove who wrote it and to prove that it has not been tampered with. This could be done by encrypting the whole assembly using the private key and then decrypting the whole assembly using the public key, when it needs to be used. However, this would end up being very slow. Instead, the Visual Basic .NET compiler takes a hash of the assembly and encrypts that using the private key. If anybody tries to tamper with the assembly the hash will cease to be valid.

Assembly Versions

Visual Basic .NET automatically keeps track of versions for us. When you build an assembly, a number signifying the version is automatically updated. There are four elements of this number: major version, minor version, build, and revision. If you look at the `AssemblyInfo.vb` file again, you will see the following near the bottom:

```
<Assembly: AssemblyVersion("1.0.*")>
```

This means that when you compile this assembly the major version will be 1, the minor version will be 0, and the build and revision number will be generated by Visual Studio .NET. Every time you recompile the assembly, Visual Basic .NET will adjust these numbers to ensure that every compilation has a unique version number. You could choose to replace the star with your own hard-coded numbers and increment them yourself, but if you're happy with Visual Basic .NET's decision then you can just leave it. If you are changing an assembly significantly, you may want to change the major or minor version—and of course, you are free to do that.

It is recommended that you set the entire version number manually, especially when you are releasing the Assembly formally (so that you have complete control), as it will be easier to manage different versions and bring in less unfortunate deployment problems.

Registering Assemblies

You've seen how an assembly can contain information to prove who wrote it (in the sense that a unique identifier is unique per publisher) and information to prove its own version. This is really useful, because it means that executables using these assemblies know what assembly author and version to look for, as well as just a filename. However, this doesn't prevent Kevin from overwriting an existing DLL with a new version—it just means that applications using the DLL will be able to tell that it's changed.

This is where the GAC comes in. The GAC can ensure that several versions of the same assembly are always available. If your application requires the `FavoritesLib` assembly version 1 and Kevin's application requires the assembly version 2, then both can go in the GAC and both can be available. Moreover, assemblies with the same name but written by different people can go in the GAC. You can guarantee that your applications will use the same assembly while running as they did when they were compiled, provided the required assembly is in the GAC.

To register an assembly into the GAC you simply need to drag the relevant DLL file into the GAC (located in the `c:\winnt\assembly directory`).

Gacutil Utility

`Gacutil.exe` is a utility provided with the .NET Framework for installing/uninstalling assemblies into the GAC via command line.

In your Visual Studio .NET Start menu item select `Visual Studio .NET Tools` and click the `Visual Studio.NET 2003 Command Prompt` shortcut.

In the console window you can use the `i` and `u` options to install and uninstall, respectively:

```
Gacutil -i favoriteslib.dll
Gacutil -u favoriteslib
```

Why Is My Assembly Not Visible in the Reference Dialog Box?

It is important to understand that the GAC is not shown in the References Dialog Box within Visual Studio. For this reason, once you have added your assembly to the GAC you will not see it and will still have to browse for it.

Visual Studio does, however, look for Assemblies to load into the Reference Dialog Box by checking keys in the Registry that map to physical paths on your drive.

Try It Out   **Getting your Assembly listed in the References Dialog box**

1. Click Start and Select Run

2. Type **regedit** and press Enter

3. In the Registry Editor locate the key
    `HKEY_LOCAL_MACHINE\SOFTWARE\Microsoft\.NETFramework\AssemblyFolders`

4. Right-click and select New ⇨ Key

5. Create the key with any name that you wish. I named mine MyAssemblies

6. Double-click (Default) value key in the pane and enter a path. I add `c:\myAssemblies`
    (see Figure 12-7)

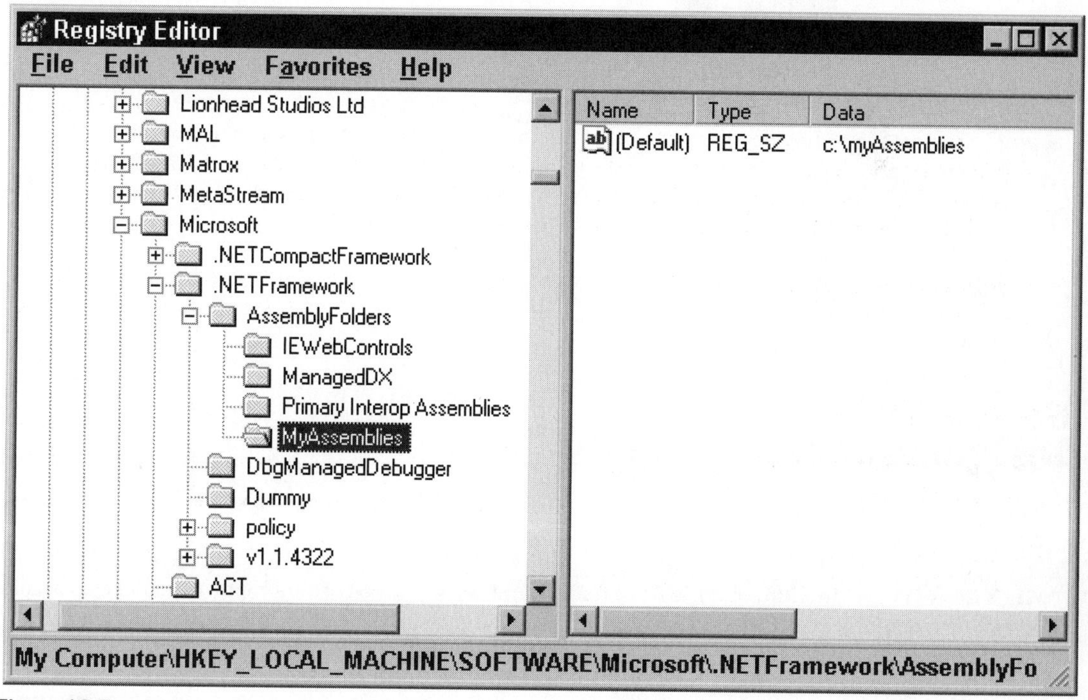

Figure 12-7

7. Open Explorer and copy and paste the `favoriteslib.dll` into a new directory named
    `myAssemblies` (see Figure 12-8)

8. You will have to restart Visual Studio .NET for this to take affect, but when you do this, you will
    see the assemblies listed in this directory from within the References Dialog Box as shown in
    Figure 12-9.

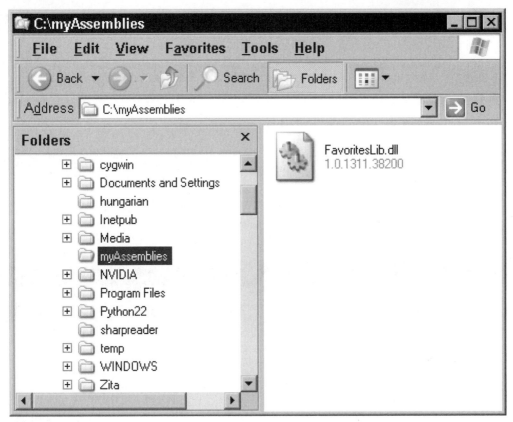

Figure 12-8

Designing Class Libraries

By now, you should be aware of how useful class libraries are, and you have also looked at the nature of classes, objects, and class libraries.

When designing an application it is best to understand what you are dealing with. Much like an architect designing a home, you will need to understand how things work (the rules, the regulations, and the recommendations) in order to know how to draw the best plan.

When software architects plan, draw out, and generate template code for components and applications, they may well use pen and paper, or a drawing tool such as Microsoft Visio that integrates with Visual Studio .NET. Visio contains various types of symbol libraries that can be used for creating schematics, flowcharts, and other diagrams. A very well-known set of descriptive symbols and diagram types is Unified Modeling Language (UML), which has its own symbols and rules for drawing software and architecture models. UML has various types of symbol libraries containing symbols that have different meaning and functions. These symbols have been derived from previous modeling symbols to form something of a fusion of styles. UML also has many types of diagrams. These diagrams range from deployment-type diagrams to component definition diagrams.

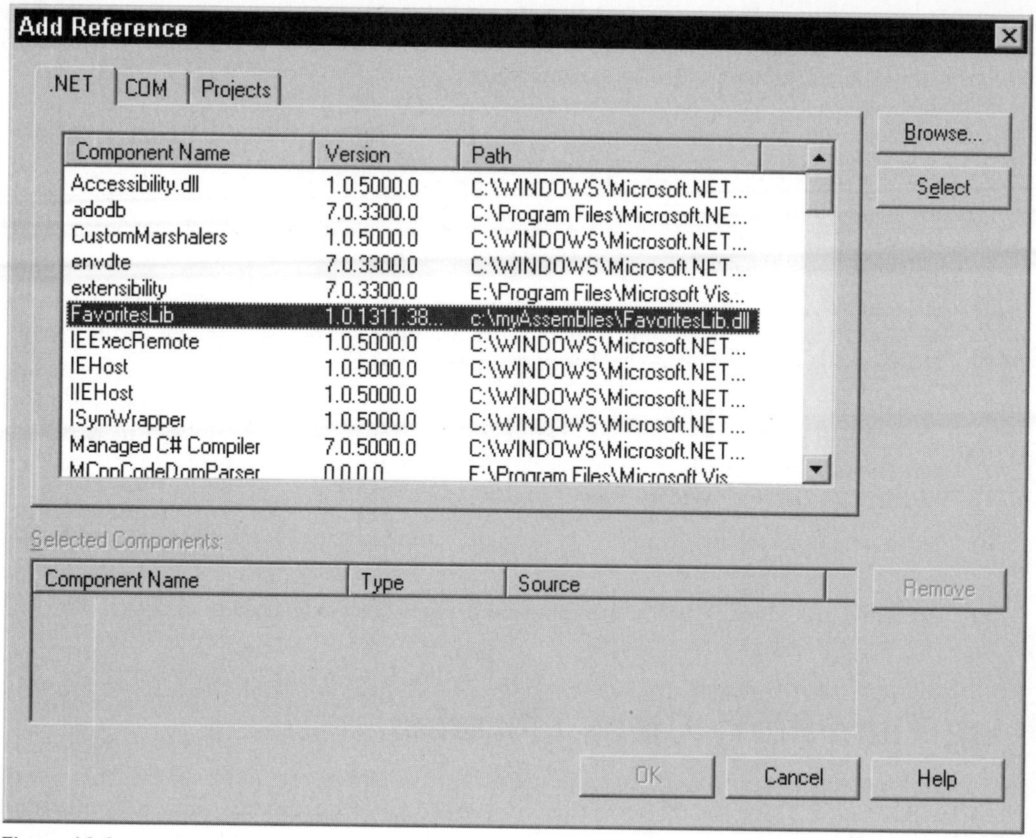

Figure 12-9

If you wish to learn more about UML then take a look at the UML Bible *(Wiley, ISBN: 0-7645-2604-9).*

If the questions, "how many parameters and methods should an object expose?" and "should an object have properties rather than methods?" are not answered correctly, your object would not be rendered completely useless, although it may be ineffective. There are, however, some things to consider.

Imagine a class library that contains over 40 methods and properties on each of its 20 or so classes. Also imagine that each class's methods contain at least 15 parameters. This component might be a little daunting—in fact, a component should never be this way.

Instead, when designing your objects try to follow the golden rule—simplicity. Simplicity is probably the most crucial element that you can have in your classes. While creating an extremely large class library is not necessarily a bad thing, using a small number of classes, aided by a few other class libraries, is by far a better solution.

When you're dealing with a large, complex set of business rules for a large system, the code within the library can be extremely complicated, often leading to debugging and maintenance nightmares. In many situations getting around the fact that many objects need to be created is a difficult task, but the point that needs to come across is that there are many situations that lend themselves to reuse. The more reusable the classes are, the smaller the end-product will be and the easier it will be to create new applications that need the same functionality provided by the components.

Every developer who uses your class library should be able to do so successfully, without any major effort or a tremendous amount of reading. You can achieve this in the following ways:

❑ Try to keep your methods to five or six parameters *maximum*, unless completely necessary. This will make coding easier.

❑ Make sure that all of those parameters and your methods have meaningful names. Try to spellout the function rather than keeping it short. As an example, it is not easy to identify the meaning of `StdNo` as it is to identify the meaning of `StudentNumber`.

❑ Do not over-exert yourself by adding every conceivable method and functional enhancement that an object can have; rather think ahead but code later. You can easily complicate matters for your developers by granting them too many choices and, at the same time, may be adding functionality that will never be used.

❑ Try to keep classes within your library down to a minimum, because better reuse comes from keeping your libraries smaller.

❑ Properties are extremely useful in a class and they enable it to be used more easily.

Using Third-Party Class Libraries

A class library compiles to a DLL file. In order to use the class library you only need the DLL, you don't need the source code. This means that you can give your DLL to other people to use and you can use other people's DLLs in your own applications. To demonstrate how to use a DLL, you're going to use the `FavoritesLib.dll` file that you created.

Using FavoritesLib.dll

You've already seen how to create references to other projects in a solution. This is a really good way to develop class libraries and applications at the same time. In this example you're going to pretend that you didn't create `FavoritesLib.dll`. You're going to modify the Favorites Tray so that it uses `FavoritesLib.dll`. This is a very quick way to demonstrate the use of DLLs, but remember that in real life you would add a reference to the DLL early on in developing the application, and then write code to use the DLL.

Try It Out   **Using FavoritesLib.dll in the Favorites Tray Application**

1. Open the Favorites Tray project.

2. Delete the following files from the project: `Favorites.vb`, `WebFavorite.vb`, and `WebFavoriteCollection.vb`.

3. Now you need to add a reference to `FavoritesLib.dll`. Right-click on the Favorites Tray project and select Add Reference. Click the Browse button.

4. Find the folder where the `FavoritesLib` project resides. `FavoritesLib.dll` will be inside the `Bin` folder that is inside the `FavoritesLib` project folder. When you have found `FavoritesLib.dll` double-click it. It will be added to the Selected Components list at the bottom of the Add Reference dialog.

5. Click OK to add the reference to the project.

6. Remember that the classes in the class library are in the `FavoritesLib` namespace, so you need to tell your code to look in that namespace for class names you use. Add the following line to the top of `Form1.vb` and `YourFavoriteMenuItem.vb`:

```
Imports FavoritesLib
```

You do not need to add it to `ExitMenuItem.vb` because `ExitMenuItem` does not use any of the classes in the library.

7. Run the program. It will work as normal, but will be using the class library now instead of classes within the application's EXE file.

How It Works

This process works in a very similar way to adding a reference to another project. You can use the classes in the class library in exactly the same way regardless of whether you reference the Class Library project or the compiled DLL. The main difference is that you cannot see or edit the class library's source code.

However, the Visual Studio .NET environment can still tell a lot about the classes even without the source code. For example, IntelliSense still works. This is because Visual Studio .NET can tell from the DLL itself what methods and properties are available on each class. You can investigate a class without using IntelliSense but using the Object Browser.

Viewing Classes with the Object Browser

To view classes that can be used within Visual Basic .NET you can use a quick and easy tool known as the Object Browser. You can also use the Object Browser to view class names and method names on objects. The Object Browser window can be viewed inside Visual Studio .NET by pressing *Ctrl+Alt+J*. It is also available by clicking the View ⇨ Other Windows ⇨ Object Browser menu.

The Object Browser is basically used for a quick reference to the classes you need to see. The Object Browser will show all assemblies that are used in the current Solution including Visual Basic Projects and pre-compiled DLLs.

The browser shows all members including methods, enumerations, and constants. Each member type is shown with a different icon. Figure 12-10 shows the `FavoritesLib.Favorite` class. You select this class by choosing the `FavoritesLib` assembly and then within that the `FavortiesLib` namespace and then within that the `Favorites` class.

Remember that an assembly can contain several namespaces and that the same namespace can be spread across several assemblies. It just happens that in Visual Basic .NET you normally have a single namespace inside a single assembly of the same name.

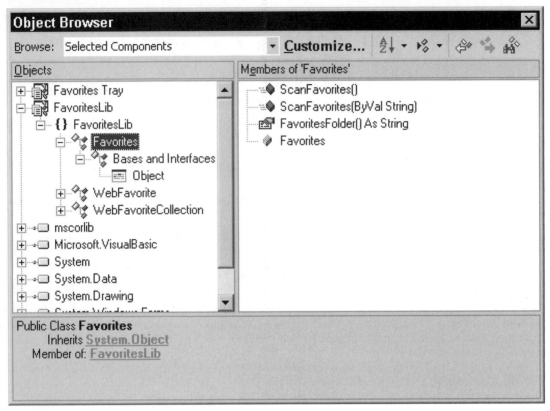

Figure 12-10

Note that in order for the Object Browser to display anything, you need an open project. The Object Browser icon representations are summarized in Figure 12-11.

The MSDN documentation contains plenty of information about classes in the .NET Framework, so you don't often need to use the Object Browser when you're only using .NET Framework classes. It is really useful, however, when you are using a DLL from a third party that does not come with documentation. Often the method and property names can give you a clue of what's happening. Of course, this underlines why it is necessary to choose good names for your classes and their members.

On other occasions, the DLL will provide short descriptions of each of its classes and members. This is done using attributes, which is a subject outside the scope of this text.

Summary

Class libraries are an integral part of Visual Basic .NET and in fact important to all of the languages in the .NET Framework. They encompass what you use and what you need to know in terms of the common language runtime and within your developments.

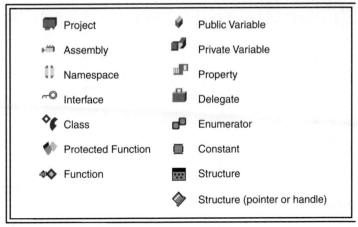

Figure 12-11

In this chapter, you have considered the nature of class libraries and how to view the properties and methods contained within them using the Object Browser. You have also seen how the .NET Framework allows developers to avoid DLL Hell through the use of keys and signatures, and looked at some of the broad issues regarding designing your own components.

In the next chapter, you will learn how to create Windows Forms controls that are components with a user interface, as opposed to class library projects, which are purely code-based. There too, you will see the importance of reusable and stable code.

Exercises

1. What are the advantages of using class libraries?

2. What is the purpose of signing an assembly?

3. What is the purpose of the Global Assembly Cache?

Creating Your Own
Custom Controls

In this book you have used many of the controls that come with the .NET Framework, from the button and the text box to the list box. You may even have tried to use some of the more advanced controls such as the DataGrid and the Treeview controls. Although at first some of them may be hard to use, they offer a lot of functionality. These controls make it easy to create user interfaces. Once you get to know how to use all their features, you will find that creating user interfaces also becomes a quicker exercise. Another important aspect that makes controls so useful is that they are reusable. You can drag and drop a Button control onto any form in any new Windows project and it *works* as a button should. The reuse factor is an important reason why Visual Basic became one of the most popular and is presently, one of the most powerful languages. Did you know that you owe much of what you experience today in Visual Studio .NET, like Windows Forms Controls, to Visual Basic? The history of Windows Forms Controls has roots in something known as VBX controls (Visual Basic Extension). This later became more widely known as ActiveX and today, revitalized and reborn into .NET as Windows Forms Controls.

In this chapter, you will:

❑   Learn what a Windows Forms Control is and how it works

❑   Create and use a Windows Forms Control

❑   Learn to add methods and events to your control

❑   Learn to code for design time and runtime

These controls are best suited for Windows Forms rather than Web Applications. To learn about Web Server controls you should turn to Chapter 18. This chapter will concentrate on the Windows Forms version.

Windows Forms Controls

Today, there are several good reasons for wanting to create Windows Forms Controls, including:

❑   You can use the same control throughout an application or in lot of different applications, thus saving on code (reuse).

❑ You can keep code relating to a control within the control's class, making the code cleaner and easier to understand. For example, you could write a button that handled its own click event—meaning you don't need to handle the event in your form's code.

In terms of reusing controls between applications, there are two main ways to do this. The first is to add the control's source file to every project where you need the control. Then, when you build the application, the control will be compiled into the main executable. This is the approach you take in this chapter, because it is simpler and will allow you to concentrate on how it works.

The second way is to build a control library. Control libraries are very similar to class libraries. In fact, they *are* class libraries that happen to contain UI driven classes. Like a class library, a control library will compile to its own assembly, which you can use in your applications. This method is attractive because it means you can distribute the assembly to other developers without giving away your source code. You can also make changes to the assembly and these will be reflected in the applications that use it—even without the applications being recompiled. The techniques for building the controls are the same regardless of whether you are using a control library or just using a control within your application project.

Creating and Testing a User Control

Creating a user control from scratch is not difficult. From one perspective, it is similar to building the Windows forms. In this section you are going to create a Windows application that uses User Controls.

Try It Out   **Building Your First Control**

1. To start with, create a new Windows Application called Controls by clicking the File menu and then clicking New ➪ Project.

2. Once the project has been created you have a blank form open and ready for you. You are not going to use this for the time being though. Instead right-click on the Controls project in the Solution Explorer and choose Add ➪ Add User Control. In the dialog box that appears, name the control MyControl and click OK. You will now have something that looks very much like a form's designer without the title bar or borders. Usually, when building a control we drag on other controls and define a way in which those controls interact. This extra behavior defines a control's purpose and makes it useful.

   You might find in the applications that you build, that you have a common need for a control that goes to a database to retrieve certain information, such as employee or customer records. If you want to build a robust control, you will need to make it as useful as possible to developers using it down the line, while requiring the minimum amount of labor to get it working. You will probably want to encapsulate the functionality of connecting to the database, querying the results, and populating the control with information, so that subsequent developers using your control do not have to know how to do this. This is a key principle of encapsulation—to make life easier for the next developer. In this way, you can also benefit from the more tangible advantage of reducing costs through quality application of code reuse.

   For your first example, you are going to create a simple control that has three basic button controls inside of it.

   When you create your own custom control that uses (hosts) existing controls inside of it, the control is known as an aggregate control.

A different message will be displayed when each button is pressed. You will then see how this control can be used in a standard Windows Forms application.

1. Building the control is actually simple indeed. All you have to do is grab three buttons off the Toolbox and place them onto the control form as shown in Figure 13-1.

2. Name the buttons `btnSayHello`, `btnSaySomething`, and `btnSaySomethingElse` (via their Name properties in the Properties window) and then change each Text property to Say "Hello, World!," Say Something, and Say Something Else, respectively.

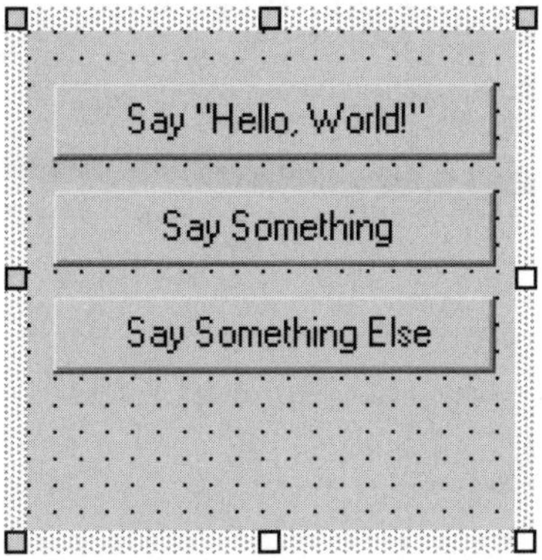

Figure 13-1

3. At the moment, this control won't do anything when the buttons are pressed—you need to wire up event code behind the Click event for each button in order for it to work. Double-click `btnSayHello` and add this code:

```
Private Sub btnSayHello_Click(ByVal sender As System.Object, _
        ByVal e As System.EventArgs) Handles btnSayHello.Click
    MessageBox.Show("Hello, world!")
End Sub
```

4. There's nothing there that you haven't already seen before. When the button is pressed, the Click event is fired and so it displays a message box. Now go back to the design view (either click on the MyControl.vb[Design]* tab or the View Designer button in the Solution Explorer's toolbar), double-click `btnSaySomething` and add this code:

```
Private Sub btnSaySomething_Click(ByVal sender As System.Object, _
        ByVal e As System.EventArgs) Handles btnSaySomething.Click
    MessageBox.Show("Something!")
End Sub
```

5. Finally, double-click `btnSaySomethingElse` in the designer and add this code:

```
Private Sub btnSaySomethingElse_Click(ByVal sender As Object, _
        ByVal e As System.EventArgs) Handles btnSaySomethingElse.Click
    MessageBox.Show("Something else!")
End Sub
```

6. The next thing you need to do is to build the project. Select Build ➪ Build Solution. Now you can test the control!

To test the control you can't just run the project. Instead, you have to put the control onto a form.

1. Open the designer for Form1, which Visual Studio .NET created when you created the Windows Application, and click on the My User Controls tab of the Toolbox. MyControl should have appeared.

2. Drag and drop a new MyControl control onto the form.

    Try running the project and clicking on the buttons. You will see that the encapsulated functionality of displaying the message boxes is now available to you.

How It Works

When you built the solution, the control was automatically added to the toolbox in the My User Controls tab. This allows you to use your user control in your project just as you would with any other control in the toolbox.

In addition to having the same visual design, all the functionality of the MyControl1 control has been made available to your form.

Exposing Properties from User Controls

A user control is implemented as a class. Therefore, anything that you can do with a class you can also do with a user control. This means that you can add properties, methods, and events to the user control that can be manipulated by whoever is consuming it. First, look at adding a new property to the control.

Your control can have two sorts of properties: those that can be manipulated from the Properties window at design time and others that have to be programmatically manipulated at runtime. For example, at design time you might want to change properties pertaining to the color or the font used to draw the control. But at runtime you might want to change properties that depend on the contents of a file that the user selected and so on. Usually, if the property is a fairly simple type such as String, Integer, or Boolean and doesn't have parameters, it can be manipulated at design time. If the property is a complex object, such as a database or file connection, or if it has parameters, you'll have to manipulate the property at runtime.

Adding Properties

Take a look at adding a property to your control. The property you're going to add is called MessageText. This will contain the text that you would like to display instead of "Hello, world!" When this property is changed you'll also want to change the text on the first of the three buttons that you have on the control.

Try It Out   Adding a New Property to MyControl

1. To add a new property you need a member variable that will store the value. Add this code to the top of `MyControl.vb`:

```
Public Class MyControl
    Inherits System.Windows.Forms.UserControl
    ' members...
    Private _messageText As String
```

2. When this property changes, you need to change the text on the first button. You'll also store the property value in the `_messageText` member that you just defined. Add this code directly after the lines you added in Step 1:

```
Public Property MessageText() As String
    Get
        Return _messageText
    End Get
    Set(ByVal Value As String)
        ' set the text...
        _messageText = Value
        ' update the button...
        btnSayHello.Text = "Say """ & _messageText & """"
    End Set
End Property
```

The reason you need so many quotes when the Text *property is set is because when you want to add a quotation mark to a string, you need to supply two extra quotes—otherwise Visual Basic .NET believes you're marking the end of the string. The text you entered here will resolve to:* Say "Whatever _messageText is set to"

3. By default you want the button value of `_messageText` to be `"Hello, world!"` The best way to do this is to explicitly set the `MessageText` property when the object is created. That way both `_messageText` and `btnSayHello.Text` will be appropriately configured from a single call. You'll need to open up the `Windows Form Designer generated code` region to find the `New` method. Add this code to the `New` method:

```
Public Sub New()
    MyBase.New()
    'This call is required by the Windows Form Designer.
    InitializeComponent()
    'Add any initialization after the InitializeComponent() call
    MessageText = "Hello, world!"
End Sub
```

4. Now, if you want to change the default text to something else, you have to make the change in only one place. Of course, this new property will have no effect unless you alter the handler for `btnSayHello.Click`. Find the handler and change this code:

```
Private Sub btnSayHello_Click(ByVal sender As System.Object, _
    ByVal e As System.EventArgs) Handles btnSayHello.Click
    MessageBox.Show(_messageText)
End Sub
```

5. To expose the new property you need to build the project. Right-click the MyControl project in the Solution Explorer and select Build. If no build errors were found the new property should be exposed.

6. Select the user control on `Form1` and scroll to the bottom of the Properties window. The new `MessageText` property will appear under the Misc category (or in the usual place if you have the properties arranged alphabetically).

How It Works

You'll notice that the default value has passed through to the designer. If you change the property in the Properties window, the text on the first button of the control will change. Also, if you run the project and press the button, the text on the message box will display whatever you entered in the `MessageText` property. When the designer needs to update the Properties window it will call into the object and request the `MessageText` property. Likewise, when you change the value it will call into the object and set the property. This also happens when the form is loaded from disk when you start up the designer.

Exposing Methods from User Controls

As you've probably guessed, if you can expose new properties for your control, you can also expose new methods. All that you need to do to make this happen is to add a public function or `Sub` to the control and then you'll be able to call it from the form that's hosting the control.

Try It Out   Adding a Method to MyControl.vb

1. Add this method to `MyControl.vb`:

```
Public Sub ResetMessageText()
    MessageText = "Hello, world!"
End Sub
```

2. This method uses the `MessageText` property to change the text of the top button back to the default setting. When this method is executed, both the text on the button and the internal member `_messageText` will be changed to reflect the new value.

3. Go back to `Form1` on the Control Test project. To make things a little easier to follow, change the `MessageText` value to Nothing using the Properties window for `MyControl1`. (That's the actual word "nothing," rather than the Visual Basic keyword.)

4. Now, add a new button to the form. Call it `btnReset` and set the Text to Reset.

5. Double-click on `btnReset`. This will create a default event handler for its `Click` event. Add this code:

```
Private Sub btnReset_Click(ByVal sender As System.Object, _
        ByVal e As System.EventArgs) Handles btnReset.Click
    MyControl1.ResetMessageText()
End Sub
```

6. Start the project and try clicking the Reset button. Notice how the text on your control changes back to Say "Hello, world!" as designed.

Exposing Events from User Controls

Now that you've seen how to expose new properties and new methods from your control, you need to take a look at how to expose events from the control. When you add events to one of your own controls, the person that uses your control can take action in their code when the event is raised.

In this part of the exercise you add an event called `HelloWorld` and you raise this event whenever the "Hello, world" button is clicked.

Try It Out — Defining Events

1. Defining an event is simply a matter of adding a statement to the class. Add this code to the top of `MyControl.vb`:

```
' members...
Private _messageText As String
' events...
Event HelloWorld(ByVal sender As Object, ByVal e As System.EventArgs)
```

In this case, you have defined an event called `HelloWorld` that takes two parameters: An `Object` representing the object that raised the event and a `System.EventArgs` object.

Although an event can have any number of parameters, all events related to Windows forms follow this model: One parameter for the object that fired it and another for the object containing the event data. When building your events you should follow this model too. That way, developers using your control won't be surprised by some weird approach that only you use.

To fire or raise an event you have to use the `RaiseEvent` keyword. This looks after the tricky aspect of actually telling the control's owner what event has been raised and passes through the appropriate parameters.

You have to give some thought as to at what point in the control's behavior the event should be fired. In this example, do you want `HelloWorld` to be fired before or after the message box has been displayed? Well, it depends. If your motivation is to provide an opportunity for the owner to change the text before it's displayed, clearly `RaiseEvent` has to be called before `MessageBox.Show`. If, on the other hand, you only want to tell the user that the message box has been displayed you call `RaiseEvent` after `MessageBox.Show`.

In the next *Try It Out* you add code to fire the event before showing the message box, giving the owner the freedom to change the `MessageText` property.

Try It Out — Raising the HelloWorld Event

1. To raise the event you need to provide the name of the event and the parameters. Add this code to `MyControl.vb`:

```
Private Sub btnSayHello_Click(ByVal sender As System.Object, _
        ByVal e As System.EventArgs) Handles btnSayHello.Click
    ' raise the event...
    RaiseEvent HelloWorld(Me, New System.EventArgs)
    MessageBox.Show(_messageText)
End Sub
```

Notice how you pass Me as the value for sender through to the event. You might expect that you were supposed to pass the value of sender that was passed into btnSayHello_Click, but remember that the sender you were given corresponds to the Button control that originated the event. This Button control is not visible to forms using your control—as far as they are concerned it is the user control that raises events, so you pass Me—representing the current user control instance.

All that remains now is to detect when the event has fired and do something. This is known as consuming an event. When a control fires an event, you can hook into the event handler. By doing this, you receive notification that the event has fired and can do something. This is one of the core concepts of the control/event methodology that you have been using throughout this book.

Try It Out   Consuming the HelloWorld Event

1. If you go back to the code for Form1 you can use the drop-down lists at the top of the window, shown in Figure 13-2, to locate and add the event handler for MyControl1. Remember, although you specifically defined a single event for this control, you still get all of the other events that were defined on the various base classes that your control class inherits from.

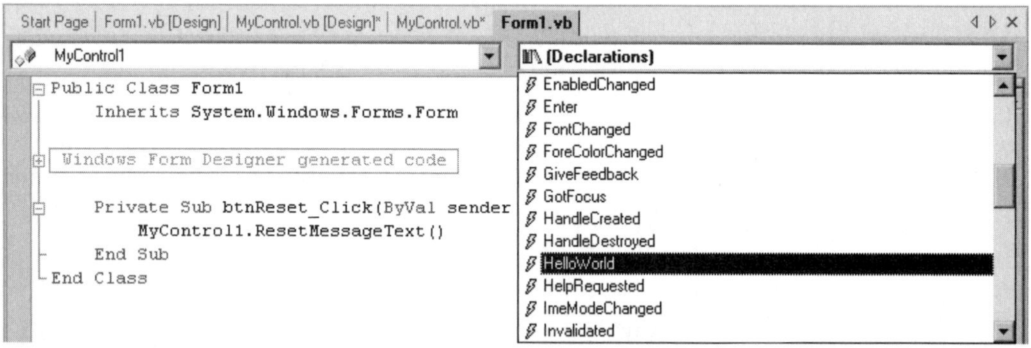

Figure 13-2

2. Of course, if you select the control and an event, you are automatically given a handler "stub" into which you can add your event-handling code. In this instance, you call the ResetMessageText method that you had built earlier from within your event handler to make sure that the text changes back to "Hello, world!" before MsgBox is called. Add this code to Form1:

```
Private Sub MyControl1_HelloWorld(ByVal sender As System.Object, _
    ByVal e As System.EventArgs) Handles MyControl.HelloWorld
    MyControl1.ResetMessageText()
End Sub
```

3. Try running the project now and you'll notice that whenever you click the button on the control the text "Hello, world!" is always displayed. This is because you're responding to the HelloWorld event and using ResetMessageText to change the message text back to the default before the message box is ever displayed.

If you need further proof that this event handler is indeed being called, try setting a breakpoint on the ResetMessageText *line. When the event is fired, Visual Studio .NET will suspend the program and show that the program does indeed get inside the event handler.*

Inheriting Control Behavior

In early versions of Visual Basic, VBX controls became a very popular technology and this drove the adoption of Visual Basic. One of the reasons for this was that when VBXs were introduced Microsoft hadn't yet launched Windows 95. Windows 95 included a greatly enhanced control library offering things like progress bars, tracker bars, and the rich text edit box. Today, the control library included in Windows 2000 and Windows XP is extremely rich, which means that the kinds of controls that you want to build are going to fall into three camps: they're either going to be a complex aggregate of many controls (like the control you just built), somehow extend the behavior of an existing control, or cause you to start completely from scratch.

The topic of creating aggregate controls is now quite straightforward, thanks to the .NET Framework. Determining the need for controls in your applications often involves looking at previous applications and finding commonality, or intuiting the advantages of making a control reusable across later projects.

For example, you might find that all your desktop applications feature the same login box that authenticates the user. This is a great candidate for reuse, but what's the best way to reuse it?

With .NET, you can create a class in a completely separate project that contains the entire form. (This was also possible before .NET but it's much easier now!) The user could then create an instance of the class and call the AuthenticateUser method. This method would display the form, capture the details, and perform the authentication. This approach is a lot easier for the consumer to use, as they don't have to build a separate form.

Now imagine that the way that authentication is performed changes. A classic example here is that the application's authentication method is integrated into the Windows Authentication scheme. Now the class that implements AuthenticateUser can do so without the dialog box. This gives even greater advantage to the consumer, as they don't have to change their code in any way to adopt the new authentication approach.

What you need to do is look at the way the functionality may be used and, if need be, implement it in a form library rather than control library. Basically, if the functionality needs to be painted on a form, so that you can put other controls on that form alongside it, the best method is as a user control, as you've just seen. If the functionality is designed to stand alone—in other words, you don't need to put other controls alongside it—implement it in a form library. You'll see how to build a form library in the next section.

The point of this discussion is to illustrate that, most of the time, if you're implementing controls there's a good chance that you'll be doing so by inheriting from an existing control and enhancing its functionality.

Enhancing Controls

Common uses for enhancing functionality include adding new properties, new methods, and encapsulating event handling code. For example, you might create a button that is linked to a TextBox control. The text box contains the name of a file on the disk and clicking the button automatically opens up the file and returns the contents of the file to the form or control that owns the button through an event. Another example would be creating a progress bar to monitor some environmental information, for example disk space.

In this example, you enhance the functionality of the button control in such a way that it has a "buddy" TextBox control and is able to return the contents of a file through an enhanced version of the button Click event.

Creating an Enhanced Button Control

1. To get started, add a new user control to the `Controls` project. Call it `FileButton`.

It's very important that you create a new user control at this point. Creating a user control puts all of the appropriate designer information in place, which means that the new control will appear properly in the Toolbox in Controls. If you create a class and then change its base class, the control will not appear in the Toolbox and you will not be able to use it with the Designer.

2. By default, this class will be derived from `System.Windows.Forms.UserControl`. You need to derive it from `System.Windows.Forms.Button` in order to get the basic button functionality that we want. You'll also eventually need access to a couple of namespaces, edit `FileButton.vb` so that it reads like this:

```
Imports System.IO
Imports System.ComponentModel
Public Class FileButton
    Inherits System.Windows.Forms.Button
        Windows Form Designer generated code
End Class
```

To implement your control, you need to add a property that lets the control know which text box it's associated with and a method to get an actual `TextBox` object from the name of a control. You'll also need to respond to the `Click` event and fire your own event.

Adding the BuddyBoxName Property

The `BuddyBoxName` property is a string containing the name of a control also contained within the form. Any class derived from `System.Windows.Forms.Control` has a `Controls` property, which contains a list of controls that the control contains. The same class also has a `Parent` property that returns the container. Therefore, you need to look in your user control's `Parent.Controls` property for the associated text box.

However, rather than storing a direct reference to the control through a `BuddyBox` property, it's more useful to store the name. This way, you can actually set the name from within the Properties window in Visual Studio .NET rather than having to do so programmatically.

Adding the BuddyBoxName Property

1. Add this code to `FileButton.vb`:

```
Public Class FileButton

    Inherits System.Windows.Forms.Button
    ' members...
    Private _buddyBoxName As String
    ' BuddyBoxName property
    Property BuddyBoxName() As String
        Get
            Return _buddyBoxName
        End Get
```

```
        Set(ByVal Value As String)
            ' Perhaps add validation code here
            _buddyBoxName = Value
        End Set
    End Property
```

2. You can now try adding this new control to your form. First, select Build ⇨ Build Solution. This will add the control to the Toolbox.

3. Now open `Form1` and add a new TextBox control and one of your new FileButton controls. Change the name of the text box to `txtFilename`.

4. Use Notepad to create a new file and save it somewhere in your computer, then set the `Text` property of `txtFilename` to the path of the new file.

5. Also, change the name of our FileButton control to `btnOpenFile` and set its `Text` property to Open. You'll see something like Figure 13-3.

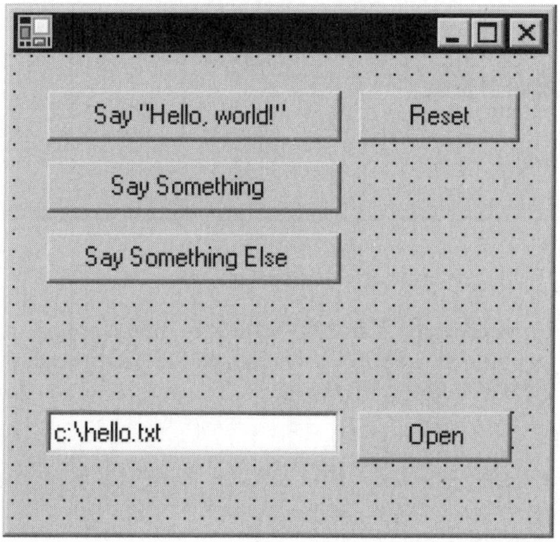

Figure 13-3

Remember your new FileButton control looks and behaves exactly like a button. You do not have to go through the hassle of trying to create a new control that looks like a button. The power of inheritance makes life very easy for you here!

6. Now, select `btnOpenFile` and take a look at the Properties window. You'll find a property called `BuddyBoxName`. Set this to `txtFilename` (in Figure 13-4 the Properties window has been set to show properties alphabetically).

Now that you have created the property and added a new control to the form, you can wire in the code that opens the file and returns the contents through the event. To respond to the `Click` event you need to create a new event that will pass the data to the owner. As already mentioned, you want to make sure that this event follows the standard format: one `Object` parameter containing a reference to the object that fired the event followed by a `System.EventArgs` parameter containing information about the event.

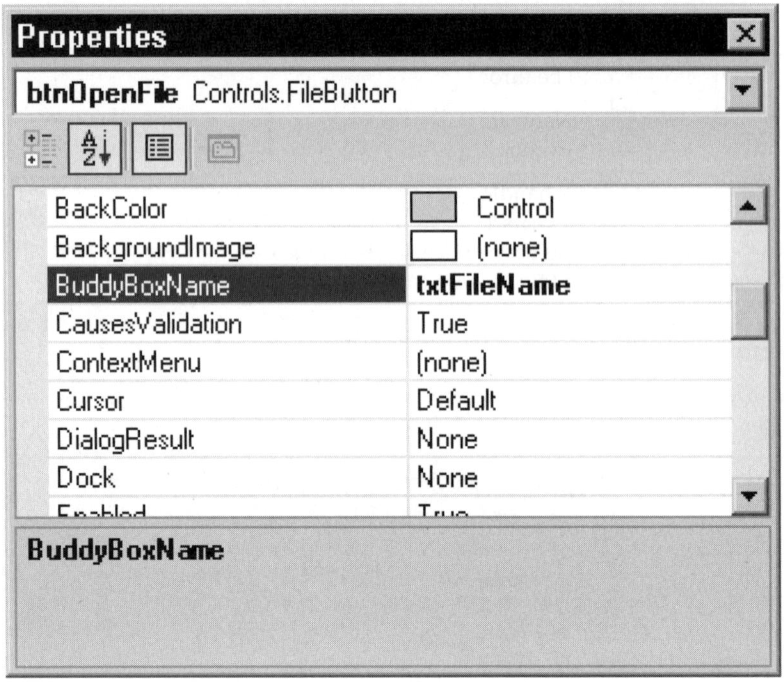

Figure 13-4

7. You're going to write a method into `FileButton` that responds to its own `Click` event. Before you can do that, you need to build a method that looks through the `Controls` collection of the parent, looking for a control with the name you gave to `BuddyBoxName`. Add this code to `FileButton.vb`:

```
' GetBuddyBox - return the actual TextBox control by looking through
' the parent's Controls property...
Public Function GetBuddyBox() As TextBox
    ' search name...
    Dim searchFor As String = BuddyBoxName.ToLower
    ' look through each control...
    Dim control As Control
    For Each control In Parent.Controls
        ' does the name match?
        If control.Name.ToLower = searchFor Then
            ' we have a match... now, cast the control
            ' to a text box and return...
            Return CType(control, TextBox)
        End If
    Next
End Function
```

8. The trick is to use the `ToLower` method, so that you're always comparing lowercase strings. Otherwise, you run into problems with case sensitivity. Notice how you prepare a lowercase version of `BuddyBoxName` right at the top of the method, so that you're not inefficiently doing

the conversion on each iteration of the loop. If you do find a control with the same name you cast it to a `System.Windows.Forms.TextBox` control and return it. If the control can't be cast, an exception will be thrown, which you'll need to handle somewhere.

9. Drop down the Class Name list in the top left corner of the editor window for `FileButton.vb` and select FileButton Events. Then select Click from the Method Name drop-down list.

10. Now, inside the `Click` handler, you call your `GetBuddyBox` method and, provided you get a control back, you retrieve its `Text` property. You can then open the file and get all of the contents back. After you have the file contents, create a new `OpenFileEventArgs` object and package the data. Add this code:

```
Private Sub FileButton_Click(ByVal sender As Object, _
        ByVal e As System.EventArgs) Handles MyBase.Click
    ' try and get the buddy box...
    Dim buddyBox As TextBox = GetBuddyBox()
    If buddyBox Is Nothing Then
        MessageBox.Show("The buddy box could not be found.")
    Else
        ' open the file and return the results...
        Dim stream As Stream = File.Open(buddyBox.Text, FileMode.Open)
        Dim reader As New StreamReader(stream)
        ' load the entire file...
        Dim contents As String = reader.ReadToEnd
        ' close the stream and the reader...
        stream.Close()
        reader.Close()
        ' do something with the contents
    End If
End Sub
```

Pause for a moment and consider what you've achieved. You are opening the specified file when the user clicks a FileButton and loading its contents into a String. Now you need to find a way to send the text to the application that is using the control. You do this by adding a public event to the FileButton control called `OpenFile`. The arguments for this event include the contents of the file.

You have already seen, however, that Windows forms events should only have two arguments. First, is the object that raised the event; second, the object that inherits from the `System.EventArgs` class and contains any other relevant information about the event. You need to create a new class that is derived from `System.EventArgs` and includes public fields for the filename and file content.

11. Now you have to create a new class derived from `System.EventArgs` that you can package the name of the file and the text of the file into. This is very easy to do. Create a new class in `Controls` called `OpenFileEventArgs` (by right-clicking the `Controls` project and selecting Add ⇨ Add Class). Then add this code:

```
Public Class OpenFileEventArgs
    Inherits System.EventArgs
    ' extend the properties of EventArgs...
    Public FileName As String
    Public FileText As String
End Class
```

12. Now you need to declare the event in the `FileButton` control. Open the code editor for `FileButton` and add this code:

```
Public Class FileButton
    Inherits System.Windows.Forms.Button
    ' event...
    Public Event OpenFile(ByVal sender As Object, _
                ByVal e As OpenFileEventArgs)
' members...
Private _buddyBoxName As String
```

13. Finally, you need to raise the event from the `FileButton` control's `Click` event handler. Add the indicated code:

```
Private Sub FileButton_Click(ByVal sender As Object, _
        ByVal e As System.EventArgs) Handles MyBase.Click
    ' try and get the buddy box...
    Dim buddyBox As TextBox = GetBuddyBox()
    If buddyBox Is Nothing Then
        MsgBox("The buddy box could not be found.")
    Else
        ' open the file and return the results...
        Dim stream As Stream = File.Open(buddyBox.Text, FileMode.Open)
        Dim reader As New StreamReader(stream)
        ' load the entire file...
        Dim contents As String = reader.ReadToEnd
        ' close the stream and the reader...
        stream.Close()
        reader.Close()
        ' do something with the contents
        ' raise the OpenFile event
        Dim args As New OpenFileEventArgs()
        args.FileName = buddyBox.Text
        args.FileText = contents
        RaiseEvent OpenFile(Me, args)
    End If
End Sub
```

Now, when a user clicks a `FileButton` control and a file opens successfully, `FileButton` will raise an `OpenFile` event.

Try It Out — Testing the Control

1. To test the control you need to make sure that you do receive the `OpenFile` event from the control. To do this, edit `Form1.vb` and use the drop-down lists to create an event handler for `btnOpenFile.OpenFile`. Then add this code:

```
Private Sub btnOpenFile_OpenFile(ByVal sender As System.Object, _
        ByVal e As OpenFileEventArgs) Handles _
        btnOpenFile.OpenFile
    MessageBox.Show(e.FileText)
End Sub
```

2. Because you defined this event as taking an `OpenFileEventArgs` object as its second parameter, this is what you'll be given. You can then gain direct access to the additional `FileText` and `FileName` properties that this class has.

3. Now, if you run the project and click the Open button, your file should be opened and your event handler will display the file contents in a message box.

Design Time or Runtime

Over the course of this discussion, I've mentioned the difference between design time and runtime. In certain circumstances, it's useful to know if your control is in design mode or run mode. For example, imagine that you have a control that establishes a database connection when a certain property is set. It might not be appropriate for that control to establish the connection when the form is being designed, but you will want it to when the project is finally run.

Usually, a control itself has a Boolean property called `DesignMode` that returns `True` if the control is in design mode or `False` if it isn't.

Creating a Control that Recognizes Design Mode

You're going to create a new control derived from `Button` that contains a timer that updates the text on the button with the current date and time, but only when the program is running. If the control is in design mode you're going to display the words "Design Mode."

Try It Out   **Creating a Control that Understands "DesignMode"**

1. Add a new user control to the project. Call it `TickButton`.

2. Change this code in `TickButton.vb`:

```
Imports System.Windows.Forms
Public Class TickButton
    Inherits System.Windows.Forms.Button
```

3. Now open the design view for `TickButton`. Drag and drop a Timer control from the Toolbox onto the new control. Set the name of the timer to ticker. Make sure that `Enabled` is set to `False` and that `Interval` is set to `100`.

4. You can detect when your control has been added to a form through the `InitLayout` method that's defined on `System.Windows.Forms.Control`. This happens both at design time and runtime. This is the best point to determine which mode you're in and, if appropriate, to start the timer. Add this code:

```
Protected Overrides Sub InitLayout()
    ' are we in design mode?
    If DesignMode = True Then
        Text = "Design Mode"
    Else
        ticker.Enabled = True
    End If
End Sub
```

One important thing to note here: In the constructor of the form, `DesignMode` *doesn't work. As the constructor is called the instant the object is created, the* `DesignMode` *property will not have been set by the .NET Framework, so the property will always return* `False`, *even if later in the control's lifetime it will return* `True`. `InitLayout` *is the best place to check.*

5. Go back to the design view of `TickButton` and double-click the Timer control. Add the following code:

```
Private Sub ticker_Tick(ByVal sender As Object, ByVal e As System.EventArgs)
Handles ticker.Tick
    ' update the text...
    Text = Now.ToString
End Sub
```

6. Build the project.

7. Now, if you open the design view for `Form1`, click on the Toolbox and then click on the My User Controls tab, the new control should appear at the bottom of the Toolbox. Draw a new `TickButton` button on your form. You'll see the text Design Mode as shown in Figure 3-5.

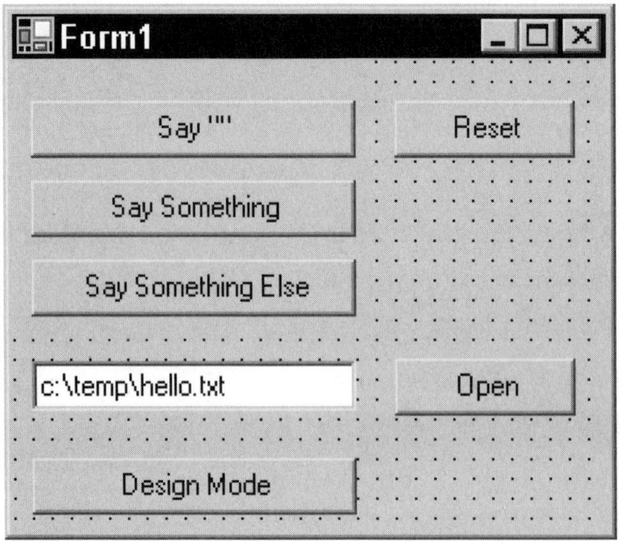

Figure 13-5

8. However, when you run the project. You will see that the Design Mode text is replaced by the runtime version, which displays the current date and time on the button.

Of course, there are many other occasions when you might want your code to behave differently at runtime or design time. An example could be that validation rules for a property will be different. In these cases, you would check the control's `DesignMode` property in exactly the same way.

Creating a Form Library

You do not always have to encapsulate this kind of functionality as a control. You could encapsulate the entire form and display it on demand. This is, in fact, what happens whenever an application wants to display the Open File or Print dialog boxes, or any other standard dialog box. You may well discover a common functionality in your applications that would be useful to add to a reusable library. For example, you might want to have a "Customer Lookup" tool available to all of your applications, or a common login window like the one discussed earlier.

Luckily, building form libraries is incredibly easy in .NET. In fact, it's not different from creating the kinds of forms that you've built so far. You just need to provide some kind of interface that allows the caller to start up the form and get values back.

Building the Form Library Project Login Form

In this section, you'll build a simple login form. Don't bother adding any functionality behind it to actually authenticate the user. Instead, concentrate on getting the form to display itself to the user.

Try It Out   Creating the Form Library Project

1. Close your existing project and create a new Class Library project and call it Forms Library.

2. Right-click References in the Solution Explorer and select Add Reference. Select System.Windows.Forms.dll from the available .NET components, click Select, and then click OK. The Reference dialog box is shown in Figure 13-6.

3. Now, create a new form by right-clicking the project within the Solution Explorer and selecting Add ➪ Add Windows Form. Call the new form LoginUser and click Open.

4. To build the form you need to change quite a few of the properties. Change these properties on the form:

   ❑ Set Text to Login User

   ❑ Set StartPosition to CenterScreen

   ❑ Set FormBorderStyle to FixedDialog

   ❑ Set MinimizeBox to False

   ❑ Set MaximizeBox to False

5. Then, add two text boxes called txtUsername and txtPassword. Set the PasswordChar property of txtPassword to *, so that entered passwords are not displayed on the screen. Empty the Text properties of both text boxes. Next, add some labels to illustrate which is the username field and which is the password field.

6. Finally, add two buttons—btnOk and btnCancel—and change their Text properties until you end up with something like the form shown in Figure 13-7.

Now that you have the basic form in place, you can wire in the logic behind the OK and Cancel buttons.

Try It Out   Add Logic to the OK and Cancel Buttons

1. Add this code to LoginUser.vb:

```
Imports System.Windows.Forms
Public Class LoginUser
    Inherits Form
    ' members...
```

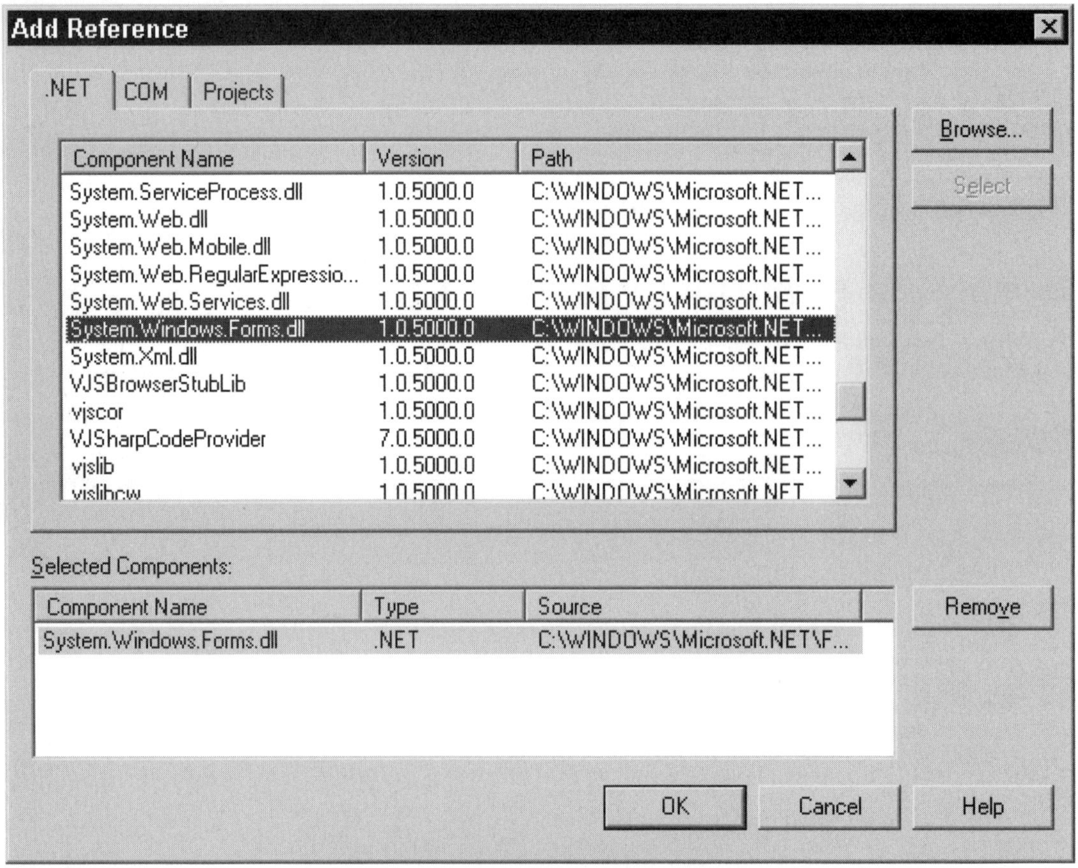

Figure 13-6

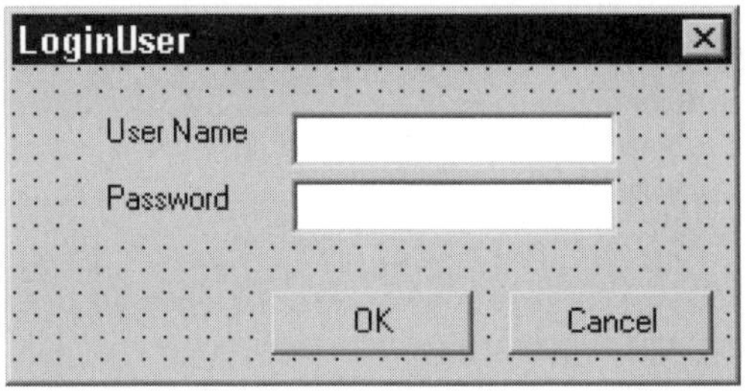

Figure 13-7

```
Public Tries As Integer
Public MaxTries As Integer = 3
Public UserId As Integer
' events...
Event LoginFailed(ByVal sender As Object, ByVal e As EventArgs)
Event LoginSucceeded(ByVal sender As Object, _
            ByVal e As LoginSucceededEventArgs)
Event LoginCancelled(ByVal sender As Object, ByVal e As EventArgs)
```

```
                        ' Go - authenticate the user...
                        Public Function Go(ByVal owner As Form) As Integer
                            ' reset ourselves...
                            UserId = 0
                            Tries = 0
                            ' show ourselves...
                            Me.ShowDialog(owner)
                            ' return the user id back...
                            Return UserId
                        End Function
                        Private Sub btnCancel_Click(ByVal sender As System.Object, _
                                ByVal e As System.EventArgs) Handles btnCancel.Click
                            RaiseEvent LoginCancelled(Me, New EventArgs())
                            Me.DialogResult = DialogResult.Cancel
                        End Sub
                        Private Sub btnOk_Click(ByVal sender As System.Object, _
                                ByVal e As System.EventArgs) Handles btnOk.Click
                            ' did we get a username?
                            If txtUsername.Text.Trim.Length > 0 Then
                                ' what password did we get?
                                If txtPassword.Text = "secret" Then
                                    ' this is a successful login!
                                    UserId = 27
                                    ' create a new event...
                                    Dim newEventArgs As New LoginSucceededEventArgs()
                                    newEventArgs.UserId = UserId
                                    RaiseEvent LoginSucceeded(Me, newEventArgs)
                                    ' hide the dialog and return...
                                    Me.DialogResult = DialogResult.OK
                                Else
                                    ' tell the username that the password was invalid...
                                    MessageBox.Show("The password you entered was invalid.")
                                    ' tell the caller that we failed...
                                    RaiseEvent LoginCancelled(Me, New EventArgs())
                                    ' add one to the number of tries...
                                    Tries += 1
                                    If Tries = MaxTries Then
                                        Me.DialogResult = DialogResult.OK
                                    End If
                                End If
                            Else
                                MessageBox.Show("You must supply a username.")
                            End If
                        End Sub
                        Windows Form Designer generated code
                End Class
```

2. The class library should have a class named `Class1.vb`. Rename this class to
   `LoginSucceededEventArgs.vb` and add this code:

```
Public Class LoginSucceededEventArgs
    Inherits EventArgs
    ' new member...
    Public UserId As Integer
End Class
```

How It Works

The first part of the class declaration includes the entire System.Windows.Forms namespace and then sets up the LoginUser class to derive from System.Windows.Forms.Form:

```
Imports System.Windows.Forms
Public Class LoginUser
    Inherits Form
```

The next part of the form defines several fields. You want one field that holds the number of attempts that the user has made to log in. You need another field to hold the maximum number of times that they are allowed to try. The last field holds the user ID that was authenticated. If the user cancels the dialog box or exceeds their maximum number of tries, the UserId will be 0.

```
' members...
Public Tries As Integer
Public MaxTries As Integer = 3
Public UserId As Integer
```

You defined three events for the form—first, when the user fails to authenticate themselves; second, when they succeed; and third, when they cancel. To receive these events you need to manually wire up event handlers, as Visual Studio .NET can't handle events raised by a form itself. It can only handle events raised by controls on a form.

```
' events...
Event LoginFailed(ByVal sender As Object, ByVal e As EventArgs)
Event LoginSucceeded(ByVal sender As Object, _
                ByVal e As LoginSucceededEventArgs)
Event LoginCancelled(ByVal sender As Object, ByVal e As EventArgs)
```

The Go method will be called by the developer who will pass in an object derived from Form. You reset your properties, display the form and, when the form has been closed, you return the user ID that you found (if any):

```
' Go - authenticate the user...
Public Function Go(ByVal owner As Form) As Integer
    ' reset ourselves...
    UserId = 0
    Tries = 0
    ' show ourselves...
    Me.ShowDialog(owner)
    ' return the user id back...
    Return UserId
End Function
```

If the user clicks the Cancel button, you raise the LoginCancelled event and close the dialog box:

```
Private Sub btnCancel_Click(ByVal sender As System.Object, _
        ByVal e As System.EventArgs) Handles btnCancel.Click
    RaiseEvent LoginCancelled(Me, New EventArgs())
    Me.DialogResult = DialogResult.Cancel
End Sub
```

Using the `DialogResult` property of the form is the proper way to close a form displayed with `ShowDialog`. In this case you're indicating that the dialog box was canceled.

If the user clicks OK, the first thing you want to do is make sure that they actually supplied a username:

```
Private Sub btnOk_Click(ByVal sender As System.Object, _
        ByVal e As System.EventArgs) Handles btnOk.Click
' did we get a username?
If txtUsername.Text.Trim.Length > 0 Then
```

For your logic, if the user enters any username with the password "secret" you authenticate them. You always give the user ID of 27.

```
' what password did we get?
If txtPassword.Text = "secret" Then
    ' this is a successful login!
    UserId = 27
    ' create a new event...
    Dim newEventArgs As New LoginSucceededEventArgs()
    newEventArgs.UserId = UserId
    RaiseEvent LoginSucceeded(Me, newEventArgs)
    ' hide the dialog and return...
    Me.DialogResult = DialogResult.OK
Else
```

`LoginSucceededEventArgs` is derived from `System.EventArgs` and will contain an extra property called `UserId`. If the user has successfully logged in using the "secret" password then a value of `UserId` will be passed to `LoginSucceededEventArgs` and the `LoginSucceeded` event fired.

If the password supplied was not "secret" you need to increment `Tries` and, if necessary, close the dialog box:

```
' tell the username that the password was invalid...
MessageBox.Show("The password you entered was invalid.")
' tell the caller that we failed...
RaiseEvent LoginCancelled(Me, New EventArgs())
' add one to the number of tries...
Tries += 1
If Tries = MaxTries Then
    Me.DialogResult = DialogResult.OK
End If
```

Finally, you round off the method definition, including the message box that tells the user to supply a username:

```
    End If
Else
    MessageBox.Show("You must supply a username.")
End If
End Sub
```

Testing the Form

To test the form, you need to jump through the same hoops you did when you first needed to test out your user controls.

1. Right-click Solution 'Forms Library' (1 project) in the Solution Explorer and select Add ⇨ New Project. Create a new Visual Basic .NET Windows Application project and call it My Application.

2. Next, you need to set up this new test application as the startup project, so right-click My Application in the Solution Explorer and select Set as StartUp Project.

3. Next, add a reference to the `Forms Library` project to `My Application`. Right-click the References entry underneath My Application and select Add Reference. Change to the Projects tab, select Forms Library, click Select, and then click OK.

4. Now you're free to create an instance of the `LoginUser` class from your application and ask it to log in the user.

5. Open up `Form1.vb` in the designer and draw on a button. Rename the button `btnLogin` and set its Text to Login.

6. Now, double-click on `btnLogin` to create an event handler for its `Click` event. Add this code:

```
Private Sub btnLogin_Click(ByVal sender As System.Object, _
        ByVal e As System.EventArgs) Handles btnLogin.Click
    ' create a new instance of the form...
    Dim login As New Forms_Library.LoginUser()
    ' get the user id back...
    Dim userId As Integer = login.Go(Me)
    ' did we get a user?
    If userId <> 0 Then
        MessageBox.Show("The logged in user has ID " & userId.ToString)
    Else
        MessageBox.Show("No user ID was returned.")
    End If
End Sub
```

7. Now run the project and click the Login button. You'll be given three chances to login. Remember, to do this successfully, enter any username along with the password "secret."

How It Works

The first thing you do is create an instance of the `LoginUser` class:

```
' create a new instance of the form...
Dim login As New Forms_Library.LoginUser()
```

Then you ask the new object to display the form through the `Go` method:

```
' get the user id back...
Dim userId As Integer = login.Go(Me)
```

By passing a reference to Me through, you're actually passing a reference to a Form object, which is then instantly passed through to the ShowDialog method of the Form object implemented by the LoginUser class. From this point, you're at the mercy of the encapsulated functionality.

When the dialog box goes away; which can be because the user canceled the dialog box, got the right password, or got the wrong password; you'll be given back the user ID as a return value from Go. If this value is 0, something went wrong and the user couldn't be logged in. Otherwise, the user could be logged in.

```
' did we get a user?
If userId <> 0 Then
    MessageBox.Show("The logged in user has ID " & userId.ToString)
Else
    MessageBox.Show("No user ID was returned.")
End If
```

It's pretty unlikely that you would implement this functionality by placing a button on a blank form that the user would click before being shown the dialog box. Rather, the application is more likely to do this automatically after its initialization routines have been completed and we could have implemented this functionality in the form's load event.

Hooking Up the Events

You will recall that you built LoginUser so that it raises events at certain times. To round off this section, take a look at how you can consume those events from within your form.

Try It Out   Receiving Events from LoginForm

1. Delete the btnLogin button that you created before, dip into the code for Form1.vb and remove the btnLogin_Click method.

2. You can tell .NET that you want to automatically capture any events that an object raises by using the WithEvents keyword. The problem with this keyword is that it can't be used in conjunction with New. In other words, you need to define a member to contain an instance of LoginForm and create one when you need it. Add this code to the top of Form1.vb:

```
Public Class Form1
    Inherits System.Windows.Forms.Form
    ' members...
    Private _userId As Integer
    Private WithEvents _login As Forms_Library.LoginUser
```

You also created another member that will hold the user ID if logging in is successful.

3. At this point, Visual Studio .NET will pick up the member that raises events and it adds that member to the two drop-down lists at the top of the code window. Select _login from the left one and then select LoginSucceeded from the right one. This is shown in Figure 13-8.

4. When you receive this event, you need to store the ID of the new user in your _userId member:

```
Private Sub _login_LoginSucceeded(ByVal sender As System.Object, _
        ByVal e As Forms_Library.LoginSucceededEventArgs) _
        Handles _login.LoginSucceeded
```

```
    ' store the user id...
    _userId = e.UserId
    ' update our caption...
    Me.Text &= " - User ID: " & _userId.ToString
End Sub
```

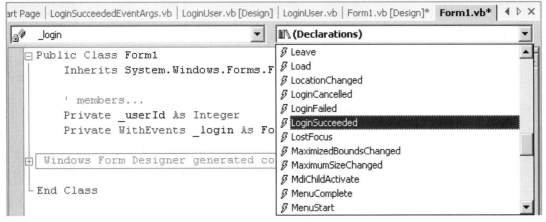

Figure 13-8

You also append the ID of the new user to the caption of the form so that you can see what happens at design time.

5. Of course, nothing is going to happen until you create an instance of `LoginUser` and call `Go`. You're going to break this up into a separate function so that, if you want, you can call it from another point in the application. (Although it's not strictly necessary here, it's good practice to break functions out in this way, as it makes the code easier to maintain.) Add this method to `Form1.vb`:

```
Private Function Login() As Boolean
    ' create an instance of login...
    _login = New Forms_Library.LoginUser()
    ' login the user...
    Dim userId As Integer = _login.Go(Me)
    ' reset our login object...
    _login = Nothing
    ' return true or false...
    If userId <> 0 Then
        Return True
    Else
        Return False
    End If
End Function
```

6. You need to physically create an instance of `LoginUser` before you can use it and in order to make sure that the event handling works, you *must* add this instance to a member variable defined using the `WithEvents` keyword, otherwise Visual Basic .NET will not be able to wire up the methods. For neatness, you also need to get rid of the object instance once you're finished. Finally, you need to return `True` or `False` to indicate whether the user properly logged in.

7. Use the drop-down lists to create an event handler for the form's `Load` event. Then, add this code:

```
Private Sub Form1_Load(ByVal sender As System.Object, _
        ByVal e As System.EventArgs) Handles MyBase.Load
    ' try and login...
    If Login() = False Then
        ' quit the application if we failed...
        MessageBox.Show("Login failed. Quitting.")
        Application.Exit()
    End If
End Sub
```

8. Now try running the application. If the login process works, you'll see an empty form with the User ID in the form's caption as shown in Figure 13-9.

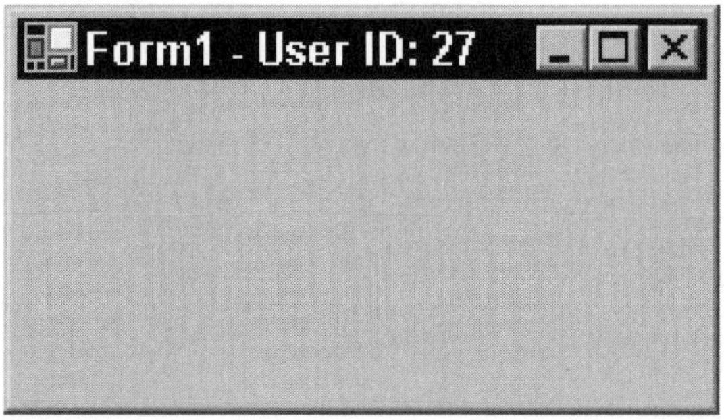

Figure 13-9

How It Works

By virtue of the fact that the caption has been changed, you know that the user successfully managed to authenticate themselves and that the user ID has indeed been properly passed through the event handler.

If the user fails to authenticate properly, you will not see the application window. Either way, the developer has been successfully able to reuse the code that provides a login dialog, which is the point of the exercise.

Although we have presented two methods for using the form here, there's no real advantage over using either as far as the developer is concerned. They still need to create an instance of `LoginUser`, still need to call it, and still need to examine the results and determine the next step that the application should make when the user can log in and when they can't.

Summary

This chapter showed two ways of packaging a user interface together with some encapsulated functionality. We looked at building user controls that aggregated a number of existing controls usefully, and how to build user controls that inherited the behavior of an existing control. In both cases, we extended the new controls with properties, methods, and events. These controls, once compiled, were shown in the ToolBox under the My User Controls tab.

We also took a look at how to create a class library that encapsulated forms with pre-built functionality, making it easy to provide a consistent interface in all of our applications that needed to implement a login form.

To summarize, you should know:

❑   What a Windows Forms Control is and how it works

❑   How to create a control

❑   How to add methods and events to your control

❑   How to code for Design Time and Runtime

Exercises

1.   How do you define an event called SomethingHappened in a user control?

2.   What keyword is used to fire (or raise) an event?

3.   How does a control know if it's design time or runtime?

14

Programming Custom Graphics

So far, in this book, you have built user interfaces entirely from existing controls. When you are writing programs with Visual Basic .NET, you also have the freedom to draw your own user interface. This gives us absolute freedom over the look and feel of our programs, and makes certain programming tasks possible.

In this chapter, you are going to look at the graphics and drawing functionality available in Visual Basic .NET. You will be introduced to the concepts by building a fairly complex drawing program, just to illustrate how simple drawing your own user interface actually is. Towards the end of the chapter, you will examine some of the multimedia features of Visual Basic .NET and learn how you can display common Internet file formats such as gif, .jpg, and .png.

In this chapter, you will:

❑   Learn about the System.Drawing namespace

❑   Use pens and brushes

❑   Learn about the Color Dialog and how to select and use colors

❑   Size and stretch images

❑   Create your own Paint program

Building a Simple Paint Program

You are going to create a simple Paint program by creating a new Windows application project and build some user controls that you will wire up to provide functionality for the application.

Creating a Project with User Controls

Your motivation for building user controls for this application is simple: It's good practice to break the application down into components. By following this technique, if you want to pull your paint functionality out of this application and into another, you can do it relatively easily.

What you are doing here with your controls is taking over the responsibility for painting them. Whenever you do this, you are creating owner drawings. Therefore, the controls you build are known as owner-draw user controls.

Try It Out   **Creating the Project**

1. Create a new Visual Basic Windows Application project in the usual way. Call it WroxPaint.

2. In the Solution Explorer, right-click the WroxPaint project and select Add ⇨ Add User Control. Change the name to PaintCanvas and click Open.

3. Make sure the Form Designer for PaintCanvas is showing, click the background of the control and from the Properties window, change the `BackColor` property to White. (To do this, use the BackColor property's drop-down list, change to the Custom tab, and click the white box in the top-left corner.)

4. Before you can use the control you need to build the project. From the menu select Build ⇨ Build Solution. This will create the new PaintCanvas control and let you use it.

5. Now, go back to the Designer for `Form1`. Click on the Toolbox and then click on the My User Controls tab and select the new PaintCanvas control.

6. Add a PaintCanvas control so that it fills up the whole form. Set its Anchor property to Top, Bottom, Left, Right: This will ensure that the control always takes up the whole window. For the sake of neatness change the Text property of the form to WroxPaint.

How Drawing Programs Work

Your computer screen is made up of pixels—hundreds of thousands of them. They are very small, but when working together they make a display on the screen. Since pixels on any given display are always of a uniform size, they are the common unit of measurement used in computer graphics.

To find out how big your desktop is, minimize all your windows and right-click on your Windows desktop. Select Properties and change to the Settings tab. The slider in the bottom-left corner controls the size of your desktop—or rather, it controls the density of pixels on your display. In Figure 14-1 you can see that my screen is set to 1,024 pixels across and 768 pixels down.

There are two very common computer graphics techniques: raster and vector. It is very useful to understand the difference between the two.

Raster Graphics

Raster graphics work a little like a physical canvas—you have a space and you fill it up with color using various tools like brushes and pens. In a raster graphics program the space is divided up into pixels. Each pixel can be a color and it's the drawing program's responsibility to set the color of each square depending on what kind of drawing tool you're using and the position and movement of the mouse.

The graphics program stores the image that you've drawn as a bitmap, this being a description of the pixels that make up the image and the color of each. A bitmap is basically a two-dimensional array of pixels. Each element in the array, accessed through a pair of (x, y) coordinates, stores a color value. If you draw a rectangle in a raster graphics package, that rectangle is abstracted to a set of pixels on the bitmap.

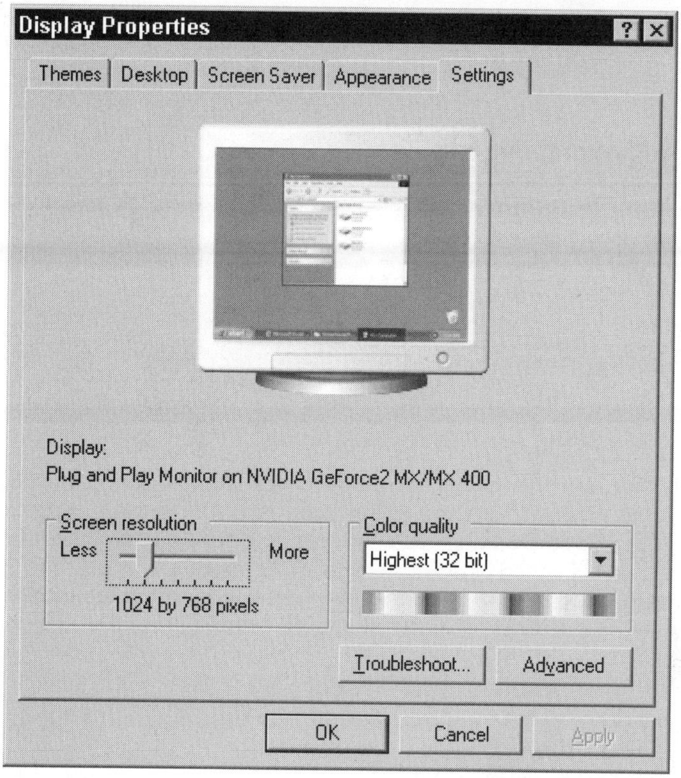

Figure 14-1

After it's been drawn you can't change the rectangle at all, other than using other tools to draw over it or draw another one.

> .jpg, .gif, and .png *images use a variation of the bitmap format to save images. However, they are compressed in particular ways to save space and download time.*

Vector Graphics

Vector graphics packages work in a different way. When you draw a rectangle onto the canvas, they physically record the fact that a rectangle exists at a given location. Vector graphics packages store a blueprint of how to draw the image, rather than storing the image that's been drawn. They do not abstract the rectangle down to a set of pixels. What this means is that you can pick it up again and move it, or change its shape or color later on because the package has an understanding of what it is.

> *A number of modern graphics packages offer a hybrid approach to this, combining raster graphics with vector graphics.*

Even in a vector graphics program, the screen itself works in pixels and is therefore a raster format. Therefore, for the program to be able to display the drawing, the picture recorded by the package has to be converted into a raster format for the display. This process is known as *rendering*.

Your paint package is going to be a vector-based drawing package—for no other reason than it makes it easier to understand how drawing works in .NET. You're going to build a set of objects that represent certain shapes—namely circles and squares—and hold them in a list.

The GraphicsItem Class

In your application, you're going to have two basic drawing types: circle and square. Each drawing type will need to have an understanding of where it appears on the canvas (and ultimately, the screen), what its color is, and whether it is filled. You'll build a base class called GraphicsItem, from which you'll derive GraphicsCircle.

Try It Out   Building GraphicsItem and GraphicsCircle

1. Create a new class named GraphicsItem by right-clicking on WroxPaint in the Solution Explorer and selecting Add ⇨ Add Class. Name the class GraphicsItem and click Open.

2. Enter this code into GraphicsItem. Remember to add the MustInherit keyword to the first line. The MustInherit keyword tells Visual Basic .NET that you cannot create instances of GraphicsItem directly. Instead, you have to create classes that inherit from it. You use the MustOverride keyword here. This has a similar meaning to MustInherit—you use it to force derived classes to add implementation for a particular method without providing any implementation in the base class. It can only be used in MustInherit classes.

```
Public MustInherit Class GraphicsItem
    ' members...
    Public Color As Color
    Public IsFilled As Boolean
    Public Rectangle As Rectangle
    ' methods...
    Public MustOverride Sub Draw(ByVal graphics As Graphics)
    ' SetPoint - add an item at the given point...
    Public Sub SetPoint(ByVal x As Integer, ByVal y As Integer, _
        ByVal graphicSize As Integer, _
        ByVal graphicColor As Color, ByVal graphicIsFilled As Boolean)
        ' set the rectangle depending on the graphic and the size...
        Rectangle = New _
            Rectangle(x - (graphicSize / 2), y - (graphicSize / 2), _
            graphicSize, graphicSize)
        ' set the color and isfilled...
        Color = graphicColor
        IsFilled = graphicIsFilled
    End Sub
End Class
```

3. Create another class named GraphicsCircle. Add this code:

```
Public Class GraphicsCircle
    Inherits GraphicsItem
    Public Overrides Sub Draw(ByVal graphics As _
        System.Drawing.Graphics)
        ' create a new pen...
        Dim brush As New SolidBrush(Me.Color)
```

```
    ' draw the circle...
    graphics.FillEllipse(brush, Me.Rectangle)
  End Sub
End Class
```

Screen and Client Coordinates

When you get into the world of building your own painting code for your user interface, you usually have to work a lot with the mouse. I have already mentioned that in Windows and .NET, the base currency of drawing is the pixel. This means that when you ask the mouse for its position (for example when verifying that the user has moved the mouse across your control or clicked one of the buttons), you get back a set of coordinates given in pixels. If the user clicks the mouse in the very top-left pixel, you'll get back coordinates of (0, 0). If you're using a 1,024×768 display and the user clicks in the very bottom-right pixel, you'll get back coordinates of (1024, 768).

Although this seems straightforward, there is a wrinkle. When you click inside a window the coordinates are adjusted depending on where the window itself is on the screen.

In Figure 14-2, Notepad is shown in the bottom-right corner of the screen. This display is configured at 1,024 pixels across and 786 pixels down, which means that the top-left corner of Notepad itself is at approximately (500, 300), according to the screen.

Figure 14-2

457

However, every window has a client area, which is the area the programmer can use to report the program's output. This client area is exclusive of the window border, the caption, menu, scrollbars, and the toolbar. When you are drawing onto the control or form (Notepad is representing your form in Figure 14-2), you are always dealing with this client area. The coordinates you use when drawing are adjusted so that the position of the window itself on the screen becomes irrelevant. These coordinates are known as client coordinates.

If you click the top-left corner of the Notepad edit area (the white part), there are actually two different coordinates that you can get:

❑   The first one will be around (510, 330), a little in and down from the top-left hand corner of the window. These are the *screen coordinates*, also known as the *absolute position*.

❑   The second pair will be around (10, 10) and these are the adjusted client coordinates. If you click the same graphic in the client, you will get (10, 10) irrespective of where the window is positioned on the screen. This is sometimes known as *relative position*.

Listening to the Mouse and Drawing GraphicsCircle Objects

For your graphics application to work you'll monitor what the user is doing with the mouse, create new objects derived from `GraphicsItem`, and store them in a big list. When it is time for you to draw, you'll go through this list and ask each `GraphicsItem` in turn to render itself on the screen.

Try It Out   Drawing

1.   In the Solution Explorer, right-click PaintCanvas and select View Code. Add these enumerations to the class. The first will be used to store the current graphics mode/tool, while the second stores the size of the pen used for drawing:

```
Public Class PaintCanvas
    Inherits System.Windows.Forms.UserControl
    ' enums...
    Public Enum GraphicTools As Integer
        CirclePen = 0
    End Enum
    Public Enum GraphicSizes As Integer
        Small = 4
        Medium = 10
        Large = 20
    End Enum
    ' Windows Forms Designer generated code
    ' ...
End Class
```

2.   Next, add these members to the class:

```
Public Class PaintCanvas
    Inherits System.Windows.Forms.UserControl
    ' enums...
    Public Enum GraphicTools As Integer
        CirclePen = 0
    End Enum
```

```
Public Enum GraphicSizes As Integer
    Small = 4
    Medium = 10
    Large = 20
End Enum
' members...
Public GraphicsItems As New ArrayList()
Public GraphicTool As GraphicTools = GraphicTools.CirclePen
Public GraphicSize As GraphicSizes = GraphicSizes.Medium
Public GraphicColor As Color = Color.Black
```

Here is what each member will do. Notice that you define a default value for these members to make initialization of the application easier:

- ❑ GraphicItems will hold a list of the GraphicsItem objects that make up the drawing.

- ❑ GraphicsTool will keep track of which graphic tool is currently being used.

- ❑ GraphicsSize will keep track of how big you want each graphic to be.

- ❑ GraphicsColor will keep track of the color of the item that you want to draw.

3. Drawing the items on the page is a two-phase process. When the user moves the mouse around on the control, you want to create new GraphicsCircle objects and add them to the GraphicsItems list. At some point, Windows will ask you to paint the control, so you'll need to go through the GraphicsItems list and draw each one in turn.

4. Add this method to PaintCanvas:

```
' DoMousePaint - respond to a mouse movement...
Private Sub DoMousePaint(ByVal e As MouseEventArgs)
    ' store the new item somewhere...
    Dim newItem As GraphicsItem
    ' what tool are you using?
    Select Case GraphicTool
        ' circlepen?
        Case GraphicTools.CirclePen
            ' create a new graphics circle...
            Dim circle As New GraphicsCircle()
            circle.SetPoint(e.X, e.Y, GraphicSize, GraphicColor, True)
            ' store this for addition...
            newItem = circle
    End Select
    ' were you given an item?
    If Not newItem Is Nothing Then
        ' add it to the list...
        GraphicsItems.Add(newItem)
        ' invalidate...
        Invalidate()
    End If
End Sub
```

5. From the left drop-down list at the top of the code editor window, select (Overrides). From the right list, select OnMouseDown. Add this code to the new event handler:

```
Protected Overrides Sub OnMouseDown( _
            ByVal e As System.Windows.Forms.MouseEventArgs)
```

```
      ' is the button down?
      If e.Button = MouseButtons.Left Then
          DoMousePaint(e)
      End If
End Sub
```

6. Again from the left drop-down list select (Overrides). Then select OnMouseMove from the right list. Add this code:

```
Protected Overrides Sub OnMouseMove( _
            ByVal e As System.Windows.Forms.MouseEventArgs)
      ' is the button down?
      If e.Button = MouseButtons.Left Then
          DoMousePaint(e)
      End If
End Sub
```

7. Finally, from the left drop-down list select (Overrides) once more. Then select OnPaint from the right list. Add this code:

```
Protected Overrides Sub OnPaint( _
            ByVal e As System.Windows.Forms.PaintEventArgs)
      ' go through the list...
      Dim item As GraphicsItem
      For Each item In GraphicsItems
          ' ask each item to draw itself...
          item.Draw(e.Graphics)
      Next
End Sub
```

8. Run the project and draw on the control by clicking and dragging the mouse over the surface.

You now have a working paint program, but you'll notice that the more you paint the more it flickers. This illustrates an important aspect of drawing, as you'll see when you fix it. For now, look at what you've done.

How It Works

When the user moves the mouse over the control, an event called MouseMove is fired. You have hooked into this event by overriding a method in the base System.Windows.Forms.UserControl class called OnMouseMove. When this happens, you check to see if the left mouse button is down and, if it is, you pass the System.Windows.Forms.MouseEventArgs object that you were given over to your private DoMousePaint method:

```
Protected Overrides Sub OnMouseMove( _
            ByVal e As System.Windows.Forms.MouseEventArgs)
      ' is the button down?
      If e.Button = MouseButtons.Left Then
          DoMousePaint(e)
      End If
End Sub
```

DoMousePaint is the method that you'll use to handle the drawing process. In this case, whenever MouseMove is received, you want to create a new GraphicsCircle item and add it to the list of vectors that make up your image.

As DoMousePaint will ultimately do more than add circles to the vector list, you need to do things in a (seemingly) counter-intuitive order. The first thing you need is to declare a variable to hold the new GraphicsItem that will be created—so declare newItem:

```
' DoMousePaint - respond to a mouse movement...
Private Sub DoMousePaint(ByVal e As MouseEventArgs)
    ' store the new item somewhere...
    Dim newItem As GraphicsItem
```

Then, you look at your GraphicTool property to determine what you're supposed to be drawing. At this point, because you only have one tool defined, this will always be a circle:

```
' what tool are you using?
Select Case GraphicTool
    ' circlepen?
    Case GraphicTools.CirclePen
        ' create a new graphics circle...
        Dim circle As New GraphicsCircle()
```

After you have the circle you call the SetPoint member, which if you recall was defined on GraphicsItem. This method is responsible for determining the point on the canvas where the item should appear. You give SetPoint the current drawing size and color, and tell it to draw a filled circle:

```
circle.SetPoint(e.X, e.Y, GraphicSize, GraphicColor, True)
```

You'll look at SetPoint *itself in more detail in a moment.*

After you have the item and have called SetPoint, you store it in NewItem and close the Select...End Select:

```
        ' store this for addition...
        newItem = circle
End Select
```

If a new GraphicsItem was stored in newItem, you have to add it to the list:

```
' were you given an item?
If Not newItem Is Nothing Then
    ' add it to the list...
    GraphicsItems.Add(newItem)
```

Finally, you have to invalidate the control. You have to do this to tell Windows that something about the appearance of the control has changed. .NET will not tell the control to paint itself unless something has told Windows that the control needs painting. Calling `Invalidate` in this way tells Windows that the appearance of the control is "invalid" and therefore needs updating:

```
        ' invalidate...
        Invalidate()
    End If
End Sub
```

Although you can invalidate the control with the `Invalidate` method, the control will be invalidated whenever Windows detects it needs redrawing. This may happen when the window is restored after being minimized, another window obscures an area that's been made visible, and so on.

That covers everything from the user dragging the mouse over the control to adding a new `GraphicsCircle` item to the list. Now what?

With the control marked as requiring painting, it's up to Windows to choose a time for the window to be painted. To increase the performance of the windowing subsystem, windows are only drawn when the system has enough "spare time" to do it. Painting is not considered to be a crucial task to the operating system. You cannot rely on painting being done immediately, or within a given time-span of your marking something as invalid. At some point in the future, the control will be asked to paint itself. You may have noticed this effect when your computer is being used heavily—an image on the screen will appear to "freeze" for a period before the display is updated.

Do not try to force Windows to paint when it doesn't want to. There is a ton of optimization code in Windows to make sure that things are painted at absolutely the best time. Invalidate when you need to flag something as needing to be redrawn and let nature take its course.

When it is ready, the `Paint` event will be called. You tap into this event by overriding the `OnPaint` method on the base `UserControl` class. All that you have to do is loop through the entire array of `GraphicsItem` objects that you've collected in `GraphicsItems` and ask each one to draw itself:

```
Protected Overrides Sub OnPaint( _
            ByVal e As System.Windows.Forms.PaintEventArgs)
    ' go through the list...
    Dim item As GraphicsItem
    For Each item In GraphicsItems
        ' ask each item to draw itself...
        item.Draw(e.Graphics)
    Next
End Sub
```

The `Paint` event passes through its parameters as a `PaintEventArgs` object. This object, among other things, contains a property called `Graphics`. This property returns a `System.Drawing.Graphics` object.

When you have hold of a graphics object, you are able to draw to the control, the form, printer, or whatever it is that's given you an object. This object contains a bundle of methods and properties that are actually used for painting. To keep in line with the principle of "only painting when needed," in typical day-to-day work you shouldn't try to create or otherwise obtain one of these objects. If you're given one then it's time to paint!

Painting is usually a matter of calling some simple methods on the Graphics object. In the case of GraphicsCircle, you call FillEllipse. This method draws and fills an ellipse (or circle, depending on which parameters you provide). Note that there's a similar method called DrawEllipse, which doesn't fill in the ellipse after it's drawn:

```
Public Overrides Sub Draw(ByVal graphics As _
        System.Drawing.Graphics)
    ' create a new pen...
    Dim brush As New SolidBrush(Me.Color)
    ' draw the circle...
    graphics.FillEllipse(brush, Me.Rectangle)
End Sub
```

The SetPoint method is responsible for populating the Color and Rectangle properties on the GraphicsCircle object—you'll see this in a minute. Painting in .NET is heavily dependent on this concept of a rectangle. This is a simple class that stores x and y coordinates for the top-left of the rectangle, and the width and height. When you draw an ellipse you provide a rectangle that describes the bounds of the ellipse.

You'll also notice that at the top of the method you created a new SolidBrush object. You then pass this brush through to the FillEllipse method. This SolidBrush object, as you have probably guessed, describes the kind of brush you want to use.

You should call the SetPoint method from inside DoMousePaint whenever you create a new GraphicsCircle object:

```
' create a new graphics circle...
Dim circle As New GraphicsCircle()
circle.SetPoint(e.X, e.Y, GraphicSize, GraphicColor, True)
```

Basically, all you're using this method for is to populate the object depending on the position of the mouse and the current graphic size and color.

The first thing you need to do in GraphicsItem.SetPoint is set up the rectangle:

```
' SetPoint - add an item at the given point...
Public Sub SetPoint(ByVal x As Integer, ByVal y As Integer, _
    ByVal graphicSize As Integer, _
    ByVal graphicColor As Color, ByVal graphicIsFilled As Boolean)
        ' set the rectangle depending on the graphic and the size...
        Rectangle = New _
            Rectangle(x - (graphicSize / 2), y - (graphicSize / 2), _
            graphicSize, graphicSize)
```

When you want to draw a circle, you provide the mid-point. Therefore, the top-left corner of the rectangle must be adjusted up and left depending on the size provided through graphicSize. You pass the top-left corner through as the first and second parameters to the rectangle's constructor. The third parameter supplied is the width and the fourth provides the height.

After you have the parameter, you need to store the color and also a flag that indicates if the circle is filled or not:

```
' set the color and isfilled...
Color = graphicColor
IsFilled = graphicIsFilled
End Sub
```

Now that you know how the painting works, let's see if you can get rid of the flickering!

Invalidation

This example was designed to flicker and slow down to illustrate an important consideration that you need to bear in mind when drawing controls: Do the least amount of work possible! Drawing to the screen is slow. The less you draw, the faster the performance of your application should be and the better it should look on the screen.

The control flickers because painting is a two-stage process. Before you're asked to paint, Windows automatically erases the region behind the area that needs to be painted. This means the whole control flashes white as everything is erased and then you fill in the details.

What you want to do is to invalidate only the area that contains the new GraphicsItem. When you invalidate the control you don't have to invalidate the whole thing. If you want, you can just invalidate a small area.

Try It Out   Invalidating a Small Area

1. In the PaintCanvas class, find the DoMousePaint method. Change the Invalidate method call at the end to this:

```
' were we given an item?
If Not newItem Is Nothing Then
    ' add it to the list...
    GraphicsItems.Add(newItem)
    ' invalidate...
    Invalidate(newItem.Rectangle)
End If
```

2. Run the project. You'll notice now that when you paint it doesn't flicker.

How It Works

After you call SetPoint on the new GraphicsCircle object, the Rectangle property is updated to contain the bounding rectangle of the circle.

This time when you call the Invalidate method, you pass in this rectangle. In this way, only a tiny area of the form is invalidated, therefore, only that tiny area is erased. After it is erased, you get the opportunity to draw your circle.

More Optimization

You'll notice that if you draw a lot on the control, after a while the edge of the line starts to become almost jagged. What you're experiencing here is that as the `GraphicsItems` list grows, more calls to `FillEllipse` end up being made. As drawing on the screen is slow, the more you have to do this, the longer the drawing process takes on aggregate. This lengthened drawing process prevents all of the `MouseMove` events from being fired and so the line appears to stutter. In the following *Try It Out* section you see how you can avoid this problem.

Try It Out   Optimized Drawing

1. Find the `OnPaint` method on the `PaintCanvas` class. Add this code:

```
Protected Overrides Sub OnPaint( _
        ByVal e As System.Windows.Forms.PaintEventArgs)
    ' go through the list...
    Dim item As GraphicsItem
    For Each item In GraphicsItems
        ' do we need to be drawn?
        If e.ClipRectangle.IntersectsWith(item.Rectangle) = True Then
            ' ask each item to draw itself...
            item.Draw(e.Graphics)
        End If
    Next
End Sub
```

2. Run the project. You should now find that the drawing process is smoother.

How It Works

The `PaintEventArgs` object contains another property called `ClipRectangle`. This rectangle describes the area of the control that has been invalidated and is known as the clipping rectangle. The `Rectangle` class contains a method called `IntersectsWith` that can tell whether two given rectangles overlap.

As you know the rectangle that describes the bounds of each of your `GraphicsItem` objects, you can use this rectangle with `IntersectsWith`. If the `GraphicsItem` overlaps, it needs drawing, otherwise you move on to the next control.

The two techniques you've seen here—only invalidating what changes and only drawing what falls into the invalidated region—are by far the two most important techniques you'll come across when painting. If you skip either of these, your control has a good chance of being sluggish and flickering.

Choosing Colors

Now that you can do some basic painting, you'll build a control that lets you choose the color that you're painting in. Like a lot of graphics programs, you'll build this so that you have a palette of different colors and you're able to choose two at a time—one for the left mouse button and one for the right.

There are a number of different ways to build this control, and perhaps the most logical is to create a control that contains a bundle of Button controls, each configured so that it displays the color that it represents. However, this example shows you how to build a control completely from scratch. The techniques that you'll learn here will be really useful if you want to roll your own controls that display a picture of something and have hot regions on them. *Hot regions* are regions that fire an event when you click them. What you're doing might seem a little obscure, but it's a great example!

Creating the ColorPalette Control

To create the color palette control, you're going to need two classes. One, derived from `UserControl` and named `ColorPalette`, which will provide the user interface (UI) for the palette itself. The other, `ColorPaletteButton`, will be used to display the actual color box on the palette.

Try It Out   Creating the ColorPalette Control

1. In the Solution Explorer, add a new class to the WroxPaint project named `ColorPaletteButton` and add the following code to it:

```
Public Class ColorPaletteButton
    ' color...
    Public Color As Color = Color.Black
    Public Rectangle As Rectangle
    ' constructor...
    Public Sub New(ByVal newColor As Color)
        Color = newColor
    End Sub
    ' SetPosition - move the button to the given position...
    Public Sub SetPosition(ByVal x As Integer, ByVal y As Integer, _
                    ByVal buttonSize As Integer)
        ' update the members...
        Rectangle = New Rectangle(x, y, buttonSize, buttonSize)
    End Sub
    ' Draw - draw the button...
    Public Sub Draw(ByVal graphics As Graphics)
        ' draw the color block...
        Dim brush As New SolidBrush(Color)
        graphics.FillRectangle(brush, Rectangle)
        ' draw an "edge" around the control...
        Dim pen As New Pen(Color.Black)
        graphics.DrawRectangle(pen, Rectangle)
    End Sub
End Class
```

2. In a similar fashion, add a user control to the WroxPaint project named ColorPalette. Double-click the background of the control to view the code editor. Add these members to the top of the class definition:

```
Public Class ColorPalette
    Inherits System.Windows.Forms.UserControl
    ' members...
    Public Buttons As New ArrayList()
    Public ButtonSize As Integer = 15
    Public ButtonSpacing As Integer = 5
    Public LeftColor As Color = Color.Black
    Public RightColor As Color = Color.White
```

Here is what the members will do:

- ❏ Buttons holds a list of the buttons on the palette.
- ❏ ButtonSize defines the size of each of the buttons on the palette.
- ❏ ButtonSpacing defines the gap between each button.
- ❏ LeftColor holds the current color that is assigned to the left mouse button.
- ❏ RightColor holds the current color that is assigned to the right mouse button.

3. Next, add this method to the class:

```
' AddColor - add a new color button to the control...
Public Function AddColor(ByVal newColor As Color) As _
      ColorPaletteButton
    ' create the button...
    Dim button As New ColorPaletteButton(newColor)
    ' add it to the list...
    Buttons.Add(button)
End Function
```

4. When you create the control you want a set of basic colors to be always available. Add this to the constructor of the class. This will create ten basic colors. To find the constructor, open the Windows Form Designer generated code region by clicking on its + sign:

```
Public Sub New()
    MyBase.New()
    'This call is required by the Windows Form Designer.
    InitializeComponent()
    ' add the colors...
    AddColor(Color.Black)
    AddColor(Color.White)
    AddColor(Color.Red)
    AddColor(Color.Blue)
    AddColor(Color.Green)
    AddColor(Color.Gray)
    AddColor(Color.DarkRed)
    AddColor(Color.DarkBlue)
    AddColor(Color.DarkGreen)
    AddColor(Color.DarkGray)
End Sub
```

Sizing the Control

Since you are handling the layout of the buttons on the control, you need to respond to the Resize event. This event is fired whenever the user changes the size of the control. You can hook into this event by overloading the OnResize method.

When Resize is fired you need to alter the position of each of the buttons, starting in the top-left corner and continuing in strips across the whole width of the control. When you've filled up one row you need to start a new row.

Try It Out   Sizing and Painting the Control

1. In the code editor for the `ColorPalette` class, select (Overrides) from the left drop-down list and `OnResize` from the right one. Add this code to the `OnResize` method:

```
' OnResize - called when the control is resized...
Protected Overrides Sub OnResize(ByVal e As System.EventArgs)
    ' variables to hold the position...
    Dim x As Integer, y As Integer
    ' go through the array and position the buttons...
    Dim button As ColorPaletteButton
    For Each button In Buttons
        ' position the button...
        button.SetPosition(x, y, ButtonSize)
        ' move for the next one...
        x += (ButtonSize + ButtonSpacing)
        ' do we need to go down to the next row?
        If x + ButtonSize > Width Then
            ' move y...
            y += (ButtonSize + ButtonSpacing)
            ' reset x...
            x = 0
        End If
    Next
    ' redraw...
    Invalidate()
End Sub
```

2. You still need to paint the control. Select (Overrides) from the left drop-down list and `OnPaint` from the right one. Add this code:

```
' OnPaint - called when the control needs painting...
Protected Overrides Sub OnPaint( _
        ByVal e As System.Windows.Forms.PaintEventArgs)
    ' loop through...
    Dim button As ColorPaletteButton
    For Each button In Buttons
        ' do we need to draw?
        If e.ClipRectangle.IntersectsWith(button.Rectangle) Then
            button.Draw(e.Graphics)
        End If
    Next
End Sub
```

3. Before you can draw the control onto `Form1`, you need to build the project. Select Build ⇨ Build Solution from the menu.

4. After the project has been built, open the Designer for `Form1`. Resize the form and the PaintCanvas control. Note, in order to be able to resize the PaintCanvas control, you'll need to modify the `Anchor` property to remove the bottom anchor. After resizing the PaintCanvas control, reset the `Anchor` property to include the bottom anchor. Add a new ColorPalette control, rename the new control paletteColor, and set its `Anchor` property to Bottom, Left, Right. Your form should now look similar to Figure 14-3.

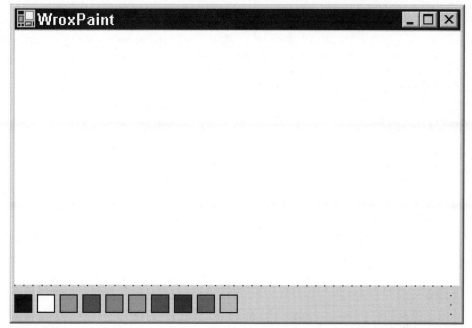

Figure 14-3

5. If you now try to rearrange the form a little, you should see that your sizing code has proven successful.

How It Works

Hopefully, the behavior of `ColorPaletteButton` shouldn't be too much of a mystery. You have members on the class that hold the color and a rectangle, and also provide a constructor that automatically populates the color:

```
Public Class ColorPaletteButton
    ' color...
    Public Color As Color = Color.Black
    Public Rectangle As Rectangle
    ' constructor...
    Public Sub New(ByVal newColor As Color)
        Color = newColor
    End Sub
```

When the button is asked to paint itself, all you do is draw one filled rectangle of the color specified in the `Color` property using the `FillRectangle` method, and for neatness you surround it with a black border using the `DrawRectangle` method:

```
    ' Draw - draw the button...
    Public Sub Draw(ByVal graphics As Graphics)
        ' draw the color block...
        Dim brush As New SolidBrush(Color)
        graphics.FillRectangle(brush, Rectangle)
```

```
    ' draw an "edge" around the control...
    Dim pen As New Pen(Color.Black)
    graphics.DrawRectangle(pen, Rectangle)
End Sub
```

When you resize the form (a subject you'll deal with soon), you pass the top-left corner of the button through to `SetPosition`. All this method does is update the `Rectangle` property:

```
' SetPosition - move the button to the given position...
Public Sub SetPosition(ByVal x As Integer, ByVal y As Integer, _
                 ByVal buttonSize As Integer)
    ' update the members...
    Rectangle = New Rectangle(x, y, buttonSize, buttonSize)
End Sub
```

The `OnResize` method is perhaps the most interesting method here. This is a common algorithm used whenever you need to manage the position of controls or other graphic objects. You know the size of each object (in your case it's a combination of `ButtonSize` and `ButtonSpacing`) and you know the bounds of the control. All you do is start in the top left and keep moving right until you have no more space, in which case you flip down to the next row.

Here is how you start—you set up a loop that iterates through all of the buttons:

```
' OnResize - called when the control is resized...
Protected Overrides Sub OnResize(ByVal e As System.EventArgs)
    ' variables to hold the position...
    Dim x As Integer, y As Integer
    ' go through the array and position the buttons...
    Dim button As ColorPaletteButton
    For Each button In Buttons
```

Throughout the loop, x and y hold the current coordinates of the top-left corner of the control. When you start this is (0, 0), or rather the very top left of the client area of the control. For each button, you call `SetPosition` passing in the current coordinates together with the size of the button:

```
        ' position the button...
        button.SetPosition(x, y, ButtonSize)
```

After each button, you move x to the right. In addition to adjusting by the size of the button, you also add a small gap to make the control more esthetically pleasing:

```
        ' move for the next one...
        x += (ButtonSize + ButtonSpacing)
```

If you detect that you don't have enough space to fit the next control completely on the current row, you adjust y down to the next row and reset x back to the beginning:

```
        ' do we need to go down to the next row?
        If x + ButtonSize > Width Then
            ' move y...
            y += (ButtonSize + ButtonSpacing)
            ' reset x...
            x = 0
        End If
    Next
```

Finally, after you've moved all of the buttons you invalidate the control so that you can see the changes.

```
    ' redraw...
    Invalidate()
End Sub
```

Responding to Clicks

Your control is going to fire an event whenever the left or right mouse button is clicked on a button. To that end, you'll be adding some events to your ColorPalette control that the control will raise. The application using this control will be able to add the event handlers and take action when the event has been raised by this control.

Try It Out **Responding to Clicks**

1. Go back to the code editor for ColorPalette. Add these event handlers to the top of the class definition:

```
Public Class ColorPalette
    Inherits System.Windows.Forms.UserControl
    ' members...
    Public Buttons As New ArrayList()
    Public ButtonSize As Integer = 15
    Public ButtonSpacing As Integer = 5
    Public LeftColor As Color = Color.Black
    Public RightColor As Color = Color.White
    ' events...
    Event LeftClick(ByVal sender As Object, ByVal e As EventArgs)
    Event RightClick(ByVal sender As Object, ByVal e As EventArgs)
```

2. You need a general-purpose method that will return the button that's positioned directly beneath the mouse. Add this method:

```
Public Function GetButtonAt(ByVal x As Integer, ByVal y As Integer) _
                As ColorPaletteButton
    ' go through each button in turn...
    Dim button As ColorPaletteButton
    For Each button In Buttons
        ' is this button in the rectangle...
        If button.Rectangle.Contains(x, y) = True Then Return button
    Next
End Function
```

3. Now, from the top left drop-down list select (Overrides) and then select OnMouseUp from the right list. (Your motivation for using MouseUp rather than MouseDown will become apparent.) Add this code:

```
Protected Overrides Sub OnMouseUp( _
        ByVal e As System.Windows.Forms.MouseEventArgs)
    ' find the button that we clicked on...
    Dim button As ColorPaletteButton = GetButtonAt(e.X, e.Y)
```

```
        If Not button Is Nothing Then
            ' select this color...
            If e.Button = MouseButtons.Left Then
                ' set the color...
                LeftColor = button.Color
                ' fire the event...
                RaiseEvent LeftClick(Me, New EventArgs())
            End If
            ' did we click with the right?
            If e.Button = MouseButtons.Right Then
                ' set right color...
                RightColor = button.Color
                ' fire the event...
                RaiseEvent RightClick(Me, New EventArgs())
            End If
        End If
    End If
End Sub
```

4. To test the new method open the Designer for `Form1`. Select the PaintCanvas control and set its Name property to canvas.

5. Open up the code editor for `Form1`. From the left drop-down menu select `paletteColor`. From the right list select `LeftClick`. Add this code to the event handler:

```
Private Sub paletteColor_LeftClick(ByVal sender As System.Object, _
    ByVal e As System.EventArgs) Handles paletteColor.LeftClick
    canvas.GraphicColor = paletteColor.LeftColor
End Sub
```

6. Try running the project. You should be able to change the color using the control palette.

How It Works

Although you've called your buttons `ColorPaletteButton`, they don't behave in the way you're used to seeing buttons behave. Button controls, like the ones you have been using till now, have the intelligence to detect when they've been clicked and fire an event to tell you what happened. Until now, your buttons have been areas on the control painted in a pretty color—you actually need to write the logic to determine when a button is clicked.

The key to this is the `GetButtonAt` method. This method takes a set of client coordinates and returns the `ColorPaletteButton` object that contains the point you asked for. In this case, you use the `Contains` method of the `Rectangle` object to see if the coordinates are contained within the rectangle.

```
Public Function GetButtonAt(ByVal x As Integer, ByVal y As Integer) _
                As ColorPaletteButton
    ' go through each button in turn...
    Dim button As ColorPaletteButton
    For Each button In Buttons
        ' is this button in the rectangle...
        If button.Rectangle.Contains(x, y) = True Then Return button
    Next
End Function
```

Of course, it could be the case that there is no button under the coordinates if the user clicks the mouse on a blank area of the control. If this is the case, GetButtonAt will return Nothing:

```
Protected Overrides Sub OnMouseUp( _
        ByVal e As System.Windows.Forms.MouseEventArgs)
    ' find the button that we clicked on...
    Dim button As ColorPaletteButton = GetButtonAt(e.X, e.Y)
    If Not button Is Nothing Then
```

As you know, the Button property of MouseEventArgs tells you which button was used, or in this case, released. If it's the left button, you update LeftColor and fire the LeftClick event:

```
        ' select this color...
        If e.Button = MouseButtons.Left Then
            ' set the color...
            LeftColor = button.Color
            ' fire the event...
            RaiseEvent LeftClick(Me, New EventArgs())
        End If
```

Alternatively, it could be the right mouse button:

```
        ' did we click with the right?
        If e.Button = MouseButtons.Right Then
            ' set right color...
            RightColor = button.Color
            ' fire the event...
            RaiseEvent RightClick(Me, New EventArgs())
        End If
    End If
End Sub
```

At the moment, PaintCanvas can only deal with one color, which is why you've only hooked up the LeftClick event. When you receive this event, you set the appropriate property on canvas and this new color will be used when creating new GraphicsCircle objects:

```
Private Sub paletteColor_LeftClick(ByVal sender As System.Object, _
        ByVal e As System.EventArgs) Handles paletteColor.LeftClick
    canvas.GraphicColor = paletteColor.LeftColor
End Sub
```

Dealing with Two Colors

In the next *Try It Out* you extend PaintCanvas so that it can deal with two colors. You'll do this by adding two public members that will track the color chosen for the left mouse button and the right mouse button. You'll also be modifying your existing code to determine if the left mouse button was clicked or if the right mouse button was clicked.

Try It Out   Dealing with Two Colors

1. You need an additional property in PaintCanvas that will let you store the alternative color. For the sake of clarity, you'll also change the name of the existing GraphicColor property to

GraphicLeftColor. Open the code editor for PaintCanvas and make these changes:

```
' members...
Public GraphicsItems As New ArrayList()
Public GraphicTool As GraphicTools = GraphicTools.CirclePen
Public GraphicSize As GraphicSizes = GraphicSizes.Medium
Public GraphicLeftColor As Color = Color.Black
Public GraphicRightColor As Color = Color.White
```

2. In DoMousePaint you need to examine the Button property of MouseEventArgs to determine which color you want to use. Make these two changes to DoMousePaint:

```
' DoMousePaint - respond to a mouse movement...
Private Sub DoMousePaint(ByVal e As MouseEventArgs)
    ' store the new item somewhere...
    Dim newItem As GraphicsItem
    ' what color do we want to use?
    Dim useColor As Color = GraphicLeftColor
    If e.Button = MouseButtons.Right Then useColor = GraphicRightColor
    ' what tool are we using?
    Select Case GraphicTool
        ' circlepen?
    Case GraphicTools.CirclePen
            ' create a new graphics circle...
            Dim circle As New GraphicsCircle()
            circle.SetPoint(e.X, e.Y, GraphicSize, useColor, True)
            ' store this for addition...
            newItem = circle
    End Select
    ' did we get given an item?
    If Not newItem Is Nothing Then
        ' add it to the list...
        GraphicsItems.Add(newItem)
        ' invalidate...
        Invalidate(newItem.Rectangle)
    End If
End Sub
```

3. At the moment, OnMouseDown and OnMouseMove will only call DoMousePaint if the left button is pressed. You need to change this so that it will accept either the left or right button. Make these changes:

```
Protected Overrides Sub OnMouseDown( _
            ByVal e As System.Windows.Forms.MouseEventArgs)
    ' is the button down?
    If e.Button = MouseButtons.Left Or e.Button = MouseButtons.Right Then
        DoMousePaint(e)
    End If
End Sub
Protected Overrides Sub OnMouseMove( _
            ByVal e As System.Windows.Forms.MouseEventArgs)
    ' is the button down?
```

```
    If e.Button = MouseButtons.Left Or e.Button = MouseButtons.Right Then
        DoMousePaint(e)
    End If
End Sub
```

4. Next, you need to change the event handler in `Form1` to set the `GraphicLeftColor` property rather than the `GraphicColor` property. Open the code editor for `Form1` and make this change:

```
Private Sub paletteColor_LeftClick(ByVal sender As System.Object, _
    ByVal e As System.EventArgs) Handles paletteColor.LeftClick
    canvas.GraphicLeftColor = paletteColor.LeftColor
End Sub
```

5. Finally, you don't have an event handler for `RightClick`. Select `paletteColor` from the left drop-down list and then select `RightClick` from the right list. Add this code:

```
Private Sub paletteColor_RightClick(ByVal sender As System.Object, _
    ByVal e As System.EventArgs) Handles paletteColor.RightClick
    canvas.GraphicRightColor = paletteColor.RightColor
End Sub
```

Now, if you run the project you should be able to assign different colors to the left and right mouse buttons and use both of the buttons to paint on the form.

Indicating the Assigned Buttons

I'm sure you've noticed that, at this point, using WroxPaint is a little confusing. There's no indication as to which color is assigned to which button. You need to resolve this issue, so what you'll do is display the letter L on the color assigned to the left button and the letter R on the color assigned to the right button.

Try It Out   Indicating the Assigned Buttons

1. First, you'll make the `ColorPaletteButton` objects aware of which button they're assigned to, if any. Open the code editor for `ColorPaletteButton` and add this enumeration to the top of the class:

```
Public Class ColorPaletteButton
    ' enums...
    Public Enum ButtonAssignments As Integer
        None = 0
        LeftButton = 1
        RightButton = 2
    End Enum
```

2. Next, add this new member that will keep track of the button's assignment:

```
Public Class ColorPaletteButton
    ' enums...
    Public Enum ButtonAssignments As Integer
        None = 0
```

```
          LeftButton = 1
          RightButton = 2
     End Enum
     ' color...
     Public Color As Color = Color.Black
     Public Rectangle As Rectangle
     Public ButtonAssignment As ButtonAssignments = ButtonAssignments.None
```

3. After the button has a way of storing what it's assigned to, you can change the Draw method to draw the L or R as appropriate. Add this code to Draw:

```
' Draw - draw the button...
Public Sub Draw(ByVal graphics As Graphics)
     ' draw the color block...
     Dim brush As New SolidBrush(Color)
     graphics.FillRectangle(brush, Rectangle)
     ' draw an "edge" around the control...
     Dim pen As New Pen(Color.Black)
     graphics.DrawRectangle(pen, Rectangle)
     ' are you selected?
     If ButtonAssignment <> ButtonAssignments.None Then
          ' create a font...
          Dim font As New Font("verdana", 8, FontStyle.Bold)
          ' what text do you use?
          Dim buttonText As String = "L"
          If ButtonAssignment = ButtonAssignments.RightButton Then _
                         buttonText = "R"
          ' what brush do you want...
          Dim fontBrush As SolidBrush
          If Color.R < 100 Or Color.B < 100 Or Color.G < 100 Then
               fontBrush = New SolidBrush(Color.White)
          Else
               fontBrush = New SolidBrush(Color.Black)
          End If
          ' draw some text...
          graphics.DrawString(buttonText, font, fontBrush, _
               Rectangle.Left, Rectangle.Top)
     End If
End Sub
```

4. To keep track of which button is selected you need to add some private members to ColorPalette. Open the code editor for this class and add this code:

```
Public Class ColorPalette
     Inherits System.Windows.Forms.UserControl
     ' members...
     Public Buttons As New ArrayList()
     Public ButtonSize As Integer = 15
     Public ButtonSpacing As Integer = 5
     Public LeftColor As Color = Color.Black
     Public RightColor As Color = Color.White
     Private leftButton As ColorPaletteButton
     Private rightButton As ColorPaletteButton
```

5. The next wrinkle you have to fix is quite verbose, but relatively straightforward. Basically, you have to make sure that a button cannot be assigned to both the left and right buttons—for no other reason than you just don't have a way of reporting that information to the user. Also, you have to mess around with the invalidation code. You'll detail that once you have the example working. Make these changes to OnMouseUp:

```
Protected Overrides Sub OnMouseUp( _
      ByVal e As System.Windows.Forms.MouseEventArgs)
      ' find the button that we clicked on...
      Dim button As ColorPaletteButton = GetButtonAt(e.X, e.Y)
      If Not button Is Nothing Then
          ' select this color...
              If e.Button = MouseButtons.Left Then
              ' make sure that this button is not the current right...
              If Not button Is rightButton Then
                  ' set the color...
                  LeftColor = button.Color
                  ' clear the existing selection...
                  If Not leftButton Is Nothing Then
                      leftButton.ButtonAssignment = _
                          ColorPaletteButton.ButtonAssignments.None
                      Invalidate(leftButton.Rectangle)
                  End If
                  ' mark the button...
                  button.ButtonAssignment = _
                      ColorPaletteButton.ButtonAssignments.LeftButton
                  Invalidate(button.Rectangle)
                  leftButton = button
                  ' fire the event...
                  RaiseEvent LeftClick(Me, New EventArgs())
              End If
          End If
          ' did we click with the right?
          If e.Button = MouseButtons.Right Then
              ' make sure this button is not the current left...
              If Not button Is leftButton Then
                  ' set right color...
                  RightColor = button.Color
                  ' clear the existing selection...
                  If Not rightButton Is Nothing Then
                      rightButton.ButtonAssignment = _
                          ColorPaletteButton.ButtonAssignments.None
                      Invalidate(rightButton.Rectangle)
                  End If
                  ' mark the button...
                  button.ButtonAssignment = _
                      ColorPaletteButton.ButtonAssignments.RightButton
                  Invalidate(button.Rectangle)
                  rightButton = button
                  ' fire the event...
                  RaiseEvent RightClick(Me, New EventArgs())
              End If
          End If
      End If
End Sub
```

6. Finally, you have to set up the first two colors added to the control as being the selected buttons when the control is started. This involves updating your `leftButton` and `rightButton` members as well as setting the `ButtonAssignment` property on the button itself. Add this code to `AddColor`:

```
' AddColor - add a new color button to the control...
Public Function AddColor(ByVal newColor As Color) As ColorPaletteButton
    ' create the button...
    Dim button As New ColorPaletteButton(newColor)
    ' add it to the list...
    Buttons.Add(button)
    ' do we have a button assigned to the left button yet?
    If leftButton Is Nothing Then
        button.ButtonAssignment = _
            ColorPaletteButton.ButtonAssignments.LeftButton
        leftButton = button
    Else
        ' how about the right button?
        If rightButton Is Nothing Then
            button.ButtonAssignment = _
                ColorPaletteButton.ButtonAssignments.RightButton
            rightButton = button
        End If
    End If
End Function
```

7. Run the project now and you should see that when you change the color selection an L and R appear on the buttons as shown in Figure 14-4.

Figure 14-4

How It Works

The first thing you did was to add an enumeration to `ControlPaletteButton` that could be used to set the state of the button:

```
' enums...
Public Enum ButtonAssignments As Integer
    None = 0
    LeftButton = 1
    RightButton = 2
End Enum
```

As you can see from the enumeration, a button can either be assigned to "no buttons" or the left or the right button.

You also added members to the ControlPalette to keep track of which button was selected. This makes your life a little easier when it comes to changing the selection. When you select a new button, you have to set the ButtonAssignment property of the old button to ButtonAssignments.None. Just being able to look in the leftButton or rightButton members as appropriate, saves you from having to look through the entire list of buttons to find the one you need to change.

The OnMouseUp method starts to look a little more complex when you add this new functionality. When you want to assign the left mouse button to a button, you have to make sure that the button is not already assigned to the right mouse button:

```
Protected Overrides Sub OnMouseUp( _
    ByVal e As System.Windows.Forms.MouseEventArgs)
    ' find the button that you clicked on...
    Dim button As ColorPaletteButton = GetButtonAt(e.X, e.Y)
    If Not button Is Nothing Then
        ' select this color...
        If e.Button = MouseButtons.Left Then
            ' make sure that this button is not the current right...
            If Not button Is rightButton Then
```

If you can set the color, you update the LeftColor property as you did before:

```
            ' set the color...
            LeftColor = button.Color
```

If another button is already assigned to the left mouse button, you need to set its ButtonAssignment property back to None. You also have to invalidate this button so that the button is redrawn and the L is removed:

```
            ' clear the existing selection...
            If Not leftButton Is Nothing Then
                leftButton.ButtonAssignment = _
                    ColorPaletteButton.ButtonAssignments.None
                Invalidate(leftButton.Rectangle)
            End If
```

Next, you set the new button's ButtonAssignment property to Left. You also invalidate the button (so that you can draw the L on this one instead) and update the _leftButton property to point at the new button:

```
            ' mark the button...
            button.ButtonAssignment = _
                ColorPaletteButton.ButtonAssignments.LeftButton
```

```
                    Invalidate(button.Rectangle)
                    leftButton = button
```

Finally, you fire the `LeftClick` event as you did before:

```
              ' fire the event...
              RaiseEvent LeftClick(Me, New EventArgs())
```

The remainder of `OnMouseUp` is the same as this, but obviously reversed to deal with the right-hand button.

When it's time to draw the button, you can check to see if a button assignment is set. If it is, you draw some text. (You've only fleetingly covered drawing text here, but you'll deal with it in more detail later in this chapter.) To draw the text, you need to create a new `System.Drawing.Font` object. Here you're creating a new 8-point Verdana font in bold:

```
  ' Draw - draw the button...
  Public Sub Draw(ByVal graphics As Graphics)
        ' draw the color block...
        Dim brush As New SolidBrush(Color)
        graphics.FillRectangle(brush, Rectangle)
        ' draw an "edge" around the control...
        Dim pen As New Pen(Color.Black)
        graphics.DrawRectangle(pen, Rectangle)
        ' are we selected?
        If ButtonAssignment <> ButtonAssignments.None Then
              ' create a font...
              Dim font As New Font("verdana", 8, FontStyle.Bold)
```

Next, you choose the text to draw:

```
              ' what text do you use?
              Dim buttonText As String = "L"
              If ButtonAssignment = ButtonAssignments.RightButton Then_
                           buttonText = "R"
```

Choosing the brush you want is quite tricky. You can't just choose a color because there's a chance it won't show up on the color that you're drawing. Instead, you have to examine the color to see whether it is a light color or a dark color. If it's dark, you choose to draw the letter in white; otherwise, you draw it in black:

```
              ' what brush do we want...
              Dim fontBrush As SolidBrush
              If Color.R < 100 Or Color.B < 100 Or Color.G < 100 Then
                    fontBrush = New SolidBrush(Color.White)
              Else
                    fontBrush = New SolidBrush(Color.Black)
              End If
```

Finally, you actually draw the text:

```
              ' draw some text...
              graphics.DrawString(buttonText, font, fontBrush, _
                         Rectangle.Left, Rectangle.Top)
        End If
  End Sub
```

Advanced Colors

So far, the only colors you've used are the ones defined by the .NET Framework, such as Color.Black and Color.Blue. The list of colors available to us on the Color structure is considerable, but you can define your own colors if you want to.

> *To find a list of predefined colors use the MSDN documentation to display "all members" of the "Color structure." Alternatively, you can use IntelliSense from within the code editor to display a list of possibilities.*

Windows defines a color as a 24-bit number, with the three bytes of the 24-bit representing a red value, a green value, and a blue value—this is commonly known as RGB. In effect, each component represents one of a possible 256 shades of red, green, and blue. By combining these shades you can get any color from a possible set of 16.7 million. For example, setting red to 255 and setting blue and green to 0 would result in bright red. Setting all components to 255 would give white. Setting all to 0 would give black, and so on.

> *If you're used to mixing paints, these color combinations may seem strange. This is because you are working with colored lights instead of colored paints—and they combine in different ways.*

To illustrate this, in the next *Try It Out* section you see how you can choose a color and then manually add that color as a button to the control palette.

Try It Out   Creating Custom Colors

1. Open the Form Designer for the ColorPalette control. In the Properties window find the BackColor property.

2. Drop down the list and change to the Custom tab. Right-click in one of the 16 bottom blank squares.

3. This will bring up the Color dialog box. Use the two controls at the top to find a color you like. In the bottom-right corner, you'll see three text boxes marked Red, Green, and Blue, as shown in Figure 14-5. Note down the values in these boxes.

4. Close the Define Color dialog box.

5. Open up the code editor for ColorPalette. In the constructor, define a new button, but replace the three values I've used here with three values you noted down. (Do this in order—the first value is the red component, the second is green, and the third is blue.)

```
Public Sub New()
    MyBase.New()
    'This call is required by the Windows Form Designer.
    InitializeComponent()
    ' add the colors...
    AddColor(Color.Black)
    AddColor(Color.White)
    AddColor(Color.Red)
    AddColor(Color.Blue)
    AddColor(Color.Green)
    AddColor(Color.Gray)
    AddColor(Color.DarkRed)
    AddColor(Color.DarkBlue)
```

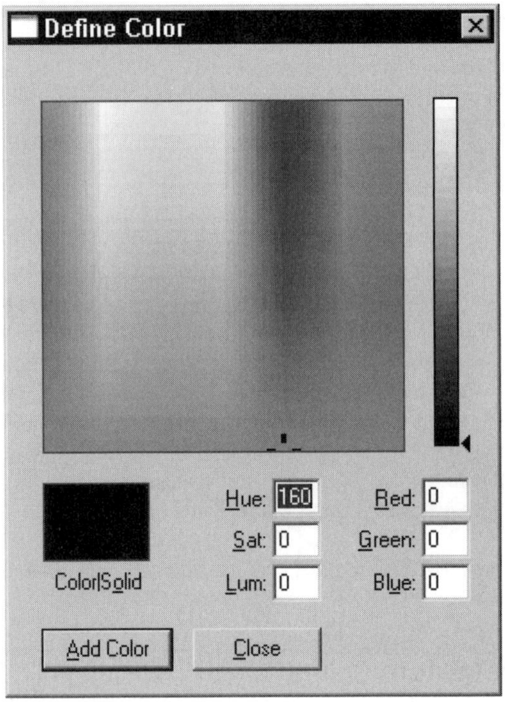

Figure 14-5

```
    AddColor(Color.DarkGreen)
    AddColor(Color.DarkGray)
    AddColor(Color.FromArgb(208, 112, 222))
End Sub
```

6. Now run the project and the color you selected should appear in the palette.

The FromArgb method is a shared method on the Color class. You can use this to define any color that you like, so long as you follow the "red, green, blue" convention Windows itself uses.

The Color Dialog Box

If you like, you can use the Color dialog box that's built into Windows to let the user add colors to the palette.

Try It Out   Using the Color Dialog Box

1. Open the Form Designer for ColorPalette. From the toolbar, select a new ColorDialog control and paint it onto the form. Change the name of the control to dlgColor.

2. Now, open the code editor for ColorPalette. Find the OnMouseUp method. Whenever the user clicks the background to the control (in other words doesn't click a button), you want to display the dialog box. Go to the bottom of the method and add an Else clause along with this code. (I've omitted some of the existing code for brevity.)

```
Protected Overrides Sub OnMouseUp( _
    ByVal e As System.Windows.Forms.MouseEventArgs)
    ' find the button that you clicked on...
    Dim button As ColorPaletteButton = GetButtonAt(e.X, e.Y)
    If Not button Is Nothing Then
    ...

    Else
        ' display the color dialog...
        If dlgColor.ShowDialog = DialogResult.OK Then
            ' add the new color...
            AddColor(dlgColor.Color)
            ' resize the palette to show the dialog...
            OnResize(New EventArgs())
        End If
    End If
End Sub
```

3. After you've added the color, you need to "fake" a `Resize` event so that the new button is actually displayed.

4. Run the project. Now if you click the background to the palette you should have the opportunity to add your own colors (see Figure 14-6).

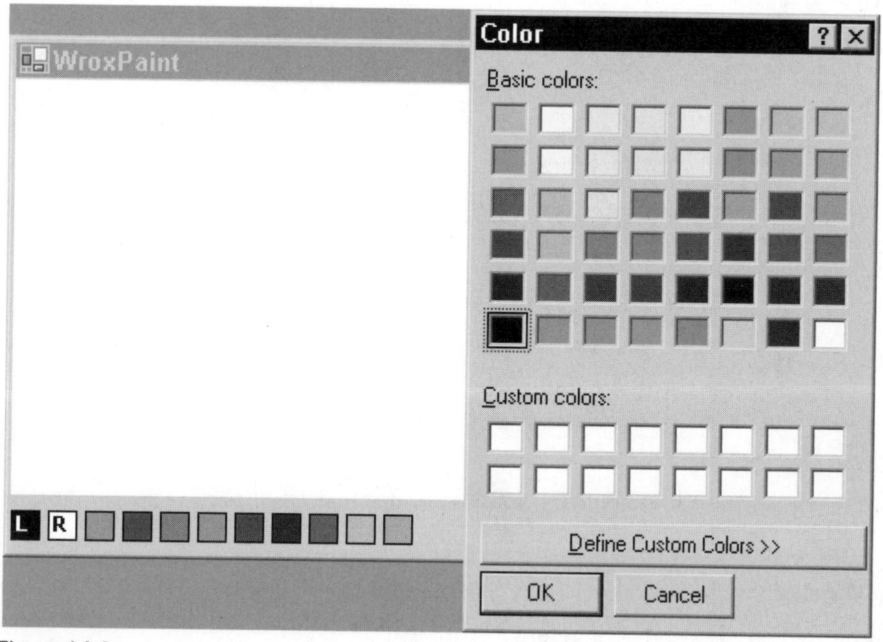

Figure 14-6

System Colors

Now you know that you can choose colors from a list of possibilities as well as define your own. The final thing you need to learn about colors is the idea of system colors.

When using Windows, the user has the ability to define all of the colors that are used for things like buttons, menus, captions, and so on. If you're building the UI for your own controls, it's reasonable to assume that from time to time you'll need to know what these colors are so that your controls have the same look and feel as the existing controls on the system.

System colors are not exposed directly, but the .NET Framework does provide a set of brushes and pens that can be used when you are drawing. Of course, you can dig into these objects to get the color out and that's what you'll do.

If you want to find a list of all the brushes and pens, look in the MSDN documentation under `System.Drawing.Brushes` class and `SystemPens` class. Alternatively, use IntelliSense when in the code editor.

In this *Try It Out*, you'll add a button to the control palette that is the same as the currently selected active caption color.

Try It Out   Adding System Colors

1. Open the code editor for `ColorPalette`. Find the constructor and add this code:

```
Public Sub New()
    MyBase.New()
    'This call is required by the Windows Form Designer.
    InitializeComponent()
    ' add the colors...
    AddColor(Color.Black)
    AddColor(Color.White)
    AddColor(Color.Red)
    AddColor(Color.Blue)
    AddColor(Color.Green)
    AddColor(Color.Gray)
    AddColor(Color.DarkRed)
    AddColor(Color.DarkBlue)
    AddColor(Color.DarkGreen)
    AddColor(Color.DarkGray)
    AddColor(Color.FromArgb(208, 112, 222))
    AddColor(CType(SystemBrushes.ActiveCaption, SolidBrush).Color)
End Sub
```

2. Run the project. You should see a new color that matches the active caption color.

How It Works

When you ask `SystemBrushes` to return a brush that could be used to paint the active caption (and remember, with Windows 2000 the caption can be graduated, so what you're actually getting is the color that appears at the far left of the caption), it will return a `Brush` object. The `Brush` object doesn't contain a `Color` property, so you use `CType` to cast it to a `SolidBrush`.

`SolidBrush` does have a `Color` property and you simply pass the value returned from this back to `AddColor` whereupon it's added to the palette.

Different Tools

Now that you have successfully cracked the nut of drawing filled circles on the page, turn your attention to building the other tools that you can use to put your applications together. The first thing you should do is to add a menu that lets you select the tool you want.

If you need a refresher on how to use the Visual Basic .NET Menu Designer, refer to Chapter 8.

Try It Out   Adding a Tools Menu

1. Open the Designer for `Form1`. Draw a new MainMenu control onto the form and rename it `mnuMain`.

2. With the `mnuMain` control selected, click on the white Type Here box that appears under the caption on `Form1`. Enter `&Tools` and press Return. Using the Properties window change the `Name` property to `mnuTools`.

3. In the new Type Here box at the bottom, enter `&Circle`. Using the Properties window change the `Name` property to `mnuToolsCircle` and set the `Checked` property to `True`.

4. Again, in the new Type Here box at the bottom, enter `&Hollow Circle`. Using the Properties window change the Name to `mnuToolsHollowCircle`. You will see the results of these steps in Figure 14-7.

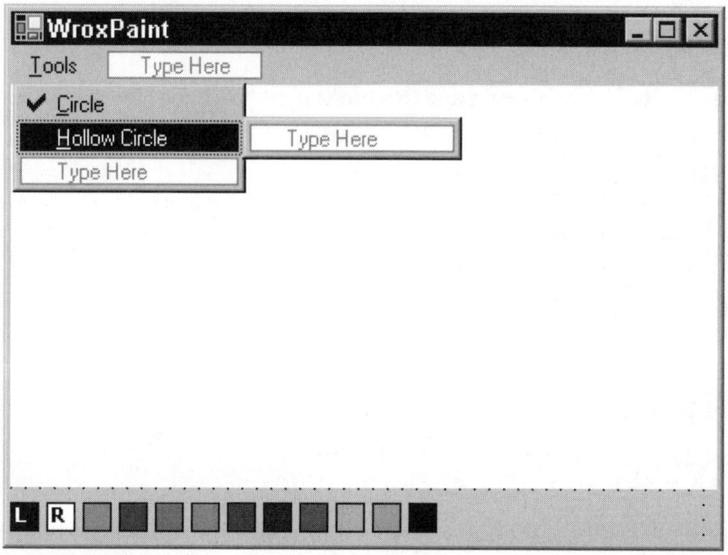

Figure 14-7

Implementing Hollow Circle

Up until now, you have used a solid circle as the graphics pen to perform the drawing on your form. In this exercise, you'll be implementing the functionality to the hollow circle graphics pen. You'll also be adding the necessary code that will allow you to select which pen you want to use from the Tools menu.

Try It Out   **Implementing Hollow Circle**

1. The first thing you need to do is change the `GraphicTools` enumeration defined in `PaintCanvas` to include the hollow circle tool. Open the code editor for `PaintCanvas` and add this code to the enumeration:

```
Public Class PaintCanvas
    Inherits System.Windows.Forms.UserControl
    ' enums...
    Public Enum GraphicTools As Integer
        CirclePen = 0
        HollowCirclePen = 1
    End Enum
```

2. Go back to the Designer for `Form1` and on the menu editor double-click the Circle menu item. This will create a `Click` handler for `mnuToolsCircle`. Add this code:

```
Private Sub mnuToolsCircle_Click(ByVal sender As System.Object, _
        ByVal e As System.EventArgs) Handles mnuToolsCircle.Click
    ' set the tool...
    canvas.GraphicTool = PaintCanvas.GraphicTools.CirclePen
    ' update the menu...
    UpdateMenu()
End Sub
```

You've yet to build the `UpdateMenu` *method, so ignore the blue wavy line that Visual Studio .NET will display indicating an error.*

3. Flip back to the Designer again and this time double-click the Hollow Circle menu item. Add this code:

```
Private Sub mnuToolsHollowCircle_Click(ByVal sender As System.Object, _
        ByVal e As System.EventArgs) Handles mnuToolsHollowCircle.Click
    ' set the tool...
    canvas.GraphicTool = PaintCanvas.GraphicTools.HollowCirclePen
    ' update the menu...
    UpdateMenu()
End Sub
```

4. Next, you need to implement the `UpdateMenu` method. Add this method below the `mnuToolsHollowCircle_Click` method:

```
' UpdateMenu - update the menu...
Private Sub UpdateMenu()
    ' go through the menu items updating the check...
    If canvas.GraphicTool = PaintCanvas.GraphicTools.CirclePen Then
        mnuToolsCircle.Checked = True
    Else
        mnuToolsCircle.Checked = False
    End If
    If canvas.GraphicTool = PaintCanvas.GraphicTools.HollowCirclePen Then
        mnuToolsHollowCircle.Checked = True
    Else
        mnuToolsHollowCircle.Checked = False
    End If
End Sub
```

5. Open the code editor for `PaintCanvas` by right-clicking on it in the Solution Explorer and select View Code. Find the `DoMousePaint` method and change this code:

```
' DoMousePaint - respond to a mouse movement...
Private Sub DoMousePaint(ByVal e As MouseEventArgs)
    ' store the new item somewhere...
    Dim newItem As GraphicsItem
    ' what color do we want to use?
    Dim useColor As Color = GraphicLeftColor
    If e.Button = MouseButtons.Right Then useColor = GraphicRightColor
    ' what tool are we using?
    Select Case GraphicTool
        ' circlepen?
        Case GraphicTools.CirclePen, GraphicTools.HollowCirclePen
            ' are we filled?
            Dim filled As Boolean = True
            If GraphicTool = GraphicTools.HollowCirclePen Then _
                filled = False
            ' create a new graphics circle...
            Dim circle As New GraphicsCircle()
            circle.SetPoint(e.X, e.Y, GraphicSize, useColor, filled)
            ' store this for addition...
            newItem = circle
    End Select
    ' were we given an item?
    If Not newItem Is Nothing Then
        ' add it to the list...
        GraphicsItems.Add(newItem)
        ' invalidate...
        Invalidate(newItem.Rectangle)
    End If
End Sub
```

6. Next, you need to change the `GraphicsCircle` class itself so that it knows when to draw a filled circle and when to draw a hollow circle. Open the code editor for `GraphicsCircle` and add this code to the `Draw` method:

```
Public Overrides Sub Draw(ByVal graphics As System.Drawing.Graphics)
    If IsFilled = True Then
        ' create a new brush...
        Dim brush As New SolidBrush(Me.Color)
        ' draw the circle...
        graphics.FillEllipse(brush, Me.Rectangle)
    Else
        'create a pen
        Dim pen As New Pen(Me.Color)
        ' use DrawEllipse instead...
        Dim drawRectangle As Rectangle = Me.Rectangle
        drawRectangle.Inflate(-1, -1)
        graphics.DrawEllipse(pen, drawRectangle)
    End If
End Sub
```

7. Finally, run the program. You should be able to select a new graphic tool from the menu and draw both filled and hollow circles, as shown in Figure 14-8.

Figure 14-8

How It Works

When the menu options are selected, click events get fired. You can respond to these messages and set the `GraphicsTool` property on the `PaintCanvas` control to a new mode:

```
Private Sub mnuToolsHollowCircle_Click(ByVal sender As System.Object, _
    ByVal e As System.EventArgs) Handles mnuToolsHollowCircle.Click
    ' set the tool...
    canvas.GraphicTool = PaintCanvas.GraphicTools.HollowCirclePen
    ' update the menu...
    UpdateMenu()
End Sub
```

When you change the mode you also need to change the check on the menu. `UpdateMenu` goes through each of the menu items in turn, switching on or off the check as appropriate:

```
' UpdateMenu - update the menu...
Private Sub UpdateMenu()
    ' go through the menu items updating the check...
    If canvas.GraphicTool = PaintCanvas.GraphicTools.CirclePen Then
        mnuToolsCircle.Checked = True
    Else
        mnuToolsCircle.Checked = False
    End If
    If canvas.GraphicTool = PaintCanvas.GraphicTools.HollowCirclePen Then
        mnuToolsHollowCircle.Checked = True
    Else
        mnuToolsHollowCircle.Checked = False
    End If
End Sub
```

Irrespective of the mode used, `PaintCanvas.DoMousePaint` still gets called whenever the mouse draws on the control. However, you do need to accommodate the new tool by changing the

`Select...End Select` block to look for `HollowCirclePen` as well as `CirclePen`. Depending on which is selected, you pass `True` ("filled") or `False` ("not filled") through to `SetPoint`:

```
' what tool are we using?
Select Case GraphicTool
    ' circlepen?
    Case GraphicTools.CirclePen, GraphicTools.HollowCirclePen
        ' are we filled?
        Dim filled As Boolean = True
        If GraphicTool = GraphicTools.HollowCirclePen Then _
            filled = False
        ' create a new graphics circle...
        Dim circle As New GraphicsCircle()
        circle.SetPoint(e.X, e.Y, GraphicSize, useColor, filled)
        ' store this for addition...
        newItem = circle
End Select
```

In `GraphicsCircle` itself, choosing whether to `FillEllipse` to draw a filled circle or use `DrawEllipse` for a hollow one is a simple determination. The only wrinkle you have to contend with is `DrawEllipse`, the width and height of the bounding rectangle have to be one pixel smaller than those used for `FillEllipse`. This is due to an idiosyncrasy in the way the Windows graphics subsystem works. You'll often find when working with graphics features that you have to experiment a little!

```
Public Overrides Sub Draw(ByVal graphics As System.Drawing.Graphics)
    If IsFilled = True Then
        ' create a new brush...
        Dim brush As New SolidBrush(Me.Color)
        ' draw the circle...
        graphics.FillEllipse(brush, Me.Rectangle)
    Else
        ' create a pen...
        Dim pen As New Pen(Me.Color)
        ' use DrawEllipse instead...
        Dim drawRectangle As Rectangle = Me.Rectangle
        drawRectangle.Inflate(-1, -1)
        graphics.DrawEllipse(pen, drawRectangle)
    End If
End Sub
```

Now that you've learned the basics of building user controls that support their own user interface, take a look at the image handling capabilities in .NET.

Images

The .NET Framework has very good support for loading and saving common image formats. In particular, you're able to load images of these types:

- ❏   `.bmp`—the standard Windows bitmap format
- ❏   `.gif`—the standard "loss-less" common Internet file format for graphic files and small images
- ❏   `.jpeg`—the standard "lossy" common Internet file format for photo-quality images

- ❑ .png—the competitor to .gif that doesn't have the tricky licensing implications
- ❑ .tiff—the standard file format for storing and manipulated scanned documents
- ❑ .wmf/.emf—the standard file formats for saving Windows metafiles
- ❑ .icon—the standard file format for program icons
- ❑ .exif—the preferred file format for storage used internally with digital cameras

Prior to .NET, developers wanting to work with the most common Internet file formats (namely, .gif and .jpeg) had to buy in third-party libraries. Now, support is built directly into the .NET Framework so from day one you can start building applications that can handle these formats. What's more surprising is that the .NET Framework also supports the saving of these files. This allows you to load a .gif file and save it as, say, a .bmp or .png file.

There are two ways in which you can use images with .NET. First, you can use the PictureBox control that you can find in the Visual Studio .NET Toolbox. This is a control that you place on a form, give a reference to an image to either at design time or runtime and it deals with painting itself. This is a quick way of getting a fixed image on a form.

The second way in which you can use images is inside your owner-draw controls. In the following exercise, you'll see how you can tweak WroxPaint so that rather than drawing on a dull, white background you're actually drawing on an image you load.

Drawing Images

The property on the control takes a System.Drawing.Image object. In addition to using the Image class with PictureBox and a few other controls in the .NET Framework, you can also use it with your own owner-draw controls.

Start by providing a way for your owner-drawn controls to display an image loaded from one of the supported image formats.

Try It Out   Setting the BackgroundImage

1. Open the Designer for Form1. Using the Toolbox draw a new OpenFileDialog control onto the form. Rename the control as dlgFileOpenBackground.

2. Using the menu designer add a new menu item called &File to the right of the &Tools menu item. Change its Name property to mnuFile. Reposition the menu to the left side of the &Tools menu item by dragging it to its new location.

3. Under the File menu add a new menu item called Open &Background Image. Rename the item as mnuFileOpenBackground.

4. Double-click the Open Background Image option. Add this code to the handler, and remember to add the new OpenBackgroundImage method:

```
Private Sub mnuFileOpenBackground_Click(ByVal sender As System.Object, _
        ByVal e As System.EventArgs) Handles mnuFileOpenBackground.Click
    OpenBackgroundImage()
End Sub
```

```
Public Sub OpenBackgroundImage()
    ' open the dialog...
    If dlgFileOpenBackground.ShowDialog() = DialogResult.OK Then
        ' create a new image that references the file...
        Dim backgroundImage As Image = _
            Image.FromFile(dlgFileOpenBackground.FileName)
        ' set the background...
        canvas.BackgroundImage = backgroundImage
    End If
End Sub
```

5. Run the project. Select File ⇨ Open Background Image from the menu and find a .bmp, .jpeg, or .gif file somewhere on your computer. (If you try to open a file from the network you may get a security exception.) The image will be displayed as shown in Figure 14-9.

Figure 14-9

How It Works

"But I didn't do anything!" You're quite right—you didn't have to write any code to support the background image. By default, the Control class that UserControl is ultimately derived from already supports a BackgroundImage property and you've set this to the image you loaded. Therefore, the base class is dealing with drawing the image.

The loading is actually done with the shared FromFile method on the Image class. This method is the easiest way of loading a file from a disk:

```
Public Sub ShowOpenBackgroundDialog()
    ' open the dialog...
    If dlgFileOpenBackground.ShowDialog() = DialogResult.OK Then
        ' create a new image that references the file...
        Dim backgroundImage As Image = _
            Image.FromFile(dlgFileOpenBackground.FileName)
```

```
            ' set the background...
            canvas.BackgroundImage = backgroundImage
        End If
    End Sub
```

Finally, when you're actually drawing on the image you may find the paint process sluggish. This is because the control is spending a lot of time drawing the image onto the control and this slows everything down. Try using a smaller image or consider this *Try It Out*—an illustration of how to manipulate images rather than providing a neat paint package!

Scaling Images

If you resize the form, you'll notice that the image is actually tiled. More importantly, if you make the control too small to accommodate the whole image the sides of the image are clipped. What you want is for the image to be scaled so that it fits the control exactly. This will involve taking over control of drawing the background image from the base Control class and providing a new implementation of the BackgroundImage property.

Try It Out   Drawing the Image Yourself

1. Open the code editor for PaintCanvas.

2. Rather than adding your code to draw the image to OnPaint, you're going to work with a different event called PaintBackground. This is called before Paint . From the left drop-down select (Overrides) and from the right drop-down select OnPaintBackground. Add this code:

```
Protected Overrides Sub OnPaintBackground( _
    ByVal pevent As System.Windows.Forms.PaintEventArgs)
    ' paint the invalid region with the background brush...
    Dim backgroundBrush As New SolidBrush(BackColor)
    pevent.Graphics.FillRectangle(backgroundBrush, pevent.ClipRectangle)
    ' paint the image...
    If Not BackgroundImage Is Nothing Then
        ' find our client rectangle...
        Dim clientRectangle As New Rectangle(0, 0, Width, Height)
        ' draw the image...
        pevent.Graphics.DrawImage(BackgroundImage, clientRectangle)
    End If
End Sub
```

3. After the OnPaintBackground event add the following code in order to enable the Resize event:

```
Protected Overrides Sub OnResize(ByVal e As System.EventArgs)
    Invalidate()
End Sub
```

4. Now run the project again. This time, the image will appear stretched or shrunken to fit the whole screen and will adjust itself as you resize the form as shown in Figure 14-10.

Figure 14-10

How It Works

All you're trying to do is take over the action of drawing the background image. As mentioned before, painting is a two-phase process: First the background is erased (the `PaintBackground` event) and second the control is given the opportunity to paint its user interface (the `Paint` event).

With the `BackgroundImage` property set, when the base class needs to draw the background it will automatically draw the image. You should stop it from doing this, otherwise you'll effectively be drawing the image twice—in other words, it'll draw the image and then you'll draw your own image on top of it.

However, you do need to mimic the functionality that erases the background, otherwise things will not work properly. To do this, you create a new `SolidBrush` that uses the current background color (`BackColor`) and paint it on the area that's marked as invalid (`ClipRectangle`):

```
Protected Overrides Sub OnPaintBackground( _
      ByVal pevent As System.Windows.Forms.PaintEventArgs)
      ' paint the invalid region with the background brush...
      Dim backgroundBrush As New SolidBrush(BackColor)
      pevent.Graphics.FillRectangle(backgroundBrush, pevent.ClipRectangle)
```

After you have painted the background you then need to draw the image. You can do this easily by using the `DrawImage` method of the `Graphics` object. But, in order to stretch the image you need to provide a rectangle that describes the bounds of the image. Once you have that, you give `DrawImage` both the image and the rectangle and the image is drawn.

```
      ' paint the image...
      If Not BackgroundImage Is Nothing Then
          ' find our client rectangle...
          Dim clientRectangle As New Rectangle(0, 0, Width, Height)
          ' draw the image...
          pevent.Graphics.DrawImage(BackgroundImage, clientRectangle)
      End If
End Sub
```

Preserving the Aspect Ratio

The problem you have now is that the image is stretched out of shape. Ideally, you want to make the image bigger or smaller while preserving the aspect ratio of the image. The aspect ratio describes the ratio between the width and height of the image.

The .NET Framework does not have any support for preserving the aspect ratio when it stretches an image. However, with a little work you can do this yourself.

Try It Out — Preserving the Aspect Ratio

1. Open the code editor for PaintCanvas again. Add this code to `OnPaintBackground`.

```
Protected Overrides Sub OnPaintBackground( _
    ByVal pevent As System.Windows.Forms.PaintEventArgs)
    ' paint the invalid region with the background brush...
    Dim backgroundBrush As New SolidBrush(BackColor)
    pevent.Graphics.FillRectangle(backgroundBrush, pevent.ClipRectangle)
    ' paint the image...
    If Not BackgroundImage Is Nothing Then
        ' find our client rectangle...
        Dim clientRectangle As New Rectangle(0, 0, Width, Height)
        ' how big is the image?
        Dim imageWidth As Integer = BackgroundImage.Width
        Dim imageHeight As Integer = BackgroundImage.Height
        ' what's the aspect ratio?
        Dim ratio As Double = _
            CType(imageHeight, Double) / CType(imageWidth, Double)
        ' scale the image...
        If imageWidth > clientRectangle.Width Then
            imageWidth = clientRectangle.Width
            imageHeight = CType(CType(imageWidth, Double) * ratio, Integer)
        End If
        If imageHeight > clientRectangle.Height Then
            imageHeight = clientRectangle.Height
            imageWidth = CType(CType(imageHeight, Double) / ratio, Integer)
        End If
        ' we just need to center the image... easy!
        Dim imageLocation As New Point( _
          (clientRectangle.Width / 2) - (imageWidth / 2), _
          (clientRectangle.Height / 2) - (imageHeight / 2))
        Dim imageSize As New Size(imageWidth, imageHeight)
        Dim imageRectangle As New Rectangle(imageLocation, imageSize)
        ' draw the image...
        pevent.Graphics.DrawImage(BackgroundImage, imageRectangle)
    End If
End Sub
```

2. Run the project. Now if you load an image it should scale and preserve the aspect ratio.

How It Works

Preserving the aspect ratio is a bit of rudimentary math coupled with throwing a few rectangles together. The first thing you need to know is how big the area that you have to fit the image into actually is. You call this `clientRectangle`.

```
Protected Overrides Sub OnPaintBackground( _
        ByVal pevent As System.Windows.Forms.PaintEventArgs)
    ' paint the invalid region with the background brush...
    Dim backgroundBrush As New SolidBrush(BackColor)
    pevent.Graphics.FillRectangle(backgroundBrush, pevent.ClipRectangle)
    ' paint the image...
    If Not BackgroundImage Is Nothing Then
        ' find our client rectangle...
        Dim clientRectangle As New Rectangle(0, 0, Width, Height)
```

Next, you need to look at the image itself to see how big it is. You then need to know the aspect ratio, which is the ratio between the width and the height. If, for example, you had an aspect ratio of 2:1 (width:height), and you had an image that was 200 pixels wide, you would know that the height had to be 100 pixels. Alternatively, if it were 25 pixels tall it would be 50 pixels wide.

```
        ' how big is the image?
        Dim imageWidth As Integer = BackgroundImage.Width
        Dim imageHeight As Integer = BackgroundImage.Height
        ' what's the aspect ratio?
        Dim ratio As Double = _
            CType(imageHeight, Double) / CType(imageWidth, Double)
```

When you calculate the aspect ratio, you want a floating-point number, so you have to convert the integer width and height values to Doubles.

Next, you look at the shape of the client area compared to the shape of the image. If the native width of the image (in other words the size before it's scaled) is wider than the width of the window, you fix the width of the image as being equal to the width of the client area. Once you've done that you use the aspect ratio to work out how tall the image should be. (Again, you've used conversions to Doubles to make sure that the calculations work properly.)

```
        ' scale the image...
        If imageWidth > clientRectangle.Width Then
            imageWidth = clientRectangle.Width
            imageHeight = CType(CType(imageWidth, Double) * ratio, Integer)
```

Alternatively, if the height of the client area is taller than the height of the image, you need to do the opposite—in other words fix the height of the image and then work out the width:

```
        Else
            imageHeight = clientRectangle.Height
            imageWidth = CType(CType(imageHeight, Double) / ratio, Integer)
        End If
```

At this point you have an adjusted width and height of the image. When you have that, to start drawing, you need to work out the upper-left corner. To do this, you divide the width of the client area by two to get the exact middle and subtract half of the width of the image from it. This gives us the x coordinate at which drawing should start. Then, you do the same for the height:

```
        ' we just need to center the image... easy!
        Dim imageLocation As New Point( _
            (clientRectangle.Width / 2) - (imageWidth / 2), _
            (clientRectangle.Height / 2) - (imageHeight / 2))
```

Once you have the location, you build a rectangle using the adjusted width and height:

```
Dim imageSize As New Size(imageWidth, imageHeight)
Dim imageRectangle As New Rectangle(imageLocation, imageSize)
```

Finally, you use `DrawImage` to actually draw the image on the screen:

```
            ' draw the image...
            pevent.Graphics.DrawImage(BackgroundImage, imageRectangle)
    End If
End Sub
```

More Graphics Methods

In this chapter, you have used a few of the graphics features available with .NET. There are some commonly used methods on the `Graphics` object that we haven't touched.

Whenever you have a `Graphics` object, either when you're building owner-draw controls or forms, try using these methods:

❑   `DrawLine` draws a single line between two points.

❑   `DrawCurve` and `DrawClosedCurve` draw a curve between a set of points.

❑   `DrawArc` draws a portion of a circle.

❑   `DrawBezier` draws a cubic Bezier curve defined by four points.

❑   `DrawPie` draws a slice of a circle (like a pie chart).

❑   `DrawPolygon` draws regular and irregular polygons from an array of points.

❑   `DrawIcon` draws Windows icons.

All of these methods use the `Brush`, `Pen`, `Point`, and `Rectangle` objects that you've seen used throughout this chapter. Each of these methods has an associated `Fill` method that fills in the shape after it's drawn it.

Summary

In this chapter you looked at how you could build your own user interface on your controls and forms. Previously, you have only been able to build your user interface by plugging other people's controls together. Here you focused on building controls derived from `System.Windows.Forms.UserControl` because you're interested in building component-based software.

After discussing the difference between vector and raster graphics, you proceeded to build a simple application that allowed the user to draw dots on the screen using the mouse. You then looked at building a separate control that provided the user with a set of colors that they could choose from when drawing. You saw how to use the Color dialog box to add new colors and how to create new colors using the Windows RGB (red, green, blue) color scheme.

Finally, you took a look at the `Image` class and saw how this could load a variety of file formats, include Windows bitmap, `.jpeg`, and `.gif`. You also saw how to scale images and preserve their aspect ratio.

To summarize, you should know how to:

❑   Use the mouse events to capture the current x, y coordinates of the mouse on the screen

❑   Invalidate only the rectangle that you are working in to prevent screen flicker

❑   Add and use named system colors as well as custom defined colors using their RGB values

❑   Use the different graphics tools such as circle and hollow circle

❑   Load, resize, and preserve the aspect ratio of images

Exercises

1.   What is a pixel?

2.   What object do you need in order to draw on a control, form, or other object?

3.   Describe the two phases of painting in Windows.

4.   What is the difference between client coordinates and screen coordinates?

5.   How can you create `Color` objects with .NET?

15

Accessing Databases

Most applications manipulate data in some way. Visual Basic .NET applications often manipulate data that come from relational databases. To do this, your application needs to interface with relational database software such as Microsoft Access, Microsoft SQL Server, Oracle, or Sybase.

Visual Studio .NET provides the data access tools and wizards to connect to these databases, and retrieve and update their data. In this chapter, you will look at these tools and wizards, and use them to retrieve data from a database.

In the next chapter you will concentrate more on writing code directly, which gives you more flexibility and control than relying on Visual Studio .NET to create it for you. With practice, writing code will also take less time than working through a wizard.

In this chapter, you will:

❑   Learn what a database really is

❑   Examine the SQL SELECT statement

❑   Examine data access components

❑   Discuss data binding in Windows Forms

❑   Use the data access wizards in Visual Studio .NET

> Note that in order to work through the exercises in this chapter, you will need Microsoft Access 2000 or higher as well as Visual Studio .NET with the Crystal Reports option installed.

What Is a Database?

Basically, a *database* consists of one or more large complex files that store data in a structured format. The database engine, in your case Microsoft Access, manages the file or files and the data within those files.

Microsoft Access Objects

The Microsoft Access database file, which has an extension of mdb contains tables, queries, forms, reports, pages, macros, and modules, which are referred to as *database objects*. That's a lot of information in one large file, but Microsoft Access manages this data quite nicely. Forms, reports, pages, macros, and modules are generally concerned with letting users work with and display data. You will be writing Visual Basic .NET applications to do this, so the only database objects you're really concerned about at the moment are tables and queries.

Tables

A *table* contains a collection of data, which is represented by one or more columns and one or more rows of data. Columns are typically referred to as *fields* in Microsoft Access and the rows are referred to as *records*. Each field in a table represents an attribute of the data stored in that table. For example, a field named First Name would represent the first name of an employee or customer. This field is an attribute of an employee or customer. Records in a table contain a collection of fields that form a complete record of information about the data stored in that table. For example, suppose a table contains two fields, First Name and Last Name. These two fields in a single record describe the name of a single person. This is illustrated in Figure 15-1.

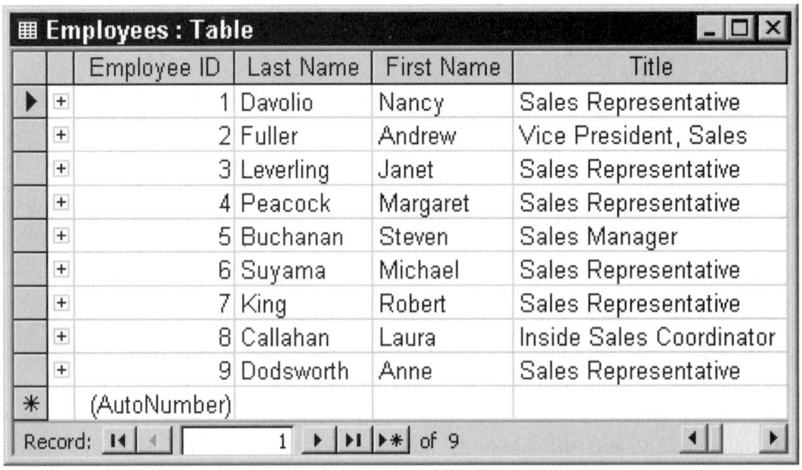

Employees : Table			
Employee ID	Last Name	First Name	Title
1	Davolio	Nancy	Sales Representative
2	Fuller	Andrew	Vice President, Sales
3	Leverling	Janet	Sales Representative
4	Peacock	Margaret	Sales Representative
5	Buchanan	Steven	Sales Manager
6	Suyama	Michael	Sales Representative
7	King	Robert	Sales Representative
8	Callahan	Laura	Inside Sales Coordinator
9	Dodsworth	Anne	Sales Representative
(AutoNumber)			

Record: 1 of 9

Figure 15-1

Queries

A *query* in a database is a group of SQL (Structured Query Language) statements that allow you to retrieve and update data in your tables. Queries can be used to select or update all of the data in one or more tables, or to select or update specific data in one or more tables.

Query objects in Microsoft Access are a hybrid of two types of objects in SQL Server—views and stored procedures. Using database query objects can make your Visual Basic .NET code simpler, because you have fewer complex SQL queries included in your code. They can also make your programs faster, because database engines can compile queries when you create them—whereas the SQL code in a Visual Basic .NET program needs to be reinterpreted every time it's used.

To really understand the implications of queries you need to learn some SQL. Fortunately, compared to *other* programming languages, SQL is really simple.

SQL SELECT Statement

SQL is an acronym for Structured Query Language. The American National Standards Institute (ANSI) defines the standards for ANSI SQL. Most database engines implement ANSI SQL to some extent and often add some features specific to the given database engine.

The benefits of ANSI SQL are that, once you learn the basic syntax for SQL, you have a solid grounding from which you can code the SQL language in almost any database. All you need to learn is a new interface for the database that you are working in. Many database vendors extended SQL to use advanced features or optimizations for their particular database. It is best to stick with the ANSI standards whenever possible in case you want to change databases at some point.

The SQL SELECT statement selects data from one or more fields in one or more records and from one or more tables in your database. Note that the SELECT statement only selects data—it does not modify the data in any way.

The simplest allowable SELECT statement is like this:

```
SELECT * FROM Employees;
```

This simply means "retrieve every field for every record in the Employees table". The * indicates "every field." Employees indicates the table name. Officially, SQL statements should end in a semi-colon. It usually doesn't matter if you forget it, though.

If you only wanted to retrieve first and last names, you can give a list of field names instead of a *:

```
SELECT [First Name], [Last Name] FROM Employees;
```

You need to enclose these field names in square brackets because these field names contain spaces. The square brackets indicate to the SQL interpreter that, even though there is a space in the name, it should treat "First Name" as one object name and "Last Name" as another object name. Otherwise the interpreter would be unable to follow the syntax.

SQL is a lot like plain English—even a non-programmer could probably understand what it means. Now say you only wanted to retrieve the employees whose last name begins with D. To do this, you add a WHERE clause to your SELECT statement:

```
SELECT [First Name], [Last Name] FROM Employees WHERE [Last Name] LIKE 'D*';
```

Lastly, if you want to retrieve these items in a particular order. You can, for example, order the results by first name. You just need to add an ORDER BY clause to the end:

```
SELECT [First Name], [Last Name] FROM Employees
                    WHERE [Last Name] LIKE 'D*' ORDER BY [First Name];
```

This means that if you have employees called Angela Dunn, Zebedee Dean, and David Dustan you will get the following result:

```
Angela     Dunn
David      Dunstan
Zebedee    Dean
```

You're specifying quite a specific command here, but the syntax is pretty simple—and very similar to how an English speaker would describe what they want. Usually, when ordering by a name, you want to order in an ascending order—A comes first, Z comes last. If you were ordering by a number, though, you might want to have the bigger number at the top—for example, so that a product with the highest price appears first. Doing this is really simple—just add DESC to the ORDER BY clause, which causes the results to be ordered in descending order:

```
SELECT [First Name], [Last Name] FROM Employees
                    WHERE [Last Name] LIKE 'D*' ORDER BY [First Name] DESC;
```

The D* means "has a D followed by anything." If you had said *D* it would mean "anything followed by D followed by anything," basically, "contains D." This would return the following:

```
Zebedee    Dean
David      Dunstan
Angela     Dunn
```

If you want to make it very clear that you want the results in an ascending order, you can add ASC *to the* ORDER BY *clause instead of* DESC. *But you don't really need to, since this is the default anyway.*

You can summarize this syntax in the following way:

```
SELECT select-list
    FROM table-name
    [WHERE search-condition]
    [ORDER BY order-by-expression [ASC | DESC]]
```

This means that you must provide a list of fields to include or use a * to select them all. You must provide a table name. You can choose to provide a search condition. You can choose to provide an order-by expression, and if you do, you can make it either ascending or descending.

SQL gets considerably more complicated when you start working with several tables in the same query. But, for various reasons, you don't need to do this all that much when working with Visual Basic .NET.

Anyway, the best way to get SQL into your head is to practice. Before moving on, please try to answer these questions in your head:

❑ How would you write a query to retrieve the Name, Description, and Price fields from a table called Product?

❑ What would you add to the query to retrieve only items with DVD in their description?

❑ How would you order the results so that the most expensive item comes first?

Queries in Access

SQL is really a basic programming language and if you are a programmer who needs to access databases, you will need to use it. However, Microsoft Access provides wizards and visual tools that enable novice programmers to write queries without knowing SQL. Even for SQL programmers, these can sometimes prove useful. These tools, demonstrated in this section, end up producing SQL statements that you can view and modify if you wish, so they can be a good way to learn more about SQL.

Creating a Customer Query

In the next *Try It Out* section, you use Access to create a simple query that will select customer information from the `Customer` table in the `Northwind.mdb` database. You'll need to ensure that the sample databases were installed when you installed Microsoft Access. You'll create this query and then view the SQL `SELECT` statement that gets generated by Access.

Try It Out   Customer Query

1. Open Microsoft Access and click the Open icon on the toobar. In the Open dialog, navigate to `C:\Program Files\Microsoft Office\Office\Samples\` and open `Northwind.mdb`, as shown in Figure 15-2. Then click the OK button.

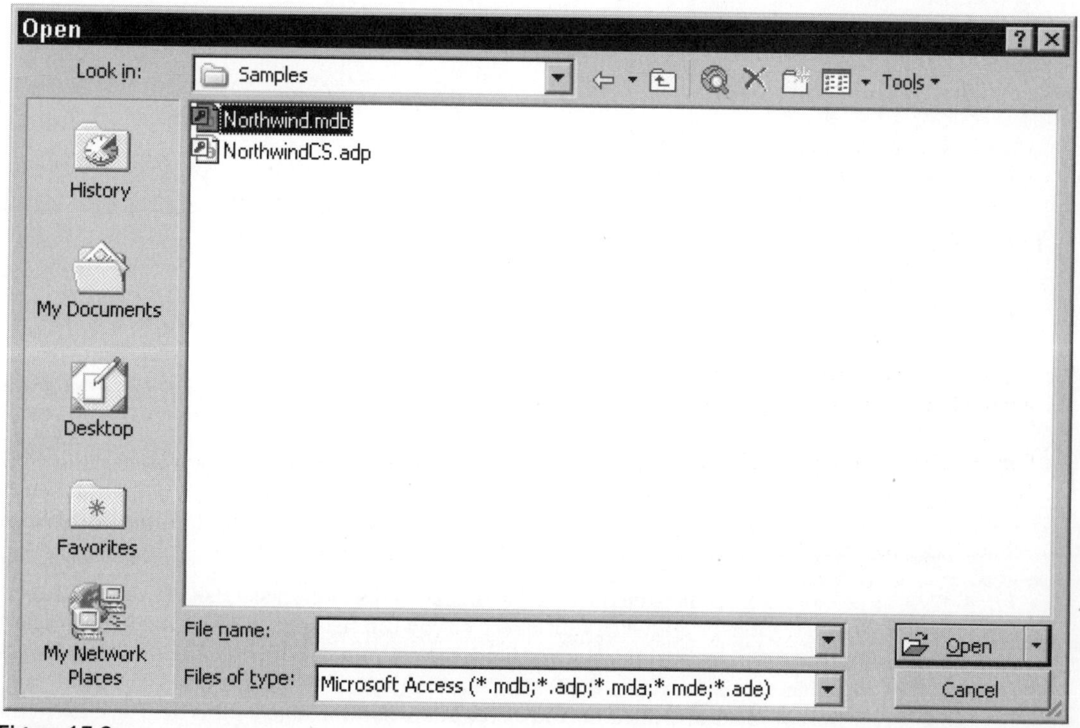

Figure 15-2

2. When the database opens, you will see two sections in the bar on the left: Objects and Groups. The Objects section lists all of your database object types, which you discussed in the section on databases. You can also use Groups to gather together related objects of any type, in any way you want (see Figure 15-3).

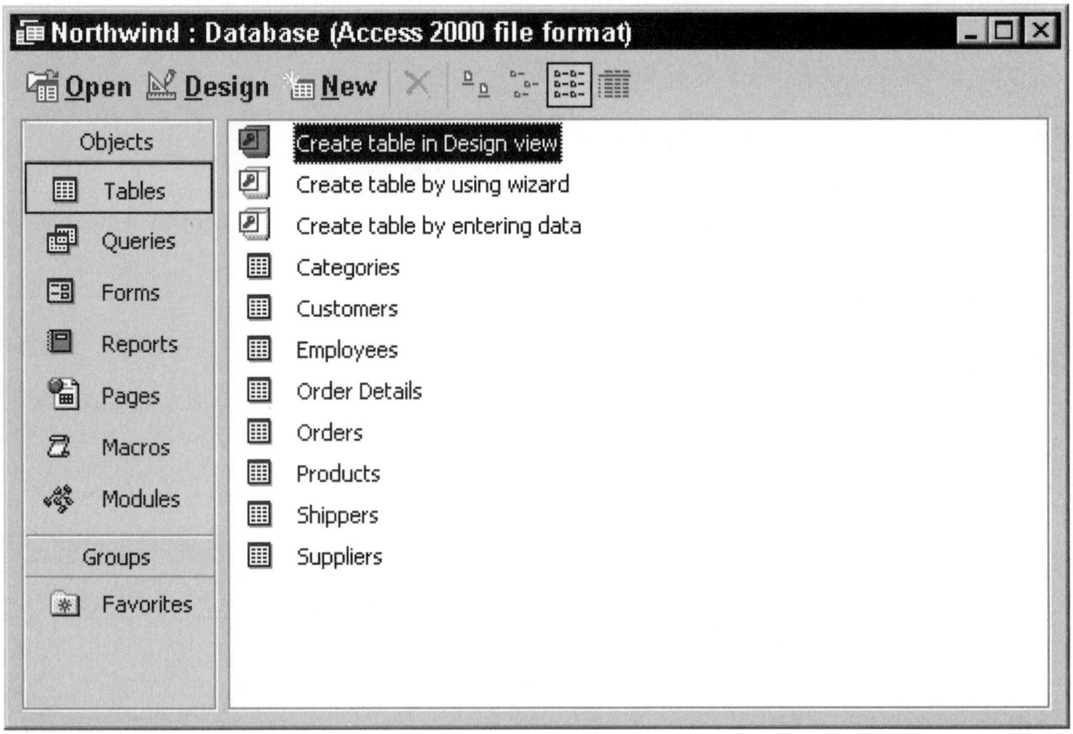

Northwind : Database (Access 2000 file format)

Open Design New

Objects
- Tables
- Queries
- Forms
- Reports
- Pages
- Macros
- Modules

Groups
- Favorites

Create table in Design view
Create table by using wizard
Create table by entering data
Categories
Customers
Employees
Order Details
Orders
Products
Shippers
Suppliers

Figure 15-3

3. Since you want to take a look at how a SQL SELECT statement is built by Access, you need to click on the Queries icon under the Objects tab.

4. You are going to build a new query so double-click **Create query in Design view** in the results window (see Figure 15-4).

5. The Show Table dialog appears and allows you to select one or more tables to be used in your query. You only want to select one table: Customers. Click on the Customers table and then click the Add button to have this table added to the Query Designer and then click the Close button to close the Show Table dialog.

6. The Customers table is displayed with all available fields plus an asterisk (*). You can select the fields that you want to be added to your query or you can select the asterisk, which will select all fields from the table. Let's just select a few fields for your query. Double-click on CompanyName in the Customers table to add it to the first column in the grid below the table. The Field and Table cells are automatically filled in. You also want to sort the data by this field so click in the Sort cell and choose Ascending to have the results of your query sorted by this field. Your screen should look like Figure 15-5.

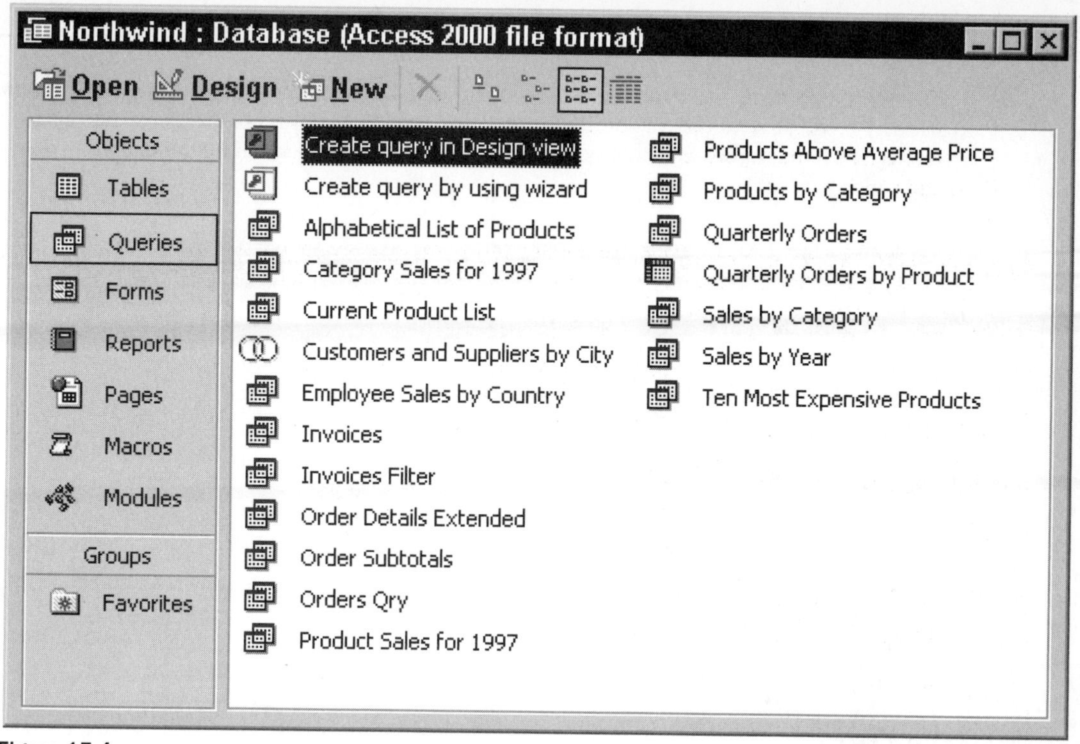

Figure 15-4

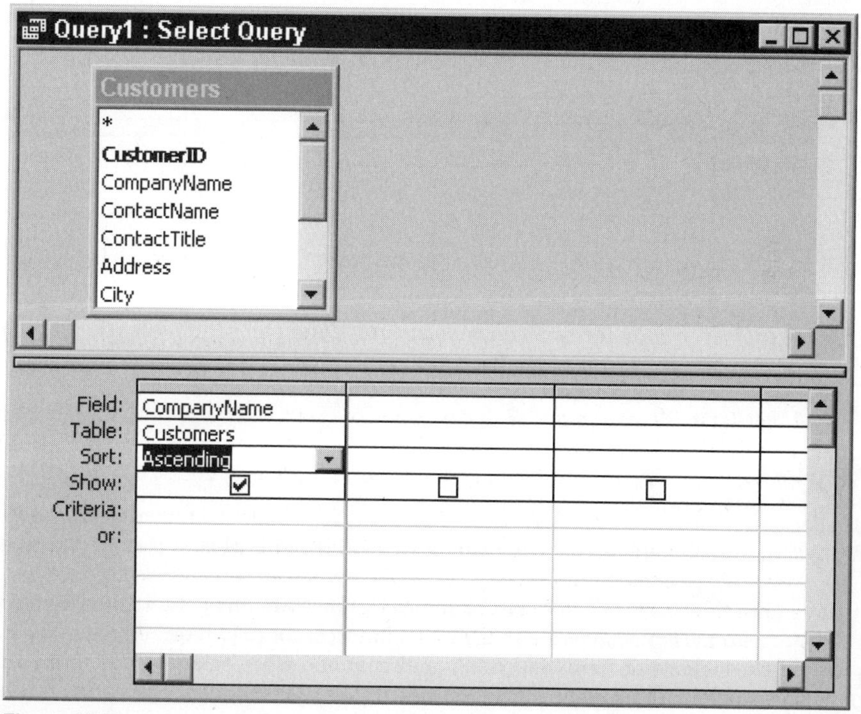

Figure 15-5

7. You have to add the ContactName field to your grid. Double-click on this field in the Customers table and it will be automatically added to the next available column in the grid. Then add ContactTitle in the same way. Your completed query should now look like the one in Figure 15-6.

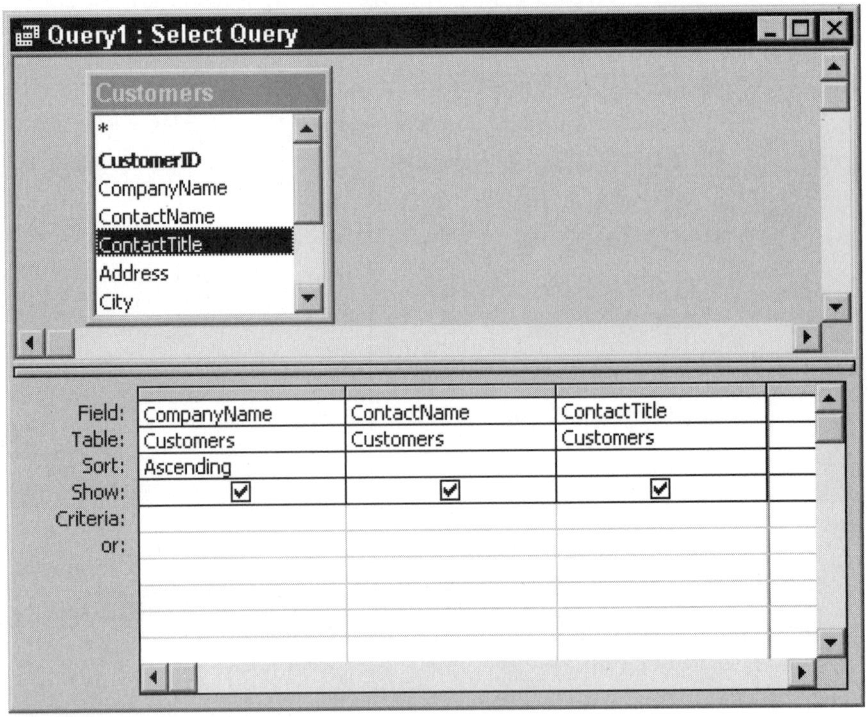

Figure 15-6

8. Click on the Save icon on the toolbar, enter the name **CustomerQuery** in the Save As dialog and click OK.

9. On the toolbar click on the run icon, indicated by !, and you should see results similar to the ones shown in Figure 15-7. Notice that the results are sorted on the CompanyName field in ascending order, as shown in the figure.

How It Works

From the choices you made, Access generates a SQL statement. To look at it you click the View menu and select the SQL View menu item. This will display the SQL statements as shown in Figure 15-8.

Notice that you have the basic SQL SELECT statement followed by the field names. Access has prefixed each field name with the table name. Remember that brackets are only required when the field names contain spaces. The table name prefix is actually only required when selecting data from multiple tables where both have a field with the same name. However, to reduce the chance of errors, Access has prefixed all fields with the table name.

CustomerQuery : Select Query

Company Name	Contact Name	Contact Title
Alfreds Futterkiste	Maria Anders	Sales Representative
Ana Trujillo Emparedados y helados	Ana Trujillo	Owner
Antonio Moreno Taquería	Antonio Moreno	Owner
Around the Horn	Thomas Hardy	Sales Representative
Berglunds snabbköp	Christina Berglund	Order Administrator
Blauer See Delikatessen	Hanna Moos	Sales Representative
Blondel père et fils	Frédérique Citeaux	Marketing Manager
Bólido Comidas preparadas	Martín Sommer	Owner
Bon app'	Laurence Lebihan	Owner
Bottom-Dollar Markets	Elizabeth Lincoln	Accounting Manager
B's Beverages	Victoria Ashworth	Sales Representative
Cactus Comidas para llevar	Patricio Simpson	Sales Agent
Centro comercial Moctezuma	Francisco Chang	Marketing Manager
Chop-suey Chinese	Yang Wang	Owner
Comércio Mineiro	Pedro Afonso	Sales Associate
Consolidated Holdings	Elizabeth Brown	Sales Representative
Die Wandernde Kuh	Rita Müller	Sales Representative
Drachenblut Delikatessen	Sven Ottlieb	Order Administrator
Du monde entier	Janine Labrune	Owner
Eastern Connection	Ann Devon	Sales Agent
Ernst Handel	Roland Mendel	Sales Manager

Record: 1 of 91

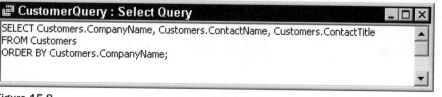

Figure 15-7

CustomerQuery : Select Query

```
SELECT Customers.CompanyName, Customers.ContactName, Customers.ContactTitle
FROM Customers
ORDER BY Customers.CompanyName;
```

Figure 15-8

The `FROM` clause in your `SELECT` statement specifies the table that data is being selected from, in this case the Customer table.

The ORDER BY clause specifies which fields should be used to sort the data, and in this case, the CompanyName field has been specified.

So how does this SQL statement actually get built? Well, when you first started creating this query you added a table name. Before any fields were added to the grid, Access generated the following SQL statement:

```
SELECT
FROM Customers;
```

Of course, this on its own is not a valid SQL statement. Once you added the first field and set the sort order for that field, the following SQL statement was generated—which is valid:

```
SELECT Customer.CompanyName
FROM Customer
ORDER BY Customers.CompanyName;
```

As you continued to add fields, the rest of the field names were added to the SQL statement until the complete SQL statement shown earlier was generated.

Let's move on now and discuss the basic data access components that are needed in Windows Forms to display data. Since you have been using Microsoft Access in your examples here, I will discuss the data access components provided in Visual Studio .NET that assist you in accessing the data in an Access database.

Data Access Components

There are three main data access components in Visual Basic .NET that you need in order to retrieve and store data from the database: OleDbConnection, OleDbDataAdapter, and DataSet. Each of these components is located in the Toolbox under the Data tab as shown in Figure 15-9. Take a brief look at each one of these components in turn.

Figure 15-9

These components are known as ADO.NET classes. In this chapter, you will simply see how to use them in a Windows application. ADO.NET will be discussed as a whole in the next chapter.

OleDbConnection

The OleDbConnection component represents an active connection to the database and provides some basic information such as the database name, location of the database, and the database driver to use to connect to the database.

In fact, the OleDbConnection connects to OLE DB, which is a database access platform that forms part of Windows. When you connect to OLE DB, you specify a database and database provider to use. When you try setting up a connection, you will specify `Northwind.mdb` and the Microsoft Access provider.

Note that there is also a SqlConnection component in the Toolbox. This works in a very similar way to the OleDbConnection. The main difference is that instead of connecting to OLE DB and then using OLE DB to connect to a database, it connects *directly* to Microsoft SQL Server databases. Because of this, SqlConnection is much faster—but can only be used to access SQL Server or the Microsoft SQL Server Desktop Engine (MSDE). SqlDataAdapter and SqlCommand are also very similar to OleDbDataAdapter and OleDbCommand—but are for use with SqlConnection. There are also components that are specific to Oracle and provide fast access to Oracle databases. Like the SQL Server counterparts, these components can only be used for Oracle. For access to older databases, a set of ODBC providers are present and allow you to access older databases that do not support the OleDb technology.

You can add an OleDbConnection component to your form and set its properties. However, you can also simply add an OleDbDataAdapter to your form and it will automatically add the OleDbConnection and prompt us to set its properties—which is what you'll be doing in the next *Try It Out*.

DataSet

The DataSet component is a cache of data that is stored in memory. It's a lot like a mini database engine, but its data exists in memory. You can use it to store data in tables, and using the DataView component you can query the data in various ways.

The DataSet is very powerful. As well as storing data in tables, it also stores a rich amount of *metadata*—or "data about the data." This includes things like table and column names, data types, and the information needed to manage and undo changes to the data. All of this data is represented in memory as XML. A DataSet can be saved to an XML file and then loaded back into memory very easily. It can also be passed in XML form over networks including the Internet.

Since the DataSet component stores all of the data in memory, you can scroll through the data both forwards and backwards, and can also make updates to the data in memory. The DataSet component is very powerful and you will be exploring this component in more detail in the next chapter. In this chapter, you will simply be using it to store data and bind it to a control on your form.

OleDbDataAdapter

The OleDbDataAdapter serves as a data bridge between the database and your DataSet object. It retrieves data from a database using an OleDbConnection and adds it to a DataSet component. You can also use it to update the database with changes made in the DataSet. In this chapter, you will be using this component to simply retrieve data from a database.

The OleDbDataAdapter connects to a database using an OleDbConnection. When you use it, you specify SQL statements for selecting, deleting, inserting, and updating the data. The OleDbDataAdapter is able to work out which command to use in order to reflect the changes made to the DataSet.

The three components just mentioned are the three basic components that you will be working with in this chapter. However let's briefly cover the rest of the components listed here.

OleDbCommand

The OleDbCommand component is used to execute SQL statements against the database. These SQL statements can be statements to select, insert, update, or delete data. The OleDbDataAdapter internally uses an OleDbCommand for each of its main functions—insert, update, and delete. However, for this chapter you do not need to be aware of them.

An OleDbCommand can also be used directly on an OleDbConnection, without requiring an OleDbDataAdapter.

DataView

The last component to be covered here is the DataView component. This component is used to create a customized view of the data in a dataset. DataView can do many of the things that a query can do, such as displaying only selected columns or rows and sorting data. You can also use it to view different states of data—for example, you could choose to view the *original* data in rows that have been changed.

> *These components are derived from classes of the same name. In the next couple of chapters, you will be exploring these components in more detail by creating objects that are derived from their respective classes.*

Data Binding

Data binding means taking data contained in a DataSet and binding it to a control. In other words, the control will receive its data from your data access components or objects, and the data will be automatically displayed in the control for the user to see and manipulate. In Visual Basic .NET, most controls support some level of data binding. Some are specifically designed for it, such as the DataGrid. In your next *Try It Out*, you will be binding data from a DataSet component to a DataGrid control so this is where you want to focus your attention.

The DataGrid Control

A *DataGrid control* is a control that is used to display data tables much like what you saw when you executed the results of your query in Access. This control displays all the data contained in the data access component that it is bound to and allows the user to edit the data if the appropriate properties are set. This section explores how data is bound to DataGrid control by setting its properties. The next chapter discusses data binding to other Windows controls in more detail.

There are two main properties in the DataGrid control that must be set in order to bind the DataSet component to it. These are the `DataSource` and `DataMember` properties.

The DataSource Property

The `DataSource` property is used to set the source of the data that will be used to supply the DataGrid control with data. The data source can be one of several components or objects such as DataSet, DataView, DataTable, or an array. In your exercise, you will be using a DataSet component to supply the DataGrid control with data.

The DataMember Property

The other property that should be set in the DataGrid control is the `DataMember` property. Like a database, a dataset can contain several tables. `DataMember` specifies which table in the dataset will be used for the binding, if more than one is available. For example, suppose a dataset contains the results of two queries listing data from the Customer and Orders tables. You must specify the table that contains the data that you want to see in your DataGrid control.

In fact, the DataGrid can display data from two tables simultaneously, and you can establish a parent–child relationship between the two tables. You won't be looking at parent-child relationships in this chapter.

That's basically all you need to do to bind data to your DataGrid control, so let's move on and put this newfound knowledge to use in a practical exercise.

In this *Try It Out*, you will be using the data access wizards in Visual Studio .NET to create the OleDbDataAdapter, OleDbConnection, and DataSet components. You will be using the `Northwind.mdb` sample database again as your data source.

Once you have populated the DataSet component, you will bind that data to your DataGrid control by setting the `DataSource` and `DataMember` properties of the DataGrid control.

Try It Out   Binding Data

1. Create a new Windows Application project called **AccessDataBinding**.

2. The first thing that you need to do in your project is to create the OleDbDataAdapter component. Click the Toolbox and select the Data tab. Locate the OleDbDataAdapter component, drag and drop it on to your form. This invokes the Data Adapter Configuration Wizard. Click the Next button to continue to the first step.

For those readers who are unfamiliar with the wizards in Visual Studio .NET, all wizards start with a Welcome screen. This Welcome screen describes what actions the wizard will perform and what information may be required on your part.

You then have the option to continue with the wizard or to cancel the wizard by clicking on the appropriate button.

3. Your OleDbDataAdapter requires a connection to the database and uses an OleDbConnection component for this (see Figure 15-10). The next step of the wizard prompts you for this

information by allowing us to choose an existing data connection if there is one or to create a new one. A *data connection* is the information used by the OleDbConnection component to connect to the database. It specifies such information as where the database is located and what OLE DB provider it should use to connect to the database.

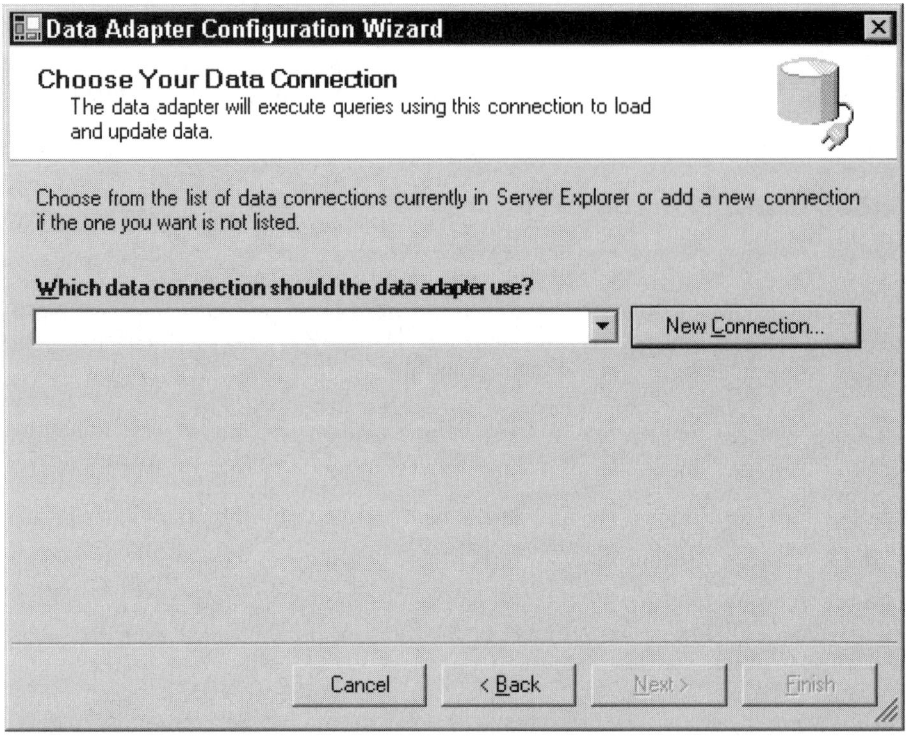

Figure 15-10

Since you do not have a data connection defined for the Northwind.mdb database you need to create a new one, so click on the New Connection button to invoke the Data Link Properties dialog.

4. By default, the Data Link Properties dialog displays the Connection tab. You need to move back a step because you are not using the default Provider. Click the Provider tab and choose Microsoft Jet 4.0 OLE DB Provider, as shown in Figure 15-11. This is the provider that you need to connect to the Northwind.mdb Microsoft Access database.

Click the Next button at the bottom of the dialog to continue to the next step. This will return you to the Connection tab, which will have changed slightly to reflect the settings for the Microsoft Jet provider.

5. The Connection tab in this dialog allows us to browse for and select the Access database that you want to use. Click the Browse button next to the text box for Select or enter a database name, and then locate and select the Northwind.mdb database. By default, this will be in the folder C:\Program Files\Microsoft Office\Office10\Samples\Northwind.mdb.

Select the Northwind.mdb database in the Open dialog and click the Open button to have this information applied to the Data Link Properties dialog, as shown in Figure 15-12.

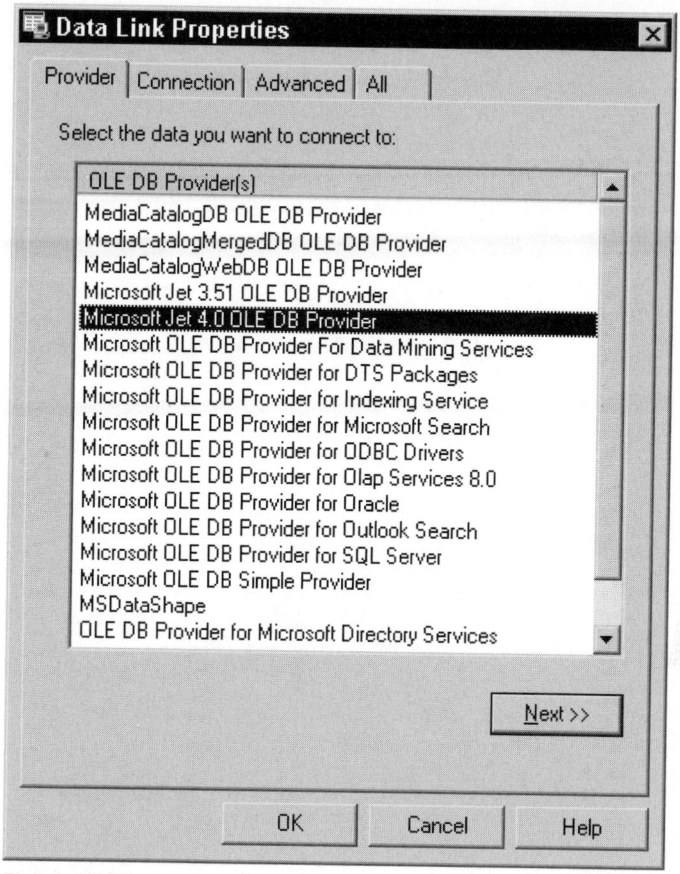

Figure 15-11

Since this database does not require a password, accept the default information for username and password, as shown in Figure 15-12.

Finally, to ensure that you have a good connection to the database, click on the Test Connection button to verify the connection. Once the connection test succeeds you will receive a message box indicating this.

If you failed to connect to the database, check to ensure you selected the Microsoft Jet 4.0 OLE DB Provider in the Provider tab and that you selected the correct database in the Connection tab.

6. That's all the information you need to connect to your database. Click the OK button in the Data Link Properties dialog to have the OleDbConnection component created and populated in the Data Adapter Configuration Wizard.

7. Click the Next button to proceed to the next step in this wizard. You now need to specify how you want to query the database for your data. Since you are using an Access database, you only have one option available: Use SQL statements as shown in Figure 15-13. Just click the Next button to continue.

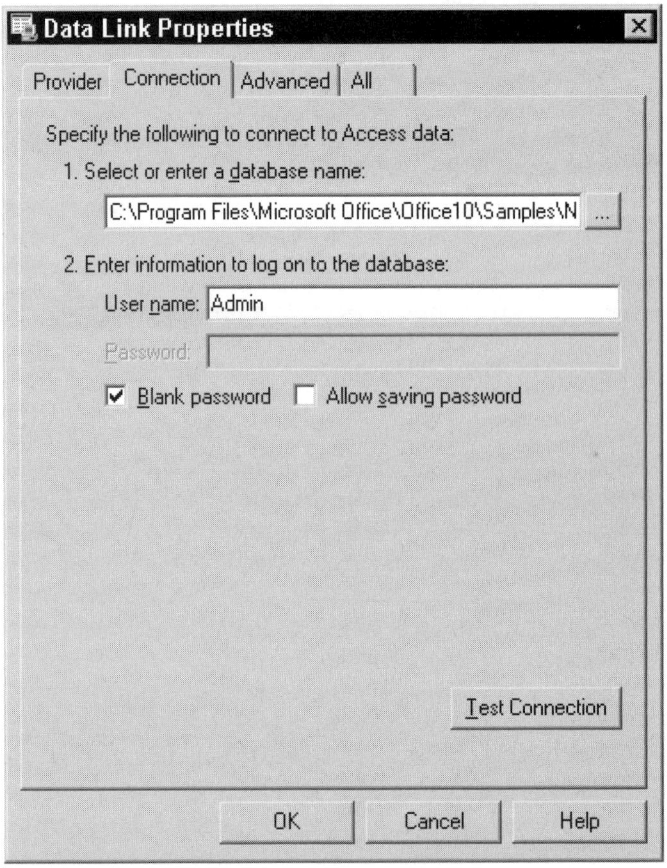

Figure 15-12

8. The next step of the Data Adapter Configuration Wizard provides several options. You can manually enter your SQL statement or you can use the Query Builder dialog box. The Advanced Options button allows you to specify what additional SQL statements should be generated to insert, update, and delete data in your database. You will use the next several steps to complete this screen of the wizard, as shown in Figure 15-14.

9. Click on the Advanced Options button to display the Advanced SQL Generation Options dialog as shown in Figure 15-15. This dialog allows you to specify that insert, update, and delete statements would be generated automatically to match the SELECT statement that you will create.

    Along with this is the option to specify how the data updates should be handled as indicated by the Use optimistic concurrency option. Having this switched on helps your applications to cope with multiple users working with the same database at the same time.

    The last option here specifies how the DataSet component should be refreshed when data in the database has been updated. When this option is checked, it will automatically add the necessary SQL statements to retrieve any changed data in the database after an insert or update. This option is disabled for Microsoft Access.

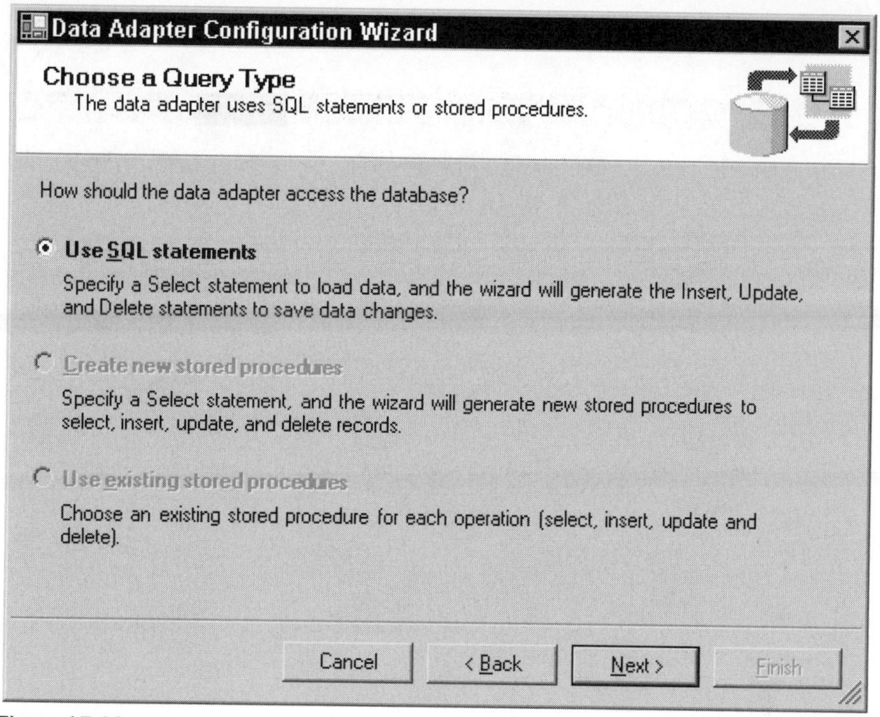

Figure 15-13

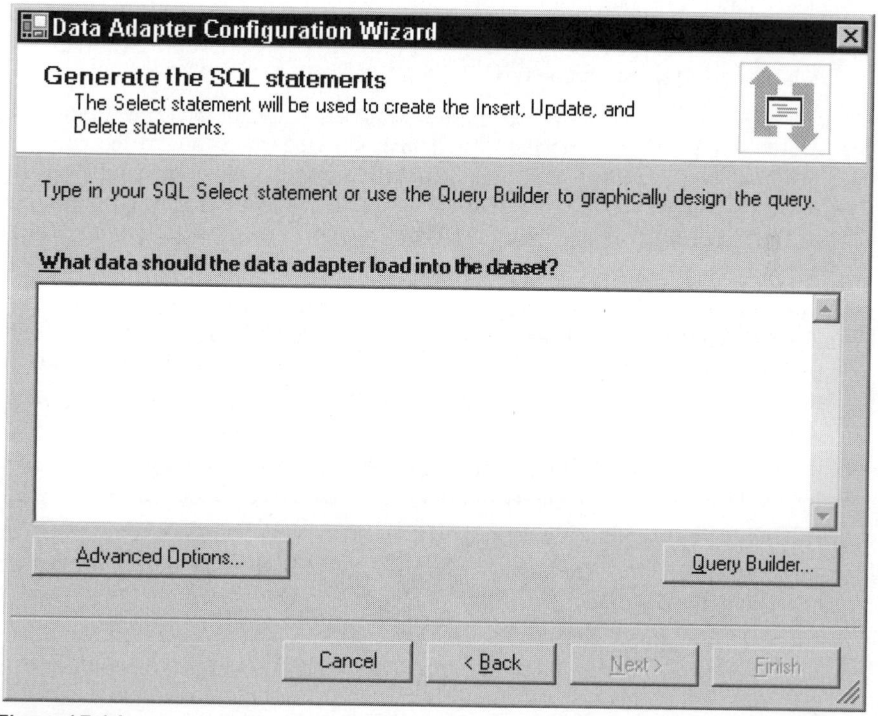

Figure 15-14

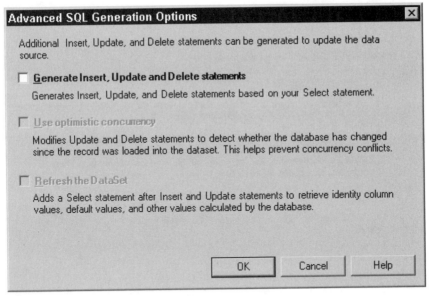

Figure 15-15

By default the first two options are selected. Since you only want to display data in your DataGrid control, you do not need to generate SQL statements that will insert, update, and delete data in your database.

Uncheck the first option and the second option will be disabled and unchecked. Then click the OK button to close this dialog box.

10. You are now back at the Generate the SQL statements step of the Data Adapter Configuration Wizard. You want to retrieve the same data as you did when you created your Access query: CompanyName, ContactName, and ContactTitle from the Customers table, ordered by CompanyName. If you are confident enough with SQL, you can just type the query into the text box. If not, you can use the Query Builder to generate the SQL for you as demonstrated by the following steps.

11. Click the Query Builder button to invoke the Query Builder dialog. The first step here is very similar to what you saw in Access as shown in Figure 15-16. You need to choose the table that you want in your SQL SELECT statement. Click the Customers table in the Add Table dialog and then click the Add button to have this table added.

12. Click Close to bring the Query Builder to the foreground. The Query Builder dialog is now shown with the Customers table added. Note that the fields in the Customers table are listed alphabetically here. In the Query Builder in Access, the fields were listed in the order that they were defined.

You want to select the fields in the order that you want them in your query, so locate and select the fields in the Customers table in the following order:

❑ CompanyName

❑ ContactName

❑ ContactTitle

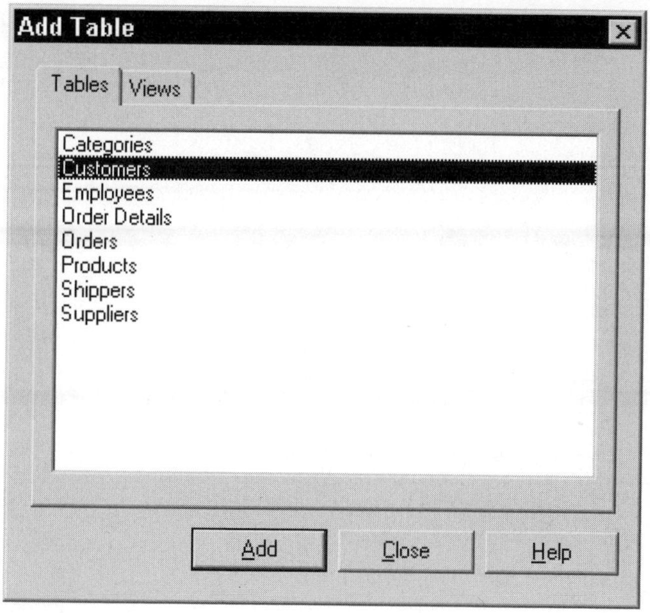

Figure 15-16

You want to sort the data by CompanyName, so click on the Sort Type column in the grid and select Ascending from the drop-down list. Your completed Query Builder dialog box should now look like the one shown in Figure 15-17.

13. Notice the SQL statement that was generated. It looks a little different from the one that Access generated in your previous *Try It Out* in that it does not have the field names prefixed with the table name. The reason for this is simply that the Query Builder in Visual Studio .NET implements ANSI SQL a little differently from the Query Builder in Access. Both SQL statements are equally valid, though—and if you were to type the SQL that Access generated, it would work fine here too.

Click the OK button to have this SQL statement added to the Generate the SQL statements step of the Data Adapter Configuration Wizard as shown in Figure 15-18.

Notice that the SQL SELECT statement has been formatted a little differently from the way it was shown in the Query Builder. Each of the field names in the SELECT statement has been placed on a separate line. Also the ORDER BY clause has been combined with the table name that you are selecting data from. Since SQL is a declarative language, all parts of the SQL statement can be on the same line or multiple lines. However, it can help to separate the parts of the SQL statement onto separate lines for readability purposes.

Click the Next button to proceed to the next step of the wizard.

14. The next screen is the last step of the wizard and displays a list of tasks that the wizard has performed for you based on the information that you have supplied.

Click the Finish button to close the Data Adapter Configuration Wizard dialog.

15. Visual Studio .Net has introduced one new dialog. This dialog prompts you as to whether or not you want the password included in your code, as shown in Figure 15-19.

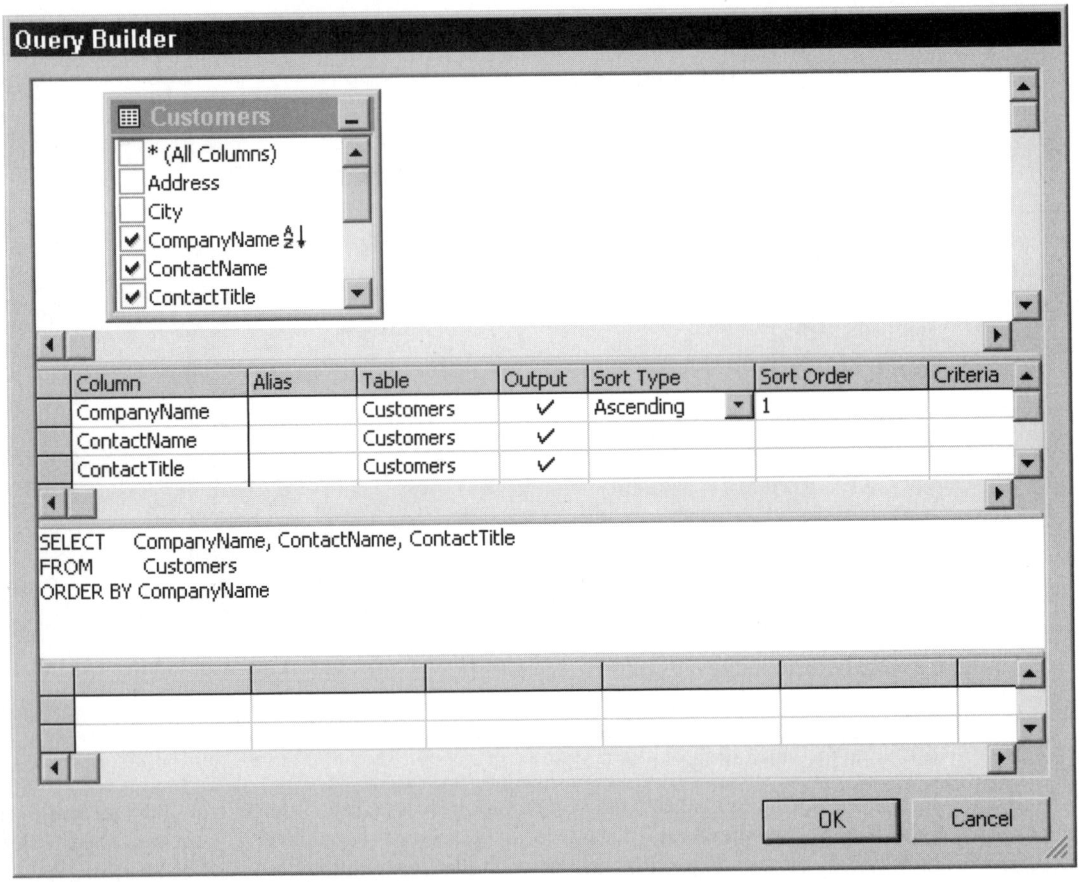

Query Builder

Column	Alias	Table	Output	Sort Type	Sort Order	Criteria
CompanyName		Customers	✓	Ascending	1	
ContactName		Customers	✓			
ContactTitle		Customers	✓			

```
SELECT    CompanyName, ContactName, ContactTitle
FROM      Customers
ORDER BY  CompanyName
```


OK   Cancel

Figure 15-17

If you choose to have the password included in your code, this could expose a security risk to your data.

Since you have no password and you are dealing with an Access database, click on the Include password button to have the wizard include the password in your code and to have the OleDbDataAdapter and OleDbConnection components added to your project.

Now that you have a means to connect to the database and a means to retrieve the data from the database, the next step is to create a component to hold the data that is retrieved. There are several options that are available to you here. You could create a DataSet component by dragging the DataSet component from the Data tab in the Toolbox and then set the various properties. Or you can have a DataSet component generated for us by the Generate DataSet wizard. Let's opt to go through this second route, which is much easier and faster.

16. Click on the Data menu and then select the Generate DataSet menu item to display the Generate Dataset dialog box shown in Figure 15-20.

This dialog does some pretty clever stuff. In previous chapters, you've seen how in Visual Basic .NET you can base new classes on existing classes. This dialog actually creates a new class,

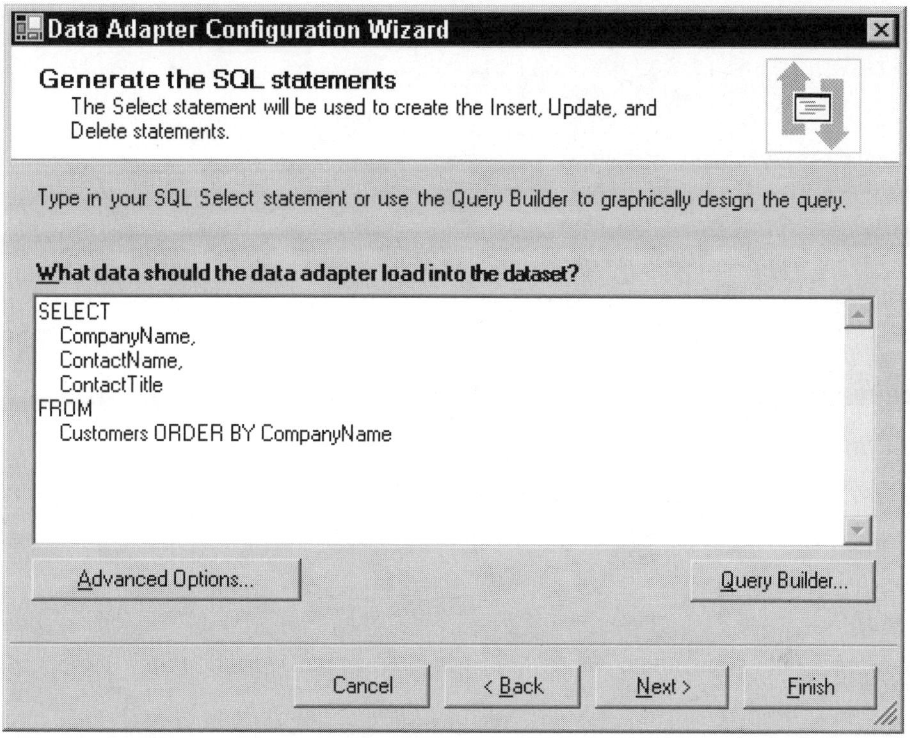

Data Adapter Configuration Wizard ☒

Generate the SQL statements
The Select statement will be used to create the Insert, Update, and Delete statements.

Type in your SQL Select statement or use the Query Builder to graphically design the query.

<u>W</u>hat data should the data adapter load into the dataset?

```
SELECT
    CompanyName,
    ContactName,
    ContactTitle
FROM
    Customers ORDER BY CompanyName
```

[<u>A</u>dvanced Options...]   [<u>Q</u>uery Builder...]

[Cancel]   [< <u>B</u>ack]   [<u>N</u>ext >]   [<u>F</u>inish]

Figure 15-18

Do you want to include the password in the connection string? ☒

The password is saved as clear text and is readable in the source code and the compiled assembly.

[Include password]   [Don't include password]   [Cancel]   [Help]

Figure 15-19

which derives from the DataSet class and adds features specifically for handling data from the selected tables. This makes the DataSet easier to work with and ensures that it contains the data you expect it to. A class that derives from DataSet in this way is called a *typed dataset*.

When you use the Generate Dataset dialog, it will find all of the tables that will be returned from available data adapters. It then enables us to select which ones you want this DataSet to contain.

Look at the fields in this dialog. The first section of this dialog presents you with the option of using an existing DataSet class in your project or creating a new one. Your project does not contain any other typed dataset classes, so you can't use this option. The New option has been selected and a default name provided. Change the name to **CustomerDataSet**.

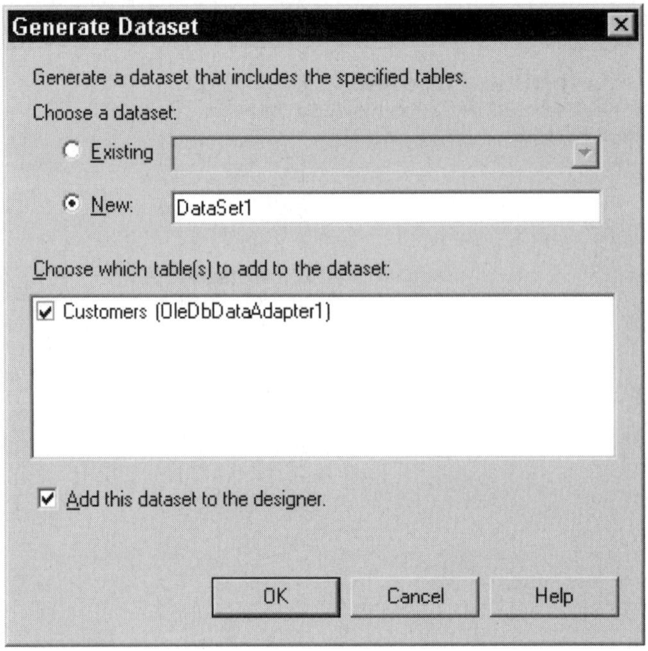

Generate Dataset

Generate a dataset that includes the specified tables.

Choose a dataset:

C Existing

⊙ New: DataSet1

Choose which table(s) to add to the dataset:

☑ Customers (OleDbDataAdapter1)

☑ Add this dataset to the designer.

OK   Cancel   Help

Figure 15-20

This dialog has read the information from the data adapter in your project and has listed the table that it will return. Again this is what you want and you will accept the default values here. If you had several data adapters in your project you would see several tables listed here.

The last section of this dialog has a check box that specifies whether you want an instance of the CustomerDataSet class that will be created added to the designer. Checking this check box generates the code in your form to have the DataSet declared and initialized. This reduces the amount of code that you have to add, so you also want to accept this default value.

Click the OK button to have the DataSet component generated and added to the project.

17. The CustomerDataSet component has been added to your project. You can see an instance of it—called CustomerDataSet1—in the component tray, underneath the form, as shown in Figure 15-21.

There is also a new item called CustomerDataSet.xsd in the Solution Explorer, as shown in Figure 15-22.

This is an XML schema that stores the information that the CustomerDataSet can contain—for example, the table and column names.

18. You now need to add code in order to have the CustomerDataSet filled with data. Double-click on the form to have the Form1_Load procedure added to the code and then add the following line of code to this procedure in order to populate the DataSet component with data:

```
Private Sub Form1_Load(ByVal sender As System.Object, _
        ByVal e As System.EventArgs) Handles MyBase.Load
    OleDbDataAdapter1.Fill(CustomerDataSet1)
End Sub
```

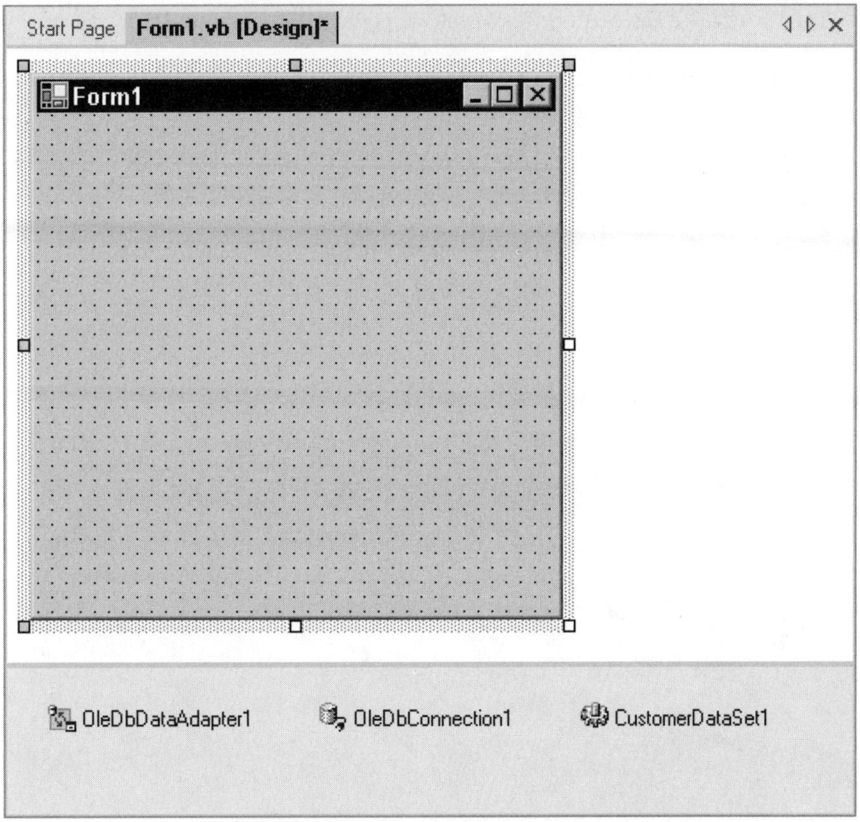

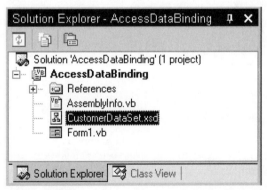

Figure 15-21

Figure 15-22

19. You now need to add a DataGrid control to your form, so that you can see the data in
CustomerDataSet1. Return to the form's designer and select the Windows Forms tab on the
Toolbox. Find the DataGrid control and add it to the form. Resize the form and the DataGrid to
a reasonable size, so that the DataGrid fills most of the form. Set its CaptionText property to
Customers.

20. The DataGrid gives us quite a few ways to control its appearance. For this example, you will set the `AlternatingBackColor` property. Select this property and pull down the drop-down menu. Select the Web tab and choose the WhiteSmoke color (or whatever color takes your fancy—a light one will work out best though).

21. The last thing that you need to do here is to bind the DataSet component to your DataGrid by setting its `DataSource` and `DataMember` properties.

Display the form in Design view and click the DataGrid control. Then in the Properties window, locate its `DataSource` property and click it. In the drop-down list, select `CustomerDataSet1`.

Next, click the `DataMember` property and in the drop-down list select Customers. Note that you could have achieved the same effect by setting the `DataSource` property to `CustomerDataSet1.Customers`, but using this method is a little clearer for people looking at the code later on. Your DataGrid should now look like Figure 15-23.

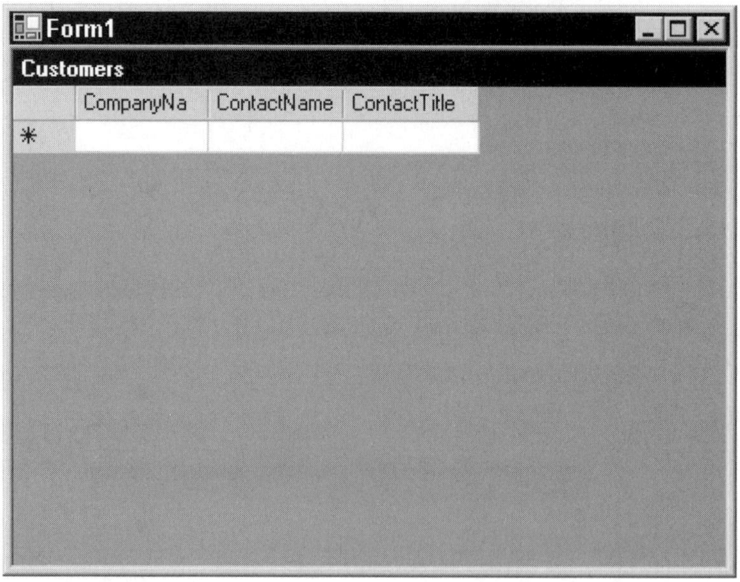

Figure 15-23

22. Now run this project to see what the final results look like. Click on the Start icon on the toolbar to run the project.

Your final results should look similar to those shown in Figure 15-24. (I have expanded the width of the form and the columns in the results so you can see the full column names and the data in the columns.)

Note how setting the `AlternatingRowColor` property has affected the grid's appearance. This can be used as a purely decorative feature, but it can also prove very useful as rows start getting longer because it helps the user to look across a row without accidentally looking at a different row.

Another built-in feature that is worth mentioning is the ability to expand the width of the columns at run-time. Users do this by hovering their mouse over the column boundary-lines in the header and dragging across. Users can also double-click the boundary line to make the column width fit the data.

Figure 15-24

Another DataGrid feature is the ability to sort the data in the DataGrid simply by clicking on the column header. You can sort the data in ascending or descending order, and a little arrow pointing up or down in the right-hand of the column indicates the order that the data has been sorted in.

Finally, the DataGrid has built-in features for editing data. Changes to data in the DataGrid are automatically reflected back to the DataSet. In this application, however, you have not written the code needed to write the changes to the DataSet back to the database.

How It Works

This chapter discussed this application as you've gone along, so you don't need to look at how it works again in detail. But a brief overview of how the application works is supplied here.

You added an OleDbDataAdapter component to the project, which automatically started the Data Adapter Configuration Wizard. Because you did not already have an OleDbConnection component in your project, you provided the information needed to build one using the Data Link Properties dialog.

You then specified the SQL SELECT statement in your OleDbDataAdapter component using the Query Builder dialog. Once you had provided this information, the OleDbDataAdpater was configured. The wizard automatically added an OleDbConnection component, based on the specifications you had given in the Data Link Properties dialog.

The next stage was to create a typed dataset that would contain the data returned by the OleDbDataAdapter. You did this using the Generate Dataset dialog box. This dialog box gathered the information provided in the OleDbConnection component and OleDbDataAdapter component in your project. You accepted the default values provided, except for the name, and then had this dialog generate DataSet component.

Next, you needed a means to populate the DataSet component with data. You double-clicked the form's surface, to generate a handler for the form's Load event, and added this line of code:

```
Private Sub Form1_Load(ByVal sender As System.Object, _
            ByVal e As System.EventArgs) Handles MyBase.Load
    OleDbDataAdapter1.Fill(CustomerDataSet1)
End Sub
```

This procedure gets executed when the form loads and this line of code populates the DataSet with data. The `Fill` method of the OleDbDataAdapter uses the SQL SELECT statement that you generated to query the database and adds the rows of data that get returned to the specified DataSet.

You then added a DataGrid control to the form and set its `DataSource` property to the DataSet component. The DataSet component is the source of your data for the DataGrid.

You then set the `DataMember` property to Customer, which is the table in the DataSet that contains the data that you want displayed. Remember that a DataSet can contain more than one table, so you must specify which table in the DataSet you want displayed in the DataGrid otherwise all tables contained in the DataSet are displayed in the DataGrid.

When the project was run the connection was made to the database, and data was retrieved and then displayed in your form with only a single line of code. This is the power of the data components and data binding at work. With one additional line of code and a few different steps when configuring the data adapter, you could have added the facility to save changes back to the database. You'll learn more about that in the next chapter.

Summary

You started this chapter by exploring what a database actually is and then looked at the SQL SELECT statement. You put this knowledge to use by creating a query in the `Northwind.mdb` database to see the SQL statements that Access generated for you.

You then took a look at the basics of binding data to controls on a form, specifically the DataGrid control. You have examined the necessary basic data access components required to retrieve and store the data from an Access database. You used the components provided in the Data tab of the Toolbox for your data access, and used the wizards to generate the necessary code to connect to the database and retrieve the data. You also added the necessary code to populate a DataSet component with the data retrieved by the OleDbDataAdapter component.

After working through this chapter, you should know:

- ❏ What a database is and the basic objects that make up a database
- ❏ How to use the SQL SELECT statement to select data from a database
- ❏ How to use the Data Adapter Configuration Wizard to create an OleDbDataAdapter component and OleDbConnection component
- ❏ How to create a DataSet component and fill it with data
- ❏ How to bind data to a DataGrid

While you have seen that the wizards provided in Visual Studio .NET make it simple to quickly bind data to the controls on a form, you sometimes need more control on how you interact with the data in a database and how you bind the data to the controls on a form. The next chapter takes a different approach to data binding by programmatically binding data to controls on a form. You will also be exploring the data access components in more detail and will learn how to set their properties and to execute their methods from your code.

Exercises

1. Do you have to prefix the field name with the table name as shown in the following SQL SELECT statement?

```
SELECT Customer.[Customer Name]
FROM Customer
```

2. How do you sort the data in a DataGrid control?

3. How do you populate the DataSet component with data?

4. What two items does the OleDbDataAdapter need before it can retrieve data from a database?

16

Database Programming with SQL Server and ADO.NET

The previous chapter introduced database programming. You obtained data from a single table in an Access database, and displayed it on a grid. You managed to give the user some cool features while writing virtually no code.

You used wizards that wrote most of the code for you—including setting up the connection, configuring the data adapter, and generating a typed dataset. This works great for simple database access using one or two tables, but writing the code yourself can give you a lot more control.

This chapter dives much deeper into the topic of database access. The database access technologies you used in the previous chapter—including components for retrieving data, storing data in memory, and binding data to controls—are collectively called *ADO.NET*. You will explore how you can use the built-in capabilities of ADO.NET to retrieve and update data from databases. You will also learn to manipulate, filter, and edit data held in memory by the DataSet.

The data you extract will be bound to the controls on your form so you will also need to explore binding more thoroughly. You will see how you can use controls to view one record at a time, for example, using text boxes and how to navigate between records using the `CurrencyManager` object.

In this chapter, you will:

- ❏   Learn about ADO.NET objects
- ❏   Bind data to controls
- ❏   Search for and sort in-memory data using ADO.NET DataView objects
- ❏   Select, insert, update, and delete data in a database using ADO.NET

You will also see in this chapter how to access SQL Server databases using the `SqlClient` data provider. As mentioned in the previous chapter, `SqlClient` is significantly faster than `OleDb`, but will only work with SQL Server databases. In order to complete the exercises in this chapter, you will need to have access to MSDE, SQL Server 7, or SQL Server 2000 and have full access to the pubs database. MSDE is a SQL Server desktop engine that comes with Visual Studio .NET and Visual Basic .NET, and Microsoft plans to take it over for Jet and Microsoft Access for desktop database applications. When this chapter uses the term *SQL Server*, the term covers SQL Server 7, SQL Server 2000, and MSDE. The database can reside in SQL Server on your local machine or in SQL Server on a network.

ADO.NET

ADO.NET is designed to provide a *disconnected architecture*. This means that applications connect to the database to retrieve a load of data and store it in memory. They then disconnect from the database and manipulate the in-memory copy of the data. If the database needs to be updated with changes made to the in-memory copy, then a new connection is made and the database is updated. The main in-memory data store is the `DataSet`, which contains other in-memory data stores such as `DataTable` objects. You can filter and sort data in a `DataSet` using `DataView` objects, as you will see later in this chapter.

Using a disconnected architecture provides many benefits, of which the most important to you is that it allows your application to scale up. This means that your database will perform just as well supporting hundreds of users as it does supporting ten users. This is made possible since the application connects to the database only long enough to retrieve or update data, thereby freeing up available database connections for other instances of your application or other applications using the same database.

ADO.NET Data Namespaces

The core ADO.NET classes exist in the `System.Data` namespace. This namespace, in turn, contains some child namespaces. The most important of these are `System.Data.SqlClient` and `System.Data.OleDb`. These provide classes for accessing SQL Server databases and OLE DB-compliant databases, respectively. You've already used classes from the `System.Data.OleDb` namespace in the previous chapter, where you used `OleDbConnection` and `OleDbDataAdapter`. In this chapter you will be using `System.Data.SqlClient` with its equivalent classes, including `SqlConnection` and `SqlDataAdapter`.

Two other child namespaces also exist in the `System.Data` namespace; `System.Data.OracleClient` and `System.Data.Odbc`. The `System.Data.OracleClient` namespace is used exclusively for Oracle databases. Like it's `SqlClient` counterpart, the `OracleClient` namespace provides optimal performance when accessing Oracle Databases. The `System.Data.Odbc` namespace provides access to older data sources that do not support the `OleDb` technology.

The `System.Data.SqlClient` and `System.Data.OleDb` namespaces are known as *data providers* in ADO.NET. There are other data providers available, for example, for Open Database Connectivity (ODBC) and Oracle. In this book you concentrate only on the standard two.

In this chapter, you will be accessing SQL Server databases using the `SqlClient` namespace. However, in ADO.NET, the different data providers work in a very similar way. So the techniques you use here can be easily transferred to the `OleDb` classes. Also, the techniques you learned in the previous chapter using `OleDb` apply to `SqlClient` too. With ADO.NET, you just use the data provider that best fits your data source—you do not need to learn a whole new interface, since all data providers work in a very similar way.

As you start working with ADO.NET you will soon come to realize how the pieces fit together and this chapter will help you in that direction.

Since the space here is limited, you focus on the specific classes that are relevant to the example programs in this chapter. The following list contains the ADO.NET classes that you will be using:

- ❑ SqlConnection
- ❑ SqlDataAdapter
- ❑ SqlCommand
- ❑ SqlParameter

Remember that these are specifically SqlClient classes, but that the OleDb namespace has very close equivalents. Whenever you want to use these classes you must import the System.Data.SqlClient namespace as shown in the following code fragment:

```
Imports System.Data.SqlClient
```

If you want to use the core ADO.NET classes such as DataSet and DataView then you must import the System.Data namespace as shown in the next code fragment:

```
Imports System.Data
```

You should already be familiar with importing different namespaces in your project. However, to be thorough you will also cover this when you go through our hands-on exercises. Now let's take a look at the main classes that exist in the System.Data.SqlClient namespace.

The SqlConnection Class

The SqlConnection class is at the heart of the classes that you will be discussing in this section, as it provides a connection to a SQL Server database. When you construct a SqlConnection object you can choose to specify a *connection string* as a parameter. The connection string contains all the information required to open a connection to your database. If you don't specify one in the constructor, you can set it using the SqlConnection.ConnectionString property. In the previous chapter, Visual Studio .NET built a connection string for you from the details you specified in the Data Link Properties dialog box. However, it is often more useful or quicker to manually write a connection string—so let's take a look at how they work.

Working with the Connection String Parameters

The way that the connection string is constructed will depend on what data provider you are using. When accessing SQL Server you will usually provide a Server and Database parameter as shown in Table 16-1.

Table 16-1 Parameters for creating a connection string to access SQL Server

Parameter	Description
Server	The name of the SQL Server that you wish to access. This is usually the name of the computer that is running SQL Server. You can use (local) or localhost if SQL Server is on the same machine as the one running the application. If you are using named instances of SQL Server, then this parameter would contain the computer name followed by a backslash followed by the named instance of SQL Server.
Database	The name of the database that you want to connect to.

You also need some form of authentication information. There are two ways that this can be done: either by providing a username and password in the connection string or by connecting to SQL Server using the NT account that the application is running under. If you want to connect to the server by specifying a username and password, you need to include additional parameters in your connection string, as shown in Table 16-2.

Table 16-2 Additional parameters when using a username and password

Parameter	Description
User ID	Username is used for connecting to the database. An account with this user ID will need to exist in SQL Server and have permission to access the specified database.
Password	The password for the specified user.

However, SQL Server can be set up to use the Windows NT account of the user who is running the program to open the connection. In this case, you don't need to specify a username and password. You just need to specify that you are using *integrated security*. (The method is called integrated security because SQL Server is integrating with Windows NT's security system and provides the most secure connection as the User ID and Password parameters need not be specified in the code). You do this using the Integrated Security parameter, which you set to True when you want the application to connect to SQL Server using the current user's NT account.

Of course, for this to work the user of the application must have permission to use the SQL Server database. This is granted using the SQL Server Enterprise Manager.

To see how these parameters function in a connection string to initialize a connection object, look at the following code fragment. It uses the SqlConnection class to initialize a connection object that uses a specific user ID and password in the connection string:

```
Dim objConnection As SqlConnection = New _
    SqlConnection("Server=localhost;Database=pubs;" & _
    "User ID=sa;Password=vbdotnet;")
```

This connection string connects to a SQL Server database. The Server parameter specifies that the database resides on the local machine. The Database parameter specifies the database that you want to access—in this case it is the pubs database. Finally, the User ID and Password parameters specify the User ID and password of the user defined in the database. As you can see, each parameter has a value assigned to it using =, and each parameter-value pair is separated by a semicolon.

Opening and Closing the Connection

Once you have initialized a connection object with a connection string as shown previously, you can invoke the methods of the SqlConnection object such as Open and Close, which actually open and close a connection to the database specified in the connection string. An example of this is shown in the following code fragment:

```
' Open the database connection...
objConnection.Open()
' ... Use the connection
' Close the database connection...
objConnection.Close()
```

Although there are many more properties and methods available in the `SqlConnection` class, the ones mentioned so far are all you are really interested in to complete the hands-on exercises and they should be enough to get you started.

SqlCommand

The `SqlCommand` class represents a SQL command to execute against a data store. The command will usually be a select, insert, update, or delete query, and can be a SQL string or a call to a stored procedure. The query being executed may or may not contain parameters.

In the example in the previous chapter, the Data Adapter Configuration Wizard generated a command object for you (although in that case it was an `OleDbCommand`). In that example, a data adapter was using the command to fill a dataset. You will look at how to write code to do this later in the chapter. For the moment, look at command objects alone. You will learn how they relate to data adapters in the next section.

The constructor for the `SqlCommand` class has several variations, but the simplest method is to initialize a `SqlCommand` object with no parameters. Then, once the object has been initialized, you can set the properties that you need to perform the task at hand. The following code fragment shows how to initialize a `SqlCommand` object:

```
Dim objCommand As SqlCommand = New SqlCommand()
```

When using data adapters and datasets there isn't much call for using command objects on their own. They will mainly be used for executing a particular delete, insert, or update, that is what you will cover in this chapter. You can also use command objects with a data reader. A *data reader* is an alternative to a `DataSet` that uses fewer system resources, but provides far less flexibility. In this book, you will concentrate on using the `DataSet` because it is the most common and useful of the two.

The Connection Property

There are certain properties that must be set on the `SqlCommand` object before you can execute the query. The first of these properties is the `Connection` property. This property is set to a `SqlConnection` object, as shown in the next code fragment.

```
objCommand.Connection = objConnection
```

For the command to execute successfully, the connection must be open at the time of execution.

The CommandText Property

The next property that must be set is the `CommandText` property. This property specifies the SQL string or stored procedure to be executed. Most databases require that you place all *string* values in single quote marks as shown here:

```
Dim objConnection As SqlConnection = New _
                    SqlConnection("server=(local);database=pubs;user
id=sa;password=")
Dim objCommand As SqlCommand = New SqlCommand()
objCommand.Connection = objConnection
```

```
objCommand.CommandText = "INSERT INTO authors " & _
                    "(au_id, au_lname, au_fname, contract) " & _
                    "VALUES('123-45-6789', 'Barnes', 'David', true)"
```

The INSERT statement is a very simple one that means: "Insert a new row into the authors table. In the au_id column put '123-45-6789', in the au_lname column put 'Barnes', in the au_fname column put 'David', and in the contract column put '1'."

This is the basic way that INSERT statements work in SQL. You have INSERT INTO followed by a table name. You then have a series of column names in parenthesis. You then have the VALUES keyword followed by a set of values, to be inserted into the columns that you've just named and in the same order.

This assumes that you know the values to be inserted when you are writing the program. This is very unlikely in most cases. Fortunately, you can create commands with parameters and then set the values of these parameters separately. Let's have a look at how to use parameters.

The Parameters Collection

Placeholders are variables prefixed with an "at" (@) sign in the SQL statement that get filled in by parameters. So if you wanted to update the authors table in the same way as above, but didn't know the values at design time, you would do this:

```
Dim objConnection As SqlConnection = New _
                    SqlConnection("server=(local);database=pubs;user
id=sa;password=")
Dim objCommand As SqlCommand = New SqlCommand()
objCommand.Connection = objConnection
objCommand.CommandText = "INSERT INTO authors " & _
                    "(au_id, au_lname, au_fname, contract) " & _
                    "VALUES(@au_id,@au_lname,@au_fname,@au_contract)"
```

Here, instead of providing values, you provided placeholders. Placeholders always start with an @ symbol. They do not need to be named after the database column that they represent, but it is often easier if they are and it helps to self-document your code.

What you need to do next is to create parameters that will be used to insert the values into the placeholders when the SQL statement is executed. You need to create and add parameters to the Parameters collection of the SqlCommand object. *Parameters* here refers to the parameters required to provide data to your SQL statement or stored procedure, and *not* the parameters that are required to be passed to a method.

You can access the Parameters collection of the SqlCommand object by specifying the Parameters property. Once you access the Parameters collection, you can use its properties and methods to create one or more parameters in the collection. The easiest way to add a parameter to a command is demonstrated in the following example:

```
Dim objConnection As SqlConnection = New _
                    SqlConnection("server=(local);database=pubs;user
id=sa;password=")
Dim objCommand As SqlCommand = New SqlCommand()
objCommand.Connection = objConnection
```

```
objCommand.CommandText = "INSERT INTO authors " & _
                         "(au_id, au_lname, au_fname, contract) " & _
                         "VALUES(@au_id,@au_lname,@au_fname,@au_contract)"
objCommand.Parameters.Add("@au_id", txtAuId.Text)
objCommand.Parameters.Add("@au_lname", txtLastName.Text)
objCommand.Parameters.Add("@au_fname", txtFirstName.Text)
objCommand.Parameters.Add("@contract", chkContract.Checked)
```

The Add method here accepts the name of the parameter and the object that you wish to add. In this case, you are using the Text property of various TextBox objects on a (fictitious) form for most of the columns. For the Contract column you use the Checked property of a CheckBox on the same form.

The ExecuteNonQuery Method

Finally, you can execute the command. To do this, the connection needs to be opened. You can invoke the ExecuteNonQuery method of the SqlCommand object. This method executes the SQL statement and causes the data to be inserted into the database. It then returns the number of rows that were affected by the query—which can be a useful way to check that the command worked as expected. To complete our code fragment, you need to open the connection, execute the query, and close the connection again.

```
Dim objConnection As SqlConnection = New _
                         SqlConnection("server=(local);database=pubs;user
id=sa;password=")
Dim objCommand As SqlCommand = New SqlCommand()
objCommand.Connection = objConnection
objCommand.CommandText = "INSERT INTO authors " & _
                         "(au_id, au_lname, au_fname, contract) " & _
                         "VALUES(@au_id,@au_lname,@au_fname,@au_contract)"
objCommand.Parameters.Add("@au_id", txtAuId.Text)
objCommand.Parameters.Add("@au_lname", txtLastName.Text)
objCommand.Parameters.Add("@au_fname", txtFirstName.Text)
objCommand.Parameters.Add("@contract", chkContract.Checked)
objConnection.Open()
objCommand.ExecuteNonQuery())
objConnection.Close()
```

SqlDataAdapter

The SqlDataAdapter class is very similar to the OleDbDataAdapter that you configured with wizards in the previous chapter. The main difference is that the OleDbDataAdapter can access any data source that supports OLE DB, while the SqlDataAdapter supports only SQL Server databases. You can use them in a very similar way though—you can configure a SqlDataAdapter using wizards, just as you configured a OleDbDataAdapter in the previous chapter (provided you are accessing a SQL Server data source). In this chapter, you look at how to configure and use SqlDataAdapter in code, but these guidelines also apply to the OleDbDataAdapter.

Data adapters act as a bridge between your data source and in-memory data objects such as the DataSet. To access the data source they use the command objects you've just looked at. These command objects are associated with connections, so the data adapter relies on command and connection objects to access and manipulate the data source.

The `SqlDataAdapter` class's `SelectCommand` property is used to hold a `SqlCommand` that retrieves data from the data source. The data adapter then places the result of the query into a `DataSet` or `DataTable`. The `SqlDataAdapter` also has `UpdateCommand`, `DeleteCommand`, and `InsertCommand` properties. These are also `SqlCommand` objects used to write the changes made to a `DataSet` or `DataTable` back to the data source. This may all seem complicated, but in fact the tools are really easy to use. You learned enough SQL in the previous chapter to write a `SelectCommand`, and there are tools called *command builders* that you can use to automatically create the other commands based on this.

Take a look at the `SelectCommand` property and then look at how you can create commands for updating, deleting, and inserting records.

The SelectCommand Property

The `SqlDataAdapter` class's `SelectCommand` property is used to fill a `DataSet` with data from a SQL Server database, as shown in Figure 16-1.

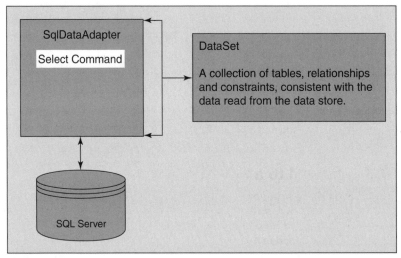

Figure 16-1

When you read data from the data store, you must set the `SelectCommand` property of the `SqlDataAdapter` class first. This property is a `SqlCommand` object and is used to specify what data to select and how to select that data. Therefore, the `SelectCommand` property has properties of its own and you need to set them just as you would set properties on a normal command. You've already seen the following properties of the `SqlCommand` object:

❑   `Connection`: Sets the `OleDbConnection` object to be used to access the data store.

❑   `CommandText`: Sets the SQL statements or stored procedure name used to select the data.

In the previous examples of `SqlCommand` objects, you used straight SQL statements. If you want to use stored procedures, you need to be aware of an additional property, `CommandType`, which sets a value that determines how the `CommandText` property is interpreted.

In this chapter you are going to concentrate on SQL statements, but stored procedures are often useful too—particularly, if they already exist in the database. If you want to use one, then set the `CommandText` property to the name of the stored procedure (remember to enclose it in quote marks because the compiler treats this as a string) and set the `CommandType` property to `CommandType.StoredProcedure`.

Setting SelectCommand to a SQL String

Take a look at how you set these properties in code. The code fragment below shows the typical settings for these properties when executing a SQL string:

```
' Declare a SqlDataAdapter object...
Dim objDataAdapter As New SqlDataAdapter()

' Assign a new SqlCommand to the SelectCommand property
objDataAdapter.SelectCommand = New SqlCommand()

' Set the SelectCommand properties...
objDataAdapter.SelectCommand.Connection = objConnection
objDataAdapter.SelectCommand.CommandText = _
    "SELECT au_lname, au_fname FROM authors " & _
    "ORDER BY au_lname, au_fname"
```

The first thing that this code fragment does is to declare a `SqlDataAdapter` object. This object has a `SelectCommand` property set to a `SqlCommand`—you just need to set that command's properties. You set the properties by first setting the `Connection` property to a valid connection object—one that already have been created before the code that you see here. Next, you set the `CommandText` property to your SQL `SELECT` statement.

Setting SelectCommand to a Stored Procedure

This next code fragment shows how you could set these properties when you execute a *stored procedure*. A stored procedure is a group of SQL statements that are stored in the database under a unique name and are executed as a unit. The stored procedure in this example (`usp_select_author_titles`) uses the same SQL statement that you used in the previous code fragment:

```
' Declare a SqlDataAdapter object...
Dim objDataAdapter As New SqlDataAdapter()

' Assign a new SqlCommand to the SelectCommand property
objDataAdapter.SelectCommand = New SqlCommand()

' Set the SelectCommand properties...
objDataAdapter.SelectCommand.Connection = objConnection
objDataAdapter.SelectCommand.CommandText = "usp_select_author_titles"
objDataAdapter.SelectCommand.CommandType = CommandType.StoredProcedure
```

The `CommandText` property now specifies the name of the stored procedure that you want to execute instead of the SQL string that was specified in the last example. Also notice the `CommandType` property. In the first example, you did not change this property because its default value is `CommandType.Text`—which is what you need to execute in SQL statements. In this example, it is set to a value of `CommandType.StoredProcedure`, which indicates that the `CommandText` property contains the name of a stored procedure to be executed.

Using Command Builders to Create the Other Commands

The `SelectCommand` is all you need to transfer data from the database into your `DataSet`. Once you've let your users make changes to the `DataSet`, you will want to write the changes back to the database. You can do this by setting up command objects with the SQL for inserting, deleting, and updating. Alternatively, you can use stored procedures. Both of these solutions require knowledge of SQL outside the scope of this book. Fortunately, there is an easier way—you can use command builders to create these commands. It only takes one more line:

```
' Declare a SqlDataAdapter object...
Dim objDataAdapter As New SqlDataAdapter()

' Assign a new SqlCommand to the SelectCommand property
objDataAdapter.SelectCommand = New SqlCommand()

' Set the SelectCommand properties...
objDataAdapter.SelectCommand.Connection = objConnection
objDataAdapter.SelectCommand.CommandText = "usp_select_author_titles"
objDataAdapter.SelectCommand.CommandType = CommandType.StoredProcedure
' automatically create update/delete/insert commands
Dim objCommandBuilder As SqlCommandBuilder = New SqlCommandBuilder
                                            (objDataAdapter)
```

Now you can use this `SqlDataAdapter` to write changes back to a database. You will look more at this later in this chapter. For know, look at the method that gets data from the database to the `DataSet` in the first place—the `Fill` method.

The Fill Method

You use the `Fill` method to populate a `DataSet` object with the data that the `SqlDataAdapter` object retrieves from the data store using its `SelectCommand`. However, before you do this, you must first initialize a `DataSet` object. Let's carry on with our previous example, however, because you don't need to use the command builder for this, you will leave it out:

```
' Declare a SqlDataAdapter object...
Dim objDataAdapter As New SqlDataAdapter()

' Assign a new SqlCommand to the SelectCommand property
objDataAdapter.SelectCommand = New SqlCommand()

' Set the SelectCommand properties...
objDataAdapter.SelectCommand.Connection = objConnection
objDataAdapter.SelectCommand.CommandText = "usp_select_author_titles"
objDataAdapter.SelectCommand.CommandType = CommandType.StoredProcedure
Dim objDataSet as DataSet = New DataSet()
```

Now you have a `DataSet` and a `SqlDataAdapter`, you can fill our `DataSet` with data. The `Fill` method has several overloaded versions, but we will be discussing the one most commonly used. The syntax for the `Fill` method is shown below:

```
SqlDataAdapter.Fill( DataSet,  string)
```

The *DataSet* argument specifies a valid `DataSet` object that will be populated with data. The *string* argument gives the name you want the table to have in the `DataSet`—remember that one `DataSet` can contain many tables. You can use any name you like, but usually it's best to use the name of the table that the data has come from in the database. This helps to self-document your code and also makes the code easier to maintain.

The following code fragment shows how you invoke the `Fill` method. The string `"authors"` is specified as the *string* argument. This is the name of the table in the data source. It is also the name you use when manipulating the in-memory version of the table:

```
' Declare a SqlDataAdapter object...
Dim objDataAdapter As New SqlDataAdapter()

' Set the SelectCommand properties...
objDataAdapter.SelectCommand.Connection = objConnection
objDataAdapter.SelectCommand.CommandText = "usp_select_author_titles"
objDataAdapter.SelectCommand.CommandType = CommandType.StoredProcedure
Dim objDataSet as DataSet = New DataSet()
' Fill the DataSet object with data...
objDataAdapter.Fill(objDataSet, "authors")
```

The `Fill` method uses the `SelectCommand.Connection` property to connect to the database. If the connection is already open, then the data adapter will use it to execute the `SelectCommand` and leave it open after it's finished. If the connection is closed then the data adapter will open it, execute the `SelectCommand`, and then close it again.

You now have the data in memory, and can start manipulating it independent of the data source. Notice that the `DataSet` class does not have `Sql` at the start of its class name. This is because you can use a `DataSet` to contain just about any data, regardless of what data source it came from. The `DataSet` is not in the `System.Data.SqlClient` namespace, it is in the parent `System.Data` namespace. The classes in this namespace are primarily concerned with manipulating data in memory, rather than obtaining data from any particular data source. Let's have a look at two of the classes in this namespace—the `DataSet` and the `DataView`.

The DataSet Class

The `DataSet` class is used to store data retrieved from a data store and stores that data in memory on the client. The `DataSet` object contains a collection of tables, relationships, and constraints that are consistent with the data read from the data store. It acts as a lightweight database engine enabling you to store tables, edit data, and run queries against it using a `DataView` object.

The data in a `DataSet` is actually disconnected from the data store and you can operate on the data independently from the data store. You can manipulate the data in a `DataSet` object by adding, updating, and deleting the records. You can then apply these changes back to the data store using a data adapter.

The data in a `DataSet` object is persisted as Extensible Markup Language (XML) (which you will discuss in detail in Chapter 18), meaning that you can save a `DataSet` as a file or easily pass it over a network. The XML is shielded from you as a developer and you should never need to edit the XML directly. All editing of the XML is done through the properties and methods of the `DataSet` class. Many developers like using XML and will sometimes choose to manipulate the XML representation of a `DataSet` directly, but this is not essential.

Like any XML document, a `DataSet` can have a schema. When you generated a typed dataset in the previous chapter, an XML Schema Definition (XSD) file was added to the Solution Explorer, as shown in Figure 16-2.

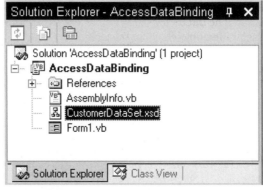

Figure 16-2

This file is an XML schema that describes the structure of the data that the `CustomerDataSet` would hold. From this, Visual Studio .NET was able to create a class that inherited from `DataSet` and that used this particular schema. A `DataSet` schema contains information about the tables, relationships, and constraints stored in the `DataSet`. Again, this is shielded from you and you do not need to know XML to work with a `DataSet`.

Since the `DataSet` contains the actual data retrieved from a data store, you can bind the `DataSet` to a control or controls to have them display (and allow editing of) the data in the `DataSet`. You did this a bit in the previous chapter and you will see more later on in this chapter.

DataView

The `DataView` class is typically used for sorting, filtering, searching, editing, and navigating the data from a `DataSet`. A `DataView` is *bindable*, meaning that it can be bound to controls in the same way that the `DataSet` can be bound to controls. Again, you learn more about data binding in code later in this chapter.

A `DataSet` can contain a number of `DataTable` objects. When you use the `SqlDataAdapter` class's `Fill` method to add data to a `DataSet`, you are actually creating a `DataTable` object inside the `DataSet`. The `DataView` provides a custom view of a `DataTable`—you can sort or filter the rows, for example, as you can in a SQL query.

You can create a `DataView` from the data contained in a `DataTable` that contains only the data that you want to display. For example, if the data in a `DataTable` contains all authors sorted by last name and first name, you can create a `DataView` that contains all authors sorted by first name and then last name. Or if you wanted, you could create a `DataView` that only contained last names or certain names.

Although you can view the data in a `DataView` in ways different from the underlying `DataTable`, it is still the same data. Changes made to a `DataView` affect the underlying `DataTable` automatically and changes made to the underlying `DataTable` will automatically affect any `DataView` objects that are viewing that `DataTable`.

The constructor for the `DataView` class initializes a new instance of the `DataView` class and accepts the `DataTable` as an argument. The following code fragment declares a `DataView` object and initializes it using the `authors` table from the `DataSet` named `objDataSet`. Notice that the code accesses the `Tables` collection of the `DataSet` object by specifying the `Tables` property and the table name:

```
' Set the DataView object to the DataSet object...
Dim objDataView = New DataView(objDataSet.Tables("authors"))
```

The Sort Property

Once a `DataView` has been initialized and is viewing the data, you can alter the view of that data. For example, suppose you want to sort the data in a different order than in the `DataSet`. To sort the data in a `DataView`, you set the `Sort` property and specify the column or columns that are to be sorted. The following code fragment below sorts the data in a `DataView` by the author's first name and then last name:

```
objDataView.Sort = "au_fname, au_lname"
```

Notice that this is the same syntax as the `ORDER BY` clause in a SQL `SELECT` statement. Like SQL `ORDER BY` clause, sorting operations on a `DataView` are always performed in an ascending order by default. If you want to perform the sort in descending order, you would need to specify the `DESC` keyword as shown in the next code fragment:

```
objDataView.Sort = "au_fname, au_lname DESC"
```

The RowFilter Property

When you have an initialized `DataView`, you can filter the rows of data that it will contain. This is very similar to specifying a `WHERE` clause in a SQL `SELECT` statement—only rows that match the criteria will remain in the view. The underlying data is not affected, though. The `RowFilter` property specifies the criteria that should be applied on the `DataView`. The syntax is very similar to the SQL `WHERE` clause. It contains at least a column name followed by an operator and the value. If the value is a string, it must be enclosed in single quote marks as shown in the code fragment below, which retrieves only the authors whose last name is `Green`:

```
' Set the DataView object to the DataSet object...
objDataView = New DataView(objDataSet.Tables("authors"))
objDataView.RowFilter = "au_lname = 'Green'"
```

If you want to retrieve all rows of authors except those whose last name is `Green`, you would specify the "not equal to" operator as shown in this example:

```
' Set the DataView object to the DataSet object...
objDataView = New DataView(objDataSet.Tables("authors"))
objDataView.RowFilter = "au_lname <> 'Green'"
```

You can also specify more complex filters as you could in SQL. For example, you can combine several criteria together using an AND operator:

```
objDataView.RowFilter = "au_lname <> 'Green' AND au_fname LIKE 'D*'"
```

This will return the authors whose last name is Green and whose first name begins with D.

The Find Method

If you want to search for a specific row of data in a DataView, you invoke the Find method. The Find method searches for data in the sort key column of the DataView. Therefore, before invoking the Find method you first need to sort the DataView on the column that contains the data that you want to find. The column that the DataView is sorted on becomes the sort key column in a DataView object.

For example, suppose you want to find the author who has a first name Ann. You would need to sort the DataView by first name to set this column as the sort key column in the DataView and then invoke the Find method as shown in the following code fragment:

```
Dim inPosition as Integer
objDataView.Sort = "au_fname"
intPosition = objDataView.Find("Ann")
```

If it finds a match, the Find method returns the position of the record within the DataView. Otherwise, the DataView returns a -1, indicating that no match was found. If the Find method finds a match, it stops looking and only returns the position of the first match. If you know there is more than one match in your data store, you could filter the data in the DataView—something covered shortly.

The Find method is not case sensitive, meaning that in order to find the author who has a first name Ann, you could enter either the text Ann or ann.

The Find method looks for an exact case-insensitive match, this means that you must enter the whole word or words of the text that you are looking for. For example, suppose you are looking for the author who has the last name of Del Castillo. You cannot enter Del and expect to find a match—you must enter all of the words that make up the author's name. Notice that the following example specifies all lowercase letters, which is perfectly fine:

```
objDataView.Sort = "au_lname"
intPosition = objDataView.Find("del castillo")
```

You have seen that a DataView can be sorted on more than one column at a time. If you want to do this, you need to supply an array of values to the Find method instead of just a single value. Let's say you want to find where Simon Watts appears in the DataView, if at all:

```
Dim intPosition As Integer
Dim arrValues(1) As Object
objDataView.Sort = "au_fname, au_lname"

' Find the author named "Simon Watts".
arrValues(0)= "Simon"
arrValues(1) = "Watts"
intPosition = objDataView.Find(arrValues)
```

The ADO.NET Classes in Action

You've now looked at the basics of the ADO.NET classes and how they allow you to retrieve and insert data into SQL Server. No doubt your head is spinning from information overload at this point, so the best way to ensure that you understand how to use all of the objects, methods, and properties that you have been looking at is to actually use them. In the next two *Try It Outs*, you'll see how to exploit the power of the DataSet object to expose data to your users. You may find that you'll want to come back and reread the previous section after you've completed the *Try It Outs*—this will help to clarify ADO.NET in your mind.

The first *Try It Out* will implement the SqlConnection, SqlDataAdapter, and DataSet classes. You will see first hand how to use these classes in a simple example where you need to retrieve read-only data and you will be displaying that data in a data grid. In fact, what you do here will be very similar to the example in the previous chapter, but you will be doing it in code instead of using wizards.

> *When writing your programs, you may often use a combination of wizards and coding to create powerful programs quickly and easily. The components created in the previous chapter by drag and drop can be manipulated in code in exactly the same way as objects created in code. In the previous chapter you used wizards almost all the time. In this chapter you will concentrate on code.*

Examining a DataSet Example

Before you dive into the details of creating the program, take a look at the data and the relationships of the data that you want to display. The data that you want comes from the pubs database in SQL Server 2000. However, if you are using SQL Server 7.0 or MSDE you should be seeing exactly the same data.

You display a list of authors, their book titles, and the price of their books. Figure 16-3 shows the tables that this data resides in and also the relationship of the tables.

You should display the author's first and last names, which reside in the authors table, and the book title and price of the book, which reside in the titles table. Because an author can have one or more books and a book can have one or more authors, the titles table is joined to the authors table via a *relationship table* called titleauthor. This table contains the many-to-many relationship of authors to books.

Having looked at the relationship of the tables and knowing what data you want, take a look at the SQL SELECT statement that you need to create to get this data:

```
SELECT au_lname, au_fname, title, price
FROM authors
JOIN titleauthor ON authors.au_id = titleauthor.au_id
JOIN titles ON titleauthor.title_id = titles.title_id
ORDER BY au_lname, au_fname
```

The first line of the SELECT statement shows the columns that you want to select. The second line shows the main table that you are selecting data from—which is authors.

The third line joins the titleauthor table to the authors table using the au_id column. Therefore, when you select a row of data from the authors table, you will get every row in the titleauthor table that matches the au_id in the authors table.

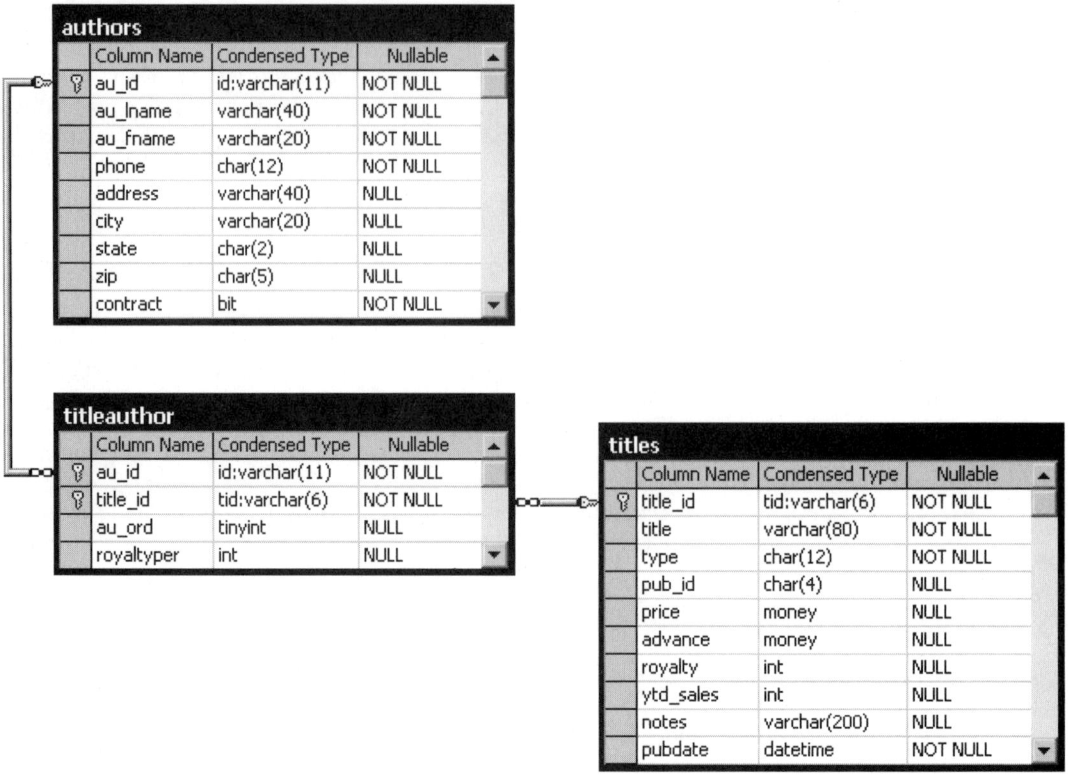

Figure 16-3

The fourth line joins the `titles` table on the `titleauthor` table using the `title_id` column. Hence, for every row of data that is selected from the `titleauthor` table, you will select the corresponding row of data from the titles table. The last line of the `SELECT` statement sorts the data by the author's last name and first name using the `ORDER BY` clause. Now, create the project.

Try It Out   DataSet Example

1. Create a new Windows Application called **DatasetExample.**

2. Set the following properties of the form:
   - ❑ Set Size to 600, 230
   - ❑ Set StartPosition to CenterScreen
   - ❑ Set Text to Bound DataSet

3. From the Toolbox, locate the DataGrid control under the Windows Forms tab and drag it onto your form. Set the properties of the DataGrid as shown:
   - ❑ Set Name to grdAuthorTitles
   - ❑ Set Location to 0, 0

❑ Set Size to 592, 203

❑ Set Anchor to Top, Bottom, Left, Right

4. First, you need to import the required namespaces. Open up the code window for your form and add these namespaces at the very top of your code:

```
' Import Data and SqlClient namespaces...
Imports System.Data
Imports System.Data.SqlClient

Public Class Form1
    Inherits System.Windows.Forms.Form
```

5. Next, you need to declare the objects necessary to retrieve the data from the database, so add the following code. Ensure that you use a user ID and password that have been defined in your installation of SQL Server:

```
Public Class Form1
    Inherits System.Windows.Forms.Form

    Dim objConnection As SqlConnection = New _
        SqlConnection("server=(local);database=pubs;user id=sa;password=")

    Dim objDataAdapter As New SqlDataAdapter()
    Dim objDataSet As DataSet = New DataSet()
```

Notice your connection string in the constructor for this object. You will need to change the server *parameter to point to the machine where SQL Server is running if it is not running on your local machine. You will also need to change the* user id *and* password *parameters to use a valid login that has been provided or that you have set up yourself. If the* user id *that you use has no password assigned, then specify the* password *argument, but do not enter anything for the actual password. For example,* password=; .

6. To add a handler for the form's Load event, select (Form1 Events) in the Class Name combo box and then select Load in the Method Name combo box. Insert the following code:

```
Private Sub Form1_Load(ByVal sender As System.Object, _
                      ByVal e As System.EventArgs) Handles MyBase.Load
    ' Set the SelectCommand properties...
    objDataAdapter.SelectCommand = New SqlCommand()
    objDataAdapter.SelectCommand.Connection = objConnection
    objDataAdapter.SelectCommand.CommandText = _
        "SELECT au_lname, au_fname, title, price " & _
        "FROM authors " & _
        "JOIN titleauthor ON authors.au_id = titleauthor.au_id " & _
        "JOIN titles ON titleauthor.title_id = titles.title_id " & _
        "ORDER BY au_lname, au_fname"
    objDataAdapter.SelectCommand.CommandType = CommandType.Text

    ' Open the database connection...
    objConnection.Open()
```

```
    ' Fill the DataSet object with data...
    objDataAdapter.Fill(objDataSet, "authors")

    ' Close the database connection...
    objConnection.Close()

    ' Set the DataGrid properties to bind it to our data...
    grdAuthorTitles.DataSource = objDataSet
    grdAuthorTitles.DataMember = "authors"

        ' Clean up
        objDataAdapter = Nothing
        objConnection = Nothing
    End Sub
```

7.   Run the project to see what you get. You should see results similar to Figure 16-4.

Figure 16-4

8.   Note that the DataGrid control has built-in sorting capabilities. If you click a column header, the data in the grid will be sorted by that column in ascending order. If you click the same column again the data will be sorted in descending order.

It should be noted that error handling has been omitted from the exercise to preserve space. You should always add the appropriate error handling to your code. Review Chapter 9 for error-handling techniques.

How It Works

To begin with, you import the following namespaces:

```
' Import Data and SqlClient namespaces...
Imports System.Data
Imports System.Data.SqlClient
```

Remember that the System.Data namespace is required for the DataSet and DataView classes, and that the System.Data.SqlClient namespace is required for the SqlConnection,

SqlDataAdapter, SqlCommand, and SqlParameter classes. You will only be using a subset of the classes just mentioned in this example, although you do require both namespaces.

Then you declare the objects that are necessary to retrieve the data from the database. These objects are declared with class-level scope so you place those declarations just inside the class:

```
Public Class Form1
    Inherits System.Windows.Forms.Form

    Dim objConnection As SqlConnection = New _
        SqlConnection("server=(local);database=pubs;user id=sa;password=")

    Dim objDataAdapter As New SqlDataAdapter()
    Dim objDataSet As DataSet = New DataSet()
```

The first object that you declare is a SqlConnection object. Remember that this object establishes a connection to your data store, which in this case is SQL Server.

The next object that you declare is a SqlDataAdapter object. This object is used to read data from the database and to populate the DataSet object.

Then, of course, the last object in your declarations is the DataSet object, which serves as the container for your data. Remember that this object stores all data in memory and is not connected to the data store.

In this particular example, there was no need to give these objects class-level scope. You only use them in one method and they could have been declared there. However, if your application enabled users to write changes back to the database then you would want to use the same connection and data adapter objects for both reading and writing to the database. In that case, having class-level scope would be really useful.

With your objects defined, you place some code to populate the DataSet in the initialization section of the form. Your SqlDataAdapter object is responsible for retrieving the data from the database. Therefore, you set the SelectCommand property of this object. This property is a SqlCommand object so the SelectCommand has all the properties of an independent SqlCommand object:

```
' Set the SelectCommand properties...
objDataAdapter.SelectCommand = New SqlCommand()
objDataAdapter.SelectCommand.Connection = objConnection
objDataAdapter.SelectCommand.CommandText = _
    "SELECT au_lname, au_fname, title, price " & _
    "FROM authors " & _
    "JOIN titleauthor ON authors.au_id = titleauthor.au_id " & _
    "JOIN titles ON titleauthor.title_id = titles.title_id " & _
    "ORDER BY au_lname, au_fname"
```

The first thing that you do here is to initialize the SelectCommand by initializing an instance of the SqlCommand class and assigning it to the SelectCommand property.

Then you set the Connection property to your connection object. This property sets the connection to be used to communicate with your data store.

The `CommandText` property is then set to the SQL string that you want to execute. This property contains the SQL string or stored procedure to be executed to retrieve your data. In this case you are using a SQL string, which was explained in detail in the `SQLDataAdapter` section earlier on.

Once all of the properties have been set, you can open our connection, fill the dataset, and then close the connection again. You open the connection by executing the `Open` method of our `SqlConnection` object:

```
' Open the database connection...
objConnection.Open()
```

You then invoke the `Fill` method of the `SqlDataAdapter` object to retrieve the data and fill your `DataSet` object. In the parameters for the `Fill` method, you specify the `DataSet` object to use and the table name—you use authors even though you are actually retrieving data from several tables:

```
' Fill the DataSet object with data...
objDataAdapter.Fill(objDataSet, "authors")
```

Once you have filled your `DataSet` object with data, you need to close the database connection and you do this by invoking the `Close` method of the `SqlConnection` object:

```
' Close the database connection...
objConnection.Close()
```

Then you set some properties of the `DataGrid` in order to bind your data to it. The first of these properties is the `DataSource` property. This property sets the data source for the `DataGrid` telling it where to get its data:

```
' Set the DataGrid properties to bind it to our data...
grdAuthorTitles.DataSource = objDataSet
grdAuthorTitles.DataMember = "authors"
```

The `DataMember` property sets the table in the `DataSource` and here you have set it to `authors`, which is the table used in your `DataSet` object.

Then you cleanup the objects that are no longer used to free memory.

```
' Clean up
objDataAdapter = Nothing
objConnection = Nothing
```

What happened when you ran the example was that the DataGrid control read the schema information from the `DataSet` object and created the correct number of columns for your data in the DataGrid control. It has also used the column names in the schema as the column names for the grid and each column has the same default width. The DataGrid has also read the entire `DataSet` object and has placed the contents into the grid.

Let's take a look at some of the `DataGrid` properties that you can use to make this a more user-friendly display of data.

Try It Out   **Changing the DataGrid Properties**

1. To make your DataGrid more user-friendly you can:

❑   Add your own column header names

❑   Adjust the width of the column that contains the book titles so that you can easily see the full title

❑   Change the color of every other row so that the data in each one stands out

❑   Make the last column in the grid (which contains the price of the books) right aligned

You can do all this by making the following modifications to your code in the `Form_Load` method:

```
' Set the DataGrid properties to bind it to our data...
grdAuthorTitles.DataSource = objDataSet
grdAuthorTitles.DataMember = "authors"
' Declare objects for the DataGrid...
Dim objDataGridTableStyle As New DataGridTableStyle()
Dim objTextCol As New DataGridTextBoxColumn()

' Set the AlternatingBackColor property...
objDataGridTableStyle.AlternatingBackColor = Color.WhiteSmoke

' Set the MappingName for the DataGridTableStyle...
objDataGridTableStyle.MappingName = "authors"

' Set the MappingName for the first column...
objTextCol.MappingName = "au_lname"
' Set the new HeaderText...
objTextCol.HeaderText = "Last Name"
' Add the column to the DataGridTableStyle...
objDataGridTableStyle.GridColumnStyles.Add(objTextCol)

' Get a new reference to the DataGridTextBoxColumn...
objTextCol = New DataGridTextBoxColumn()
' Set the MappingName for the second column...
objTextCol.MappingName = "au_fname"
' Set the new HeaderText...
objTextCol.HeaderText = "First Name"
' Add the column to the DataGridTableStyle...
objDataGridTableStyle.GridColumnStyles.Add(objTextCol)

' Get a new reference to the DataGridTextBoxColumn...
objTextCol = New DataGridTextBoxColumn()
' Set the MappingName for the third column...
objTextCol.MappingName = "title"
' Set the new HeaderText...
objTextCol.HeaderText = "Book Title"
' Set the Width of the column...
objTextCol.Width = 304
' Add the column to the DataGridTableStyle...
objDataGridTableStyle.GridColumnStyles.Add(objTextCol)
```

```
    ' Get a new reference to the DataGridTextBoxColumn...
    objTextCol = New DataGridTextBoxColumn()
    ' Set the MappingName for the fourth column...
    objTextCol.MappingName = "price"
    ' Set the new HeaderText...
    objTextCol.HeaderText = "Retail Price"
    ' Set the Alignment within the column...
    objTextCol.Alignment = HorizontalAlignment.Right
    ' Format the value to the local currency
    objTextCol.Format = "c"
    ' Add the column to the DataGridTableStyle...
    objDataGridTableStyle.GridColumnStyles.Add(objTextCol)

    ' Add the DataGridTableStyle to the DataGrid...
    grdAuthorTitles.TableStyles.Add(objDataGridTableStyle)

    ' Clean up
    objDataAdapter = Nothing
    objConnection = Nothing
End Sub
```

2. Run your project again. You should now see results similar to Figure 16-5. You can compare this figure with Figure 16-4 and see a world of difference. It's amazing what setting a few properties will do and how it makes this a more user-friendly display.

	Last Name	First Name	Book Title	Retail Price
▶	Bennet	Abraham	The Busy Executive's Database Guide	$19.99
	Blotchet-Halls	Reginald	Fifty Years in Buckingham Palace Kitchens	$11.95
	Carson	Cheryl	But Is It User Friendly?	$22.95
	DeFrance	Michel	The Gourmet Microwave	$2.99
	del Castillo	Innes	Silicon Valley Gastronomic Treats	$19.99
	Dull	Ann	Secrets of Silicon Valley	$20.00
	Green	Marjorie	The Busy Executive's Database Guide	$19.99
	Green	Marjorie	You Can Combat Computer Stress!	$2.99
	Gringlesby	Burt	Sushi, Anyone?	$14.99

Bound DataSet

Figure 16-5

How It Works

Since the DataGrid control is already populated with data at this point, you can access the table that it has drawn through the `DataGridTableStyle` class.

To start, you declare some objects that will allow you to access the table styles for the datagrid. The `DataGridTableStyle` class represents the table drawn by the DataGrid control and enables you us to customize the columns in the datagrid:

```
    ' Declare objects for the DataGrid...
    Dim objDataGridTableStyle As New DataGridTableStyle()
    Dim objTextCol As New DataGridTextBoxColumn()
```

The first thing that you do here is to alternate the background color of each row of the data. This helps them to stand out and makes it easier to see the data in each column for a single row. The `Color` structure provides a large list of color constants, as well as a few methods that can be called to generate colors:

```
' Set the AlternatingBackColor property...
objDataGridTableStyle.AlternatingBackColor = Color.WhiteSmoke
```

You now need to specify the mapping name that is used to map this table to a data source. This is the table name contained in your `DataSet` object:

```
' Set the MappingName for the DataGridTableStyle...
objDataGridTableStyle.MappingName = "authors"
```

Now you can set the properties for a particular column using the `DataGridTextBoxColumn` class. This class hosts a TextBox control in a cell of the datagrid, but it can also be used to set the column names in a DataGrid control, which is how you are using it here.

The first thing that you do is map the column name in your `DataSet` object to the column name in your datagrid by setting the `MappingName` property. Then you set the `HeaderText` property to give the column header a more meaningful name. Finally, you apply this class to the `DataGridTableStyle` object by adding it to the `GridColumnStyles` property:

```
' Set the MappingName for the first column...
objTextCol.MappingName = "au_lname"
' Set the new HeaderText...
objTextCol.HeaderText = "Last Name"
' Add the column to the DataGridTableStyle...
objDataGridTableStyle.GridColumnStyles.Add(objTextCol)
```

You repeat the same process for the next column, but you must first reinitialize your `DataGridTextBoxColumn` object as shown in the first line of code:

```
' Get a new reference to the DataGridTextBoxColumn...
objTextCol = New DataGridTextBoxColumn()
' Set the MappingName for the second column...
objTextCol.MappingName = "au_fname"
' Set the new HeaderText...
objTextCol.HeaderText = "First Name"
' Add the column to the DataGridTableStyle...
objDataGridTableStyle.GridColumnStyles.Add(objTextCol)
```

You repeat the same process for the third column. Here, however, you have an additional line of code. This column contains the title of the book, so you expand the default width of the column, which can be done by setting the `Width` property. You have specified a column width of 304 here. There is no magic process for determining the width of a column; you simply need to set it, then test your code, and make adjustments as necessary:

```
' Get a new reference to the DataGridTextBoxColumn...
objTextCol = New DataGridTextBoxColumn()
' Set the MappingName for the third column...
objTextCol.MappingName = "title"
```

```
' Set the new HeaderText...
objTextCol.HeaderText = "Book Title"
' Set the Width of the column...
objTextCol.Width = 304
' Add the column to the DataGridTableStyle...
objDataGridTableStyle.GridColumnStyles.Add(objTextCol)
```

The last column that you set here is the column for the price of a book. Since this column contains a money value you align the data in this column to the right, which can be done by setting the `Alignment` property. The `HorizontalAlignment` enumeration has three values for aligning text: `Left`, `Center`, and `Right`. You have chosen `Right` since you want your text aligned to the right of the column. Then you specify the format of the data in the column by specifying a value of `c`. This will use the culture information of the computer where the program is running to format the data in this column to the appropriate currency:

```
' Get a new reference to the DataGridTextBoxColumn...
objTextCol = New DataGridTextBoxColumn()
' Set the MappingName for the fourth column...
objTextCol.MappingName = "price"
' Set the new HeaderText...
objTextCol.HeaderText = "Retail Price"
' Set the Alignment within the column...
objTextCol.Alignment = HorizontalAlignment.Right
' Format the value to the local currency
objTextCol.Format = "c"
' Add the column to the DataGridTableStyle...
objDataGridTableStyle.GridColumnStyles.Add(objTextCol)
```

The last thing that you need to do is apply the style changes made in the `DataGridTableStyle` object to the actual DataGrid control itself. You do this by adding this object to the `TableStyles` property of the datagrid:

```
' Add the DataGridTableStyle to the DataGrid...
grdAuthorTitles.TableStyles.Add(objDataGridTableStyle)
```

You have now seen how to bind the `DataSet` object to a control, in this case a DataGrid control. In the next *Try It Out*, you will be expanding on this knowledge by binding several controls to a `DataView` object and using the `CurrencyManager` object to navigate the data in the `DataView` object. However, before you get to that, read about data binding and how you can bind data to simple controls, such as TextBox and how to navigate the records.

Data Binding

The DataGrid control is a great tool for displaying all your data at one time. You can also use it for editing, deleting, and inserting rows, provided you have the logic to write changes back to the data source. However, you often use a control to display a single-column value from one record at a time. In cases like these you need to bind individual pieces of data to simple controls, such as a textbox, and only display a single row of data at a time. This type of data binding not only gives you more control over the data, but also increases the complexities of your programs, as you must write the code to bind the data to the controls and also write the code to navigate between records. This section takes a look at what is involved in binding data to simple controls and also how to manage the data bindings.

In this discussion, *simple controls* refer to controls that can display only one item of data at a time, such as Textbox, a Button, a CheckBox, or a RadioCheck. Controls such as ComboBox, ListBox, and DataGrid can contain more than one item of data and are not considered simple controls when it comes to data binding. Generally speaking, non-simple controls have particular properties intended for binding to a data object, such as a `DataTable` or `Array`. When binding to simple controls, you are actually binding a particular item of data to a particular property. This is usually the Text property, but it does not need to be.

BindingContext and CurrencyManager

Each form has a built-in `BindingContext` object that manages the bindings of the controls on the form. Since the `BindingContext` object is already built into each form, you don't need to do anything to set it up. The `BindingContext` object manages a collection of `CurrencyManager` objects. Whenever you add a data source to a form a new `CurrencyManager` is automatically created. This makes working with data-bound controls very convenient and simple.

The `CurrencyManager` is responsible for keeping the data-bound controls in sync with their data source and with other data-bound controls that use the same data source. This ensures that all controls on the form are showing data from the same record. The `CurrencyManager` manages data from a variety of objects such as `DataSet`, `DataView`, `DataTable`, and `DataSetView`.

If you have multiple data sources in your form, you can create a `CurrencyManager` object and set a reference to the appropriate `CurrencyManager` object in the collection managed by the `BindingContext` object. You then have the capability to manage the data in the data-bound controls.

Using the `DataSet` object that you used in the previous example you can define and set a reference to the `CurrencyManager` that manages the data source containing the authors table. The following code fragment first declares an object using the `CurrencyManager` class.

Then you set your `CurrencyManager` object to your `DataSet` object (`objDataSet`) contained in the `BindingContext` object. You use the `CType` function to return an object that is explicitly converted. The `CType` function accepts two arguments: the expression to be converted and the type to which you want to convert the expression. Since you want to convert the expression to a `CurrencyManager` object, you have specified `CurrencyManager` for the type argument:

```
Dim objCurrencyManager As CurrencyManager
objCurrencyManager = _
    CType(Me.BindingContext(objDataSet), CurrencyManager)
```

Once you have a reference to the data-source object, you can manage the position of the records using the `Position` property as shown in the following example. This example advances the current record position in the `objDataSet` object by one record:

```
objCurrencyManager.Position += 1
```

If you wanted to move backward one record, you would use the following code:

```
objCurrencyManager.Position -= 1
```

To move to the first record contained in the `DataSet` object, you would use the following code:

```
objCurrencyManager.Position = 0
```

The `Count` property of the `CurrencyManager` contains the number of records in the `DataSet` object managed by the `CurrencyManager`. Therefore, in order to move to the very last record, you would use the following code:

```
objCurrencyManager.Position = objCurrencyManager.Count - 1
```

Notice that this code specified the `Count` property minus 1. Since the `Count` property contains the actual number of records and the `DataSet` object has a base index of zero you must subtract 1 from the `Count` property to get to the last record.

Binding Controls

When you bind a data source to a control, you set the `DataBindings` property for that control. This property accesses the `ControlBindingsCollection` class. This class manages the bindings for each control and it has many properties and methods. The method of interest here is the `Add` method.

The `Add` method creates a binding for the control and adds it to the `ControlBindingsCollection`. The `Add` method has three arguments and its syntax is shown here:

```
object.DataBindings.Add( propertyname,  datasource,  datamember)
```

In this syntax note the following:

❑   `object` represents a valid control on your form

❑   The *propertyname* argument represents the property of the control to be bound

❑   The *datasource* argument represents the data source to be bound and can be any valid object that contains data such as a `DataSet`, `DataView`, or `DataTable`

❑   The *datamember* argument represents the data field in the data source to be bound to this control

An example of how the `Add` method works is shown in the following code. This example binds the column name `au_fname` in the `objDataView` object to the `Text` property of a text box named `txtFirstName`:

```
txtFirstName.DataBindings.Add("Text", objDataView, "au_fname")
```

Sometimes, after a control has been bound, you may want to clear the bindings for that control. To do this you can use the `Clear` method of the `ControlBindingsCollection`. The `Clear` method clears the collection of all bindings for this control. An example of this method is shown in the following code fragment:

```
txtFirstName.DataBindings.Clear()
```

Now that you have had a look at the `BindingContext`, `CurrencyManager`, and `Control-BindingsCollection` objects, learn how all of these pieces fit and work together in a practical hands-on exercise.

Binding Example

The following *Try It Out* will demonstrate not only how to use the `BindingContext`, `CurrencyManager`, and `ControlBindingsCollection` objects, but also how to use the `DataView`, `SqlCommand`, and `SqlParameter` classes.

> *You will be using the query from the last example as the base for your new query and will display all authors' first and last names, as well as their book titles, and the prices of their books. However, this example, unlike the the last one, displays only one record at a time.*

You will use the `CurrencyManager` object to navigate the records in the `DataView` object and provide the functionality to move forward and backward, as well as to the first and last records.

Try It Out   Binding Simple Controls

1. Create a new Windows Application project called BindingExample.

2. Drag a ToolTip control from the toolbox and drop it on your form to have it added to the designer. Set the various form properties as follows:

    ❑ Set FormBorderStyle to FixedDialog

    ❑ Set MaximizeBox to False

    ❑ Set MinimizeBox to False

    ❑ Set Size to 430, 360

    ❑ Set StartPosition to CenterScreen

    ❑ Set Text to Binding Controls

3. You are going to add objects to the form, so that the form ends up looking like Figure 16-6. The steps that follow provide property settings to produce an exact replica of this form. However, the "cosmetic" properties are not important—if you wish, you can approximate the layout visually. It is crucial, however, to use the same control names as are used here in your own application.

4. Add a GroupBox control to the form. Set the GroupBox1 properties according to the following list:

    ❑ Set Location to 8, 8

    ❑ Set Size to 408, 128

    ❑ Set Text to Authors && Titles

> *Note that to have an ampersand (&) displayed in the GroupBox title you have to write &&; this is because a single & causes the character following it to be underlined.*

5. Using the table list add the required controls to `GroupBox1` and set their properties:

    ❑ Add a Label control. Name it Label1 and set Location = 8, 26; Size = 64, 16; Text = Last Name

    ❑ Add a Label control. Name it Label2 and set Location = 8, 50; Size = 64, 16; Text = First Name

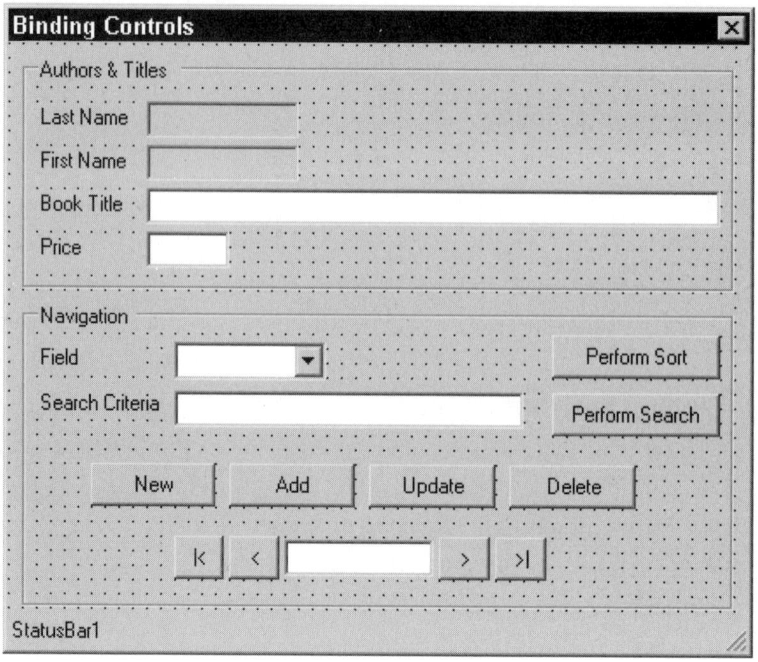

Figure 16-6

- ❏ Add a Label control. Name it Label3 and set Location = 8, 74; Size = 56, 16; Text = Book Title

- ❏ Add a Label control. Name it Label4 and set Location = 8, 98; Size = 64, 16; Text = Price

- ❏ Add a TextBox control. Name it txtLastName and set Location = 72, 24; Size = 88, 20; Text = *nothing*; ReadOnly = True

- ❏ Add a TextBox control. Name it txtFirstName and set Location = 72, 48; Size = 88, 20; Text = *nothing*; ReadOnly = True

- ❏ Add a TextBox control. Name it txtBookTitle and set Location = 72, 72; Size = 328, 20; Text = *nothing*

- ❏ Add a TextBox control. Name it txtPrice and set Location = 72, 96; Size = 48, 20; Text = *nothing*

6. Now add a second GroupBox and set its properties according to this list:

- ❏ Set Location to 8, 144

- ❏ Set Size to 408, 168

- ❏ Set Text to Navigation

7. In GroupBox2, add the following controls:

- ❏ Add a Label control. Name it Label5 and set Location = 8, 23; Size = 64, 16; Text = Field

- ❏ Add a Label control. Name it Label6 and set Location = 8, 48; Size = 80, 16; Text = Search Criteria

- ❑ Add a ComboBox control. Name it cboField and set Location = 88, 21; Size = 88, 21; DropDownStyle = DropDownList

- ❑ Add a TextBox control. Name it txtSearchCriteria and set Location = 88, 48; Size = 200, 20; Text = *nothing*

- ❑ Add a TextBox control. Name it txtRecordPosition and set Location = 152, 130; Size = 85, 20; Text = *nothing*; TabStop = False; TextAlign = Center

- ❑ Add a Button control Name it btnPerformSort and set Location = 304, 16; Size = 96, 24; Text = Perform Sort

- ❑ Add a Button control. Name it Perform Search and set Location = 304, 48; Size = 96, 24; Text = Perform Search

- ❑ Add a Button control. Name it btnNew and set Location = 40, 88; Size = 72, 24; Text = New

- ❑ Add a Button control. Name it btnAdd and set Location = 120, 88; Size = 72, 24; Text = Add

- ❑ Add a Button control. Name it btnUpdate and set Location = 200, 88; Size = 72, 24; Text = Update

- ❑ Add a Button control. Name it btnDelete and set Location = 280, 88; Size = 72, 24; Text = Delete

- ❑ Add a Button control. Name it btnMoveFirst and set Location = 88, 128; Size = 29, 24; Text = |<; ToolTip on ToolTip1 = Move First

- ❑ Add a Button control. Name it btnMovePrevious and set Location = 120, 128; Size = 29, 24; Text = <; ToolTip on ToolTip1 = Move Previous

- ❑ Add a Button control. Name it btnMoveNext and set Location = 240, 128; Size = 29, 24; Text = >; ToolTip on ToolTip1 = Move Next

- ❑ Add a Button control. Name it btnMoveLast and set Location = 272, 128; Size = 29, 24; Text = >|; ToolTip on ToolTip1 = Move Last

8. Finally, add a StatusBar control. Leave its name as the default StatusBar1 and its default location and size.

9. When you are done, your completed form should look like the one shown in Figure 16-6.

10. Again, you need to add references to the namespaces needed. To do this, switch to the code view and then insert the following lines of code at the very top:

```
' Import Data and SqlClient namespaces...
Imports System.Data
Imports System.Data.SqlClient
```

11. Next, you need to declare the objects that are global in scope to this form, so add the following code:

```
Public Class Form1
    Inherits System.Windows.Forms.Form

    ' Declare objects...
    Dim objConnection As SqlConnection = New _
```

```
            SqlConnection("server=(local);database=pubs;user id=sa;password=;")
      Dim objDataAdapter As SqlDataAdapter = New SqlDataAdapter( _
            "SELECT authors.au_id, au_lname, au_fname, " & _
            "titles.title_id, title, price " & _
            "FROM authors " & _
            "JOIN titleauthor ON authors.au_id = titleauthor.au_id " & _
            "JOIN titles ON titleauthor.title_id = titles.title_id " & _
            "ORDER BY au_lname, au_fname", objConnection)
      Dim objDataSet As DataSet
      Dim objDataView As DataView
      Dim objCurrencyManager As CurrencyManager
```

Be sure to update the connection string to match your settings for the user id *and* password, *and also set the* Server *to the machine where SQL Server is running if it is not your local machine.*

12. The first procedure that you need to create is the `FillDataSetAndView` procedure. This procedure, along with the following ones, will be called in your initialization code. Add the following code to the form's class just below your object declarations:

```
Private Sub FillDataSetAndView()
    ' Initialize a new instance of the DataSet object...
    objDataSet = New DataSet()

    ' Fill the DataSet object with data...
    objDataAdapter.Fill(objDataSet, "authors")

    ' Set the DataView object to the DataSet object...
    objDataView = New DataView(objDataSet.Tables("authors"))

    ' Set our CurrencyManager object to the DataView object...
    objCurrencyManager = CType(Me.BindingContext(objDataView), CurrencyManager)
End Sub
```

13. The next procedure that you need to create is one that will actually bind the controls on your form to your `DataView` object:

```
Private Sub BindFields()
    ' Clear any previous bindings...
    txtLastName.DataBindings.Clear()
    txtFirstName.DataBindings.Clear()
    txtBookTitle.DataBindings.Clear()
    txtPrice.DataBindings.Clear()

    ' Add new bindings to the DataView object...
    txtLastName.DataBindings.Add("Text", objDataView, "au_lname")
    txtFirstName.DataBindings.Add("Text", objDataView, "au_fname")
    txtBookTitle.DataBindings.Add("Text", objDataView, "title")
    txtPrice.DataBindings.Add("Text", objDataView, "price")

    ' Display a ready status...
    StatusBar1.Text = "Ready"
End Sub
```

14. Now you need a procedure that will display the current record position on your form:

```
Private Sub ShowPosition()
    'Always format the number in the txtPrice field to include cents
    Try
        txtPrice.Text = Format(CType(txtPrice.Text, Decimal), "##0.00")
    Catch e As System.Exception
        txtPrice.Text = "0"
        txtPrice.Text = Format(CType(txtPrice.Text, Decimal), "##0.00")
    End Try
    ' Display the current position and the number of records
    txtRecordPosition.Text = objCurrencyManager.Position + 1 & _
    " of " & objCurrencyManager.Count()
End Sub
```

15. You've added some powerful procedures to your form. But at the moment there is no code to call them. You want these procedures, as well as some other code, to execute every time the form loads. So return to the Form Designer, double-click the Form Designer, and add the following to the `Form_Load` method (note that you must click on an area outside of the GroupBox controls):

```
Private Sub Form1_Load(ByVal sender As System.Object, _
                    ByVal e As System.EventArgs) Handles MyBase.Load
    ' Add items to the combo box...
    cboField.Items.Add("Last Name")
    cboField.Items.Add("First Name")
    cboField.Items.Add("Book Title")
    cboField.Items.Add("Price")

    ' Make the first item selected...
    cboField.SelectedIndex = 0

    ' Fill the DataSet and bind the fields...
    FillDataSetAndView()
    BindFields()

    ' Show the current record position...
    ShowPosition()
End Sub
```

16. Next, you'll add the code for your navigation buttons. You will need to switch back and forth between the design and code views, double-clicking each button and then adding the code or you can select the buttons in the Class Name combo box and then select the `Click` event in the Method Name combo box. Add the code to the procedure for the `btnMoveFirst` button first:

```
Private Sub btnMoveFirst_Click(ByVal sender As Object, _
            ByVal e As System.EventArgs) Handles btnMoveFirst.Click
    ' Set the record position to the first record...
    objCurrencyManager.Position = 0

    ' Show the current record position...
    ShowPosition()
End Sub
```

17. Add code to the `btnMovePrevious` button next:

```
Private Sub btnMovePrevious_Click(ByVal sender As Object, _
         ByVal e As System.EventArgs) Handles btnMovePrevious.Click
    ' Move to the previous record...
    objCurrencyManager.Position -= 1

    ' Show the current record position...
    ShowPosition()
End Sub
```

18. The next procedure that you want to add code to is the `btnMoveNext` procedure:

```
Private Sub btnMoveNext_Click(ByVal sender As Object, _
         ByVal e As System.EventArgs) Handles btnMoveNext.Click
    ' Move to the next record...
    objCurrencyManager.Position += 1

    ' Show the current record position...
    ShowPosition()
End Sub
```

19. The final navigation procedure that you need to code is the `btnMoveLast` procedure:

```
Private Sub btnMoveLast_Click(ByVal sender As Object, _
         ByVal e As System.EventArgs) Handles btnMoveLast.Click
    ' Set the record position to the last record...
    objCurrencyManager.Position = objCurrencyManager.Count - 1

    ' Show the current record position...
    ShowPosition()
End Sub
```

20. At this point you have entered a lot of code and are probably anxious to see the results of your work. Run the project to see how your `DataView` object gets bound to the controls on the form and to see the `CurrencyManager` object at work as you navigate through the records.

Once your form displays, you should see results similar to Figure 16-7. The only buttons that work are the navigation buttons, which change the current record position. Test your form by navigating to the next and previous records and moving to the last record and the first record. Each time you move to a new record the text box between the navigation buttons will be updated to display the current record.

Once on the first record, you can try to move to the previous record but nothing will happen because you are already on the first record. Likewise, you can move to the last record and try to navigate to the next record and nothing will happen because you are already on the last record.

If you hover your mouse pointer over the navigation buttons, you will see a ToolTip indicating what each button is for. This just provides a nice user interface for your users.

It should be noted that error handling has been omitted from the exercise to preserve space. You should always add the appropriate error handling to your code. Please review Chapter 9 for error-handling techniques.

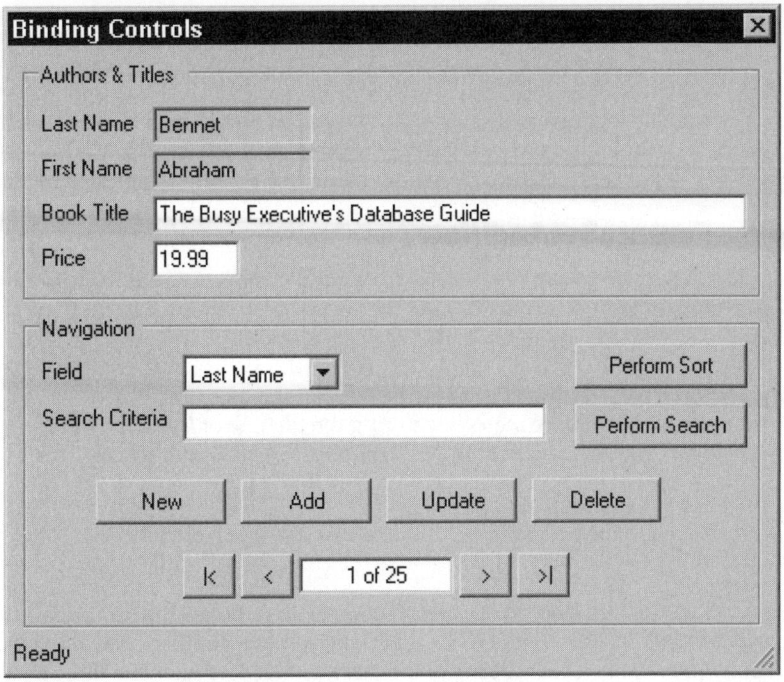

Figure 16-7

How It Works: Namespaces and Object Declaration

As usual you import the `System.Data` and `System.Data.SqlClient` namespaces. Next, you declare the objects on your form. The first three objects should be familiar to you as you used them in your last project.

Take a closer look at the initialization of the `SqlDataAdapter` object. You use a constructor that initializes this object with a string value for the `SelectCommand` property and an object that represents a connection to the database. This constructor saves you from writing code to manipulate the `SqlDataAdapter` properties—it's already set up.

The `SELECT` statement that you are using here is basically the same as in the previous project, except that you have added a couple more columns in the *select list* (the list of columns directly following the word `SELECT`).

The `au_id` column in the select list has been prefixed with the table name `authors`, because this column also exists in the `titleauthor` table. Therefore, you must tell the database which table to get the data from for this column. This is the same for the `title_id` column, except that this column exists in the `titles` and `titleauthor` tables:

```
' Initialize a new instance of the OleDbDataAdapter object...
objDataAdapter = New OleDbDataAdapter( _
    "SELECT authors.au_id, au_lname, au_fname, " & _
    "titles.title_id, title, price " & _
    "FROM authors " & _
```

```
                    "JOIN titleauthor ON authors.au_id = titleauthor.au_id " & _
                    "JOIN titles ON titleauthor.title_id = titles.title_id " & _
                    "ORDER BY au_lname, au_fname", objConnection)
```

The last two objects are new but were discussed in the section on binding. You use the `DataView` to customize your view of the records returned from the database and stored in the dataset. The `CurrencyManager` object controls the movement of your bound data as you saw in the previous section.

How It Works: FillDataSetAndView

The first procedure you created was the `FillDataSetAndView` procedure. This procedure will be called several times throughout your code and will get the latest data from the database and populate your `DataView` object.

The first thing you need to do is initialize a new instance of the `DataSet` object. You do this here because this procedure might be called more than once during the lifetime of the form. If it is, you do not want to add new records to the records already in the dataset—you always want to start afresh:

```
    Private Sub FillDataSetAndView()
        ' Initialize a new instance of the DataSet object...
        objDataSet = New DataSet()
```

Next, you execute the `Fill` method on `objDataAdapter` to populate the `objDataSet` object. Then you specify that your `DataView` object will be viewing data from the authors table in the `DataSet` object. Remember that the `DataView` object allows you to sort, search, and navigate through the records in the dataset:

```
        ' Fill the DataSet object with data...
        objDataAdapter.Fill(objDataSet, "authors")

        ' Set the DataView object to the DataSet object...
        objDataView = New DataView(objDataSet.Tables("authors"))
```

Once you have initialized your `DataView` object, you initialize the `CurrencyManager` object. Remember that the `BindingContext` object is built into every Windows form and contains a collection of `CurrencyManagers`. The collection contains the available data sources and you choose the `DataView` object:

```
        ' Set our CurrencyManager object to the DataView object...
        objCurrencyManager = _
            CType(Me.BindingContext(objDataView), CurrencyManager)
```

How It Works: BindFields

The next procedure that you create (`BindFields`) actually bind the controls on your form to your `DataView` object. This procedure first cleared any previous bindings for the controls and then set them to your `DataView` object.

> It is important to clear the bindings first as, once you modify the `DataView` object by adding, updating, or deleting a row of data, the `DataView` object will only show the changed data. Therefore, after you update the database with your changes, you must repopulate your `DataView` object and rebind your controls. If you didn't do this then the data that is actually in the database and the data that is in the `DataView` may not be the same.

Using the `DataBindings` property of the controls on you form, you executed the `Clear` method of the `ControlBindingsCollection` class to remove the bindings from them. Notice that the controls that you have bound are all the text boxes on your form that will contain data from the `DataView` object:

```
Private Sub BindFields()
    ' Clear any previous bindings to the DataView object...
    txtLastName.DataBindings.Clear()
    txtFirstName.DataBindings.Clear()
    txtBookTitle.DataBindings.Clear()
    txtPrice.DataBindings.Clear()
```

Once you have cleared the previous bindings, you can set the new bindings back to the same data source, our `DataView` object. You do this by executing the `Add` method of the `ControlBindingsCollection` object returned by the `DataBindings` property. The `Add` method has three arguments as can be seen in the following code.

❑   The first argument is the *propertyname* and specifies the property of the control to be bound. Since you want to bind your data to the `Text` property of the text boxes, you have specified `"Text"` for this argument.

❑   The next argument is the *datasource* argument and specifies the data source to be bound. Remember that this can be any valid object that contains data such as `DataSet`, `DataView`, or `DataTable`. In this case you are using a `DataView` object.

❑   The last argument specifies the *datamember*. This is the data field in the data source that contains the data to be bound to this control. Notice that you have specified the various column names from your `SELECT` statement that you executed in the previous procedure:

```
    ' Add new bindings to the DataView object...
    txtLastName.DataBindings.Add("Text", objDataView, "au_lname")
    txtFirstName.DataBindings.Add("Text", objDataView, "au_fname")
    txtBookTitle.DataBindings.Add("Text", objDataView, "title")
    txtPrice.DataBindings.Add("Text", objDataView, "price")
```

The last thing that you do in this procedure is to set a message in the status bar using the `Text` property of `StatusBar1`:

```
    ' Display a ready status...
    StatusBar1.Text = "Ready"
End Sub
```

How It Works: ShowPosition

The `CurrencyManager` object keeps track of the current record position within the `DataView` object.

The price column in the titles table in pubs is defined as a `Currency` data type. Therefore, if a book is priced at $40.00, the number that you get is 40—the decimal portion is dropped. The `ShowPosition` procedure seems like a good place to format the data in the `txtPrice` text box, as this procedure is called whenever you move to a new record:

```
Private Sub ShowPosition()
'Always format the number in the txtPrice field to include cents
```

```
Try
    txtPrice.Text = Format(CType(txtPrice.Text, Decimal), "##0.00")
Catch e As System.Exception
    txtPrice.Text = "0"
    txtPrice.Text = Format(CType(txtPrice.Text, Decimal), "##0.00")
End Try

' Display the current position and the number of records
txtRecordPosition.Text = objCurrencyManager.Position + 1 & _
                         " of " & objCurrencyManager.Count()
End Sub
```

This part of the function is enclosed in a `Try...Catch` block in case the `txtPrice` is empty. If `txtPrice` is empty the `Format` function throws an exception and defaults the price to 0. The second line of code in this procedure uses the `Format` function to format the price in the `txtPrice` text box. This function accepts the numeric data to be formatted as the first argument and a format string as the second argument. In order for the format function to work correctly, you need to convert the string value in the `txtPrice` field to a Decimal value using the `CType` function.

The last line of code displays the current record position and the total number of records that you have. Using the `Position` property of the `CurrencyManager` object, you can determine which record you are on. The `Position` property uses a zero-based index so the first record is always 0. Therefore, you have specified the `Position` property plus 1, in order to display the true number.

The `CurrencyManager` class's `Count` property returns the actual number of items in the list and you are using this property to display the total number of records in the `DataView` object.

How It Works: Form_Load

Now that you've looked at the code for the main procedures, you need to go back and look at your initialization code.

You have a combo box on your form that will be used when sorting or searching for data. This combo box needs to be populated with data representing the columns in the `DataView` object. You specify the `Add` method of the `Items` property of the combo box to add items to it. Here you are specifying text that represents the columns in the `DataView` object in the same order as they appear in the `DataView` object:

```
'Add any initialization after the InitializeComponent() call

' Add items to the combo box...
cboField.Items.Add("Last Name")
cboField.Items.Add("First Name")
cboField.Items.Add("Book Title")
cboField.Items.Add("Price")
```

Once you have loaded all of the items into your combo box, you select the first item. You do this by setting the `SelectedIndex` property to 0. The `SelectedIndex` property is zero-based so the first item in the list is 0.

```
' Make the first item selected...
cboField.SelectedIndex = 0
```

Next, you call the `FillDataSetAndView` procedure to retrieve the data and then call the `BindFields` procedure to bind the controls on your form to your `DataView` object. Finally, you call the `ShowPosition` procedure to display the current record position and the total number of records contained in your `DataView` object:

```
' Fill the DataSet and bind the fields...
FillDataSetAndView()
BindFields()

' Show the current record position...
ShowPosition()
```

How It Works: Navigation Buttons

The procedure for the `btnMoveFirst` button causes the first record in the `DataView` object to be displayed. This is accomplished using the `Position` property of the `CurrencyManager` object. Here you set the `Position` property to 0 indicating that the `CurrencyManager` should move to the first record:

```
' Set the record position to the first record...
objCurrencyManager.Position = 0
```

Because your controls are bound to the `DataView` object they will always stay in sync with the current record in the `DataView` object and display the appropriate data.

Once you have repositioned the current record, you need to call the `ShowPosition` procedure to update the display of the current record on your form:

```
' Show the current record position...
ShowPosition()
```

Next, you add the code for the `btnMovePrevious` button. You move to the prior record by subtracting 1 from the `Position` property. The `CurrencyManager` object will automatically detect and handle the beginning position of the `DataView` object. It will not let you move to a position prior to the first record; it will just quietly keep its position at 0:

```
' Move to the previous record...
objCurrencyManager.Position -= 1
```

Again, after you have repositioned the current record being displayed, you need to call the `Show-Position` procedure to display the current position on the form.

In the `btnMoveNext` procedure, you increment the `Position` property by 1. Again, the `Currency-Manager` will automatically detect the last record in the `DataView` object and will not let you move past it:

```
' Move to the next record...
objCurrencyManager.Position += 1
```

You call the `ShowPosition` procedure to display the current record position.

When the btnMoveLast procedure is called, you move to the last record in the DataView object. You do this by setting the Position property equal to the Count property minus one. Then you call the ShowPosition procedure to display the current record:

```
' Set the record position to the last record...
objCurrencyManager.Position = objCurrencyManager.Count - 1

' Show the current record position...
ShowPosition()
```

Now that you have built the navigation, let's move on to add sorting functionality to this project.

Try It Out   **Including Sorting Functionality**

1.   Double-click on the Perform Sort button on the form in design mode to have the empty procedure added to the form class or select the button in the Class Name combo box and then select the Click event in the Method Name combo box. Insert the following code in the btnPerformSort_Click event procedure:

```
Private Sub btnPerformSort_Click(ByVal sender As Object, _
        ByVal e As System.EventArgs) Handles btnPerformSort.Click
    ' Determine the appropriate item selected and set the
    ' Sort property of the DataView object...
    Select Case cboField.SelectedIndex
        Case 0 'Last Name
            objDataView.Sort = "au_lname"
        Case 1 'First Name
            objDataView.Sort = "au_fname"
        Case 2 'Book Title
            objDataView.Sort = "title"
        Case 3 'Price
            objDataView.Sort = "price"
    End Select

    ' Call the click event for the MoveFirst button...
    btnMoveFirst_Click(Nothing, Nothing)

    ' Display a message that the records have been sorted...
    StatusBar1.Text = "Records Sorted"
End Sub
```

2.   Let's test out this newest functionality. Click the start button to compile and run it. Select a column to sort on and then click the Perform Sort button. You should see the data sorted by the column that you have chosen. Figure 16-8 shows the data sorted by book price.

How It Works

The first thing that you do in this procedure is to determine which field you should sort on. This information is contained in the cboField combo box.

```
' Determine the appropriate item selected and set the
' Sort property of the DataView object...
```

```
Select Case cboField.SelectedIndex
    Case 0 'Last Name
        objDataView.Sort = "au_lname"
    Case 1 'First Name
        objDataView.Sort = "au_fname"
    Case 2 'Book Title
        objDataView.Sort = "title"
    Case 3 'Price
        objDataView.Sort = "price"
End Select
```

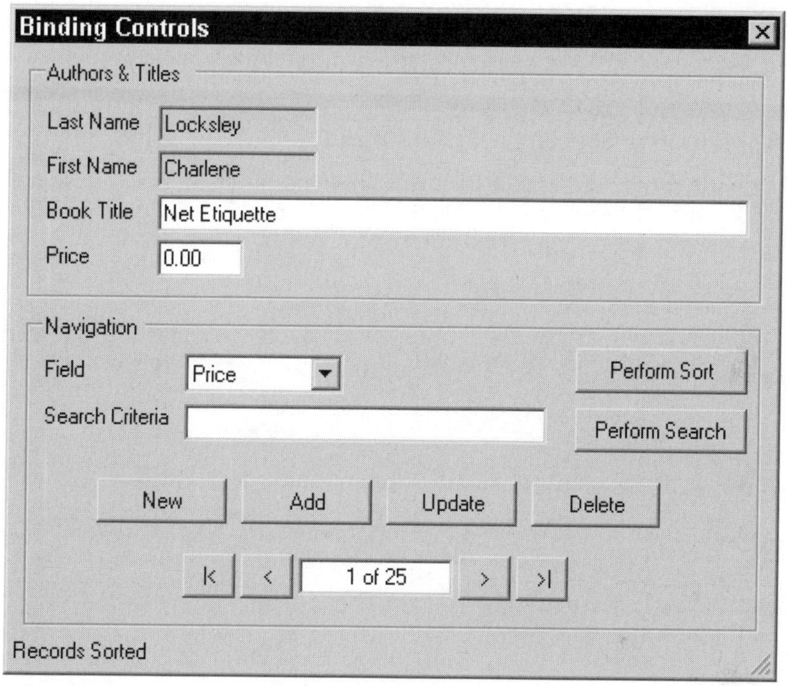

Figure 16-8

Using a `Select Case` statement to examine the `SelectedIndex` property of the combo box, you can determine which field the user has chosen. Once you have determined the correct entry in the combo box, you can set the `Sort` property of the `DataView` object using the column name of the column that is to be sorted. Once the `Sort` property has been set, the data will be sorted.

Once the data has been sorted, you move to the first record and there are a couple of ways you can do this. You could set the `Position` property of the `CurrencyManager` object and then call the `ShowPosition` procedure, or you can simply call `btnMoveFirst_Click` procedure, passing it `Nothing` for both arguments. This is the procedure that would be executed had you actually clicked the Move First button on the form.

The `btnMoveFirst_Click` procedure has two arguments, `ByVal sender As Object` and `ByVal e As System.EventArgs`. Since these arguments are required, you need to pass something to them, so you pass the `Nothing` keyword. The `Nothing` keyword is used to disassociate an object variable from an object. Thus, by using the Nothing keyword you satisfy the requirement of passing an argument to the procedure, but not pass any actual value:

```
' Call the click event for the MoveFirst button...
btnMoveFirst_Click(Nothing, Nothing)
```

After the first record has been displayed, you display a message in the status bar indicating that the records have been sorted. You do this by setting the Text property of the status bar as you have done before.

Note that another way would be to have a procedure called MoveFirst and call that from here *and* from the btnMoveFirst_Click procedure. Some developers would opt for this instead of having to pass Nothing to a procedure. Now take a look at what's involved in searching for a record.

Try It Out   Including Searching Functionality

1.   Double-click the Perform Search button or select the button in the Class Name combo box and then select the Click event in the Method Name combo box and add the following to the btnPerformSearch_Click event procedure:

```
Private Sub btnPerformSearch_Click(ByVal sender As Object, _
        ByVal e As System.EventArgs) Handles btnPerformSearch.Click
    ' Declare local variables...
    Dim intPosition As Integer

    ' Determine the appropriate item selected and set the
    ' Sort property of the DataView object...
    Select Case cboField.SelectedIndex
        Case 0 'Last Name
            objDataView.Sort = "au_lname"
        Case 1 'First Name
            objDataView.Sort = "au_fname"
        Case 2 'Book Title
            objDataView.Sort = "title"
        Case 3 'Price
            objDataView.Sort = "price"
    End Select

    ' If the search field is not price then...
    If cboField.SelectedIndex < 3 Then
        ' Find the last name, first name, or title...
        intPosition = objDataView.Find(txtSearchCriteria.Text)
    Else
        ' otherwise find the price...
        intPosition = objDataView.Find(CType(txtSearchCriteria.Text, Decimal))
    End If
    If intPosition = -1 Then
        ' Display a message that the record was not found...
        StatusBar1.Text = "Record Not Found"
    Else
        ' Otherwise display a message that the record was
        ' found and reposition the CurrencyManager to that
        ' record...
```

```
        StatusBar1.Text = "Record Found"
        objCurrencyManager.Position = intPosition
    End If

    ' Show the current record position...
    ShowPosition()
End Sub
```

2. Rest the searching functionality that you have added. Run the project and select a field in the Field combo box that you want to search on and then enter the search criteria in the Search Criteria textbox. Finally, click the Perform Search button.

    If a match is found, you will see the first matched record displayed along with a message in the status bar indicating that the record was found, as shown in Figure 16-9. If no record was found you will see a message in the status bar indicating the record was not found.

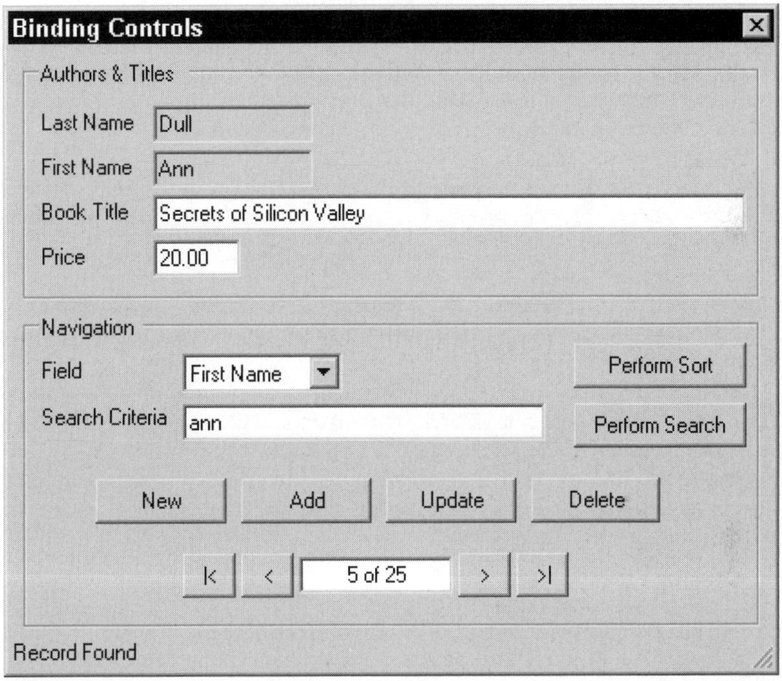

Figure 16-9

How It Works

This procedure is a little more involved as there are multiple conditions that you must test for and handle, such as a record that was not found. The first thing that you do in this procedure is to declare a variable that will receive the record position of the record that has been either found or not found.

```
    ' Declare local variables...
    Dim intPosition As Integer
```

Next, you sort the data based on the column that is used in the search. The Find method will search for data in the sort key. Therefore, by setting the Sort property, the column that is sorted on becomes the sort key in the `DataView` object. You use a `Select Case` statement just as you did in the previous procedure:

```
' Determine the appropriate item selected and set the
' Sort property of the DataView object...
Select Case cboField.SelectedIndex
    Case 0 'Last Name
        objDataView.Sort = "au_lname"
    Case 1 'First Name
        objDataView.Sort = "au_fname"
    Case 2 'Book Title
        objDataView.Sort = "title"
    Case 3 'Price
        objDataView.Sort = "price"
End Select
```

The columns for the authors' first and last names as well as the column for the book titles all contain text data. However, the column for the book price contains data that is in a currency format. Therefore, you need to determine which column you are searching on, and if that column is the price column, you need to format the data in the `txtSearchCriteria` text box to a decimal value.

Again, you use the `SelectedIndex` property of the `cboField` combo box to determine which item has been selected. If the `SelectedIndex` property is less than 3 then you know that you have to search on a column that contains text data.

You then set the `intPosition` variable to the results returned by the `Find` method of the `DataView` object. The `Find` method accepts the data to search for as the only argument. Here you are passing it the data contained in the `Text` property of the `txtSearchCriteria` text box.

If the `SelectedIndex` equals 3 you are searching for a book with a specific price and this requires you to convert the value contained in the `txtSearchCriteria` text box to a decimal value. `CType` function accepts an expression and the data type that you want to convert that expression to and returns a value, in this case a decimal value. This value is then used as the search criteria by the `Find` method.

```
' If the search field is not price then...
If cboField.SelectedIndex < 3 Then
    ' Find the last name, first name or title...
    intPosition = objDataView.Find(txtSearchCriteria.Text)
Else
    ' otherwise find the price...
    intPosition = objDataView.Find(CType(txtSearchCriteria.Text, Decimal))
End If
```

Once you have executed the `Find` method of the `DataView` object, you need to check the value contained in the `intPosition` variable. If this variable contains a value of 1 then no match was found. Any value other than 1 points to the record position of the record that contains the data.

So, if the value in this variable is 1 you display a message in the status bar that says that no record was found.

If the value is greater than 1 you display a message that the record was found and position the `DataView` object to that record using `Position` property of the `CurrencyManager` object:

```
StatusBar1.Text = "Record Found"
objCurrencyManager.Position = intPosition
```

It is worth noting that the `Find` method of the `DataView` object performs a search looking for an exact match of characters. There is no "wildcard" search method here, so you must enter the entire text string that you want to search for. The case, however, does not matter, so the name "Ann" is the same as "ann" and you do not need to be concerned with entering proper case when you enter your search criteria.

The last thing that you do in this procedure is to show the current record position, you do this by calling the `ShowPosition` procedure.

Now all that is left is to include the functionality to add, update, and delete records. Take a look at what is required to add a record first.

Try It Out   Adding Records

1.   First, you need to add just two lines of code to the `btnNew_Click` procedure, as shown:

```
Private Sub btnNew_Click(ByVal sender As Object, _
          ByVal e As System.EventArgs) Handles btnNew.Click
    ' Clear the book title and price fields...
    txtBookTitle.Text = ""
    txtPrice.Text = ""
End Sub
```

2.   The next procedure that you add code to is the `btnAdd_Click` procedure. This procedure is responsible for adding a new record and has the largest amount of code by far among any of the procedures you have coded or will code in this project. The reason for this is the relationship of book titles to authors and the primary key used for book titles:

```
Private Sub btnAdd_Click(ByVal sender As Object, _
          ByVal e As System.EventArgs) Handles btnAdd.Click
    ' Declare local variables and objects...
    Dim intPosition As Integer, intMaxID As Integer
    Dim strID As String
    Dim objCommand As SqlCommand = New SqlCommand()

    ' Save the current record position...
    intPosition = objCurrencyManager.Position
    ' Create a new SqlCommand object...
    Dim maxIdCommand As SqlCommand = New SqlCommand _
        ("SELECT MAX(title_id) AS MaxID " & _
        "FROM titles WHERE title_id LIKE 'DM%'", objConnection)

    ' Open the connection, execute the command
    objConnection.Open()
    Dim maxId As Object = maxIdCommand.ExecuteScalar()
```

```
' If the MaxID column is null...
If maxId Is DBNull.Value Then
    ' Set a default value of 1000...
    intMaxID = 1000
Else
    ' otherwise set the strID variable to the value in MaxID...
    strID = CType(maxId, String)
    ' Get the integer part of the string...
    intMaxID = CType(strID.Remove(0, 2), Integer)
    ' Increment the value...
    intMaxID += 1
End If

' Finally, set the new ID...
strID = "DM" & intMaxID.ToString

' Set the SqlCommand object properties...
objCommand.Connection = objConnection
objCommand.CommandText = "INSERT INTO titles " & _
    "(title_id, title, type, price, pubdate) " & _
    "VALUES(@title_id,@title,@type,@price,@pubdate);" & _
    "INSERT INTO titleauthor (au_id, title_id) VALUES(@au_id,@title_id)"

' Add parameters for the placeholders in the SQL in the
' CommandText property...

' Parameter for the title_id column...
objCommand.Parameters.Add("@title_id", strID)

' Parameter for the title column...
objCommand.Parameters.Add("@title", txtBookTitle.Text)

' Parameter for the type column
objCommand.Parameters.Add("@type", "Demo")
' Parameter for the price column...
objCommand.Parameters.Add("@price", txtPrice.Text).DbType _
                            = DbType.Currency

' Parameter for the pubdate column
objCommand.Parameters.Add("@pubdate", Date.Now)

' Parameter for the au_id column...
objCommand.Parameters.Add _
            ("@au_id", BindingContext(objDataView).Current("au_id"))

' Execute the SqlCommand object to insert the new data...
Try
    objCommand.ExecuteNonQuery()
Catch SqlExceptionErr As SqlException
    MessageBox.Show(SqlExceptionErr.Message)
End Try

' Close the connection...
objConnection.Close()
```

```
' Fill the dataset and bind the fields...
FillDataSetAndView()
BindFields()

' Set the record position to the one that you saved...
objCurrencyManager.Position = intPosition

' Show the current record position...
ShowPosition()

' Display a message that the record was added...
StatusBar1.Text = "Record Added"
```
End Sub

3. Run your project. Find an author that you want to add a new title for and then click the New button. The Book Title and Price fields will be cleared and you are ready to enter new data to be added as shown in Figure 16-10. Take note of the number of records that are in the DataView (25).

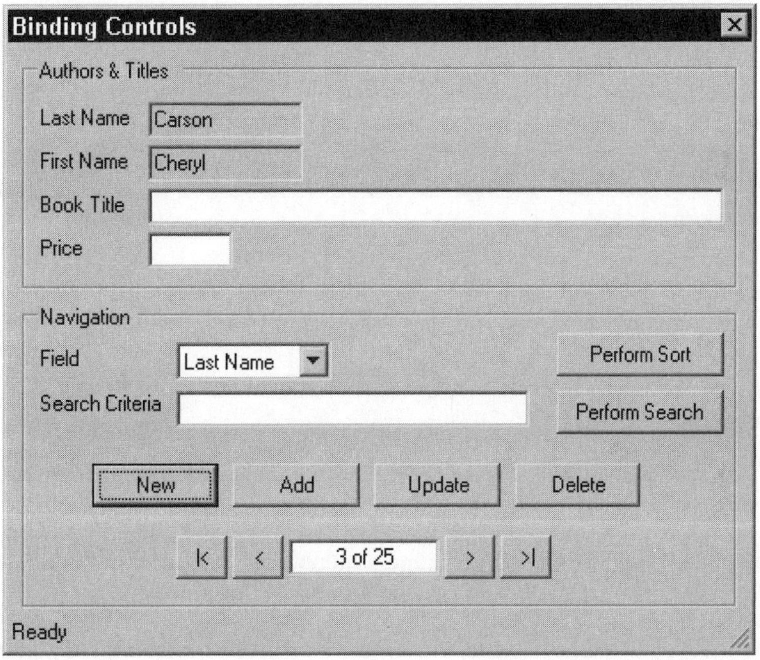

Figure 16-10

4. Now enter a title and price for the new book and click the Add button. You will see a message in the status bar indicating that the record has been added and you will also see that the number of records has changed (to 26) as shown in Figure 16-11.

Now that you have added a record, examine what you actually did.

How It Works

Remember that the only data that you can add is a new book title and its price. So instead of selecting the data in each of these fields, deleting it, and then entering the new data, you can simply click the New

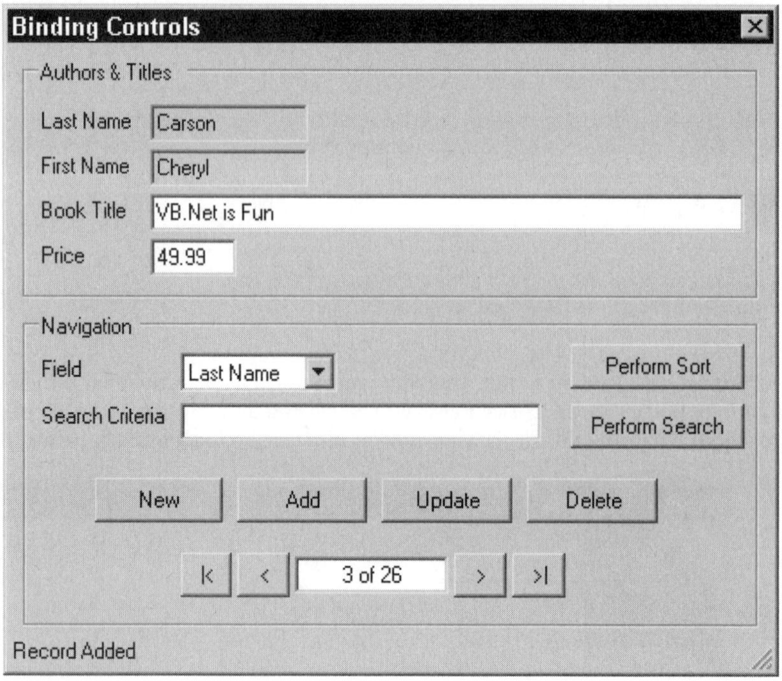

Figure 16-11

button. The job of the New button is to clear the book title and price fields for you. All you need to do here is to set the Text properties of these text boxes to an empty string as shown here:

```
' Clear the book title and price fields...
txtBookTitle.Text = ""
txtPrice.Text = ""
```

The primary key used in the titles table is not the database's Identity column. Identity columns use a sequential number and automatically increments the number for you when a new row is inserted. Instead of an Identity column, the primary key is made up of a category prefix and a sequential number. This means that you must first determine the maximum number used in a category and then increment that number by 1 and use the new number and category prefix for the new key.

The first thing that you do in the btnAdd_Click event procedure is declare your local variables and objects that will be used here. The intPosition variable will be used to save the current record position and the intMaxID variable will be used to set and increment the maximum sequential number for a category. The strID will be used to store the primary key from the authors table and to set the new key for the authors table. Finally, the objCommand object will be used to build a query to insert a new record into the titleauthor and titles tables.

Before you do anything, you want to save the position of the current record that you are on. This enables you to go back to this record once you reload the DataView object, which will contain the new record that you will add in this procedure:

```
intPosition = objCurrencyManager.Position
```

You need to execute a command on the database in order to work out the ID for your new title. You use a SqlCommand object to do this. You pass in a SQL string and the connection that you use throughout our program. This SQL string will select the maximum value in the title_id column, where the title_id value begins with the prefix of DM.

There is no category for demo so you add all of the test records under this category and use the category prefix of DM, enabling you to quickly identify the records that you have inserted just in case you want to manually get rid of them later.

Because the function you are using in MAX is an *aggregate function* (meaning that it is a function that works on groups of data), the data that is returned will be returned without a column name. Therefore, you use the AS keyword in the SELECT statement and tell SQL Server to assign a column name to the value, in this case MaxID. You use a LIKE clause in the SELECT statement to tell SQL Server to search for all values that begin with DM:

```
Dim maxIdCommand As SqlCommand = New SqlCommand( _
    "SELECT MAX(title_id) AS MaxID " & _
    "FROM titles WHERE title_id LIKE 'DM%'", objConnection)
```

This sets up your command object but doesn't execute it. To execute it you need to open the connection and then call one of the SqlCommand execute methods. In this case you use ExecuteScalar:

```
' Open the connection, execute the command
objConnection.Open()
Dim maxId As Object = maxIdCommand.ExecuteScalar()
```

ExecuteScalar is a useful method when you have a database command that returns a single value. Other commands you've used so far have returned a whole table of values (you have used these as the SelectCommand of a data adapter), or no values at all (you have executed these with Execute-NonQuery). In this case you are only interested in one number so you can use ExecuteScalar. This returns the first column of the first row in the result set. In this case there is only one column and one row, so that is what you get.

You check for a Null value returned from the command, so you compare the resulting Object against the Value property of the DBNull class:

```
' If the MaxID column is null...
If maxId Is DBNull.Value Then
```

If the expression evaluates to True, then you have no primary key in the titles table that begins with DM so you set the initial value of the intMaxID variable to a value of 1000. You have chosen 1000 because all of the other primary keys contain a numeric value of less than 1000:

```
' Set a default value of 1000...
intMaxID = 1000
```

If the column value evaluates to False, then you have at least one primary key in the titles table that begins with DM. In this case you need to obtain the integer portion of this ID in order to work out what integer to use for our ID. To do this, you must convert your maxId Object to a String:

```
Else
    ' otherwise set the strID variable to the value in MaxID...
    strID = CType(maxId, String)
```

Then you can extract the integer portion of the key by using the Remove method of the string variable, strID. The Remove method removes the specified number of characters from a string. You specify the offset at which to begin removing characters and the number of characters to be removed. This method returns a new string with the removed characters. In this line of code, you are removing the prefix of DM from the string so that all you end up with is the integer portion of the string. You then use the CType function to convert the string value that contains a number to an Integer value, which you place in the intMaxID variable. Finally, you increment it by one to get the integer portion of the ID that you will use:

```
        ' Get the integer part of the string...
        intMaxID = CType(strID.Remove(0, 2), Integer)
        ' Increment the value...
        intMaxID += 1
    End If
```

Now that you've got the integer part, you build a new primary key in the strID variable by concatenating the numeric value contained in the intMaxID variable with the prefix DM:

```
        ' Finally, set the new ID...
        strID = "DM" & intMaxID.ToString
```

Next, you build the SQL statements to insert a new row of data into the titles and titleauthor tables. If you look closely, there are two separate INSERT statements in the CommandText property of your objCommand object. The two separate INSERT statements are separated by a semicolon, which enables you to concatenate multiple SQL statements. The SQL statements that you built use placeholders that will get filled in by the SqlParameter objects.

> *Note that because of the relationship between the titles table and the authors table, you must first insert a new title for an author into the titles table and then insert the relationship between the title and the author in the titleauthor table. You'll notice that our INSERT statements specify the columns that you want to insert data into and then specify the values that are to be inserted, some of which are represented by placeholders.*

You have seen the properties of the SqlCommand object before. This time, however, you are using properties rather than the constructor. You set the Connection property to a SqlConnection object and then set the CommandText property to the SQL string that you want to execute, in this case, the two separate INSERT statements:

```
        objCommand.Connection = objConnection
        objCommand.CommandText = "INSERT INTO titles " & _
            "(title_id, title, type, price, pubdate) " & _
            "VALUES(@title_id,@title,@type,@price,@pubdate);" & _
            "INSERT INTO titleauthor (au_id, title_id) VALUES(@au_id,@title_id)"
```

You then add entries to the Parameters collection property for each of your placeholders in the preceding SQL statements. Where the same parameter name is used twice in the CommandText property—as title_id is here—you only need one SqlParameter object:

```
        ' Add parameters for the placeholders in the SQL in the
        ' CommandText property...

        ' Parameter for the title_id column...
        objCommand.Parameters.Add("@title_id", strID)
```

```
      ' Parameter for the title column...
      objCommand.Parameters.Add("@title", txtBookTitle.Text)

      ' Parameter for the type column
      objCommand.Parameters.Add("@type", "Demo")

      ' Parameter for the price column...
      objCommand.Parameters.Add _
                      ("@price", txtPrice.Text).DbType = DbType.Currency

      ' Parameter for the pubdate column
      objCommand.Parameters.Add("@pubdate", Date.Now)

      ' Parameter for the au_id column...
      objCommand.Parameters.Add("@au_id", _
  BindingContext(objDataView).Current("au_id"))
```

For the `@title_id` parameter, you use the `strID` variable that you created and set earlier in this method. For the `@title` parameter, you use the text in the Book Title text box entered by the user. For the `@price` parameter you use the text in the Price text box. However, the `Text` property is a `String`. SQL Server cannot automatically convert between a `String` and a `Currency` data type, so you particularly specify that the parameter is of the `DbType.Currency` data type.

For `@au_id` you need to use the ID of the currently selected author. There are no bound controls for the `au_id` column, so you need to use some code to obtain the value. Take a close look at this particular statement:

```
      BindingContext(objDataView).Current("au_id")
```

Here you are getting the form's `BindingContext` for the `objDataView` data source, which is the one you're using for all of your bound controls. When you're accessing a `DataView` through `BindingContext`, the `Current` property returns a `DataRowView` object. This object represents the view of the particular row that the user is currently looking at. You are then able to select a particular column from that row, thus giving you a specific value. Here, of course, you are obtaining the `au_id` column.

The remaining parameters mark the new record as a Demo record and timestamp the record with the current date and time:

```
      ' Parameter for the type column
      objCommand.Parameters.Add("@type", "Demo")

      ' Parameter for the pubdate column
      objCommand.Parameters.Add("@pubdate", Date.Now)
```

Once you have added all of your parameters, you execute the command using the `ExecuteNonQuery` method. This causes your SQL statements to be executed and the data inserted. Once the new data has been inserted you close the database connection.

This is the one spot in your code that is really subject to failure so very basic error handling is included here. You execute your `INSERT` statement inside the `Try` block of your error handler and if an error is encountered, the code in the `Catch` block will be executed. The code there simply displays a message box that shows the error encountered:

```
' Execute the SqlCommand object to insert the new data...
Try
    objCommand.ExecuteNonQuery()
Catch SqlExceptionErr As SqlException
    MessageBox.Show(SqlExceptionErr.Message)
Finally
    ' Close the connection...
    objConnection.Close()
End Try
```

Then the `FillDataSetAndView` and `BindFields` procedures are called to reload the `DataView` object and to clear and rebind your controls. This ensures that you get all new data added, updated, or deleted from the tables in SQL Server.

You then reposition the `DataView` object back to the record that was being displayed by setting the `Position` property of the `CurrencyManager` using the `intPosition` variable. This variable was set using the current record position at the beginning of this procedure.

The position that you set here is only approximate. It does not take into account any records that have been inserted or deleted by someone else or you. It is possible that the title you just inserted for a specific author could be returned prior to the title that was displayed before. If you need more detailed control over the actual record position, you will need to add more code to handle finding and displaying the exact record that was displayed; however, this is beyond the scope of this book.

After you have repositioned the record that is being displayed, you call the `ShowPosition` procedure to show the current record position.

Finally, you display a message in the status bar indicating that the record has been added.

The next procedure that you code is the `btnUpdate_Click` procedure. This procedure is a little simpler because all you need to do here is to update the titles table. You do not have to select any data to build a primary key.

Try It Out   Updating Records

1. To the `btnUpdate_Click` event procedure, add the following code:

```
Private Sub btnUpdate_Click(ByVal sender As Object, _
        ByVal e As System.EventArgs) Handles btnUpdate.Click
    ' Declare local variables and objects...
    Dim intPosition As Integer
    Dim objCommand As SqlCommand = New SqlCommand()

    ' Save the current record position...
    intPosition = objCurrencyManager.Position

    ' Set the SqlCommand object properties...
    objCommand.Connection = objConnection
```

```
objCommand.CommandText = "UPDATE titles " & _
        "SET title = @title, price = @price WHERE title_id = @title_id"
objCommand.CommandType = CommandType.Text

' Add parameters for the placeholders in the SQL in the
' CommandText property...

' Parameter for the title field...
objCommand.Parameters.Add("@title", txtBookTitle.Text)

' Parameter for the price field...
objCommand.Parameters.Add("@price", txtPrice.Text).DbType _
                        = DbType.Currency

' Parameter for the title_id field...
objCommand.Parameters.Add _
            ("@title_id", BindingContext(objDataView).Current("title_id"))

' Open the connection...
objConnection.Open()

' Execute the SqlCommand object to update the data...
objCommand.ExecuteNonQuery()

' Close the connection...
objConnection.Close()

' Fill the DataSet and bind the fields...
FillDataSetAndView()
BindFields()
' Set the record position to the one that you saved...
objCurrencyManager.Position = intPosition

' Show the current record position...
ShowPosition()

' Display a message that the record was updated...
StatusBar1.Text = "Record Updated"
End Sub
```

2. Run your project. You can update the price of the book that you have just added or you can update the price of another book. Choose a book, change the price in the Price field, and then click the Update button.

Once the record has been updated, you will see the appropriate message in the status bar and the record will still be the current record, as shown in Figure 16-12.

How It Works

As always, the first thing that you do is to declare your variables and objects. You need one variable to save the current record position and one object for the SqlCommand object. Next, you save the current record position just as you did in the last procedure.

By adding the following code, you set the Connection property of the SqlCommand object using your objConnection object. Then you set the CommandText property using a SQL string. The SQL string

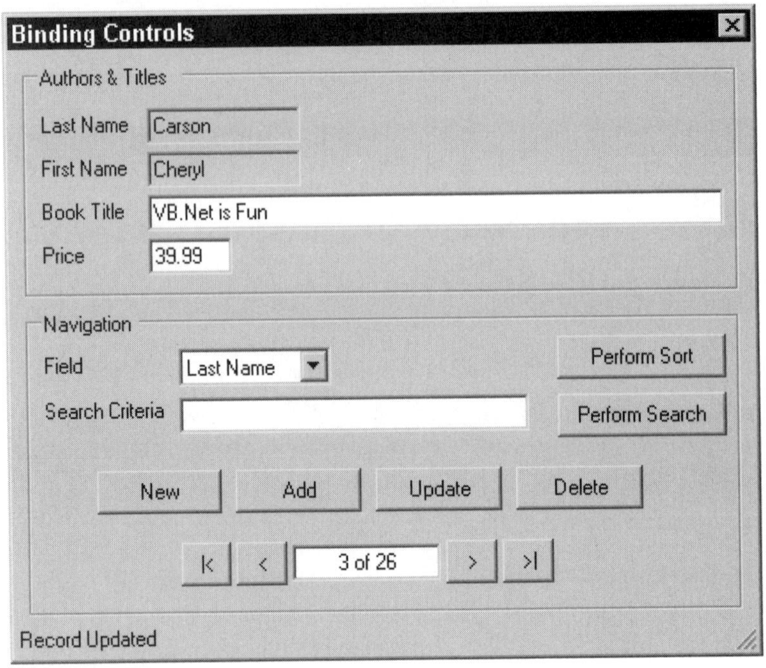

Figure 16-12

here contains an UPDATE statement to update the title and price columns in the titles table. Notice that there are three placeholders in this UPDATE statement. Two placeholders are for the title and price, and one is for the title_id in the WHERE clause:

```
' Set the SqlCommand object properties...
objCommand.Connection = objConnection
    objCommand.CommandText = "UPDATE titles " & _
            "SET title = @title, price = @price WHERE title_id = @title_id"
objCommand.CommandType = CommandType.Text
```

Again, once you have set the CommandText property, you set the CommandType property to indicate that this is a SQL string.

You now add the appropriate parameters to the Parameters collection. The first parameter that you need to add is for the title column in your UPDATE statement. You have seen parameters several times before. The title of the book is coming from the Text property of the txtBookTitle text box on your form.

The second parameter is for the price in your UPDATE statement. This parameter will be used to update the price of a book and the data is coming from the txtPrice text box on your form. Once again, you need to explicitly set the DbType for this parameter.

This last parameter is for your WHERE clause in the UPDATE statement. The data for the Value property is coming directly from the form's BindingContext, as the au_id did in the Adding Records example.

The rest of the procedure is similar to the btnAdd_Click event procedure.

The final procedure that you need to code is btnDelete_Click.

Try It Out   Deleting Records

1.   To include delete functionality in your project, add the following code to the `btnDelete_Click` event procedure:

```
Private Sub btnDelete_Click(ByVal sender As Object, _
        ByVal e As System.EventArgs) Handles btnDelete.Click
    ' Declare local variables and objects...
    Dim intPosition As Integer
    Dim objCommand As SqlCommand = New SqlCommand()

    ' Save the current record position - 1 for the one to be
    ' deleted...
    intPosition = Me.BindingContext(objDataView).Position - 1

    ' If the position is less than 0 set it to 0...
    If intPosition < 0 Then
        intPosition = 0
    End If

    ' Set the Command object properties...
    objCommand.Connection = objConnection
    objCommand.CommandText = "DELETE FROM titleauthor " & _
            "WHERE title_id = @title_id;" & _
            "DELETE FROM titles WHERE title_id = @title_id"

    ' Parameter for the title_id field...
    objCommand.Parameters.Add _
            ("@title_id", BindingContext(objDataView).Current("title_id"))

    ' Open the database connection...
    objConnection.Open()

    ' Execute the SqlCommand object to update the data...
    objCommand.ExecuteNonQuery()

    ' Close the connection...
    objConnection.Close()

    ' Fill the DataSet and bind the fields...
    FillDataSetAndView()
    BindFields()

    ' Set the record position to the one that you saved...
    Me.BindingContext(objDataView).Position = intPosition

    ' Show the current record position...
    ShowPosition()

    ' Display a message that the record was deleted...
    StatusBar1.Text = "Record Deleted"
End Sub
```

2.   That's it for this project so test this newest functionality. Run your project and choose any book that you want to delete and then click on the Delete button. Keep in mind though that the pubs

database is a sample database for everyone to use and it's probably a good idea to delete a book that you have added. Before you delete a book, however, take note of the record count that is displayed on the form (see Figure 16-13).

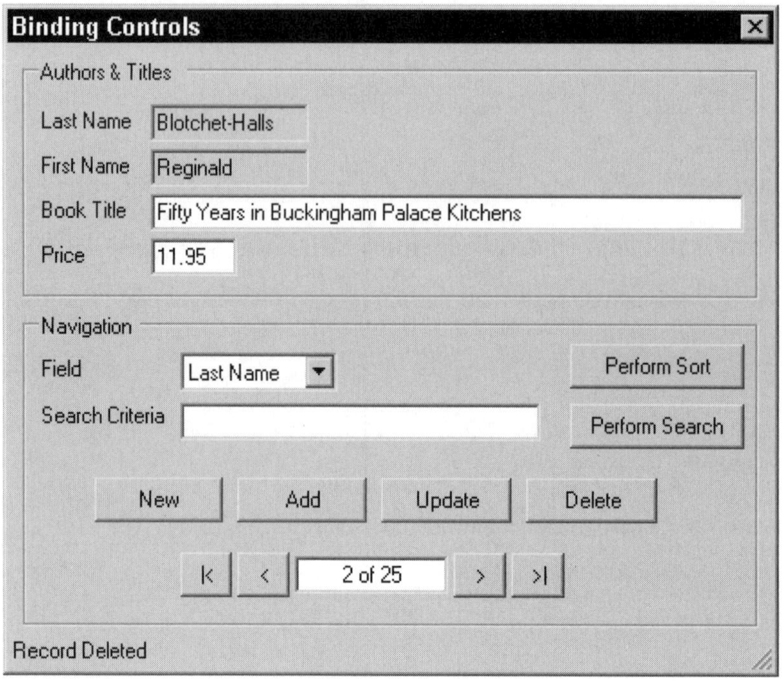

Figure 16-13

After the delete has been performed you will see one less record in the record count on the form.

How It Works

This procedure is a little more involved than the `btnUpdate_Click` procedure because of the relationship of titles to authors. Remember that there is a relationship table to join authors and titles. You must delete the row in the titleauthor relationship table before you can delete the row of data in the titles table. Therefore, you need two `DELETE` statements in your SQL string.

Notice that this time, after you have declared your variables, you have specified the `Position` property minus 1. This will allow for the user to be on the last record and deleting it. You have also allowed for the user to be on the first record as you check the value of the `intPosition` variable. If it is less than `0` you know that the user was on the first record and so you set it to `0`; this means that when you restore the record position later, it will once again be on the first record.

Notice also that you have not used the `CurrencyManager` object this time. Instead, you used the `BindingContext` object and specified the `objDataView` object as the object to be manipulated. Remember that the `BindingContext` object is automatically part of the form and there is nothing you need to do to have it added. The reason for using the `BindingContext` object here is to demonstrate how to use it, so that you know that you do not have to use the `CurrencyManager` object to navigate the records contained in the `objDataView`:

```
' Declare local variables and objects...
Dim intPosition As Integer
Dim objCommand As SqlCommand = New SqlCommand()

' Save the current record position - 1 for the one to be
' deleted...
intPosition = Me.BindingContext(objDataView).Position - 1

' If the position is less than 0 set it to 0...
If intPosition < 0 Then
    intPosition = 0
End If
```

When you set the properties of your `SqlCommand` object, the SQL string specified in the `CommandText` property contains two `DELETE` statements separated by a semicolon. The first `DELETE` statement deletes the relationship between the titles and authors table for the book being deleted. The second DELETE statement deletes the book from the titles table:

```
' Set the Command object properties...
objCommand.Connection = objConnection
objCommand.CommandText = "DELETE FROM titleauthor " & _
    "WHERE title_id = @title_id;" & _
    "DELETE FROM titles WHERE title_id = @title_id"
```

Again, you used placeholders for the primary keys in the `WHERE` clause of your `DELETE` statements.

This statement only uses one parameter. The next line sets it up in the normal way:

```
' Parameter for the title_id field...
objCommand.Parameters.Add("@title_id", _

BindingContext(objDataView).Current("title_id"))
```

The rest of the code is the same as the code for the previous two methods and should be familiar to you by now. That wraps up this project and this chapter. Hopefully, you will walk away with some valuable knowledge about data binding and how to perform inserts, updates, and deletes using SQL to access a database.

Before you leave, remember that error handling is a major part of any project. Except for one place in our code, it has been omitted to preserve space. You have also omitted data validation, so trying to insert a new record with no values could cause unexpected results and errors.

Summary

This chapter has taken a look at a few very important ADO.NET classes, particularly the `SqlConnection`, `SqlDataAdapter`, `SqlCommand`, and `SqlParameter` classes. You saw first hand how valuable these classes can be when selecting, inserting, updating, and deleting data. These particular classes are specifically for accessing SQL Server, but similar principles apply to the OLE DB counterparts.

You also saw the `DataSet` and `DataView` classes from the `System.Data` namespace put to use, and used both of these classes to create objects that were bound to the controls on your forms. Of particular interest to this discussion is the `DataView` object, as it provides the functionality to perform sorting and searching of data. The `DataView` class provides the most flexibility between the two classes as you can also present a subset of data from the `DataSet` in the `DataView`.

You saw how easy it is to bind the controls on your form to the data contained in either the `DataSet` or `DataView`. You also saw how to manage the navigation of the data in these objects with the `Currency-Manager` class. This class provides quick and easy control over the navigation.

This chapter has demonstrated using manual control over the navigation of data on the form and manual control over the insertion, update, and deletion of data in a data store. You should use the techniques that you have learned in this chapter when you need finer control of the data, especially when dealing with complex table relationships such as you have dealt with here.

To summarize, after reading this chapter you should:

❏ Feel comfortable using the ADO.NET classes discussed in this chapter

❏ Know when to use the `DataSet` class and when to use the `DataView` class

❏ Know how to manually bind controls on your form to either a `DataSet` or `DataView` object

❏ Know how to use the `CurrencyManager` class to navigate the data in a `DataSet` or `DataView` object

❏ Know how to sort and search for data in a `DataView` object

Exercises

1. When is it better to bind to a `DataView` object instead of straight to a `DataSet` object?

2. When using the `SqlCommand` object, you set the `CommandText` property to a SQL string to be executed. How can you use a stored procedure instead of a SQL string?

3. What do the words beginning with @ mean in the following SQL string?

```
objCommand.CommandText = "INSERT INTO titles " & _
    "(title_id, title, type, price, pubdate) " & _
    "VALUES(@title_id,@title,@type,@price,@pubdate);" & _
    "INSERT INTO titleauthor (au_id, title_id) VALUES(@au_id,@title_id)"
```

4. When binding a control, when is it necessary to first clear the binding as shown in the following example?

```
txtLastName.DataBindings.Clear()
txtLastName.DataBindings.Add("Text", objDataView, "au_lname")
```

Web Forms

No matter how hard you try, you can't escape the presence of the Web; it is becoming a vital part of many of the things you do. With Visual Basic .NET, you can write Web applications in a way that's quite similar to writing Windows applications.

In the previous chapter, you took a look at binding data to controls in Windows Forms. This chapter discusses programmatically binding data to controls in Web forms. You will not only take a look at data binding, but will also take a look at the major differences between Windows Forms and Web forms and how it affects data binding.

When you deal with Web applications the term *thin client* is often used, as the client can be any browser such as Microsoft Internet Explorer or Netscape Navigator and requires very few resources as most of the processing is done on the server. You will explore how this type of client/server architecture affects you as a developer and learn what you need to know to ramp up on creating Web forms.

In this chapter, you will:

- ❏ Look at a basic overview of thin client architecture
- ❏ Learn about Web forms architecture and how it differs from Windows Forms
- ❏ Understand ADO.NET objects as they relate to the `System.Data.SqlClient` namespace and ASP.NET applications
- ❏ Work with data binding in Web forms
- ❏ Sort data
- ❏ Update data

Remember that in order to develop and run the code in this chapter, you will need to have IIS 5.x or 6.0 and the .NET Framework installed on the machine that you intend to run it on. In addition, error handling has been omitted from all of the Try It Outs *in this chapter to save space. You should always add the appropriate error handling to your code. Review Chapter 9 for error handling techniques.*

Thin Client Architecture

When dealing with a Windows Forms application you have a compiled program that must be distributed to the user's desktop before they can use it. Depending upon the application, there may also be one or more supporting DLLs or other executables that also need to be distributed along with the application.

In thin client architecture there is typically no program or DLL to be distributed. Users merely need to start their browser and enter the URL of the Web site that they want to access. The server hosting the Web site is responsible for maintaining all resources that are required by the Web application. The resources are used at the server and provide functionality to the Web site.

All code required in a thin client architecture is stored in one central location, the server hosting the Web site. Any update that is made to the code is immediately available the next time a user requests a Web page that was updated.

Thin client architecture provides several key benefits. First and foremost is the cost of initial distribution of the application; there is none. In traditional client/server architecture, the program would have to be distributed to every client that wants to use it, which could be quite a time-consuming task if the application is used in offices throughout the world.

Another major benefit is the cost of distributing updates to the application; again there are none. All updates to the Web site and its components are distributed to the Web server. Once an update is made it is immediately available to every user the next time they access the updated Web page. In traditional client/server architecture, the updated program would have to be distributed to every client and the updates could take days or weeks to roll out. This allows a new version of an application to be distributed instantly to all the users without having to touch a single desktop.

Another major benefit is that you can make changes to the back-end architecture and not have to worry about the client. Suppose, for example, that you want to change the location of the database from a low-end server to a new high-end server. The new server would typically have a new machine name. In a traditional client/server application, the machine name of the database server is stored in the code or registry setting. You would need to modify either the code or registry setting for every user who uses the application. In thin client architecture, you simply need to update the setting of the Web server to point to the new database server and you are in business, and so are all of the clients.

You can see that in a thin client architecture model, any client with a browser can access your Web site and immediately have access to updates. In fact, if your changes were transparent to the user, the client wouldn't even know that changes have been made.

Now that you have a basic understanding of thin client architecture, look at how Web forms work.

Web Forms Versus Windows Forms

In this section, you take a high-level look at how both Windows Forms and Web forms work so that you can compare the differences in architecture between the two. This will give you an idea of the challenges that you face when working with Web forms. You look at some differences in the development environment when working with Web forms.

Windows Forms Overview

When you execute a program that uses Windows Forms, you click on a desktop icon or navigate to the appropriate Programs group folder and click on the icon that represents the program that you want to execute. The Windows operating system then loads the program, executes the code, and displays the form.

Suppose that you are working with data in the authors' table in the sample pubs database. Your form displays a combo box listing all the states that authors live in. When you select a state in the combo box, the code in your form sends a query to the database to retrieve all authors for that state and display them in a data grid.

All of this happens in a blink of the eye and happens right there in the code in the form on your local computer. The form not only contains the code to handle the events of the controls, but also the code to perform the data retrieval. This is not the case with Web forms.

Web Forms Overview

When you execute a Web form, you must first open a browser and enter the URL of the Web site, which is usually on a Web server somewhere. *Internet Information Server (IIS)* is invoked and it looks at the page that you want to be displayed and it executes the appropriate ASP.NET Web page. The code in the Web page is processed; retrieving the data for the combo box, building the HTML for the Web form, and then sending this data to the browser.

Now that the Web form is displayed in the browser, you can select a US state from the combo box listing all the states that authors live in. When you select a state, the Web form will post a request back to the Web server for the appropriate data. IIS in turn loads the same Web page again for our Web form and determines that you now want to select all authors who live in a particular state. It will send the query to the database to retrieve all the authors in that state. IIS will then build the HTML for your Web form and send the data to your browser.

As you can see, when dealing with resources that are not located on the client, there are a lot of round trips back and forth between the browser and the Web server. This is something that you must keep in mind when you write Web applications. You want to reduce the number of trips to the server to as few as possible because each trip requires the user to wait and requires resources on the server. That's why it is important to perform validation of input fields on the client side; you don't need to make a trip to the server to validate fields.

Web Form Code

By now you are familiar with the Visual Studio .NET development environment and know that you can view a Windows Form in design mode or view the code behind the form. You know that you can double-click a control on the form and the appropriate event handler will be added to your code.

Design Mode

Web forms offer the same flexible functionality and more. When you open a new Web Application project you are presented with a Web form in design mode. You can drag and drop controls from the Toolbox onto the form as shown in Figure 17-1.

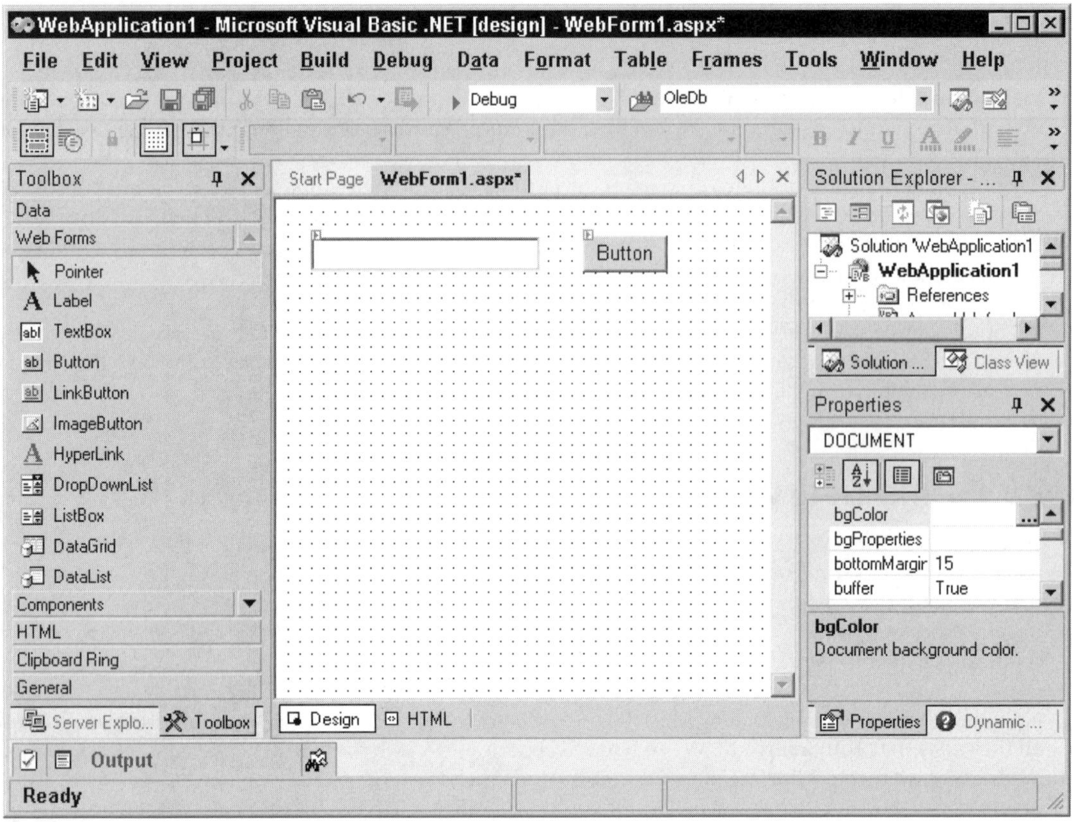

Figure 17-1

Notice at the bottom of the Web form that there are two tabs, one for Design mode and one for HTML mode. That's right, the source HTML behind the form can be viewed and manipulated. Figure 17-2 shows what the HTML looks like.

HTML View

The Design and HTML views define only how the page looks. To define how it behaves you need to write Visual Basic .NET code. The Visual Basic .NET code goes into a separate file called the code behind file.

The Code Behind the Web Form

The code behind the Web form looks very similar to what you have seen in your Visual Basic .NET projects. Figure 17-3 shows what the code looks like.

Now that you have seen how Web forms look in the development environment and how you can view the code, take a look at the controls that are available. While you'll progress fairly quickly here, keep in mind that you will be getting first-hand experience building Web forms and each step will be thoroughly explained.

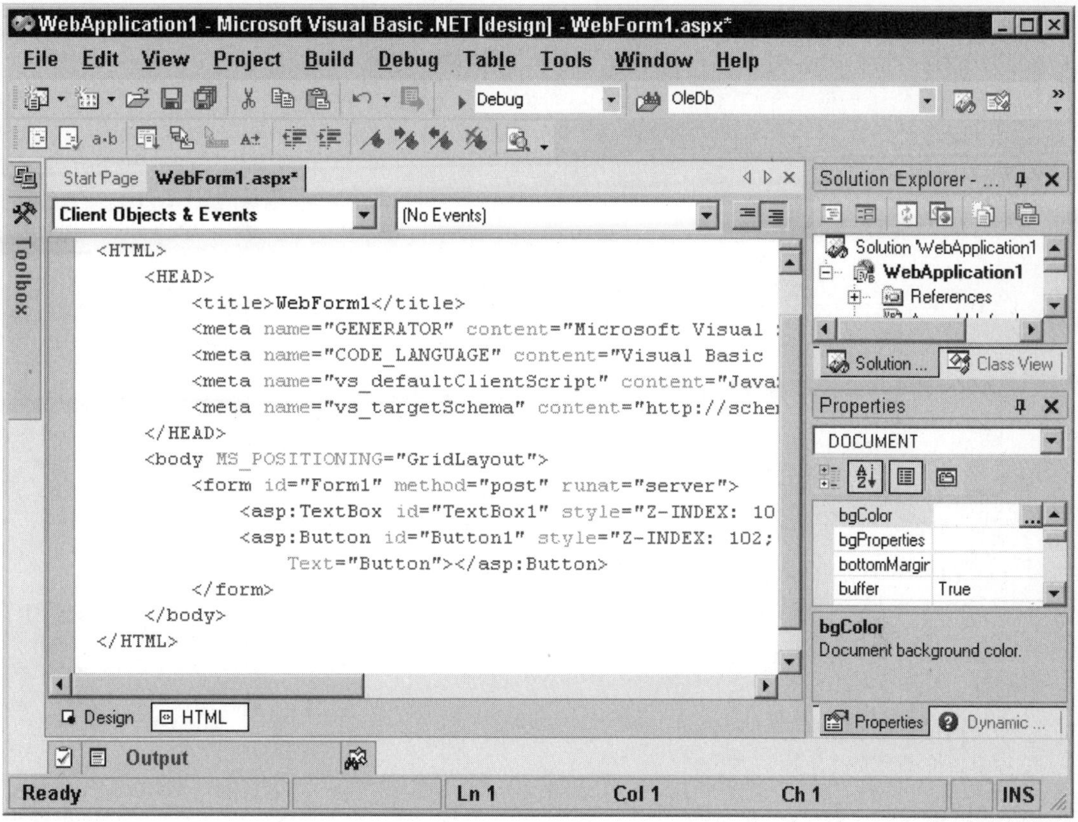

Figure 17-2

Web Form Controls

Web form controls are broken down into two separate categories in the Toolbox in the development environment: Web Forms and HTML, as shown in Figure 17-4.

First, take a look at the HTML Server controls.

HTML Controls

HTML controls are the controls that you see in today's Web applications and include such controls as TextBox, Label, Button, and Table. These are the controls that are used in standard HTML pages. Of course, there are many more but these are the most recognizable.

Under normal circumstances, you cannot manipulate these controls at runtime from your Visual Basic .NET code. However, Visual Studio .NET puts a twist on these controls by allowing you to convert them into HTML Server controls. When you convert an HTML control to an HTML Server control, this control then becomes available in your server-side code and has properties and methods exposed that can be programmed against. However, as far as the Web browser is concerned, it's still plain HTML. The

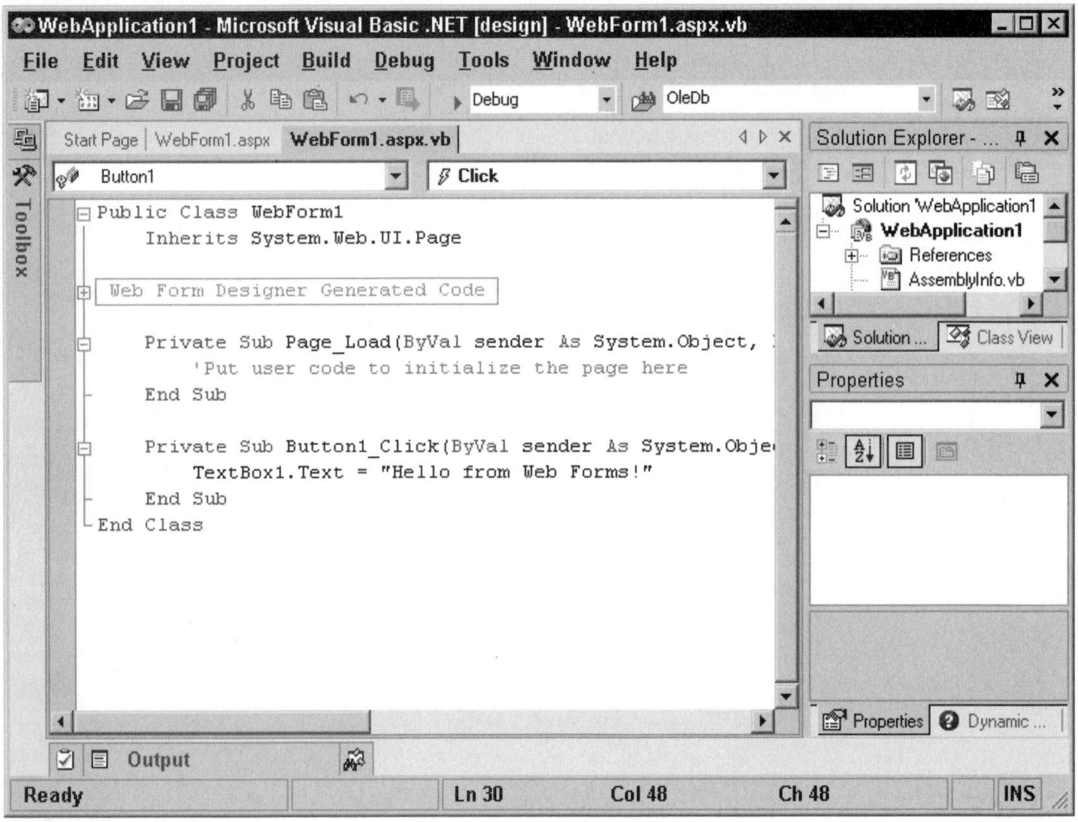

Figure 17-3

ASP.NET environment does the work of making it appear as normal HTML to the browser and a proper codeable object to us.

> *Note that although HTML controls are not accessible from our server-side Visual Basic .NET code, they are accessible from client-side JavaScript and VBScript code. You will be using client-side VBScript to demonstrate this in the following sections.*

The conversion process can be performed in one of two ways and the difference between an HTML control and an HTML Server control is very distinguishable on the Web form in design mode. You can convert an HTML control to an HTML Server control by right-clicking the control in design mode and choosing the Run As Server Control menu item.

This will cause one or more attributes to be added to the control. At a minimum, the RUNAT=SERVER property will be added. In addition, depending on the control the asp prefix may be added to the control and an ID property may be assigned. This property allows you to access the control in code using this ID, which is basically the same as the Name property.

> *You could also perform the conversion from HTML control to HTML Server control manually, by viewing the HTML and modifying the controls in the HTML code. However, this is not a simple process and you should let the development environment do the work for you.*

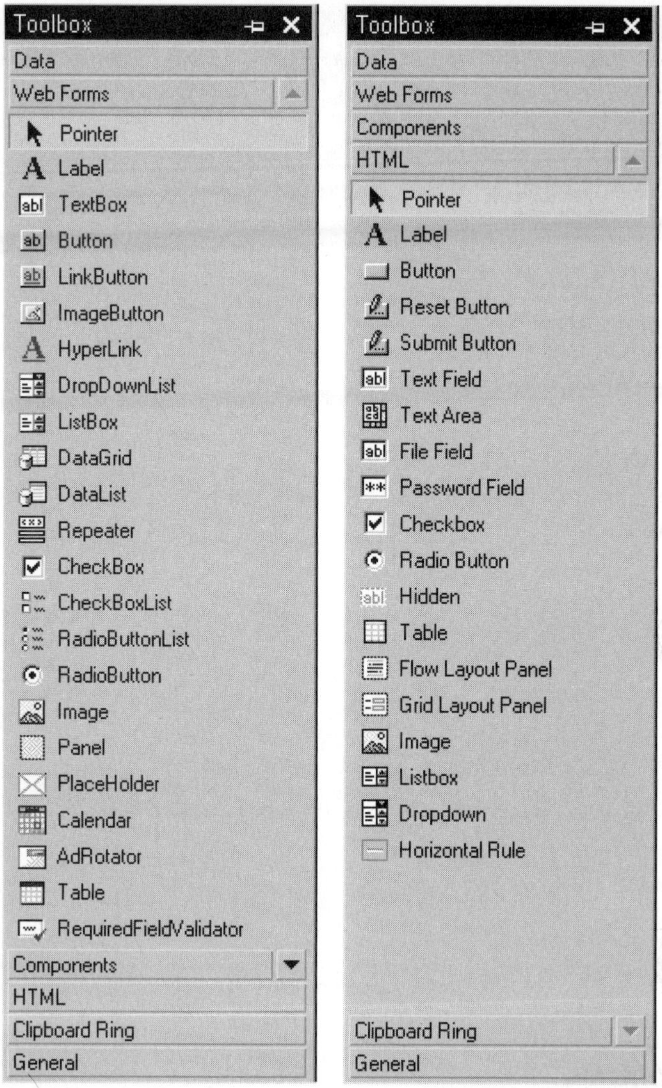

Figure 17-4

Figure 17-5 shows two sets of HTML controls, each has a TextBox and a Button. The first set of controls are HTML Server controls and the second set are HTML controls. The little green arrow icon on the top left corner of the controls distinguishes them as HTML Server controls.

Now that you have seen the two controls in design mode, take a look at the HTML behind the scenes for these controls. Figure 17-6 shows how the HTML for these two sets of controls differs.

Notice that the first TextBox control contains the ID and run at attributes, indicating that this control is an HTML Server control. The second TextBox control has neither of these properties, indicating that it is a standard HTML control and cannot be manipulated from your Visual Basic .NET code.

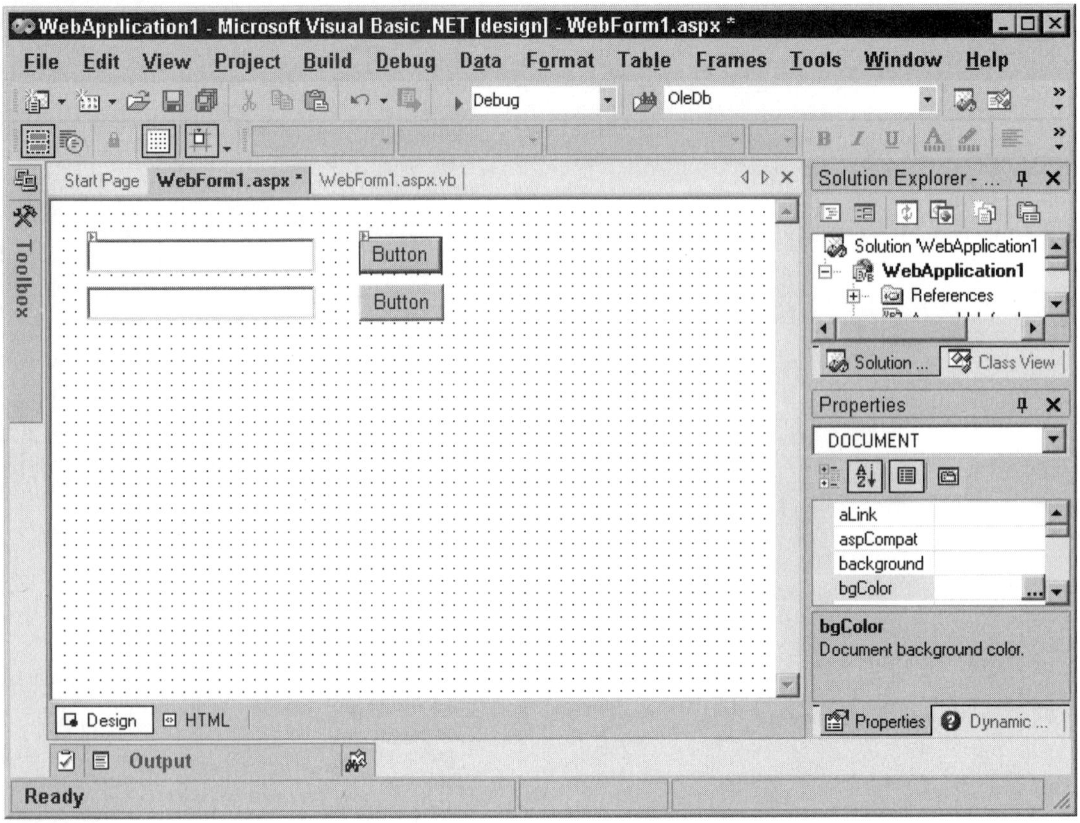

Figure 17-5

The first button on the form is an `asp:Button` HTML Server control. The second button is a regular HTML control. The code difference between the two buttons is another good reason to let the development environment handle the transition from HTML control to HTML Server control.

Web Server Controls

Web Server controls are the rich controls that behave very much like the Windows controls you've used throughout the book. When I say these are *rich controls*, I mean that they have lots of properties that can be set to customize the look and feel of the control. They can be bound to data and they expose their events to you in the development environment so that you can insert event handlers and write code to run when these events occur (such as when a user clicks on a button).

While the number of controls under the Web Forms tab in the Toolbox is far less than the number of controls found in the Windows Forms tab of the Toolbox, they are in fact very important to you as a developer. As just mentioned, they are capable of being bound to data, which is very important when writing Web applications. They can also be programmed in the same familiar environment to which you have become accustomed as shown in Figure 17-3, discussed earlier in this chapter.

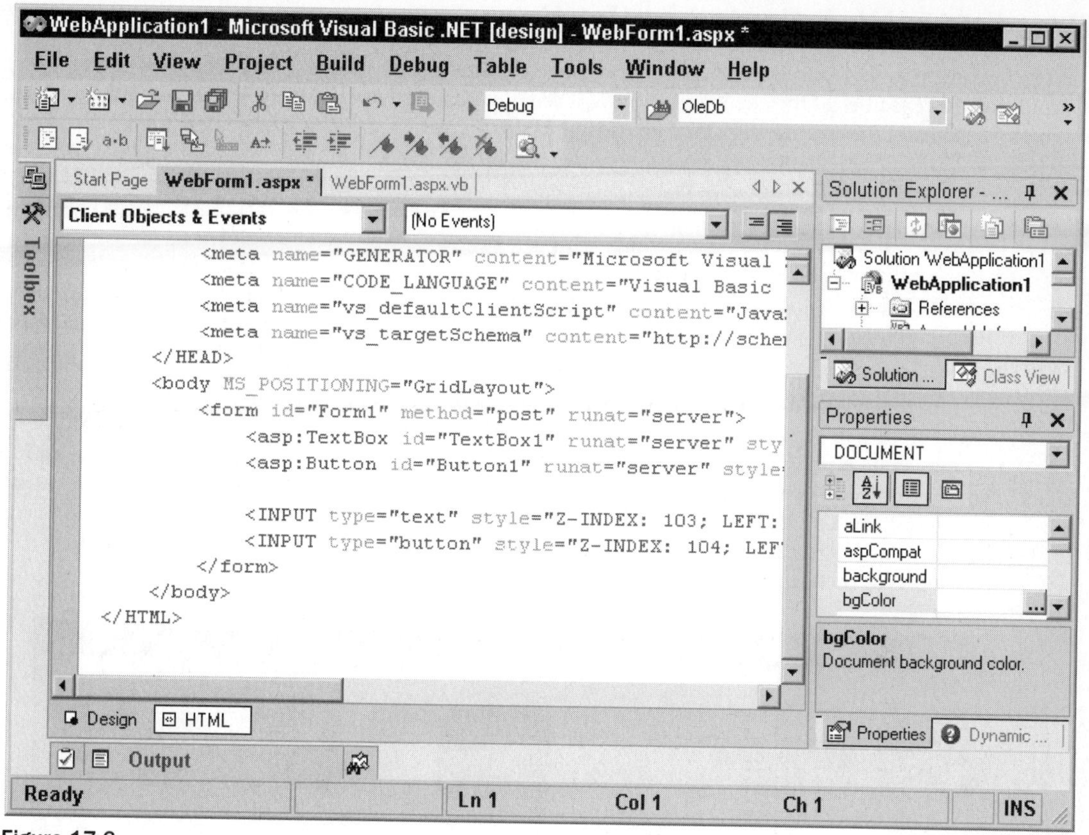

Figure 17-6

Notice that Figure 17-3 shows the Visual Basic .NET code behind the Web form and looks very similar to the code behind Windows Forms. This makes coding a Web form very similar to coding a Windows Form.

There are controls in the Web Forms tab in the Toolbox that are not found in a Windows Forms project. These include items such as validator controls, CheckBoxList, and RadioButtonList controls. *Validator controls* are typically used to perform client-side validation of data (although server-side validation can also be performed) and there are many validator controls that will do validation such as ensuring a field contains data, a field contains data in a certain range, a field contains data that compares to certain values, and so on. The CheckBoxList and RadioButtonList controls are particularly useful as, when bound to data, they can be used to automatically build a list of items from a `DataSet` object.

Web Applications

In this section, you will walk through the basic steps required to create a Web application. You will also be exploring the basic parts of a Web form, the controls available, the code behind the form, and how the Web form works.

Creating a Web Form Application

The Web form in this exercise will contain two sets of controls, one whose code executes at the server side and one that executes at the client side. You will see how to add these controls, write code for them, and explore the basic processing steps that are taking place.

Web Form Creation

1. Bring up the New Project dialog box, shown in Figure 17-7. As usual, select Visual Basic Projects from the Project Types list, but this time, select ASP.NET Web Application from the Templates list. Enter the name of **Client/server Processing** after the server in the Location box.

2. The Location text box contains the Web server on your local machine by default and this is fine for this exercise. You can also replace your machine name with the text localhost, which basically refers to the local machine. This allows the application to be developed on any machine without any changes to the project. However, you can use the Browse button and choose another Web server. Keep in mind though, that the Web server that you choose must be running IIS 5.x or later and it must have the .NET Framework installed on it. Be sure IIS is up and running at this point so the project can be created. Click the OK button to have this application created.

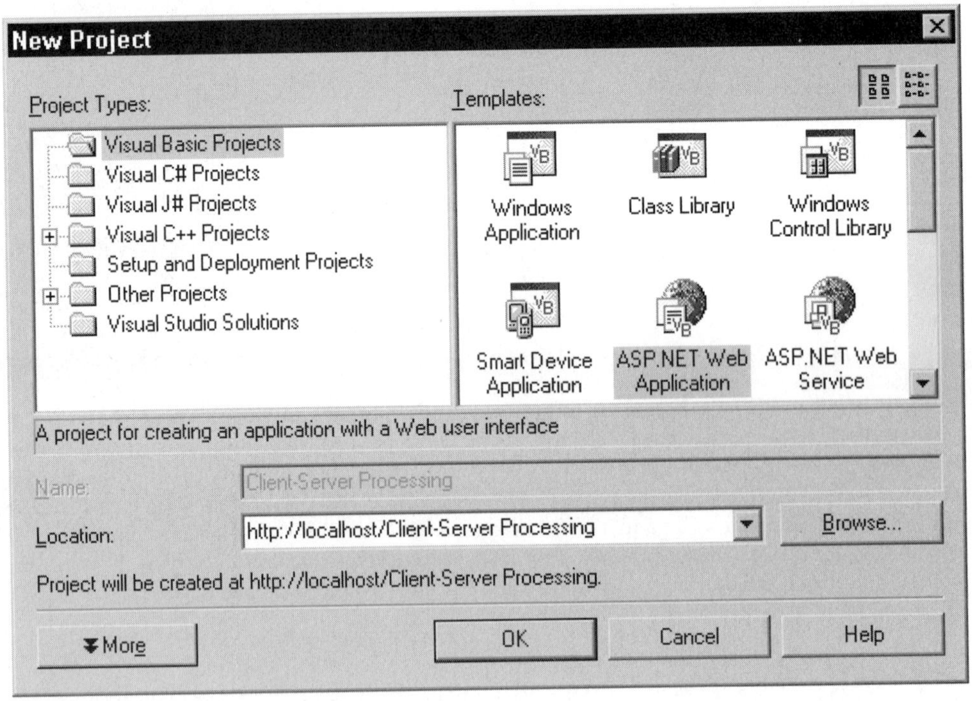

Figure 17-7

Visual Studio .NET will not only create the physical directory for this project, but also a virtual directory in IIS for this project and the files for this project.

The physical directory will be created in the default location where IIS was installed. For example, if IIS was installed using the default location, then your physical directory will be created as `C:\Inetpub\wwwroot\Client-Server Processing`. The virtual directory is used by IIS to specify your Web site. This is the address that you enter in a browser to get to your Web site.

3. By default, your Web page uses a grid layout as shown in Figure 17-8. As the message says on the page, you can change this layout mode by clicking on the pageLayout property in the Properties window and choosing FlowLayout. However, for our purposes, the GridLayout will do just fine.

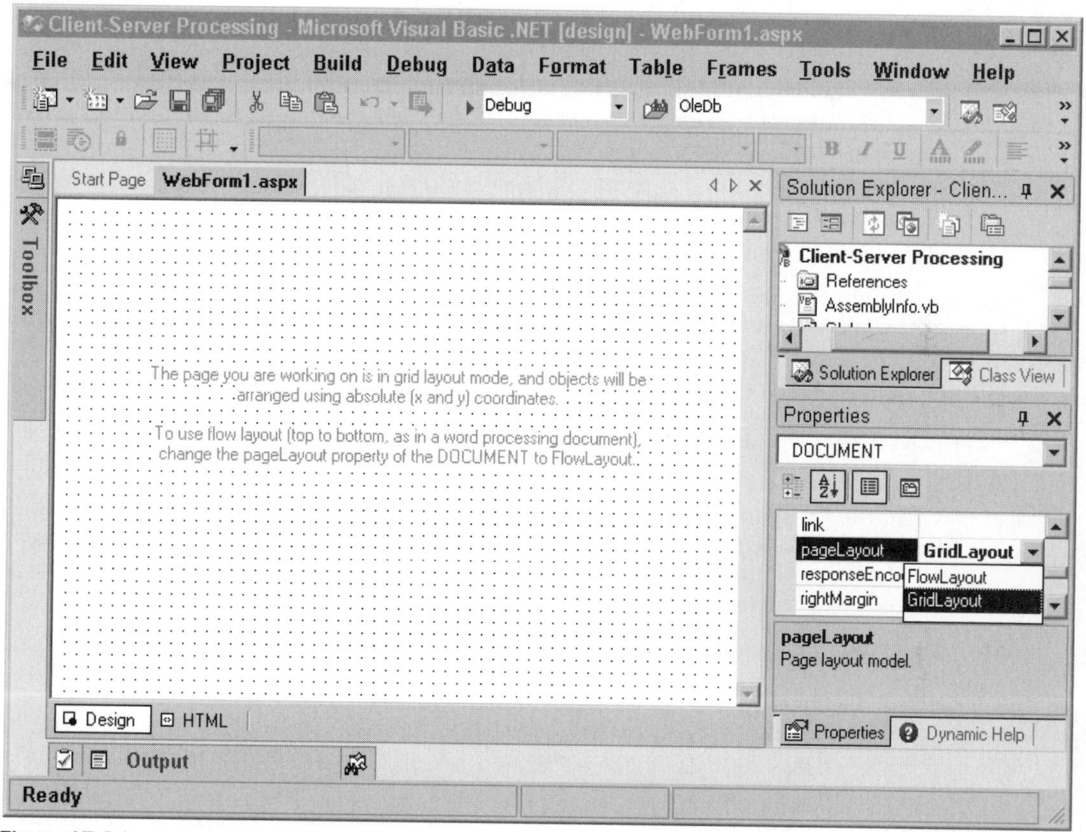

Figure 17-8

4. The default title that is displayed in the browser when you run your project is the URL for the page being displayed. You want something more meaningful here so click on the form and then in the Properties window set the title property to **Client/Server Processing.**

5. You want to add some HTML controls to this form so bring up the Toolbox. Then click on the HTML tab and add the controls listed here to your Web form:

    ❑   Add a Text Field control. Name it **txtServerTextField** and set these properties: Size = 30; Style = Z-INDEX: 101; LEFT: 10px; POSITION: absolute; TOP: 15px.

❑ Add a Button control. Name it **btnServerButton** and set these properties:
Style = Z-INDEX: 102; LEFT: 238px; WIDTH: 93px; POSITION: absolute; TOP: 14px;
HEIGHT: 24px; Value = Server-Side

❑ Add a Text Field control. Name it **txtClientTextField** and set these properties:
Size = 30; Style = Z-INDEX: 103; LEFT: 10px; POSITION: absolute; TOP: 46px

❑ Add a Button control. Name it **btnClientButton** and set these properties:
Style = Z-INDEX: 104; LEFT: 238px; WIDTH: 93px; POSITION: absolute; TOP: 45px;
HEIGHT: 24px; Value = Client-Side

❑ Add a Button control. Name it **btnClearButton** and set these properties:
Style = Z-INDEX: 105; LEFT: 238px; WIDTH: 93px; POSITION: absolute; TOP: 78px;
HEIGHT: 24px; Value = Clear Fields

6. You now want to convert the first Text Field and Button controls from HTML controls to HTML Server controls. Right-click on the first Text Field and choose Run As Server Control from the context menu.

Visual Studio .NET will convert this control to an HTML Server control and you will see a little green arrow icon in the upper left corner of the control. This is your indication that this is an HTML Server control.

7. Next, right-click the first button and again choose Run As Server Control from the context menu. Again, you will see the icon in the upper left corner of the control once it has been converted.

Your completed Web form should look similar to the one shown in Figure 17-9.

8. Before you begin, you want to run the project so you can get a feel of what the completed form will look like in a browser. Click on the Start icon on the toolbar or select the Debug ⇨ Start.

9. You should see your Web form displayed in a browser just like the one shown in Figure 17-10. Of course, since you have not added any code yet, there will be no functionality and clicking the buttons will not perform any actions. Notice that there is no identifiable difference between the HTML Server controls and the HTML controls as displayed on the form. The difference comes in the code that generates these controls and how you program them.

10. Close your browser so you can start looking at the code that has been generated so far.

Try It Out   **The HTML**

1. Click on the HTML tab at the bottom of the Web form. You can now view the HTML behind the form. The following HTML has been autogenerated and contains the necessary HTML to generate this Web form:

```
<%@ Page Language="vb" AutoEventWireup="false" Codebehind="WebForm1.aspx.vb"
Inherits="Client_Server_Processing.WebForm1"%>
<!DOCTYPE HTML PUBLIC "-//W3C//DTD HTML 4.0 Transitional//EN">
<HTML>
    <HEAD>
        <title>Client/Server Processing</title>
        <meta name="GENERATOR" content="Microsoft Visual Studio .NET 7.1">
        <meta name="CODE_LANGUAGE" content="Visual Basic .NET 7.1">
        <meta name="vs_defaultClientScript" content="JavaScript">
        <meta name="vs_targetSchema"
```

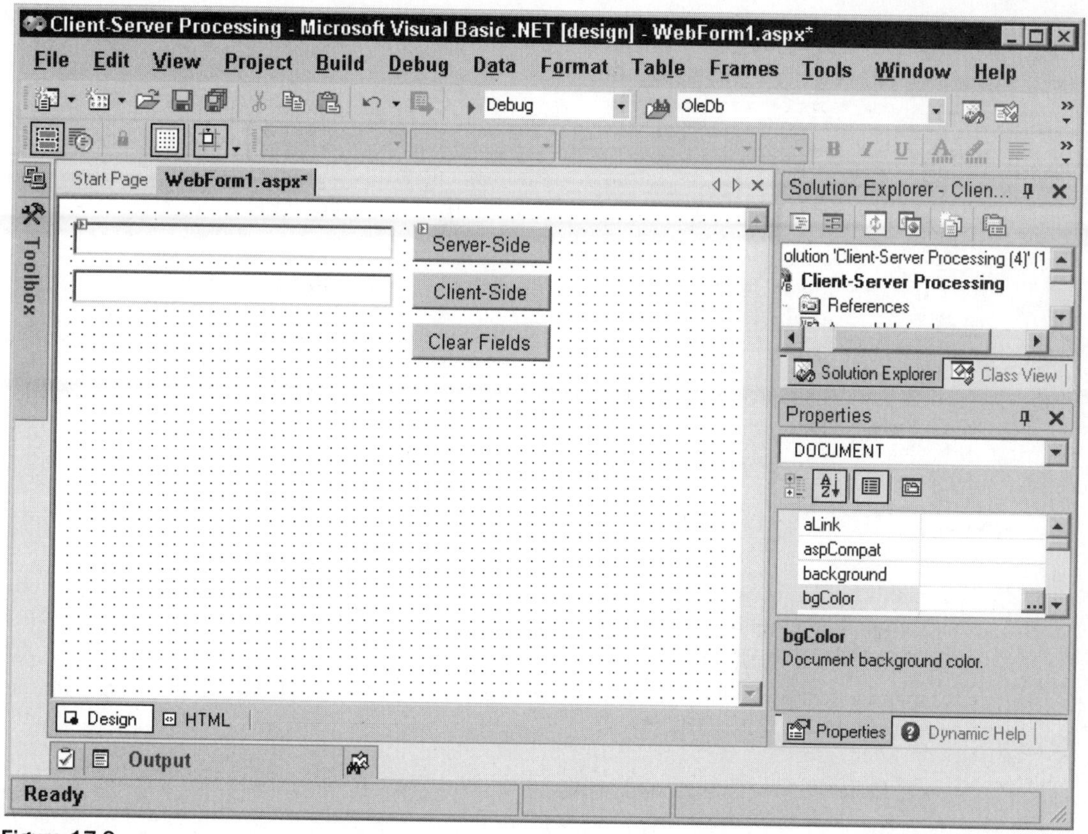

Figure 17-9

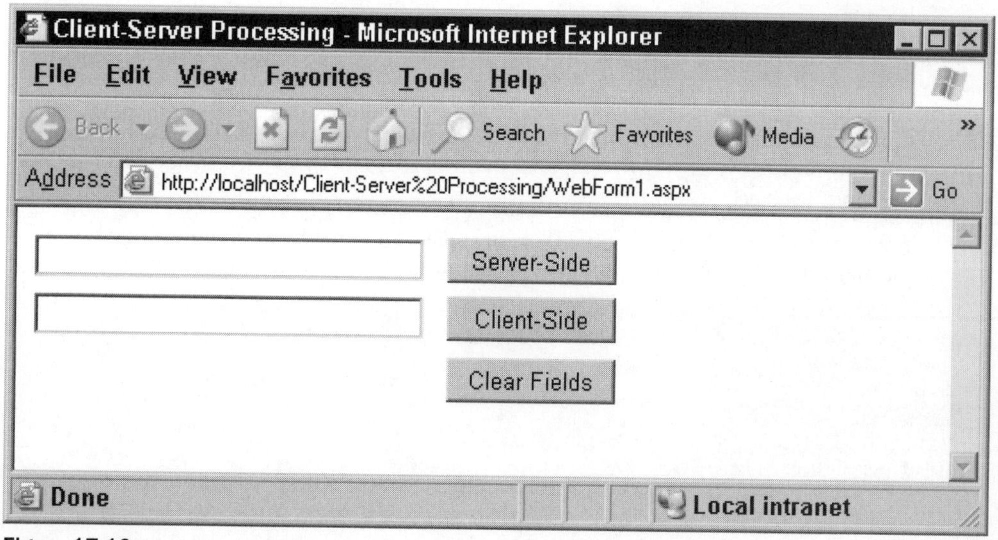

Figure 17-10

```
content="http://schemas.microsoft.com/intellisense/ie5">
    </HEAD>
<body MS POSITIONING="GridLayout">
    <form id="Form1" method="post" runat="server">
        <INPUT id="txtServerTextField" style="Z-INDEX: 101; LEFT: 10px;
POSITION: absolute; TOP: 15px" type="text" size="30" name="Text1"
runat="server">
        <INPUT id="btnServerButton" style="Z-INDEX: 102; LEFT: 238px; WIDTH: 93px;
POSITION: absolute; TOP: 14px; HEIGHT: 24px" type="button" value="Server-Side"
runat="server">
        <INPUT id="txtClientTextField" style="Z-INDEX: 103; LEFT: 10px;
POSITION: absolute; TOP: 46px" type="text" size="30">
        <INPUT id="btnClientButton" style="Z-INDEX: 104; LEFT: 238px; WIDTH: 93px;
POSITION: absolute; TOP: 45px; HEIGHT: 24px" type="button"value="Client-Side">
        <INPUT id="btnClearButton" style="Z-INDEX: 105; LEFT: 238px; WIDTH: 93px;
POSITION: absolute; TOP: 78px; HEIGHT: 24px" type="button"
value="Clear Fields">
    </form>
</body>
</HTML>
```

2. Since this book is about Visual Basic .NET, change the default client-side language that will be used from JavaScript to VBScript. Note that doing this will limit the browser that is supported to IE, since Netscape does not support VBScript.

    Change the following line of HTML. Click on any white space in HTML mode to bring up the properties for the DOCUMENT:

    ```
    <meta name=vs_defaultClientScript content="JavaScript">
    ```

    Click in the box for the defaultClientScript property and you will see a list of available languages for the client script. Choose VBScript from the list. Your altered line of HTML should now look like this:

    ```
    <meta name=vs_defaultClientScript content="VBScript">
    ```

3. You want to add some client-side code to execute when the page loads in the browser to set the Value property of your HTML text field. In order to do this you need to add an event handler for the Window object.

    In the Object combo box, select the Window object and then in the Event combo box, select the onload event. The following code will be added to your project:

    ```
    <script id=clientEventHandlersVBS language=vbscript>
    <!--

    Sub window_onload

    End Sub

    -->
    </script>
    ```

Notice that the `language` property has been specified automatically and is VBscript. This is because you modified the <META> element for the default client script.

4.   Place the following line of code in the `Window_OnLoad` procedure. This will cause the text field to contain the value shown in the code when this page is loaded:

```
Sub window_onload
    document.all.txtClientTextField.value = "Click the button ==>"
End Sub
```

5.   You now want to add the appropriate client-side code for the two Client-Side buttons in our Web form. Unlike server-side controls or in Visual Basic .NET, you cannot double-click the control in Design mode to have the procedure added. You must be in HTML mode, select the control in the Object combo box and then select the appropriate event in the Event combo box.

In the Object combo box select `btnClientButton` and in the Event combo box select the OnClick event. The following code will be added to your project:

```
Sub btnClientButton_onclick

End Sub
```

6.   You want to add some code in the `btnClientButton_onclick` procedure to change the text that is displayed in the client-side Text Field. When you click this button the text that is displayed in the client-side Text Field will change. Add the following code to this procedure:

```
Sub btnClientButton_onclick
    document.all.txtClientTextField.value = _
            "Client-side processing performed"
End Sub
```

7.   Now add the procedure for `btnClearButton`. Select `btnClearButton` in the Object combo box and then select the `OnClick` event in the Event combo box. The procedure for this button will be added just below the previous procedure.

8.   You want the code in `btnClearButton_onclick` to clear both Text Fields on the form. Add the following code to your project:

```
Sub btnClearButton_onclick
    document.all.txtServerTextField.value = ""
    document.all.txtClientTextField.value = ""
End Sub
```

How It Works

The first line of code that you see is the @ Page directive. This directive defines the page-specific attributes for the page such as the language used and the class name of the code behind the Web form. This directive can be placed anywhere in the Web page but it is common practice to place this directive at the top.

Note that Visual Studio .NET has done most of this for us. If you are happy with what Visual Studio .NET has done automatically, you don't need to understand all of the following details.

The @ Page directive is enclosed in server-side script tags. The beginning server-side script tag is specified with the less than and percent symbol (<%). The ending server-side script tag is specified with the percent symbol and a greater than sign (%>). You place all server-side code between these symbols:

```
<%@ Page Language="vb" AutoEventWireup="false" Codebehind="WebForm1.aspx.vb"
Inherits="Client_Server_Processing.WebForm1"%>
```

There are many attributes that can be specified in the @ Page directive but focus your attention on the ones that are in your code:

❏ The first attribute is the Language attribute, which specifies the language to be used while compiling code contained in the server-side script blocks (<% %>).

❏ The AutoEventWireup attribute is used to specify whether the page events are automatically enabled. This value is True by default, but in this case, Visual Studio .NET has set this value to False.

❏ The Codebehind attribute specifies the name of the file that contains the Visual Basic .NET code for your Web form. This file is a separate file from the Web form and contains all of the Visual Basic .NET code for your form.

❏ The Inherits attribute specifies the code-behind class in the code-behind file that this form inherits.

The next line of HTML is the <!DOCTYPE> element. You don't need to worry about this element, but it defines the document type definition for the page and the version of HTML that this document was written for:

```
<!DOCTYPE HTML PUBLIC "-//W3C//DTD HTML 4.0 Transitional//EN">
```

The next few lines of code are the HTML elements that start your Web form. Every Web form starts with the <HTML> element followed by the <HEAD> element that describes the header section of the Web page.

Notice that the first line of HTML code in the <HEAD> section is the <TITLE> element. This is the text that is displayed in the title bar when your page is displayed in a browser:

```
<HTML>
  <HEAD>
    <title>Client/Server Processing</title>
```

Following the <TITLE> element are several <META> elements. These elements contain information about the page and can be used by some search engines to index the page. They are also used to convey information about the page to the server and to the client browser and are used by Visual Studio .NET as you write code for this Web form.

The first <META> element specifies that this page is a Visual Studio .NET-generated page. The next <META> element specifies that the language that this page was generated with was Visual Basic .NET. The third <META> element specifies the default client-side language for the page (VBScript). The fourth <META> element is used to specify the target browser for this page (IE5):

```
<meta content="Microsoft Visual Studio .NET 7.1" name="GENERATOR">
<meta content="Visual Basic .NET 7.1" name="CODE_LANGUAGE">
```

```
    <meta content="VBScript" name="vs_defaultClientScript">
    <meta content="http://schemas.microsoft.com/intellisense/ie5"
name="vs_targetSchema">
```

<META> elements are normally optional but are used here by Visual Studio .NET for various tasks and documentation as you saw when you changed the client-side scripting language and then inserted our client-side script block.

Notice in the previous code that there is a closing tag for the <HEAD> element (</HEAD>). Most HTML elements have a closing tag which is the element name preceded by a forward slash. The <META> elements just happen to be one of those HTML elements that do not require a closing element.

The next two lines of code are the starting elements for the <BODY> element and the <FORM> element. The <BODY> element defines the start of the body of our page and the <FORM> element defines the start of your form.

```
<body MS_POSITIONING="GridLayout">
<form id=Form1 method=post runat="server">
```

Almost every HTML element has multiple properties that can be specified to further define how that element will render the HTML that you see. If you click on the <BODY> element and look in the Properties window, you will see all of the available attributes that can be set for the <BODY> element.

The <FORM> element has its ID property set, which allows you to access this element in your code. It also has the Method property set with a value of POST, which means that this form will post the values to the server when you submit this form. The other Method option is GET, which you do not use very often because it shows the values in the form in the URL address bar of the Web browser. The RUNAT property distinguishes the code from client-side code and ensures that the form is run on the server side and the resulting HTML is sent to the client.

The next two elements are <INPUT> elements. The <INPUT> element creates a variety of input controls on a page and uses the Type property to distinguish what type of control should be built. The first type of control being built here is the Text Field control as specified by the Type property of text and the second type of control being built is the button control:

```
<INPUT id=txtServerTextField style="Z-INDEX: 101; LEFT: 10px;
    POSITION: absolute; TOP: 15px" type=text size=30
    runat="server">
<INPUT id=btnServerButton style="Z-INDEX: 102; LEFT: 238px;
    WIDTH: 93px; POSITION: absolute; TOP: 14px; HEIGHT: 24px"
    type=button value=Server-Side runat="server">
```

Remember that these controls were modified to be HTML Server controls and can be distinguished as such by the RunAt property, which has been set to use a value of server. The Style property is used to position these controls at absolute x and y coordinates on the page because you are using a MS_POSITIONING property value of GridLayout. The Z-Index property indicates the stacking order of the elements and only applies to elements that specify the Position property.

The Size property in the first <INPUT> control is used to specify how wide the Text Field should be. The Value property in the second <INPUT> control is used to specify the text on the button. The next three

`<INPUT>` controls are for the second text field and the last two buttons. Notice the absence of the `RunAt` property indicates that these controls are strictly HTML controls:

```
<INPUT id=btnClientButton style="Z-INDEX: 104; LEFT: 238px;
        WIDTH: 93px; POSITION: absolute; TOP: 45px; HEIGHT: 24px"
        type=button value=Client-Side>
<INPUT id=txtClientTextField style="Z-INDEX: 103; LEFT: 10px;
        POSITION: absolute; TOP: 46px" type=text size=30>
<INPUT id=btnClearButton style="Z-INDEX: 105; LEFT: 238px;
        WIDTH: 93px; POSITION: absolute; TOP: 78px; HEIGHT: 24px"
        type=button value="Clear Fields">
```

Again, you see the `Style` property has been set for you to position these controls at absolute x and y coordinates. These were set when you positioned these controls on the Web form.

The code in your page is wrapped up by specifying the closing elements for the `<FORM>`, `<BODY>`, and `<HTML>` elements.

```
        </FORM>
    </body>
</HTML>
```

There are several client-side events that happen when a Web page loads in a browser and one of those events is the `OnLoad` event for the `Window` object. The `Window` object represents an open window in a browser. One `Window` object is created for each page that gets loaded into a browser. For example, your page will cause one Window object to be created. If your page contained frames, then one Window object for the page as a whole and one Window object for each frame in the page would be created.

The text field is defined inside the `<FORM>` element, meaning that the form is the parent of this control. You cannot access this text field directly you must access it though its parent. So what does this mean? When you access a control inside a form, you must first specify the form name followed by the control name as shown in the following code fragment:

```
form1.txtClientTextField.value = "Click the button ==>"
```

However, the form itself is a child of the `Document` object and the text field is considered a child of the `Document` object. You access the `Document` object by using the name document. All controls in your page are considered children of the `Document` object so you can actually access the text field as shown in the next code fragment.

Notice that in this example you have specified the `All` collection of the `Document` object. This will retrieve all elements that are contained in the `Document` object. You then follow this using the `ID` of your text field:

```
document.all.txtClientTextField.value = "Click the button ==>"
```

Which method should you use? This depends on the complexity of your Web forms. If all controls are located inside your form then you can use the first method. However, I find it easier to use one method, which reduces confusion and keeps the code in your Web page consistent, so I typically use the second method.

Note that at the moment, you have no server-side code. Every time a user views this page, the server will send the same HTML and VBScript code to the browser and the browser will interpret it. In the next stage you will write some code that executes on the server.

Client/Server Processing Using Visual Basic .NET

1. Right-click on WebForm1.aspx in the Solution Explorer window and then select the View Code option, you will see the form class code for this form. Opening up all the plus signs will display the Visual Basic .NET code and allows you to write server-side code:

```
Public Class WebForm1
    Inherits System.Web.UI.Page

#Region " Web Form Designer Generated Code "

    'This call is required by the Web Form Designer.
    <System.Diagnostics.DebuggerStepThrough()> Private Sub InitializeComponent()

    End Sub
    Protected WithEvents btnServerButton As
System.Web.UI.HtmlControls.HtmlInputButton
    Protected WithEvents txtServerTextField As
System.Web.UI.HtmlControls.HtmlInputText

    'NOTE: The following placeholder declaration is required by the Web Form
Designer.
    'Do not delete or move it.
    Private designerPlaceholderDeclaration As System.Object

    Private Sub Page_Init(ByVal sender As System.Object, ByVal e As
System.EventArgs) Handles MyBase.Init
        'CODEGEN: This method call is required by the Web Form Designer
        'Do not modify it using the code editor.
        InitializeComponent()
    End Sub

#End Region

    Private Sub Page_Load(ByVal sender As System.Object, ByVal e As
System.EventArgs) Handles MyBase.Load
        'Put user code to initialize the page here
    End Sub

End Class
```

2. Modify the Page_Load method as shown in the following code. This will cause the Value property in the server-side text field control to be set here in code and the resulting HTML sent to the browser. Note that you can only manipulate server-side controls here; you cannot manipulate client-side (HTML) controls:

```
Private Sub Page_Load(ByVal sender As Object, _
        ByVal e As System.EventArgs) Handles MyBase.Load
    'Put user code to initialize the page here
    txtServerTextField.Value = "Click the button ==>"
End Sub
```

3. You also want to add some code to the HTML Server button. The easiest way to have the appropriate procedure added to our code is to switch to the Web form in Design mode and double-click on the button. Once you do, the following procedure will be added to your class.

Add the following line of code to this procedure. This will change the text in the `Value` property of your text field when the server processes this procedure:

```
Private Sub btnServerButton_ServerClick(ByVal sender As _
        System.Object, ByVal e As System.EventArgs) _
        Handles btnServerButton.ServerClick
    txtServerTextField.Value = "Server-side processing performed"
End Sub
```

How It Works

As you can see, this is very similar to the code you see while coding Windows Forms, as you have a public class. Instead of the class inheriting from `System.Windows.Forms.Form`, this class inherits from `System.Web.UI.Page`, which renders a Web form instead of a Windows form.

Since you converted two HTML controls to HTML Server controls, you see the code that has been added to your class inside the designer generated code so that you may access these controls in code:

```
Protected WithEvents txtServerTextField As _
        System.Web.UI.HtmlControls.HtmlInputText
Protected WithEvents btnServerButton As _
        System.Web.UI.HtmlControls.HtmlInputButton
```

The next bit of code was also autogenerated and should not be modified. Like its counterpart in a Windows form, this code is used to initialize and build the resulting HTML that gets sent to the browser.

The `Page_Load` method (on the server) is where you place any code that you need to run before the page is sent from the server to the browser. Here you can set the various properties of the two HTML Server controls, before the HTML is sent to the browser.

You added code to display some initial text in the first text field on the form. You could do this by setting the `Value` property while viewing the Web form in either Design mode or HTML mode, simply by clicking on the code and modifying the `Value` property in the Properties window. However, you modified the property by adding the following code:

```
txtServerTextField.Value = "Click the button -->"
```

That's all the code you need to add and now you are ready to test.

Try It Out   **Testing Your Web Form**

1. Click on the Start icon on the toolbar or click on the Debug ⇨ Start menu option.

   The form that is displayed should look similar to the one shown in Figure 17-11. Before you begin testing notice the title in the title bar. This is the text that you specified in the <TITLE> element. This is always followed by a dash and the text `Microsoft Internet Explorer` (when using Internet Explorer).

Figure 17-11

2. Click on the Server-Side button and you will see the text in the text field changes from `Click the button ==>` to `Server-side processing performed`. The Web form was posted back to the server to process the request as indicated by a flicker of the browser and the text in the status bar shows that it is processing the Web page. This is because the Button and Text Field controls were defined as server-side controls, so the server must process the events for these controls and build the HTML to be sent back to the browser.

3. Now click on the Client-Side button. Notice that the text changed in this Text Field to `Client-side processing performed` and the form did not get posted back to the server to process the request because the status bar did not indicate that it was processing the Web page. This change in the text was made at the client in your client-side script and your Web page should now look like the one shown in Figure 17-12.

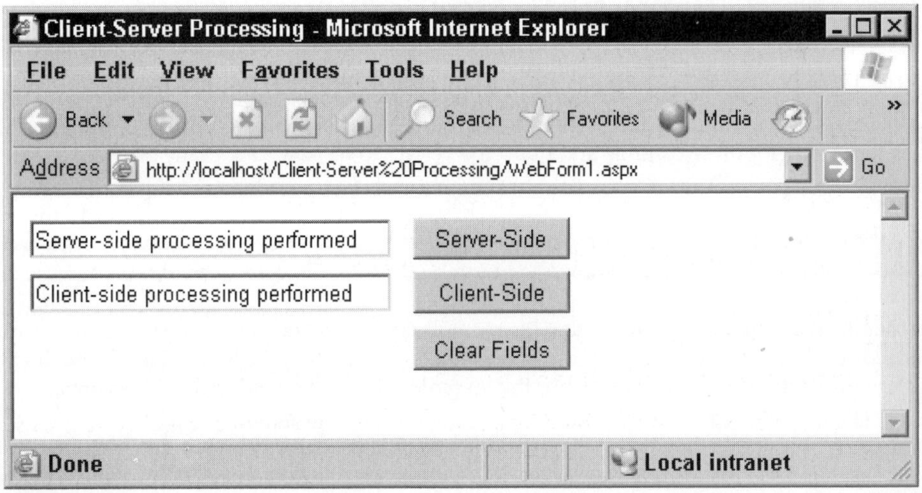

Figure 17-12

4.   Click on the Server-Side button again. Your Web page should now look like the one shown in Figure 17-13, again indicating that the form was posted back to the server for processing.

Figure 17-13

How It Works

If you view the source in the browser for this Web page, you will see the client-side script that you coded. To view the source, right-click on an empty area of the page and choose View Source from the context menu or select View ⇨ Source from the browser's menu.

You will see the scripts that you coded and the HTML that you saw in HTML mode when working with your Web form. There is also some HTML and script that has been added by Visual Studio .NET, which allows this Web form to be posted back to the server for processing.

Visual Studio .NET automatically generates this code when the Web page is compiled and provides the appropriate event handlers to post the form back to the server.

When you clicked on the Server-Side button, the Web form was posted back to the server to process the request. This is because button and text field were defined as server-side controls and the server must process the events for these controls and build the HTML to be sent back to the browser.

In contrast, when the Client-Side button was clicked, the form did not get posted back to the server to process the request. This change in the text was made at the client in your client-side script and your Web page should now look like the one shown in Figure 17-13.

To further illustrate the point that the first button will post the form back to the server for processing, the Server-Side button was clicked again. You should have noticed that the text in the second Text Field had been changed back to its original state, but the text in the first Text Field looked the same.

The reason for this is that the form was posted back to the server for processing, which caused the text in the first Text Field to indicate that the Server-Side button was clicked. The server built a new page, with the new text, and then sent the resulting HTML back to the browser. Your script that executes on the `Window_OnLoad` event caused the text in the second text field to be set back to its original state.

You can further test this by clicking on the Clear Fields button, which will cause all Text Fields to be cleared and then clicking on the Server-Side button again. You will see the same results as you saw previously.

This *Try It Out* has shown you how a Web form is built, sent to the client for processing, and posted back to the server for processing. The next couple of *Try It Outs* that you go through will further demonstrate how a Web form is posted back to the server for processing.

Data Binding in Web Forms

After having a first hand look at how a Web form is built and processed, you now want to move on and incorporate data access into your Web forms. You will be using a DataGrid control in your Web form to display authors' names, book titles, and the price of their books. The next two *Try It Outs* will use the DataGrid control, but each one will incorporate different functionality for it.

You can always use the wizards to set up and perform data binding but you will be focusing on how to do this through code as you did in the last chapter. This allows you to see what is actually going on behind the scenes and provides you with greater control over how updates are applied. There are several different ways that you can perform data binding in a Web form. One way is to place all of your code in the Web form class, which is the code behind the Web form. Another way is to place your code in a server-side script block within the HTML in the Web form itself. You will be taking a look at both methods in the remaining *Try It Outs* in this chapter. You could also mix your code between the Web form class and server-side script blocks but you will not be covering that method here.

Since data binding itself is basically the same for a Web form as it is for a Windows Form you will forgo all of the details that you have covered it in the last chapter. However, if you need to refresh your memory, peruse the *Data Binding* section in the previous chapter.

The thing to keep in mind as you start to work with bound data in your Web forms is the fact that each time you need to perform some sort of operation on the data (such as editing it), the Web form gets posted back to the server for processing. For example, suppose you need to sort the data, the Web form is posted back to the server for this operation to take place. Once the Web form is posted back to the server, it is built from scratch, the appropriate logic executed, and the resulting HTML sent back to the browser.

All of these round trips take time to process and can be costly when dealing with large amounts of data. You did not have to worry about this round trip processing with Windows Forms as the form did not have to be rebuilt, only the fields are refreshed with the new data.

There is a solution to this problem and it lies with XML. You can use XML on the client and perform all of this sorting there. However, this is a topic that is beyond the scope of this book. Further details on this can be found in *Professional VB .NET 2nd Edition* (ISBN 1-86100-716-7).

When building Web forms for a production application, keep in mind the processing that must take place and always try to reduce the amount of data that must be sent back and forth between the client and the server.

DataGrid Example

This *Try It Out* will use a DataGrid control in a Web form and you will bind data to it through code. The functionality that you will incorporate in this DataGrid will allow the user to sort the data in it by clicking on the header for a specific column. The Web form will then post the request back to the server for processing and the Web form will be rebuilt and then sent back to the client.

Once again, you will be using the pubs database in SQL Server for our data. You will be using the `System.Data.SqlClient` namespace to access SQL Server. Remember that this namespace has been optimized for use exclusively with SQL Server and will provide better performance than the `System.Data.OleDb` namespace.

The data binding that you will perform in this exercise will be written exclusively in the Web form class, the code-behind the Web form. This is the environment with which you are most familiar—when coding Windows Forms and will demonstrate how you can use this class.

Try It Out	DataGrid Sorting

1. Create a new ASP.NET Web Application project called **DataGrid Sorting**. Remember that the Location combo box specifies the Web server that this project will use. The project folder will be placed on that Web server under the WWW Root folder.

2. In the Toolbox, click on the Web Forms tab and drag the DataGrid control from the Toolbox onto your form. Position the DataGrid near the upper-left corner of the form. The exact position is not important here.

3. You have seen how to set the properties of a control while in Design mode, so let's explore how to set the properties while in HTML mode. At the bottom of the Web form, click on the HTML tab to view the HTML behind your form.

4. Click on the line of code that defines the DataGrid control. The partial line of code that will be generated is shown here.

```
<asp:DataGrid id="DataGrid1"
```

Notice that the Properties window reflects that your cursor is on the DataGrid control and displays its properties. This is another easy way to set the properties for this control.

5. Set the following properties of the DataGrid control in your project:

- ❑ Set (ID) to grdAuthors*
- ❑ Set AllowSorting to True
- ❑ Set AlternatingItemStyle-BackColor to Any light color you like
- ❑ Set AutoGenerateColumns to True
- ❑ Set BackColor to White or any other light color you prefer
- ❑ Set CellPadding to 3
- ❑ Set Font-Name to Verdana
- ❑ Set Font-Size to 8pt

❑   Set GridLines to None

❑   Set HeaderStyle-BackColor to Maroon or any other dark color you prefer

❑   Set HeaderStyle-Font-Bold to True

❑   Set HeaderStyle-ForeColor to White

After setting these properties you can switch to Design mode and see how these settings affect the look of the DataGrid, which should look like Figure 17-14.

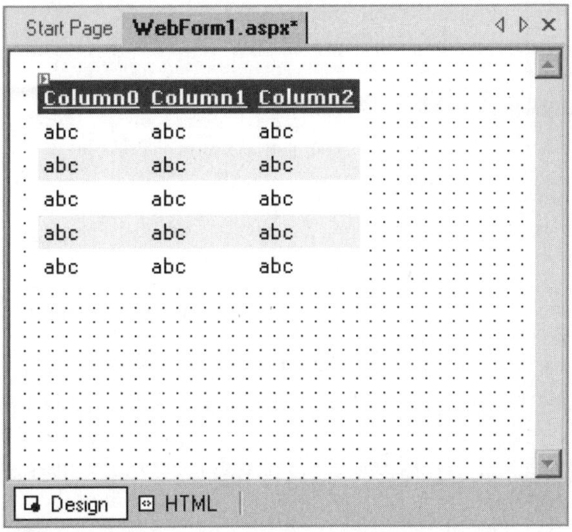

Figure 17-14

6.   There is one last item that you want to change in the HTML. Switch back to HTML mode and set the <TITLE> element to DataGrid Sorting. This will be the title that is displayed in your browser:

```
<title>DataGrid Sorting</title>
```

7.   In the Solution Explorer window, right-click on WebForm1.aspx and choose View Code from the context menu to view the code behind.

The first thing that you need to do here is to import the necessary namespaces to access SQL Server. Add the following namespaces to your code:

```
Imports System.Data
Imports System.Data.SqlClient

Public Class WebForm1
```

8.   Next you need to declare a Connection object that is global in scope to this class, so add the following code:

```
Public Class WebForm1
    Inherits System.Web.UI.Page


    ' Declare a Connection object that is global in scope...
    Dim objConnection As SqlConnection
```

9. Add the following code to the `Page_Load` method:

```
'Put user code to initialize the page here

    ' Initialize the Connection object...
    objConnection = New SqlConnection("Server=localhost;" & _
        "Database=Pubs;User ID=sa;Password=vbdotnet;")

    ' Only bind the data the first time the page is built...
    ' Subsequent post backs will be to sort the data in the grid...
    If Not (IsPostBack) Then
        BindGrid("Last Name")
    End If
```

Don't forget to update the connection information (server, password, and user ID) so that it will connect to your SQL Server or MSDE database.

10. The next method that you code is `BindGrid`, which you call from `Page_Load`:

```
Sub BindGrid(ByVal strSortField As String)
    ' Declare objects...
    Dim objDataSet As DataSet
    Dim objDataAdapter As SqlDataAdapter

    ' Set the SQL string...
    objDataAdapter = New SqlDataAdapter( _
        "SELECT au_lname AS 'Last Name', au_fname AS 'First Name', " & _
        "title AS 'Book Title', price AS 'Retail Price' " & _
        "FROM authors " & _
        "JOIN titleauthor ON authors.au_id = titleauthor.au_id " & _
        "JOIN titles ON titleauthor.title_id = titles.title_id " & _
        "ORDER BY au_lname, au_fname", objConnection)

    ' Initialize the DataSet object and fill it...
    objDataSet = New DataSet()
    objDataAdapter.Fill(objDataSet, "Authors")

    ' Declare a DataView object, populate it,
    ' and sort the data in it...
    Dim objDataView As DataView = _
        objDataSet.Tables("Authors").DefaultView
    objDataView.Sort = strSortField

    ' Bind the DataView object to the DataGrid control...
    grdAuthors.DataSource = objDataView
    grdAuthors.DataBind()
```

```
      ' Clean up...
      objDataView = Nothing
      objDataSet = Nothing
      objDataAdapter = Nothing
   End Sub
```

11. The next method will be called when you click on a column in the `DataGrid` to be sorted and will pass the column name on to `BindGrid`.

To have this procedure inserted into your code, click on the Class Name combo box and select grdAuthors. Then click on the Method Name combo box and select SortCommand.

```
Private Sub grdAuthors_SortCommand(ByVal source As Object, _
         ByVal e As _
         System.Web.UI.WebControls.DataGridSortCommandEventArgs) _
         Handles grdAuthors.SortCommand
   ' Bind the DataGrid using the sort column requested
   BindGrid(e.SortExpression)

End Sub
```

12. That's all the code you need to make this project functional. Let's test it out now! Click the Run button on the Visual Studio .NET toolbar. This will start up a Web browser. When the browser loads your Web page (and this might take a few moments while the data is being retrieved from the database), you should see results similar to Figure 17-15.

13. At this point, you can test the functionality of the DataGrid control by clicking on a column header. The Web form is posted back to the server and the page will start executing from the top. The first procedure that is executed is the `Page_Load` procedure, followed by the `grdAuthors_SortCommand` procedure. `grdAuthors_SortCommand` calls the `BindGrid` procedure, passing it the column to be sorted on.

You will then see the `DataGrid` redisplayed, sorted by the column that you clicked on.

As you can see, you implemented some very useful functionality here and it did not take a lot of code. You were also able to do this by a method that you are already familiar with, that is writing code in a form class.

How It Works

To begin with, you added the necessary namespaces to utilize SQL Server functionality:

```
Imports System.Data
Imports System.Data.SqlClient
```

Then you declared a `SqlConnection` object that was global in scope to this class. This will allow you to access this object in multiple procedures in the class. As you learned in previous chapters, you use `SqlConnection` when you are accessing SQL Server or MSDE:

```
   ' Declare a Connection object that is global in scope...
   Dim objConnection As SqlConnection
```

One of the first procedures that executes when a Web page loads is the `Page_Load` procedure. This is where you want to place the code to initialize your connection to the database. This procedure will be

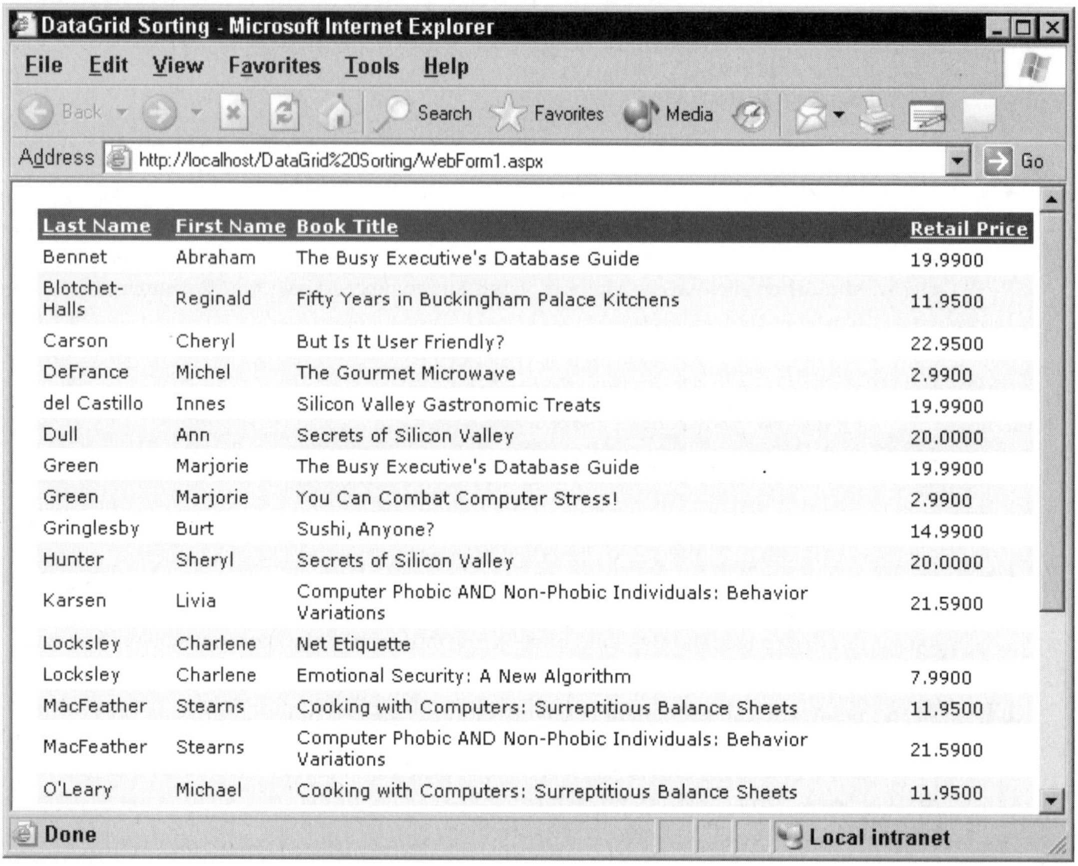

Figure 17-15

called every time this page is loaded and executed:

```
' Initialize the Connection object...
objConnection = New SqlConnection("Server=localhost;" & _
    "Database=Pubs;User ID=sa;Password=vbdotnet;")
```

The IsPostBack property returns a True or False value indicating whether the page has been posted back from a client request or whether the page is being loaded for the first time. The value is returned as True when the client posts the page back to the server for processing.

If this is the initial load of the page, then you want to call the BindGrid procedure and pass it a sort parameter of "Last Name." This will cause the data to be sorted by the Last Name column before it is bound to the DataGrid if this is the first time that the screen has loaded.

If this is not the initial load of the page, IsPostBack will be True and the following code will not execute:

```
If Not (IsPostBack) Then
    BindGrid("Last Name")
End If
```

The `BindGrid` method will extract the data from the SQL Server, sort it, and bind it to your DataGrid control. Notice that this procedure has one parameter defined (`strSortField`) and that is for the sort field.

When you are working with ASP.NET, always consider whether code in Page_Load should only execute if the page is executing for the first time. Otherwise, your application will end up being quite slow.

The first thing that you did in `BindGrid` was to declare some objects that will be needed. You covered the `DataSet` class and the `SqlDataAdapter` class's counterpart (`OleDbDataAdapter`) in Chapters 15 and 16. These two classes perform the exact same function and that is to act as a data bridge between your application and the database:

```
Sub BindGrid(ByVal strSortField As String)
    ' Declare objects...
    Dim objDataSet As DataSet
    Dim objDataAdapter As SqlDataAdapter
```

You then initialized the `SqlDataAdapter` object and set the SQL string to be executed. In the last chapter, you saw how you could modify the DataGrid control by setting the column headers to text that was more meaningful. This time you are using the SQL statement to return more meaningful column names.

When you select a column from a table, you can assign what is known as a column alias to that column. You do this by specifying the `AS` keyword in your `SELECT` statement following the column that has been selected and assigning a new name to that column. Notice that your column names are enclosed in single quotes because there are spaces in the column names. If you did not include spaces in the alias column names then you would not have to enclose them in single quotes.

You are assigning a column alias to every column selected in this `SELECT` statement. Note that this `SELECT` statement is very similar to the one that you used in the beginning of the last chapter:

```
        ' Set the SQL string...
        objDataAdapter = New SqlDataAdapter( _
        "SELECT au_lname AS 'Last Name', au_fname AS 'First Name', " & _
        "title AS 'Book Title', price AS 'Retail Price' " & _
        "FROM authors " & _
        "JOIN titleauthor ON authors.au_id = titleauthor.au_id " & _
        "JOIN titles ON titleauthor.title_id = titles.title_id " & _
        "ORDER BY au_lname, au_fname", objConnection)
```

Remember that, when the dataset has been populated with data it will contain not only the data, but the structure of the data also. This means that it will contain column names and the name of the table that the data was selected from. Hence, the new column names that you assigned in the `SELECT` statement will be propagated down to the `DataSet` object.

Once you have populated your dataset, you declare a `DataView` object and populate it with the data contained in the dataset. You need to do this because the `DataSet` object does not allow you to sort the data within the object.

```
        Dim objDataView As DataView = _
            objDataSet.Tables("Authors").DefaultView
```

After you have populated the `DataView` object, you can sort the data in it using the `Sort` property. You do that here by using the `strSortField` parameter that was passed into this procedure:

```
objDataView.Sort = strSortField
```

The `DataGrid` control, like the Windows controls that you have worked with up to this point, has events that are fired and you can place code inside the procedures for these events.

When you click on a header column in the datagrid, the Web form will be posted back to the server and the `grdAuthors_SortCommand` procedure will be executed.

The e parameter in this procedure contains the `SortExpression` property, which returns the column name that the user clicked on and wants to sort by:

```
Private Sub grdAuthors_SortCommand(ByVal source As Object, _
          ByVal e As _
          System.Web.UI.WebControls.DataGridSortCommandEventArgs) _
          Handles grdAuthors.SortCommand
    ' Bind the DataGrid using the sort column requested
    BindGrid(e.SortExpression)

End Sub
```

Remember that the `BindGrid` procedure retrieves the data from SQL Server, populates the `DataView` object, sorts the data, and finally binds the `DataGrid` control with the sorted data. This procedure simply calls the `BindGrid` procedure to sort on the column that the user has selected.

When you ran the project, you should have noticed that the column headers matched the column names in our SQL statement and were underlined, indicating that they were hyperlinks that performed an action. In this case, they execute JavaScript that will post the form data back to the server for processing. This JavaScript was automatically built for us and will handle the steps necessary to post this Web form back to the server. Once the datagrid is sent to the browser, it is nothing more than HTML—you can check by viewing the source code in your browser.

Updating Data with a DataGrid

In the first *Try It Out* in this chapter, you wrote client-side script in your HTML that would load the initial contents and change the contents of a text field on your Web form. You have seen how to write client-side script in our HTML and in the next *Try It Out*, you will be taking this one step further by showing you how to write server-side script in your HTML.

Not only will you write server-side script to extract data and bind it to a DataGrid, but you will also be writing code to handle the various events from the DataGrid, such as editing and updating a row of data in it. This will give you an opportunity to explore an alternative method of handling the events of the controls on your form and also show you how to bind data to your controls using script.

Writing a server-side Visual Basic .NET code that is embedded in HTML in order to bind data is not that much different from writing code in a form class to bind data. You still have to define your data objects, access the database, and bind your controls. You have the same procedures that you did in a form class and you will be using the same language, Visual Basic .NET. There are a few minor differences, because you are mixing server-side code in with HTML, and this section points out the differences as you go along.

In this *Try It Out*, you will build a Web form that contains a DataGrid that allows you to update the rows of data within it. Once the updates are made, you will be able to apply the updates or cancel them by clicking on a hyperlink as you did when you sorted the data.

All of the updates to SQL Server are made using server-side script with the updated data. Therefore, you will be using the classes in the `System.Data.SqlClient` namespace.

In addition to writing server-side script, you will be exploring more details about the `DataGrid` control as you provide the functionality to edit and update rows of data. This will involve manually defining the columns to be bound and also specifying templates for the data in a column. *Templates* allow you to provide labels and text boxes in a cell in the DataGrid to display and allow editing of the data. You can apply styles to the data so that it is displayed in different fonts and colors, and you can also apply special formatting of the data, such as formatting numeric values into currency values.

You will be displaying the same data that you saw in the last *Try It Out*. However, your SELECT statement will be slightly different, as you will see.

Try It Out   DataGrid Updates

1. Create a new ASP.NET Web Application called **DataGrid Updates**.

2. In the Toolbox, click on the Web Forms tab and drag the `DataGrid` control onto your form. Position it near the upper left corner of the form. Again, the exact position is not important here.

3. Switch to HTML mode by clicking on the HTML tab. Find and click on the DataGrid control and then set its properties according to the following list (the important ones are bold here):

    ❑   **Set (ID) to grdAuthors**

    ❑   Set AlternatingItemStyle-BackColor to WhiteSmoke

    ❑   **Set AutoGenerateColumns to False**

    ❑   Set BackColor to White

    ❑   Set CellPadding to 3

    ❑   **Set DataKeyField to title_id**

    ❑   Set Font-Name to Verdana

    ❑   Set Font-Size to 8pt

    ❑   Set GridLines to None

    ❑   Set HeaderStyle-BackColor to Maroon

    ❑   Set HeaderStyle-Font-Bold to True

    ❑   Set HeaderStyle-ForeColor to White

4. Now add the following event handlers to the `DataGrid` control:

```
<asp:DataGrid id=grdAuthors
    style="Z-INDEX: 101; LEFT: 13px; POSITION: absolute; TOP: 12px"
    runat="server"
    AlternatingItemStyle-BackColor=WhiteSmoke
    AutoGenerateColumns=false
    BackColor=White
    CellPadding=3
    DataKeyField="title_id"
    Font-Name=Verdana
    Font-Size=8pt
    GridLines=None
    HeaderStyle-BackColor=Maroon
    HeaderStyle-Font-Bold=true
    HeaderStyle-ForeColor=White
    OnEditCommand="EditGridData"
    OnCancelCommand="CancelGridData"
    OnUpdateCommand="UpdateGridData">
</asp:DataGrid>
```

5. Place the following lines of HTML directly below those you just entered (before the `</asp:DataGrid>` close tag). This defines the start and end of the Columns collection for the `DataGrid` control:

```
<Columns>

</Columns>
```

6. Next you need to add the columns between the `<Columns>` and `</Columns>` elements. The first column that you need to add is a column for the edit commands:

```
<Columns>
    <asp:EditCommandColumn
        EditText="Edit Row"
        CancelText="Cancel Edit"
        UpdateText="Update Row"
        ItemStyle-Wrap="False"/>
</Columns>
```

7. The rest of the columns that you want to add are: the first column of bound data in the DataGrid (the ID, which you will keep hidden), the author's last name, author's first name, title of the book, and finally the price of the book:

```
    ItemStyle-Wrap="False"/>

<asp:BoundColumn
    DataField="title_id"
    Visible="False"/>

<asp:BoundColumn
    DataField="au_lname"
    HeaderText="Last Name"
```

```
          ReadOnly="True"
          ItemStyle-Wrap="False"/>

      <asp:BoundColumn
        DataField="au_fname"
        HeaderText="First Name"
        ReadOnly="True"
        ItemStyle-Wrap="False"/>

      <asp:TemplateColumn
        HeaderText="Title"
        ItemStyle-Wrap="False">
        <ItemTemplate>
          <asp:Label runat="server"
            Text='<%# DataBinder.Eval (Container.DataItem, "title") %>'/>
        </ItemTemplate>

        <EditItemTemplate>
          <asp:TextBox runat="server"
          ID="edit_title"
          Font-Name="Verdana"
          Font-Size="8pt"
          Width="400"
          Text='<%# DataBinder.Eval(Container.DataItem, "title") %>'/>
        </EditItemTemplate>
      </asp:TemplateColumn>

      <asp:TemplateColumn
        HeaderText="Price"
        HeaderStyle-Font-Bold="True"
        ItemStyle-HorizontalAlign=Right>
        <ItemTemplate>
          <asp:Label runat="server"
          Text='<%# DataBinder.Eval(Container.DataItem, "price", "{0:C2}")%>'/>
        </ItemTemplate>
        <EditItemTemplate>
          <asp:TextBox runat="server"
          ID="edit_price"
          Font-Name="Verdana"
          Font-Size="8pt"
          Width="50"
          Text='<%# DataBinder.Eval(Container.DataItem, "price", "{0:C2}") %>'/>
        </EditItemTemplate>
      </asp:TemplateColumn>
</Columns>
```

8. The last bit of HTML code that you want to add is the code to set the title in the page. Find the `<TITLE>` element at the beginning of the page and add a title of **DataGrid Updates**:

```
<title>DataGrid Updates</title>
```

9. Since you will not be using the form class for any code in this exercise, you need to remove the @ `Page` directive. Remove this line of code from your project. Leaving it in will prevent the `Page_Load` and `Page_Unload` events from firing in our server-side script in your HTML page.

10. Next, you want to import the namespaces that are required when accessing data in a data store. These are the same namespaces that you used in the last *Try It Out*. Place them at the top of the page:

```
<%@ Import Namespace="System.Data.SqlClient" %>
<%@ Import Namespace="System.Data" %>
```

11. You need to add a server-side script block between the ending </HEAD> element and before the <BODY> element. Right-click between these two elements and select Insert Script Block ⇨ Server. The following code is inserted into your project:

```
<script runat=server>

</script>
```

12. You want to set the language for this script block, so click on the first line of this script block and notice that the Properties window displays all available properties for this script block. Set the language property to Visual Basic. Your script block should now show the language property and it should be set to vb:

```
<script runat=server language=vb>

</script>
```

13. The first line of code that you need to place inside this script block is the declaration for our Connection object as shown below. This is the same Connection object that you used in the last *Try It Out* and, again, you are using the SqlConnection class for this object:

```
' Declare a Connection object that is global
' in scope to this script...
Dim objConnection As SqlConnection
```

14. The Page_Load procedure is one of the first procedures to be executed, so insert the following code in the script block as well:

```
Sub Page_Load(Sender As Object, E As EventArgs)
    objConnection = New _
        SqlConnection("Server=localhost;Initial Catalog=Pubs;" & _
        "User ID=sa;Password=vbdotnet;")

    If Not (IsPostBack)
        BindGrid()
    End If
End Sub
```

Remember that you need to specify the User ID and Password parameters that are defined in your database.

15. Now you want to add the `BindGrid` procedure to the script block. As mentioned previously, this procedure will not perform any sorting this time so you have not specified any parameters in this procedure:

```
Sub BindGrid()
   Dim objDataSet As DataSet
   Dim objDataAdapter As SqlDataAdapter

   objDataAdapter = New SqlDataAdapter( _
      "SELECT au_lname, au_fname, titles.title_id, title, price " & _
      "FROM authors " & _
      "JOIN titleauthor ON authors.au_id = titleauthor.au_id " & _
      "JOIN titles ON titleauthor.title_id = titles.title_id " & _
      "ORDER BY au_lname, au_fname", _
      objConnection)
   objDataSet = New DataSet()
   objDataAdapter.Fill(objDataSet, "Authors")

   grdAuthors.DataSource = objDataSet
   grdAuthors.DataBind()

End Sub
```

16. Next, you want to add the `EditGridData` procedure to the script block. You defined this event handler in the `DataGrid` control:

```
Sub EditGridData(Sender As Object, E As DataGridCommandEventArgs)
   grdAuthors.EditItemIndex = CType(E.Item.ItemIndex, Integer)
   BindGrid()
End Sub
```

17. `CancelGridData`, which should also be added to the script block, is necessary if the user chooses to cancel the update:

```
Sub CancelGridData(Sender As Object, E As DataGridCommandEventArgs)
   grdAuthors.EditItemIndex = -1
   BindGrid()
End Sub
```

18. Finally, the `UpdateGridData` procedure will be called when the user clicks on the Update Text link for the row of data that they are editing. Both this and the event handler for `CancelGridData` were added to the `DataGrid` control at the start of this *Try It Out*:

```
Sub UpdateGridData(Sender As Object, E As DataGridCommandEventArgs)
   Dim objCommand As SqlCommand
   Dim objTextBox As TextBox

   Dim strSQL As String = "UPDATE titles " & _
      "SET title = @Title, price = @Price " & _
      "WHERE title_id = @ID"

   objCommand = New SqlCommand(strSQL, objConnection)
```

```
        objCommand.Parameters.Add(New SqlParameter("@ID", _
                SqlDbType.VarChar, 6))
        objCommand.Parameters.Add(New SqlParameter("@Title", _
                SqlDbType.VarChar, 80))
        objCommand.Parameters.Add(New SqlParameter("@Price", _
                SqlDbType.Money, 8))

        objCommand.Parameters("@Id").Value = _
                grdAuthors.DataKeys(CType(E.Item.ItemIndex, Integer))

        objTextBox = E.Item.FindControl("edit_title")
        objCommand.Parameters("@Title").Value = objTextBox.Text
        objTextBox = E.Item.FindControl("edit_price")

        If objTextBox.Text.Substring(0, 1) = "$" Then
            objTextBox.Text = objTextBox.Text.Remove(0, 1)
        End If
        objCommand.Parameters("@Price").Value = objTextBox.Text

        objCommand.Connection.Open()

        objCommand.ExecuteNonQuery()

        grdAuthors.EditItemIndex = -1

        objCommand.Connection.Close()

        BindGrid()

    End Sub
```

You are now ready to run this project and test it out, but before you do, you'll go through what you have actually done during the addition of the previous code.

How It Works

When you write server-side script while in HTML mode, you do not have access to the events for the DataGrid control as you did when you wrote code in the form class. Therefore, you need to add these events for the DataGrid to your code manually. These event handlers will post the form back to the server and instruct the server on which procedures are to be executed. You are specifying the event name, followed by the procedure in your script that it should execute:

```
OnEditCommand="EditGridData"
OnCancelCommand="CancelGridData"
OnUpdateCommand="UpdateGridData">
```

You needed to add some columns since you are not allowing the DataGrid to automatically generate the columns. You began by adding a column for the edit commands. This special column, defined by the HTML asp:EditCommandColumn, will automatically provide hyperlinks that will execute JavaScript when you click on the text. The JavaScript will be automatically generated.

```
<asp:EditCommandColumn
    EditText="Edit Row"
    CancelText="Cancel Edit"
```

```
UpdateText="Update Row"
ItemStyle-Wrap="False"/>
```

The first property in this column is `EditText` and defines the text that is displayed in the column. The next two properties, `CancelText` and `UpdateText`, will display the corresponding text in this column once you click the Edit Row hyperlink.

The `ItemStyle-Wrap` property indicates whether the text in this column can wrap over two or more lines. By setting this property to `False`, you prevent the text from wrapping and so the width of the column will expand to allow all of the text to be displayed on one line.

The next column is the first column of bound data in the DataGrid. This column is defined by the HTML `asp:BoundColumn` and will bind the column of data from your `DataSet` object as specified in the `DataField` property.

```
<asp:BoundColumn
    DataField="title_id"
    Visible="False"/>
```

The `DataField` property specifies the column of data in the `DataSet` object that should be bound to this column. The second property (`Visible`) specifies whether the column should be shown in the grid. You have set this property to `False` indicating that this column is hidden. The reason for this is that you need the data for this row as it provides the primary key for the row and will be posted back to the server when you perform updates.

Next, you added a column for the author's last name, followed by one for the author's first name. The `HeaderText` property is used to change the text that is displayed in the header. Remember that by default the text that is displayed in the header is the column name. Since the column name doesn't make much sense to the end user, you specify text that is meaningful. In the last *Try It Out*, you did this in the SELECT statement by assigning column aliases. The method you choose is entirely up to you and one method is not better than the other. However, this method provides better self-documentation within the code:

```
<asp:BoundColumn
    DataField="au_lname"
    HeaderText="Last Name"
    ReadOnly="True"
    ItemStyle-Wrap="False"/>

<asp:BoundColumn
    DataField="au_fname"
    HeaderText="First Name"
    ReadOnly="True"
    ItemStyle-Wrap="False"/>
```

The `ReadOnly` property will let the `DataGrid` control know that this column cannot be edited.

The fourth column you added was the one for the title of the book. You must specify a definition for your own edit fields, which is what you are doing here with the `asp:TemplateColumn`. This column type allows you to customize the controls in a column in the DataGrid:

```
<asp:TemplateColumn
    HeaderText="Title"
    ItemStyle-Wrap="False">
```

You specify the `HeaderText` and `ItemStyle` properties just as you did for the other columns. Then you specify the `ItemTemplate` for the data that is displayed. This property sets the template to be used to display the data in a read-only format. This is how you will initially see the data in the DataGrid. You need to specify an `ItemTemplate`—when the data is in read-only mode, and an `EditItemTemplate` to control how the data is displayed when you edit a row of data:

```
<ItemTemplate>
<asp:Label runat="server"
    Text='<%# DataBinder.Eval (Container.DataItem, "title") %>'/>
</ItemTemplate>
```

Within the `ItemTemplate` property you define a `Label` control as indicated by the `asp:Label` code. You set its `Text` property using the `DataBinder.Eval` method, which evaluates a binding expression against an object. The `Container.DataItem` method is used to extract the title column from the `DataSet` object and place the contents into this label.

Notice that you use the standard ASP.NET data binding tags (`<%#` and `%>`) to encapsulate your data binding expression. The `Eval` method of the `DataBinder` class is used to parse and evaluate a data binding expression at runtime.

The `EditItemTemplate` is used to specify the control to display when a column is being edited. Within this template, you have defined a text box and have set the various properties of it, the first of which is the ID property. You assign an ID property to this control to make it easier to access in our server-side script:

```
<EditItemTemplate>
<asp:TextBox runat="server"
    ID="edit_title"
    Font-Name="Verdana"
    Font-Size="8pt"
    Width="400"
    Text='<%# DataBinder.Eval(Container.DataItem, "title") %>'/>
</EditItemTemplate>
</asp:TemplateColumn>
```

The other properties set the font name, font size, and the width of the text box. The last property here sets the text in the textbox and again uses the `DataBinder.Eval` method.

Finally, you added a column for the price of the book. You may have noticed in the last *Try It Out* that you did not format the price of the books. However, you want to do it this time to demonstrate the formatting options when binding data. The `Text` property of the `Label` and `TextBox` controls has special formatting being applied to the data using an overloaded version of the `Eval` method:

```
Text='<%# DataBinder.Eval(Container.DataItem, "price", "{0:C2}")%>'/>
```

The `DataFormatString` of {0:C2}, indicates that the data should be formatted in the currency format and that it should contain two decimal places. This property has two parts separated by a colon. The part before the colon specifies the index of the data in a zero-based list. Since you have no list you have specified a value of 0.

The second part contains the format character to be used, in this case C for currency and the number following the format character, which is specified when formatting currency or decimal values. You have specified a value of 2, indicating that two digits are required to be present after the decimal. If a price has no cents then two zeros will be inserted.

When importing namespaces in an ASPX page, you must use the @ Import directive. This directive imports the namespace that you specify. You added the following code shown to your project where the @ Page directive was defined:

```
<%@ Import Namespace="System.Data.SqlClient" %>
<%@ Import Namespace="System.Data" %>
```

Remember that the Page_Load procedure is one of the first procedures to be executed and this is where you placed our code in the last *Try It Out* to initialize your Connection object. Therefore, you must code this procedure in your script as shown. The first thing that you do in this procedure is to initialize your Connection object:

```
Sub Page_Load(Sender As Object, E As EventArgs)
    objConnection = New _
        SqlConnection("Server=localhost;Initial Catalog=Pubs;" & _
        "User ID=sa;Password=;")
```

The last part of the procedure should also look familiar to you as you are using IsPostBack property to determine if this is the first time this page has been loaded. Remember that this property returns a value of False only if this is the first time this page is loaded:

```
    If Not (IsPostBack)
        BindGrid()
    End If
End Sub
```

You are calling the same procedure as you did in your last *Try It Out*, which is the BindGrid procedure. Notice that this time, however, you have no parameters. This is because you are not performing any sorting in this *Try It Out*. When the data is displayed it will be sorted by the author's last name and first name because you used the ORDER BY clause in your SELECT statement.

The BindGrid procedure will not perform any sorting this time, so you have not specified any parameters in this procedure. The first thing that you do in this procedure is to declare the objects that you need. Again, you are using the DataSet and SqlDataAdapter classes to declare your objects:

```
Sub BindGrid()
    Dim objDataSet As DataSet
    Dim objDataAdapter As SqlDataAdapter
```

Next, you initialize the SqlDataAdapter object setting the SQL string to be executed. Your SELECT statement looks a little different from the last *Try It Out*, as you are not using column aliases. You have an ORDER BY statement and you are also selecting an extra column. This new column, title_id is the primary key column in the titles table. When you update a book title and price, you need this data to let you know which row of data to update:

```
objDataAdapter = New SqlDataAdapter( _
    "SELECT au_lname, au_fname, titles.title_id, title, price " & _
    "FROM authors " & _
```

```
"JOIN titleauthor ON authors.au_id = titleauthor.au_id " & _
"JOIN titles ON titleauthor.title_id = titles.title_id " & _
"ORDER BY au_lname, au_fname", _
objConnection)
```

Next, you initialize the `DataSet` object and then populate it by executing `Fill` method of the `SqlDataAdapter` object:

```
objDataSet = New DataSet()
objDataAdapter.Fill(objDataSet, "Authors")
```

You then bind the DataGrid to the `DataSet` object by specifying the `DataSource` property and setting it to your `DataSet` object. Then you call the `DataBind` method of the DataGrid to actually perform the binding.

```
grdAuthors.DataSource = objDataSet
grdAuthors.DataBind()

End Sub
```

When you click on the Edit Text hyperlink in the DataGrid for a specific row, it will cause the Web form to be posted back to the server for processing. This will allow the server to format the selected row in the DataGrid for editing, which causes the text boxes to be displayed with the current data in it. The following `EditGridData` procedure contains the necessary code to make this happen.

```
Sub EditGridData(Sender As Object, E As DataGridCommandEventArgs)
    grdAuthors.EditItemIndex = CType(E.Item.ItemIndex, Integer)
    BindGrid()
End Sub
```

The `EditItemIndex` property determines which row in the DataGrid should be edited. When you set this property, the DataGrid will display text boxes in this row of data for editing.

You set this property using the `DataGridCommandEventArgs` that are passed to this procedure when the Web form is posted back to the server. This class contains information about the events raised and lets you know on which row of data the event was raised. Using the `Item` property you can determine which row of data the user wants to edit. You use the `CType` function just to ensure the value in the `ItemIndex` property is converted to an `Integer` value since this is what the `EditItemIndex` property expects.

Finally, you call the `BindGrid` procedure to reload the DataGrid with data and to set it up for editing. The selected row will have the text boxes added because the `EditItemIndex` property is set.

Once a user has started editing a row of data, they have the option of either canceling the edit or updating the data. This next procedure (`CancelGridData`) will be executed if the user chooses to cancel the update. You do this simply by setting the `EditItemIndex` property to 1. This causes the text boxes for this row of data to be removed. Then you call the `BindGrid` procedure to reload the DataGrid:

```
Sub CancelGridData(Sender As Object, E As DataGridCommandEventArgs)
    grdAuthors.EditItemIndex = -1
    BindGrid()
End Sub
```

The `UpdateGridData` procedure will be executed if the user decides to update the data. The first thing that you do in this procedure is to declare the objects that you need. Here you are declaring a `SqlCommand` object that will be used to execute the UPDATE statement to update the row of data in the database and a `TextBox` object to retrieve the data that is being updated from the DataGrid:

```
Sub UpdateGridData(Sender As Object, E As DataGridCommandEventArgs)
    Dim objCommand As SqlCommand
    Dim objTextBox As TextBox
```

You then declare and set the SQL string that will be used to update the database. The `SqlCommand` class uses parameters in your SQL string as shown here and as you saw in the previous chapter. These parameters are defined with an at (@) sign followed by the name of the parameter:

```
Dim strSQL As String = "UPDATE titles " & _
    "SET title = @Title, price = @Price " & _
    "WHERE title_id = @ID"
```

You initialize the `SqlCommand` object next, specifying the SQL string variable and the `SqlConnection` object:

```
objCommand = New SqlCommand(strSQL, objConnection)
```

You start adding parameters to the `SqlCommand` object next. This should look familiar as you added parameters to the `SqlCommand` object in the previous chapter. Here you initialize and add a new parameter all in one step. You pass the parameter several arguments, the first of which is the parameter name. Then you specify the data type for the parameter followed by the size of the data type.

The first parameter is a SQL `VarChar` data type, which contains string data. You have specified that this parameter can contain a maximum of six characters:

```
objCommand.Parameters.Add(New SqlParameter("@ID", _
        SqlDbType.VarChar, 6))
```

The second parameter is also a SQL `VarChar` data type and you have specified that this parameter can contain a maximum of 80 characters:

```
objCommand.Parameters.Add(New SqlParameter("@Title", _
        SqlDbType.VarChar, 80))
```

The third and final parameter contains a SQL `Money` data type. Remember that instead of specifying the maximum value here, you must specify the storage size for this parameter in SQL Server, which is 8 bytes:

```
objCommand.Parameters.Add(New SqlParameter("@Price", _
        SqlDbType.Money, 8))
```

Now that your parameters have been defined, you populate these parameters with data. The `@ID` parameter is populated with the data in the `DataKeys` property of the DataGrid. You get the correct data by specifying the `Item` property, which contains the row of data that you are editing:

```
objCommand.Parameters("@Id").Value = _
        grdAuthors.DataKeys(CType(E.Item.ItemIndex, Integer))
```

Next, you must find the control with the name of `edit_title`. You do this by using the `FindControl` method of the `Item` property of the `DataGridCommandEventArgs` class. Once you find the control, you assign it to the `TextBox` object that you defined earlier. This allows you to access the data that was placed in the text box when the data was edited.

Using the `Text` property of the `TextBox` object, you assign the data in that control to the parameter `@Title`:

```
objTextBox = E.Item.FindControl("edit_title")
objCommand.Parameters("@Title").Value = objTextBox.Text
```

You perform the same process to find the edit_price textbox. However, before assigning the value in the `TextBox` object to the parameter you first check for and remove the dollar sign, if one is present. This is not a valid character for the `Money` data type and will cause an error if you try to assign it to the `@Price` parameter.

Using the `Left` function, you check for the presence of the dollar sign in the first position, and if present, remove it using the `Right` function. The `Left` function returns the specified number of characters in the left portion of a string, while the `Right` function returns the specified number of characters to the right of a string.

When you use the `Substring` function in your code as shown next, you are only returning the left-most character in the string because you have specified an offset of 0 and a length of 1 in the call to the function. Then you use the `Remove` function to remove the first character.

Once you have checked for, and if necessary, removed the dollar sign, you assign the value in this `TextBox` object to the `@Price` parameter:

```
objTextBox = E.Item.FindControl("edit_price")
If objTextBox.Text.Substring(0, 1) = "$" Then
    objTextBox.Text = objTextBox.Text.Remove(0, 1)
End If
objCommand.Parameters("@Price").Value = objTextBox.Text
```

At this point, you are ready to execute our SQL string to update the database so you open your `SqlConnection` object first. Then you execute the SQL string by executing the `ExecuteNonQuery` method of the `SqlCommand` object:

```
objCommand.Connection.Open()

objCommand.ExecuteNonQuery()
```

You then set the `EditItemIndex` of the DataGrid to 1, to indicate that no row is to be in edit mode and then call the `BindGrid` procedure to have the DataGrid repopulated with data. Once the `DataGrid` is repopulated with data it will reflect the updated row of data.

```
grdAuthors.EditItemIndex = -1

objCommand.Connection.Close()
```

```
    BindGrid()

  End Sub
```

Now you can go on to test your project!

Try It Out — Testing the DataGrid Updates Project

1. Start the project. Once the Web form has been loaded in the browser, you should see results similar to Figure 17-16.

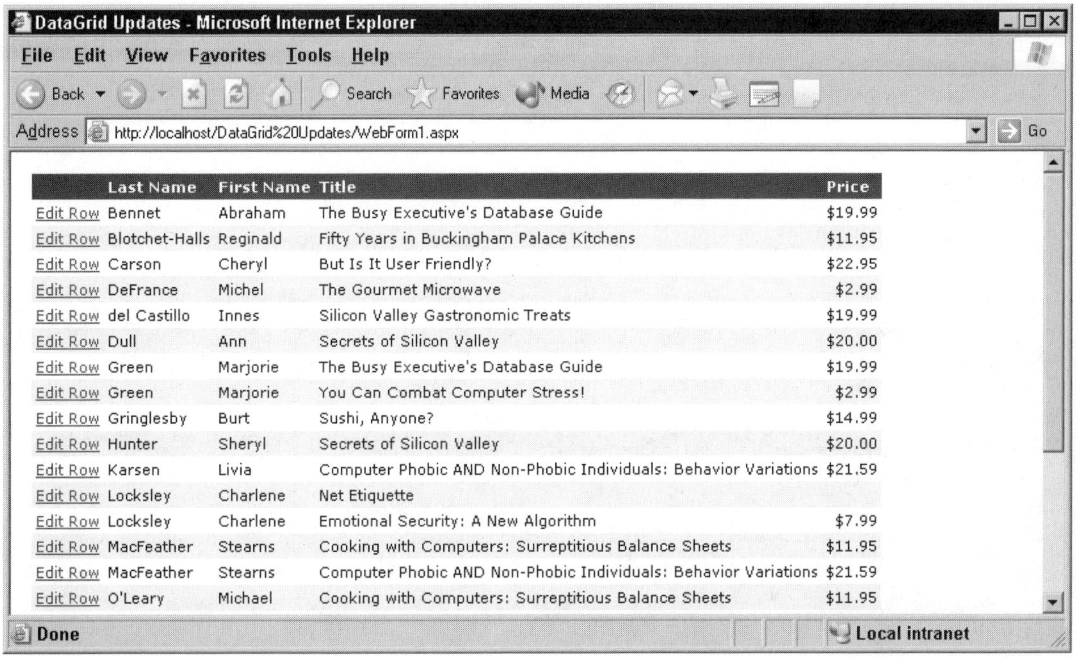

	Last Name	First Name	Title	Price
Edit Row	Bennet	Abraham	The Busy Executive's Database Guide	$19.99
Edit Row	Blotchet-Halls	Reginald	Fifty Years in Buckingham Palace Kitchens	$11.95
Edit Row	Carson	Cheryl	But Is It User Friendly?	$22.95
Edit Row	DeFrance	Michel	The Gourmet Microwave	$2.99
Edit Row	del Castillo	Innes	Silicon Valley Gastronomic Treats	$19.99
Edit Row	Dull	Ann	Secrets of Silicon Valley	$20.00
Edit Row	Green	Marjorie	The Busy Executive's Database Guide	$19.99
Edit Row	Green	Marjorie	You Can Combat Computer Stress!	$2.99
Edit Row	Gringlesby	Burt	Sushi, Anyone?	$14.99
Edit Row	Hunter	Sheryl	Secrets of Silicon Valley	$20.00
Edit Row	Karsen	Livia	Computer Phobic AND Non-Phobic Individuals: Behavior Variations	$21.59
Edit Row	Locksley	Charlene	Net Etiquette	
Edit Row	Locksley	Charlene	Emotional Security: A New Algorithm	$7.99
Edit Row	MacFeather	Stearns	Cooking with Computers: Surreptitious Balance Sheets	$11.95
Edit Row	MacFeather	Stearns	Computer Phobic AND Non-Phobic Individuals: Behavior Variations	$21.59
Edit Row	O'Leary	Michael	Cooking with Computers: Surreptitious Balance Sheets	$11.95

Figure 17-16

2. Choose a row of data to edit and click on the Edit Row hyperlink. This should result in a figure similar to Figure 17-17.

3. At this point, you have two choices: cancel the edit or update the row of data. If you chose to cancel it you would click on the Cancel Edit hyperlink.

4. If you chose to edit the row of data, you would make your changes and then click on the Update Row hyperlink. Figure 17-18 reflects that the fourth row of data was updated by slightly changing the book title and changing the price.

How It Works

Notice that the first column in the DataGrid contains the text `Edit Row`. This was the first column that you defined in your DataGrid and it has a hyperlink that will execute JavaScript to post this form back to the server.

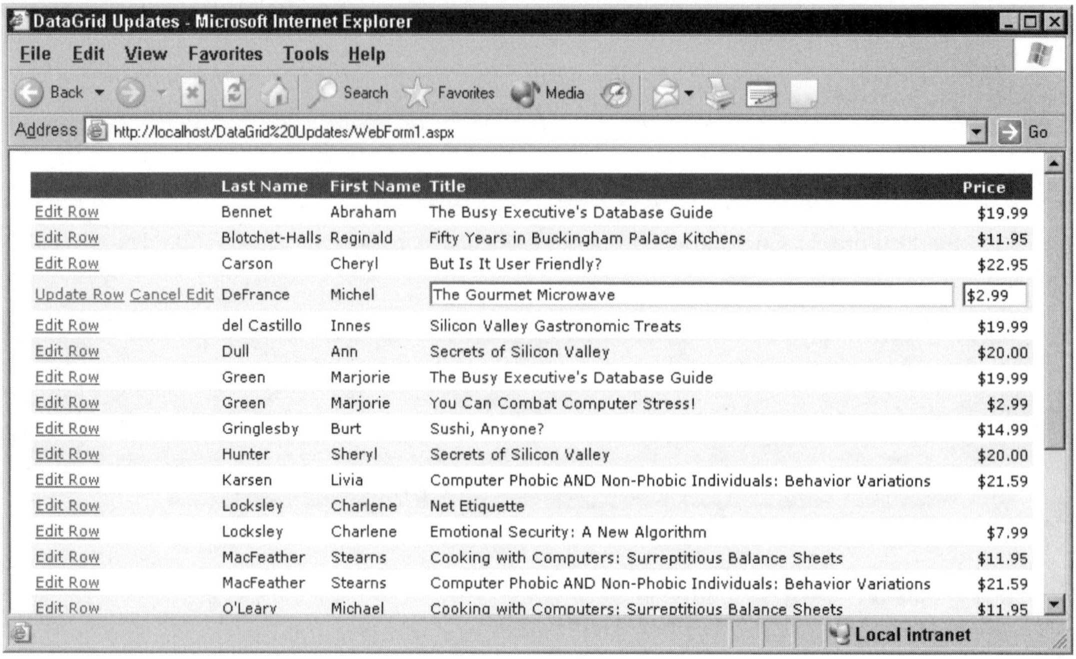

Figure 17-17

Figure 17-18

When you click on the Edit Row hyperlink, the form gets posted back to the server and the EditGridData procedure is executed. This procedure sets the EditItemIndex property of the row to be edited. Once the BindGrid procedure is called, the DataGrid will be built and this row will be displayed with text boxes in columns that allow editing.

When you click on the Cancel Edit hyperlink, the JavaScript will be executed, which in turn will post the form back to the server for processing. The CancelGridData procedure will then be executed and the EditItemIndex property set to a value of −1, which will cause this row to be displayed normally when you call the BindGrid procedure.

Editing rows and choosing the Update Row hyperlink causes the appropriate JavaScript to be executed, which in turns submits this form back to the server for processing. Once at the server, the UpdateGridData procedure gets executed, which updates the database for this row of data. Once the updates are made, the EditItemIndex property is once again set to a value of 1, indicating that this row should no longer be edited. The BindGrid procedure is once again executed and the DataGrid is populated with data, reflecting the updates made.

While you did not provide sorting capability in this *Try It Out*, you could very easily do so by incorporating the code from the previous example.

This *Try It Out* has shown you how to provide update capabilities to a DataGrid. In the process, you have seen how to add template columns to it to control the size and look of the text boxes that are displayed when editing a row of data. You have also seen how to format the text in a column in the DataGrid.

Along with all of this, you have seen how easy it is to write server-side script in your HTML. While the differences are small some of them are significant. For example, you do not have a means to insert the empty procedures for the events of the DataGrid control that you need, so you must code them all by hand. In my opinion it is best to use the Web Form class and not to mix the HTML code with the server script.

Summary

This chapter has introduced you to Web forms and how they differ from Windows Forms. You can see that there is a lot of processing going on when working with Web forms, as the form and its data is posted back to the server whenever you need to update data or change how it is displayed. One of the major benefits of this processing is that the JavaScript, required to handle posting the Web form back to the server, is automatically generated for you.

Having coded two projects that performed data binding, you have seen how to perform data binding through code in both a form class and server-side script. Although there were not a whole lot of differences between the two, being exposed to these two methods can only benefit you in the long run. Knowing how to code both methods will better prepare you for the real world.

While this chapter did not cover data binding using the wizards, they are available for use when coding Web forms. You should be able to apply the same principles to Web forms as you did when using the wizards in Windows Forms back in Chapter 15.

To summarize, you should now know:

❑ Windows Forms and Web forms differ when it comes to retrieving data and presenting it to the user

❑ How to perform sorting and updating in a DataGrid

❑ How to write server-side script in your Web form to bind data to a datagrid on a Web form

❑ How to perform sorting and updating with a DataGrid in a Web form

Exercises

1. How do Web Server controls differ from HTML controls?

2. Can HTML controls also be programmed at the server?

3. What does the IsPostBack property do?

4. Can you mix the code that you use? For example, can you write server-side code in a form class and also write server-side code in a script block in the HTML?

18

Creating Web Server Controls

In Chapter 13, you looked at how to create your own custom controls for WinForm applications. It provides tremendous flexibility and reuse when creating your user interface. A Web server control (WSC) is meant for the same purpose. In fact, a custom control is to WinForms as WSCs are to your Internet browser. They both offer themselves as a reusable UI component.

These ideas come from components known as ActiveX controls and even further back in history: the Visual Basic Extensions (VBX). The VBX is now long gone, but it was the forerunner to ActiveX and WinForm controls. The ActiveX control created a large market in third-party software and promoted components and reuse. All Windows applications could use them, whether they are the freely provided ones that come with .NET, or created by vendors who create controls like bar charts and trends. They had a major role to play in Visual Basic becoming one of the largest used languages.

The WSC is a new and small technology in this large component market place, but is set to become a much larger player in the future. Similar to the form-based controls used earlier, the WSC offers all the benefits, but now these benefits can also be applied to Web development.

A WSC is an exciting addition to the Visual Basic .NET language and this chapter will introduce how to create your own.

In this chapter, you will:

- ❑ Learn what a WSC control is
- ❑ Create your own WSC
- ❑ Interact with JavaScript and learn the difference between client- and server-side code
- ❑ Learn how to prevent a Web form from posting back to the server

Introducing the Web Server Control

As the name suggests, a WSC lives and works on the server. It does not execute on the client directly. The products of a WSC are technologies, such as HTML and JavaScript. These are rendered to the client from the server, just like normal HTML. Therefore, the Visual Basic .NET code that you write for the WSC never executes in the browser. To facilitate the understanding of this, have a look at Figure 18-1, which shows the client–server architecture behind this technology. In the figure, you will see that the WSC generates browser technologies to the client by using Visual Basic .NET. You can see that you will need a good understanding of HTML, JavaScript, Visual Basic Script, and other open-standard technologies such as CSS and XSL to create remarkable controls. The current version of the .NET Framework does not help you very much in the client-side area.

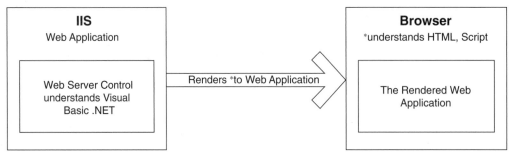

Figure 18-1

As I just pointed out, a WSC is server centric and all the detail you need to look at lies on the server.

Web forms and Web user controls work in a similar way. They too deliver HTML and other browser technologies to the client.

With respect to the Web classes, .NET has tried to formalize and abstract how you create Web pages. If you write an HTML page in Notepad, you could have all, many, or no tags whatsoever. The majority of browsers look for tags that are in the document and processes it. Therefore, in Notepad, if you were to write the following in a file named `myfile.htm` and open it in your browser, your browser would render the text.

```
Hello World
```

If you were to write:

```
<b>Hello World</b>
```

The browser would render the text in a bold font.

There is no <head> or <body> tag. But you know that a good HTML writer should have all these proper tags. The Web side of .NET has taken this "good practice" and made it work for you. When you create a Web form, it automatically has a <head> and <body> tag. It also has a <form> tag.

The Web form is what could be called the outer container. It contains the content of other abstractions, such as a User Control and the WSC.

The User Control is similar to a WSC, with regard to the fact that it is also contained within a Web form. However, a user control is more like a code snippet than a component. A User Control is a snippet of HTML that will be inserted into the <body> tag of the Web form that it is loaded into. Although a User

Control can be packaged inside an Assembly and extracted manually, it is not a component. A WSC is based on the idea that it is a component and therefore is different from a User Control. So what makes the WSC what it is? A WSC is just another class in an assembly. The class, however, has to inherit from one or more of the control classes provided by the .NET Framework. The standard interface to derive a Web server Control from is System.Web.UI.WebControls.WebControl. The complete hierarchy all the way to System.Object is shown in Figure 18-2. How it appears next to things such as the Web form is also shown. You will see that a Web form is not actually a Framework class. It is a template name given to a class when derived from System.Web.UI.Page. (I have omitted the HTMLControls namespace.)

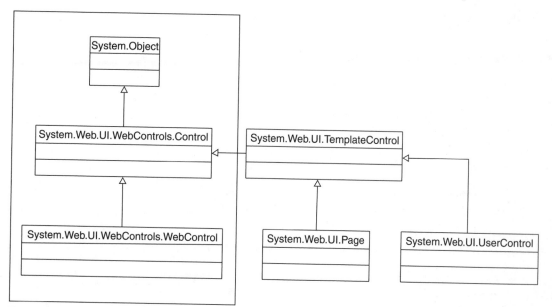

Figure 18-2

The System.UI.Page class extends the System.UI.Control class in a way that makes it useful as a page. This means that it handles the post-back for events and writes out the form tag and other page-oriented data. It is still very much like a WSC. The WSC that you create would normally extend the System.UI.WebControl class with a notion of a control such as a TextBox or Button. This is exactly what the server controls that are installed with .NET do. System.Web.UI.WebControls.Button also inherits from System.Web.UI.WebControls.WebControl just like the one you will create in the next section.

Creating the MessageBox Web Server Control

In your first coding example, you create a WSC that solves a specific problem. Rather than a useless sample, this one will hopefully prove to be quite useful. The control that you build here will display text on your Web form in its initial state. Once you get toward the end of the chapter, you'll have implemented functionality in this control to make it display information either on your Web form or in a MessageBox dialog box.

Creating the Web Server Library Project

1.   Create a New Web Control Library project named MessageBox by clicking on the File menu, then clicking on the New menu item and then the Project sub menu item. Select the Web Control Library icon in the Template's pane.

2.   Open the `WebCustomControl1.vb` class so that you see the code window. You will see default boiler plate code. Notice that it inherits from `System.Web.UI.WebControls.WebControl`.

3.   Now you have a default Web Control Library project that consists of one WSC class.

4.   Rename `WebCustomControl1` to the name MessageBox so that it looks like the following code. There are three occurrences.

```vb
Imports System.ComponentModel
Imports System.Web.UI

<DefaultProperty("Text"), _
    ToolboxData("<{0}:MessageBox runat=server></{0}:MessageBox>")> _
Public Class MessageBox
    Inherits System.Web.UI.WebControls.WebControl

    Dim _text As String

    <Bindable(True), Category("Appearance"), _
        DefaultValue("")> Property [Text]() As String
        Get
            Return _text
        End Get

        Set(ByVal Value As String)
            _text = Value
        End Set
    End Property

    Protected Overrides Sub Render(ByVal output As System.Web.UI.HtmlTextWriter)
        output.Write([Text])
    End Sub

End Class
```

At this point, you have successfully created a simple control. You did not have to do much. Next you will test the control before you start adding more functionality.

Creating a Test Application

If you run the project, you get an error dialog box like the one in Figure 18-3. To run the project and see your server control, you must create a Web application as a test project.

Creating a Test Web Application

1.   Add a New ASP.NET Web application to your solution and name it TestWebApplication. Your solution should now have two projects.

> **Microsoft Development Environment** ⚠ ☒
>
> A project with an Output Type of Class Library cannot be started directly.
>
> In order to debug this project, go to the Debugging tab under Configuration Settings in Project Properties, and set the Start Action to Start External Program or Start URL. Alternatively, you can add a non-library project to this solution that uses a reference to this project and set it as the startup project.
>
> **OK**

Figure 18-3

2. Next you must add a reference to the MessageBox Web server control. First, you need to build the solution by clicking on the Build menu and then clicking on the Build Solution menu item. Then, right-click on the Toolbox in the Web forms tab and select Add/Remove Items.

3. In the Customize Toolbox dialog box, click the Browse button and browse to your project's bin folder and select `MessageBox.dll` as in Figure 18-4. After clicking the OK button, Visual Studio .NET adds a new icon in your Toolbox for the MessageBox.

Customize Toolbox ☒

.NET Framework Components | COM Components

Name	Namespace	Assembly Name
☑ MainMenu	System.Windows.Forms	System.CF.Windows.Forms (7.0.5000.0)
☑ MainMenu	System.Windows.Forms	System.Windows.Forms (1.0.5000.0)
☐ ManagementInstaller	System.Management.Instrum...	System.Management (1.0.5000.0)
☐ MarshalByValueCom...	System.ComponentModel	System (1.0.5000.0)
☐ MenuItemArray	Microsoft.VisualBasic.Compa...	Microsoft.VisualBasic.Compatibility (7.0.5...
☐ Message	System.Messaging	System.Messaging (1.0.5000.0)
☑ MessageBox	MessageBox	MessageBox (1.0.1411.9541)
☑ MessageQueue	System.Messaging	System.Messaging (1.0.5000.0)
☐ MessageQueueInstal...	System.Messaging	System.Messaging (1.0.5000.0)
☑ MonthCalendar	System.Windows.Forms	System.Windows.Forms (1.0.5000.0)

MessageBox
 Language: Invariant Language (Invariant Country)
Version: 1.0.1411.9541 (Retail)

Browse...

OK | Cancel | Reset | Help

Figure 18-4

4. Drag the control marked as MessageBox from the toolbox onto your Web form. You should see the control with the text [MessageBox "MessageBox1"] displayed on the form.

5. Build the Project.

Altering the Text Property and Running the Project

1. Select the WSC and set the Text property to **This is the MessageBox Server Control.**

2. There is one last thing you must do before you can run the project. If you do not set the Web application as the default project, you will still get the error dialog box as in Figure 18-3. Make sure the Web application is the default Startup project by right-clicking on TestWebApplication in the Solution Explorer and selecting Set as `Startup Project`.

3. Now, if you run the project, Internet Explorer will load with your Web form and you will see your Web server control.

Completing the Render Method

By default, the `Render()` method contains one line of code. This line of code purely writes out the value of the Text property to the browser.

This line of code is generally rather useless and is merely a placeholder for you to add your own custom rendering. By default, this line does not even render the other properties that you will see in your Test Application.

Change the BackgroundColor Property

1. Go to `WebForm1.aspx` in your test application and select the MessageBox WSC that you placed on it earlier. Next, go to the Properties window (Press F4, if it is not visible.)

2. Change the `backgroundColor` property to another color.

3. Run the application by pressing F5.

4. You will not see a change. Now sort this out by adding some code to the `Render()` method.

5. What you need to do is add two more lines of code to the Render procedure in your control to wrap the existing line. Add the code below to your `MessageBox` class.

```
Protected Overrides Sub Render(ByVal output As System.Web.UI.HtmlTextWriter)
    Me.RenderBeginTag(output)
    output.Write([Text])
    Me.RenderEndTag(output)
End Sub
```

The new lines of code force the control to render the main Web server to the browser. If you run the project now, you will see the change we expected earlier.

Altering the Default Behavior of the Visible Property

For optimization purposes, setting the Visible property to `False` will not render the control to the client at all. Why should it? If it is invisible, then it should not be in the HTML. However, what if you don't want it to be visible when it *first* loads in the browser, but do want it visible when a button is clicked, after it's loaded?

For the MessageBox sample, you need to have the show/hide triggered by an event. This event would most likely be when the user clicks on a button. One good scenario would be something like the following. The User clicks on a Submit button, the MessageBox displays a Message asking the user "Are you sure?" and presents an OK and Cancel button.

One obvious way to accomplish this is to code it in a Button Web server control. This would fire an event, which will run code on the server that will make it visible. Then, if you used server buttons, it would want to post-back to the server. How would you deny this? Also, if the server button posted the form, it would be too late to render the MessageBox, as the post has already happened.

The default behavior left as it is, means that the client would not be able to show/hide the control. It would have to post-back to the server. Since you want the client to control the visibility of the control, it must therefore exist on the client, for the client to manage it.

To solve this problem, you need to do three things. The first is to alter the default behavior of the Visible property. We will be doing this by adding code to our control to add a CSS style of Display to the HTML and setting its property to None. This causes the control to be rendered in the HTML, but it remains hidden.

Try It Out   Overriding the Visible Property

1. To get the Visible property to render the control to the HTML source, but without showing it in Internet Explorer takes a little extra code.

2. Add two private fields to your MessageBox class. The _visible property will hold the state of Boolean and the _displayAttribute property will hold a vital piece of magic required for the client.

```
Dim _visible As Boolean
Dim _displayAttribute As String
```

3. Then add the following override:

```
<Bindable(True), Category("Appearance"), DefaultValue("")> Overrides Property
[Visible]() As Boolean
        Get
             Return _visible
        End Get
        Set(ByVal Value As Boolean)
             _visible = Value
             'Set the _visibleAttribute to the HTML attribute required
             If Value Then
             Me.Attributes.CssStyle.Add("display", "")
             _displayAttribute = ""
        Else
             Me.Attributes.CssStyle.Add("display", "none")
             _displayAttribute = "none"
        End If
    End Set
End Property
```

4. Now if you run the project, you will not see the server control in the browser. However, if you view source HTML, you will see that the HTML for the control is there but is hidden by the `display` attribute. (Note: If you still see the control, stop your project and build just the MessageBox control and then run your project again.)

```
<input type="hidden" name="VIEWSTATE"
value="dDwxNjYxMjA5MjY1Ozs+fj9WWkASA4O1JFOgt66fkhu36T0=" />
<span id="MessageBox1" style="display:none;color:#C04000;background-
color:#FFC080;border-style:Solid;Z-
INDEX:101;LEFT:24px;POSITION:absolute;TOP:24px;display:none;">This is the
MessageBox Server Control</span>
```

Adding Client Script to Control Visibility

Now that you have altered the visibility, you need to implement two more changes. This involves the event and the controlling of the post-back. In sequence, you need to know what will trigger the event, show the MessageBox, and then deny the post-back if the user clicks Cancel.

Now that you have altered the `Visible` property to output the HTML and hide/show it based on its value, you must implement client-side script to control it. But who will control it?

Creating a Client-Side Event to Control the MessageBox

1. Add the following code to the `MessageBox` class to handle the `ClientController`. The `ClientController` will store the name of the control, assigned the responsibility for the MessageBox's visibility.

```
Dim _clientController As String
<Bindable(True), Category("Appearance"), DefaultValue("")> Property
ClientController() As String
     Get
            Return _clientController
        End Get
        Set(ByVal Value As String)
            _clientController = Value
        End Set
     End Property
```

2. Next alter the `Render()` method.

```
Protected Overrides Sub Render(ByVal output As System.Web.UI.HtmlTextWriter)
        Me.RenderBeginTag(output)
        output.Write([Text])
        If (Not _clientController Is Nothing) And _
            (ClientController <> "") Then
            output.Write("<script language='JavaScript' for=" & _
                _clientController & _
                " event=onclick> Show" & _
                Me.ClientID & "(); </script>")
```

```
            output.WriteLine("")
            output.Write("<script language='JavaScript'>")
            output.Write("function Show" & Me.ClientID & _
            "() {")
            output.Write("if (document.getElementById('" & _
            Me.ClientID & _
            "').style.display == '')" & _
            ".{ document.getElementById('" & _
            Me.ClientID & _
            "').style.display = 'none'; }" & _
            " else { document.getElementById('" & _
            Me.ClientID & "').style.display = ''; }")
            output.Write("}</script>")
        End If
        Me.RenderEndTag(output)
    End Sub
```

3. The Render() method outputs two <script> blocks which provides control to the ClientController to show/hide the MessageBox Server control on the client without posting back to the server.

4. The first block creates a click event handler for the ClientController, and the second <script> block contains the JavaScript code to show/hide the control. To see this for yourself, compile the project and go to WebForm1 in the Test Application.

5. Add an HTML button (not a server control) to your form.

6. With the button selected, change its id property to htmlbutton1.

7. Next, select the MessageBox WSC and change the new ClientController property to htmlbutton1. The ClientController value must correspond to the id of an HTML button found on the form. Figure 18-5 shows the modified ClientController property.

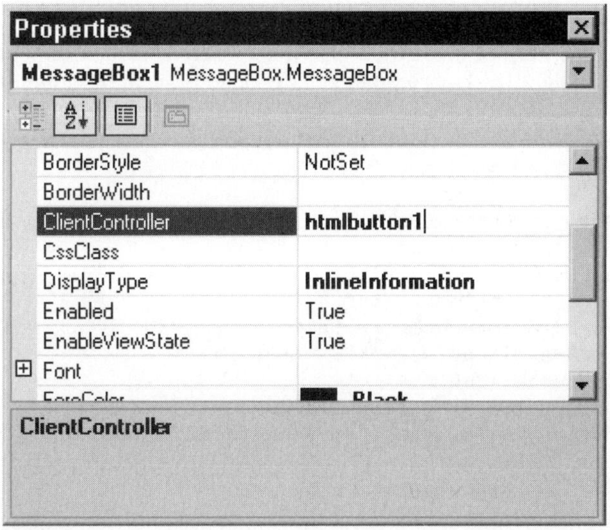

Figure 18-5

8. Press *F5* and click the button a few times. It will toggle the visibility of the MessageBox without posting back to the server.

Try It Out   **Implementing Display Methods**

For customization, this simple Messagebox will implement three different ways to display itself. First, it will display a normal MessageBox dialog with some information and an OK button. You will call this `PopUpInformation`. The second display method will show a pop-up MessageBox dialog once again, but this time with OK and Cancel buttons. You will call this `PopupConfirmation`. Lastly, you will implement an inline version of the first display method. This will show a message inside the normal flow of the HTML, as you have already seen. You will call this `InlineInformation`.

1. For this, you need a `DisplayType` property, a `DisplayEnumeration` for the different displays, and a field to hold the state. Add the following code to your MessageBox class:

```
Dim _displayType As DisplayEnumeration
    Enum DisplayEnumeration
        PopupInformation
        PopupConfirmation
        InlineInformation
    End Enum

    <Bindable(True), Category("Appearance"), DefaultValue("")> _
    Property DisplayType() As DisplayEnumeration
        Get
            Return _displayType
        End Get
        Set(ByVal Value As DisplayEnumeration)
            _displayType = Value
        End Set
    End Property
```

2. Now modify the `Render()` method. You must insert a `Case` statement to output the required script based on the `DisplayType` and add code to prevent the submitting of the form.

```
Protected Overrides Sub Render(ByVal output As System.Web.UI.HtmlTextWriter)
    Me.RenderBeginTag(output)
        output.Write([Text])
        If (Not _clientController Is Nothing) And _
            (ClientController <> "") Then
            output.Write("<script language='JavaScript' for=" & _
                _clientController & _
                " event=onclick> Show" & _
                Me.ClientID & "(); </script>")
        output.WriteLine("")
        output.Write("<script language='JavaScript'>")
        output.Write("function Show" & Me.ClientID & _
            "() {")
            Select Case _displayType
                Case DisplayEnumeration.InlineInformation
                    output.Write("if (document.getElementById('" & _
                    Me.ClientID & _
```

```
                            "').style.display == '')" & _
                            "{ document.getElementById('" & _
                            Me.ClientID & _
                            "').style.display = 'none'; }" & _
                            " else { document.getElementById('" & _
                            Me.ClientID & "').style.display = ''; }")
                    Case DisplayEnumeration.PopupInformation
                            output.Write("alert('" & Text & "');")
                    Case DisplayEnumeration.PopupConfirmation
                            output.Write("AllowSubmit = confirm('" & _
                            Text & "');")
                    Case Else
                            output.Write(" ")
                End Select
                output.Write("}</script>")
                output.Write("<script language=JavaScript>")
                 output.Write("var AllowSubmit = true;")
                 output.Write("function CanISubmit()")
                 output.Write(" { return AllowSubmit; }")
                 output.Write("</script> ")
            End If
            Me.RenderEndTag(output)
    End Sub
```

3. Next, click on the Class Name drop-down list in the code editor for the MessageBox class and select (Overrides). Then in the Method Name drop-down list, select the OnInit method. Add the following code to the OnInit() method as shown:

```
Protected Overrides Sub OnInit(ByVal e As System.EventArgs)
    Me.Page.RegisterOnSubmitStatement("OnSubmit", _
            " return AllowSubmit ; ")
End Sub
```

How it Works

Let us take a closer look at the code in the Render() method. This first portion of code checks to see if the ClientController property contains a valid value. This is important as you use the name entered here for your client-side script.

```
If (Not _clientController Is Nothing) And _
(ClientController <> "") Then
```

Next, you write a script block to the client. The script block uses the JavaScript For keyword to map the click event to a function.

```
output.Write("<script language='JavaScript' for=" & _
_clientController & _
        " event=onclick> Show" & _
        Me.ClientID & "(); </script>")
```

The code outputs the following JavaScript. You can see this by viewing the HTML source in your browser. Notice that the name from the ClientController property has been used in the For attribute of the <script> tag. The onclick attribute points to a function named ShowMesseageBox1(). The name of the JavaScript method was created by using `Me.ClientID`, which provides the ID of the MessageBox Server control as it will be named inside the browser on the client.

```
<script language='JavaScript'
for=htmlbutton1 event=onclick>
     ShowMessageBox1();
</script>
```

The next portion of code decides what the `JavaScript:ShowMessage1()` method will actually do. It outputs the body portion of the `JavaScript:ShowMessage1()` method, based on the `DisplayType` Property.

```
output.Write("<script language='JavaScript'>")
output.Write("function Show" & Me.ClientID & _
"() {")
Select Case _displayType
Case DisplayEnumeration.InlineInformation
          output.Write("if (document.getElementById('" & _
              Me.ClientID & _
              "').style.display == '')" & _
              "{ document.getElementById('" & _
              Me.ClientID & _
              "').style.display = 'none'; }" & _
              " else { document.getElementById('" & _
              Me.ClientID & "').style.display = ''; }")
Case DisplayEnumeration.PopupInformation
            output.Write("alert('" & Text & "');")
     Case DisplayEnumeration.PopupConfirmation
            output.Write("AllowSubmit = confirm('" & _
              Text & "');")
     Case Else
            output.Write(" ")
End Select
output.Write("}</script>")
```

As an example, the resulting JavaScript for the `DisplayEnumeration.InlineInformation` is:

```
<script language='JavaScript'>function ShowMessageBox1()
{
    if (document.getElementById('MessageBox1').style.display=='')
    {
    document.getElementById('MessageBox1').style.display='none';
    }
    else
    {
    document.getElementById('MessageBox1').style.display = '';
    }
}
</script>
```

The JavaScript `document.getElementByID('MessageBox1').style.display` is used to set the HTML display type, and the whole function is written as a toggle to show and then hide the control.

The last portion of code controls the post-back handler of the Web form, which is the parent of the control.

```
output.Write("<script language=JavaScript>")
output.Write("var AllowSubmit = true;")
output.Write("function CanISubmit()")
output.Write(" { return AllowSubmit; }")
output.Write("</script> ")
```

In this code, you register a JavaScript method that returns Boolean value. The CanISubmit() function controls the value of this variable. The JavaScript outputted looks like this:

```
<script language=JavaScript>
var AllowSubmit = true;
function CanISubmit()
{
    return AllowSubmit;
}
</script>
```

The RegisterOnSubmitStatement() is provided to us by the System.Web.UI.Page object and is vital for the whole thing to work. It must be inside the OnInit() event as it needs to know about the added statement before it renders the <Form> tag.

```
Protected Overrides Sub OnInit(ByVal e As System.EventArgs)
    Me.Page.RegisterOnSubmitStatement("OnSubmit", _
            " return AllowSubmit ; ")
End Sub
```

The RegisterOnSubmitStatement() changes the <form> tag from this:

```
<form name="Form1" method="post" action="WebForm1.aspx"
id="Form1">
```

to this (Notice that the onsubmit attribute returns the Boolean variable):

```
<form name="Form1" method="post" action="WebForm1.aspx"
id="Form1"
language="javascript"
onsubmit=" return AllowSubmit;">
```

To test your newest functionality, compile the MessageBox control by clicking on the Build menu and then clicking on the Build Solution menu item. Then, run your project. When you click the button on your Web form, you'll see a MessageBox dialog displayed with the message that has been set in the Text property of the MessageBox control and an OK button. Close the Web form in the IDE, click on the MessageBox control on your Web form. Notice that the default value for the DisplayType property is PopupInformation. Change this property to PopupConfirmation and then run your project again. Now when you click the button on your Web form, you'll see a MessageBox dialog with both the OK and Cancel buttons. Close the Web form once again.

Now change the DisplayType property of the MessageBox control to InlineInformation and run your project once again. Notice that when you click the button on your Web form, the information in the

`Text` property of your MessageBox control is displayed on your Web form as it was when you first built this control.

Your sample can be connected to an HTML control or a server control. You can try it by adding a Web form control and adding its name to the `ClientController` property of the `MessageBox`. It will also work with a `TextBox` or any other control that supports the JavaScript `onClick` event handler.

Summary

In this chapter, you created a MessageBox Web Server Control. Although you did not look closely at the namespaces it derives from, or much detail surrounding it, you saw how to create one and how it works in principle. I hope that you have gained a small insight into this type of development, but the road is far from the end, as many books could be written on this topic.

To summarize, you should know how to:

❑ Override the `Render` method on `System.Web.UI.WebCntrols.WebControl`

❑ Send JavaScript to the browser from a within a control

❑ Create your own properties in the control

❑ Use an enumeration to preset the values for a property in your control

❑ Stop a Web form from posting back to the server

Exercises

1. Which namespace class does a WSC directly inherit from?
2. How did you register a script for the `onSubmit` method from a WSC?
3. Why did you need to override the `Visible` property?

19

Visual Basic .NET and XML

Put simply, Extensible Markup Language, or XML as it is known, is a language used for exchanging data between applications. Although it has been around for some time, XML has established itself as the de facto data exchange standard for Internet applications. XML is not only used on the Internet, but it is now being used to simply exchange data between different platforms and applications.

In this chapter, you are not going to get bogged down in the details regarding XML, for example, its validation and "well-formedness". Instead, XML is going to be introduced generally and then you will look at its role with Visual Basic. After that, you will focus on using XML inside an application.

In this chapter, you will:

- ❏ Gain a deeper understanding of XML and what it looks like
- ❏ Learn how to read and write XML files
- ❏ Learn how to serialize and deserialize XML data
- ❏ Learn how to navigate through an XML document
- ❏ Learn how to change existing XML data and add new data to an XML document

Understanding XML

The need for XML is simple. In commercial environments, applications need to exchange information in order to integrate. This integration is more applicable to the line-of-business software that a company may have, rather than desktop productivity applications like Microsoft Office. For example, a company may have invested in a piece of software that allows it to track the stock in its warehouse—that piece of software would be an example of line-of-business software.

Integration has traditionally been very difficult to do, and XML together with Web services (which is discussed in the next chapter) is designed to reduce the difficulty and cost involved in software integration. In reducing the difficulty of software integration, there is a knock-on benefit in terms of the ease with which more general data/information exchange can occur.

For example, imagine you are a coffee retailer who wants to place an order with a supplier. The "old school" technique of doing this is to phone in or fax your order. However, this introduces a human element into the equation. It is likely that your own line-of-business applications (telling you what products you have sold) are suggesting that you buy more of a certain machine or certain blend of coffee. From that suggestion, you formulate an order and "transmit" it to your supplier. In the case of phone or fax, a human being at the supplier then has to transcribe the order into his or her own line-of-business system for processing.

An alternative way of carrying out this order would be to get the "suggestion" that has been raised by your line-of-business system to create an order automatically in the remote system of your supplier. This makes life easier and more efficient for both you and the management of your chosen supplier. However, getting to a point where the two systems are integrated in this way requires a lot of negotiation, coordination, and cost. Thus, it is only relevant for people doing a lot of business with each other.

Before the Internet, for two companies to integrate in this way, specific negotiations had to be undertaken to set up some sort of proprietary connection between the two companies. With the connection in place, data is exchanged not only to place the order with the supplier, but also for the supplier to report the status of the order back to the customer. With the Internet, this proprietary connection is no longer required—provided both parties are on the Internet, data exchange can take place.

However, without a common language for this data exchange, the problem is only half solved. XML is this common language. As the customer, you can create an XML document that contains the details of the order. You can use the Internet to transmit that order written in XML to the supplier, either over the Web, through e-mail, or by using Web services. The supplier receives the XML document, decodes it, and raises the order in their system. Likewise, if the supplier needs to report anything back to the customer, he or she can construct a different document (again using XML), and use the Internet to transmit it back again.

The actual structure of the data contained within the XML document is up to the customer and supplier to decide. (Usually it's for the supplier to decide upon and the customer to adhere to.) This is where the "extensible" in XML comes in—any two parties who wish to exchange data using XML are completely free to decide exactly what the documents should look like.

This does not sound amazing as companies in the past and even today still use comma-separated files. These files had a format and worked within the same "philosophy." So what does XML have that the previous formats did not?

XML is a lot more descriptive and it can be validated against a schema. A schema defines what the XML document or fragment should look like. Even without a schema, XML can potentially describe itself well enough for others to ascertain what the data is. In line with the benefits of previous file formats, XML is also a text-based format. This means that XML can be moved between platforms using Internet technologies like e-mail, the Web, FTP, and other file copy techniques. Traditional software integration was difficult when moving data between platforms, such as between Windows, UNIX, Mac, AS/400, OS/390, or any other platform, and so the fact that it's text-based adds to making it easier to send these across platforms.

What Does XML Look Like?

If you have any experience with HTML, XML is going to look familiar to you. In fact, both have a common ancestor in Standard General Markup Language (SGML). In many ways, XML is not a language as the name suggests, but is rather a set of rules for defining your own markup languages that allow the exchange of data. XML is not a standalone technology either; in fact, a whole lot of different related specifications form what you can and cannot do with XML. I am referring to specifications like the following (not the best late-night reading):

- ❑ URI (Uniformed Resource Identifiers) `www.ietf.org/rfc/rfc2396.txt`
- ❑ UTF-8 (Unicode Transformation Format) `www.utf-8.com/`
- ❑ XML (Extensible Markup Language) `www.w3.org/TR/REC-xml`
- ❑ XML Schema `www.w3.org/XML/Schema`
- ❑ XML Information Set `www.w3.org/TR/xml-infoset/`

Although the specifications may not beat a book such as this in terms of format, layout, and ease of understanding, it has a whole lot to offer the XML fan. If you feel up to it, you can read more about XML after this introduction.

XML is tag based, meaning that the document is made up of tags that contain data. Here is how you might choose to describe this book in XML:

```
<Book>
    <Title>Beginning VB.NET 2003</Title>
    <ISBN>0764556584</ISBN>
    <Publisher>Wiley</Publisher>
</Book>
```

In XML, you delimit tags using the < and > symbols. There are two sorts of tags. An example of a start tag is `<Title>` and that of an end tag is `</Title>`. Together the tags and the content between them are known as an element. In the previous example, the `Title` element is written like this:

```
<Title>Beginning VB.NET 2003</Title>
```

while the ISBN element looks like this:

```
<ISBN>0764556584</ISBN>
```

and the Publisher element looks like this:

```
<Publisher>Wiley</Publisher>
```

Note that elements can contain other elements. In this case, for example, the `Book` element contains three sub-elements:

```
<Book>
    <Title>Beginning VB.NET 2003</Title>
    <ISBN>0764556584</ISBN>
    <Publisher>Wiley</Publisher>
</Book>
```

Note: Instead of the term elements, many use terms such as trees and nodes.

If you were given this XML document, you would need to have an understanding of its structure. Usually, the company that designed the structure of the document will tell you what it looks like. In this case, someone might tell you that if you first look for the `Book` element and then the `Title` element, you will determine the title of the book. The value between the `<Title>` start tag and the `</Title>` end tag is the title, in this case `Beginning VB.NET 2003`.

As in HTML, XML can also potentially use what are known as attributes. *Attributes* are descriptive to the node (element) wherein it is located. Here is the same XML fragment as the previous one, but this time using attributes:

```
<Book>
   <Title  ISBN="0764556584 ">Beginning VB.NET 2003</Title>
   <Publisher>Wiley</Publisher>
</Book>
```

XML is largely common sense, which is one of the things that make it so simple. For example, I believe you can guess what this document represents, even though you may have only just started thinking about XML:

```
<Books>
   <Book>
      <Title>Beginning VB.NET 2003</Title>
      <ISBN>0764556584</ISBN>
      <Publisher>Wiley</Publisher>
   </Book>
   <Book>
      <Title>Professional Visual Basic.Net</Title>
      <ISBN>1861005555</ISBN>
      <Publisher>Wiley</Publisher>
   </Book>
</Books>
```

XML for Visual Basic Newcomers

As a newcomer to programming and Visual Basic, it is unlikely that you will be undertaking projects that involve complex integration work. If XML is so popular because it makes systems integration so much easier, how is it relevant to a newcomer?

The answer to this question is that, besides being a great tool for integration, XML is also a great tool for storage and general data organization. Before XML, the two ways that an application could store its data were by using a separate database, or by having its own proprietary file format with code that could save into and read from it.

In many cases, a database is absolutely the right tool for the job, because you need the fast access, shared storage, and advanced searching facilities that a database like Access or SQL Server gives you. In other cases, such as with a graphics package or word processor, building your own proprietary format is the right way to go. The reasons for this may be you want the application to be light and do not want to have the hassle of showing the user how to set up and maintain a database, or simply do not want to deal with the licensing implications of needing a separate application to support yours.

XML gives you a new way of storing application data, though it is still based on the concept of defining your own proprietary application storage format. The key difference, in contrast to formats such as `.doc` files for Word documents, however, is that the XML storage format is a universal standard.

The Address Book Project

You're going to build a demonstration application that allows you to create an XML file format for an address book. You'll be able to create a list of new addresses in your list and save the whole lot as an XML file on your local disk. You'll also be able to load the XML file and browse through the addresses one by one.

Creating the Project

As always, the first thing you have to do is create a new project.

Try It Out   **Creating the Project**

1.   Open Visual Studio .NET and select File ⇨ New Project from the menu. Create a new Visual Basic .NET Windows Application project and call it Address Book.

2.   The Form Designer for Form1 will open. Change its `Text` property to Address Book. Now add 10 text boxes (clearing the `Text` property for each), twelve labels, and a button to the form so that it looks like Figure 19-1.

3.   The text boxes should be named as follows, in the order given:

   1. txtFirstName
   2. txtLastName
   3. txtCompanyName
   4. txtAddress1
   5. txtAddress2
   6. txtCity
   7. txtRegion
   8. txtPostalCode
   9. txtCountry
   10. txtEmail

4.   The button should be named btnSave. Finally, the Label control marked (number) should be called lblAddressNumber.

That's all you need to do with respect to form design. Let's move on and write some code to save the data as an XML file.

The SerializableData Class

Your application is going to have two classes: `Address` and `AddressBook`. `Address` will be used for storing a single instance of a contact in the address book. `AddressBook` will store your entire list of addresses and provide ways for you to navigate through the book.

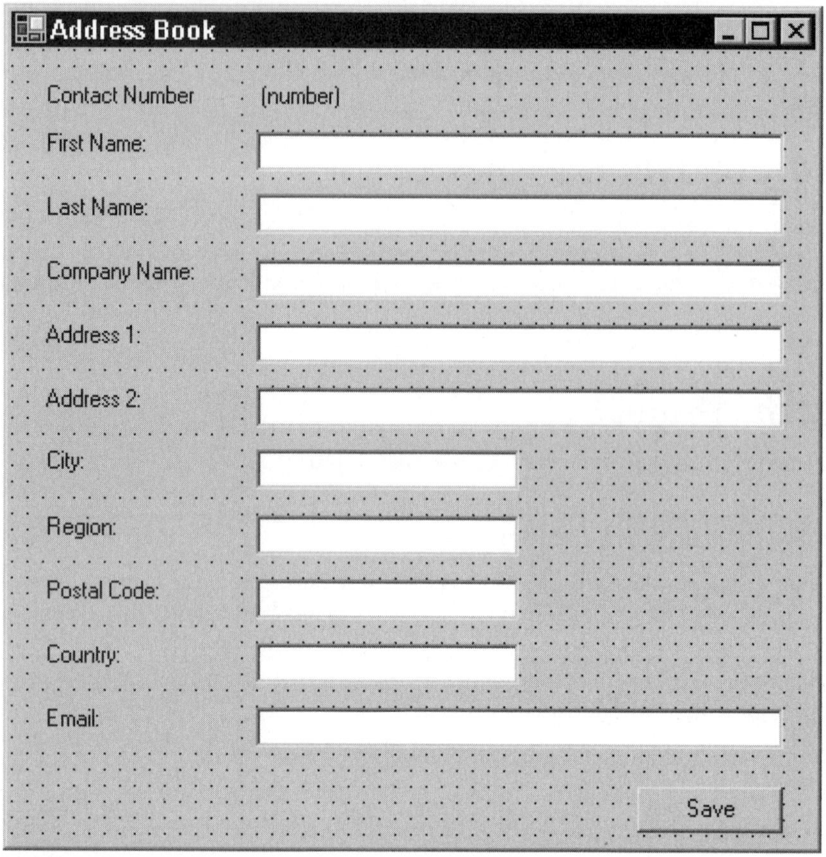

Figure 19-1

Both of these classes will be inherited from another class called `SerializableData`. This base class will contain the logic needed for saving the addresses to disk and loading them back again. In XML parlance, the saving process is known as *serialization* and the loading process is known as *deserialization*. In the following section, you're going to build the `SerializableData` and `Address` classes so that you can demonstrate saving a new address record to disk.

Try It Out   Building SerializableData

1. The first class you need to build is the base `SerializableData` class. Using the Solution Explorer, right-click on the Address Book project and select Add ➪ Add Class. Call the new class SerializableData and click Open.

2. At the top of the class definition, add these namespace import directives:

```
Imports System.IO
Imports System.Xml.Serialization
Public Class SerializableData
End Class
```

3. Next, add these two methods to the class:

```
' Save - serialize the object to disk...
Public Function Save(ByVal filename As String)
    ' make a temporary filename...
    Dim tempFilename As String
    tempFilename = filename & ".tmp"
    ' does the file exist?
    Dim tempFileInfo As New FileInfo(tempFilename)
    If tempFileInfo.Exists = True Then tempFileInfo.Delete()
    ' open the file...
    Dim stream As New FileStream(tempFilename, FileMode.Create)
    ' save the object...
    Save(stream)
    ' close the file...
    stream.Close()
    ' remove the existing data file and
    ' rename the temp file...
    tempFileInfo.CopyTo(filename, True)
    tempFileInfo.Delete()
End Function
' Save - actually perform the serialization...
Public Function Save(ByVal stream As Stream)
    ' create a serializer...
    Dim serializer As New XmlSerializer(Me.GetType)
    ' save the file...
    serializer.Serialize(stream, Me)
End Function
```

4. Create a new class called `Address`. Set the class to derive from `SerializableData`, like this:

```
Public Class Address
    Inherits SerializableData
End Class
```

5. Next, add the members to the class that will be used to store the address details:

```
Public Class Address
    Inherits SerializableData
    ' members...
    Public FirstName As String
    Public LastName As String
    Public CompanyName As String
    Public Address1 As String
    Public Address2 As String
    Public City As String
    Public Region As String
    Public PostalCode As String
    Public Country As String
    Public Email As String
End Class
```

6. Go back to the Form Designer for Form1 and double-click the Save button to have the `Click` event handler created. Add this code to it:

```
Private Sub btnSave_Click(ByVal sender As System.Object, _
        ByVal e As System.EventArgs) Handles btnSave.Click
    ' create a new address object...
    Dim address As New Address()
    ' copy the values from the form into the address...
    PopulateAddressFromForm(address)
    ' save the address...
    Dim filename As String = DataFilename
    address.Save(filename)
' tell the user...
    MsgBox("The address was saved to " & filename)
End Sub
```

7. Visual Studio will highlight the fact that you haven't defined the `DataFilename` property or the `PopulateAddressFromForm` method by underlining these respective names. To remove these underlines, first add the `DataFileName` property to the `Form1` code:

```
' DataFilename - where should we store our data?
Public ReadOnly Property DataFilename() As String
    Get
        ' get our working folder...
        Dim folder As String
        folder = Environment.CurrentDirectory
        ' return the folder with the name "Addressbook.xml"...
        Return folder & "\AddressBook.xml"
    End Get
End Property
```

8. Now you need to add the `PopulateAddressFromForm` method to your `Form1` code:

```
' PopulateAddressFromForm - populates Address from the form fields...
Public Sub PopulateAddressFromForm(ByVal address As Address)
    ' copy the values...
    address.FirstName = txtFirstName.Text
    address.LastName = txtLastName.Text
    address.CompanyName = txtCompanyName.Text
    address.Address1 = txtAddress1.Text
    address.Address2 = txtAddress2.Text
    address.City = txtCity.Text
    address.Region = txtRegion.Text
    address.PostalCode = txtPostalCode.Text
    address.Country = txtCountry.Text
    address.Email = txtEmail.Text
End Sub
```

9. Run the project and fill in an address.

10. Click the Save button. You will see a MessageBox dialog informing you where the file has been saved to.

11. Go to the folder that this XML file has been saved into using Windows Explorer. Double-click it, and Internet Explorer should open and list the contents. What you see should be similar to the contents listed below:

```
<?xml version="1.0"?>
<Address xmlns:xsd="http://www.w3.org/2001/XMLSchema"
xmlns:xsi="http://www.w3.org/2001/XMLSchema-instance">
  <FirstName>Thearon</FirstName>
  <LastName>Willis</LastName>
  <CompanyName>Wiley</CompanyName>
  <Address1>123 Main Street</Address1>
  <Address2 />
  <City>Anytown</City>
  <Region>USA</Region>
  <PostalCode>12345</PostalCode>
  <Country>US</Country>
  <Email>thearon@nowhere.com</Email>
</Address>
```

How It Works

First of all, look at the XML that has been returned. For this discussion, you can ignore the first line starting `<?xml` because all that is doing is saying, "Here is an XML version 1.0 document." You can also ignore the `xmlns` attributes on the first and second lines as this is just providing some extra information about the file. At this level it is something that you can let .NET worry about and you don't need to get involved with. With those two parts removed, this is what you get:

```
<Address>
  <FirstName>Thearon</FirstName>
  <LastName>Willis</LastName>
  <CompanyName>Wiley</CompanyName>
  <Address1>123 Main Street</Address1>
  <Address2 />
  <City>Anytown</City>
  <Region>USA</Region>
  <PostalCode>12345</PostalCode>
  <Country>US</Country>
  <Email>thearon@nowhere.com</Email>
</Address>
```

You can see how this is pretty similar to the code described previously in this chapter—you have start tags and end tags and when taken together these tags form an element. Each element contains data, and it's pretty obvious to see that, for example, the `CompanyName` element contains `Thearon`'s company name.

You'll notice that there is an `Address` tag both at the start and the bottom of the document. All other elements are enclosed by these tags. This means that each of the elements in the middle belongs to the `Address` element. The `Address` element is the first element in the document and is therefore known as the top-level element or root element.

It's worth noting that an XML document can only have one root element; all other elements in the document are child elements of this root.

Look at the `<Address2 />` line. By placing the slash at the end of the tag, what you're saying is that the element is empty. You could have written this as `<Address2></Address2>`, but this would have used up more storage space in the file. The `XmlSerializer` class itself chooses the naming of the tags, which is discussed later in this chapter.

Now you know what was created, but how did you get there? Follow the path of the application from the clicking of the Save button.

The first thing this method did was to create a new `Address` object and call the `PopulateAddress-FromForm` method. (This method just reads the `Text` property for every text box on the form and populates the matching property on the `Address` object.)

```
Private Sub btnSave_Click(ByVal sender As System.Object, _
    ByVal e As System.EventArgs) Handles btnSave.Click
    ' create a new address object...
    Dim address As New Address()
    ' copy the values from the form into the address...
    PopulateAddressFromForm(address)
```

Then, you asked the `DataFilename` property (which you wrote in Step 7 of this *Try It Out*) to give you the name of a file that you can save the data to. You do this by using the `Environment.Current-Directory` property to return the folder that the address book is executing in and then tacking `"\AddressBook.xml"` to the end of this directory pathway. This is going to be the convention you use when saving and loading files with your application—you won't bother about giving the user an opportunity to save a specific file. Rather, you'll just assume that the file you want always has the same name and is always in the same place:

```
    ' save the address...
    Dim filename As String = DataFilename
```

You then call the `Save` method on the `Address` object. This method is inherited from `SerializableData`, and in a moment you'll take a look at what this method actually does. After you've saved the file, you tell the user where it is:

```
    address.Save(filename)
    ' tell the user...
    MsgBox ("The address was saved to " & filename)
End Sub
```

It's the two `Save` methods on `SerializableData` that are the really interesting part of this project. The first version of the method takes a filename and opens the file. The second version of the method actually saves the data using the `System.Xml.Serialization.XmlSerializer` class, as you'll soon see.

When you save the file, you want to be quite careful. You have to save over the top of an existing file, but you also want to make sure that if the file cannot be saved for any reason, you don't end up trashing the only good copy of the data the user has. This is a fairly common problem with a fairly common solution—you save the file to a different file, wait until you know that everything has been saved properly, and then replace the existing file with the new one.

To get the name of the new file, you just tack `.tmp` onto the end. So, if you had the filename given as `C:\MyPrograms\AddressBook\AddressBook.xml`, you would actually try and save to

`C:\MyPrograms\AddressBook\AddressBook.xml.tmp`. If this file exists, you delete it by calling the `Delete` method:

```
' Save - serialize the object to disk...
Public Function Save(ByVal filename As String)
    ' make a temporary filename...
    Dim tempFilename As String
    tempFilename = filename & ".tmp"
    ' does the file exist?
    Dim tempFileInfo As New FileInfo(tempFilename)
    If tempFileInfo.Exists = True Then tempFileInfo.Delete()
```

Once the existing file is gone, you can create a new file. This will return a `System.IO.FileStream` object:

```
    ' open the file...
    Dim stream As New FileStream(tempFilename, FileMode.Create)
```

You then pass this stream to another overloaded `Save` method. You'll go through this method in a moment, but for now, all you need to know is that this method will do the actual serialization of the data.

Then, you close the file:

```
    ' close the file...
    stream.Close()
```

Finally, you replace the existing file with the new file. You have to do this with `CopyTo` (the `True` parameter you pass to this method means "overwrite any existing file") and finally delete the temporary file:

```
    ' remove the existing data file and
    ' rename the temp file...
    tempFileInfo.CopyTo(filename, True)
    tempFileInfo.Delete()
End Function
```

The other version of `Save` looks like this:

```
' Save - actually perform the serialization...
Public Function Save(ByVal stream As Stream)
    ' create a serializer...
    Dim serializer As New XmlSerializer(Me.GetType)
    ' save the file...
    serializer.Serialize(stream, Me)
End Function
```

The `System.Xml.Serialization.XmlSerializer` class is what you use to actually serialize the object to the stream that you specify. In this case, you're using a stream that points to a file, but later in the chapter you'll use a different kind of file.

`XmlSerializer` needs to know ahead of time what type of object it's saving. You use the `GetType` method to return a `System.Type` object that refers to the class that you actually are saving, which in this case is `Address`. The reason why `XmlSerializer` needs to know the type is because it works by iterating through all of the properties on the object—looking for ones that are both readable and writable (in other words, ones that are not flagged as read-only or write-only). Every time it finds one, it writes it to the stream, which in this case means it subsequently gets written to the `AddressBook.xml` file.

`XmlSerializer` bases the name of the element in the XML document on the name of the matching property. For example, the `FirstName` element in the document matches the `FirstName` property on `Address`. In addition, the top-level element of `Address` matches the name of the `Address` class. In other words, the root element name matches the class name.

`XmlSerializer` is a great way of using XML in your programs because you don't need to mess around creating and manually reading XML documents—it does all the work for you.

Loading the XML File

Now you can load the address back from the XML file on the disk. In this next *Try It Out* exercise, you'll be adding the methods necessary to deserialize the XML back into data that you can work within your application.

Try It Out   Loading the XML File

1. Using the Solution Explorer, open the code editor for `SerializableData`. Add these two methods:

```
' Load - deserialize from disk...
Public Shared Function Load(ByVal filename As String, _
                ByVal newType As Type) As Object
    ' does the file exist?
    Dim fileInfo As New FileInfo(filename)
    If fileInfo.Exists = False Then
        ' create a blank version of the object and return that...
        Return System.Activator.CreateInstance(newType)
    End If
    ' open the file...
    Dim stream As New FileStream(filename, FileMode.Open)
    ' load the object from the stream...
    Dim newObject As Object = Load(stream, newType)
    ' close the stream...
    stream.Close()
    ' return the object...
    Return newObject
End Function
Public Shared Function Load(ByVal stream As Stream, _
                ByVal newType As Type) As Object
    ' create a serializer and load the object....
    Dim serializer As New XmlSerializer(newType)
    Dim newObject As Object = serializer.Deserialize(stream)
    ' return the new object...
    Return newobject
End Function
```

2. Go back to the Form Designer for Form1. Delete the Save button (you don't need it anymore) and replace it with a new button. Set the `Text` property to **Load** and set the `Name` to **btnLoad**.

3. Double-click the Load button and add this code to the event handler:

```
Private Sub btnLoad_Click(ByVal sender As System.Object, _
        ByVal e As System.EventArgs) Handles btnLoad.Click
    ' load the address using a shared method on SerializableData...
    Dim newAddress As Address = _
        SerializableData.Load(DataFilename, GetType(Address))
    ' update the display...
    PopulateFormFromAddress(newAddress)
End Sub
```

4. You'll also need to add this method to Form1:

```
' PopulateFormFromAddress - populates the form from an
' address object...
Public Sub PopulateFormFromAddress(ByVal address As Address)
    ' copy the values...
    txtFirstName.Text = address.FirstName
    txtLastName.Text = address.LastName
    txtCompanyName.Text = address.CompanyName
    txtAddress1.Text = address.Address1
    txtAddress2.Text = address.Address2
    txtCity.Text = address.City
    txtRegion.Text = address.Region
    txtPostalCode.Text = address.PostalCode
    txtCountry.Text = address.Country
    txtEmail.Text = address.Email
End Sub
```

5. Run the project and click the Load button. The address should be loaded from the XML file and displayed on the screen. After the load button, you should see what you typed in and saved previously as shown in Figure 19-2.

How It Works

Deserialization is the opposite of serialization. It can be used for loading the XML data from the file, whereas before you saved the XML data to the file. (Note that here I'm using the word file for simplification. In fact, you can serialize to and deserialize from any kind of stream.)

Whenever you ask `XmlSerializer` to deserialize an object for you, it will create a new object. You can use this functionality to get `XmlSerializer` to create a new object for you rather than having to create one yourself. This is a good candidate for an overloaded method on the `SerializableData` object. You create an overloaded method called `Load`, the first version of which takes a filename and also a `System.Type` object. This `Type` object represents the type of object you ultimately want to end up with. Specifically, you'll need to pass in a `Type` object that tells `XmlSerializer` where to find a list of properties that exist on your `Address` object.

Since `XmlSerializer` doesn't save .NET class namespaces or assembly information into the XML file, it relies on an explicit statement saying what class the file contains; otherwise things get ambiguous.

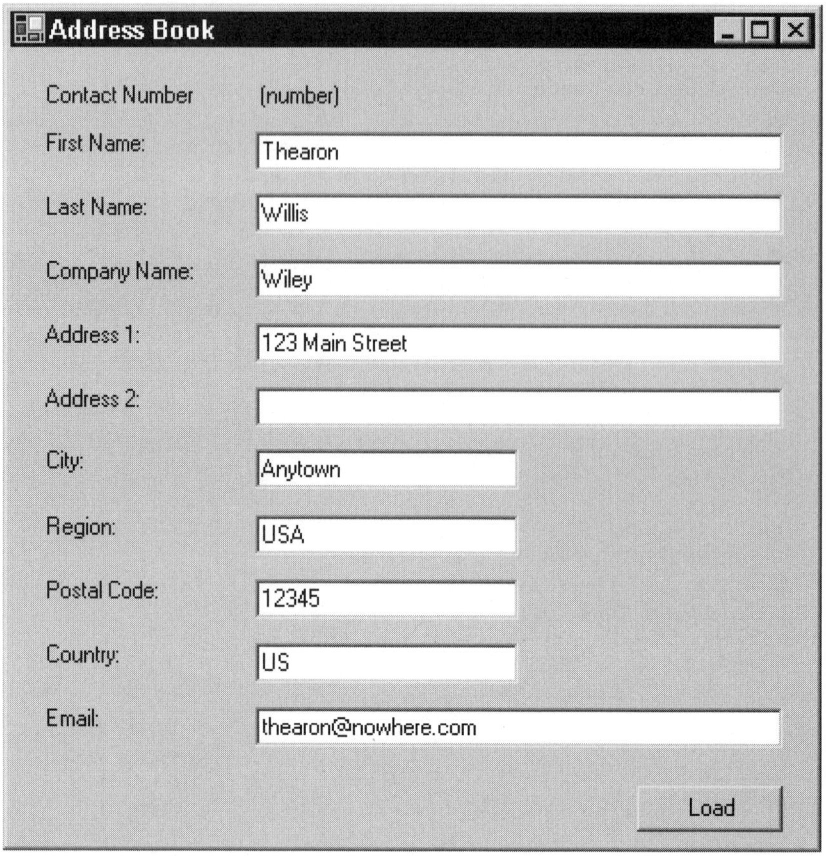

Figure 19-2

(Imagine you might have 100 assemblies on your machine, each containing a class called `Address`. How could `XmlSerializer` know which one you mean?)

Obviously, when the method is called, the first thing you do is check to see if the file exists. If it doesn't, you'll return a blank version of the object that you asked for:

```
' Load - deserialize from disk...
Public Shared Function Load(ByVal filename As String, _
                ByVal newType As Type) As Object
    ' does the file exist?
    Dim fileInfo As New FileInfo(filename)
    If fileInfo.Exists = False Then
        ' create a blank version of the object and return that...
        Return System.Activator.CreateInstance(newType)
    End If
```

If the file does exist, you open it and pass it to the other version of `Load`, which you'll see in a moment. You then close the file and return the new object to the caller:

```
' open the file...
Dim stream As New FileStream(filename, FileMode.Open)
' load the object from the stream...
Dim newObject As Object = Load(stream, newType)
' close the stream...
stream.Close()
' return the object...
Return newObject
End Function
```

The other version of `Load` uses the `XmlSerializer` again and, as you can see, it's no more complicated than when you used it last time. Except, of course, that the `Deserialize` method returns a new object to you:

```
Public Shared Function Load(ByVal stream As Stream, _
                ByVal newType As Type) As Object
    ' create a serializer and load the object....
    Dim serializer As New XmlSerializer(newType)
    Dim newObject As Object = serializer.Deserialize(stream)
    ' return the new object...
    Return newobject
End Function
```

When it's deserializing, `XmlSerializer` goes through each of the properties on the new object that it has created, again looking for the ones that are both readable and writable. When it finds one, it takes the value stored against it in the XML document and sets the property. The result: You are given a new object, fully populated with the data from the XML document.

Once you've called `Load` and have gotten a new `Address` object back, you pass the new object to `PopulateFormFromAddress`:

```
Private Sub btnLoad_Click(ByVal sender As System.Object, _
        ByVal e As System.EventArgs) Handles btnLoad.Click
    ' load the address using a shared method on SerializableData...
    Dim newAddress As Address = _
        SerializableData.Load(DataFilename, GetType(Address))
    ' update the display...
    PopulateFormFromAddress(newAddress)
End Sub
```

Changing the Data

To prove that nothing funny is going on, you'll change the XML file using Notepad and try clicking the Load button again.

Try It Out   Changing the Data

1. Open up Windows Notepad and load the XML file into it. Inside the `FirstName` element, change the name that you entered to something else; save the file and exit Notepad.

2. Go back to the Address Book program. Click the Load button again and the new name that you entered will be loaded.

How It Works

What you've done here is to prove `XmlSerializer` does indeed use the `AddressBook.xml` file as the source of its data. You changed the data, and when you loaded the `Address` object again, the `FirstName` property had indeed been changed to the new name that you entered.

Sending E-mail

For this next *Try It Out*, you'll see how you can integrate this application with Outlook and Outlook Express using the e-mail data from your addresses. You'll be using the `Process` class to start the program (Outlook or Outlook Express) associated with the `mailto` protocol as you see in a few moment.

Try It Out   Sending E-mail from the Client

1. Go back to the Form1 designer and, using the Toolbox, draw a LinkLabel control underneath the E-mail label. Set its `Text` property to Send E-mail and change its `Name` property to lnkSendEmail as shown in Figure 19-3.

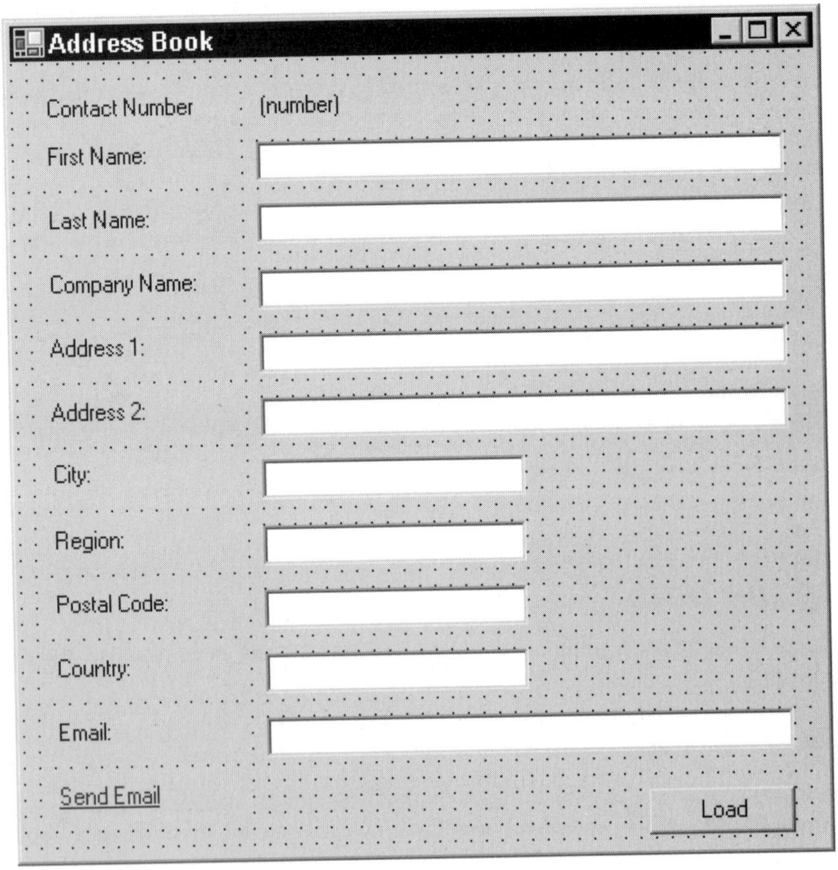

Figure 19-3

Note that this will work with a normal Button control, too.

2. Double-click the LinkLabel control. This will create an event handler for the `LinkClicked` event. Add this code:

```
Private Sub lnkSendEmail_LinkClicked(ByVal sender As System.Object, _
    ByVal e As System.Windows.Forms.LinkLabelLinkClickedEventArgs) _
    Handles lnkSendEmail.LinkClicked
        ' start the e-mail client...
        System.Diagnostics.Process.Start("mailto:" & txtEmail.Text)
End Sub
```

3. Run the project and click the Load button. Ensure that you have an e-mail address entered in the E-mail field and then click the Send E-mail link. Outlook (or your e-mail application) should display a new mail message with the To field filled in with your e-mail address.

How It Works

Windows has a built-in ability to decode Internet addresses and activate the program that is associated with them.

When Outlook or Outlook Express is installed, it registers a protocol called `mailto` with Windows. When Internet Explorer is installed, it registers a protocol called HTTP—and I'm sure you'll recognize HTTP from when you've browsed the Web.

If you were to close the mail message, click the Start button from the Windows task bar, select Run and enter "mailto:" followed by the email address from your program and then click OK, the same mail message would appear.

In your code, you take the current value of the txtEmail field and put `mailto:` at the beginning. This turns the e-mail address into a URL. You then call the shared `Start` method on the `System .Diagnostics.Process` class, passing it this URL:

```
Private Sub lnkSendEmail_LinkClicked(ByVal sender As System.Object, _
    ByVal e As System.Windows.Forms.LinkLabelLinkClickedEventArgs) _
    Handles lnkSendEmail.LinkClicked
        ' start the e-mail client...
        System.Diagnostics.Process.Start("mailto:" & txtEmail.Text)
End Sub
```

The `Start` method behaves in exactly the same way as the Run dialog box. Both tap into Windows' built-in URL-decoding functionality. In this case, you've used this functionality to integrate your application with Outlook. However, if you had specified a protocol of `http:` rather than `mailto:`, your application could have opened a Web page. Likewise, if you had supplied a path to a Word document, or Excel spreadsheet, the application could open those too. Note that when you're working with a file, you don't need to supply a protocol—for example, you only need to do this:

```
c:\My Files\My Budget.xls
```

Creating a List of Addresses

The purpose of this exercise is to build an application that allows you to store a list of addresses in XML. At the moment you can successfully load and save just one address, so now you have to turn your attention to managing a list of addresses.

The class you're going to build to do this is called `AddressBook`. You'll inherit this from `SerializableData` because ultimately you want to get to a point where you can tell the `AddressBook` object itself to load and save to the XML file without you having to do anything.

Try It Out   **Creating AddressBook**

1.   Using Solution Explorer, create a new class called `AddressBook`.

2.   First, add this namespace declaration:

```
Imports System.Xml.Serialization
Public Class AddressBook
End Class
```

3.   Second, set the class to inherit from `SerializableData`:

```
Imports System.Xml.Serialization
Public Class AddressBook
    Inherits SerializableData
End Class
```

4.   To store the addresses, you're going to use a `System.Collections.ArrayList` object. You also need a method that you can use to create new addresses in the list. Add the following member and method to the class:

```
Imports System.Xml.Serialization
Public Class AddressBook
    Inherits SerializableData
    ' members...
    Public Items As New ArrayList()
    ' AddAddress - add a new address to the book...
    Public Function AddAddress() As Address
        ' create one...
        Dim newAddress As New Address()
        ' add it to the list...
        Items.Add(newAddress)
        ' return the address...
        Return newAddress
    End Function
End Class
```

5.   Open the code editor for Form1. Add these members to the top of the class:

```
Public Class Form1
    Inherits System.Windows.Forms.Form
```

```
    ' members...
    Public AddressBook As AddressBook
    Private _currentAddressIndex As Integer
```

6. Next, add this property to Form1:

```
' CurrentAddress - property for the current address...
ReadOnly Property CurrentAddress() As Address
    Get
        Return AddressBook.Items(CurrentAddressIndex - 1)
    End Get
End Property
```

7. Then, add this property to Form1:

```
' CurrentAddressIndex - property for the current address...
Property CurrentAddressIndex() As Integer
    Get
        Return _currentAddressIndex
    End Get
    Set(ByVal Value As Integer)
        ' set the address...
        _currentAddressIndex = Value
        ' update the display...
        PopulateFormFromAddress(CurrentAddress)
        ' set the label...
        lblAddressNumber.Text = _
        _currentAddressIndex & " of " & AddressBook.Items.Count
    End Set
End Property
```

8. Double-click the form to create the Load event for Form1 and add this code:

```
Private Sub Form1_Load(ByVal sender As System.Object, _
        ByVal e As System.EventArgs) Handles MyBase.Load
    ' load the address book...
    AddressBook = _
        SerializableData.Load(DataFilename, GetType(AddressBook))
    ' if the address book only contains one item, add a new one...
    If AddressBook.Items.Count = 0 Then AddressBook.AddAddress()
    ' select the first item in the list...
    CurrentAddressIndex = 1
End Sub
```

9. Now that you can load the address book, you need to be able to save the changes. From the left drop-down list, select (Overrides). From the right list, select OnClosed. Add this code to the event handler, and also add the SaveChanges and UpdateCurrentAddress methods:

```
Protected Overrides Sub OnClosed(ByVal e As System.EventArgs)
    ' save the changes...
    UpdateCurrentAddress()
    SaveChanges()
End Sub
```

```
' SaveChanges - save the address book to an XML file...
Public Sub SaveChanges()
    ' tell the address book to save itself...
    AddressBook.Save(DataFilename)
End Sub
' UpdateCurrentAddress - make sure the book has the current
' values currently entered into the form...
Private Sub UpdateCurrentAddress()
    PopulateAddressFromForm(CurrentAddress)
End Sub
```

Before running the project, it's very important that you delete the existing AddressBook.xml *file. If you don't,* XmlSerializer *will try to load an* AddressBook *object from a file containing an* Address *object and an exception will be thrown.*

10. Run the project. Don't bother entering any information into the form because the save routine won't work—I've deliberately introduced a bug to illustrate an issue with XmlSerializer. Close the form and you should see the exception thrown as shown in Figure 19-4.

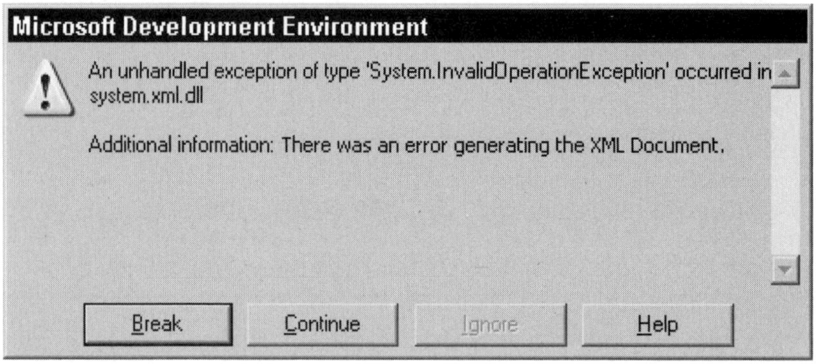

Figure 19-4

How It Works (or Why It Doesn't!)

When the form is loaded, the first thing you do is ask SerializableData to create a new AddressBook object for the AddressBook.xml file. As you deleted this before you ran the project, this file won't exist and, as you recall, you rigged the Load method so that if the file didn't exist it would just create an instance of whatever class you asked for. In this case, you get an AddressBook:

```
Private Sub Form1_Load(ByVal sender As System.Object, _
        ByVal e As System.EventArgs) Handles MyBase.Load
    ' load the address book...
    AddressBook = _
      SerializableData.Load(DataFilename, GetType(AddressBook))
```

However, the new address book won't have any addresses in it. You ask AddressBook to create a new address if the list is empty:

```
    ' if the address book only contains one item, add a new one...
    If AddressBook.Items.Count = 0 Then AddressBook.AddAddress()
```

At this point, you'll either have an `AddressBook` object that has been loaded from the file and therefore contains a set of `Address` objects, or you'll have a new `AddressBook` object that contains one blank address. You set the `CurrentAddressIndex` property to 1, meaning the first item in the list:

```
    ' select the first item in the list...
    CurrentAddressIndex = 1
End Sub
```

The `CurrentAddressIndex` property does a number of things. First, it updates the private `_currentAddressIndex` member:

```
' CurrentAddressIndex - property for the current address...
Property CurrentAddressIndex() As Integer
    Get
        Return _currentAddressIndex
    End Get
    Set(ByVal Value As Integer)
    ' set the address...
    _currentAddressIndex = Value
```

Then, it uses the `CurrentAddress` property to get the `Address` object that corresponds to whatever `_currentAddressIndex` is set to. This `Address` object is passed to `PopulateFormFromAddress` whose job it is to update the display:

```
        ' update the display...
        PopulateFormFromAddress(CurrentAddress)
```

Finally, it changes the `lblAddressNumber` control, so that it displays the current record number:

```
        ' set the label...
        lblAddressNumber.Text = _
        _currentAddressIndex & " of " & AddressBook.Items.Count
    End Set
End Property
```

You'll just quickly look at `CurrentAddress`. This property's job is to turn an integer index into the corresponding `Address` object stored in `AddressBook`. However, because `AddressBook` works on the basis of an `ArrayList` object that numbers items from 0, and your application starts numbering items at 1, you have to decrement your index value by one to get the matching value from `AddressBook`:

```
' CurrentAddress - property for the current address...
ReadOnly Property CurrentAddress() As Address
    Get
        Return AddressBook.Items(CurrentAddressIndex - 1)
    End Get
End Property
```

All good so far, but why is `XmlSerializer` throwing an exception? Well, the problems occur when you close the application. This fires the `OnClosed` method, which ultimately calls the `Save` method of `AddressBook`.

As you know, to save an object to disk, `XmlSerializer` scans through each of the properties looking for ones that are readable and writable. So far, you've only used `XmlSerializer` with `System.String`, but when the object comes across a property that uses a complex type, like `Address`, it uses the same principle—in other words, it looks through all of the properties that the complex type has. If properties on that object return complex types, it will drill down again. What it's doing is looking for simple types that it knows how to turn into text and write to the XML document.

However, some types cannot be turned into text and at this point `XmlSerializer` chokes. The `ArrayList` object that you're using to store a list of addresses had some properties that cannot be converted to text, which is the reason why the exception is being thrown. What you need to do is provide an alternative property that `XmlSerializer` can hook into in order to get a list of addresses and tell it not to bother trying to serialize the `ArrayList`.

Ignoring Members

Although `XmlSerializer` cannot cope with certain data types, it has no problems with arrays. You've also seen that `XmlSerializer` has no problems with your `Address` class, simply because this object doesn't have any properties of a type that `XmlSerializer` cannot support. What you'll do is provide an alternative property that returns an array of `Address` objects and tells `XmlSerializer` to keep away from the `Items` property because `XmlSerializer` cannot deal with `ArrayList` objects.

Try It Out   Ignoring Members

1. Open the code editor for `AddressBook`. Find the `Items` property and prefix it with the `System.Xml.Serialization.XmlIgnore` attribute:

```
Public Class AddressBook
    Inherits SerializableData
    ' members...
    <XmlIgnore()>Public Items As New ArrayList
```

2. Now, add this new property to the `AddressBook` class:

```
' Addresses - property that works with the items
' collection as an array...
Public Property Addresses() As Address()
    Get
        ' create a new array...
        Dim addressArray(Items.Count - 1) As Address
        Items.CopyTo(addressArray)
        Return addressArray
    End Get
    Set(ByVal Value As Address())
        ' reset the arraylist...
        Items.Clear()
        ' did you get anything?
        If Not Value Is Nothing Then
            ' go through the array and populate items...
            Dim address As Address
```

```
            For Each address In Value
                Items.Add(address)
            Next
        End If
    End Set
End Property
```

3. Run the project and then close the application; this time everything functions correctly. Run the project again, and this time around enter some data into the address fields. Close the application and you should now find that `AddressBook.xml` does contain data. (I've removed the `xmlns` and `?xml` values for clarity here.)

```
<AddressBook>
  <Addresses>
    <Address>
      <FirstName>Thearon</FirstName>
      <LastName>Willis</LastName>
      <CompanyName>Wiley</CompanyName>
      <Address1>123 Main Street</Address1>
      <Address2 />
      <City>Anytown</City>
      <Region>USA</Region>
      <PostalCode>12345</PostalCode>
      <Country>US</Country>
      <Email>thearon@nowhere.com</Email>
    </Address>
  </Addresses>
</AddressBook>
```

How It Works

The XML that got saved into your file proves that your approach works, but why?

At this point, your `AddressBook` object has two properties: `Items` and `Addresses`. Both are read/write properties, so both are going to be examined as candidates for serialization by `XmlSerializer`. As you know, `Items` returns an `ArrayList` object and `Addresses` returns an array of `Address` objects.

However, you marked `Items` with the `XmlIgnore` attribute. This means, not surprisingly, that `XmlSerializer` will ignore the property, despite the fact that it is readable and writable. Instead, it will move on to the `Addresses` property.

The `Get` portion of the `Addresses` property is what interests you. All you do is create a new array of `Address` objects and use the `CopyTo` method on the ArrayList to populate it:

```
' Addresses - property that works with the items
' collection as an array...
Public Property Addresses() As Address()
    Get
        ' create a new array...
        Dim addressArray(Items.Count - 1) As Address
        Items.CopyTo(addressArray)
        Return addressArray
```

```
      End Get
      Set(ByVal Value As Address())
          ...
      End Set
   End Property
```

When `XmlSerializer` gets an array of objects that it can deal with, all it does is iterate through the array serializing each of these contained objects in turn. You can see this in the XML that you received—the structure of the XML contained within the `Addresses` element exactly matches the structure of the XML you saw when you tested the process and wrote a single `Address` object to the file:

```
<AddressBook>
  <Addresses>
    <Address>
       <FirstName>Thearon</FirstName>
       <LastName>Willis</LastName>
       <CompanyName>Wiley</CompanyName>
       <Address1>123 Main Street</Address1>
       <Address2 />
       <City>Anytown</City>
       <Region>USA</Region>
       <PostalCode>12345</PostalCode>
       <Country>US</Country>
       <Email>thearon@nowhere.com</Email>
    </Address>   </Addresses>
</AddressBook>
```

Loading Addresses

If you're lucky, loading addresses should just work! Close the program and run the project again. You will see a record as shown in Figure 19-5.

You already set up the project to load the address book the first time you ran the project after creating the `AddressBook` class itself. This time, however, `AddressBook.Load` can find a file on the disk and so rather than creating a blank object, it's getting `XmlSerializer` to deserialize the lot. As `XmlSerializer` has no problems in writing arrays, you can assume it has no problem reading them.

It's the `Set` portion of the `Addresses` property that does the magic this time. One thing you have to be careful with this property is that, if you have passed a blank array (in other words `Nothing`), you try to prevent exceptions being thrown:

```
' Addresses - property that works with the items
' collection as an array...
Public Property Addresses() As Address()
    Get
        ...
    End Get
    Set(ByVal Value As Address())
        ' reset the arraylist...
        Items.Clear()
        ' did you get anything?
```

```
          If Not Value Is Nothing Then
              ' go through the array and populate items...
              Dim address As Address
              For Each address In Value
                  Items.Add(address)
              Next
          End If
      End Set
  End Property
```

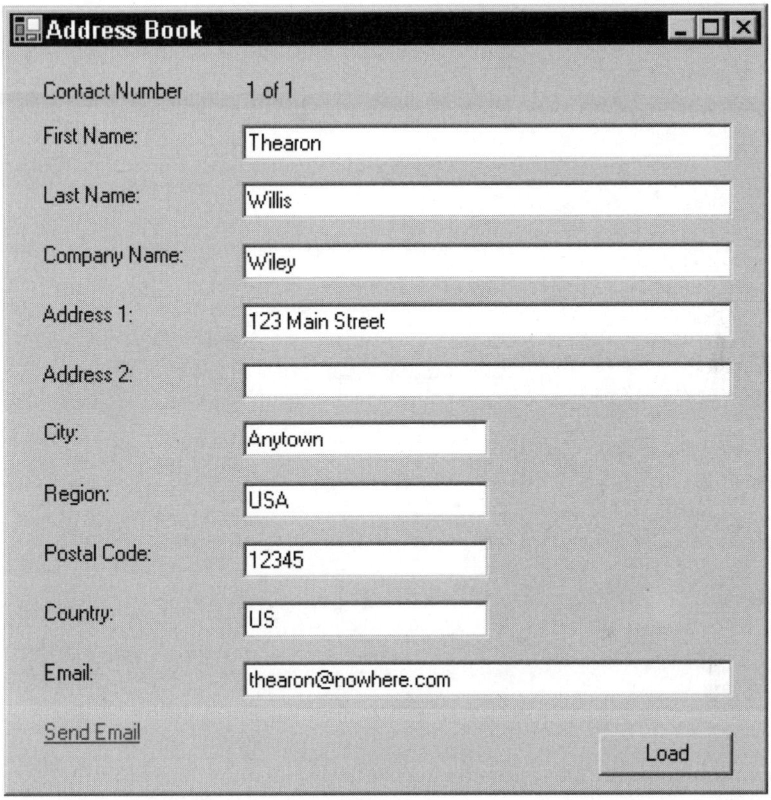

Figure 19-5

For each of the values in the array, all you have to do is take each one in turn and add them to the list.

Adding New Addresses

Next, you'll look at how you can add new addresses to the list. In this *Try It Out* exercise, you'll be adding four new buttons to your form. Two buttons will allow you to navigate through the list of addresses and two buttons will allow you to add and delete addresses.

Try It Out   **Adding New Addresses**

1. Open the Form Designer for Form1, remove the Load button before adding the four new buttons shown in Figure 19-6.

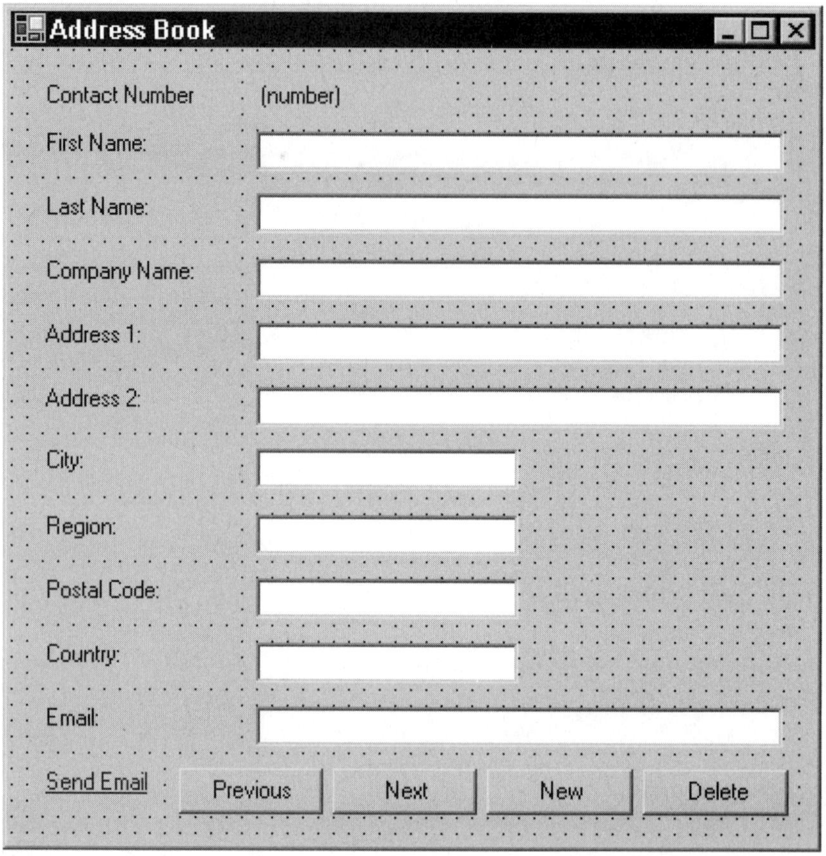

Address Book

Contact Number   (number)

First Name:

Last Name:

Company Name:

Address 1:

Address 2:

City:

Region:

Postal Code:

Country:

Email:

Send Email   Previous   Next   New   Delete

Figure 19-6

2. Name the buttons in turn as btnPrevious, btnNext, btnNew, and btnDelete and set their Text properties to Previous, Next, New, and Delete, respectively.

3. Double-click on the New button to create a Click handler. Add this code to the event handler and also add the AddNewAddress method:

```
Private Sub btnNew_Click(ByVal sender As System.Object, _
        ByVal e As System.EventArgs) Handles btnNew.Click
    AddNewAddress()
End Sub
Public Function AddNewAddress() As Address
    ' save the current address...
    UpdateCurrentAddress()

    ' create a new address...
```

```
        Dim newAddress As Address = AddressBook.AddAddress
        ' update the display...
        CurrentAddressIndex = AddressBook.Items.Count
        ' return the new address...
        Return newAddress
End Function
```

4. Run the project. Click New and a new address record will be created. Enter a new address.

5. Close down the program and the changes will be saved. Open up `AddressBook.xml` and you should see the new address.

How It Works

This time you have a new address object added to the XML document. It is contained within the `Addresses` element so you know that it is part of the same array.

The implementation was very simple—all you had to do was ask `AddressBook` to create a new address and then you update the `CurrentAddressIndex` property so that it equaled the number of items in the `AddressBook`. This had the effect of changing the display so that it changed to record 2 of 2 ready for editing.

However, it is important that, before you actually do this, you save the changes that the user might have made. With this application, you are ensuring that any changes the user makes will always find themselves being persisted into the XML file. Whenever the user closes the application, creates a new record, or moves backward or forward in the list, you want to call `UpdateCurrentAddress` in order that any changes will be saved:

```
Public Function AddNewAddress() As Address
    ' save the current address...
    UpdateCurrentAddress()
```

After you've saved the changes, it is then safe to create the new record and show it to the user:

```
    ' create a new address...
    Dim newAddress As Address = AddressBook.AddAddress
    ' update the display...
    CurrentAddressIndex = AddressBook.Items.Count
    ' return the new address...
    Return newAddress
End Function
```

Navigating Addresses

Now that you can add new addresses to the address book, you need to wire up the Next and Previous buttons so that you can move through the list. In this exercise, you'll be adding the code that will read the next or previous address from the array of addresses maintained by the `AddressBook` class. Before reading the next or previous address, however, you'll also want to ensure that any updates made to the current address are updated and you'll be calling the appropriate procedures to update the current address before navigating to a new address.

Navigating Addresses

1. Open the Form Designer for Form1. Double-click the Next button to create a new `Click` handler. Add this code and the associated `MoveNext` method:

```
Private Sub btnNext_Click(ByVal sender As System.Object, _
    ByVal e As System.EventArgs) Handles btnNext.Click
    MoveNext()
End Sub
Public Sub MoveNext()
    ' get the next index...
    Dim newIndex As Integer = CurrentAddressIndex + 1
    If newIndex > AddressBook.Items.Count Then
        newIndex = 1
    End If
    ' save any changes...
    UpdateCurrentAddress()
    ' move the record...
    CurrentAddressIndex = newIndex
End Sub
```

2. Next, flip back to the Form Designer and double-click the Previous button. Add this code:

```
Private Sub btnPrevious_Click(ByVal sender As System.Object, _
    ByVal e As System.EventArgs) Handles btnPrevious.Click
    MovePrevious()
End Sub
Public Sub MovePrevious()
    ' get the previous index...
    Dim newIndex As Integer = CurrentAddressIndex - 1
    If newIndex = 0 Then
        newIndex = AddressBook.Items.Count
    End If
    ' save changes...
    UpdateCurrentAddress()
    ' move the record...
    CurrentAddressIndex = newIndex
End Sub
```

3. Run the project. You should now be able to move between addresses.

How It Works

All you've done here is wire up the buttons so that each one changes the current index. By incrementing the current index, you move forward in the list. By decrementing it, you move backward.

However, it's very important that you don't move outside the bounds of the list (in other words, try to move to a position before the first record or to a position after the last record), which is why you check the value and adjust it as appropriate. When you move forward (`MoveNext`) you flip to the beginning of the list if you go off the end. When you move backward (`MovePrevious`) you flip to the end if you go off the start.

In both cases, you make sure that before you actually change the `CurrentAddressIndex` property, you call `UpdateCurrentAddress` to save any changes:

```
Public Sub MoveNext()
    ' get the next index...
    Dim newIndex As Integer = CurrentAddressIndex + 1
    If newIndex > AddressBook.Items.Count Then
        newIndex = 1
    End If
    ' save any changes...
    UpdateCurrentAddress()
    ' move the record...
    CurrentAddressIndex = newIndex
End Sub
```

Deleting Addresses

To finish off the functionality of your address book, you'll deal with deleting items. When deleting items, you must take into account that the item you are deleting is the last remaining item. In this case, you'll have to provide the appropriate code to add a new blank address. This *Try It Out* will provide this and all necessary functionality to properly delete an address.

Try It Out   Deleting Addresses

1. Go back to the Form Designer for Form1 and double-click the Delete button. Add this code to the event handler, and also add the `DeleteAddress` method:

```
Private Sub btnDelete_Click(ByVal sender As System.Object, _
        ByVal e As System.EventArgs) Handles btnDelete.Click
    ' ask the user if they are ok with this?
    If MsgBox ("Are you sure you want to delete this address?", _
        MsgBoxStyle.Question Or MsgBoxStyle.YesNo) = _
        MsgBoxResult.Yes Then
        DeleteAddress(CurrentAddressIndex)
    End If
End Sub
' DeleteAddress - delete an address from the list...
Public Sub DeleteAddress(ByVal index As Integer)
    ' delete the item from the list...
    AddressBook.Items.RemoveAt(index - 1)
    ' was that the last address?
    If AddressBook.Items.Count = 0 Then
        ' add a new address?
        AddressBook.AddAddress()
    Else
        ' make sure you have something to show...
        If index > AddressBook.Items.Count Then
            index = AddressBook.Items.Count
        End If
    End If
```

```
    ' display the record...
    CurrentAddressIndex = index
End Sub
```

2. Run the project. You should be able to delete records from the address book. Note that if you delete the last record, a new record will automatically be created.

How It Works

The algorithm you've used here to delete the records is an example of how to solve another classic programming problem.

Your application is set up so that it always has to display a record. That's why, when the program is first run and there is no AddressBook.xml, you automatically create a new record. Likewise, when an item is deleted from the address book, you have to find something to present to the user.

To physically delete an address from the disk, you use the RemoveAt method on the ArrayList that holds the Address objects.

```
' DeleteAddress - delete an address from the list...
Public Sub DeleteAddress(ByVal index As Integer)
    ' delete the item from the list...
    AddressBook.Items.RemoveAt(index - 1)
```

Again, notice here that, because you're working with a zero-based array, when you ask to delete the address with an index of 3, you actually have to delete the address at position 2 in the array.

The problems start after you've done that. It could be that you've deleted the one remaining address in the book. In this case, because you always have to display an address, you create a new one:

```
' was that the last address?
If AddressBook.Items.Count = 0 Then
    ' add a new address?
    AddressBook.AddAddress()
```

Alternatively, if there are items in the address book, you have to change the display. In some cases, the value that's currently stored in CurrentAddressIndex will be valid. For example, if you had five records and are looking at the third one, the _currentAddressIndex will be 3. If you delete that record, you have four records, but the third one as reported by _currentAddressIndex will still be 3 and valid. However, as 4 has now shuffled into 3's place you need to update the display.

It could be the case that you've deleted the last item in the list. When this happens, the index isn't valid because the index would be positioned over the end of the list. (You have four items in the list, delete the fourth one, you only have three, but _currentAddressIndex would be 4, which isn't valid.) So, when the last item is deleted, the index will be over the end of the list, so you set it to be the last item in the list:

```
Else
    ' make sure you have something to show...
    If index > AddressBook.Items.Count Then
        index = AddressBook.Items.Count
    End If
End If
```

Whatever actually happens, you still need to update the display. As you know, the `Current-AddressIndex` property can do this for you:

```
    ' display the record...
    CurrentAddressIndex = index
End Sub
```

Testing at the Edges

This brings me onto a programming technique that can greatly help you test your applications. When writing software, things usually go wrong at the "edge." For example, you have a function that takes an integer value, but in order for the method to work properly, the value supplied must lie between 0 and 99.

Once you're satisfied that your algorithm works properly when you give it a valid value, test some values at the "edge" of the problem (in other words, at the boundaries of the valid data). For example: −1, 0, 99, and 100. In most cases, if your method works properly for one or two of the possible valid values, it will work properly for the entire set of valid values. Testing a few values at the edge will show you where potential problems with the method lie.

A classic example of this is with your `MoveNext` and `MovePrevious` methods. If you had a hundred addresses in your address book and only tested that `MoveNext` and `MovePrevious` worked between numbers 10 and 20, it most likely would have worked between 1 and 100. However, the moment you move past 100 (in other words "go over the edge"), problems can occur. If you hadn't handled this case properly by flipping back to 1, your program would have crashed.

Integrating with the Address Book Application

So far you've built an application that is able to save and load its data as an XML document. You've also taken a look at the document as it's been changing over the course of the chapter, so by now you should have a pretty good idea of what an XML document looks like and how it works.

The beginning of this chapter pitched XML as a technology for integrating software applications. It then went on to say that for newcomers to Visual Basic, using XML for integration is unlikely to be something that you would do on a day-to-day basis and so you've been using XML to store data. In the rest of this chapter, I'm going to demonstrate why XML is such a good technology for integration. What you'll do is build a separate application that, with very little work, is able to read in and understand the proprietary data format that you've used in `AddressBook.xml`.

Using XML is an advanced topic—so if you would like to learn more about the technology and its application, try the following books:

- ❑ *Beginning XML, 2nd Edition* (ISBN 1-86100-559-8)
- ❑ *Visual Basic .NET and XML: Harness the Power of XML in VB.NET Applications* (ISBN 0-471-12060-X)

Demonstrating the Principle of Integration

Before you build the application that can integrate with your address book application, you should try and understand the principles involved. Basically, XML documents are good for integration because they can be easily read, understood, and changed by other people. Old-school file formats require detailed documentation to understand and often don't "evolve" well. (By that I mean when new versions of the format are released, software that worked with the old formats often breaks.)

XML documents are typically easily understood. Imagine you had never seen or heard of your address book before and look at this XML document:

```
<Addresses>
  <Address>
      <FirstName>Thearon</FirstName>
      <LastName>Willis</LastName>
      <CompanyName>Wiley</CompanyName>
      <Address1>123 Main Street</Address1>
      <Address2 />
      <City>Anytown</City>
      <Region>USA</Region>
      <PostalCode>12345</PostalCode>
      <Country>US</Country>
      <Email>thearon@nowhere.com</Email>
  </Address>
</Addresses>
```

Common sense tells you what this document represents. You can also perceive how the program that generated it uses it. In addition, you can use various tools in .NET to load, manipulate, and work with this document. To an extent, you still need to work with the people that designed the structure of the document, especially when more esoteric elements come into play, but you can use this document to some meaningful effect without too much stress.

Providing you know what structure the document takes, you can build your own document or add new things to it. For example, if you know that the Addresses element contains a list of Address elements, and that each Address element contains a bunch of elements that describe the address, you can add your own Address element using your own application.

To see this happening, you can open the AddressBook.xml file in Notepad. You need to copy the last Address element (complete with the contents) to the bottom of the document, but make sure it remains inside the Addresses element. Change the address data to something else. Here's mine:

```
<?xml version="1.0"?>
<AddressBook xmlns:xsd="http://www.w3.org/2001/XMLSchema"
xmlns:xsi="http://www.w3.org/2001/XMLSchema-instance">
  <Addresses>
    <Address>
      <FirstName>Thearon</FirstName>
      <LastName>Willis</LastName>
      <CompanyName>Wiley</CompanyName>
      <Address1>123 Main Street</Address1>
      <Address2 />
      <City>Anytown</City>
      <Region>USA</Region>
      <PostalCode>12345</PostalCode>
      <Country>US</Country>
      <Email>thearon@nowhere.com</Email>
    </Address>
```

```
   <Address>
     <FirstName>Margie</FirstName>
     <LastName>Willis</LastName>
     <CompanyName />
     <Address1>123 Main Street</Address1>
     <Address2 />
     <City>Anytown</City>
     <Region>USA</Region>
     <PostalCode>12345</PostalCode>
     <Country>US</Country>
     <Email />
   </Address>
 </Addresses>
</AddressBook>
```

Finally, if you save the file and run the address book application, you should find that you have two addresses and that the last one is the new one that you added. What this shows is that, providing you understand the format of the XML that the application uses, you can manipulate the document and gain some level of integration.

Reading the Address Book from Another Application

To further illustrate, what you'll do now is build a completely separate application from Address Book that's able to load in the XML file that Address Book uses and do something useful with it. Specifically, you'll extract all of the addresses in the file and display a list of names together with their matching e-mail addresses.

Try It Out   Reading Address Book Data

1. Create a new Visual Basic .NET Windows Application project. Call it Address List.

2. On Form1, draw a ListBox control. Change its IntegralHeight property to False, its Dock property to Fill and its Name to lstEmails, as shown in Figure 19-7.

3. Double-click the form's title bar. Add this code to the XE:

"Address Book project (example):Form1 class:Load event"\r"Load4" Load event handler.

Remember to add this namespace declaration:

```
Imports System.Xml
Public Class Form1
    Inherits System.Windows.Forms.Form
Private Sub Form1_Load(ByVal sender As System.Object, _
        ByVal e As System.EventArgs) Handles MyBase.Load
    ' where do we want to get the XML from...
    Dim filename As String = _
        "c:\Visual Studio Project\AddressBook\bin\AddressBook.xml"
    ' open the document...
    Dim reader As New XmlTextReader(filename)
    ' move to the start of the document...
    reader.MoveToContent()
```

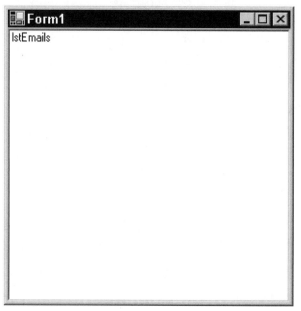

Figure 19-7

```
' start working through the document...
Dim addressData As Collection, elementName As String
Do While reader.Read
    ' what kind of node to we have?
    Select Case reader.NodeType
        ' is it the start of an element?
        Case XmlNodeType.Element
            ' if it's an element start, is it "Address"?
            If reader.Name = "Address" Then
                ' if so, create a new collection...
                addressData = New Collection()
            Else
                ' if not, record the name of the element...
                elementName = reader.Name
            End If
        ' if we have some text, try storing it in the
        ' collection...
        Case XmlNodeType.Text
            ' do we have an address?
            If Not addressData Is Nothing Then
                addressData.Add(reader.Value, elementName)
            End If
        ' is it the end of an element?
        Case XmlNodeType.EndElement
            ' if it is, we should have an entire address stored...
            If reader.Name = "Address" Then
                ' try to create a new listview item...
                Dim item As String
```

```
                Try
                    item = addressData("firstname") & _
                        " " & addressData("lastname")
                    item &= " (" & addressData("email") & ")"
                Catch
                End Try
                ' add the item to the list...
                lstEmails.Items.Add(item)
                ' reset...
                addressData = Nothing
            End If
        End Select
    Loop
End Sub
```

I've assumed in this code listing that your AddressBook.xml *will be in* C:\Visual Studio Project\AddressBook\bin. *If yours is not, change the filename value specified at the top of the code.*

4. Run the project; you should see something like what is shown in Figure 19-8. Notice that addresses that don't have an e-mail address display fine as the Email element in your XML file contains an empty string value instead of a null value that is typically found in databases.

Figure 19-8

How It Works

To fully appreciate the benefit of this exercise (and therefore the benefit of XML), imagine that before writing the application you'd never seen the XML format used by the Address Book application. Since XML is a text-based format, you're able to open it in a normal text editor, read it, and make assumptions about how it works. You know that you want to get a list of names and e-mail addresses, and you understand that you have an array of Address elements, each one containing the three elements you need: FirstName, LastName, and Email. All that remains is to extract and present the information.

Since announcing .NET, Microsoft has made a big play about how it is built on XML. This shows in the .NET Framework support for XML—there is a dazzling array of classes for reading and writing XML documents. The XmlSerializer object that you've been using up until now is by far the easiest one to use, but it relies on your having classes that exactly match the document structure. Therefore, if you are given a document from a business partner, you won't have a set of classes that matches the document. As a result, you need some other way to read the document and fit it into whatever classes you do have.

In your Address List project, you don't have applicable `AddressBook` or `Address` classes, so you have to use some classes to "walk" through a file. The one you're using is `System.Xml.XmlTextReader`. This class provides a "pointer" that starts at the top of the document and, on command, moves to the next part of the document. (Each of these parts is called a node.) The pointer will stop at anything, and this includes start tags, end tags, data values, and whitespace.

So, when you start walking, the first thing `XmlTextReader` will tell you about is this node:

```
<?xml version="1.0" ?>
```

When you ask it to move on, it will tell you about this node:

```
<AddressBook xmlns:xsi="http://www.w3.org/2001/XMLSchema-instance"
xmlns:xsd="http://www.w3.org/2001/XMLSchema">
```

Then, you ask it to move on again, it will tell you about this node:

```
<Addresses>
```

Then about `<Address>`, `<FirstName>`, `Thearon`, `</FirstName>`, and `<LastName>`, and so on until it gets to the end of the document. In between each one of these, you may or may not be told about whitespace nodes. By and large, you can ignore these.

What your algorithm has to do then is get hold of an `XmlTextReader` and start moving through the document one piece at a time. When you first start, the pointer will be set ahead of the first node in the document. Each call to `Read` moves the pointer along one node, so the first call to `Read` that you see at the start of the `Do While` loop actually sets the pointer to the first node:

```
Private Sub Form1_Load(ByVal sender As System.Object, _
            ByVal e As System.EventArgs) Handles MyBase.Load
    ' where do you want to get the XML from...
    Dim filename As String = _
        "c:\MyPrograms\AddressBook\AddressBook.xml"
    ' open the document...
    Dim reader As New XmlTextReader(filename)
    ' move to the start of the document...
    reader.MoveToContent()
    ' start working through the document...
    Dim addressData As Collection, elementName As String
    Do While reader.Read
```

You can use the `NodeType` property of `XmlTextReader` to find out what kind of node you're looking at. If you have an `Element` node, this maps directly onto a start tag in the document. You can use the `Name` property to get the name of the tag. When you find the `<Address>` start tag, you create a new collection called `addressData`. If the start tag that you're looking at isn't the `<Address>` tag, you store the name in `elementName` for later use:

```
            ' what kind of node to we have?
            Select Case reader.NodeType
                ' is it the start of an element?
                Case XmlNodeType.Element
                    ' if it's an element start, is it "Address"?
```

```
If reader.Name = "Address" Then
    ' if so, create a new collection...
    addressData = New Collection()
Else
    ' if not, record the name of the element...
    elementName = reader.Name
End If
```

Alternatively, the node you get might be a lump of text. If this is the case, you check to see if addressData points to a Collection object. If it does, you know that you are inside an Address element. Remember, you've also stored the name of the element that you are looking at inside elementName. This means that if elementName is set to FirstName, you know you're in the FirstName element and therefore the text element you're looking at must be the first name in the address. You then add this element name and the value into the collection for later use:

```
' if we have some text, try storing it in the
' collection...
Case XmlNodeType.Text
' do we have an address?
If Not addressData Is Nothing Then
    addressData.Add(reader.Value, elementName)
End If
```

As you work through the file, you'll get to this point for each of the elements stored in the Address element. Effectively, by the time you reach </Address>, addressData will contain entries for each value stored against the address in the document.

To detect when you get to the </Address> tag, you need to look for EndElement nodes:

```
' is it the end of an element?
Case XmlNodeType.EndElement
```

When you get one of these, if Name is equal to Address, you know that you have reached </Address>, and this means that addressData should be fully populated. You form a string and add it to the list:

```
' if it is, you should have an entire address stored...
If reader.Name = "Address" Then
    ' try to create a new listview item...
    Dim item As String
    Try
        item = addressData("firstname") & _
                " " & addressData("lastname")
        item &= " (" & addressData("email") & ")"
    Catch
    End Try
    ' add the item to the list...
    lstEmails.Items.Add(item)
    ' reset...
    addressData = Nothing
End If
```

You'll notice that in your Try...Catch you won't do anything if an exception does occur. To keep this example simple, you're going to ignore any problems that do occur. Specifically, you'll run into problems if the Address element you're looking through has sub-elements missing—for example, you might not always have an e-mail address for each address as was shown in Figure 19-8.

You then continue the loop. On each iteration of the loop, XmlTextReader.Read will be called, which advances the pointer to the next node. If there are no more nodes in the document, Read returns False and the loop stops:

```
        End Select
    Loop
End Sub
```

I hope that this example has illustrated the power of XML from a software integration perspective. With very little work, you've managed to integrate the Address Book and Address List applications together.

If you want to experiment with this a little, try adding and deleting addresses from the Address Book. You'll need to close the program to save the changes to AddressBook.xml, but each time you start Address List you should see the changes you made.

Summary

This chapter introduced the concept of XML. XML is a language based on open standards that can be used as a tool for software integration. Within a single organization, XML can be used to easily transport data across platforms. It also allows two organizations to define a common format for data exchange and, because XML is text-based, it can easily be moved around using Internet technologies like e-mail, the Web, and FTP. XML is based on building up a document composed of tags and data.

XML is primarily used for integration work to make the tasks of data transportation and exchange easier, and you, as a newcomer to Visual Basic and programming in general, are unlikely to do integration work (as it is typically done by developers with lots of experience). Nevertheless, this chapter has "dipped your toes in" so to speak, by focusing on using the System.Xml.Serialization.XmlSerializer class to save entire objects to disk (known as serialization). This same object was used to load objects from disk (known as deserialization). You built a fully functional address book application that was able to use an XML file stored on the local computer as its primary source of data.

To conclude the chapter and demonstrate that XML is a great tool for software integration work, you wrote a separate application that was able to load and make sense of the XML document used by the Address Book application.

To summarize, you should:

❑ Have a better understanding of XML and know what it looks like

❑ How to serialize and deserialize XML data into objects

❑ How to manipulate XML data in your applications

❑ How to use the XMLTextReader class to walk through an XML document

Exercises

1. What does XML stand for?

2. What is XML primarily used for?

3. What kinds of data can XmlSerializer work with?

4. How do you stop XmlSerializer working with a property that it might otherwise try and serialize?

5. Which class can be used to iterate through an XML document one node at a time?

20

Web Services and .NET Remoting

Industry watchers have been predicting for some time that Web services are going to be the "next big thing" in Internet development. This chapter introduces the concept of Web services and shows you how to build your own. This chapter also looks at .NET Remoting and offers some guidance for choosing between .NET Remoting and XML Web services.

In this chapter, you will:

❑   Get an overview of SOAP, the method used to exchange data with Web services

❑   Build multiple Web services

❑   Learn how to test the Web services using the built-in test harness

❑   Build front-end applications that consume Web services

❑   Get an overview and hands on experience with .Net Remoting

What Is a Web Service?

When you use the Internet, the two things you most likely use it for are sending (and receiving) e-mail and surfing the Web. These two applications are, by far, the most popular uses of the Internet .

However, from time to time as Internet usage grows, new technologies and applications that have the potential to change forever the way you use the Internet are released. In recent times, Napster has been a commercial product that has grown from nothing to "ridiculously huge" in a very short space of time. (In fact, the rate of growth of Napster, until the various court decisions that clipped its wings took hold, was far in excess of the rate of growth of the Web itself!) Naturally, its fall from grace was just as fast!

Building upon the success of the World Wide Web as you know it today, Web service has the potential to be "the next big thing."

The Web is a great way to share information. However, the problem with the Web as it is today is that in order to use it you have to be a human. Web sites are built to be read with human eyes and interpreted with the human mind. Web services, on the other hand, are built to be read and interpreted by computer programs, not by humans. Web services are, in effect, Web sites for computers to use. These Web sites tend to be dynamic in nature, so they don't contain static unchanging content, but can react and adapt to choices and selections. For example, I might want to use a Web service that accepts a quantity in U.S. dollars and returns the number of equivalent Euros.

Why is this a good thing? Well, when building computer systems in a commercial information technology environment, the most costly factor always involved is integrating disparate computer systems. Imagine you have two pieces of software; one, used to keep track of stock in your warehouse, the other used to capture customer orders. These two pieces of software were developed by different companies and bought at different times. However, when an order is placed using the second piece of software, that software should be able to tell the warehousing software that a quantity of a particular product has been sold. This may trigger some autonomous action in the warehousing software, such as placing an order to replenish the stock or asking someone to go and pick it off the shelf.

When two pieces of software work together, you call it *integration*. But, integration is rarely easy and on large installations it often involves hiring teams of consultants and spending thousands of dollars on custom-written integration software.

Without going into too much detail, Web services make integration far, far easier. By making something that much easier, you inevitably make it far, far cheaper and that's why it's predicted to be the next big thing. Not only will companies who are already integrating have a more cost-effective option than before, but also companies will be able to integrate their computer systems in previously unseen ways. Web services will also provide opportunities for new businesses wanting to introduce specialized services with relative ease.

The commercial pros and cons of Web services together with a discussion of the movers and shakers in this particular space are beyond the scope of this book. However, if you would like to learn more, take a look at www.webservicesarchitect.com/.

How Does a Web Service Work?

First of all, Web services are based upon completely open standards that are not tied to any particular platform or any particular company. Part of their attraction is that it doesn't matter whether you deploy your Web service on Solaris, Unix, Mac, or Windows—anyone will be able to connect to and use your Web service. This is the same with normal Web sites—you do not care what platform the Web sites you visit every day actually run on, as long as they work.

Second, the .NET implementation of Web services are entirely based around a programming paradigm that developers have been falling in love with for years: object orientation. If you're used to using objects (and by Chapter 20 of this book, you should be!) you'll have absolutely no problems with Web services.

The principle behind a Web service is that you build a class that has methods in it. However, the traditional method of deployment and instantiation does not apply. Here is what happens traditionally:

❑ A developer builds an object

❑ That object is installed (copied onto a computer)

- ❑ A piece of software running on that *same* computer creates an instance of the class (the "object")
- ❑ The piece of software calls a method on the object
- ❑ The object does something and returns a value
- ❑ The piece of software receives the value and does something with it

But here is what happens with a Web service:

- ❑ A developer builds an object
- ❑ That object is copied onto a server computer running a Web server (like Microsoft IIS)
- ❑ A piece of software running on a *different, remote* computer (usually located somewhere on the Internet) asks the Web server to run a particular method on the class
- ❑ The server creates an instance of the class and calls the method
- ❑ The server returns the results of the method to the calling computer
- ❑ The piece of software on the remote computer receives the value and does something with it

You can see that the technique is very similar, but there's a disconnection between the server that the object is actually installed on and the computer that wants to use the object. In fact, with a Web service there is a huge process gulf (namely, the Internet) between the client of the object and the object itself. A solution to handle this disconnection is provided by the standards used by and specifically developed for Web services.

Simple Object Access Protocol

As Web services are, in effect, "Web sites for computers to use," they've been built on the same technology that's made the World Wide Web so popular, specifically, the Hypertext Transfer Protocol (HTTP) standard that powers all Web servers.

When you're dealing with "Web sites for people to read," the client (browser) and server usually exchange a mixture of documents. Hypertext Markup Language (HTML) documents, and their extension technologies like Dynamic HTML and JavaScript, describe the page layout and text on the page and common image formats like GIF and JPEG are used to exchange images.

However, when you're dealing with "Web sites for computers to use," you only exchange one kind of document. These documents are known as SOAP documents.

When a client application wants to ask the Web service for some information, such as the current stock level for a product, or the status of an order, or to get the computer at the end of the connection to do something like convert currencies or place an order, the application constructs a SOAP request document. Using the HTTP protocol, this document is sent over the Internet to the Web server that powers the Web service. This document contains all the information that the Web service needs to determine what has been asked for. As Web services work on the common object/method paradigm, the request document includes things like the name of the method and any data that should be passed through to the method as parameters.

At the server end, the Web service receives the SOAP request, deserializes it, and runs the appropriate piece of software. (You're going to build some of these appropriate pieces of software in this chapter.) During the call, the method generates a SOAP response document that contains the information to be passed back to the caller. Like the request document, this new document is transferred using HTTP through the Web server.

SOAP documents are constructed with XML. This means that if you read a SOAP document, it'll look very similar to the sort of document that you saw in Chapter 19. However, at the level of Visual Basic, you don't need to look too hard at the SOAP documents . As you work through the chapter, you'll see some of the SOAP response documents that come back from the server, but you won't be seeing any of the request documents.

You know that Web service technology is not tied to a specific platform, so from a developer's perspective the value of choosing one platform over another is determined by how transparent this SOAP document construction and transfer work actually is or what is available at the site where development will take place. .NET is very good for both building and using Web services—you don't have to go within a hundred yards of a SOAP document. (This is why in this chapter you're not going to dwell on SOAP too much, even though without SOAP you wouldn't be able to do anything you can do in this chapter.) On the other hand, other platforms will be equally good for building Web services, but you need to jump through a few more hoops to create powerful Web services.

Obviously, this chapter is concerned with how Web services work with .NET. But first, have a close look at Figure 20-1 as it provides a simple form of the architecture behind Web services.

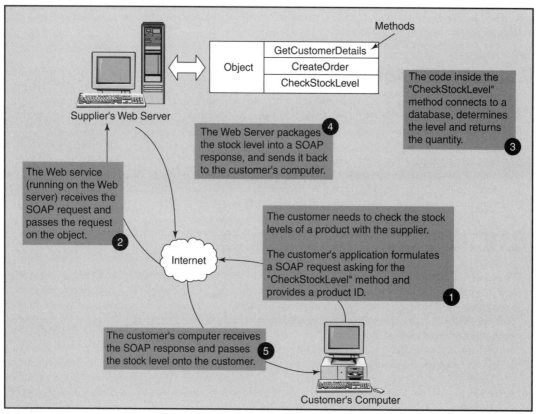

Figure 20-1

Building a Web Service

Building Web services with Visual Studio .NET is a breeze! In this section, you'll build a simple Web service and will be introduced to some of the concepts involved. Specifically, you'll see how to include the appropriate attributes to expose a method as a Web service method. You'll also learn how to test your Web methods using the test harness built into Web services.

A Web Services Demonstration

A Web service is basically a class that sits on the server. Some of the methods on that class are marked in a special way, and it's by looking for these special marks that .NET knows which methods to publish on the service. You'll see how this works as you go through the first *Try It Out* in this chapter. Anyone wishing to use the Web service can then call these methods on the remote Web service, as if the method existed in a class installed on their local computer. You'll also see a method that allows us to test the Web service from within Internet Explorer.

Try It Out   **A Demonstration Web Service**

1. Open Visual Studio and select File ➪ New ➪ Project from the menu.

2. Make sure Visual Basic Projects is selected in the left box and select ASP.NET Web service from the right list. Enter the name as **DemoService** and click OK (see Figure 20-2).

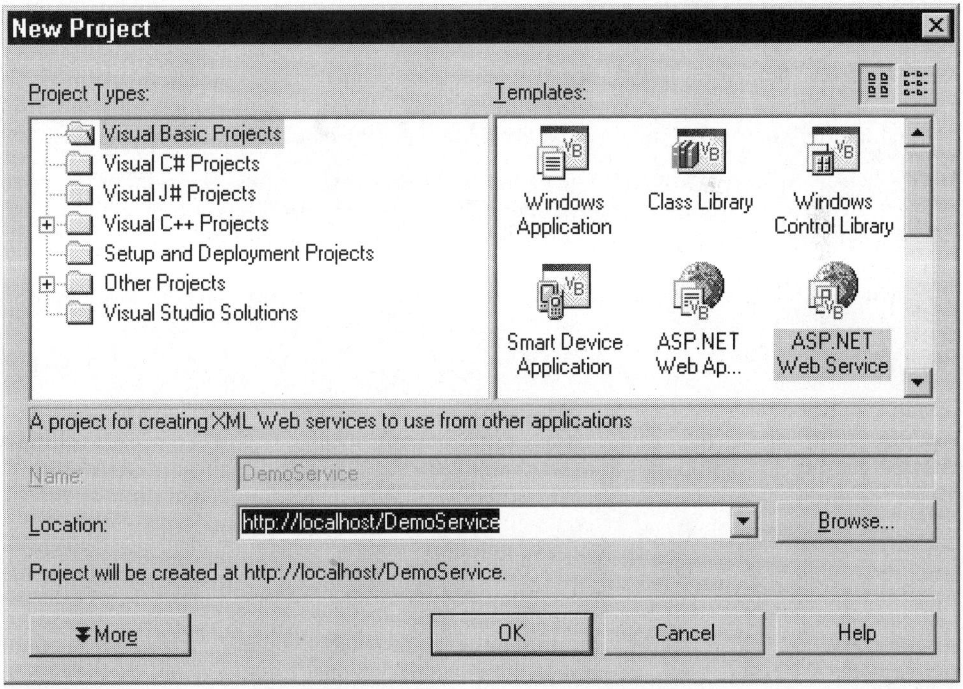

Figure 20-2

Web services are based on ASP.NET technology, so the project will be created in the same way as the Web applications you worked with in Chapter 17. If you have problems creating the project, look back at that chapter for troubleshooting information.

Visual Studio .NET will create a new virtual directory and create a new page called `Service1`. `asmx`, where `.asmx` stands for Active Server Methods. (The extra x comes from the original name of ASP.NET: ASP+. The x is the plus sign turned through 45 degrees.) This page represents one service and a Web service project (or site) can contain many different services.

3. Using the Solution Explorer, right-click Service1.asmx and select View Code. When Visual Studio .NET created the page, it puts an example method on the service called `HelloWorld`. This is commented out at the moment, so remove the comments such that the code looks like the code shown here:

```
' WEB SERVICE EXAMPLE
' The HelloWorld() example service returns the string Hello World.
' To build, uncomment the following lines then save and build the project.
' To test this web service, ensure that the .asmx file is the start page
' and press F5.
'
<WebMethod()> _
Public Function HelloWorld() As String
    Return "Hello World"
End Function
```

Run the project by selecting Debug ⇨ Start from the menu. The project will be compiled and Internet Explorer will open and display the Service1.asmx page. This is the test interface. On this initial page, all of the methods supported by the service appear in a bulleted list at the top of the page.

4. Click the HelloWorld link. This will open another page that lets you run the method. This page contains the Web method name, a button to invoke the Web method for testing, and the protocols supported for this Web method. Notice that two protocols are listed: SOAP and HTTP POST.

5. Click the Invoke button. This will open another browser window. This window contains the SOAP response from the server as shown in the code here:

```
<?xml version="1.0" encoding="utf-8" ?>
<string xmlns="http://tempuri.org/DemoService/Service1">Hello World</string>
```

How It Works

Just as in Web forms where you have a class behind the `.aspx` page, you also have a class behind each `.asmx` page with Web services. This class is the one that you enabled the `HelloWorld` method on. If you look at the definition for the class, you'll see that it's inherited from `System.Web.Services`.`WebService`:

```
Public Class Service1
    Inherits System.Web.Services.WebService
```

The `WebService` class is responsible for presenting the pages that you clicked through in Internet Explorer to invoke the `HelloWorld` method. (You can use another browser to test the service, but Visual

Studio .NET chooses Internet Explorer by default.) These pages are known as the test interface. Methods on the class that you want exposed to the Web service must be marked with the `WebMethod` attribute. You can see this attribute defined at the beginning of the method (note that it must be encased in a similar fashion to HTML tags):

```
<WebMethod()> _
Public Function HelloWorld() As String
    HelloWorld = "Hello World"
End Function
```

When the test interface starts, it displays the methods flagged to be exposed on the server. When you click through to the page tied to a specific method, the test interface presents a form that you can use to invoke it.

When the method is invoked, to the method it "feels" just like a normal call—in other words there's nothing special about writing Web services and everything that you've learned so far still applies.

You already know that Web services are powered by SOAP. When you click the Invoke button, the SOAP message that's returned to the caller (in this case, that is your Internet Explorer) contains the response. You can see that this is indeed the value you returned from the method buried within a block of XML:

```
<?xml version="1.0" encoding="utf-8" ?>
< string xmlns="http://tempuri.org/DemoService/Service1"> Hello World </string>
```

The structure of the XML that makes up the SOAP message, by and large, is not important. However, when you're working through more examples, I'll point out where the actual results can be found.

Adding More Methods

Let us build some methods that illustrate your Web service actually doing something. In this next *Try It Out* exercise, you'll be adding a Web method that will calculate the square root of the number that you pass into it. You'll be adding the Web method and writing the code to calculate the square root, as well as testing this new Web method.

Try It Out   Adding a SquareRoot Method

1. Open the code editor for `Service1.asmx`. Add this new method to the `Service1` class below the existing `HelloWorld` method:

```
Public Function GetSquareRoot(ByVal number As Double) As Double
    Return Math.Sqrt(number)
End Function
```

If you can't type into the code window, it means that the instance of Internet Explorer that Visual Studio .NET opened is still running. Close down the test interface windows and any extra windows displaying the SOAP responses and the project should stop running. Alternatively, select Debug ⇨ Stop Debugging from the menu.

2. Run the project. You'll notice that the new method does not appear in the list at the top of the page. In fact, you will see the same screen that was shown previously. This is due to the fact that you didn't mark the method with the `WebMethod` attribute. I did this to show you that a class can contain methods that, although public, are not exposed on the Web service. Close the browser and add the `WebMethod` attribute:

```
<WebMethod()> _
Public Function GetSquareRoot(ByVal number As Double) As Double
    Return Math.Sqrt(number)
End Function
```

3. Run the project again and you should see the new method at the top of the page.

4. Click on the GetSquareRoot link. This time, the Invoke form should offer a way to enter a number because of the method parameter. Without entering a number, click Invoke.

5. When the new browser appears, you won't see a SOAP response, but instead you'll see something that looks like this:

```
System.ArgumentException: Cannot convert to System.Double.
Parameter name: type ---> System.FormatException: Input string was not in a
correct format.
   at System.Number.ParseDouble(String s, NumberStyles style, NumberFormatInfo
info)
   at System.Double.Parse(String s, NumberStyles style, IFormatProvider
provider)
   at System.Convert.ToDouble(String value, IFormatProvider provider)
   at System.String.System.IConvertible.ToDouble(IFormatProvider provider)
   at System.Convert.ChangeType(Object value, Type conversionType,
IFormatProvider provider)
   at System.Convert.ChangeType(Object value, Type conversionType)
   at System.Web.Services.Protocols.ScalarFormatter.FromString(String value,
Type type)
   --- End of inner exception stack trace ---
   at System.Web.Services.Protocols.ScalarFormatter.FromString(String value,
Type type)
   at
System.Web.Services.Protocols.ValueCollectionParameterReader.Read(NameValue
Collection collection)
   at System.Web.Services.Protocols.HtmlFormParameterReader.Read(HttpRequest
request)
   at System.Web.Services.Protocols.HttpServerProtocol.ReadParameters()
   at System.Web.Services.Protocols.WebServiceHandler.Invoke()
   at System.Web.Services.Protocols.WebServiceHandler.CoreProcessRequest()
```

You'll see this kind of message whenever you enter invalid information into the Invoke form. In this case, it's telling us that it cannot convert to `System.Double`, which should be a big giveaway that it can't convert an empty string to a floating-point value.

6. Close the browser window and enter 2 into the number field. Click Invoke and you'll get this response:

```
<?xml version="1.0" encoding="utf-8" ?>
<double
xmlns=" http://tempuri.org/DemoService/Service1">1.4142135623730952</double>
```

How It Works

If you look in the SOAP message that was returned, you'll find a double value that's as close as you can get to the square root of 2.

```
<?xml version="1.0" encoding="utf-8" ?>
<double
xmlns="http://tempuri.org/DemoService/Service1">1.4142135623730952</double>
```

So you know that the method works. You should have also seen by now that building simple Web services is not hard. This was Microsoft's intent with the Web services support in .NET—the plumbing to build a service is remarkably easy. Everything you've learned about creating classes, building methods with parameters, and returning values is paying dividends here because there's virtually no learning curve to climb. You can concentrate on building the logic behind the Web service, which, after all, is the bit you get paid to do!

The Picture Server Service

As building simple Web services is so straightforward, you'll move on relatively quickly to building a proper application that does something practical with a Web service. You'll also look at building a desktop client application that uses the Web service, because up to now all you've used is the test interface provided by the `WebService` class. The specific example you'll use will be to build a Web service that allows an application to view pictures placed on a remote server.

Creating the Project

In this section, you will:

❑ Set up a folder on your Web service server (this could be your local machine or a remote machine where the Web service will run) that contains pictures downloaded from a digital camera. You'll divide this folder into subfolders for different events, for example, "Deborah's Graduation," "Trip to Boston," and so on.

❑ Build aWeb service that can interrogate the folder to return a list of subfolders. You'll also be able to return a list of the files in each subfolder.

❑ When you do return a file, you'll also return details on the file, such as graphic format, width, height, and so on.

❑ Set up the Web site so that you can view the pictures you find using a Web browser.

That doesn't sound like anything you can't do using an ASP.NET Web site. However, what you can do with the Web service that you cannot do with a standard Web site is build your own custom front-end Windows Forms application. With a Web site, you are tied to using HTML and a Web browser to present the information on the server to the user.

Try It Out   **Creating the Project**

1. Select File ➪ New ➪ Project from the menu to create a new ASP.NET Web service project and call it PictureService. When the project loads, you don't want to use the default `Service1.asmx` file. Using the Solution Explorer right-click `Service1.asmx` and select Delete. Click OK when asked.

2. Using the Solution Explorer again, right-click the PictureService project. Select Add ⇨ Add Web service. Enter the name of the service as Service and click Open. The Solution Explorer should now contain `Service.asmx`.

3. Now that you've created this new `.asmx` page, when you run the project you want this to be the one that gets loaded into Internet Explorer. In the Solution Explorer, right-click the `Service.asmx` entry and select Set as Start Page.

4. To make the pictures available over the Web site you need to create a folder called `Pictures`, directly within the folder that theWeb service itself runs out of. There is a problem however, thanks to the way Visual Studio .NET works with IIS, this folder will vary widely from installation to installation. To ensure that you get the right folder, what you need to do is get the Web service itself to tell us the folder it is running from.

5. Now, right-click `Service.asmx` in the Solution Explorer and select the View Code menu item. Find the `HelloWorld` method again, remove the comments from the code, and alter the code so that it looks like this:

```
Public Class Service
    Inherits System.Web.Services.WebService
    ' WEB SERVICE EXAMPLE
    ' The HelloWorld() example service returns the string Hello World.
    ' To build, uncomment the following lines then save and build the
    ' project. To test this web service, ensure that the .asmx file is
    ' the start page and press F5.
    '
    <WebMethod()> _
    Public Function HelloWorld() As String
        Return_
        Server.MapPath(Context.Request.ServerVariables.Item("script_name"))
    End Function
End Class
```

6. Run the project. As usual, when Internet Explorer starts, click the HelloWorld method link. Click the Invoke button when the page loads. TheWeb service should now tell you the full path of `Service.asmx`:

```
<?xml version="1.0" encoding="utf-8" ?>
    <string xmlns=" http://tempuri.org/PictureService/Service">
        c:\inetpub\wwwroot\PictureService\Service.asmx
    </string>
```

7. You can see that, on my computer, the folder containing `Service.asmx` is `c:\inetpub\wwwroot\PictureService`. You'll refer to this folder as the service root folder from this point on. Now, open a copy of Windows Explorer (that's the normal file Explorer, not Internet Explorer). Go to the service root folder and create a new subfolder called Pictures, as shown in Figure 20-3.

8. Now you'll need to find some pictures to use with the service. I am going to use some that a friend of mine took with his digital camera, but you can use any picture you like as long as they are in either GIF or JPEG format.

Figure 20-3

9. Divide the pictures into a set of three subfolders under the Pictures folder. Use any folder name that you like for your three subfolders.

How It Works

At this point, you should have both a Web service and a load of pictures that you can use with the service. In a moment, you'll start building methods on the service that are able to return the folders to the user.

The only piece of code you wrote in this section was the code that returned the complete path of `Service.asmx`:

```vb
<WebMethod()> _
Public Function HelloWorld() As String
    Return _
    Server.MapPath(Context.Request.ServerVariables.Item("script_name"))
End Function
```

This is quite an advanced ASP.NET trick (Web services are, after all, based on ASP.NET technology) and is beyond the scope of the book. However, what I can tell you is that all pages running on ASP.NET are able to make many determinations about their environment, including the physical path in which the server is located.

For more information on building Web sites with ASP.NET, check out Beginning ASP.NET 1.1 with VB.NET 2003 *(ISBN: 0-7645-5707-6).*

Returning Arrays

In the first part of this chapter, you looked at a Web service that returned single values from each method call, for example, a string or a number.

Chapter 20

In some cases you want to return arrays of information. This is particularly true when you ask the Web service for a list of the picture subfolders. You want to return an array of string values, each one containing the name of a folder.

Try It Out   Returning a List of Picture Subfolders

1. Open the code editor for `Service.asmx` again. Delete the `HelloWorld` method.

2. You need a reference to the `System.IO` namespace for this exercise, so go to the top of the code listing and add this new namespace reference:

```
Imports System.Web.Services
Imports System.IO
```

When you're building methods, you're going to need a way to get the full path to your `Pictures` folder. This uses the work you did before to find the service root folder, but with an extra bit of code to actually get the full path to the `Pictures` folder. Add this property to `Service`:

```
' PictureFolderPath - readonly property to return the picture
' folder...
Public ReadOnly Property PictureFolderPath() As String
    Get
        ' get the full path of this asmx page...
        Dim asmxPath As String, picturePath As String
        asmxPath = _
    Server.MapPath(Context.Request.ServerVariables.Item("script_name"))
        ' get the service path - everything up to and including
        ' the "\"
        Dim servicePath As String = _
            asmxPath.Substring(0, asmxPath.LastIndexOf("\") + 1)
        ' append the word "Pictures" to the end of the path...
        picturePath = servicePath & "Pictures"
        ' return the path...
        Return picturePath
    End Get
End Property
```

3. Having the name of the folder is just half the battle. In order to do anything useful, you need an object that lets you search through the folder looking for subfolders. `System.IO.DirectoryInfo` is the class for such an object, so add this property to `Service`:

```
' PictureFolder - property to the DirectoryInfo containing
' the pictures...
Public ReadOnly Property PictureFolder() As DirectoryInfo
    Get
        Return New DirectoryInfo(PictureFolderPath)
    End Get
End Property
```

4. Now you can actually build the `GetPictureFolders` Web method:

```
' GetPictureFolders - return an array of the picture folders...
<WebMethod(Description:="Return an array of the picture folders")> _
Public Function GetPictureFolders() As String()
    ' get hold of the picture folder...
    Dim pictureFolder As DirectoryInfo = Me.PictureFolder
    ' get the array of subfolders...
    Dim pictureSubFolders() As DirectoryInfo = _
        pictureFolder.GetDirectories()
    ' create a string array to accommodate the names...
    Dim folderNames(pictureSubFolders.Length - 1) As String
    ' now, loop through the folders...
    Dim pictureSubFolder As DirectoryInfo, index As Integer
    For Each pictureSubFolder In pictureSubFolders
        ' add the name...
        folderNames(index) = pictureSubFolder.Name
        ' next...
        index += 1
    Next
    ' finally, return the list of names...
    Return folderNames
End Function
```

5. Run the project and when Internet Explorer appears, click on the GetPictureFolders link. When prompted, click Invoke and you should see something similar to the following. Of course, the folders returned will be the folders that you created:

```
<?xml version="1.0" encoding="utf-8" ?>
<ArrayOfString xmlns:xsi="http://www.w3.org/2001/XMLSchema-instance"
xmlns:xsd="http://www.w3.org/2001/XMLSchema"
xmlns="http://tempuri.org/PictureService/Service">
    <string>Deborah's Graduation</string>
    <string>Trip to Boston</string>
    <string>Trip to Ottawa</string>
</ArrayOfString>
```

How It Works

You can see by the results that you do, indeed, have an array of strings returned. You know this because first, you have the ArrayOfString tag appearing in the string and second, you actually have the three strings for your three folders.

```
<?xml version="1.0" encoding="utf-8" ?>
<ArrayOfString xmlns:xsi="http://www.w3.org/2001/XMLSchema-instance"
xmlns:xsd="http://www.w3.org/2001/XMLSchema"
xmlns="http://tempuri.org/PictureService/Service">
    <string>Deborah's Graduation</string>
    <string>Trip to Boston</string>
    <string>Trip to Ottawa</string>
</ArrayOfString>
```

The PictureFolderPath property is quite important, since you'll frequently use this in your methods. The first thing you do is to get hold of the complete path to the Service.asmx file that's powering the service:

```
' PictureFolderPath - readonly property to return the picture
' folder...
Public ReadOnly Property PictureFolderPath() As String
    Get
        ' get the full path of this asmx page...
        Dim asmxPath As String, picturePath As String
        asmxPath = _
    Server.MapPath(Context.Request.ServerVariables.Item("script_name"))
```

However, this string will return something like:

```
c:\inetpub\wwwroot\PictureService\Service.asmx
```

and what you ultimately want is:

```
c:\inetpub\wwwroot\PictureService\Pictures
```

Therefore, you have to clip off the `Service.asmx` at the end and replace it with `Pictures`. To do this, you use the Substring method of the String class to extract just the portion of the path that you need and return it in the `servicePath` variable. The substring that you want to extract starts at position 0 of the string and ends with the last backslash in the path. Using the `LastIndexOf` method of the `String` class you can easily find the position of the last backslash in the path. You then add 1 to that position to ensure that the last backslash is included in the string returned:

```
        ' get the service path - everything up to and including
        ' the "\"
        Dim servicePath As String = _
            asmxPath.Substring(0, asmxPath.LastIndexOf("\") + 1)
```

Next, you want to append the Pictures folder to the `servicePath` variable and return the complete path from the property:

```
        ' append the word "Pictures" to the end of the path...
        picturePath = servicePath & "Pictures"
        ' return the path...
        Return picturePath
    End Get
End Property
```

`System.IO.DirectoryInfo` is a class that can help you learn more about a folder on the computer or the network. You create a new property called `PictureFolder` that returns a `DirectoryInfo` object based on the value returned by the `PictureFolderPath` property:

```
' PictureFolder - property to the DirectoryInfo containing
' the pictures...
Public ReadOnly Property PictureFolder() As DirectoryInfo
    Get
        Return New DirectoryInfo(PictureFolderPath)
    End Get
End Property
```

Once you have that, you can create your `GetPictureFolders` method. Notice that you have included a description for your `WebMethod` attribute. This description is displayed on your Service page under the GetPictureFolders link and helps to document the Web methods available to be consumed. The first thing this Web method does is use the `PictureFolder` property to get hold of the `DirectoryInfo` object that points to `c:\inetpub\wwwroot\PictureService\Pictures`. You have to use the `Me` keyword because you have a local variable with the same name. This removes the ambiguity of the call and makes sure that when you ask for `PictureFolder` you actually go off to find the value of the property, rather than returning the current value of `pictureFolder`, which would be an empty string:

```
' GetPictureFolders - return an array of the picture folders...
<WebMethod(Description:="Return an array of the picture folders")> _
Public Function GetPictureFolders() As String()
    ' get hold of the picture folder...
    Dim pictureFolder As DirectoryInfo = Me.PictureFolder
```

The `GetDirectories` method will return an array of `DirectoryInfo` objects, one for each of the subfolders:

```
    ' get the array of subfolders...
    Dim pictureSubFolders() As DirectoryInfo = _
        pictureFolder.GetDirectories()
```

Once you have this array, you can use its `Length` property to determine how many subfolders the `Pictures` folder actually has. You can then use this folder to create an empty array of the correct length:

```
    ' create a string array to accommodate the names...
    Dim folderNames(pictureSubFolders.Length - 1) As String
```

With the array in place, you can loop through the `pictureSubFolders` array and copy the name of each folder into the `folderNames` array:

```
    ' now, loop through the folders...
    Dim pictureSubFolder As DirectoryInfo, index As Integer
    For Each pictureSubFolder In pictureSubFolders
        ' add the name...
        folderNames(index) = pictureSubFolder.Name
        ' next...
        index += 1
    Next
```

Finally, you can return the array back to the caller:

```
    ' finally, return the list of names...
    Return folderNames
End Function
```

Here is a quick point—why do you appear to have some inconsistency in naming between directories and folders? Well, with the introduction of Windows 95, Microsoft decided that directories as they had been called for decades should actually be called folders. However, the group in charge of the `DirectoryInfo` class in the .NET team apparently believed that directory was a better name than folder. If you noticed, you've always called folders "folders" and the .NET Framework has always called folders "directories." Providing that each party sticks to their own convention, things shouldn't get confusing.

Returning Complex Information

So far, whenever you've returned anything from a Web service, you've only returned simple values, albeit that you now know how to return arrays of simple values. With a little work, however, you can return complex structures of information from the Web service.

In this section, you want to return a list of the pictures that are contained within each folder. However, unlike with the picture subfolders where you only needed to know the name, for each picture you would like to return the following information:

The filename of the picture (for example, `PIC00001.jpg`)

❑ The complete URL that points to the picture (for example, `http://localhost/PictureService/Pictures/Trip to Boston/PIC00001.jpg`)

The name of the folder that contains the picture (for example, `Trip to Boston`)

❑ The size of the image (for example 26,775 bytes)

❑ The date the image was created (for example, 6/26/2002)

❑ The format of the image (for example, JPG)

Try It Out   Returning Complex Information

1. To return a set of information, you need to create a structure that you can populate with the information you want. To do this, add a new class to the project by right-clicking on the PictureService project in the Solution Explorer and selecting Add ➪ Add Class. Call it PictureInfo. You want to create a structure rather than a class (although in this particular case either will do), so change `Class` and `End Class` to `Structure` and `End Structure` and add these members:

```
Public Structure PictureInfo
    ' members...
    Public Name As String
    Public Url As String
    Public FolderName As String
    Public FileSize As Integer
    Public FileDate As Date
    Public ImageFormat As String
End Structure
```

2. To get the pictures contained within a folder, you'll create a new Web method that takes the name of the folder as a parameter. Open the code editor for `Service.asmx` and add this code:

```vb
' GetPicturesInFolder - return an array of pictures from the folder...
<WebMethod(Description:="Return an array of pictures from the folder")> _
Public Function GetPicturesInFolder(ByVal folderName _
    As String) As PictureInfo()
    ' get hold of the folder that we want...
    Dim pictureSubFolder As DirectoryInfo
    pictureSubFolder = _
            New DirectoryInfo(PictureFolderPath & "\" & folderName)
    ' we need to get the URL of the picture folder...
    Dim pictureFolderUrl As String
    pictureFolderUrl = _
        Context.Request.ServerVariables.Item("script_name")
    ' manipulate the URL to return an absolute URL to the Pictures folder
    pictureFolderUrl = "http://" & _
        Context.Request.ServerVariables.Item("server_name") & _
        pictureFolderUrl.Substring(0, pictureFolderUrl.LastIndexOf("/") + 1) & _
        "Pictures"
    ' get the list of files in the subfolder...
    Dim pictureFiles() As FileInfo = pictureSubFolder.GetFiles
    ' create somewhere to put the picture infos...
    Dim pictureList(pictureFiles.Length - 1) As PictureInfo
    ' loop through each picture...
    Dim pictureFile As FileInfo, index As Integer
    For Each pictureFile In pictureFiles
        ' create a new pictureinfo object...
        Dim pictureInfo As New PictureInfo()
        pictureInfo.Name = pictureFile.Name
        pictureInfo.FolderName = folderName
        pictureInfo.Url = pictureFolderUrl & "/" & _
            folderName & "/" & pictureFile.Name
        pictureInfo.FileSize = pictureFile.Length
        pictureInfo.FileDate = pictureFile.LastWriteTime
        pictureInfo.ImageFormat = _
        pictureFile.Extension.Substring(1).ToUpper
        ' add it to the array...
        pictureList(index) = pictureInfo
        index += 1
    Next
    ' return the list of pictures...
    Return pictureList
End Function
```

3. Run the service. When Internet Explorer loads, click on the GetPicturesInFolder link. When prompted, enter the name of the folder whose images you want to return, such as Trip to Boston.

4. When you click Invoke you'll get a list of files back. In my Trip to Boston folder, I have eight images, so the document I get back is relative to this. Here is an abbreviated version of the document containing information regarding two of the files:

```xml
    <?xml version="1.0" encoding="utf-8" ?>
<ArrayOfPictureInfo xmlns:xsi="http://www.w3.org/2001/XMLSchema-instance"
xmlns:xsd="http://www.w3.org/2001/XMLSchema"
xmlns="http://tempuri.org/PictureService/Service">
    <PictureInfo>
```

```
    <Name>PIC00001.jpg</Name>
    <URL>http://localhost/PictureService/Pictures/Trip to
Boston/PIC00001.jpg</URL>
    <FolderName>Trip to Boston</FolderName>
    <FileSize>26775</FileSize>
    <FileDate>2002-06-26T17:30:48.0000000-04:00</FileDate>
    <ImageFormat>JPG</ImageFormat>
  </PictureInfo>
  <PictureInfo>
    <Name>PIC00002.jpg</Name>
    <URL>http://localhost/PictureService/Pictures/Trip to
Boston/PIC00002.jpg</URL>
    <FolderName>Trip to Boston</FolderName>
    <FileSize>2071</FileSize>
    <FileDate>2002-06-26T15:31:55.0330592+01:00</FileDate>
    <ImageFormat>JPG</ImageFormat>
  </PictureInfo>
</ArrayOfPictureInfo>
```

How It Works

Once you have a folder name, you can get a DirectoryInfo object from it and use a method called GetFiles to return an array of System.IO.FileInfo objects that describe each file. However, you have to mate the folder name with the value returned by PictureFolderPath. This way, if you ask for Trip to Boston, you'll get a folder name of c:\inetpub\wwwroot\PictureService\Pictures\Trip to Boston:

```
' GetPicturesInFolder - return an array of pictures from the folder...
<WebMethod(Description:="Return an array of pictures from the folder")> _
Public Function GetPicturesInFolder(ByVal folderName _
    As String) As PictureInfo()
    ' get hold of the folder that we want...
    Dim pictureSubFolder As DirectoryInfo
    pictureSubFolder = _
        New DirectoryInfo(PictureFolderPath & "\" & folderName)
```

When the user has used the service to learn what pictures are available on the server, you'll expect them to use a Web browser to download them. That's why you put your Pictures folder within the c:\inetpub\wwwroot\PictureService folder itself—IIS will share the folders and files without you having to do any extra configuration work.

However, the URL that you need on the client has to be an absolute name that includes the name of the server and the http:// part. If you ask the Web service to return the name of its own .asmx file, you get a relative URL like this: /PictureService/Service.asmx.

```
' we need to get the URL of the picture folder...
Dim pictureFolderUrl As String
pictureFolderUrl = _
    Context.Request.ServerVariables.Item("script_name")
```

Now you want to build the absolute URL to the Picture folder in the pictureFolderUrl variable. To do this you start by adding a text string of "http://" followed by the server name where the Web service is running. Next you use the SubString method of the String class to extract just the virtual directory name of the Web service and then append the text string of `Pictures` to finally end up with a string like `"http://localhost/PictureService/Pictures"`:

```
' manipulate the URL to return an absolute URL to the Pictures folder
pictureFolderUrl = "http://" & _
    Context.Request.ServerVariables.Item("server_name") & _
    pictureFolderUrl.Substring(0, pictureFolderUrl.LastIndexOf("/") + 1) & _
    "Pictures"
```

The next thing you need is a list of the files that the folder contains:

```
' get the list of files in the subfolder...
Dim pictureFiles() As FileInfo = pictureSubFolder.GetFiles
```

For each file in the folder, you're going to create and populate a new `PictureInfo` structure. You'll be returning these in an array, so next you create that array:

```
' create somewhere to put the picture infos...
Dim pictureList(pictureFiles.Length - 1) As PictureInfo
```

Now you can start looping through the files. For each one, you create a new `PictureInfo` and populate it. When you come to populate the `ImageFormat` member, you want to chop off the initial period (hence the need for `Substring`) and then convert the remaining characters to uppercase (hence `ToUpper`):

```
' loop through each picture...
Dim pictureFile As FileInfo, index As Integer
For Each pictureFile In pictureFiles
    ' create a new pictureinfo object...
    Dim pictureInfo As New PictureInfo()
    pictureInfo.Name = pictureFile.Name
    pictureInfo.FolderName = folderName
    pictureInfo.Url = pictureFolderUrl & "/" & _
        folderName & "/" & pictureFile.Name
    pictureInfo.FileSize = pictureFile.Length
    pictureInfo.FileDate = pictureFile.LastWriteTime
    pictureInfo.ImageFormat = _
    pictureFile.Extension.Substring(1).ToUpper
```

Once you have the image information you can put it into its position in the array:

```
' add it to the array...
pictureList(index) = pictureInfo
index += 1
Next
```

Finally, you return the results to the caller:

```
' return the list of pictures...
Return pictureList
End Function
```

That's it! Your service only needs those two methods. So now let's look at how you can use this Web service with your applications.

The Picture Server Client

So far in this chapter you've seen how to create Web services and how to manipulate them using the browser interface that the .NET Framework creates for you. This browser interface is actually a test interface—it's not what you would expect people using your Web service to use.

The principle behind Web services is that they enable software to integrate—therefore, when you actually want to use a Web service, you effectively build the functionality that the service offers into your own applications.

In this section, you're going to build a desktop Windows application that can display a list of the picture subfolders on the remote server. The user can select one of these folders and see the list of files contained within. Clicking on one of the images will show the image in Internet Explorer.

(As a special treat, you're going to host Internet Explorer inside your own application!)

> *Using a Web service is often known as consuming a Web service.*

Web Services Description Language

To consume a Web service, you can use something called a Web Services Description Language (WSDL) document. This is an XML document that contains a list of all of the methods available on the Web service. It details the parameters for each method and what each method is expected to return.

Your `WebService` class automatically creates a WSDL document for you, but because WSDL is an accepted industry standard, it is good practice for all Web services on any platform to expose a WSDL document. Theoretically (Web services are still too new to say that in practice this always works!), if you have the WSDL document for a Web service running on .NET or on another platform, you'll be able to build a Visual Basic .NET application that can use the Web service it belongs to.

Creating the Client

First, you'll create the client. As you're going to use Internet Explorer inside your application, you'll also customize the Toolbox to include the Microsoft Web Browser control.

Try It Out   Creating the Client

1. In Visual Studio .NET, create a new Windows Application project called PictureClient.

2. When the Designer for the new Form1 loads, right-click on the open Toolbox and select Add/Remove Items.

    The control you're going to add is Internet Explorer. This isn't a cut-down browser—the object you use is the same one that the standalone Internet Explorer itself uses to display Web content.

However, .NET is pretty new and Internet Explorer is an old product still based on old COM technology. There isn't a specific .NET version of Internet Explorer available, as this would involve a complete rewrite of it, and Internet Explorer is a pretty complicated application in its own right, although this rewrite may happen in the future. You can use old style COM controls as well as the new .NET controls in your Windows forms. However, you must go through the following steps to add them to a project.

When the Customize Toolbox dialog box appears, make sure the COM Components tab is selected and scroll down until you find Microsoft Web Browser. Check this and click OK, as shown in Figure 20-4.

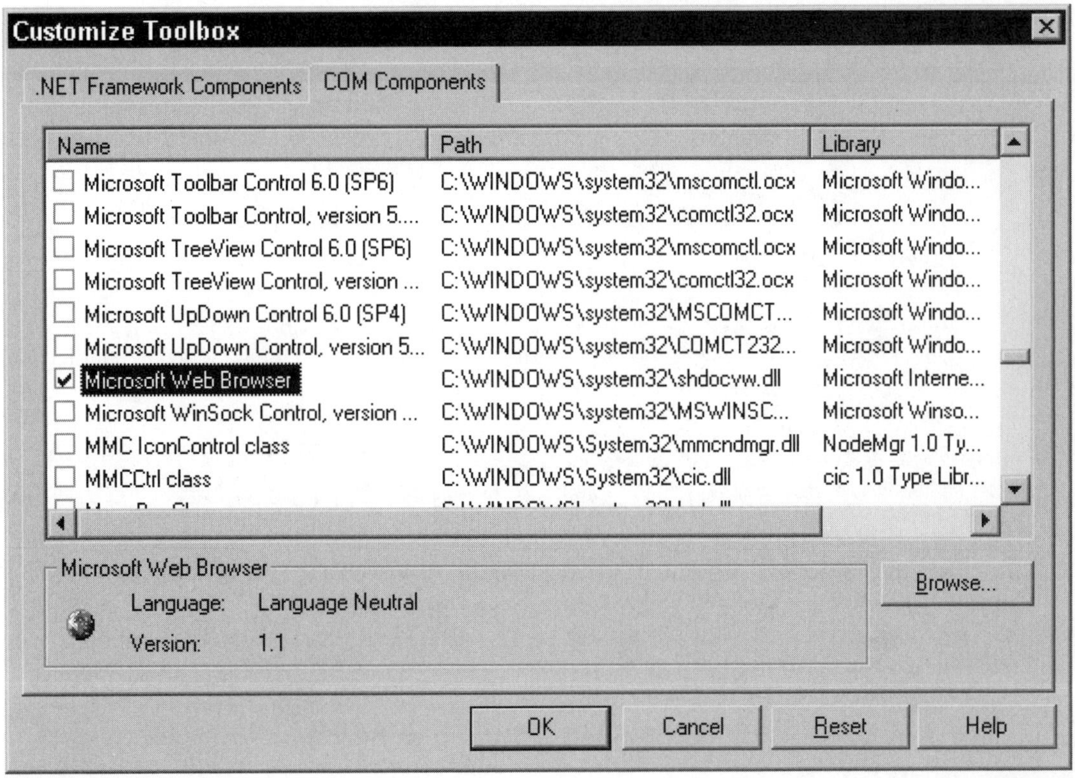

Figure 20-4

3. At the bottom of the Toolbox you'll now find a Microsoft Web Browser control.

4. Select the Web Browser item from the ToolBox and draw the control onto the form, as shown in Figure 20-5.

5. Using the Properties window change the name of the control to iePicture. Also, set its `Anchor` property to Top, Bottom, Left, Right.

6. You're going to use the browser to display the pictures, but it seems a shame not to verify that it actually works as a fully functioning Web browser. So add some code to show how the

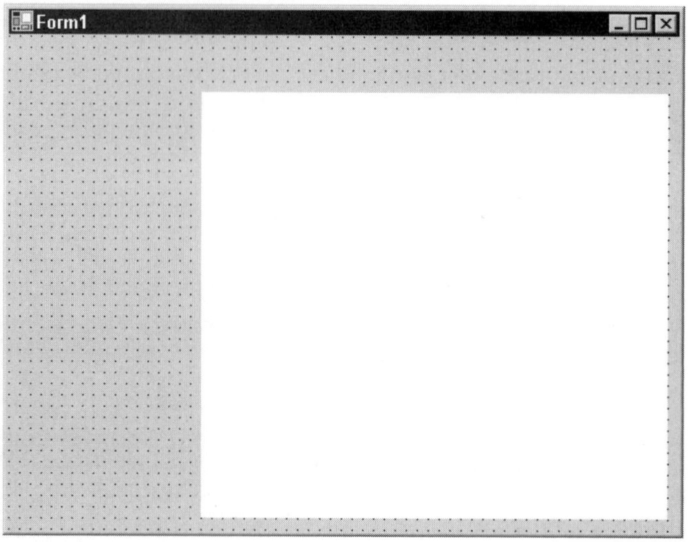

Figure 20-5

full-blown features of Internet Explorer can be utilized within Windows Forms in .NET. Double-click on the background of the form and add this code to the Load event handler:

```
Private Sub Form1_Load(ByVal sender As System.Object, _
        ByVal e As System.EventArgs) Handles MyBase.Load
    ' set the browser to a default page...
    iePicture.Navigate2("http://www.google.com/")
End Sub
```

7. Run the project and you should see Google's home page. Try entering some search terms and you'll notice that this browser behaves in exactly the same way as the full Internet Explorer does.

If you try using the browser you'll notice you don't have a toolbar, so if you want to go back a page, right-click on the page and select Back.

Adding a Web Reference

To use a Web service you need to add a Web reference to the project. This will prompt Visual Studio .NET to go away and create some classes for you that will let you call methods on the Web service. The two classes that are created are PictureInfo and Service.

Try It Out   Adding a Web Reference

1. Right-click the PictureClient project named and select Add Web Reference. This will open the Add Web Reference dialog box shown in Figure 20-6. In the drop-down box indicated by the URL label, type the full name of your Web service location, http://wsthearon/ PictureService/Service.asmx, where wsthearon is replaced with the name of your computer and then click the Go button.

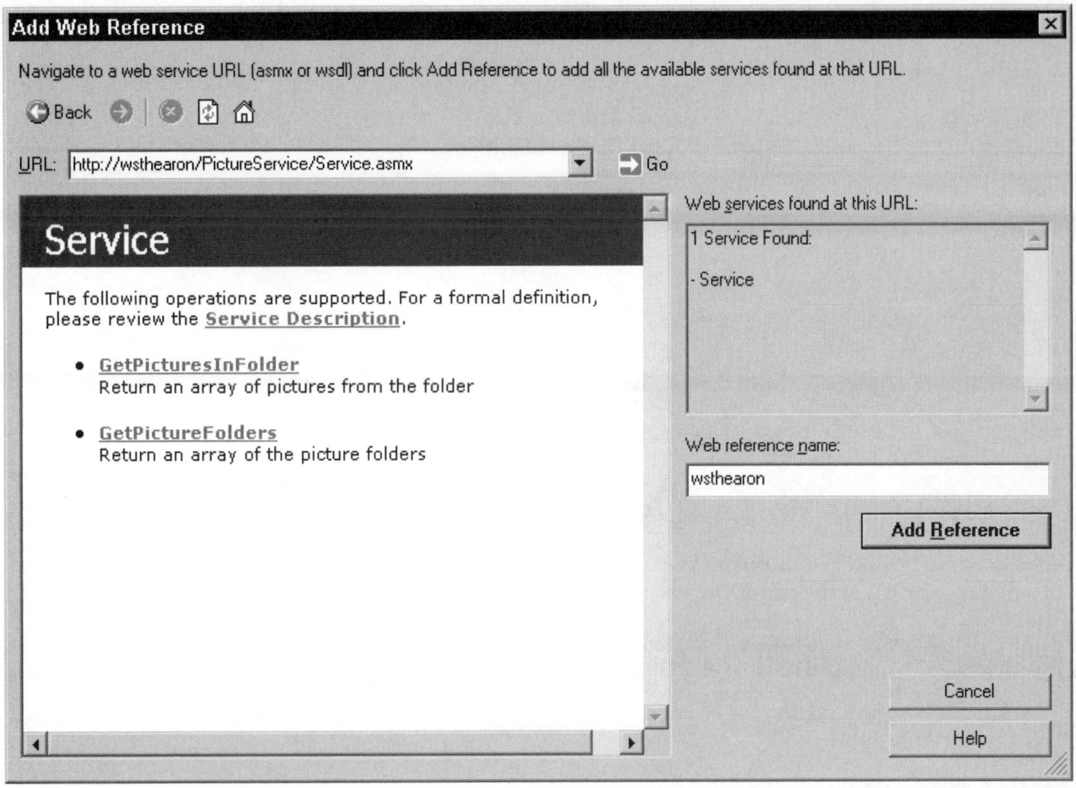

Figure 20-6

2. When it finds the service, you will see the Service page listing the available Web methods that you saw in your previous exerices. If you have typed the URL incorrectly you will get a "Page not found" message. When you have located the correct URL click the Add Reference button.

3. A new Web reference will be added to the Solution Explorer and this will match the name of the server (your computer name). Right-click the new reference and select Rename. Change the name to PictureService, as shown in Figure 20-7.

How It Works

At this point, Visual Studio .NET has successfully added a reference to the remote (or local) server. It has also created a new class for you called `PictureService.Service`. By creating instances of this object (as you're about to see) you can call methods on the Web service.

The name that you choose when you renamed the Web service in Solution Explorer acts as the namespace for the new class.

In this case, you've used `PictureService`, *but if you hadn't renamed it from, say,* `localhost`, *the new class that exposes the Web service methods would be called* `localhost.Service`.

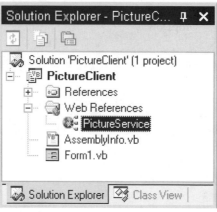

Figure 20-7

Displaying the Folder List

You can now call methods on the Web service. You start by adding a drop-down list to the project that will display a list of the remote picture subfolders by calling the GetPictureFolders method.

Try It Out   **Displaying the Folder List**

1.   Open the Designer for Form1. Draw on a ComboBox control at the top of the form, as shown in Figure 20-8.

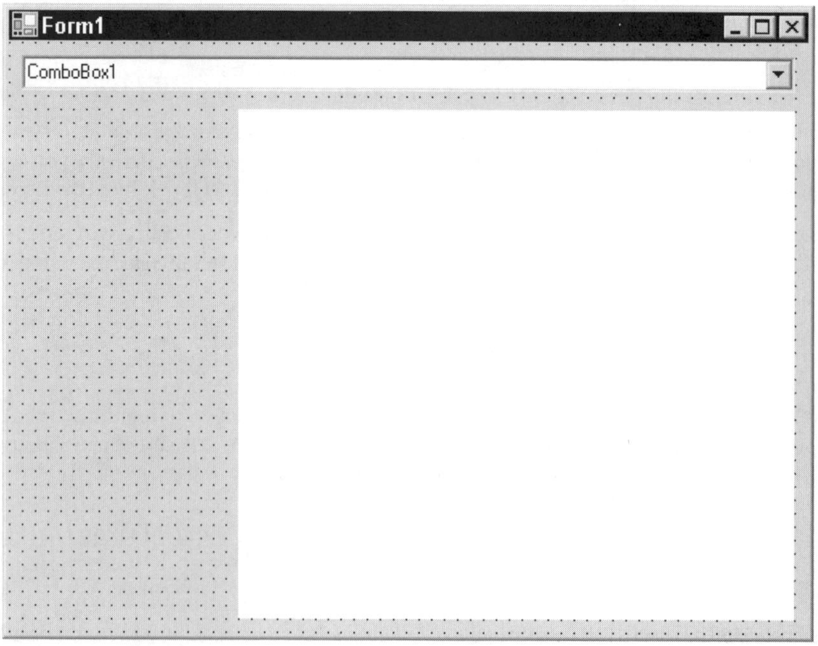

Figure 20-8

2. Using the Properties window, change the Name property to cboFolders. Clear the `Text` property. Change the DropDownStyle to DropDownList and the AnchorProperty to Top, Left, Right.

3. Double-click on the form background to open the `Load` event handler for the form. When you start the application you'll want to run the remote `GetPictureFolders` method. Add this code replacing the previous code that you added:

```
Private Sub Form1_Load(ByVal sender As System.Object,_
        ByVal e As System.EventArgs) Handles MyBase.Load
    ' get the pictures...
    Try
        ' create a connection to the service...
        Dim service As New PictureService.Service()
        ' get a list of the folders...
        Dim folderNames() As String
        folderNames = service.GetPictureFolders
        ' go through the list and add each name...
        Dim folderName As String
        For Each folderName In folderNames
            cboFolders.Items.Add(folderName)
        Next
    Catch ex As Exception
        HandleException(ex)
    End Try
End Sub
```

4. You'll notice a blue wavy line appear under `HandleException`. This is to indicate an error, since you haven't built this method yet, add it now:

```
' HandleException - handle a Web service exception...
Private Function HandleException(ByVal e As Exception)
    ' loop through the inner exceptions...
    Do While Not e.InnerException Is Nothing
        e = e.InnerException
    Loop
    ' report the problem...
    MessageBox.Show("An exception occurred." & e.Message)
End Function
```

Remember, if you need a refresher on how exceptions work, take a look at Chapter 9.

5. Run the project. You'll notice the form takes a while to appear (the first connection to a Web service is often slower than the rest as it takes .NET a short time to get its "house in order" before establishing the connection), but when it does, the folder names will be available if you drop down the list.

How It Works

That was not complicated! .NET abstracts away a lot of the complexity involved in consuming a Web service.

You start with a `Try...Catch` block:

```
Private Sub Form1_Load(ByVal sender As System.Object,_
        ByVal e As System.EventArgs) Handles MyBase.Load
    ' get the pictures...
    Try
```

It is very important that when consuming a Web service you use exception handling around any code that could cause an exception. A lot of things can go wrong while connecting to a Web service and passing data between service and client, and if anything does go wrong you'll get an exception.

Next, you create an instance of the `PictureService.Service` class that Visual Studio created for you. At this point you have not connected to the Web service—you have just prepared things for when you do:

```
        ' create a connection to the service...
        Dim service As New PictureService.Service()
```

The beauty of Web services in .NET is that calling methods on a remote object is no different from calling methods on an object installed on your local machine. Here, you call `GetPictureFolders` and get back an array of strings:

```
        ' get a list of the folders...
        Dim folderNames() As String
        folderNames = service.GetPictureFolders
```

Once you have the array, you loop through each of the strings and add the folder name to the ComboBox list:

```
        ' go through the list and add each name...
        Dim folderName As String
        For Each folderName In folderNames
            cboFolders.Items.Add(folderName)
        Next
```

If an exception is thrown, you call `HandleException`:

```
    Catch ex As Exception
        HandleException(ex)
    End Try
End Sub
```

That is all you have to do to call the Web service. But, before you go on, look at `HandleException`.

The SOAP standard dictates that whenever the service detects a problem, it must use an exception-handling model to tell the client about the problem.

Notice, the word, "model." Web services can be deployed on any platform and that platform may well not have the great exception-handling functionality that .NET has. But the principle is the same—shout about the problem and hope someone hears it.

When .NET detects that an exception has been thrown on the server, it will wrap that exception in its own "problem on the server" exception. The actual exception that occurred on the server will be buried within the `InnerException` property, so `HandleException` has the logic to keep stepping down through the buried exceptions until it gets the one that the server actually threw:

```
' HandleException - handle a Web service exception...
Private Function HandleException(ByVal e As Exception)
    ' loop through the inner exceptions...
    Do While Not e.InnerException Is Nothing
        e = e.InnerException
    Loop
    ' report the problem...
    MessageBox.Show("An exception occurred." & e.Message)
End Function
```

You can test out the exception handling by stopping the IIS service. To do this, click the Start button at the bottom of your screen and select Run and enter this command:

```
net stop iisadmin
```

You'll see a list of services that depend on the IIS Admin Service and you'll be prompted as to whether or not you want to continue. Enter *Y* and press *Return*. If you now run the project, you will see an exception like the one shown in Figure 20-9.

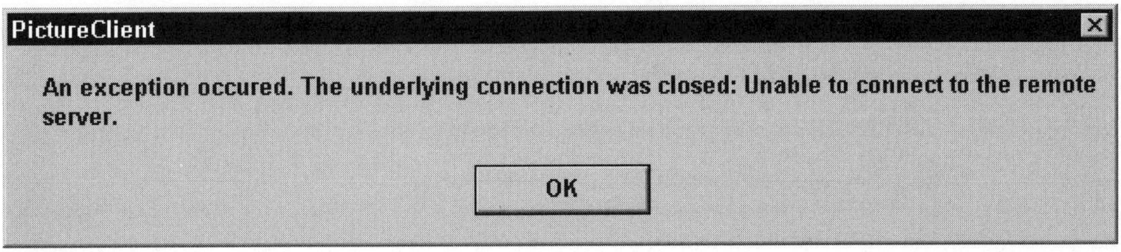

PictureClient   ☒

An exception occured. The underlying connection was closed: Unable to connect to the remote server.

OK

Figure 20-9

> *This exception can also occur if your URL cannot be located due to its nonexistence and/or network connection problems in general.*

To Start the IIS service once again, you type:

```
net start iisadmin
```

If you would like to restart IIS though for any reason, the command below is more useful:

```
iisreset
```

Displaying the File List and Choosing Files

When you change the selected folder, you want to connect to the Web service once more and get a list of the files in the folder you requested. You'll do this by extracting the folder name from the ComboBox and calling the `GetPicturesInFolder` Web method. You'll then take that list of pictures returned from the Web method and populate a list box.

Try It Out   Displaying the File List

1. To display the file list, you need to create a new class that encapsulates the `PictureInfo` structures you're going to get back from the server. Create a new class using the Solution Explorer by right-clicking on the PictureClient project and selecting Add ➪ Class. Call it PictureItem.

    Add this code to `PictureItem`:

```
Public Class PictureItem
    Public PictureInfo As PictureService.PictureInfo
    ' Constructor...
    Public Sub New(ByVal info As PictureService.PictureInfo)
        PictureInfo = info
    End Sub
    ' ToString - provide a better representation of the object...
    Public Overrides Function ToString() As String
        Return PictureInfo.Name
    End Function
End Class
```

2. Go back to the Designer for Form1. Add a ListBox control to the form. Change its `Name` property to `lstFiles`. Set its `IntegralHeight` property to `False` and its `Anchor` property to `Top`, `Bottom`, `Left`. Your form should look like Figure 20-10.

3. Double-click on the `cboFolders` drop-down list. This will create a new `SelectedItem-Changed` handler. Add this code:

```
Private Sub cboFolders_SelectedIndexChanged(ByVal sender As _
        System.Object, ByVal e As System.EventArgs) _
        Handles cboFolders.SelectedIndexChanged
    ' what folder did we select?
    Dim folderName As String =_
        cboFolders.Items(cboFolders.SelectedIndex)
    ' clear the files list...
    lstFiles.Items.Clear()
    ' connect to the service again and get the files back...
    Try
        ' connect...
        Dim service As New PictureService.Service()
        ' get the files back...
        Dim pictureList() As PictureService.PictureInfo
        pictureList = service.GetPicturesInFolder(folderName)
        ' add the pictures to the list...
        Dim pictureInfo As PictureService.PictureInfo
        For Each pictureInfo In pictureList
            ' just add the name...
            lstFiles.Items.Add(New PictureItem(pictureInfo))
        Next
    Catch ex As Exception
        HandleException(ex)
    End Try
End Sub
```

Figure 20-10

4. After you've done that, go back to the Designer for Form1 and double-click on the lstFiles list. Add this code to the new event handler:

```
Private Sub lstFiles_SelectedIndexChanged(ByVal sender As _
        System.Object, ByVal e As System.EventArgs) Handles _
        lstFiles.SelectedIndexChanged
    ' get the pictureitem...
    Dim item As PictureItem = lstFiles.Items(lstFiles.SelectedIndex)
    If Not item Is Nothing Then
        ' tell ie to show the picture...
        iePicture.Navigate2(item.PictureInfo.Url)
    End If
End Sub
```

5. Try running the project and selecting a picture from the list on the left. Internet Explorer should load the image.

How It Works

The ListBox control in Windows Forms works best if you can supply a custom-built object for each item. In this case, you build a separate object that contains an instance of a PictureInfo object and overload the `ToString` method available on all objects in .NET to return the `Name` property of `PictureInfo`:

```
Public Class PictureItem
    Public PictureInfo As PictureService.PictureInfo
    ' Constructor...
    Public Sub New(ByVal info As PictureService.PictureInfo)
        PictureInfo = info
    End Sub
    ' ToString - provide a better representation of the object...
    Public Overrides Function ToString() As String
        Return PictureInfo.Name
    End Function
End Class
```

When the item gets added to the list the ListBox will call `ToString` on the object to get the value that should be displayed in the list. If you wanted, rather than returning Name, you could return the URL, in which case the list would appear as a list of URLs rather than a list of names.

One thing that's worth noting—the `PictureInfo` you have on the client is not the same object that you had on the server. Visual Studio .NET has also automatically created the `PictureInfo` class just like it did for the `Service` class. (This is why on the client `PictureInfo` is a class, whereas on the server it's actually a structure.)

When the drop-down list selection changes you find the currently selected item, which is the folder name, and clear the file list:

```
Private Sub cboFolders_SelectedIndexChanged(ByVal sender As _
            System.Object, ByVal e As System.EventArgs)_
            Handles cboFolders.SelectedIndexChanged
    ' what folder did we select?
    Dim folderName As String = _
        cboFolders.Items(cboFolders.SelectedIndex)
    ' clear the files list...
    lstFiles.Items.Clear()
```

You then open up a `Try...Catch` so that you can manage any problem that occurs:

```
    ' connect to the service again and get the files back...
    Try
```

Connecting the service is just a matter of creating `Service` object again:

```
        ' connect...
        Dim service As New PictureService.Service()
```

Calling `GetPicturesInFolder` and providing the folder name retrieves the list of files contained in the folder as an array of `PictureInfo` objects. If the folder doesn't exist on the server, the service itself will throw an exception and this will find its way back and be perceived as an exception in your own code that `HandleException` can deal with:

```
        ' get the files back...
        Dim pictureList() As PictureService.PictureInfo
         pictureList = service.GetPicturesInFolder(folderName)
```

When you have the array, you create new `PictureItem` objects and add them to the file list:

```
        ' add the pictures to the list...
        Dim pictureInfo As PictureService.PictureInfo
        For Each pictureInfo In pictureList
            ' just add the name...
            lstFiles.Items.Add(New PictureItem(pictureInfo))
        Next
    Catch ex As Exception
        HandleException(ex)
    End Try
End Sub
```

When the selection on the file list itself changes, the currently selected item will be a `PictureItem` object. You can use the `PictureInfo` property of this object to get hold of the `PictureInfo` that was returned by the server, and then use the `Url` property of `PictureInfo` to find the URL that relates to the selected file and tell Internet Explorer to display that URL. You also check to make sure that item is not `Nothing` as this would cause an exception if the user clicked on the `lstFiles` control when no files were displayed:

```
Private Sub lstFiles_SelectedIndexChanged(ByVal sender As _
        System.Object, ByVal e As System.EventArgs)_
        Handles  lstFiles.SelectedIndexChanged
    ' get the pictureitem...
    Dim item As PictureItem = lstFiles.Items(lstFiles.SelectedIndex)
    If Not item Is Nothing Then
        ' tell ie to show the picture...
        iePicture.Navigate2(item.PictureInfo.Url)
    End If
End Sub
```

.NET Remoting

.NET Remoting is similar to Web services in that it is used to connect to a service located elsewhere (on the same or different computer). Just like XML Web services, IIS can also expose an assembly for remoting. .NET Remoting can also use SOAP, the standard protocol of Web services. From these few aspects it is extremely similar.

Where .NET Remoting becomes independent, is when you look at the fact that it can also communicate via the Transmission Control Protocol (TCP) Channel and allows you to customize what is transported and how. The data that is transported can also be sent in binary form, which you cannot do with Web services. .NET Remoting is lot more flexible, but does not replace the need for Web services. Web services is regarded as the extensible, open standards based means of communicating between different programming environments and operating systems, where Remoting is more specific to .NET, but offers much more flexibility.

Since this is a beginner's guide you will not go deep into any .NET Remoting details, but you do need to know a few things.

One of these things is a term known as *marshalling*. In simple terms, marshalling is what happens when an object or value is transported (marshaled) from one process to another. It can also be marshaled from a process on one machine to a process on another machine. Marshalling is a vital part of .NET Remoting. So much so, that anything that travels across boundaries (such as the process boundary) must inherit from `MarshByRefObject` (MBRO).

Another aspect to understand is the difference between a server and a client. A *server* is typically the application that registers a type on a channel and a port. The server having registered the type then creates an instance of it when the client requests it. The server passes the instance back to the client. The *client* on the other hand sends a request to a channel and a port. The request is to create a type. You can see by this explanation that it is important that the server and client communicate on the same channel and the same port. The way in which .NET Remoting does this is by using a Uniformed Resource Identifier (URI) in the form of:

```
<transport>://<machine>:<portnumber><name>
```

In your sample you will see the following URI being used, where `wsthearon` is the name of your computer.

```
tcp://wsthearon:8000/MyPongEngine
```

If you chose to use HTTP as the transport, then the URI could have been:

```
http://localhost:8000/MyPongEngine
```

The port number used here could be anything, as long as the server and client knows the same number.

You will soon see this in action. Without further explanation for now, you will create your small .NET Remoting example. As the architecture described in Figure 20-11 suggests, .NET Remoting requires a server and a client. You will first create the server application.

Try It Out   Creating the Pong Server and PongEngine project

1. Create a new ClassLibrary project named PongEngine.

2. Rename the `Class1.vb` file created by default in the PongEngine project to Pinger.vb.

3. Add a Console Application project to the solution named PongServer.

4. Next, add two references to the PongServer project.

   ❏ Add a reference to the PongEngine project inside the solution.

   ❏ Add a reference to `System.Runtime.Remoting` found as one of the standard References in the References Dialog box (see Figure 20-12).

5. Your solution and its projects should now look like the Solution Explorer shown in Figure 20-12.

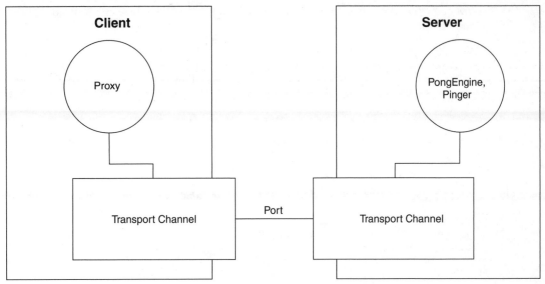

Figure 20-11

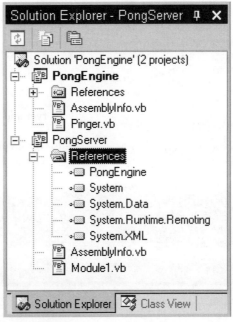

Figure 20-12

6. Now open the class named `Pinger.vb` in the PongEngine ClassLibrary project and change the code to look like this:

```
Public Class Pinger
    Inherits MarshalByRefObject

    Public ReadOnly Property Name() As String
        Get
            Return Environment.MachineName
        End Get
    End Property
End Class
```

7. Now add the following code to `Module1.vb` in the PongServer project:

```
Imports System.Runtime.Remoting
Imports System.Runtime.Remoting.Channels
Imports System.Runtime.Remoting.Channels.Tcp

Module Module1
    Sub Main()
        Dim channel As TcpChannel = New TcpChannel(8000)
        ChannelServices.RegisterChannel(channel)

RemotingConfiguration.RegisterWellKnownServiceType(GetType(PongEngine.Pinger),_
            "MyPongEngine", WellKnownObjectMode.SingleCall)
        Console.Write("PongEngine Registered." + Environment.NewLine)
        Console.Write("Server Active . . .")
        Console.Read()
    End Sub
End Module
```

8. Now right-click on the PongServer project and choose Set As Startup Project from the context menu.

9. Run the project and you should see the console application as shown in Figure 20-13.

Figure 20-13

How It Works

At this point all you have really done is create a Class Library and a Console Application. The strange code using the `Remoting` namespace does not seem to do much. If you see the Console window as in Figure 20-13, then it is working. But what has it done?

The server has created and registered a channel on port 8000. It uses this channel and port number for communications. You are specifying that you require a channel and a port. This port number could be any number as long as the server and client (which you will create next) use the same number.

```
Dim channel As TcpChannel = New TcpChannel(8000)
ChannelServices.RegisterChannel(channel)
```

Next, the code registered your Pinger type on this port. This provides .NET Remoting with the schema or interfaces so that it knows what it should create when a client makes the request. This effectively exposes it to the outside world via TCP and of course through port 8000. Your code has also given it a friendly name MyPongEngine.

```
RemotingConfiguration.RegisterWellKnownServiceType(GetType(PongEngine.Pinger),_
     "MyPongEngine", WellKnownObjectMode.SingleCall)
```

The WellKnownObjectMode.SingleCall enumeration used in the previous code specifies that it will be destroyed after a call is made to the object. This means that a new object would be created for every call you make on it. A term often used for this kind of behavior is *stateless*.

Next, you will create a client to talk to PongServer. But before that you need to create a proxy.

Generating the Proxy

A proxy is required for your client, as you need to provide the client something that defines the PongEngine interface. You could use the actual PongEngine.dll and make a reference to it within your client application, but since the client will never create the PongEngine on the machine it is located on, you do not need all the code that is inside it. All you need is the interface. A proxy is the interfaces for a real assembly. It looks like the real assembly but it is not. It does not contain the code. It is made up of the interface definitions and the code to make it a proxy. A client references the proxy instead of the real assembly. The actual object is always created on the server (which is where the channel is registered).

Try It Out — Generating the Proxy

1. To generate a proxy for PongEngine.dll open Visual Studio .NET Command Prompt. You do this by navigating to the Program Files folder where Visual Studio .NET is installed and then clickining on Visual Studio .NET Tools followed by clicking on the Visual Studio .NET Command Prompt icon. The Visual Studio .NET Command Prompt icon executes a batch file which sets up your environment to include the appropriate paths to execute the command line tools installed with Visual Studio .NET.

2. Next, change your current working directory to the bin path where the PongEngine.dll was compiled. An example is shown in Figure 20-14.

3. Then type in the following command line:

```
soapsuds -ia:PongEngine -oa:PongEngine_proxy.dll
```

soapsuds.exe comes with the framework and can be found in the sdk directory:

```
<installdir>\Microsoft Visual Studio .NET 2003\SDK\<version>\Bin
```

Running the command creates a new Assembly named PongEngine_proxy.dll

Visual Studio .NET 2003 Command Prompt
Setting environment for using Microsoft Visual Studio .NET 2003 tools.
(If you have another version of Visual Studio or Visual C++ installed and wish
to use its tools from the command line, run vcvars32.bat for that version.)
C:\Documents and Settings\Thearon>cd "C:\Documents and Settings\Thearon\My Documents\Beginning VB.Net 3rd Edition\PongEngine\bin"
C:\Documents and Settings\Thearon\My Documents\Beginning VB.Net 3rd Edition\PongEngine\bin>soapsuds -ia:PongEngine -oa:PongEngine_proxy.dll
C:\Documents and Settings\Thearon\My Documents\Beginning VB.Net 3rd Edition\PongEngine\bin>_

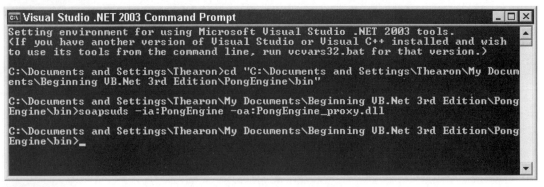

Figure 20-14

4. To see that there is indeed a difference between the new Assembly and the original you can view the two assemblies in ILDASM. Still in the Visual Studio .NET command prompt type **ildasm**. This will open the ildasm application.

5. Drag and drop the `PongEngine_proxy.dll` onto ILDASM. You will see the entries as shown in Figure 20-15.

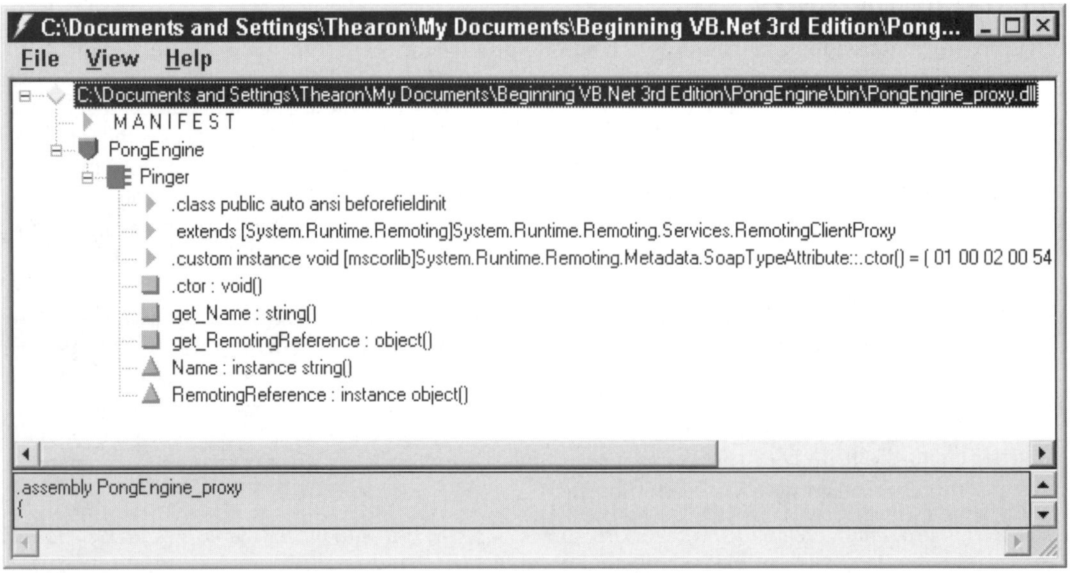

C:\Documents and Settings\Thearon\My Documents\Beginning VB.Net 3rd Edition\Pong...
File View Help
C:\Documents and Settings\Thearon\My Documents\Beginning VB.Net 3rd Edition\PongEngine\bin\PongEngine_proxy.dll
MANIFEST
PongEngine
Pinger
.class public auto ansi beforefieldinit
extends [System.Runtime.Remoting]System.Runtime.Remoting.Services.RemotingClientProxy
.custom instance void [mscorlib]System.Runtime.Remoting.Metadata.SoapTypeAttribute::.ctor() = (01 00 02 00 54
.ctor : void()
get_Name : string()
get_RemotingReference : object()
Name : instance string()
RemotingReference : instance object()
.assembly PongEngine_proxy
{

Figure 20-15

You can open another instance by opening another ildasm window and dragging the original Assembly onto the second copy. You should now have two instances open showing the two different assemblies. You will immediately realize that they are different.

You can think of the proxy as the "dumb" representative of the original Assembly. It deploys with the client so that it can reference the correct Object, but not the actual one.

Try It Out   **Creating a Remoting Client**

1. Create a new Console Application project named PongClient.

2. Add a reference to `System.Runtime.Remoting` found in the References dialog box by right-clicking on the Project and selecting Add Reference.

3. Next you need to add a reference to the proxy of the PongEngine that you created previously. Open the Add References dialog box again and click the Browse button. Locate and select the `PongServer_proxy.dll` file that you created.

4. Your project and its references should now look like the one shown in Figure 20-16.

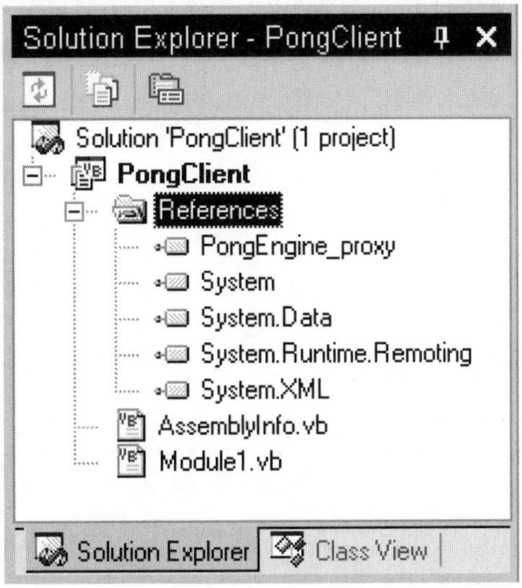

Figure 20-16

5. Next you need to add the code that creates the `PongEngine.Pinger` type. Add the following code to `Module1.vb` in the PongClient project. Don't forget to change the machine name of `wsthearon` to your machine name.

```vb
Imports System.Runtime.Remoting.Services.RemotingClientProxy
Module Module1
    Sub Main()
        Dim client As PongEngine.Pinger

        Console.Write("Trying to obtain Type from Server . . ." + _
        Environment.NewLine)
        client = CType(Activator.GetObject(GetType(PongEngine.Pinger),_
        "tcp://wsthearon:8000/MyPongEngine"), PongEngine.Pinger)
        Console.Write("Type Created and returned" + Environment.NewLine)
        Console.Write("The object returned:" + client.Name + _
        Environment.NewLine)
        Console.Read()
    End Sub
End Module
```

6. You'll need to start the PongServer application by navigating to the bin folder where the executable was compiled and double clicking on PongServer.exe.

7. Next, run the PongClient project and the client should connect to the server and provide the name of the server machine (see Figure 20-17).

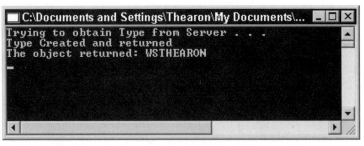

Figure 20-17

How It Works

If you copy PongClient.exe and PongEngine_proxy.dll to another machine on the network that has the .Net Framework installed and run it from there, it will still return the name of the machine the server is running on. This is due to .NET Remoting, which marshals the object and its values through the network. Have a look at the code:

```
Dim client As PongEngine.Pinger
client = CType(Activator.GetObject(GetType(PongEngine.Pinger), _
"tcp://wsthearon:8000/MyPongEngine"), PongEngine.Pinger)
```

The code here first defines a variable of type PongEngine.Pinger and then creates the object by using the Activator class. There are two parameters used from Activator.GetObject call: the type that should be created, and the URI pointing to where the object resides.

You will then see this wrapped by the CType function. This is because Activator.GetObject call returns a System.Object and you have to cast it to the type you want.

If you did not cast System.Object to your Pinger class, then you would not see the ReadOnly Property Name, as it does not exist on System.Object. This is why you need the proxy, so the client can know what the object looks like. You say that the client knows the interface.

Summary

In this chapter, you were introduced to Web services and .NET Remoting. Web services work by allowing a developer to expose an object that is accessible through a Web server. Web services are based on open standards like SOAP and WSDL and are underpinned by tried-and-tested technologies like HTTP and XML.

You started off this chapter by building a basic Web service that could return some information and also do something useful—namely, return the square root of a number that you gave it. As a more practical example, you then built a Web service that allowed the consumer to download a list of pictures from the service. With the service in place, you built a simple client application that connected to the Web service and called methods on the remote object. This also briefly demonstrated how to utilize the COM interoperability layer on .NET in order to actually put Internet Explorer inside your application.

Finally, you went through the creation of a Server and a Client using .NET Remoting. You created a class library and used it from another machine. .NET Remoting is a powerful way of creating machine communications and more. You could use .NET Remoting for networking support in your next game (did you wonder why it was named PongEngine?), or any other machine-to-machine communication that requires quick interoperation.

To summarize, you should know:

- ❑   What a Web service is and how it works
- ❑   How to create Web methods in a Web service and test them with the test harness built into a Web service
- ❑   How to create a client application that accesses a Web service
- ❑   What .Net Remoting is and generally how it works
- ❑   The different protocols used by Web services and .Net Remoting

Exercises

1.   What's the difference between a Web site and a Web service?
2.   What is SOAP?
3.   How do you mark a method as being available on a Web service?
4.   What kind of information can you return from a Web service method?
5.   What's unusual about the way the Internet Explorer control is used in Windows Forms?
6.   Can a server and a client run on the same machine when using .NET Remoting?
7.   What .NET Framework utility is used to create a proxy assembly?

21

Deploying Your Application

Deploying an application can be a complicated process, especially when dealing with large complex applications. A wealth of knowledge is required on nearly every aspect of a development. A large software installation for Windows requires you to have knowledge from registry settings, mime types, and configuration files to database creation and manipulation. Companies tend to rely on dedicated deployment software for these large installations, together with key people who understand the processes involved. However, Visual Studio .NET does provide some basic deployment functionality, which is tremendously helpful for the standard developer and smaller installations.

Under the Visual Studio .NET banner, you can create many different types of applications, from desktop to Web applications and services. All of these have varying degrees of complexity or peculiarities when it comes to installation time.

Since this is a beginner's guide, this chapter will not go into depth on specifics regarding the deployment of the different applications, but rather provide an overview to it.

In this chapter, you will:

❑   Learn concepts and terminology
❑   Create a setup program with Visual Studio .NET
❑   Implement `Dotnetfx.exe` redistributable
❑   Deploy private and shared assemblies

What Is Deployment?

Deployment is the art of delivering a copy of an application to other machines so that it runs in the new environment. It is the larger architectural view for what you may know as an installation or a setup. There is a subtle difference between these words.

Deployment is the art of distribution. It is concerned with how something is distributed. In other words, distribution is the way in which something is distributed and how.

The installation or setup is a process, where you load, configure, and install the software. So an *installation* is what you do to configure the software, and *deployment* is how you get it where you want it.

With this terminology, a CD is a deployment mechanism as is the Internet. The two deployment mechanisms may have different installation requirements. As an example, if an installation is on a CD, you may have all the additional dependant software on that CD. This would be fine for a CD but perhaps not for delivery via the Internet. Another example (that may affect the Installation option) is where you may have written an installation in JavaScript. This may work fine when executed on a machine by the user having the correct Windows User Rights, but would not work through Internet Explorer. These kinds of considerations are important to consider when deciding your best deployment option. The type of installations you require could also be different per application.

Before I show you how Visual Studio helps you deploy applications, let me introduce you to some basic options.

No Touch Deployment

No touch deployment is the concept of sending an application or its referenced assemblies via the Internet to the client without a formal installation program. In line with terminology, the .NET runtime becomes the installer. This can be useful for smaller applications or a combination of Web and desktop functionality. It is also a very easy thing to do. By copying an executable to your Web server and simply accessing it via the browser, you are effectively allowing the client to download and execute the application. There are a few limitations, such as security restrictions, but still it is a useful deployment option in some circumstances.

Try It Out   Running an Application from the Web

1. Copy an existing Windows application executable from an exercise in one of the previous chapters to your Web directory. (This could be an existing virtual directory that you have on your machine.)

   In Chapter 17, you created a virtual directory for the Web forms examples. You can copy a .NET executable to this directory via Windows Explorer (c:\inetpub\wwwroot\client-server processing) *or create a new one.*

2. Open your internet browser and type http://localhost/<vdir><appname> where <vdir> is the name of the virtual directory and <appname> is the application executable including the extension. If you used the same directory as the Web forms example, this would be http://localhost/client-server%20processing/WroxPaint.exe.

3. The application will be downloaded and executed. Depending on your configuration, there may be a standard security message that gets displayed, see Figure 21-1, and there is a limitation on accesing files and the registry, but otherwise it will run normally.

XCOPY Deployment

XCOPY deployment gets its name from the MS DOS XCOPY command. XCOPY is a copy procedure that would copy a directory and all files including subfolders. This is commonly associated with Web

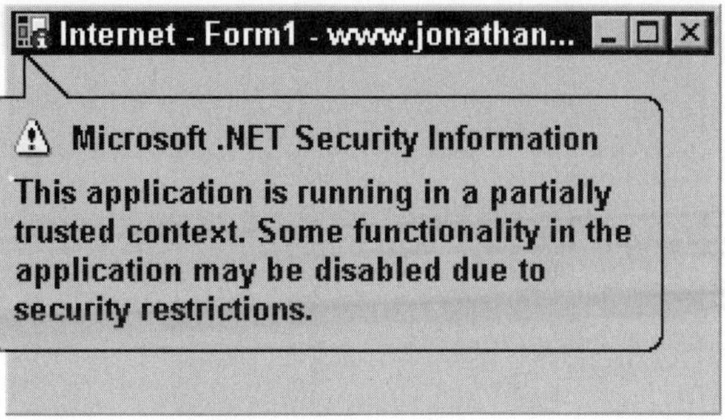

Figure 21-1

applications, but with .NET it can also apply to a desktop application. Since a standard .NET assembly does not need any form of registration, it fully supports this option. XCOPY does not work with shared assemblies because they require installation (If they are used from the Global Assembly Cache). You learn more about shared assemblies later in this chapter.

Creating a Visual Studio .NET Setup Application

Visual Studio .NET supports the Windows Installer. But what is it? The Windows Installer service is a general platform for installing applications in Windows and gets installed with Visual Studio .Net. It provides a lot of functionality such as uninstall capabilities and transactional installation options (the ability to rollback if something fails) as well as other general features. Many of these features are either built in, and you do not have to do anything, or they are configurable and/or extensible.

The Visual Studio .NET Windows Installer support has made it relatively easier to create a simple installation. Visual Studio has provided templates in the New Project dialog box for this purpose.

Visual Studio .NET exposes four templates for creating Windows installer projects:

❑   Setup Project for desktop or general setup

❑   Web Setup Project for Web applications or Web services

❑   Merge Module, a package that can only be merged into another setup

❑   Cab Project creates a package that can be used as a type of install

Finally, Visual Studio .NET also has a Setup Wizard Project, which aids you in creating one of the windows installer templates listed here.

Creating a Setup Application for Paint

In the following *Try It Out* section, you create a setup application for the Paint program from Chapter 14. You will need the executable (compiled version) of the program.

Try It Out   **Creating a Setup Application**

1.   Open Visual Studio and create a New Blank Solution named Deployment.

2.   Add a new setup project to the Solution called MyInstaller (see Figure 21-2).

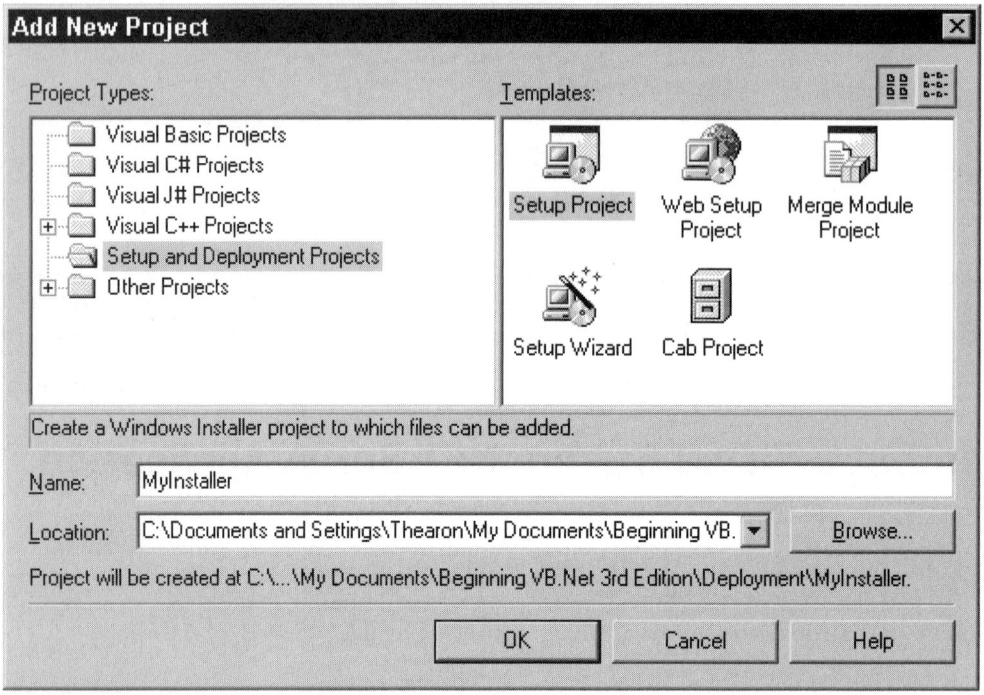

Add New Project   ✕

Project Types: Templates:

    📁 Visual Basic Projects
    📁 Visual C# Projects   🖥️   🖥️   📑
    📁 Visual J# Projects
  ⊞ 📁 Visual C++ Projects   Setup Project   Web Setup   Merge Module
    📁 Setup and Deployment Projects   Project   Project
  ⊞ 📁 Other Projects
                                        🖥️   🗄️

                                    Setup Wizard   Cab Project

Create a Windows Installer project to which files can be added.

Name: MyInstaller

Location: C:\Documents and Settings\Thearon\My Documents\Beginning VB. ▼   Browse...

Project will be created at C:\...\My Documents\Beginning VB.Net 3rd Edition\Deployment\MyInstaller.

                              OK   Cancel   Help

Figure 21-2

When Visual Studio creates the project it adds a Designer. There are three main folders in the left pane of the Designer: Application Folder, User's Desktop, and User's Program Menu.

3.   Right-click the Application Folder node in the Designer and select Add ➪ File.

4.   Next, browse for the Paint program's executable `WroxPaint.exe`. Once you select the Paint program, you see the file listed in the right pane of the Designer.

5.   Next, you must repeat steps 3 and 4, but this time, right-click and add the file to the User's Programs menu.

6.   Build the project.

7.   Right-click the project in the Solution Explorer and select Install. You see that a Windows Installer will be loaded. This is the Setup project you have just created.

How it Works

When you created the setup application, Visual Studio created a Windows Installer. Changes you made, like adding the Paint program to the project, included the file in the Installer database.

In this sample you added one executable, it is also possible to add many other types of files, including text files, help files, and other assemblies.

When you built the project, three files were created:

❑   The msi file

❑   An installation loader named setup.exe

❑   A setup.ini file

You can see these files in your <application directory>\debug folder. If you do not know the path, you can see it by selecting the Solution and looking at the Path property in the Properties window of Visual Studio.

Assemblies as Installers

Sometimes when you create an assembly, whether it is a library or a custom control, the code may depend on other resources. Perhaps it needs a specific file or a directory or maybe a database with a few tables. The Windows Installer in Visual Studio has a wonderful way for extending the installation. The extension can be coded within the assembly itself and can be called and executed by the installation process. This is a great way to aid a component to encapsulate its functionality.

Traditionally, when you write a component that accesses a database, the database is usually installed with the installation process and is separate from the assembly. The assembly, if used without the installation (copied onto a system), could be rendered useless. Consider for a moment a component that stores contact information. The component stores the data in a database. Imagine if you could simply reference the assembly and not worry about installing the database. If Microsoft Data Access Components (MDAC) is installed on the system, the assembly would install the database itself. This is indeed possible. A component can be written to do this without the installer. You could write a method to install itself, but .NET has an interface for this. What is more, the Windows Installer knows this interface and can work with it. The interface that you concentrate on for this sample is known as System.Configuration. Install.Installer. The sample, although a simple demonstration, exposes what is possible with this Interface.

Creating an Assembly Installer

Before you begin creating an assembly installer in the next *Try It Out* section, make sure you have the setup project you created earlier open in Visual Studio.

Try It Out   Creating an Assembly Installer

1.   Add a new Class Library project to the Solution and name it InstallerHelper.

2.   Delete the Class1.vb file that is created by default.

3.   Right-click the project in the Solution Explorer and select Add ➪ Add New Item. A dialog box appears showing icons for the various files you could add to the project.

4. Select the installer class and click the Open button. Visual Studio adds a file named `Installer1.vb` to your project.

5. Open the file so that you see the code in the editor. You see boiler plate code for the class. Note that this class inherits from `System.Configuration.Install.Installer`. The code is shown as follows. I have omitted the code inside the region for brevity.

```
Imports System.ComponentModel
Imports System.Configuration.Install

<RunInstaller(True)> Public Class Installer1
    Inherits System.Configuration.Install.Installer

 #Region " Component Designer generated code "
End Class
```

6. Next, you need to add some code to this class. You add a simple `EventLog` entry to the `AfterInstall` event, as shown here. This event will be fired at the appropriate time and write an entry to the event log during the installation process:

```
<RunInstaller(True)> Public Class Installer1
        Inherits System.Configuration.Install.Installer

    #Region " Component Designer generated code "

        Private Sub Installer1_AfterInstall(ByVal sender As Object, _
          ByVal e As System.Configuration.Install.InstallEventArgs) _
          Handles MyBase.AfterInstall
                System.Diagnostics.EventLog.WriteEntry("MyInstaller", _
                "Installation Complete")
        End Sub
    End Class
```

7. Build the project.

Try It Out Adding the Installer to an Installation

1. Now that you have an Installer in an assembly, you need to add it to the installation. Open the designer for the `MyInstaller` project by right-clicking the project name in the Solution Explorer window and selecting View ⇨ File System.

2. Right-click the node named `Application Folder` and select Add ⇨ Project Output. You are presented with the dialog box as shown in Figure 21-3.

3. In the dialog box shown in Figure 21-3, select the `InstallerHelper` project from the drop-down-list and select Primary Output. Click the OK button when done. This adds the output from the `InstallerHelper` project (the `InstallerHelp Assembly`) to the `MyInstaller` project to be installed.

4. Next, you need to create a custom action for the installer. Right-click on the project in the Solution Explorer and select View ⇨ Custom Actions. You see the editor now as a root node named Custom Actions and four folders named `Install`, `Commit`, `Rollback`, and `Uninstall`.

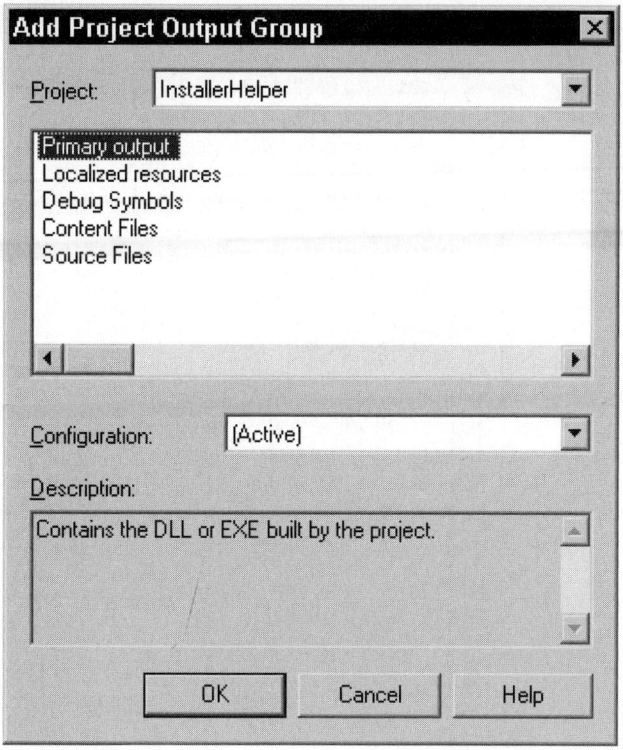

Figure 21-3

5. Right-click the top node named `Custom Actions` in the Editor and select Add Custom Action to open another dialog box where you can select one of three folders. Double-click the Application Folder item and select the item named Primary Output from InstallerHelper and then click the OK button.

6. Build the entire solution.

7. Install the MyInstaller by right clicking the project in the Solution Explorer and selecting Install. It will first uninstall the last installation and then install this newly built version.

8. Once you have completed the setup, open your Event Viewer from Control Panel ⇨ Administrative tools. Figure 21-4 shows you that the installer, assembly, and an event log entry should exist.

How it Works

The assembly named `InstallerHelper` that you created contains a class that inherits from `System.Configuration.Install.Installer`. When you added the assembly to the installation, the installation knows that it contains this class. It registers an instance of this class to listen for the events. When the events are raised your `Installer` class is notified, which fires your code. You could write mostly any kind of code you wish in these events including calling other classes and perhaps even creating a database.

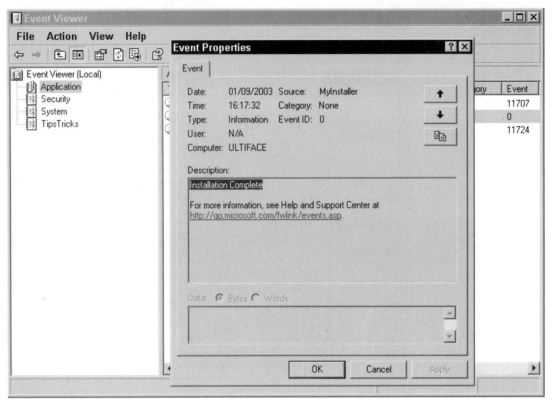

Figure 21-4

The Core of Deployment

Up to now, you have probably done this installation on your machine where you have .NET. However, since your application uses .NET, the .NET runtime is required on the client. If you had to install it on a machine where .NET was not installed, your application would fail. In this section, you learn about deploying .NET to a machine so that your application can run as you expect.

Distributing .NET

You do not have to install Visual Studio .NET as this is your development environment, nor do you have to install the .NET SDK, as this contains more development type tools and files that would not be required by your application. Instead, .NET has an installation for the files that enable .NET applications to run. These files are packaged as `dotnetfx.exe`.

> You can download `dotnetfx.exe` *from the Microsoft downloads Web site. It is approximately 24MB in size and can be found at http://msdn.microsoft.com/library/default.asp?url=/downloads/list/netdevframework.asp.*

The `dotnetfx.exe` installation installs the framework files that hold all the assemblies that you have been learning and coding against. These files include `System.dll` and `System.Windows.Forms.dll`, which are required by default by a Desktop application.

At this point you have two options:

❑ Provide the `dotnetfx.exe` installation to your client so that users can install .NET before your application. This is known as a prerequisite.

❑ Install the .NET runtime from within the installation for your application.

Many larger companies with many applications to install would probably want to consider the first option as it would make smaller installations. A prerequisite CD with the `dotnextfx.exe` install is usually an option as many other types of installs may be required such as MDAC. Putting this all together in one place as prerequisites makes a lot of sense.

You may also want to use the first option if you are providing a download from your Web site. The `dotnetfx.exe` redistributable is a large file.

> Note that if your application uses a database, as you learned in Chapters 15 and 16, you will need to install MDAC. This is also available on the Microsoft downloads Web site. It is not included in `dotnetfx.exe`.

Using a Bootstrap Loader

By default, your setup project is using the Windows bootstrap loader. The project creates this `Setup.exe` and `Setup.ini` files together with your `msi` file. It is known as a bootstrap loader as it is the file that boots or launches the installation.

The windows bootstrap loader checks to see whether .NET is installed on the machine. If it does not exist, a message is displayed and the setup is cancelled. This is only useful as a means to prevent your application from being installed on a machine where you know it will fail.

Microsoft has released another bootstrap loader that can install the .NET runtime if it does not exist. It has been included with the source code to this book. The two files are:

❑ `setup.exe`

❑ `settings.ini`

Try It Out — Changing the Default Bootstrap Loader

1. Right-click your setup project in the Solution Explorer and select Properties. You will see the Project Properties dialog box.

2. Change the value for the Bootstrapper option to None as shown in Figure 21-5.

3. Rebuild the Project.

4. Open Windows Explorer and navigate to where the Setup project resides on your file system.

5. In Windows Explorer, the debug folder now only contains the `myInstaller.msi` file. The bootstrap files are excluded.

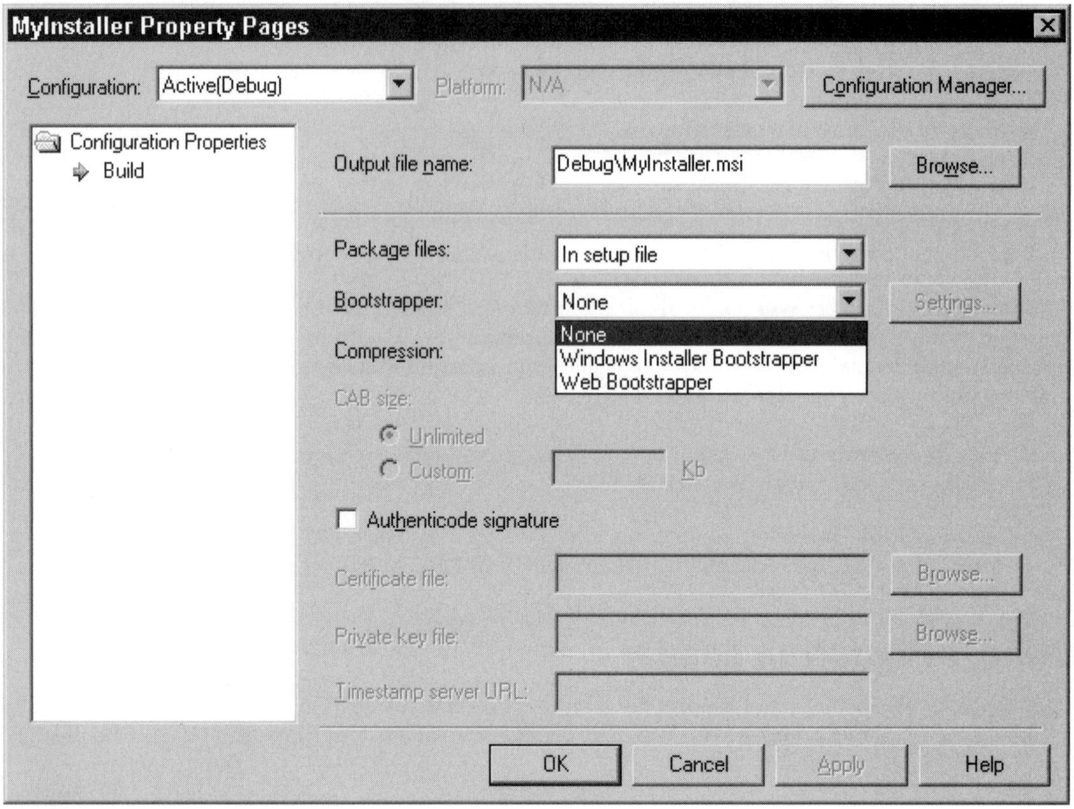

Figure 21-5

6. Next, you need to copy the new bootstrap loader to this directory. The new bootstrap loader are the two files named `setup.exe` and `settings.ini` found with the source for this book.

7. Copy `dotnetfx.exe` to the same directory. You should have four files in this directory now.

8. Next you need to alter the `settings.ini` file. You can do this by opening the file in Notepad

9. Inside the `settings.ini` alter the `Msi` section so that it has the name of the `msi` file for your setup project. If you named it correctly, it would be called `MyInstaller.msi`. Refer to Figure 21-6 to see the change I made.

10. Now you can run the `setup.exe` application.

Note you will receive an error if `dotnetfx.exe` *is not in the same directory as your bootstrap loader and* `msi` *package.*

How It Works

When you changed the bootstrap loader for the Setup project to None, Visual Studio did not create the standard bootstrap loader. Therefore, the `setup.exe` and `setup.ini` files that you saw earlier were not present. You did this so that you could add the new files manually.

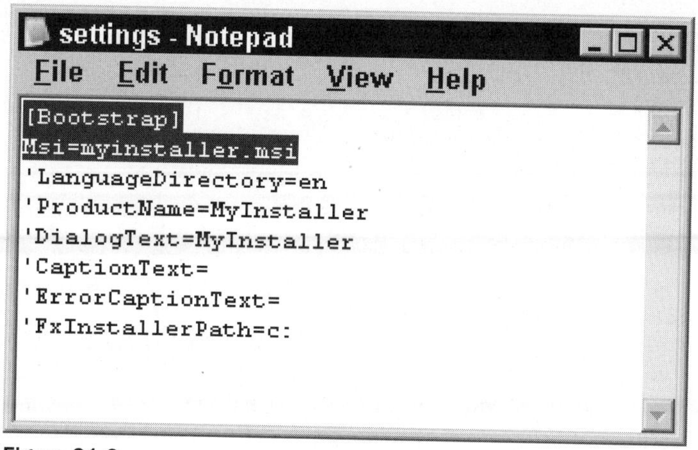

Figure 21-6

Note that if you change the bootstrap loader setting back to the Windows Installer Bootstrapper inside Visual Studio, it deletes the bootstrap files that you placed there manually.

After copying the new bootstrap loader, you altered the `settings.ini` file to point to your `msi` file. `setup.exe` is now able to launch your `msi` file after the .NET runtime has been installed.

Deploying Different Solutions

Deploying applications is actually a large and complex thing, made easier by various tools. But if you consider, for a moment, a large suite of applications, something like Microsoft Office, you will notice that there can be a vast amount of files. All these files require explicit locations or registry entries. They all tie together to make the application work. As well as being a large installation, there can also be many other complexities, such as database creation: What happens if the database exists? What happens with the data that is already there? This kind of activity, commonly referred to as migration, could potentially mean a lot of work for an installation expert.

When you have multiple applications types, it can also make an installation complex, and detailed knowledge of the different applications is required for a successful installation. The following section discusses some items regarding the different deployment scenarios surrounding the different types of applications that can be created with Visual Studio .NET

Private Assemblies

Private assemblies are installed in a directory named `bin` located under the application directory. These files are private to the application. There are a few benefits in doing this.

❑ No versioning is required, as long as it is the same version as the one with which the application was built.

❑ It is not a shared assembly and therefore it cannot be updated by another application (at least it is not meant to).

- You can manually replace the assembly as long as it is the same version.

- It enables XCOPY deployment (the ability to simply copy and paste files to a location and it works).

- You can make changes to the assembly, and if two different applications use it, you could update the one independantly from the other.

- There is no configuration or signing (see next section) to do. It just works.

- It is great for small utility Assemblies and/or application specific code.

Private assemblies have the following negatives:

- When you have multiple applications using one assembly, you have to deploy the assembly to the bin directory of each application.

- You would normally have to include the assembly in each setup project where it is used.

- Versioning is not enforced like a shared assembly is.

- It is not strongly named, which means someone could spoof your Assembly.

   Spoofing an assembly is when someone creates an assembly that looks identical to yours and replaces yours with the spoof copy. This spoof copy could do malicious things.

Shared Assemblies

Shared assemblies are actually more stable and have a thorough approach to assembly deployment. It can also behave like a private assembly, so all the benefit of that approach applies here too. The traditional shared assembly is different because of the extra work you need to do and the extra capabilities it then gains.

A shared assembly is like going back in time. In Windows 3.1, the main deployment location for these kinds of DLLs was the Windows system directory. Then you were advised to have these files in the local application path as it made for easier installation and uninstallation. Today it goes back to the system directory in a new guise named the Global Assembly Cache (GAC). However, the strong naming of assemblies is a definite stepup.

In the first example, you installed the executable by browsing for the file and adding it to the Application folder in the Setup Designer. A private assembly works in the same way. To install a shared assembly you have to add the file to a new folder named Global Assembly Cache. By default, this folder is not visible in the three default folders that are listed. To add the GAC folder you must right-click the node named "File System on Target Machine" and select Add Special Folder ⇨ Global Assembly Cache.

   Note that any project type can use a shared assembly, including a Web application.

Following is a list of the main benefits of a shared assembly:

- It is signed and cannot be spoofed.

- It has strong versioning support and configuration options.

❑   It is stored in one central location and does not need to be copied to the bin directory of every application that uses it.

❑   You can have many different versions running side-by-side.

Shared assemblies have the following negatives:

❑   You have to sign the assembly.

❑   You have to be careful not to break compatibility with existing applications or you have to configure the different versions.

❑   Configuration can be a nightmare depending on the requirements.

Deploying Desktop Applications

In the first example project, you created a setup for a desktop application. All that you installed was the one executable. It had no dependencies other than the .NET Framework, which is always required. In a more complete application, you may have various assemblies, WinForm controls, or other files that you have created for the application. Installing a private assembly with the Setup project means that you include the file in the same way that you included the `Paint.exe` file in the first example.

Deploying Web Applications

A Web application, when using private assemblies, can be simple to deploy. You can use the Visual Studio .NET Web Application setup project to create a simple Web setup. The setup creates a virtual directory and copies the files you specify to the physical directory location.

You do not need to deploy the Visual Basic code files. These are compiled into an Assembly in the bin directory. Only `aspx`, `ascx`, `js`, `css`, *and other HTML files or scripting files are required.*

Deploying XML Web Services

A Web service is deployed in much the same way as a Web application is deployed. It also has a virtual directory. The files that it requires are somewhat different though. You need to deploy the `asmx` and `discovery` files together with the assembly.

Advanced Deployment Options

This section introduces some deployment-related topics. These are simply a collection of general topics that will either aid your general understanding of deployment or help when you are creating one.

Configuring the .NET Runtime for an Application

Different .NET runtime versions can be installed side-by-side (SxS). This means that a client can have two or more versions of the framework installed at one time. By default, the application runs against the version it was compiled for; however, you can alter this behavior by modifying the Application configuration file. The Application configuration file is a XML based settings file that has the following naming convention:

Convention: *AppFileName.Extention*.Config

Example: MyApp.exe.Config

This file having the same name as the application must also be located in the same directory as the application. Inside this file you can specify the runtime version. The following code specifies that the application must use the 1.1.4322 version (version 1.1).

```
<configuration>
<startup>
    <supportedRuntime version="v1.1.4322" />
</startup>
</configuration>
```

To support the 1.0 version the supportedRuntime value must be as follows:

```
<supportedRuntime version="v1.0.3705" />
```

The usual scenario for this change would be from the setup process. The setup would detect and decide which version to use and then alter the configuration file. The Windows Installer templates cannot do this by default. To do this more advanced feature you have to extend the setup or use a different installation process.

Configuring the .NET Runtime for a Web Application

Unfortunately, a Web application works differently. You cannot use the Web.Config to accomplish this redirection. Instead, you configure Web applications via IIS. Figure 21-7 shows the IIS Properties for a Web site and you will see that the ISAPI extension is ASP.NET_1.1.4322.5. This is version 1.1 of the framework.

> *To get the properties for the Web site shown in Figure 21-7, Open IIS, found in Control Panel ➪ Administrative Tools. Then you need to right-click on the Web sites node in the tree and select Properties.*

To alter the version that the Web application runs on, you must change this ISAPI extension to point to one of the following directories:

❑   %windir%\Microsoft.Net\Frameworks\v1.0.3705 for version 1.0

❑   %windir%\Microsoft.Net\Frameworks\v1.1.4322 for version 1.1

There is a limitation here though. All virtual directories use the version you specify here because all virtual directories inherit the settings of the main Web site. In a Web server scenario where different domains are configured and used, a different framework version can be used.

To alter the version, simply click on the Add button on the ISAPI filters tab, enter in any name and browse for the aspnet_asapi.dll file located in one of the directories listed previously.

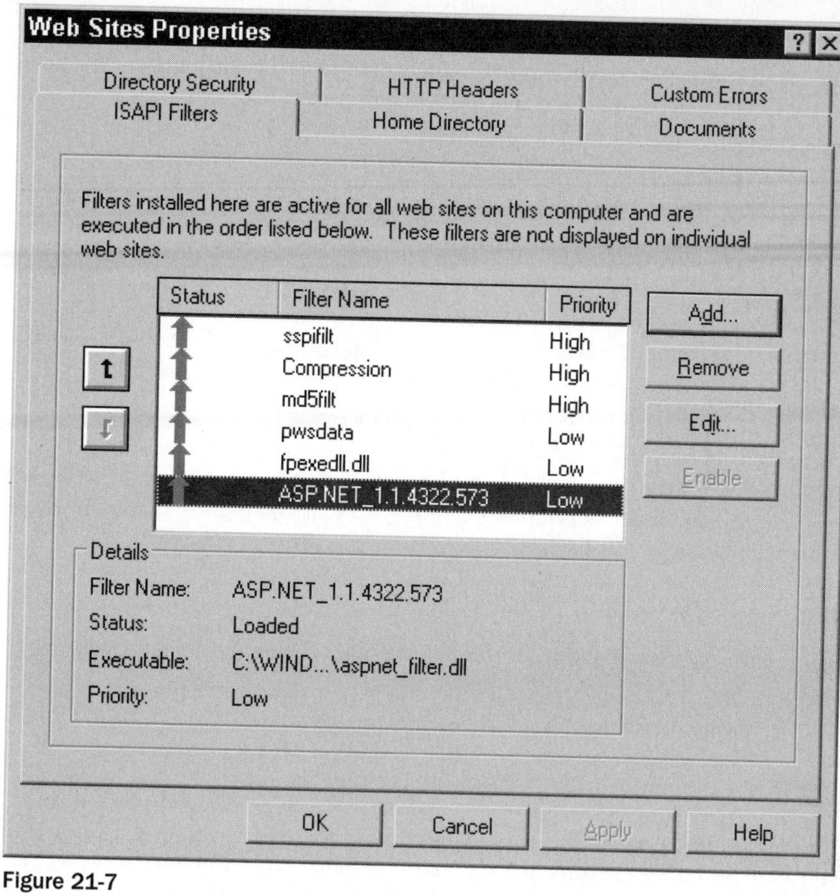

Figure 21-7

Useful Tools

There are a few tools that either come with .NET or are in Windows already for you to use. This section briefly points to these tools. When creating an installation, you also need to test it by installing it on various machines. Sometimes when things do not go according to plan you may need to do some or all of the activities by hand to see if it was the cause of the problem. As an example, perhaps you suspect that the `ASPNET_WP.dll` process has become unstable or broken in some fashion and it has affected the installation. In this scenario, you may wish to restart IIS before you run the `install`. In a similar vein, perhaps an Assembly that was supposed to be registered in the GAC as a shared Assembly cannot be found by the client, perhaps then you may want to register it manually to check if there was a problem with the registration.

ASPNET_RegIIS

The `aspnet_regiis.exe` command line tool can be found in the `<sysdir>\Microsoft.NET\ Framework\<version>` directory. This tool makes it an easy task to reinstall various aspects of the ASP.NET runtime.

Chapter 21

IISReset

IISRESET simply restarts IIS without requiring you to open the IIS management console. Simply open a DOS prompt and type `iisreset` and it will immediately restart IIS.

ILDasm

If you wish to inspect the MetaData of an Assembly, ILDASM is the tool for the job. With the tool, you can inspect everything from the Namespaces to the version.

GACUtil

This is a command line tool for registering/un-registering Assemblies from the Global Assembly Cache. The `/I` option is for registering the Assembly and the `/u` option for unregistering.

RegAsm

This utility is used for creating the necessary COM information from an Assembly. This is used when you need to expose an Assembly for COM Interop. The regasm tool includes switches for registering/un-registering type libraries.

InstallUtil

InstallUtil is a command line tool for executing the Installer classes within an Assembly. This can execute the InstallerHelper sample you did earlier in this chapter.

Summary

Well, I hope you enjoyed looking at some general aspects of deployment. In the first section of this chapter, you were introduced to some terminology and then you saw how to create a simple Setup Application inside Visual Studio. You also learned how to change the bootstrap loader for the setup so that you could install the .NET runtime. Most importantly though, you were introduced to various aspects surrounding an installation, such as extending an install with Visual Basic .NET code and general tools that are used in the creation of installs. These tools are peripheral, but helpful when things go wrong. Ultimately, I hope you learned that there is potentially a lot to learn in this area, from getting to know more about the features of the Windows Installer templates, to learning how to do more with the `System.Configuration.Install` Namespace.

Now that you have finished this chapter, you should know how to:

❑ Create a Visual Studio .NET Setup Application

❑ Change the Default Bootstrap Loader

❑ Create an Installer class for the Setup Application

❑ Use general Deployment terms such as XCOPY, No Touch Deployment, Shared versus Private Assemblies

❑ Configure which version of the .NET runtime is used for a Desktop and Web application

Exercises

1. What is XCOPY deployment?

2. What is a Bootstrap Loader?

3. What is the difference between a private and a shared Assembly?

4. What is the full Namespace of the Installer class we inherited from to create our InstallHelper?

5. Name three tools that could be useful when creating or installing a setup application?

22

Building Mobile Applications

Over the last few years, mobile or smart devices, have been increasing in processor speed and memory capacity. The general overall performance characteristics of a modern hand-held device runs at a faster speed than the desktop PC of 5 years ago, which shows the enormous bounds that computing has evolved to over the past decade. Development was previously done in C++ and later within Visual Basic. Many believe that the mobile device industry needs a boost from a 'killer app' and more functional applications. With Visual Studio .NET 2003 now supporting the mobile cause, it could be you who creates the next killer application in Visual Basic. NET.

The .NET Compact Framework (.NET CF) works with the Windows CE operating system that was launched in 1996. In fact, .NET CF works with my older IPAQ, which was a nice surprise when I hooked it up. Windows CE is a modified and lighter version of the Windows API and Windows kernel, and it was created from scratch. Windows CE made development for smart device applications more like that of a traditional computer. All the standard Windows functionality, such as the API, COM, and OLE (object linking and embedding) is supported by Windows CE. The Pocket PC is only a wrapper that sits on top of Windows CE to provide a different user interface. In the same vein, the .NET Compact Framework is a wrapper for the API that exists in Windows CE. The .NET Framework you have been learning about in this book does not cover all Windows APIs; the .NET CF version has even fewer namespaces and objects to work with. However, this does not mean that it is not a good framework to work with. In fact, working with .NET CF is so similar to what you have learned throughout this book, it's quite exciting as your knowledge for writing software for these devices is basically at the same level.

In my opinion, the .NET Compact Framework and the Visual Studio .NET integration is a significant jump for the smart device. The development integration into Visual Studio .NET significantly simplifies application development for these devices by providing you with a similar development experience to a standard Windows development. It broadens the exposure of programming for a smart device to the general developer community. For example, developing a form for a pocket PC looks and feels the same as developing a form for Windows. The drag and drop of UI components onto a form is there together with the standard code editor, which potentially will work with any .NET language. Of course, this is not where the similarity ends. The .NET Framework exposed for mobile devices is a subset of the standard .NET Framework, therefore classes look the same. Since it is a subset, not all the .NET Framework namespaces and classes are available, but a lot of functionality is still there. From a UI perspective, many familiar controls are available to a form targeting a device, such as the TreeView, Textbox, StatusBar, MenuBar,

TabControl, RadioButton, and so on. Most of the traditional controls that you would expect are available and at the time of this writing, there were 28 different controls.

In this chapter, you will:

- ❑ Create a HelloWorld Pocket PC application
- ❑ See some of the differences between the Compact Framework and the .NET Framework
- ❑ Use the `WebRequest` and `WebResponse` objects to get a Really Simple Syndication (RSS) file and display it on the Pocket PC

Building Your First CF Application

The smart device application is one of many templates that Visual Studio .NET has for the Compact Framework. Most of these templates are wrapped inside a wizard called the Smart Device Application Wizard. The different templates that this wizard exposes include:

- ❑ Windows application
- ❑ Class Library
- ❑ Nongraphical application
- ❑ Empty project

The targeted platforms for these projects are either the Pocket PC or Windows CE. A simple difference between these two on a software level is the fact that the Pocket PC has an extra GUI library that sits on top of Windows CE to alter the appearance of the system. The most significant aspect of the Pocket PC UI is that it runs a window size of 246×295 and the standard Windows CE core runs at 640×443. Both types of devices run Windows CE as the core operating system. When building for the Pocket PC the user interface is significantly different than the standard Windows CE. The Windows CE looks pretty much like a standard Windows user interface from a desktop system.

Creating a Pocket PC Application

Your first application will be a Pocket PC application written in the standard HelloWorld introduction. To create a Windows application you must first choose the correct template and options in the Wizard.

Try It Out   Creating a Windows Application

1.   In Visual Studio .NET, select the File New Project menu. This will display the standard New Project dialog box.

2.   Select the Visual Basic project type on the left and then find the icon that includes a mobile phone and a smart device in its graphics on the right, it is named Smart Device Application. Click the OK button. The selection is shown in Figure 22-1.

3.   The Smart Device Application Wizard appears on screen showing you some options for the project to create. Select Pocket PC for the target platform and select Windows Application for the Project Type. Click OK.

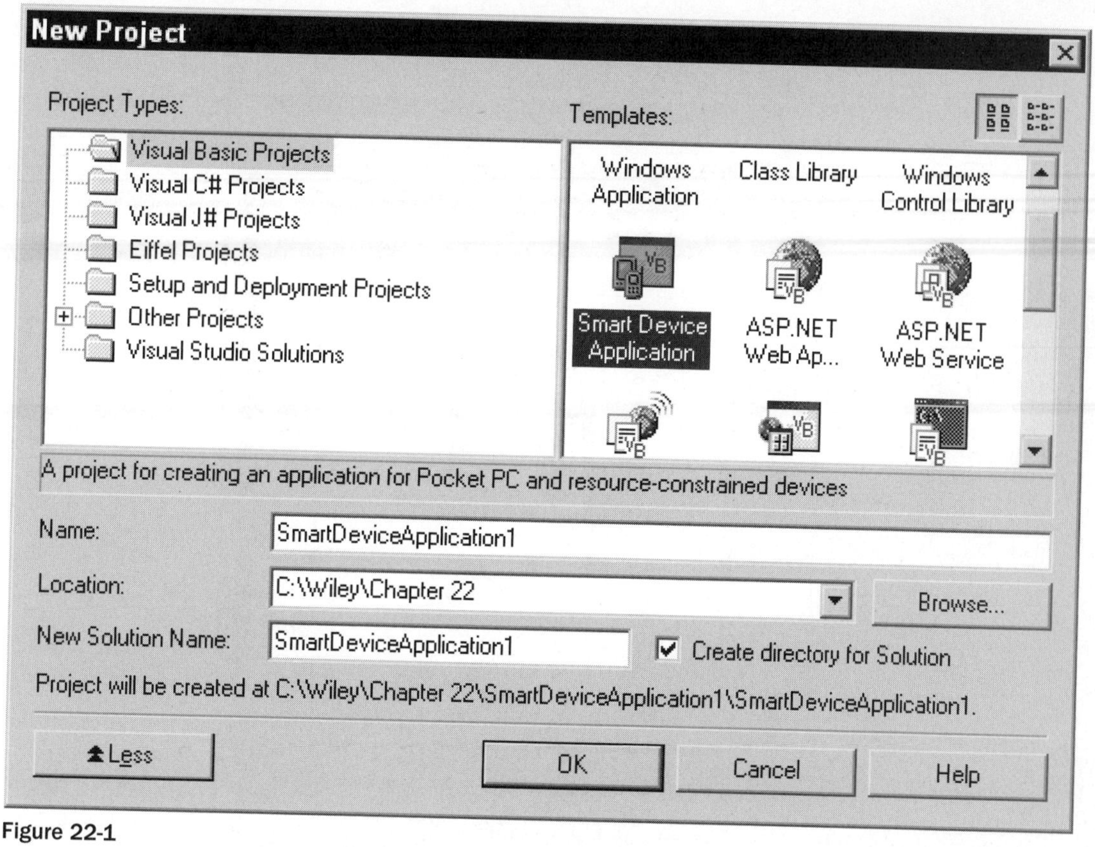

Figure 22-1

4. When the project is created you will be presented with a standard Pocket PC form.

5. Now drag a button onto the form as you have learned before with a standard Windows Form application. You will add some code behind this button.

6. Double-click the button. In the `click` event type the following code:

```
MessageBox.Show(Hello World)
```

7. Now press *F5* (Run) as you would in any application. When you do, the dialog box shown in Figure 22-2 will be presented to you. Select the Pocket PC 2002 Emulator option.

8. You will have to wait a while for the application to be copied, but once done, your application will run inside an emulated Pocket PC environment. Clicking the button will display a MessageBox.

If you have problems with the running of your Pocket PC application, consult www.microsoft.com/ downloads/details.aspx?FamilyID=7ec99ca6-2095-4086-b0cc-7c6c39b28762 &DisplayLang=en *for a download of the Windows CE utilities.*

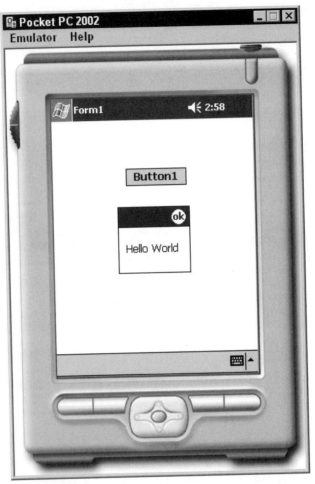

Figure 22-2

How It Works

When you create a new smart device application, Visual Studio loads the appropriate .NET Compact Framework references and its environment. Although it looks and feels extremely similar to a standard Windows Forms application, there is indeed a different world occurring underneath the template.

The first time you run or debug your application, the emulator accepts the application executable as well as the .NET runtime for the Pocket PC. This enables it to execute your application. Unless there is a change in the runtime version or if you perform a soft or hard reset in the emulator, the runtime files are only copied the first time you run it. Thereafter, the applications you are debugging are only transported to the emulator. When you have a Pocket PC device attached to your PC, the same will occur. The Pocket PC emulator runs just like a physical device would run. If you were to choose between the Windows CE and the Pocket PC as different targets, you would get either the Windows CE emulator (Figure 22-3) or the Pocket PC emulator (Figure 22-4).

Behind the scenes, the .NET Compact Framework has an execution engine that caters for almost the same amount of functionality as the .NET runtime that you know. It supports Garbage collection, JIT compilation, as well as the Common Type system. All these factors make for a standard development environment and once again show the benefits of the .NET Framework.

The standard functionality even extends to debugging. You can put a break point in your code and it will halt execution as with standard coding exercises. The debugging includes:

1. Call Stack Window

2. Watch Window

3. Immediate Window

4. Breakpoints

Sometimes a connection between the device and Visual Studio .NET can be lost or broken causing your application not to deploy or run. Microsoft documentation recommends that you do not close the emulator between debugging sessions. However, on certain occasions I found that I needed to either perform a soft reset conducted from the Menus in the emulator or by closing the emulator.

Understanding the Environment

Now that you have had a small introduction to the basics of creating a smart device application, I will try to outline what you have to work with when you are creating an application. There are some standard controls, a subset of the .NET Framework classes and the .NET Compact Framework execution engine is copied over to the device when you run your application. This section attempts to formalize these ideas and include more about the environment for your Smart Device Application developments to give you a better understanding of the capabilities of your environment.

Common Language Runtime

The common language runtime for the .NET Compact Framework maintains its usefulness in the following areas. That is, it supports these functional aspects:

❑ Garbage collection

❑ Common type system

❑ Just-in-time compilation

❑ Unmanaged code execution such as Windows CE API

❑ Platform independence from MSIL (Microsoft Intermediate Language)

❑ Above the MSIL layer, Visual Basic .NET and C# can be used as languages

❑ Standard Visual Basic .NET exception handling, type safety, and object-oriented capabilities

ASP.NET, COM, security for unmanaged code, and the remoting infrastructure are not supported by the .NET Compact Framework.

The Compact Framework Classes

The .NET Compact Framework classes are different from what you are used to, but similar in its design, naming of classes, and structure. The differences are mainly due to what has been left out and some inclusions not required on a desktop.

One of the most significant differences across the .NET Framework classes is the reduced set of overrides. Most methods within the classes come with only a subset of the overrides available for the standard .NET Framework. This means that code written against the standard .NET Framework class library may need to be altered when targeted at the smart device, because some overrides may not be available. As an example, the standard .NET Framework comes with 12 overrides for `MessageBox` `.Show()`, but the CF version comes with three. In some cases this will be irrelevant, but in other cases, when you do not have certain information for the exposed overrides, reworking code may be required.

The framework classes for Windows CE Form controls are also a subset of the standard Windows Forms control. A complete list of controls available to a smart-device is shown in Table 22-1.

Table 22-1 Controls found in the .NET Compact Framework

Name	Name
Button	CheckBox
ComboBox	ContextMenu
DataGrid	DomainUpDown
HscrollBar	ImageList
InputPanel	Label
ListBox	ListView
MainMenu	NumericUpDown
OpenFileDialog	Panel
PictureBox	ProgressBar
RadioButton	SaveFileDialog
StatusBar	TabControl
TextBox	Timer
ToolBar	TrackBar
TreeView	VScrollBar

The most notable of missing controls include the CheckedListBox, ColorDialog, and the NotifyIcon controls.

Large portions of the .NET Framework class library are not found in the CF version; they include the sections mentioned in Table 22-2.

Table 22-2 Missing .NET Framework library portions

Name	Description
System.Reflection.Emit	Building and emitting of MSIL is not supported
System.Runtime.Remoting	The .NET communications and transport mechanisms are not supported with exception to HTTP based communications found in System.Web
GDI+ from System.Drawing namespace	All Graphics functionality for GDI+ has been removed as it is not supported by Windows CE
System.Drawing.Printing	Printing functionality

There have also been some rudimentary additions to the .NET Compact Framework that are not in the standard .NET Framework class library (see Table 22-3).

Table 22-3 Additional .NET Framework library portions

Name	Description
System.NET.irDA	Infrared communications support
System.Data.SqlClient and System.Data.SqlServerCE	SQL CE support
Microsoft.WindowsCE.Forms	Includes the InputPanel Control
System.Windows.Forms	Contains controls known as System.CF.Windows.Forms described in Table 22-1
System.Web.UI.MobileControls	Controls for Mobile Applications include Calendar and Image controls

Really Simple Syndication on the Pocket PC

Really Simple Syndication (RSS) has been growing in popularity over the last few years. RSS is an XML standard for declaring content entries for small content feeds. It is a really a simple format and has taken communities by storm. The XML formatted according to the RSS specification (http://blogs.law .harvard.edu/tech/rss) is either found as a physical file or is obtained via a Web site that handles the request and sends the content over the Internet to the client. Some community Web sites provide you with the infrastructure you would need to publish and host a Web log. There are also Web frameworks, libraries, and tools for creating, publishing, and viewing the content. Even nonprogrammers can have a Web log.

In this section, I will show you how to build a small RSS reader that fetches the RSS content and displays it on your Pocket PC. This is tremendously easy to do. In order to accomplish this let me first give you a run down of the RSS format.

The RSS format

The XML format declares that the XML must have a root element of <rss>, which identifies the document. This is shown in the following sample snippet. The <rss> element contains one <channel> element and then many <item> elements that hold the content.

```
<rss>
    <channel>
    <item/>
    </channel>
</rss>
```

The majority of the elements declared by the RSS specification are optional; however, a minimum set of elements does exist to make it somewhat functional. I will not explain all the elements here as the specification outlines it extremely well.

The <channel> element should at least contain the following children:

❑ Item (at least 1)

❑ Title

❑ Link

❑ Description

The <item> tag should at least contain the following children:

❑ Title

❑ Link

❑ Description

Here is an example of a well-formed RSS file and the format of my Web log, which you are going to retrieve and display on your Pocket PC.

```
<rss>
    <channel>
    <title>Jonathan Crossland Weblog</title>
    <link>http://www.jonathancrossland.com</link>
    <description>Tech Rants and Raves</description>
    <language>en-gb</language>
    <item>
        <title>Active Directory Event</title>
        <pubDate>GMT Formatted date</pubDate>
        <description>
            <![CDATA[ <br/> My Content ]]>
        </description>
```

```
            <link>My Link</link>
               <category>My Category</category>
          </item>
       </channel>
    </rss>
```

Creating an RSS Reader Application

1. Start a new smart device application in Visual Studio.

2. Add a class to the project and name it RssReader.

3. Design the form. Add a Tab Control to the form and add two Tabs named Content and Source. Set the text for the tabs to the same names (see Figure 22-3).

4. Add a text box to the tab named `txtSource` and position it on the second tab (named Source), and set its `Multiline` property to `True`. You can make it fill the available area by dragging and sizing it manually. There is no `Docking` property.

5. Design the form. You will need another text box, this one named `txtUrl`, a button named `btnGo`, a combo box named `cboTitles`, a label named `lblTitle`, and a text box named `txtContent`. See Figure 22-3 for the layout. They should be positioned on the tab named Content.

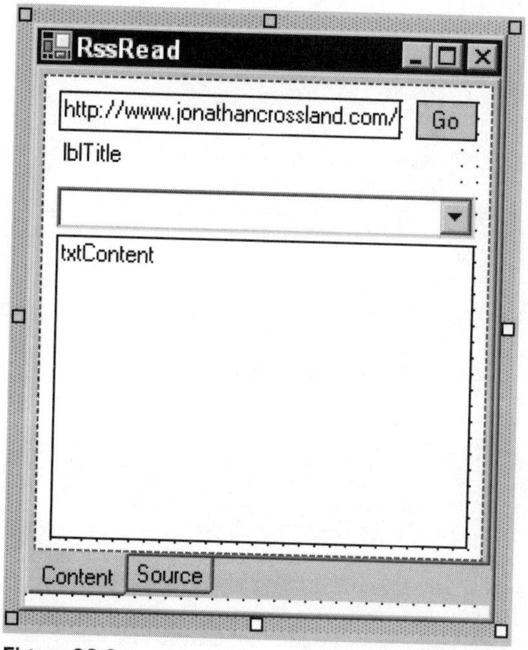

Figure 22-3

6. Next, you need to add some code to retrieve an XML document. For this you will create a function inside the `RssReader` class named `Read()`. The function and the code inside the class is shown here:

```
Imports System.Net
Imports System.Text
Imports System.IO

Public Class RssReader
    Public Function Read(ByVal url As String) As String
        Dim strSource As New StringBuilder("")

        Dim request As WebRequest = request.Create(url)
        Dim response As WebResponse = request.GetResponse()
        'get the stream of data
        Dim streamReader As New StreamReader(_
        response.GetResponseStream(), _Encoding.ASCII)
        'Read the contents of the stream and return to caller
        Return streamReader.ReadToEnd()

    End Function
End Class
```

7. Behind the `Click` event of the button named `btnGo`, add the following code to call the `RssReader.Read` method:

```
Private Sub btnGo_Click(ByVal sender As System.Object, _
    ByVal e As System.EventArgs) Handles btnGo.Click

    Dim url As String = txtUrl.Text

    Dim reader As RssReader = New RssReader
    Dim content As String = reader.Read(url)
    txtSource.Text = content
    doc = New System.Xml.XmlDocument
    doc.LoadXml(content)

    Dim node As XmlNode
    Dim titlenodes As XmlNodeList = doc.GetElementsByTagName("title")

    For Each node In titlenodes
        If node.ParentNode.Name = "channel" Then
            lblTitle.Text = node.InnerText
        End If
        If node.ParentNode.Name = "item" Then
            cboTitles.Items.Add(node.InnerText)
        End If
    Next
End Sub
```

8. Add an `Imports` declaration to the top of the class and add a variable underneath the class declaration. Both lines are highlighted in the following code:

```
Imports System.Xml
Public Class Form1
    Inherits System.Windows.Forms.Form
    Friend WithEvents Content As System.Windows.Forms.TabPage
    Friend WithEvents Source As System.Windows.Forms.TabPage
```

```
Friend WithEvents TabControll As System.Windows.Forms.TabControl
Friend WithEvents MainMenu1 As System.Windows.Forms.MainMenu

Dim doc As System.Xml.XmlDocument

'Other code including the code for the btnGo click event.
End Class
```

9. Next, you need to add some code to get the description from the `<item>` selected from the combo box and display it in the text box named `txtContent`. The following code must be added to the cboTitles `SelectedIndexChanged` event:

```
Private Sub cboTitles_SelectedIndexChanged(ByVal sender As System.Object,_
    ByVal e As System.EventArgs) Handles cboTitles.SelectedIndexChanged
        Dim node As XmlNode
        Dim titlenodes As XmlNodeList = doc.GetElementsByTagName("title")

        For Each node In titlenodes
            If node.ParentNode.Name = "item" And _
                node.InnerText = cboTitles.Text Then
                txtContent.Text = node.ParentNode.Item("description").InnerText
                Exit For
            End If
        Next
End Sub
```

10. Now you can run your project, type a URL in the `txtUrl` such as www.jonathancrossland .com/rss.xml and you will be presented with the contents.

If you cannot establish a connection to the Internet you will need to configure the emulator network settings. There is a section named Configuring the Emulator for Internet Access *later in this chapter.*

How It Works

This small example has shown that it is possible to retrieve an XML-based file via the Internet and manipulate it when it is returned. The .NET Compact Framework provided you with the `WebRequest` and `WebResponse` classes that you could also use for a desktop application. However, although you will be able to use the code in this sample for a desktop application as well, the original library I created for a desktop client was not usable on the smart device. You can see this quite clearly if you refer to one of your existing libraries in a smart device application.

The original library that I created for a desktop client has not been shown here; however, it used object serialization and had classes for each of the elements in the RSS specification. Object serialization, which made the library efficient in manipulating the XML was one of the problems for the .NET Compact Framework, where this functionality does not exist. This all makes it necessary to learn the limitations of the Compact Framework before attempting to use a library that may not work when used on a smart device. The limitations do not end there. In fact, in nearly every class there were methods and classes that could not be found in the .NET Compact Framework.

If you noticed that the `UserAgent` property on the `WebRequest` object is not in the .NET Compact Framework, you would have also realized that far too much is not there to actually go into detail. This poses two distinct situations. Even though the language, syntax, and form design is the same, the fact that the libraries are different is a problem. It was a problem for me, as I had many occasions where something frustrated me because it was not there. On the positive side, there is actually a lot in the .NET Compact Framework; you just have to get to know the limitations and that comes with practice.

On a positive note, you did create an RSS reader (although a simple example). The application used the `WebRequest` and `WebResponse` objects that exist in the .NET Framework and they were used in the same way. The `WebRequest` was issued and a `WebResponse` was received from the URL specified, just like as it would for a library targeted for a desktop PC.

```
Dim request As WebRequest = request.Create(url)
Dim response As WebResponse = request.GetResponse()
```

The URL came from the text box on screen, which pointed to an RSS-formatted XML file. The `WebRequest` returned the XML in this file located on the server. You can see the returned XML in its entirety on the Source tab, where you dumped the contents of the `WebResponse` that was created by the `WebRequest`.

```
Dim reader As RssReader = New RssReader
Dim content As String = reader.Read(url)
txtSource.Text = content
```

The XML was manipulated as an `XMLDocument`, which was easy enough for this small sample.

```
doc = New System.Xml.XmlDocument
doc.LoadXml(content)
```

The code then extracted the `<title>` elements and filled a drop-down box on screen with the titles of each of the Web log entries. When a title was selected from the drop-down list, the code dumped the description element contents into the `txtContent` text box as you received it.

A professional version of this application may use the Internet Explorer control or a way of formatting the HTML in a more readable way.

Configuring the Emulator for Internet Access

To get your Pocket PC on the Internet you have to make sure that your Internet settings are correct. The emulator and your Pocket PC will gain access via ActiveSync.

These connection settings only work with Windows CE 2000 and higher.

In ActiveSync, you must make sure that the Allow network (Ethernet) and Remote Access Service (RAS) server connection with This Desktop Computer option is checked. You will find this in the ActiveSync Connection Settings dialog located by selecting the File ⇨ Connection Settings menu. Figure 22-4 shows this dialog box.

Summary

Building software for smart devices has never been easier than with the .NET Compact Framework. The ease and familiarity of your everyday programming language and Visual Studio .NET Environment also

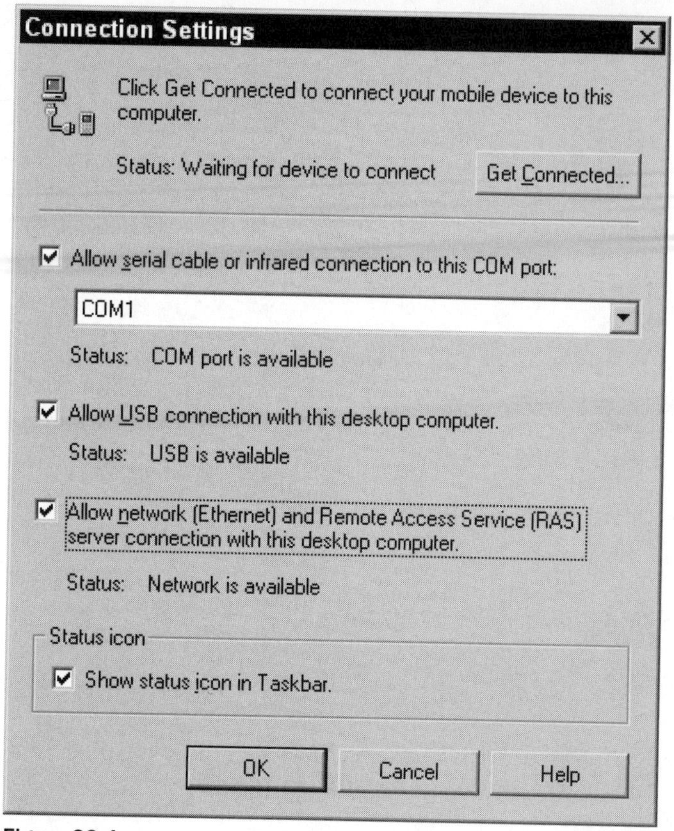

Figure 22-4

negates the need to learn new tools and languages. There are limitations, however. In a more functionally rich application, you will probably need to access the Windows CE API as the .NET Compact Framework does not have all the answers and functionality.

You should know how to:

❑ Create small applications that run on the Pocket PC

❑ Some of the limitations and features of the Compact Framework

Exercises

1. What is the default screen resolution for the Pocket PC?

2. Name two controls that are available on both Windows Forms and Windows CE Forms.

3. The InputPanel control can be used on a standard Windows Form. True or False?

Appendices

A

Where to Now?

Now that you have come to the end of this book, you should have a relatively good idea of how to write code using Visual Basic .NET. The topics and example code covered in this book have been designed to provide you with a firm foundation, but it is just the beginning of your journey. In fact, this book is just one of the many steps you are going to take on your road to becoming a full fledged Visual Basic .NET programmer. Although you have come a long way, there is still a lot further to go, and that is certain as you probably still have many questions.

The problem now is, where do you get these questions answered and, of course, "What next?"

This appendix offers you some advice on what your possible next step(s) could be. As you can imagine, there are a number of different routes open to any one person. The path you choose will probably depend on what your goal is or what you are being asked to do by your employer. Some of you will want to continue at a more general level with some knowledge about all aspects of Visual Basic .NET, while others may want to drill down into more specific areas.

Well, it is extremely important not to take a long break before carrying on with Visual Basic .NET. You will find that if you do so, you will quickly forget what you have learned. The trick is to practice. You can do this in a number of ways.

- ❑ Continue with the samples from this book. Try to add more features and more code to it. Try to merge and blend different samples together.

- ❑ You may have an idea for a new program. Go on and write it.

- ❑ Try to get a firm understanding of the terminology.

- ❑ Read as many articles as you can. Even if you do not understand them at first, bits and pieces will come together.

- ❑ Make sure you communicate your knowledge, if you know other programmers, get talking and ask questions.

- ❑ Consult our online and offline resources for more information.

The rest of this appendix lists available resources both online and offline to help you decide where to go next.

Online Resources

Basically, there are thousands of places you can go online for help with any problems you may have. The good news is that many of them are free. Whenever you come across a problem, and unfortunately you will, there are always loads of people out there willing to help. These unknown souls include others who were at the same stage as you and may have had a similar problem, or experts with a great deal of knowledge. The key is not to be intimidated and to use these resources as much as you like. Remember everyone was a complete beginner at some point and has had many of the same experiences as you.

In this section, we are going to begin by examining the P2P site provided by Wrox and then follow on with some of the more general sites around. If you can't find what you want through any of the sites listed here or if you have some time and want to explore, just search for Visual Basic .NET and you will be on your way!

P2P.Wrox.com

P2P provides programmer-to-programmer support on mailing lists, forums, and newsgroups in addition to a one-to-one e-mail system. You can join any of the mailing lists for author and peer support in Visual Basic .NET (plus any others you may be interested in).

You can choose to join the mailing lists and you can receive a weekly digest of the list. If you don't have the time or facilities to receive mailing lists, you can search the online archives using subject areas or keywords.

Should you wish to use P2P for online support, go to `http://p2p.wrox.com`. On P2P you can view the groups without becoming a member. These lists are moderated so you can be confident of the information presented. Also, junk and spam mail are deleted and your e-mail is protected by the unique Lyris system from Web-bots that can automatically cover up newsgroup mailing list addresses.

Microsoft Resources

Probably one of the first sites you'll intuitively turn to is the Microsoft site (`www.microsoft.com`). It makes sense as it is full of information, including support, tips, hints, downloads, and newsgroups (`news://msnews.microsoft.com/microsoft.public.dotnet.languages.vb`).

There are also a number of sites on MSDN that you may find to be very helpful, including the following:

- ❑ Microsoft Developer Network site: `http://msdn.microsoft.com`.
- ❑ Microsoft Visual Basic site: `http://msdn.microsoft.com/vbasic/`.
- ❑ Microsoft Visual Studio site: `http://msdn.microsoft.com/vstudio/`.
- ❑ .NET download site: `http://msdn.microsoft.com/netframework/downloads`.
- ❑ GotDotNet: `www:gotdotnet.com`.

Other Resources

As said earlier, there are hundreds of sites online that discuss both Visual Basic and Visual Basic .NET. These sites give everything from news on moving from Visual Basic 6 to Visual Basic .NET, to listings of up and coming conferences worldwide. Although you can do a search for Visual Basic .NET, the number of sites returned can be extremely overwhelming. We are going to quickly look at two of these possible sites, one for the United Kingdom and another for the United States.

In the United Kingdom, www.vbug.co.uk offers a wealth of information on Visual Basic .NET. This is the Web site for the Visual Basic Users Group (VBUG), which you can join. Besides the Web site, this group holds meetings and an annual conference, plus provides a magazine. There is a listing of further links on the Web site, and you may want to use this to start your search over the Internet.

In the United States you can get a journal, *The Visual Studio Magazine*, from a similar user group. Again, this journal is backed by meetings and four yearly conferences along with a Web site, http://www.devx.com/vb/, which can give e-mail updates. On the Web site, you have access to a number of different areas both in Visual Basic and other related and non-related .NET areas.

Of course, these are just two among the many out there to try to get you started. Some of you may decide to use these two and many of you may choose others as your favored sites, it's all up to you! What you need to remember though is that the Internet is not the only place to find information, so we will go on to look at some resources not found on the Web.

Offline Resources (Books)

Wrox Press is committed to providing books that will help you develop your programming skills in the direction that you want. We have a selection of tutorial-style books that build on the Visual Basic .NET knowledge gained here. These will help you to specialize in particular areas. Here are the details of a few key titles.

Professional VB .NET, 2nd Edition

(Wrox Press, ISBN 0-7645-4400-4)

This book takes a deeper look at all aspects of Visual Basic .NET and is probably the most logical of "next steps." It provides the next level from this book; however, it will be worth practicing your programming skills beforehand.

Topics include:

- ❑ Introducing the common language runtime
- ❑ Changes to data types, variables, error handling, and window creation in Visual Basic .NET
- ❑ Object inheritance
- ❑ Threading (having different methods executing at the same time)
- ❑ Integration with COM

- ❏ Using XML
- ❏ ADO.NET
- ❏ Web forms
- ❏ Web services
- ❏ Remoting
- ❏ Creating Windows services

Beginning ASP.NET Databases Using VB .NET

(Wrox Press, ISBN 0-7645-4375-X)

In Chapters 15 and 16, we began investigating how Visual Basic .NET can be used to access and program with databases. Databases are ubiquitous and all programmers need to know how to build programs to interact with them, so you'll probably want to develop your skills in this area. This book will provide a comprehensive beginner-level guide to this topic.

This book is for people with some basic experience of Visual Basic .NET and ASP.NET, who want to begin programming database applications with Visual Basic .NET for the Web.

This book covers:

- ❏ Connecting to SQL Server and Access databases
- ❏ Reading and editing data from a Web interface
- ❏ Using Web server controls to display and manipulate data
- ❏ How to use reusable class libraries for data access code

B

Architecture and Design Patterns

The term *architecture*, applied to software, is a broad term with many definitions. Most of these definitions come from the background of the person attempting to explain it and therefore offer subtleties in terminology and function. Definitions range from explaining in fine detail to sweeping overviews, specific language terminology to language and platform independence. In the spirit of explaining the term (not for confusion), I will offer my definition, which I hope will provide some insight into what architecture is in general. In this appendix, I will explain it in more detail.

> *Architecture is the conceptual "look and feel" of an entire software system, composed of architectural elements and their relationships. Architectural elements is a broad term, which can define anything from an object to a file on disk. Their relationships could be anything from the network protocols to object inheritance.*

The architecture of a system is tremendously important as architecture defines the how, why, where, and next. Over many years, a great number of knowledgeable people have studied and worked in an environment where architecture has been the forefront of thinking and many design techniques, technologies, methodologies, and best practices have been born. In the arena of architectural design, we come across terms such as Object Oriented (OO), Analysis and Design (AD), Unified Modeling Language (UML), and Design Patterns. In this appendix, I will communicate two of these areas, Architecture as a general topic and then Design Patterns as this has had increasing support over recent years and is directly beneficial to you at a coding level.

Understanding Architecture

Architecture is the landscape of a system. It is the infrastructure and the connection points between various aspects of the system. A good metaphor is to align software architecture to that of the architecture of a city. Architecture is applied to city planning, road infrastructure, as well as to individual buildings. Architecture arguably is not the specifics of what type of appliances and furnishings will be found in different living quarters, this is the work of an interior designer. Architecture is also not concerned with the type of doors or windows that are prevalent on each building, but may set standards for a certain range or type to be used. Architecture will also not be concerned with the number of rooms in each building, but may require the total living, working, and relaxation areas to be a certain number or percentage. In the planning of a city, the city planner, architect, road engineers, and builders, each have different responsibilities and motivations. A builder will be concerned about the quality of individual aspects of the building, building standards, and codes. An architect would promote, alter, negotiate, and communicate any standards and have them applied. Architecture applied to a city, also includes piping, electricity networks, and sewers beneath the city, which if not done correctly would render the city useless.

I will turn the metaphor on its head for a moment and explain from a software point of view. If we erect a software component and imagine it as a building in a city, we need to respect the environment, the land on which it stands, and how it will interact with the rest of the city. What will an executable, perhaps a Windows Application be akin to in our metaphor? Well, it would be a very large building inside our city. Most of the roads would be cul-de-sac, as it does not expose interfaces (doors, windows) to the outside world. Let's leave the metaphor for now and get back to the real world.

Here is a portion of a specification for a new product.

"Create software to convert a value between Celsius and Fahrenheit. This will be used by Web clients and will be available on our public Web site."

So what do you think is required here? There is a wide range of choices for the implementation including variations and they may include the following:

❑   A Windows application used from the Web using no touch deployment

❑   A Web form that does the calculation

❑   A Web server control that could be used in any project

❑   A class library containing two functions `ToCelsius()` and `ToFahrenheit()`

❑   A Web service exposing the functionality

One main difference between the architecture and just implementing something is the thought and motivations behind problems and what the solutions mean. As a developer, you may have created the first choice, a Windows application that calculated Celsius to Fahrenheit, but what if the class library with the functions were more suitable? The motivation behind the building of a class library was that it may have been thought that it was going to be reused in other sections of the system and not only in your part of it. But that may just be circumstantial or a choice that someone may or may not make. There are, however, more tangible and more realistic motivations behind certain decisions.

Understanding the motivations behind software architecture or the choices made within its design will make its definition clearer as well as provide you with that larger view. But what are the motivations and why are they important? We will look at some motivations such as change, reuse, and agility next to demonstrate what kinds of problems architecture faces.

Change and Evolving Requirements

The common problem for all of us in this industry is a little word called *change*. Usually a lot of work goes into changing an existing piece of software to do something else. In the real world of our city metaphor, imagine that a road network needed to be added to the city to increase traffic flow. Congestion is a problem and the roads are not coping. A new network of bridges and raised roads would cost the city an arm and a leg. In software the same thing is occurring. We build components that cope with certain conditions, but somewhere in its future, certain issues will require the component to be altered. It can be even worse if no components were used at all. Changes in software can be costly.

Reuse of Architectural Elements

To minimize change and eliminate reoccurring work, reusable components have been created. Reusable components are not an exact science as there is no formula that makes a component reusable. Instead, it is the evaluation of repetitive actions, tasks, and abstracting those into something that can be used in more than one location. Somewhere, at some time, someone thought it would be a good idea to have the concept of a brick, which revolutionized the building industry.

Every day in the software industry someone out there is building a hierarchy, something that will populate a tree-view control. As an example, someone may be writing software to capture a family tree. A component could be written that is generically available to all authors of such software. The component could look like Figure B-1. However, a component could be written to deal with hierarchy as a whole or generically as in Figure B-2. What is the best option here? It is difficult to know without analyzing the situation and the environment that it would be contained in. It may be something completely different.

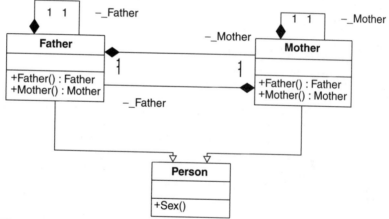

Figure B-1

The difference between designs 1 and 2 shown in Figures B-1 and B-2, respectively, is the terminology and the level of abstraction. In the first design, the classes are named `Father`, `Mother`—based on and derived from `Person`. This has *humanized* the component. This terminology restricts the use of the component within systems that do not deal with hierarchy in genealogy. The second design, expresses a more generic form of hierarchy. There is no specific human quality and it seems as if it could be used in a different context.

Designing something like this is extremely hard and can be broken into two well-known types, one-many (one to many) and many-many (many to many). Traditionally, software is based on the fact that there is "one parent and many children" as is the case with a tree-view control. The tree-view control does not cope with a multi-parent scenario very well.

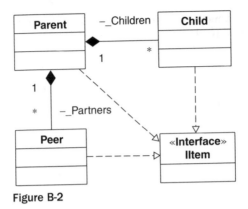

Figure B-2

There are two main points that this demonstrates. Although tree-view control is extremely reusable, it does not cover all requirements. It suggests that there are scales or levels of reuse, which indeed there are. The second aspect that the example communicates is the fact that a design could be limited or expanded simply on the basis of terminology. It is important to note though, that different levels of abstraction are required for different situations. After all, we would not feel comfortable using one name for everything. The term *Item* is sometimes not good enough and we will need to use *Person* or a more specific term.

Agility in Software Systems

In software we can do a lot of things because it is all conceptual and virtual. There are a lot of beneficial abstractions that we can create to make a task or concept easier. Agility is one of the main characteristics of a reusable component. The more agile a component is, the more places it can be used in. The term *agile* means flexible and pliable. It is something that software as a whole would love to become. Research is currently going into areas of artificial intelligence, learning systems, and fuzzy logic, but there are things you can do today.

Being agile is to think and design something carefully so that it can be used later in an evolving system, but how do you make something agile?

Overriding Methods

Arguably, this can be done by elaborating on an interface by exposing more combinations or more methods that do things differently. As an example, overriding is a wonderful way to make a component agile. In the .NET Framework you have many choices of different parameters for a method you need to supply. You can either create an object by using a parameter in its constructor, or not. You can use different parameters based on the data you have at the time. When you design a component, you could add different methods that require different parameters and thus make it more agile.

Object-Oriented Techniques

Another way of making something agile is by using object-oriented techniques such as polymorphism, where two objects are derived from the same interface, thus allowing a known method to be executed on both objects even if you do not know what the objects are. This means that you can get an object, cast it to the known interface, and call a method on it. The parameter of the method would be of type `System.Object` or the base type. This makes code not only more agile but also harder to negotiate.

Abstraction and Layering

Another well-used means of making a system more agile is by having components, levels of abstraction, and a concept known as *layers*. This was first introduced to you in Chapter 12. Layers are conceptually horizontal as shown in Figure B-3, and there are even specific names that have been given to well-known layers, such as Data Layer, Business Layer, and so on. The idea behind a layer is that one or more components are responsible for a particular functional aspect of the system. A data layer contains components that are only responsible for creating, maintaining, and executing data-oriented aspects. A business layer would only be concerned with aspects of business, rules, procedures, and processes. The business layer shown in Figure B-3 uses the layer beneath it to access data when it is required.

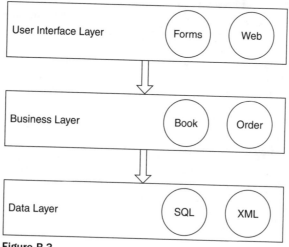

Figure B-3

Meeting Expectations with Patterns

I have demonstrated the need for meeting the architectural motivations of change, reuse, and agility. But when you are designing a software system, these aspects need to be thought about and integrated into the actual implementation. I too have suggested that there are techniques such as object-oriented techniques, layering, and terminology, but what I omitted from the description was a word that describes all these kinds of techniques, which has come to be known as *Patterns*. The term pattern actually comes from the metaphor we have been using. It comes from repetitive patterns in buildings and city architecture. In building a city, there are many repetitive themes such as walls, doors, and roads. What makes a road a road? Is it the fact that it allows vehicles on it? Or is it simply because it is a relatively smooth surface with lines on it? The pattern for a road can be defined as all of those things. The "road pattern" would be composed of a description, a set of guidelines, and definitions. It would even have implementation details about the type of surfacing that is required. In software, patterns in this form have evolved to make developing repetitive conceptual implementations an easier task.

Patterns also come at different levels. As an example, layering described earlier is a pattern at an architectural level, where interface inheritance, or overriding, is a pattern applied at the level of construction.

Over the past decade, software patterns as a term and a practice has gained a tremendous following of developers, architects, and engineers. I too, am a firm believer that software patterns will provide answers to the software development sector for many more years to come. It is imperative that we all learn what others have learned and apply the knowledge to our systems, but it is beyond the scope of this book to outline, document, and explain the different patterns. I will, however, end this section with an explanation of how it fits into software architecture and its development.

The role of patterns is to first create terminology and categorizations of concepts and to provide a guideline. A concept such as an Array and a Collection is different. A pattern would differentiate these two types of coding concepts by a set of rules and definitions. A Collection amongst other things has a Count property, an Add() and Remove() method, whereas an Array does not. Instead, an Array has a Length property and the language syntax allows the Array to be organized and dimensioned. The Collection has an interface by which it can be recognized. This is its *Pattern*. Other types also have patterns, whether it is a constructor that has to be named the same as the class name, or the Dispose method used with Garbage Collection. The entire .NET Framework libraries are pattern oriented as they abide by pattern rules. All Collections will look the same. Although different types of collections may look and behave in a slightly different way, the core is the same. Why is this so vital?

If a developer codes a new type of Collection, with the core being the same, another developer understanding the Collection pattern would easily identify it as a Collection. Identifying the Collection is 50 percent of understanding it, as it makes the code easier to read. If you do not understand the code, it could be because you have not identified the patterns, or perhaps, it has no pattern. Patterns must be the next step for all those who wish to write software geared for reuse, agility, and change.

Summary

This appendix on Software Architecture and Patterns only provided a way of thinking when dealing with the terms. It has not explained everything in detail, but I hope that you understand that the larger view of a system is important, and that architecture and patterns are two of the tools that can be used. I also hope that it has become apparent to you that the .NET Framework uses patterns and therefore things look the same in different libraries even though the functionality may be different.

The next step is to learn all you can about your language, Visual Basic .NET, and then to learn skills such as patterns and architecture as it will aid you in understanding the different aspects of software. The door to the building is now open and it is up to you to learn more about the city. A search for patterns and architecture on the Wiley Web site will provide you with a wealth of learning sources for these topics. One of the best books I would recommend is *Pattern-Oriented Software Architecture* (Volume 1 and 2) published by Wiley (ISBN 0-471-95869-7 and 0-471-60695-2).

An Introduction to Code Security

Over recent years, security holes, vulnerabilities, and attacks have been increasing. These malicious attacks have come in many guises, from a virus to insecure components. As a developer or as a publisher of software components, you need to be sure that your software does not aid attackers. Imagine for a moment a component that reads and writes to a file on disk. You create the component with this functionality perhaps to save and load an XML-based file. The interface accepts a filename as a parameter and the content of the file is passed as a string. An attacker, knowing the interface could call the method and pass in a different filename and his content, thus using your component to write a file of his choice. This is not a good scenario, especially when your component may be deployed on a third-party network. Another well-known exploit is interface spoofing where a component is created to look and behave in the same way as an existing component. When the original version is replaced by a hacker with a spoof copy, any malicious act could be done when the component is called. In this case, imagine you have two components named A and B. Component A calls a method on B. If component B were replaced by a spoofed copy, thus having the same method call, the attacker's code would be executed instead of the original code. This means that on initial inspection it would look like your code conducted the malicious activity. This is known as a *luring* attack.

Another example of a luring attack is to use IISHelp that is installed with IIS in Windows. Administrators are told not to install or remove this and for good reason. Within IISHelp located in the `C:\WINDOWS\Help\iisHelp\iis\misc` directory is a file named `default.asp`. Inside this file is a portion of code that looks at the `QueryString` for the index `"JumpUrl"`. When the value for `JumpUrl` is not null, it redirects the page to the URL specified in the `QueryString`, thus allowing an attacker to navigate to another file on the drive or in the virtual directory. Therefore, if you type `http://yourdomain/iishelp/iis/misc/default.asp?jumpurl=http://www.wiley.com` in your browser you get the Wiley Web site inside the IISHelp. Now, at first this may not look to be so serious, but consider what may be exploited if it is combined with other hacking techniques. If you enter the following `http://yourdomain/iishelp/iis/misc/default.asp?jumpurl=c:` you get the C drive inside your browser. So what does all this mean? Well, it means that a simple application or component or even an ASP file can aid an attacker to accomplish a malicious deed.

The traditional Windows security mechanisms rely on the use of Roles and Groups and their permissions. This has been known as principle- or role-based security. In this model you have the ability to verify a user based on username, and the ability to delegate another user or impersonate an existing user. Role-based security has management tools to support it and the .NET Framework also provides mechanisms in the System.Security namespace to deal with it. Administrators define groups and insert users in these groups. It is then up to you to write software that looks at these groups. The two main elements for role-based security are the WindowsPrincipal and the WindowsIdentity classes in the System.Security namespace. Although role-based security has some benefits, it does not cover all scenarios. Role-based security will not prevent a spoofed copy of a component from being executed. For this kind of security, .NET has created a new abstraction named Code Access Security.

Code Access Security is not based on the identity of the user, but rather on the identity of the assembly. The origin and authenticity of the assembly itself is the focus, which means that certain security breaches, such as spoofing, can be avoided. This brings security down to a component level and even though a user may have the rights to execute a particular component, the assembly may not have the appropriate rights to execute for the user. This .NET abstraction sits on top of the Windows operating system and is concerned with where the code is coming from rather than who the user is or to which group the user belongs. Administrators have greater control over the code itself.

In this appendix you are going to look at Code Access Security and specifically learn the following topics:

❑ How policies, code groups, and permission sets work
❑ How to demand and assert a permission
❑ How to create a Membership Policy and have it applied

Evidence

The key concept in the Code Access Security abstraction is evidence. In short, *evidence* is the proof of the origin of a piece of code.

Evidence comes in various forms, from zone to publisher certificates, and it determines which policies are applied to it by the runtime. Here is the full list of evidence types provided by the .NET Framework.

1. Zone
2. URL
3. Strong name
4. Hash
5. Site
6. Application directory
7. Publisher certificates

Evidence is acquired by looking at the environment and metadata of an assembly. The assembly loader determines whether the assembly was loaded from a URL or from a particular zone and so on, and uses this evidence to establish the security policy to apply. (Policies are discussed next.) First, in the preceding list is the zone. The zone evidence is the proof of where the assembly was loaded from in terms of zones in Internet Explorer. The zones include Local Intranet, Trusted Sites, Internet, Restricted

`Sites,` and `Local Machine.` You can see this portrayed in code within the `System.Security` `.SecurityZone` enumeration.

URL is the next type of evidence and is associated with the zone as a collective piece of information. The URL could be any valid URI and is retrieved from the CodeBase. You can gain access to this by looking at the `System.Reflection.Assembly.CodeBase` interface for an assembly. The following code snippet shows how to retrieve the assembly and the CodeBase information for the type `System.Object`. The CodeBase or URL evidence is collectively used in the URL, Site, and Zone Evidence types as they all are concerned with the location from which the assembly is loaded:

```
Dim t As Type
Dim asm As System.Reflection.Assembly

t = Type.GetType("System.Object")
asm = System.Reflection.Assembly.GetAssembly(t)
Console.Write(asm.CodeBase.ToString())
Console.ReadLine()
```

Site evidence is simply the HostName of a URL, therefore, `www.wiley.com` and `www.wrox.com` are both valid HostNames for site evidence. A URL that points to a physical directory is not regarded as site evidence. MyComputer is therefore never associated with site evidence, but always with the local file system. The application directory evidence is also associated with the MyComputer zone and is thus also a location-oriented form of evidence.

The remaining types—Publisher Certificates, Strong Name, and Hash—are all aimed at providing a more secure way of determining the origin of the code. A URL is not entirely safe because an attacker could publish a component on a site that you have deemed trustworthy. A strong name is also known as signing, which is a broader term. Signing encompasses all three of these types of evidence. Strong name signing is when a hash is created consisting of two parts: a public and a private key. It is recommended that the key be stored in a safe place allowing only the publisher access to it. The key is embedded into an assembly and can be signed by Visual Studio .NET or using the command-line tool sn.exe. In Visual Studio .NET, the `Assembly.Info` file that is in all project templates can hold attributes for signing. These include the `AssemblyDelaySign` and `AssemblyKeyFile` attributes. The hash and publisher certificates are also forms of signing an assembly. All three are aimed at allowing code to be verified by a system because it comes from a trusted publisher. The most valuable option for reaching this endeavor is the publisher certificate.

In code, you can access the evidence for an assembly, as the assembly loader would use it. To get the evidence information for an assembly, you can write a simple piece of code to output it to a console window. The following code is a snippet and can be pasted into a console application:

```
Dim t As Type
Dim asm As System.Reflection.Assembly

t = Type.GetType("System.Object")
asm = System.Reflection.Assembly.GetAssembly(t)
Dim i As IEnumerator = asm.Evidence.GetEnumerator
While i.MoveNext
    Console.Write(i.Current)
End While
Console.ReadLine()
```

The preceding code serializes the data from the evidence type and shows the XML in the console window. It looks like the XML presented here:

```
<System.Security.Policy.Zone version="1">
    <Zone>MyComputer</Zone>
</System.Security.Policy.Zone>
<System.Security.Policy.Url version="1">
    <Url>file://C:/windows/microsoft.net/framework/v1.1.4322/mscorlib.dll</Url>
</System.Security.Policy.Url>
<StrongName version="1"
            Key="00000000000000000400000000000000"
            Name="mscorlib"
            Version="1.0.5000.0"/>
<System.Security.Policy.Hash version="1">
<RawData> - a long byte array value - </RawData>
</System.Security.Policy.Hash>
```

Security Policy Levels and Code Groups

Now that you have been introduced to evidence for an assembly, you need to look at how it is enforced by the .NET runtime.

In execution of an application, the runtime loads assemblies based on types and the interfaces that are invoked. The assembly is interrogated for evidence as described in the previous section. A policy is executed on the basis of the evidence that is found for an assembly.

There are four policy levels built into the .NET Framework, represented in the `System.Security` `.PolicyLevel` class:

❑   User

❑   Machine

❑   Enterprise

❑   AppDomain

Each of these levels, with exception to the AppDomain, has an associated XML file located on the file system as follows:

❑   User—`Documents and Settings\Jonathan\Application Data\Microsoft\CLR Security Config\v1.1.4322`

❑   Machine—`<windir>\microsoft.net\framework\v1.1.4322\config\ security.config`

❑   Enterprise—`<windir>\microsoft.net\framework\v1.1.4322\config\ enterprisesec.config`

❑   AppDomain—specified programmatically

Underneath each policy level the hierarchy continues with code groups called Named, Permission, and Policy Assemblies. This can be seen clearly in the .NET Configuration Tool. You can find the tool in Administrative Tools inside Control Panel.

A security policy is enforced and the tree consisting of code groups is traversed. The evaluation is done first on the policy level when it intersects the permissions from each level. This means that all levels must grant permission in order for the overall consent to be given. If any level denies a requested permission, the request is denied. As an example, an assembly loaded will be granted file access only if the enterprise, machine, user, and AppDomain all grant access. In this example, if file access is granted to the assembly by intersecting the policy level permission set, it then traverses the tree to the code group. The first code group it encounters is the `All Code Group`. This group always returns `True`, which means permission is granted. This is due to the fact that as the name suggests, the membership condition is all code, which means that it applies to all code. Membership conditions are used to determine whether code should belong to a particular code group. If a membership condition for a code group is evaluated to be `True`, then that code group is applied.

You will notice that membership to a Code Group is based on the evidence that the Assembly presents which is in fact a form of Membership Condition.

The membership conditions for code groups are listed in Table C-1.

Table C-1 Descriptions of membership conditions

Membership	Description
AllMembership	Applies to all code
ApplicationDirectoryMembership	Applies to code that is loaded from within the Application directory
HashMembership	Code which has a hash value embedded in a known position in the Assembly
PublisherMembership	Verifies that the Publisher has a valid certificate
SiteMembership	The code must originate from the site specified
StrongNameMembership	ECMA signing. A public/private key pair
URLMembership	Belonging to a valid URL
ZoneMembership	Internet Explorer Based Zones such as Internet

After a code group has been determined, the permissions within that code group are applied. As an example, the Machine (PolicyLevel)—All_Code (code group)—My_Computer_Zone (code group)—Microsoft_Strong_Name (Code Group) allows the FullTrust Permission Set. FullTrust means access to all resources and no restrictions are enforced. The Restricted_Zone Code Group, however, allows the Nothing Permission Set. Permission Sets are explained next.

Permission Sets

Permission Sets are collections of permissions given a name that can be associated at the code group level. A single permission in a Permission Set could include file IO, Web access, and other types of resource-oriented permissions. By default there are a few Permission Sets on your system, containing preset permissions:

❑   FullTrust

❑   Execution

❑   Nothing

❑   LocalIntranet

❑   Internet

❑   SkipVerification

A Permission Set is easy to view in the .NET Configuration Tool. Table C-2 shows the default permissions for LocalIntranet and gives a closer look inside the security permissions.

Table C-2 Permission Sets

Permission Set Name	Security Description
FullTrust	Unrestricted Access
SkipVerification	Does not undergo any verification but does not execute the code
Execution	Executes the code
Nothing	No Permissions are set
LocalIntranet	A Typical IE Zone Permission Set which includes unrestricted access to UI, allows DNS querying, and declares Safe Printing
Internet	Similar to LocalIntranet but permits less. Example: DNS Querying cannot be conducted and only has access to it's own Clipboard instance
Everything	This Permission Set allows all built in Permissions to be granted as opposed to FullTrust, which would also include custom permissions.

Summary

Now that you have received a taste of code groups, policies, and how Code Access Security works, you need to further understand how to code and use it. You can limit how your code is used and executed and provide the system administrator a more complete way of securing portions of code.

In your code you can request or deny permissions at will. You can either explicitly request a permission in code with attributes known as declarative style or you can code inline within methods known as

Imperative style. You can obtain a wealth of information within the MSDN documentation as well as within books like *.NET Security Programming* (ISBN: 0-471-22285-2) and other Internet resources.

Code Access Security is an abstraction that you cannot leave out of your learning, as it is important for the next era of computing. As developers, security aspects need our attention to close the door to attackers. Some of the most well-known exploits come from utilizing someone else's code that was not written with prevention in mind.

Exercise Answers

Chapter 1: Welcome to Visual Basic .NET

1. Combo boxes are given the prefix cbo. Labels are prefixed with lbl. Text boxes are prefixed with txt.

2. If you search for the word *MessageBox* with the Help Filter setting at No Filter, you'll return many more topics than if you searched with it set to Visual Basic and Related. The drawback is that you get topics that are only relevant if you're working in C# or C++ . Be sure to select the right Help Filter setting for your needs.

3. You can create a keyboard hot key by using an ampersand (&) in the Text property before the correct letter. To create a hot key for Cancel button, you enter &Cancel as the Text property.

Chapter 2: The Microsoft .NET Framework

1. The premise behind .NET is to create an abstraction away from the underlying operating system and processor. Microsoft's motivation for doing this is to relieve the dependence on the Windows platform itself.

2. .NET is very similar to Java, but whereas Java from day one has said "write once, run on many platforms," .NET is saying "write in many languages, run on one platform . . . for now." Large similarities lie in the fact that they both have Garbage Collection mechanisms and are compiled to an intermediate language as an abstraction from the processor that is targeted.

3. The Framework Class Library is a vast set of classes that abstracts the various subsystems of the operating system into a set of easy-to-use classes that you can use in your programs. These classes are also categorized by means of Namespaces.

4. Interoperation (or interop) is the principle of accessing software not built with a .NET language or compiled for the .NET Framework. A good example is COM component written in Visual Basic 6. The Visual Basic 6 compiler does not compile for the .NET runtime and therefore, interop would be needed to access the Visual Basic 6 compiled code.

5. Code is compiled from the source language into Microsoft Intermediate Language or MSIL. When the code is executed, it is further compiled from MSIL into the native language understood by the processor. This extra compilation is known as Just-in-Time compilation.

Chapter 3: Writing Software

1. Code written in camel casing has a hump, for example, `camelCasing`.

2. In day-to-day programming, you're more likely to use integer variables than decimal variables. Integers are usually used to keep track of the state of the program, whereas you'll probably find that you rarely want to perform calculations.

3. You use `As String` like this:

    ```
    Dim s As String
    ```

4. Here is the answer:

    ```
    n *= 64
    ```

5. An algorithm is a step-by-step description of *how* the problem that can be solved in software is going to be solved. It's the base currency of all software and good algorithm skills are essential if you want to become a good programmer.

Chapter 4: Controlling the Flow

1. Equal to (=), not equal to (<>), less than (<), less than or equal to (<=), greater than (>), and greater than or equal to (>=).

2. The `String.Compare` method can be used to perform case insensitive string comparisons in an `If` statement. In a `Select Case` statement you use `ToLower` or `ToUpper`.

3. If you have a set of objects provided in an array you can use a `For Each...Next` loop to automatically loop through each item in the array.

4. In the case of a `For` loop you can use the `Exit For` statement. For `Do` loops, you can use `Exit Loop`.

5. A `Select Case` statement is useful for making decisions based on a set of possible values. It is more efficient and easier to read than using combinations of `If...End If` statements.

Chapter 5: Working with Data Structures

1. An array is a set of similar data that is held in a list. Providing an index can access individual items in this list.

2. The differences are subtle, but the two main differences are that you don't have to use the `New` keyword with a structure before you can use it and you cannot inherit from a structure. It's also relatively tricky to convert from one to the other once you've chosen and started using the structure/class, so it's worth choosing wisely before you write a lot of code based on it.

3. The best way to build a collection is to inherit a new class from `System.Collections.CollectionBase` and provide implementations for `Add` and `Remove` methods and provide an `Item` property. This approach makes working with lists of classes, or structures that you build, very easy for both yourself and other developers.

4. An enumeration is a list based on a simple data type such as an integer or a string that limits the values that can be stored in a specific variable.

5. A Hashtable is a way of associating a key with a value. You can build a Hashtable up by adding items and giving each item a specific key. Coming back to the Hashtable later on with a specific key will unlock the item and make it available to you again.

Chapter 6: Building Windows Applications

1. The button's `MouseEnter` event is fired when the mouse pointer "enters" a control. As the mouse pointer leaves the `MouseLeave` event is fired.

2. You can lock your controls to the form by using the Format ⇨ Lock Controls menu option.

3. Controls should be named whenever you need to refer to them from code. You should choose a convention for naming, and in this chapter you've made the control names descriptive of what the control itself does. You also prefix the name with the type of control (`btnOK` for example) and make sure you follow camel casing.

4. The Toolbar and Status bar controls automatically dock themselves to an edge of the form. When the form is resized, these docked controls stay in their relative positions glued to whatever edge they're attached to.

5. Separators are created by setting the Style property of a toolbar button to Separator.

Chapter 7: Displaying Dialog Boxes

1. The answer to this question is shown in the following code fragment. Since you did not want to display an icon in the message box, you specified `Nothing` where you would have normally have specified a constant from the `MessageBoxIcon` enumeration:

```
MessageBox.Show("This is your message.", "caption goes here", _
MessageBoxButtons.OKCancel, Nothing, MessageBoxDefaultButton.Button2)
```

To display the same message using `MsgBox`, write this:

```
MsgBox("This is your message.", _
   MsgBoxStyle.OKCancel + MsgBoxStyle.DefaultButton2, _
   "caption goes here")
```

2. Set the `FileName` property to the file name that should be displayed in the Name drop-down box before calling the `ShowDialog` method.

3. Set the `ForeColor` property of the text box to the `Color` property of the `ColorDialog`.

4. Yes and No. Remember that the `SaveFileDialog` is merely a means to specify where the file should be saved. It does not actually save the file; you use the `StreamWriter` class for this. However, clicking the Save button in the dialog box when a file already exists will cause a prompt to be displayed. Clicking the Yes button in this prompt will cause the `SaveFileDialog` control to return a `DialogResult` of `OK`. Then your code would overwrite the existing file.

5. No, the FontDialog control is smart enough to display the same font again. The reason for this is that the FontDialog control never goes out of scope until you end the program. However, if you

created your own object and displayed the Font dialog box as shown in the following code fragment, the same font that was previously selected would not be displayed:

```
' Declare and set a font object...
Dim objFont As FontDialog = New FontDialog()

' Show the dialog...
If objFont.ShowDialog() = DialogResult.OK Then
    ' If OK then set the font in the text box...
    txtFile.Font = objFont.Font
End If

' Clean up...
objFont = Nothing
```

You would need to set the `Font` property to the font that was previously selected before calling the `ShowDialog` method. The reason for this is that the Font object that you declared goes out of scope as soon as you are done with it because you set it to `Nothing`:

```
' Declare and set a font object...
Dim objFont As FontDialog = New FontDialog()

' Set the Font property before calling the ShowDialog method...
objFont.Font() = txtFile.Font

' Show the dialog...
If objFont.ShowDialog() = DialogResult.OK Then
    ' If OK then set the font in the text box...
    txtFile.Font = objFont.Font
End If

' Clean up...
objFont = Nothing
```

Chapter 8: Creating Menus

1. Use an ampersand in the text. For example, to specify an access key of *F* for the File menu, you specify the text `&File`. If a menu or menu item contains an ampersand in the name you need to specify two consecutive ampersands in order not to have it interpreted as an access key. For example, suppose you had the menu item *Tools & Tips*. In order to have the first T as the access key and the ampersand in the text displayed correctly, you would need to specify the text `&Tools && Tips`.

2. Absolutely! As long as it is in the list of shortcuts in the drop-down list in the `ShortCut` property. The shortcut that you assign here will be the shortcut executed for this menu item.

3. Yes. You use the same properties as you did when you did this in the menu.

4. Yes. When creating a context menu item, a text area appears to the right and to the bottom of the context menu item that you are working on.

5. Yes, however, keep in mind that menus should be short and to the point. If you have too many menu items, it will be hard to locate the correct menu item. You should consider splitting a long menu into two or more separate menus.

Chapter 9: Debugging and Error Handling

1. The Visual Studio .NET development environment will underline syntax errors caused by improper use of methods and properties of objects and for variables not declared when the `Option Explicit` option or statement is turned on, which is turned on by default.

2. Yes. To set a conditional breakpoint click the line of code where you want the breakpoint such as a variable and then click on the Debug ➪ New Breakpoint menu item to invoke the New Breakpoint dialog box. In the New Breakpoint dialog box, click the Condition button to invoke the Breakpoint Condition dialog box and enter the condition in which you want the breakpoint activated. For example, to break when the `intLineCount` variable is equal to 5, enter `intLineCount = 5` in the Breakpoint Condition dialog box.

3. It shows all variables and objects "visible" to the current function or procedure executing and allows you to change these values.

4. Click the Step Over icon on the Debug toolbar or click the Debug ➪ Step Over menu item.

5. Yes. You can test for specific errors as shown in the following code:

```
Try
    intX = 1
    intY = 0
    intResult = intX / intY
Catch e As DivideByZeroException
    ...
    error handling code here
    ...
Catch e As OverflowException
    ...
    error handling code here
    ...

Finally
    ...
    code here always executes
    ...
End Try
```

6. This is a logic error. The code compiles (so it is not a syntax error) and runs without raising any complaints (so it is not an execution error). However, there is something in your code that means the program doesn't do what you want it to (your *logic* is flawed).

The reason for this problem is the following line:

```
Loop While currentLine <> Nothing
```

which assumes that if there are no characters in a line, you have reached the end of the file. You could have found this line by stepping through the program and finding that this was the line where the program made the wrong decision to stop reading the file. The way to fix it is to change the condition so that it uses a more reliable test:

```
Loop While myReader.Peek <> -1
```

This condition now peeks ahead at the file and checks if there is any more data to read. If there is no data, the Peek method returns -1—so you go around the loop *until* the Peek method returns -1. Then you stop looping and carry on with the rest of the program.

Chapter 10: Building Objects

1. A private member can only be accessed by functions, methods, and properties defined on the same class. A public member is accessible to anyone consuming the class.

2. A property describes something about the object (Property), whereas a method does something to the object (Behavior). On a class representing a TV, the current channel should be described as a property because it's a fact about the state of the TV, whereas if you wanted to turn the TV on you would use a method because that's something you're doing to the object.

3. A constructor is a block of code that gets called whenever the object is created. They are useful whenever you need the object to be in a certain state before the consumer starts using it.

4. All classes in .NET inherit from System.Object.

5. Overriding is providing a new implementation for a method or a property that already exists on the base class (the class that the new class inherits from). It is known as overriding because your new implementation is called over the base version. Unless you specifically call the base version, it will not be executed.

Chapter 11: Advanced Object-Oriented Techniques

1. The advantage of a class library is that objects, and therefore the functionality encapsulated within them, can easily be reused in other applications. All you have to do is build the classes in a separate library (or move them from existing projects into new class libraries) and include references between library and application.

2. The menu items you added had to know which WebFavorite instance they related to in order that Internet Explorer could be told to open the proper URL. Creating a new class inherited from MenuItem means that you can add a new property for storing the WebFavorite instance.

3. When a developer wants to work with your classes, it's useful to have a separate class optimized for moving around lists. Creating a new class inherited from System.Collections .CollectionBase and adding a few properties makes this very easy for them.

4. Trick question! There is no way to determine the time that will elapse between the final reference to an object being released and the object being cleaned up by the Garbage Collector.

5. The Dispose method should be called by the consumer as soon as the resources used by the object are no longer required. The Garbage Collector automatically calls the Finalize method.

Chapter 12: Building Class Libraries

1.   Class libraries enable you to reuse code without having access to the original source, or recompiling the reused code into every program that uses it. There are lots of other advantages of course, but these are the main ones.

2.   To prove that it was written by a specific person or organization. Some functionality, such as registering it in the GAC (Global Assembly Cache), requires an Assembly to be signed.

3.   To store copies of a given version of an assembly and to prevent conflicts with assemblies that have the same name but for some reason do different things. It's also a useful way of sharing assemblies between applications.

Chapter 13: Creating Your Own Custom Controls

1.   At a minimum, an event should be defined by:

```
Event SomethingHappened(ByVal sender As Object, _
ByVal e As System.EventArgs)
```

However, an event can have any number of additional parameters.

2.   To raise an event, you use the `RaiseEvent` keyword and supply the event that you want to raise along with values for the event parameters. For example, to raise the `SomethingHappened` event, you would write something like this:

```
RaiseEvent SomethingHappened(Me, New System.EventArgs)
```

3.   A control has a property called `DesignMode`, which is `True` if the control is in design mode and `False` if it is in run mode.

Chapter 14: Programming Custom Graphics

1.   A pixel (or picture element) is a tiny dot. Pixels are grouped together into bitmaps whereupon a programmer can set the color of each pixel individually in order to build up a picture.

2.   Whenever you want to draw with .NET, you need to be given a `System.Drawing.Graphics` object. This object exposes most of the methods you need in order to draw shapes and images.

3.   Whenever a "thing" in Windows (control, form, menu, whatever) needs painting it is invalidated. Windows knows which windows are invalidated and which ones need drawing. In the first phase, the invalid area is erased. In the second phase you get the opportunity to paint your user interface.

4.   Client coordinates do not change when the user moves the form around on the desktop. Your client area always starts at (0, 0) irrespective of where the form is on the screen. Screen coordinates on the other hand describe any point on the screen starting at (0, 0) in the top-left.

5.   `System.Drawing.Color` objects come from a number of sources. You can either use shared properties on the `Color` object to get hold of common system colors, for example, `Color.Blue` or `Color.Red`. Alternatively, you can use `Color.FromArgb` and provide a red component, a

blue component, and a green component to make up any color that you wish. Finally, you can use the `SystemBrushes` and `SystemPens` classes to get hold of brushes and pens used for painting in the user-defined Windows user interface object colors.

Chapter 15: Accessing Databases

1. No. You only need to prefix the field name with the table name when you are selecting data from multiple tables and the tables contain the same field names.

2. Once the `DataGrid` is displayed, simply click the column header of the column that you want sorted to have the data sorted in ascending order. Clicking the same again will sort the data in that column in descending order.

3. Use the `Fill` method of the `OleDbDataAdapter` as shown in the following code fragment:

   ```
   OleDbDataAdapter1.Fill(DataSet1)
   ```

4. An `SqlCommand` component and a SQL `SELECT` statement.

Chapter 16: Database Programming with SQL Server and ADO.NET

1. When you need just a subset of data from the `DataSet` object or you need the ability to sort or search for data.

2. You simply need to specify the stored procedure name and set the `CommandType` property to indicate that the `CommandText` property contains a stored procedure as shown in the following code fragment:

   ```
   objCommand.CommandText = "usp_sel_authortitles"
   objCommand.CommandType = CommandType.StoredProcedure
   ```

3. They represent placeholders for data that will be inserted by the `SqlParameter` objects in the `Parameters` collection.

4. If the control has been previously bound as was done in the Binding Example program.

Chapter 17: Web Forms

1. Web form controls provide a more feature-rich object model and can be programmed at the server. This allows you to bind data to these controls and also to use Visual Basic .NET code, which you are most familiar with.

2. Yes and No. HTML controls cannot be programmed at the server. However, HTML controls can be converted to HTML Server controls by right-clicking the control while in Design mode and choosing the Run As Server Control from the context menu. This will convert the "pure" HTML control to a server-side control, which can be programmed again at the server.

3. The `IsPostBack` property returns a `True`/`False` value indicating whether the page has been posted back from a client request or whether the page is being loaded for the first time.

4. Yes. However, remember that if you want to write code in a server-side script block, that is for an event for a control, you must specify the event in the control and then specify the procedure name that should be executed.

The following example control specifies the procedure to be executed when the `OnClick` event is fired. When you click the button in a form, the form will be posted back to the server and the procedure `Button1_Click` in server-side script will be executed:

```
<asp:Button id=Button1 runat="server" Text="Server-Side" OnClick=Button1_Click>
```

Chapter 18: Creating Web Server Controls

1. A Web Server Control inherits from `System.Web.UI.WebControls.WebControl`. The sample uses the code given below:

```
Page.RegisterOnSubmitStatement("OnSubmit", _ " return AllowSubmit ; ")
```

2. The `System.Web.UI.Page` class is available to your Web Server Control by specifying the `Me` keyword.

3. You needed to override the `Visible` property, because its default behavior when set to `False`, is not to render the control to the browser at all. The sample required that the control be rendered but not seen, until shown. This prevented a trip back to the server when you wanted to show the control to the user on the client.

Chapter 19: Visual Basic .NET and XML

1. Extensible Markup Language

2. XML is an open standard that's primarily used in software integration. It allows an application vendor to define its own text-based format for data that can be transferred around the network and Internet and, with a little cooperation, could be easily understood by third parties.

3. `XmlSerializer` ultimately wants to work with simple data types such as strings, integers, Booleans, and doubles. It can work with complex structures and classes, provided that each of the properties it tries to work with ultimately ends up as a simple type.

4. By putting the `System.Xml.Serialization.XmlIgnore` attribute before a property or public member variable, you can tell `XmlSerializer` not to bother trying to work with the property.

5. `System.Xml.XmlTextReader` is the object that you used to work through an XML document node by node.

Chapter 20: Web Services and .NET Remoting

1. A Web site is designed to be used by a human being. A Web service is designed to be used by a piece of computer software.

2. SOAP, or Simple Object Access Protocol, is the open standard that defines how Web services and client applications exchange information. Requests are made of the Web service through a SOAP

request document, which is an XML document transferred over a Web server like Microsoft IIS. When the service wants to return a value, it's packaged in another XML document called a SOAP response document.

3. To mark a method as being available on a Web service, you use the `WebMethod` attribute at the beginning of the method definition.

4. You can return all kinds of information from a Web service, including simple values and arrays of simple values. If you want to return a set of information (such as customer record or information about a picture), you can package the results as a separate structure or class.

5. There is no .NET version of Internet Explorer because Microsoft hasn't gotten around to porting it from COM to .NET technologies. When you want to use the Internet Explorer control in your applications, you have to use the COM interoperability layer. Luckily, Visual Studio does this for you, so if you want to use any old COM controls in your project, you just have to add them to the Toolbox.

6. Yes, both the client and server can run on the same machine.

7. `Soapsuds.exe`.

Chapter 21: Deploying Your Application

1. XCOPY deployment gets its name from the `XCOP` DOS command. It is when files are copied from one location to another as an installation. There would be no installation, registry entries, or any other kind of configuration except for the copying of files.

2. A Bootstrap Loader is a small application that runs and launches the setup program or MSI package.

3. A private assembly can usually be used in an XCOPY situation and is private to the application that uses it. The private assembly exists in the same directory or a sub-directory (usually bin). If you wanted to use the assembly in another application you would need to make a copy of the assembly for the other application, thus two copies of the assembly would exist.

   A shared assembly is a signed assembly registered in the Global Assembly Cache (GAC) and can be referenced and used by many applications on the same machine.

   Both private and shared assemblies can, however, be versioned and signed.

4. `System.Configuration.Install.Installer`

5. GACUtil.exe, RegAsm, ILDasm are three useful tools.

Chapter 22: Building Mobile Applications

1. The default screen resolution for the Pocket PC is 246×295.

2. The TextBox and ScrollBar controls are available for both Windows Forms and Windows CE Forms. Other examples are the Button, ComboBox, ListBox, PictureBox, and TreeView controls.

3. The answer is False. An InputPanel is only available to mobile devices.

Differences Between .NET Framework Versions 1.0 and 1.1

Version 1.1 of the .NET Framework has seen some enhancements over Version 1.0 and also some new features. This appendix highlights both.

Interestingly enough, when you install Version 1.1 of the .NET Framework on a clean machine, both Versions 1.0 and 1.1 are installed and operate in a side-by-side mode. This enables you to install and run legacy applications written against the 1.0 .NET Framework and new applications written against the 1.1 .NET Framework.

The 1.1 Version of the .NET Framework is touted to be both backward and forward compatible with existing and new .NET applications. However, the documentation is careful to point out that most, but not all, of the existing applications written against the 1.0 .NET Framework will run against the new .NET Framework.

Enhanced Features

Before learning about the new features in the .NET Framework, you should explore what has been enhanced and note any "gotchas" along the way. This section touches on some of the major enhancements. The MSDN library that gets installed with Visual Studio .NET 2003 provides a complete list of enhancements.

Security

Security is a major concern at Microsoft and not just with their operating systems but with all of their products. This translates into some security changes not only in the .NET Framework but also in Visual Studio .NET 2003.

Passwords

One of the first things that developers upgrading from Visual Studio .NET to Visual Studio .NET 2003 will notice is the warning dialog box when using one of the connection objects (OleDbConnection,

SqlConnection, and so on) from the Data tab in the Toolbox. This warning dialog box warns you that the password in the connection string being built will be placed in your code and compiled assembly in plain text. This dialog box gives you an opportunity to either include or not to include the password in your code, or to cancel the operation of building the connection string altogether.

It has always been a best practice among developers concerned with security issues to encrypt passwords and store them in the registry and not to place them in their code. This serves multiple purposes, but the main one is security. Microsoft has recognized this best practice and the problems related to placing plain text passwords in code, hence the change mentioned here.

Web Services Protocols

One of the main security enhancements in the 1.1 .NET Framework that may break existing .NET code is the use of the HttpPost and HttpGet protocols from various applications to Web services. These protocols have been turned off by default in the 1.1 Version of the .NET Framework and will cause applications that use these protocols to access Web services to stop working.

To correct this problem, you'll need to uncomment the lines for these two protocols in the following section of your machine.config file, which are shown, commented out in the following code fragment:

```
<webServices>
 <protocols>
      <add name="HttpSoap1.2"/>
      <add name="HttpSoap"/>
      <!-- <add name="HttpPost"/> -->
      <!-- <add name="HttpGet"/> -->
      <add name="HttpPostLocalhost"/>
      <add name="Documentation"/>
 </protocols>
 </webServices>
```

Connection Strings

It was possible in the 1.0 .NET Framework to set the SQLPermision.AllowBlankPassword=false in the security.config file. It was expected to disallow blank and no password parameters in a connection string. However, this did not work and blank and no password parameters were allowed for the SlqConnection object. Version 1.1 fixes this problem and your applications will now fail as expected.

The default behavior for the OleDbConnection object was to allow blank passwords in the connection string in Version 1.0. This default behavior has been changed in 1.1 of the .NET Framework and now requires passwords to be passed in the connection string. This will cause existing applications that do not need to supply passwords, such as connecting to Microsoft Access databases, to fail.

To work around this configuration change, you'll need to modify your security.config file to allow blank passwords for OleDbConnection objects.

ADO.NET

This section covers some of the major changes in ADO.NET that can help you write more efficient code and also some of the issues that have been fixed.

DataReader

The DataReader classes (`OleDbDataReader`, `SqlDataReader`, and so on) now contain a `HasRows` property that can be called to determine whether the `DataReader` retrieved any rows from the data source. This enables you to quickly check a property of the `DataReader` class to determine if data is present without having to call the `Read` method to make this determination.

Also, if you executed multiple SQL statements against the database and one or more of the SQL statements failed, you would receive an exception when closing the `OleDbDataReader` object in 1.0 of the .NET Framework. This has been fixed in 1.1 and no exception is now raised.

Namespaces

The `System.Data.Odbc` namespace was available in Version 1.0 of the .NET Framework but had to be downloaded from Microsoft if you wanted to use it. This namespace now ships and gets installed with Version 1.1 of the .NET Framework.

Visual Studio Projects

This last section here really doesn't fall into an enhancement category but does need a mention as it can be a "gotcha" scenario.

When you open an existing project in Visual Studio .NET 2003 that was created with Visual Studio .NET, it will prompt you to convert the project in the Visual Studio .NET 2003 format. The dialog box that is displayed warns you that after a project has been converted it cannot be opened, edited, built, or run in the previous version of Visual Studio .NET and the 1.0 .NET Framework.

Heed this warning! Even if you do not make any changes to your code, the project will be converted once you answer Yes in the dialog box, and now you will not be able to open or edit the project in the previous version of Visual Studio .NET.

Additional Information

There are many other changes in the 1.1 Version of the .NET Framework. Consult the MSDN library that gets installed with Visual Studio .NET 2003 for a complete list of changes.

You can also view the following link for a comprehensive list of backward compatible changes for the 1.1 .NET Framework that will cause problems with your existing applications written for the 1.0 .NET Framework: www.gotdotnet.com/team/changeinfo/Backwards1.0to1.1/default.aspx.

For a forward breaking list of changes go to:

www.gotdotnet.com/team/changeinfo/Forwards1.0to1.1/default.aspx.

New Features

This section of the appendix highlights some of the new features of the 1.1 NET Framework. Having read this book up to this point you'll undoubtedly have discovered some of the newer features already (for example, support for mobile applications).

Namespaces

One of the changes that you saw in the last section was the inclusion of the `System.Data.Odbc` namespace in the .NET Framework, which was an optional download for version 1.0 Framework developers. One of the new features in Version 1.1 is the inclusion of `System.Data.OracleClient` namespace for accessing Oracle databases.

Like its `System.Data.SqlClient` namespace counterpart, the `System.Data.OracleClient` namespace contains the major classes for working with data; `OracleConnection`, `OracleCommand`, `OracleDataReader`, and so on. This namespace also includes some classes that are specific to Oracle and are used to access some data types specific to Oracle. Examples include the `OracleBFile` class used to work with the `BFILE` data type and the `OracleLob` class, which is used to work with the `LOB` data type.

The `System.Data.OracleClient` namespace, like its `System.Data.SqlClient` namespace counterpart, will offer better performance over the `System.Data.Odbc` namespace and can only be used to access Oracle databases.

ASP.NET Mobile Controls

As you saw in Chapter 22, the 1.1 Version of the .NET Framework and Visual Studio .NET 2003 now includes support for ASP.NET Mobile Controls and ASP.NET Mobile Web Applications. Mobile devices include items such as personal data assistants (PDA) and cell phones.

With native support for ASP.NET Mobile Controls, you extend the reach of your .NET applications even further and build true enterprise applications that have a wide reach. You can apply the same skills that you have acquired for working with ASP.NET to ASP.NET Mobile Web applications.

Perhaps the biggest advantage of ASP.NET Mobile Controls is the ability to let you write code for mobile devices without having to worry about targeting and writing code for a specific device. This relieves you of the responsibility of having to worry about the details of every type of mobile device that your code might run on.

Visual Studio .NET 2003 and the 1.1 Version of the .NET Framework will take care of the details of properly executing and rendering your applications on each of the various types of devices.

Side-by-Side Execution

Side-by-side execution refers to the ability to install multiple instances of an application or component on a single computer and have each installation access a different version of any required component or the common language runtime (.NET Framework).

This is made possible through the use of the application configuration file that is specific to and gets installed with each application. You can create and set the `supportedRuntime` and `requiredRuntime` elements in the application configuration file to tell .NET which version of the Framework to run on.

It should also be noted that existing applications written for the 1.0 Version of the .NET Framework will automatically be run on the 1.1 Version of the .NET Framework once a computer has been upgraded with

Version 1.1 or Version 1.1 is installed on a new computer and your existing application is installed afterwards.

If you want your application to be specifically run on Version 1.0 of the .NET Framework then you must include the `supportedRuntime` and `requiredRuntime` elements in your application configuration file.

Your application configuration file takes on the name of your application's executable with a `.config` extension. For example, suppose your application's executable is named `SalesForcast.exe`. Then your application configuration file will need to be named `SalesForcast.config`.

Because each application has the ability to include an application configuration file, multiple installations of the same application can be installed on a computer to different directories. The application configuration file must reside in the same directory as the application's executable.

This allows you to simultaneously run different versions of the same application and have each application target different versions of the .NET Framework or even different versions of required components.

Summary

This appendix has highlighted some of the major enhancements and new features of the 1.1 Version of the .NET Framework. It has also brought to your attention some enhancements that can cause problems with your existing application when you upgrade your computer with the 1.1 .NET Framework.

For a complete and comprehensive list of enhancements and new features available in the 1.1 Version of the .NET Framework please review the MSDN library that gets installed with Visual Studio .NET 2003 or visit the Microsoft .NET Framework home page at: `http://msdn.microsoft.com/netframework/`.

Index

Index